European Union

A key textbook for undergraduate and postgraduate students of contemporary European politics, *European Union: Power and policy-making*, fourth edition, offers a comprehensive and accessible analysis of the European Union's policy process.

Intended to advance understanding of the EU as a now mature and ongoing policy system, this book addresses the central issues relating to the distribution of power and influence in the European Union including:

- Theoretical perspectives
- The roles of key institutions in the processing of policy problems
- Different channels of representation
- The EU as a policy-making state.

Written by a distinguished group of international scholars, this new edition will also appeal to the worldwide community of researchers on the EU.

New to this edition:

- New chapters such as: The Politics of Multispeed Europe, The Distribution of Power Among Institutions, EU Agencies, Covert Integration in the European Union, and Political Representation and Democracy in the EU
- New authors and theoretical approaches on many topics such as differentiated integration, opt-outs and multispeed integration, negotiation and coalition building, the interplay of judicial and legislative policy-making, power distribution, agency behaviour, integration by subterfuge, and the democratic deficit
- Fully updated data and content throughout.

Jeremy Richardson is joined by a co-editor, Professor Sonia Mazey, for the fourth expanded edition of this highly regarded textbook on the EU.

Jeremy Richardson is Emeritus Fellow at Nuffield College, Oxford, UK, and Adjunct Professor at the National Centre for Research on Europe, University of Canterbury, New Zealand. He is also Founder and Co-editor of the *Journal of European Public Policy*.

Sonia Mazey is a Professor and Pro-Vice-Chancellor of the College of Business and Law, University of Canterbury, New Zealand, and formally a Fellow of Keble College, Oxford, UK.

D1421954

"Like its predecessors, the fourth edition of *European Union: Power and policy-making* will be a truly indispensable tool for teaching and research. Jeremy Richardson, and Sonia Mazey as his new co-editor, further expanded this highly regarded EU textbook to cover 20 timely chapters on key institutional and policy issues."

Gerda Falkner, Director, Institute for European Integration Research,
University of Vienna, Austria

"European integration has gained in complexity in recent years. Though it is increasingly contested, its influence on public policy has not been waning, far from it. This textbook, now a classic, manages to provide readers with information on recent developments, together with insights on how contributions from leading scholars in the field can improve our understanding of the changes under way. A 'must read' for advanced students, as well as for all those who want to make sense of the EU scene."

Renaud Dehousse, Director, Centre for European Studies,
Sciences Po, Paris, France

"*European Union: Power and policy-making* occupies a unique place among EU textbooks, presenting an in-depth and comprehensive discussion of all important institutions, processes and issues in today's EU. This edition, as the previous ones, remains essential reading for advanced students of the European Union. The list of contributors reads as a 'who's who' in the field of EU politics."

Sebastiaan Princen, Professor of Governance and Policymaking in the European
Union, Utrecht University, the Netherlands

"This fourth edition of *European Union: Power and policy-making* is, if anything, even more impressive than the earlier three editions. It contains a number of essays which make significant contributions to the study of the EU, and assist understanding of the Union in a comparative context. It is absolutely essential for any student of the EU, and indeed for any student of comparative politics."

B. Guy Peters, Adjunct Professor, Graduate School of Public and
International Affairs, University of Pittsburgh, USA

European Union

- Power and policy-making

Fourth edition

Edited by Jeremy Richardson and Sonia Mazey

Routledge
Taylor & Francis Group

LONDON AND NEW YORK

First edition published 1996
by Routledge

Third edition published 2006
by Routledge

Fourth edition published 2015
by Routledge
2 Park Square, Milton Park, Abingdon, Oxon, OX14 4RN

and by Routledge
711 Third Avenue, New York, NY 10017

Routledge is an imprint of the Taylor & Francis Group, an informa business

British Library Cataloguing-in-Publication Data

A catalogue record for this book is available from the British Library

Library of Congress Cataloging-in-Publication Data

European Union : power and policy-making / [edited by] Jeremy Richardson,
  Adjunct Professorial Fellow at the University of Canterbury and Emeritus
  Fellow, Nuffield College, Oxford, Sonia Mazey, Pro-Vice Chancellor and
  Associate Dean of Commerce at the College of Business and Economics,
  University of Canterbury — Fourth edition.
    pages cm
  1. European Union.   2. European Union countries—Politics and government.
I. Richardson, J. J. (Jeremy John)   II. Mazey, Sonia.
  JN30.E942 2015
  341.242'2—dc23
  2014027181

ISBN: 978-0-415-71550-8 (hbk)
ISBN: 978-0-415-71552-2 (pbk)
ISBN: 978-1-315-73539-9 (ebk)

Typeset in Century Old Style
by Apex CoVantage, LLC

Printed and bound in Great Britain by
TJ International Ltd, Padstow, Cornwall

To Lil and Jim Mazey who thought we could do no wrong and that the EU did everything wrong. We greatly miss their love, and hope that, wherever they are, there is no form of regional integration.

Contents

CONTENTS

Contents

Notes on contributors

Henrik Enderlein is Professor of Political Economy, Hertie School of Governance, Berlin, Germany.

Mark Franklin is John R. Reitemeyer Professor Emeritus Trinity College, Connecticut, USA.

Gregory W. Fuller is Professorial Lecturer at American University's School of International Service in Washington, D.C., USA.

Ole Funke is Desk Officer European Directorate-General, German Ministry of Foreign Affairs, Germany.

Adrienne Héritier holds a joint chair of political science in the Department of Political and Social Science and the Robert Schuman Centre for Advanced Studies at the European University Institute in Florence, Italy.

Sara B. Hobolt holds the Sutherland Chair in European Institutions and professor at the European Institute, London School of Economics and Political Science, UK.

Liesbet Hooghe is W.R. Kenan Distinguished Professor in Political Science at the University of North Carolina at Chapel Hill and Chair in Multilevel Governance at the VU University Amsterdam, Netherlands.

Christian B. Jensen is Assistant Professor of Political Science at the University of Nevada, Las Vegas, USA.

Erik Jones is Professor and Director of European and Eurasian Studies at The Johns Hopkins University School of Advanced International Studies, Washington, D.C., USA, and Bologna, Italy, and is Senior Research Fellow at Nuffield College, Oxford, UK.

Michael Keating holds the Chair of Scottish Politics at the University of Aberdeen, UK.

Christoph Knill is Professor of Political Science, University of Munich, Germany.

Sandra Kröger is a lecturer in European politics at the University of Exeter, UK.

Johannes Lindner is Head of Division of the EU Institutions and Fora Division in the Directorate General International and European Relations of the European Central Bank, Frankfurt, Germany.

Sonia Mazey is a Professor and Pro-Vice-Chancellor of the College of Business and Law, University of Canterbury, New Zealand.

Daniel Naurin is Professor of Political Science at the Centre for European Research (CERGU) and the Department of Political Science, University of Gothenburg, Sweden.

Jeremy Richardson is an Emeritus Fellow at Nuffield College, Oxford, UK, and Adjunct Professor at the National Centre for Research on Europe, University of Canterbury, New Zealand.

Berthold Rittberger is Professor of International Relations, University of Munich, Germany.

Frank Schimmelfennig is Professor of European Politics, Center for Comparative and International Studies, ETH Zurich, Switzerland.

Susanne K. Schmidt is Professor of Political Science, University of Bremen, and former Dean of the Bremen International School of Social Sciences (BIGSSS), Germany.

Jonathan B. Slapin is Associate Professor of Political Science and Director of the Center for International and Comparative Studies at the University of Houston, Texas, USA.

Michael Smith is Professor of European Politics at Loughborough University, UK.

Michaël Tatham is Associate Professor of Comparative Politics at the University of Bergen, Norway.

Mark Thatcher is Professor of Comparative and International Politics, London School of Economics, UK.

Robert Thomson is Professor of Politics, University of Strathclyde, Glasgow, UK.

Thomas Winzen is a post-doctoral researcher at the Center for Comparative and International Studies, ETH Zurich, Switzerland.

Arndt Wonka is Senior Researcher and Field Coordinator at the Bremen International Graduate School of Social Sciences (BIGSSS), Germany.

Preface

The first edition of this volume was published in 1996. That year saw the start of another Intergovernmental Conference (IGC) dominated by many of the familiar debates which have dogged the European Community and European Union since the historic first steps towards European integration taken in 1951. The 1996 agenda included such issues as the powers and organisation of the main European institutions, namely the Council, Commission, European Parliament (and national parliaments), and European Court of Justice; the power relations between these institutions; problems of enlargement; the role of non-governmental actors such as interest groups and citizen groups; the alleged democratic deficit; and, perhaps above all, the erosion of national sovereignty in the face of steady Europeanization. Over a decade and a half later, this agenda looks very familiar, albeit that the weighting of issues has changed. Thus, at the time of writing, July 2014, the successes of anti-European parties in the 2014 Euro-elections will undoubtedly cause greater emphasis to be placed on sovereignty issues.

It is conventional wisdom to describe the EU as a *sui generis* political system. We do not dispute that but argue that the EU is no longer a *new* political system. It has moved from adolescence to maturity and exhibits rather a high degree of stability. As was argued in the Preface to the third edition of this book, cries of 'Europe in crisis' and of Europe having lost its way were as familiar in 2005 as they were in 1996, at least suggesting a degree of agenda stability! Today's doomsters are no more likely to be right than they were in 1996 or 2005. They fail to appreciate the resilience of the EU, its capacity to adapt and learn, and its ability to change when needed. The key players are, generally, intelligent actors, capable of knowing when to touch the brake rather than the accelerator. Moreover, two main factors will enable the EU to continue, broadly, on its historic path. First, economic prosperity will, at some point, return to Europe. Thus, the EU should be able to rely on the old adage that rising prosperity buys off discontent. Secondly, we need to remember that the EU policy process, being mature, is very much about 'low politics' technical issues, not about high salience issues (such as immigration) that grab the headlines and turn voters against Europe. Thirdly, there is a very strong and varied coalition of pro-European actors who will mobilise against any major repatriation of EU public policy to the member states.

Thus, the main purpose of this new Edition is, as before, to explain to students of European integration the ways in which power is exercised in the EU. Our focus is on the policy-making process, as the ultimate arena of power on all societies. What role do the institutions and other actors play in deciding what European policy is about and determining the actual content of the now massive amount of EU 'legislation'? How does the EU 'policy engine' work?

As always, a huge debt is owed to our contributors. Each Edition has brought together a team of internationally recognised researchers. The team has changed with each new edition, as fresh perspectives are introduced. This fourth edition is no exception as we bid farewell to a number of valued colleagues and welcome many new ones. Each team has exhibited two overriding traits: sheer professionalism combined with a sophisticated understanding of what makes the EU 'tick'. As Editors, we owe our contributors a very personal debt, however, for their forbearance over the delays in completing the volume, as we managed the repair process to our home following the Christchurch earthquakes. At times, we became more concerned with house foundation designs rather than how codecision was working out, but our contributors' collective will won out in the end!

Jeremy Richardson and Sonia Mazey,
Christchurch, NZ,
July 2014

Part I

STATE BUILDING, DIFFERENTIATED INTEGRATION AND A MULTISPEED EUROPE

Chapter 1

The EU as a policy-making state

A policy system like any other?

JEREMY RICHARDSON

> Studying the EU ... it is natural to understand European integration as the progressive realization of an emerging system of authoritative rule at the supranational level.
> —Caporaso and Wittenbrick (2006: 472)

'Europeanization' and EU state building[1]

One of the main attributes of a modern political system is the ability to make what David Easton termed 'authoritative allocations of values' for society (Easton 1965). By this he meant policy outputs that are 'produced by ... or [that] are closely associated with those who hold positions of authority in the system and [that] thereby set the goals toward which the energies and resources of the system may be directed' (Easton 1965: 350). In practice this means an ability to formulate and implement public policy programmes governing the operation of society. Hix and Høyland, whilst rejecting the notion of the European Union (EU) as a state, see the EU as a political system in the manner described by Easton. Drawing on work by Almond and Easton in the mid-1950s they extract four key characteristics of a political system, as follows:

1   There is a stable and clearly defined set of institutions for collective decision-making and a set of rules governing relations between and within these institutions.
2   Citizens seek to realize their political desires through the political system, either directly or through intermediary organizations such as interest groups and political parties.
3   Collective decisions in the political system have a significant impact on the distribution of economic resources and the allocation of values across the whole system.
4   There is continuous interaction between these political outputs, new demands on the system, new decisions and so on.

(Hix and Høyland 2011: 12–13)

Easton produced a simplified model of a political system, as follows (Easton 1965: 32; see Figure 1.1).

Easton might not have intended it, but it is possible to substitute 'state' for 'system' in his model. Thus, if it is to persist over time, a state has as its key functions the

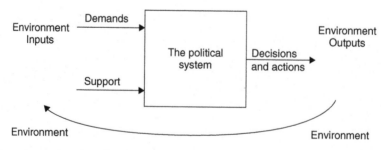

Figure 1.1 Easton's political systems model

generation of support, the processing of demands and the production of outputs (public policies) which in turn have an effect on the level of support and the generation of new demands via a feedback loop. Since the EU's inception, these interrelated processes have been very evident.

One can adapt Easton's simplified model of a political system and construct a simplified model of the EU policy-making state, as shown in Figure 1.2.

The main problem with Easton's model is that the political system is something of a black box, out of which decisions and actions emerge. The 'EU black box' is extremely productive in terms of 'decisions and actions'. As Hix and Høyland note, the EU now produces approximately 150 pieces of new legislation each year, more than in most other democratic polities (2011: 13). Moreover, the *range* of policy areas in which the EU has at least some remit is now quite vast. It is difficult to find a policy area which is not influenced in *some* way by the EU. However, this is not to suggest that Europeanization of public policy is uniform (for examples of variation in Europeanization of policy sectors; see Richardson 2012a; Rittberger and Shimmelfennig, in this volume). Thus, no scholars deny that Europeanization has taken place. However, what is now meant by the much used term Europeanization?

In fact, the term Europeanization is replete with definitional problems. In particular, as Caporaso points out, authors (including himself, he admits) often use the term Europeanization in two opposing senses, the creation of governance structures at the European level *and* the impact of the EU on domestic politics (Caporaso 2007: 27). However, Radaelli (2003) notes that Lawson has used 'Europeanization' rather differently than many authors have. Lawson identifies a *de jure transfer of power* to the EU in various sectors (albeit with a *de facto* lack of authority). He argues that 'Europeanization may also be interpreted as the transfer of power from national governments to supranational institutions' and views 'Europeanization as the shift in policy hegemony from national capitals to Brussels' (Lawton 1999: 94). He is not claiming that the power shift is absolute: 'Supranational authorities in Brussels play an increasing role in the shaping and policing of policy in Europe, but national institutions retain considerable authority

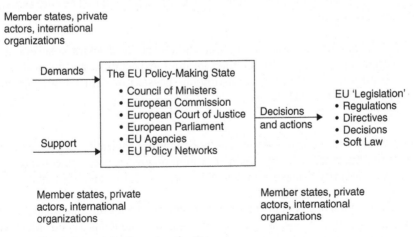

Figure 1.2 Easton's model adapted to the EU

and popular legitimacy' (Lawton 1999: 94). Lawton goes on to suggest that *policy-style* changes follow from the shift in power to Brussels:

> This shift in authority from the national to the EU level signifies a merging, rather than a convergence of European policy styles. A single European approach emerges, which is either a hybrid of previous national methods or mirrors a particular national policy style. European policy-making thus becomes a process dominated by supranational institutions.
>
> (1999: 94)

The notion of an emerging Euro-level policy style was earlier suggested by Mazey and Richardson. Labeling the style 'promiscuous policy-making' they argued that 'the emerging "European policy style" is likely to emphasize complex bargaining, complex coalition building, and consensus building in policymaking arenas somewhat distant from domestic institutional settings' (Mazey and Richardson 1995: 338). Apart from suggesting a new policy style, Lawton is really describing the construction of a completely new policymaking *venue* at the regional level. The creation and expansion of this venue have some inevitable consequences for member states and private actors who seek to extract policy gains from participation at this new policy-making venue. (For a discussion of venues and venue shift, see Baumgartner 2007; Baumgartner and Jones: 1993; Bouwen and McCown 2007; Broscheid and Coen 2007; Stephenson 2012.)

Without in any way wishing to claim that authors who use the term *Europeanization* in the sense of domestic adaptation are wrong to do so, I argue that it is also important to focus on the other 'face' of Europeanization in the sense that Lawton uses the term, namely the shift in the *locus* of public policy-making power to the EU level. By Europeanization I mean '*the processes by which the key decisions about public policies are gradually transferred to the European level (or for new policy areas, emerge at the European level)*'. My use of the term *Europeanization* is based on Ernst Haas's (1958) seminal *The Uniting of Europe*. Caporaso sees Haas's work as the research exemplar of the first wave of European integration (and integration theory) '... which was dominated by bottom-up thinking, i.e. the causal flow was predominantly from state and society of the member states to the regional organization' (Caporaso, 2007: 24). The core assertion in Haas's analysis was that

> [p]olitical integration is the process whereby political actors in several distinct settings are persuaded to shift their loyalties, expectations and political activities toward a new center, whose institutions possess or demand jurisdiction over pre-existing national states.
>
> (1958: 16)

Similarly, Olsen notes that some scholars 'portray Europeanization as the institutionalization at the European level of a distinct system of governance with common institutions and the authority to make, implement and enforce European-wide binding policies' (2007: 76).

Does the creation of a system of governance with common institutions and the authority to make binding decisions, as Olsen put it, mean that the EU is a state? Most writers are reluctant to answer yes, although sometimes resort to terms such as 'proto-state' in order to indicate that the EU does exhibit at least *some* state-like characteristics. One of the problems in answering the question is that there are many different conceptions of the state. As Caporaso argues, the answer one gives depends heavily on which definition of the state one has adopted. He relies on the concept 'forms of the state' developed by Cox (1983, 1986). 'Forms of state' is an umbrella concept within which many specific state structures can be accommodated. Caporaso treats '. . . each state form less as a discrete category and more as an emphasis, something to be accented rather than something to sort into a category . . . At best, we can think of different state forms . . .' (1996: 31). In his view, the EU exhibits aspects of different definitions of the state (Caporaso 1996: 34). For example, it has traditionally been argued that states possess a monopoly over the use of legitimate violence. Thus, 'the Westphalian state is the Weberian ideal in which monopolies of legitimate violence, rational bureaucracies and centralized policy-making authority correspond to territorially exclusive political orders' (Caporaso 1996: 34). If one were to accept that a monopoly of the legitimate use of violence is a central feature of any definition of the state, then, of course, the EU could not be described as a state. However, it is reasonable to argue that modern Western states rarely, if ever, rely on the threat (let alone actual use) of violence as a tool. The rule of law and an increasingly complex array of sanctions, incentives, and consensus-building processes are the common tools of government, not 'legitimate' violence. Western states seem extremely reluctant to use violence as a means of governing. In trying to decide what the EU is, we should not use as a yardstick, a rather crude concept of the state. In fact, it is odd that we cling to a 'monopoly of the legitimate use of violence' as the defining characteristic of the state at a time when there is so much emphasis on so-called new governance, the core aspect of which is actually relatively weak states sharing power with a wide range of other stakeholders. Indeed, it is possible to argue that new governance is not new at all as modern democracies have long practiced the processes of gover*nance* rather than govern*ment* (Richardson 2012b: 311–324).

In suggesting that the EU is clearly not a state, analysts might be making exactly the same mistake that Zweifel suggested is commonly made when claiming that the EU has a 'democratic deficit'. Zweifel compared the EU with the US and Switzerland on various measures of democracy and concluded that ' [w]hile there is much room for improvement, the EU does *not* suffer from a democratic deficit greater than that of the world's most liberal democracies' (2002: 812). Thomson's analysis of state sovereignty in international relations often refers to a 'monopoly on legitimate *coercion*' (1995: 214, emphasis added) which perhaps best captures the reality of power in modern Western states. The state still possesses strong powers to shape or control behaviour and to *coerce* people and organizations into some form of compliance, but this tends not to rest on the threat of legitimate violence by the state. Moreover, as Thomson suggests, one should not subscribe to some idealized model of state power and control. As she puts it '. . . there never was a time when state control over anything, including violence, was assured or secure . . . Sovereignty is not about state control but about state *authority*' (Thomson 1995: 216, emphasis added). Caporaso goes on to identify two other key conceptions of the state, *regulatory* and *postmodern*, which seem much more appropriate yardsticks by which to assess the EU (1996: 39–48).

One of the enduring puzzles about the EU is that everyone recognizes that it is hugely important, yet by conventional indicators, such as taxation revenue and spending totals, it is tiny and should, in theory, be quite weak. However, as Majone has argued, the European Commission has found that *regulation* is a very effective policy instrument, if only because the Commission does not bear the costs of any regulation (Majone 1994: 87). He also argues that the shift towards economic and social regulation has become widespread across many states (Majone 1996: 54–55). In that sense, characterizing the EU as a 'regulatory state' is not so radical. Not only has the amount of EU regulation increased hugely over time, but also

> [a] good part of national regulations are today of European origin or are produced in order to implement European legislation. As explanatory variables of the growth of statutory regulation in the member states, EC directives are even more significant than . . . American influences, privatization policies and the crisis of the Keynesian welfare state.
>
> (Majone 1996: 56)

Caporaso fleshes out the concept of an EU regulatory state as follows: 'The regulatory state is (in this case) essentially an international and arguably supranational state specializing in the control and management of international externalities' (1996: 9).

Idema and Kelemen, in criticizing the literature on 'new modes of governance' in the EU, point to the *coercive* powers of the EU as a regulatory state (although not using the term *coercion*). They place great emphasis on the link between the growth of EU regulation and what they see as '. . . the pervasive increase in the formality and judicialization of EU policy making' (Idema and Kelemen 2006: 109). They see a tendency to produce detailed and inflexible regulations as deeply rooted in the EU's political system, with a predilection for 'judicial enforcement of strict legal norms' (Idema and Kelemen 2006: 115). Moreover, they see member states as active parties in this aggrandizement of power by the EU. Far from the EU forcing member states to relinquish power, they argue that

> [m]ember states favour this approach because they fear becoming the 'sucker' that implements costly EU policies while others shirk. Therefore, they regularly support strict EU laws that can be readily monitored and enforced by the Commission, the ECJ and national courts . . . member states have an incentive to create rights for private parties and to enlist national courts to apply them.
>
> (Idema and Kelemen 2006: 116)

Insofar as EU policy-makers emphasize new modes of governance (often so-called soft law), this might simply be the EU velvet glove which hides the mailed fist of the 'strict legal norms' described by Idema and Kelemen. Moreover, by adopting this policy style (described as 'adversarial legalism' by Kagan [2001]) the EU has acquired for itself a kind of 'surrogate legitimate use of coercion' by relying on the considerable powers of national courts. If we accept the notion of the EU as a regulatory state, what next? Caporaso argues that

> We should not expect the EU to look like a traditional nation-state at all, nor its future development to follow the beaten path from intergovernmental relations to confederation to federation . . . the regulatory state is not the Westphalian

state, the extractive state, or the social democratic state, its future contours are not likely to resemble these states more than at present.

(1996: 41)

His suggestion that we need to 'think out of the box' when envisioning the EU state has also been advocated by Skocpol (2008) in her classic work 'Bringing the State Back In'. Thus, she argues that 'above the level of national states, the growth of international federations and institutional undertakings by the United Nations and other transnational bodies can be understood as new kinds of state building' (Skocpol, 2008: 116).

Caporaso's third conception of the state, the postmodern state, also has particular attractions when considering if the EU is some kind of state. Caporaso suggests that

> [t]he post-modern state contrasts most strongly with the Westphalian state. It is abstract, disjointed, increasingly fragmented, not based on stable and coherent coalitions of issues or constituencies, and lacking a clear public space within which competitive visions of the good life and pursuit of self-interested legislation are discussed and debated.
>
> (1996: 45)

He captures well the 'messiness' of the EU when he notes that (a) politics and governance occupy different sites, (b) process and activity become more important than structure and fixed institutions and (c) the state becomes not so much a thing as a set of spatially detached activities, diffused across the Member States but reflecting no principled – let alone constitutional – considerations (Caporaso 1996: 45).

The postmodern state can be expected to be more changeable than the Westphalian state, not least because it responds to changes in public policy. This link between policy and politics has been noted by Skocpol, too, as an aspect of state building. She is surely right to argue that

> [a]fter new public policies come into existence, they *reshape* subsequent political processes in various ways. The steps taken to implement new or adjusted public programs are likely to modify the capacities of governmental organizations; so state capacities change.
>
> (Skocpol 2008: 116)

The difficulty in capturing the 'stateness' of the EU is that it really is a *sui generis* political system. Moreover, it is based not on force (legitimate use of violence) but on two quite different principles. The first principle is that member states have decided, voluntary, to give up ever-increasing amounts of their sovereignty. This behaviour is often driven by uncertainty. As Peter Haas argued, the politics of uncertainty lead to a certain mode of behaviour, namely that policy-makers, when faced with 'the uncertainties associated with many modern responsibilities of international governance turn to new and different channels of advice, often with the result that international policy coordination is advanced' (1992: 14). Whilst wise counsels in the EU usually prevail, in the sense that stakeholders recognize that compromise and mutual gains go hand in hand, the EU is also characterized by considerable conflict. Indeed, external perceptions of the EU are often couched in terms of disunity and chaos. There are often bitter policy disputes (note the fundamental conflict over the response to the 2011 sovereign debt crisis), yet the policy game continues, because exit for any one player is either politically impossible or very costly (see Jensen and Slapin, in this volume). This feature is not unique to the EU and is quite normal in bargaining situations. Cooperation and conflict go hand in hand. The EU policy process is rather like a football match in which each player in the team wants the game played according to his or her own set of rules yet accepts that he or she has to be on the team nevertheless. It is certainly not chaos, even though it might appear so to outsiders, and it 'works' in the sense that the EU manages to produce a huge and increasingly varied amount of public policy output.

The second principle of the EU state is the rule of law, especially the doctrine of the supremacy of EU law and direct effect. There is no effective challenge to the doctrine of the supremacy of EU law over national law, and it is a fundamental principle of the EU 'state'. Once agreement is reached and a proposal is passed into EU law, that law can be enforced in various ways, not by an EU police force or an EU army but enforceable nevertheless. Thus, we see replicated at the EU level what is perfectly familiar at the level of nation-states. Laws have enormous force, and compliance does not require physical violence from the state to enforce them. That is not to say that all EU laws are obeyed, no more than all federal laws in the US are obeyed.

My argument is that the EU meets at least the original Latin meaning of *state*, namely meaning 'public order or organization', and has over time acquired for itself most of the features of western democratic states, apart from (what I regard as a somewhat outdated feature of modern states) the monopoly of the legitimate use of violence. Above all, it has acquired for itself, in very many policy areas, the central function of a modern state, the power to decide on public policies that were hitherto the province of member states. In that sense the EU has acquired quite a high degree of sovereignty and by so doing has begun to look very state-like or, as I put it, a *policy-making state* (Richardson 2012a). This shift in the *locus* of power to the EU as a policy-making state obviously does cause adaptation at member state (and sub-state) level but the phenomenon is perhaps best termed *Euro-adaption* rather than Europeanization. As Laffan *et al.* suggest, the defining characteristic of the Union is the enmeshing of the national and the European, or the embedding of the national in the European (2000: 74–78). This has led to what they term a system of 'international governance', with the EU, as an arena of public policy, presenting 'a challenge to national political systems because they are confronted with the need to adapt to a normative and strategic environment that escapes total control' (Laffan *et al.* 2000: 84–87). The EU is, of course, a complex and (like national policy systems) to some degree a unique policymaking system. Its multinational and neo-federal nature, the extreme openness of decision-making to lobbyists, and the considerable weight of national politico-administrative elites within the process, create an unpredictable and multilevel policymaking environment. Even the relationships among key institutions – such as the Commission, the European Parliament (EP), the Council of Ministers (CM) and the European Court of Justice (ECJ) – has been in a considerable state of flux for many decades, with each treaty reform producing a new 'institutional settlement'. Borrás and Radaelli see the treaties as 'governance architectures', defined as 'strategic and long-term political initiatives of international organizations on cross-cutting policy issues locked in commitments about targets and processes' (2011: 464. For an excellent analysis of the treaty reform process see Part II, 'Treaties', in Jones *et al.* [2012: 79–178]). These governance architectures typically combine old and new organizational structures (Borrás and Radaelli 2011: 464). The governance architecture of the EU has been a long-running cause of dispute. Describing the EU governance as a 'loosely coupled multi level system', Benz warns that 'hardly stabilized by institutional rules, governance depends to a considerable extent on strategic actions among participants' (2010: 224). The EU policy process has exhibited, at best, some stable patterns of cross-national coalition building and, at worst, some of the extreme aspects of a garbage can (Cohen *et al.* 1972) model of decision-making (see the following discussion).The EU policy process is undoubtedly 'messy', but we should be a little cautious in seeing it as especially unusual or indeed especially bad. It may be ugly but many aspects are perfectly familiar to policy analysts (see Mazey and Richardson, in this volume). 'Ugly but familiar' is probably a fair description.

The EU policy style: consensual promiscuity

The very 'messiness' of the EU as a policy system makes it difficult to formulate reliable descriptions – let alone theoretical models – which capture more than a few aspects of the policy process as a whole or which apply to all cases. However, one of the central features of the EU policy process, which seems to hold good for a high percentage of cases, is that it 'works' only by mobilizing a large number of public and private actors, from different nations and policy domains and, somehow, persuading them to move from the status quo to a new policy settlement. Hence the popularity of theoretical approaches that focus on the key role that policy communities and policy networks play in the EU. Analysing EU policy-making via this actor-based or 'stakeholder perspective' also enables us to utilize related approaches to the study of policymaking which emphasize the importance of ideas, knowledge and expertise, rather than pure 'interest'. Elsewhere in this volume, contributors analyse the roles of 'official' or 'public' stakeholders (e.g. national governments, the Commission, the EP, the ECJ). However, all of these actors are influenced by ideas, knowledge and private interests. Thus, more than 40 years ago E.E. Schattschneider reminded us that the supreme instrument of political power was the ability to determine what politics was about (Schattschneider 1960). The EU agenda-setting process is especially problematic because of its transnational nature and because of the wide range of state and non-state actors involved in the EU policy process. As Princen points out, '. . . agenda setting is a combination of political activism and outside events . . .' which produces a degree of unpredictability (2012: 38; see also Princen [2007] and Peters [1994]). Moreover, as with nation-states, the EU's policy agenda is permeable to extraterritorial influences – from non-EU states such as the US, Japan and China but also from international standard-setting bodies and organisations such as the World Health Organization (Richardson 1994), the Organisation for Economic Co-operation and Development (Dostal 2004) and via the EU's participation in global regulatory agencies such as the World Trade Organization (Poletti 2011). Such complex policy-making arrangements can, under certain circumstances, privilege the role of experts and technocrats in agenda setting, who are increasingly transnational in their focus and activities. Thus, analysis of the role of 'communities' of experts – so-called epistemic communities (see the following discussion) is important in understanding policy dynamics in the EU. The policy community/network approach, in contrast, appears to have some utility in assisting our understanding of the ways in which agenda issues are translated or 'processed' into technical and workable EU legislative proposals, especially in areas of 'low politics' (Hoffmann 1966). Once big problems are 'unpacked' into more manageable technical issues, stakeholders can bargain and negotiate in a more cooperative manner. The essence of policy community politics is consensus building. Thus, as Richardson and Jordan argued (in their case, describing British policy-making),

> [i]n describing the tendency for boundaries between government and groups to become less distinct through a whole range of pragmatic developments, we see policies being made (and administered) between a myriad of interconnecting, interpenetrating organizations. It is the relationship involved in committees, *the policy community* of departments and groups, the practices of cooption and the consensual style, that perhaps better account for policy outcomes than do examinations of party stances, of manifestos or of parliamentary influence.
>
> (1979: 73–74)

Other related concepts from public policy, which attempt to integrate analyses of ideas and interests – such as Sabatier's 'advocacy coalitions' (discussed later) and Kingdon's 'policy streams' (discussed later) are also useful in assisting our understanding dynamics of the EU, especially if we view the EU policy process as essentially a multi-arena, multilevel game. They may enable us to better understand how all decision-makers in the EU, public or private, national or supranational, come to 'frame' problems (Rein and Schön 1991). Interestingly, in terms of our earlier reference to coercion, Fischer sees the construction of 'social meanings' (akin to framing) as a more basic strategy for generating support in a democratic system than coercion. Thus, although coercion can help to counter political resistance, 'the most basic strategy for support in democratic systems is the evocation of social and political interpretations that legitimize the desired course of action' (Fischer 2003: 55).

The 'level of analysis' question is, of course, important. Thus, it may be a mistake to look for only one model of the EU policy process. As Scharpf argued, '. . . competition among poorly fitting and contested generalizations could be overcome if European studies made use of a plurality of simpler and complimentary concepts, each of which is meant to represent the specific characteristics of certain subsets of multi-level interactions . . .' (Scharpf 2010: 214). Within the EU, policy can be determined at a number of levels and the policy process goes through a number of stages. Also, particular policy areas may themselves be episodic, exhibiting different characteristics at different times. Different models of analysis may be useful at different levels the EU and at different stages of the policy process. For example, if we were to conceptualize the EU policy process into four stages – agenda setting, policy formulation, policy decision, and policy implementation – we might need to utilize rather different conceptual tools in order to understand fully the nature of the processes in each stage. The epistemic communities approach might be particularly useful in understanding stage 1, the policy community/network model for stage 2, institutional analysis for stage 3, and inter-organisational behaviour and implementation analysis for stage 4. Even then, reality is likely to be much more messy, suggesting that we need a fairly eclectic use of concepts and models. 'Grand theory' must await a much stronger empirical base, bearing in mind that there are major cross-sectoral variations in EU policy styles. (For examples of cross-sectoral variation, see Richardson 2012a).

It is also important to note that the EU policy-making system as a whole might vary over time. Thus, just as the pace and nature of the integration process is not constant, so the nature of the policy process within it can vary over time. For example it is now conventional wisdom that the (allegedly weaker) Commission is rather less inclined to resort to regulation, reflecting the increased resistance from business groups to further costly regulations and the rise of Euro-scepticism more generally (see Wonka, in this volume). The annual output of directives has declined, and there is an alleged shift towards new policy instruments that emphasize cooperation, voluntary action, demonstration projects, good practice, benchmarking, and so forth. The introduction of the so-called Open Method of Coordination (OMC) following the Lisbon summit in 2000 can be seen as a *process* reform (Borrás and Jacobsson 2004: 188) designed to meet criticisms of old-style, top-down, and *dirigiste* legislation. Thus, it is essentially intergovernmental, there is no role for the ECJ, with the Council and the Commission 'relying to a larger extent on political rather than legal logic' (Borrás and Jacobsson 2004: 188). Thus, policy styles can change, sometimes dramatically (Richardson 2000). In the context of the EU, Sable and Zeitlin use the concept of 'experimentalist governance' to capture the emergence of a new style of governing the EU. Thus,

> [i]n this decision-making design, framework goals (such as full employment, social inclusion, 'good water status', a unified energy grid) and measures for gauging their achievement are established by joint action of the Member States and EU institutions. Lower-level units (such as national ministries or regulatory authorities and the actors with whom they collaborate) are given the freedom to advance these ends as they see fit. Subsidiarity in this architecture implies that in writing framework rules the lower-level units should be given sufficient autonomy in implementing the rules to be able to propose changes to them. But in return for this autonomy, they must report regularly on their performance, especially as measured by the agreed indicators, and participate in a peer review in which their results are compared with those pursuing other means to the same general ends. Finally, the framework goals, metrics, and procedures themselves are periodically revised by the actors who initially established them, augmented by such new participants whose views come to be seen as indispensable to full and fair deliberation.
>
> (Sabel and Zeitlin 2008: 273–74)

This more flexible approach of OMC and the spread of experimentalist governance should not be seen as having obliterated old-style EU regulation, however. The greater emphasis on 'softer' policy instruments may actually disguise the continuation and extension of old-style regulation (see Idema and Kelemen 2006; Rittberger and Richardson 2003). The shift towards softer policy instruments has been accompanied by an intensification of consultation of stakeholders (see Mazey and Richardson, in this volume). The more the policy-making legitimacy of the EU has been challenged, the more the Commission has mobilized stakeholder participation in the process. Interestingly, the expansion of consultation also appears as a feature of OMC. Thus, 'OMC seeks to mobilize the participation of a wide range of actors, public as well as private. In terms of actor constellation, the OMC is multi-level, involves other than state actors, and is designed to foster co-operative practices and networking' (Borrás and Jacobsson 2004: 189).

While big constitutional issues and meta-policy issues are, of course, important, and certainly absorb the interest of national governments, the 'European policy game' continues to be played at the detailed policy level and continues to attract the attention and efforts of a plethora of interest groups and others in the manner predicted by the neo-functionalists. Low politics this may be, in the Hoffmann (1966) terminology, but it is probably the nine-tenths of the EU 'policy iceberg' that is below the water line. Also, we need to remember that the EU is no longer a 'new' policy system. In terms of institutional design, it has been in a state of flux, but the key point, for our purposes, is that it has been churning out public policy for a very long time. There is a huge amount of so-called low politics activity within the EU (just as there is in any of the member states), much of it revising and reforming existing EU policies as well as extending the EU's into yet more policy areas (for example, see Greer 2012). This policy-making activity is not simply a question of intergovernmental relations – if only because such a wide range of non-governmental organizations is so obviously involved, at both the national, the EU, and the extra-EU level. EU policies are not simply the outcome of interstate bargaining, even if the policy process usually appears to culminate in the CM. It is a long and complex process involving many different types of actors, most of whom are involved in a series of 'nested games' (Tsebelis 1990), in serial coalition building, and a constant process of bargaining (see Farrell and Héritier 2005).

All governmental systems, including that of the EU, devise procedural mechanisms (formal and informal institutions, formal and informal rules) to bring stakeholders together to thrash out solutions to which they can sign up. There is a *procedural logic* which brings policy actors together in some kind of ad hoc or permanent relationship – hence, the popularity in public policy analysis of variants of the policy network approach which emphasizes bargaining and consensus rather than hierarchy. The very fact that it is now more difficult, in the face of Euro-scepticism, to introduce new Euro legislation, simply further incentivizes Euro-level policy-makers to redouble their efforts to incorporate as many private actors as they can. As Mazey and Richardson suggest in this volume, the trend is for more and more participation in the EU policy process. Similarly, Sable and Zeitlin argue that 'the diffusion of procedural commitments to transparency and participation in EU networked governance has had a democratizing destabilization effect in terms of stimulating demands to widen the circle of actors and alternatives in policy making at the national as well as at the European level' (Sabel and Zeitlin 2008: 315–16). The number of actors now involved in the EU policy process is so great, and the rate of ad hoc coalition formation so rapid, such that the EU policy style is best characterized as *consensual promiscuity*.

A simple picture of policy-making in which a limited number of 'recognized' stakeholders in a tightly drawn policy community granted the franchise for a given area of public policy is difficult to sustain when the number and range of stakeholders expands rapidly. Within the EU (and, again, similar trends can be seen at the national level), the pattern appears to be an increase in the number of stakeholders (public and private) demanding and getting participation in EU policy-making, and an extension of the range of policy sectors from which they are drawn, for each particular example of consultation (Richardson 2000). This gradual shift in emphasis – from a world of policy-making characterized by tightly knit policy communities to a more loosely organized and therefore less predictable policy process – is very familiar in the US. The seminal work (on either side of the Atlantic) is still Heclo's 1978 analysis, which began to redirect us towards policy *dynamics* rather than policy stability. Just as many authors (including this one!) were emphasizing stable policy communities, Heclo had observed a trend which appears to be still running strongly at both the national and international levels – namely that policy problems often eventually escape the confined and exclusive 'worlds' of professionals and are resolved in a much looser configuration of participants in the policy process. Heclo argued that the nature of power in Washington had begun to change. Exercising power was not as much fun as it used to be in the 'clubby' days of Washington politics (Heclo 1978: 94). Politics was less 'clubbable' because more and more groups had entered the policy process. Thus, 'as proliferating groups have claimed a stake and clamoured for a place in the policy process, they have helped diffuse the focus of political and administrative leadership' (Heclo 1978: 94–95). The process had gone so far, he argued:

> With more public policies, more groups are being mobilized and there are more complex relationships among them. Since very few policies ever seem to drop off the public agenda as more are added, congestion among those interested in issues grows, the chances for accidental collisions increase, and the interaction tends to take on a distinctive group-life of its own in the Washington community. One scene in a recent Jacques Tati film pictures a Paris traffic circle so dense with traffic that no one can get in or out; instead, drivers spend their time socialising with each other as they drive in endless circles. Group politics in Washington may be becoming such a merry-go-round.
>
> (Heclo 1978: 97)

In the context of the EU, all we need do is substitute Brussels for Washington. Correctly, Heclo argued that we needed to rethink our notions of political power as existing concepts of power and control were not well suited to the 'loose-jointed' power play of influence that was emerging. In a now classic formulation, he argued that

> [o]bviously questions of power are still important. But for a host of policy initiatives undertaken in the last twenty years it is all but impossible to identify clearly who the dominant actors are. Who is controlling those actions that go to make up our national policy on abortions, or on income redistribution, or consumer protection, or energy? Looking for the few who are powerful we tend to overlook the many whose webs of influence provoke and guide the exercise of power. These webs, or what I will call 'issue networks', are particularly relevant to the highly intricate and confusing welfare policies that have been undertaken in recent years.
>
> (Heclo 1978: 102)

Asking 'Who runs this place?' is a singularly difficult question within the EU. The safe answer is usually 'Many people run this place'. Even Heclo, however, was reluctant to accept a total-disorder thesis, making at least two important qualifications to the model of confusion, diffuse power, and lack of accountability. He pointed out a paradox of disorder *and* order when he argued that there was a second tendency cutting in the opposite direction to the widening group participation in public policy. In the midst of the emergence of the loose-issue networks cited earlier we could also see what he called 'policy as intramural activity'. Thus, 'expanding welfare policies and Washington's reliance on indirect administration have encouraged the development of specialized subcultures composed of highly knowledgeable policy-watchers ... what they (*the participants*) all have in common is the detailed understanding of specialized issues that comes from sustained attention to a given policy debate' (Heclo 1978: 49). It is to the role of knowledge and expertise in bringing some order to the apparently chaotic EU policy process that we now turn.

Policy-making under uncertainty: knowledge and mutual gains

The EU is faced with 28 different policy systems, each reflecting national power structures (and national policy networks). They bring to the Brussels table their own public policy traditions in terms of policy and regulatory styles. The EU is, therefore, a huge cauldron of policy proposals, ideas, and traditions from which EU public policy must be distilled. If European integration via EU public policy is to take place, national policy arrangements must be challenged in some way and new Euro-level policy settlements agreed. Although the processes of EU policy formulation and implementation are generally consensual, there are, of course, some aspects of an impositional policy style in the EU (Richardson 1982). Thus, Qualified Majority Voting (QMV) in the end 'imposes' decisions on the losers in any policy conflict, and ECJ decisions are difficult to ignore. EU legislation is neither symbolic nor cheap talk. It matters materially to a whole host of actors, not least national governments but also many private actors. It is not surprising therefore that the range of potential actors active in the EU policy process is enormous (they know that it is best to shoot where the ducks are!), and the patterns of interaction are sometimes unpredictable.

Garbage can politics

With so many actors and so many ideas, how, then, does policy change take place within the EU in the absence of a European government or at least a stable 'governing' coalition? In a key passage, Adler and Haas argue that it is useful to turn the study of the political process into a question about who learns what, when, to whose benefit, and why (1992: 370). Perceiving the policy process as centrally concerned with ideas, knowledge, and their use is both helpful and consistent with our concern with actor-based models of the policy process. The work by Peter Haas and his colleagues is of particular relevance to the workings of the EU. Although concerned with international cooperation (and therefore approaching the EU from an international relations perspective) Haas's comment that 'a related question/debate is the extent to which state actors fully recognize and appreciate the anarchic nature of the system and, consequently, whether rational choice, deductive-type approaches or interpretative approaches are most appropriate' is very apposite to our own task here (1992: 2). Acting rationally in situations of very high uncertainty and in the absence of crucial information about the policy positions of other stakeholders is difficult. Indeed, actors may be totally unaware of other stakeholders in the process, let alone of the policy preferences and strategies of those actors. The total 'system' is large and amorphous, with large numbers of part-time participants and a wide range of ideas floating around in some ethereal fashion. In these situations, processes may resemble the 'garbage can' model of decision-making developed by Cohen *et al.* in 1972 and elaborated by Kingdon (1984). The central feature of the original garbage can model is that 'decision situations' (or what Cohen *et al.* termed 'organized anarchies') are characterized by three general properties. First, there are problematic preferences. The organization operates based on a variety of inconsistent and ill-defined preferences (Cohen *et al.* 1972: 1) Their description of organisational life fits well with what we already know about some aspects of the EU, namely that 'it [the organisation] can be described better as a loose collection of ideas than as a coherent structure; it discovers preferences through action more than it acts on the basis of preferences' (Cohen *et al.* 1972: 1). The second characteristic of decision situations is unclear technology. Although the organization manages to survive and even produce, its own processes are not well understood by its members. A succession of Inter-Governmental Conferences (IGCs) has considered demands for the simplification of the EU policy process and for greater predictability of decision pathways, but the EU policy process remains complex and opaque. Thus, following the 2014 EU elections in France in which the far right gained nearly 25 per cent of the vote, President Hollande complained that the EU project had become 'remote and incomprehensible'. Europe had to become simple and clear, he argued. In fact, the EU is just like any other decision-making organization. Over time it changes its procedures in the light of past practice and experience and it has a capacity for policy learning that leads to a continuous process of policy and institutional adjustment. In practice, organizations such as the national governments and the EU operate 'on the basis of simple trial-and-error procedures, the residue of learning from the incident of past experience, and pragmatic inventions of necessity' (Cohen *et al.* 1972: 1). Third, there is fluid participation in that participants vary in the amount of time and effort they devote to different domains. In practice, it is useful to view an organization as '*a collection of choices looking for problems, issues and feelings looking for decision situations in which they might be aired, solutions looking for issues to which they might be the answer, and decision-makers looking for work*' (Cohen *et al.* 1972: 2).

Recognizing that organizations can learn is a key aspect of Peter Haas's argument, namely that the politics of uncertainty leads to a certain mode of behaviour – namely that policy-makers, when faced with 'the uncertainties associated with many modern responsibilities of international governance turn to new and different channels of advice, often with the result that international policy co-ordination is advanced' (1992: 12).

One common source of advice that policy-makers seek out is so-called epistemic communities which Haas defines as

> [a]n epistemic community is a network of professionals with recognised expertise and competence in a particular domain and an authoritative claim to policy-relevant knowledge within that domain or issue-area. Although an epistemic community may consist of professionals from a variety of disciplines and backgrounds, they have (1) a shared set of normative and principled beliefs, which provide a value-based rationale for the social action of community members; (2) shared causal beliefs, which are derived from their analysis of practices leading or contributing to a central set of problems in their domain and which then serve as the basis for elucidating the multiple linkages between possible

policy actions and desired outcomes; (3) shared notions of validity-that is, inter-subjective, internally defined criteria for weighing and validating knowledge in the domain of their expertise; and (4) a common policy enterprise-that is, a set of common practices with a set of problems to which their professional competence is directed, presumably out of the conviction that human welfare will be enhanced as a consequence.

(1992: 3)

Under conditions of uncertainty actors not only turn to new sources of advice; they are also prepared to engage in negotiation processes even when there is disagreement over basic goals or even core beliefs. The key role of epistemic communities in this process, which may well lead to changes in actors' preferences, relates directly to the principle that policy-makers are operating under conditions of uncertainty. Thus,

[g]iven the technical uncertainties regarding an issue and the legitimacy of claims to expertise of members of an epistemic community, especially those placed close to the decision-making process, their influence may cause the perceived interests of key players in different countries to grow closer together, along with their understanding of underlying causal relationships. In this situation, the epistemic community members may come to act as a coordinated set of common interpretative filters.

(Sebenius 1992: 354)

It is the knowledge-based (or at least perceived knowledge-based) nature of epistemic communities that provides these networks of actors with the potential to influence the policy process. Authoritativeness, and therefore legitimacy, is the key currency of these types of networks.

Interestingly, Haas sees some kind of 'logic' in this process of policy coordination via epistemic communities. The situation in which policy-makers find themselves leads almost naturally to the use of experts of various kinds. Just as it has been argued in Britain that there is a 'logic of negotiation' (Jordan and Richardson 1982; see also Mazey and Richardson, in this volume), so the dynamics of uncertainty, interpretation and institutionalization at the international level drive policy-makers towards the use of epistemic communities. Haas argues that 'in international policy coordination, the forms of uncertainty that tend to stimulate demands for information are those which arise from the strong dependence of states on each other's policy choices for success in obtaining goals and those which involve multiple and only partly estimable consequences of action' (1992: 3–4). Uncertainty gives rise to demands for information – particularly about 'social or physical processes, their interrelationship with other processes, and the likely consequences of actions that require considerable scientific or technical expertise' (Haas 1992: 4). In a key passage, Haas argues that epistemic communities play a central role in the policy process:

Epistemic communities are one possible provider of this sort of information and advice. As demands for such information arise, networks or communities of specialists capable of producing and providing the information emerge and proliferate. The members of a prevailing community become strong actors at the national and transnational level as decision-makers solicit their information and delegate responsibility to them. A community's advice, though, is informed by its own broader world view. To the extent to which an epistemic community consolidates bureaucratic power within national administrations and international secretariats, it stands to institutionalise its influence and insinuate its view into broader international politics.

Members of transnational epistemic communities can influence state interests either by directly identifying them for decision-makers or by illuminating the salient dimensions of an issue from which the decision-makers may then deduce their interests. The decision-makers in one state may, in turn, influence the interests and behaviour of other states, thereby increasing the likelihood of convergent state behaviour and international policy coordination, informed by the causal beliefs and policy preferences of the epistemic community. Similarly, epistemic communities may contribute to the creation and maintenance of social institutions that guide international behaviour. As a consequence of the continued influence of these institutions, established patterns of cooperation in a given issue-area may persist even though systematic power concentrations may no longer be sufficient to compel countries to coordinate their behaviour.

(Haas 1992: 5)

However, no one (not even Haas) is arguing that epistemic communities explain everything about the policy process. The influence of epistemic communities is over the *form* of policy choices – 'the extent to which state behavior reflects the preferences of these networks remains strongly conditioned by the distribution of power internationally' (Haas 1992: 7). As Héritier and Farrell suggest, epistemic communities sometimes lead to an acceleration of regional integration and sometimes not. They, too, see power and bargaining as very important, although they conclude that epistemic factors are a key negotiating resource in many contexts. Thus, epistemic communities 'may fundamentally reshape the parameters within which political actors bargain – and do this while bargaining is taking place' (Farrell and Héritier 2005: 288).

Although the (often indirect) power of epistemic communities is considerable, it is constrained by the need of policy-makers – at both the EU and national levels – to involve and bargain with other powerful actors, particularly conventional interest groups. For example, epistemic communities in the cancer research field are very active in trying to influence policy-makers, but the latter also have to deal with the well-resourced and powerful tobacco industry. One should be cautious, therefore, in arguing that knowledge and ideas are paramount. As Jacobsen argued in his now-classic article, the flaw in the 'power of ideas' arguments is their failure to take account of the fact that ideas and interests cannot be separated (1995: 309). As Campbell also emphasizes, 'arguing that ideational conditions affect policy-making outcomes does not mean that interests are unimportant' (1998: 400). Like Jacobsen, he argues that it is the interaction of ideas and interests that is important. It is to the often-messy processes in which ideas and actors interact that we now turn.

The 'primeval soup' of the EU and the importance of advocacy coalitions

As Kingdon suggests, the phrase 'an idea whose time has come' captures a fundamental reality about 'an irresistible movement that sweeps over our politics and our society pushing aside everything that might stand in its path' (1984: 1). He identifies a number of possible actors in the agenda-setting process, including the mobilization of relevant publics by leaders, the diffusion of ideas in professional circles among policy elites, particular bureaucrats, changes in party control or in intra-party ideological balances brought about by elections. The processes involved in agenda-setting are identified as being of three kinds – problems, policies, and politics (Kingdon 1984: 17). His objective is to move the analysis from the usual political science preoccupation with pressure and influence and instead to explore the world of ideas. Using a revised version of the Cohen *et al.* (1972) garbage can model, Kingdon analyses three 'process streams' flowing through the system–streams of problems, policies, and politics, largely independent of each other. He likens the generation of policy to a process of biological natural selection. Thus,

> many ideas are possible in principle and float around in a 'policy soup' in which specialists try out their ideas in a variety of ways…proposals are floated, come into contact with one another, are revised and combined with one another, and floated again . . . the proposals that survive to the status of serious consideration meet several criteria, including their technical feasibility, their fit with dominant values and the current national mood, their budgetary workability, and the political support or opposition they might experience. Thus the selection system narrows the set of conceivable proposals and selects from that large set a short list of proposals that is actually available for serious consideration.
>
> (Kingdon 1984: 21)

He argues that the separate streams of problems, policies, and politics come together at certain critical times. Solutions are joined to problems, and both of them are joined to favourable political forces. The timing of this coupling is influenced by the appearance of 'policy windows': these windows are opened either by the appearance of compelling problems or by happenings in the political stream (Kingdon 1984: 21). Again, this seems to fit the EU rather well. For example both in energy policy (Eberlein 2012) and competition policy (Blauberger 2012), the Commission has been adept at exploiting windows of opportunity in order to bring about policy change.

Kingdon cites one of his (US) respondents as saying that it is almost impossible to trace the origin of a proposal: 'This is not like a river. There is no point of origin' (1984: 77). There is an almost uncanny resemblance between this description of US policy making and the perceptions of key actors in the EU policy process. Identifying just where a policy 'started' in the EU is extremely difficult – hence, the common response from those intimately involved in the EU policy process that 'policies seem to come from nowhere'. Kingdon is at pains to point out, however, that the processes he describes are not entirely random. (Just as Heclo [1978] was not ready to accept the total disorder notion.) Thus 'some degree of pattern is evident in these fundamental sources: processes within each stream, processes that structure couplings, and general constraints on the system' (Kingdon 1984: 216).

One reason why the process is not random is, of course, that policy problems and policy ideas both help determine actor preferences and attract coalitions of actors. As we have argued, the EU policy process is at least 'mature' in the sense that it has produced a mass of public policy and continues to generate yet more policy proposals and outputs. The institutional rules have been uncertain and the balance between EU institutions has been in a state of flux, but the policy game has carried on just the same. Essentially, EU policy-making is institutionalized 'repeat social interaction'. As Busch argues, situations of repeat social interactions pose special problems for game theorists and rational choice analysts (1999: 36). He quotes Hechter as arguing that game theory 'must not be judged solely by the mathematical elegance of its solutions, but by its capacity to shed light on those real world collective action problems' (Hechter 1990: 248). Busch sees ideational factors as one way out of trying to explain repeated games. He cites work by Garrett and Weingast, arguing that ideas can play a potentially pivotal role as 'shared beliefs may act as "focal points" around which the behaviour of actors converges' (1993: 176). Sabatier also argues that (within a policy sub-system)

> actors can be aggregated into a number of advocacy coalitions composed of people from various organizations who share a set of normative and causal beliefs and who often act in concert. At any particular point in time, each coalition adopts a strategy(s) envisaging one or more institutional innovations which it feels will further its objectives.
>
> (Sabatier 1988: 133)

An advocacy coalition can include actors from a variety of positions (elected and agency officials, interest group leaders, researchers) who share a particular belief system, that is a set of basic values, causal assumptions and problem perceptions, and who show a non-trivial degree of coordination over time. Sabatier developed the model partly in response to the complexity of policy sub-systems. Using the US air-pollution control sub-system as an example, he found that it contained a large diverse set of actors. Normally, he argues, the number of advocacy coalitions would be quite small – in a quiescent sub-system' there might be only a single coalition; in others, between two and four (Sabatier 1988: 140). To Sabatier, it is shared beliefs which provide the principal 'glue' of politics. Indeed, he emphasizes stability of belief systems as an important characteristic of policy sub-systems. Policy change within a sub-system can be understood as the product of two processes: first, the efforts of advocacy coalitions within the sub-system to translate the policy cores and the secondary aspects of their belief systems into governmental programmes and, second, the systemic events, for example changes in socio-economic coalitions, outputs from other sub-systems, and changes in the system-wide governing coalition, affect the resources and the constraints on the sub-system actors, that is policy change takes place when there are significant 'perturbations' external to the sub-system (Sabatier 1988: 148). One of his hypotheses seems especially relevant to more recent developments in the EU. Thus, he suggests that 'policy-orientated learning across belief systems is most likely when there exists a forum which is a) prestigious enough to force professionals from different coalitions to participate and b) dominated by professional norms' (Sabatier 1988: 148). As Mazey and Richardson argue in this volume, Commission officials develop institutionalized structures which do just this, that is bring together groups of policy actors (be they epistemic communities, advocacy coalitions, or different policy communities). As Sabatier suggests, the purpose of these structures is

> to force debate among professionals from different belief systems in which their points of view must be aired before peers. Under such conditions, a desire for professional credibility and the norms of scientific debate will lead to a serious analysis of methodological assumptions, to the gradual elimination of the more improbable causal assertions and invalid data, and thus probably to a greater convergence of views over time concerning the nature of the problem and the consequences of various policy alternatives.
>
> (1988: 156)

In the context of the EU, Sabel and Zeitlin suggest that there is widespread agreement that the EU's '. . . regulatory successes are possible because decision making is at least in part deliberative: actors' initial preferences are transformed through discussions by the force of the better argument' (Sabel and Zeitlin 2008: 272). Again, we see a suggestion that EU policy-makers are intent on securing *agreement* and *stability* and recognize that this process must involve the participation of the various of stakeholders in the policy area or policy sub-system. It is worth noting that to actors, a *stable outcome* can count as a 'win' almost as significant as gaining their own particular preference. For example, it can be argued that polluters can adjust to most regulatory changes over time and that what they really abhor is constant *change* in their regulatory environment. The concept of *stakeholder* is important, as ultimately it determines who (rather than what) 'matters' in any particular case and can ultimately lead to some kind of broadly based 'ownership' of EU policies. Identifying stakeholders also facilitates the continuation of policy-making business during implementation and the inevitable re-steering of policies as implementation problems emerge (see Knill, in this volume). In fact, *stakeholder* is a term commonly used by the Commission when describing the consultation process. A particularly acute problem for the EU is that the number of stakeholders is very large indeed and it is a difficult managerial task to construct coherent policy communities. Also, the 'glue' holding coalitions together might be rather weak – hence the common feature of temporary, *ad hoc* coalitions of actors not sharing a common intellectual base, policy frame, or belief system. Thus, one actor might be bitterly opposed to another actor's position in one policy domain, only to join forces in a coalition with that very same actor in another policy domain, exhibiting a functional promiscuity in relationships.

Multiple policy-making 'venues' and the erosion of national sovereignty

The very fact that EU policy-making is a collective exercise involving large numbers of participants, often in intermittent and unpredictable relationships, is likely to re-enforce the process by which national sovereignty is being eroded, as well as the capacity for consistent EU-level political leadership. The likelihood of any one government or any one national system of policy actors (e.g. governments and interest groups combined) imposing their will on the rest is low. National governments know this. We can, therefore, expect to see the emergence of two apparently contradictory trends. First, the need to construct complex transnational coalitions of actors will force all actors to become less focused on the nation-states as the 'venue' for policy-making. Just as many large firms have long since abandoned the notion of the nation-state, so will other policy actors; they will seek to create and participate in a multi-layered system of transnational coalitions. Second, the 'politics of uncertainty' will lead national governments and national interest groups to try to coordinate their Euro strategies. In that sense, Euro policy-making may bring them closer together.

One reason for the difficulty in maintaining stable national coalitions is that membership of the EU presents all policy actors with a choice of venue for the resolution of policy conflicts. As Baumgartner and Jones argue, political actors are capable of strategic action by employing a dual strategy of controlling the prevailing image of the policy problem and also seeking out the most favourable venue for the consideration of issues (1991: 1046). In this sense, the EU policy process represents a different order of multiple access points for policy actors when compared with many of the policy systems of the member states. Many of them, such as Britain and France, have traditionally operated rather centralized policy-making systems with, consequently, relatively few national 'venues' for exercising influence. The EU policy process is more akin to the US system, where interests have a wide range of venues to engage in the policy process. Unified and centralized policy systems may encourage cohesion in policy communities in part because all the players know that there are relatively few options for exercising influence elsewhere: this is not the case within the EU, where several 'venues' are available to actors who have lost out in any one of them. The tendency of the EU policy process to pass through periods of stability and periods of dramatic institutional change – in the episodic fashion suggested earlier – will also lead to instability in actor relationships. As Baumgartner and Jones suggest, changes in institutional structures (a feature of the EU) can also often lead to dramatic and long-lasting changes in policy outcomes (1993: 12).

Conclusion: perpetual policy-making and muddling through

As always, Fritz Scharpf has a perceptive view on how the EU works. Referring specifically to the integrative role of the ECJ, he noted the phenomenon of 'perpetual momentum of integration through law' (2012: 127). However, this particular aspect of EU integration is but one (albeit crucial) part of a much broader phenomenon of perpetual policy-making. Within this meta-characteristic, we can identify three factors which, together, appear to guarantee perpetual policy-making, namely neofunctionalist spillover, policy as its own cause, and what Charles Lindblom termed the science of muddling through.

Neofunctionalism and spillover

The concepts of neo-functionalism and spillover as explanations of the process of European integration have been subject to academic analysis for decades. Space does not permit adding to that analysis here (however, for an excellent contribution, see Niemann

2006). Suffice to say that there is now evidence aplenty of what Ernst Haas termed 'the expansive logic of sector integration'. He saw interdependence between economies and policy sectors as inevitably leading to more integration, with integration starting with the least controversial sectors and spreading to others, hence the term *spillover*. This spillover process is not even, however, with some sectors, such as steel (Dudley and Richardson 2012) and agriculture (Daugbjerg 2012) being Europeanized very early, others such as energy (Eberlein 2012) and migration (Niemann 2012) being rather slow but then having a 'growth spurt', and others, such as health, at the heart of national welfare states, being some of the slowest to become Europeanized (Greer 2012). To Haas, Europeanization (or in his terms, integration) seemed unstoppable. Once the process starts, it has no end, as *technical* pressures will lead to adjacent sectors also being integrated. Europeanization begets more Europeanization because, in the end, all policy problems are linked, hence the term *spillover* or *functional spillover*. As he put it, '[s]ector integration . . . begets its own impetus toward extension to the entire economy even in the absence of group demands and their attendant ideologies' (Haas 1958: 297). With hindsight, it seems that Haas possibly anticipated the rationale for what Rhodes (1995) terms 'the treaty base game', whereby the Commission finds some (often unlikely or tenuous) Treaty base for action'. This innovation has underpinned much on the Commission's policy entrepreneurship over many decades. For example Rhodes notes that the Treaty of Rome made only highly ambiguous provisions for EU social or employment policy and that the various articles that did offer some scope for policy innovation were insufficient basis for the Community to advance policy in this sector (2010: 287–8). He argues that many of the employment policy advances from the 1960's onwards were based on alternative articles such as Articles 100 (EEC), the internal market provision, and 235 (EEC) the 'flexible clause' that allowed the Council to adopt by unanimity any provisions directly related to the aims of the Community (Rhodes 2010: 288). The treaty base game is not the sole prerogative of the Commission, however. The ECJ also resorted to the treaty base game, creating health services policy by making decisions based on internal market provisions. The member states participate in this game too. For example a majority of member states have combined with the Commission to use Article 118a rather frequently as the legal basis for social Directives. More recently, higher education policy intervention is now being justified in terms of the EU's strategy for jobs and growth.

Policy as its own cause

The EU is, of course, still in the making (and will ever be so) but it has been in existence long enough for a considerable *corpus* of EU public policy to have been amassed. This is an obvious point to make, but it is of profound importance for the EU policy process. The mere *existence* of such a large and varied mass of public policy is itself a crucial factor in the continued expansion of the EU as a policy state. Whatever the outcome of the current (2014) wave of anti-EU opinion across the member states, it is very unlikely that much, if any, existing EU public policy will be entirely repatriated. One can imagine some especially politically salient policies, such as freedom of movement of workers, being amended. However, it is more difficult to imagine the EU totally withdrawing from a policy area in which it has become embedded, not least because powerful interests, currently benefitting in some way from existing EU policy, will act like a magnetic field around existing policy in order to keep it in place.

However, policies are rarely static once introduced. There seems to be an inevitable process of refinement and amendment taking place. Noting this phenomenon, Wildavsky formulated a 'law of large solutions in public policy'. He did so in answer to some enduring questions in public policy studies such as

> Why do public policy problems never seem to be solved? Why don't organizations that promote public policies seem to learn from experience? If they do try, why do their actions lead to ever larger numbers of unanticipated consequences? If bureaucracies are the principal opponents of change, as is often alleged, how can they also be its chief sponsors? Why, in a word, do supposed solutions turn into perplexing problems?
>
> (Wildavsky 1979: 62)

Wildasky's answer to these sensible questions is simple, namely 'because the Law of Large Solutions in Public Policy – when the solution dwarfs the problem as a source of worry – is *inexorable*' (1979: 62, emphasis added). His thesis was that policy solutions create their own effects which gradually displace the original difficulty. This was especially true for big problems as they usually create 'solutions so large that they become the dominate cause of the consequences with which public policy must contend' (Wildavsky 1979: 63). EU agricultural policy (CAP) is a very good example of Wildavsky's thesis at work. Thus, CAP was such a huge policy solution that it has fuelled decades of further policy-making to try to fix some of the problems it created (Daugbjerg 2012). More spectacularly, are the consequences of monetary union. The euro crisis produced major policy change in this sector in order to avoid the collapse of the euro (Hodson 2012). Crises of various types often act as the 'spark' for policy innovation. I can think of no cases where such 'sparks' have lead to *less* Europeanization. Crises are manna from heaven to those institutions and interests seeking more Europeanization and are classic windows of opportunity as predicted by Kingdon (1984). Those policy-makers who seek more Europeanization simply need to be patient. The *inexorable march of problems*, as Kingdon put it, will sooner or later generate a crisis of some sort, followed by subsequent crises. At some point a favourable window of opportunity will arise. As Zahariadis has argued, EU policy outputs 'depend on the interaction of problems, solutions, and politics during open policy windows' (2008: 525). As is nearly always the case in the EU, there will be an advocacy coalition hanging around in the EU garbage can, ready with a 'Europeanization' solution.

To Wildavsky, the main problem seemed to be one of size. He was surely right to see 'big solutions' as inevitably generating 'big problems', although he was also careful to not say that large problems have no big solutions or that small solutions are always preferable. However, big problems do involve large numbers of actors. As he put it,

> [t]he Law of Large Solutions implies that the greater the proportion of the population involved in a policy problem, and the greater proportion of the policy space occupied by a supposed solution, the harder it is to find a solution that will not become its own worst problem.
>
> (Wildavsky 1979: 63)

In a telling sentence, he remarks 'the evils that worry us now spring directly from the good things that we tried to do before'. He cites, in particular, the business of economic regulation as teeming 'with examples of the solution (regulation of prices and conditions by government) becoming the problem – higher prices, barriers to entry, shortages' (Wildavsky 1979: 63). The EU has exhibited exactly the same regulatory phenomenon. Thus, the EU as the regulatory state *par excellence* has now been engaged in over a decade of trying to fine tune the EU 'regulatory iceberg' in response to countervailing pressures from regulatees who have mobilized against what they see as some perverse effects of previous EU regulatory innovations. Dissatisfaction with existing EU policy is not unique to regulatory issues, of course. Noting that the number of pages of secondary legislation in the EU is over 80,000 pages, and that the dominant picture is not one of inertia but of change, Selck demonstrated that there is an apparent desire on the part of many EU legislative actors to depart from the *status quo* (2005: 1055–70). As Wildavsky put more broadly, *policy is its own cause*.

Wildavsky also drew attention to the importance of policy *interdependence*. Once we get so many big policy programmes, the total policy space becomes densely rather than lightly packed, for 'as large programs proliferate, they begin to exert strong effects on each other, increasing reciprocal relations and mutual causation' (Wildavsky 1979: 64). Moreover, 'interdependence . . . increases faster than knowledge grows. For each additional program that interacts with every other, an exponential increase in consequences follows' (Wildavsky 1979: 65). Thus, a phenomenon which EU scholars tend to as unique (spillover) is actually perfectly well known in national policy systems.

The science (or art?) of muddling through

The trajectory of European integration, and the construction of a dense European policy system, has certainly been uneven, but the remarkable thing about the EU is that both phenomena have continued over time. In its own way, the Union has become adept at what Lindblom saw as a key feature of modern policy-making, the so-called science of muddling through. He was at pains to point out that, in the real world, there are severe limits to truly *rational* decision-making. Important possible outcomes are neglected, important alternative potential policies are neglected, and important affected values are neglected (Lindblom 1959: 81). In practice, he argued, '*agreement* on policy becomes the only practicable test of a policy's correctness' (Lindblom 1959: 84, emphasis added). This process of 'muddling through' is essentially an *incremental* process. Thus, 'democracies change their policies entirely through incremental adjustments. Policy does not move in leaps and bounds' (Lindblom 1959: 84). That this muddling-through process for making EU policy has produced a complex and inconsistent pattern of public policies and a very 'messy' institutional structure, even including opt-outs for certain member states, should occasion no surprise. In effect, the EU has become a gigantic 'frame-reflection' machine – namely, a set of rather fluid institutional arrangements for what Schön and Rein termed the 'resolution of intractable policy controversies'. As they suggest, 'when controversies are situated in messy and politically contentious policy arenas, they actually lend themselves . . . to pragmatic solution' (Schön and Rein 1994: xviii). Actors come to the table with hugely different policy frames, yet more or less workable (albeit untidy) solutions emerge. The most remarkable feature of the EU is not that it is institutionally messy but that so much EU public policy is now in place, despite the multitude of interests and policy frames in play in the EU policy game. Somehow, the EU works as a policy-making system. In part, this is because actors have usually been able to focus on specific policy issues even when deadlocked over the constitutional fundamentals of the EU and its future. High politics disputes can hide a lot of 'business as usual' for low politics. As Stone Sweet suggests, 'European integration is fundamentally about how large numbers of actors, operating in relatively separate arenas, were able to produce new forms of exchange and collective governance for themselves' (2004: 236). 'Low politics' works quite effectively in contrast to high politics, in part because of the use of subterfuge as a policy style. Thus, as Héritier suggests, 'subterfuge is a typical pattern of European policy making in view of an imminent deadlock' (1999: 97). As she argues in this volume, a key aspect of EU policy-making is 'backstage' activity. Thus, what she terms 'covert integration' occurs outside the formal central political arena, through various mechanisms of integration. Falkner has also emphasized mechanisms for bringing about policy innovation in the EU, even in the face of opposition from member states, particularly sidelining of all or some of the Council delegations, and re-forming policy preferences (Falkner 2012). In a sense, the EU is a rather good example of Hood's observation that 'elements of the garbage may at least in some circumstances be better viewed as a design recipe than an unintended condition' (1999: 77).

I conclude by reverting to Lindblom. Just like its member states, the EU will continue to 'muddle through', in the sense that it will continue as a productive policy-making machine, often incrementally, but sometimes more radically when circumstances force the many stakeholders to embrace new frames and ideas as a response to what Kingdon called 'the inexorable march of problems'. At the time of writing (June 2014) it is clear that the rise of Euro-sceptic parties is a clear example of an inexorable problem (namely a rift between EU leaders and their peoples) that has reached the point where it must be addressed. It presents a major challenge to EU policy-makers but I have no doubt the EU will continue to 'muddle through'. Obituaries for the EU project are definitely premature.

Note

1   This section draws heavily on an extract (about 2,500 words) from pages 1–14 in chapter 1, 'Supranational State Building in the European Union', and an extract (1,500 words) from pages 337–39 and 349–52 in chapter 17, 'The Onward March of Europeanization: Tectonic Movement and Seismic Events', by Jeremy Richardson from *Constructing a Policy-Making State?: Policy Dynamics in the EU*, edited by Jeremy Richardson (2012a). Free permission, author's own material; by permission of Oxford University Press.

References

Adler, E. and Haas, P. (1992) 'Conclusion: Epistemic Communities, World Order and the Creation of a Reflective Research Program', *International Organization* 46(1): 367–90.

Baumgartner, F. (2007) 'EU Lobbying: a View from the US', *Journal of European Public Policy*, 14(3): 482–88.

Baumgartner, F. R. and Jones, B. D. (1991) 'Agenda Dynamics and Policy Subsystems', *Journal of Politics* 53(4): 1044–74.

Baumgartner, F. R. and Jones, B. (1993) *Agendas and Instability in American Politics*, Chicago: Chicago University Press.

Benz, A. (2010) 'The European Union as a Loosely Coupled Multi-level System', in Enderlein, H., Wälti, S. and Zürn, M. (Eds), *Handbook on Multi-level Governance*, Cheltenham: Edward Elgar: 214–26.

Blauberger, M. (2012) 'Competition Policy: The Evolution of Commission Control', in Richardson, J. (Ed), *Constructing a Policy-Making State? Policy Dynamics in the EU*, Oxford: Oxford University Press, 49–68.

Borrás, S. and Jacobsson, K. (2004) 'The Open Method of Co-ordination and New Patterns of Governance in the EU', *Journal of European Public Policy* 11(2): 185–208.

Borrás, S. and Radaelli, C. (2011) 'The Politics of Governance Architectures: Creation, Change and Effects of the Lisbon Strategy', *Journal of European Public Policy* 18(4): 463–84.

Bouwen, P. and McCown, M. (2007) 'Lobbying versus Litigation: Political and Legal Strategies of Interest Representation in the European Union', *Journal of European Public Policy* 14(3): 422–43.

Broscheid, A. and Coen, D. (2007) 'Lobbying Activity and for a Creation in the EU: Empirically Exploring the Nature of the Policy Good', *Journal of European Public Policy* 14(3): 346–65.

Busch, A. (1999) 'From "Hooks" to "Focal Points": The Changing Role of Ideas in Rational Choice Theory', in D. Braun and A. Busch (Eds), *Public Policy and Political Ideas*, Cheltenham: Edward Elgar.

Campbell, J.L. (1998) 'Institutional Analysis and the Role of Ideas in Political Economy', *Theory and Society* 27: 377–409.

Caporaso, J. (1996) 'The European Union and Forms of State: Westphalian, Regulatory or Post-Modern?', *Journal of Common Market Studies* 34(1): 29–52.

Caporaso, J. (2007) 'The Three Worlds of Integration Theory' in Graziano P. (Ed.), *Europeanization: New Research Agendas*, Basingstoke: Palgrave Macmillan, 23–34.

Caporaso, J. and Wittenbrick, J. (2006) ' The New Modes of Governance and Political Authority in Europe', *Journal of European Public Policy* 13(4): 474–80.

Cohen, M., March, J. and Olsen, J. (1972) 'A Garbage Can Model of Organizational Choice', *Administrative Science Quarterly* 17(1): 1–25.

Cox, R. (1983) 'Gramsci, Hegemony, and International Relations: An Essay in Method', *Millennium: A Journal of International Studies* 12(2): 162–75.

Cox, R. (1986) 'Social Forces, States, and World Orders: Beyond International Relations Theory', in Keohane, R. (Ed), *Neorealism and its Critics*, New York: Columbia University Press.

Daugbjerg, C. (2012) 'Globalization and Internal Policy Dynamics in the Reform of the Common Agricultural Policy', in Richardson, J. (Ed), *Constructing a Policy-Making State? Policy Dynamics in the EU*, Oxford: Oxford University Press, 88–103.

Dostal, M. (2004) 'Campaigning on Expertise: How OECD Framed EU Welfare and Labour Market Policies – and Why Success Could Trigger Failure', *Journal of European Public Policy* 11(3): 440–60.

Dudley, G. and Richardson, J. (2012) 'From The Treaty of Paris to Globalization: Steel and its "Escape" from Europe', in Richardson, J. (Ed), *Constructing a Policy-Making State? Policy Dynamics in the EU*, Oxford: Oxford University Press, 69–87.

Easton, D. (1965) *A Systems Analysis of Political Life*, New York: John Wiley.

Eberlein, B, (2012) 'Inching towards a Common Energy Policy: Entrepreneurship, Incrementalism, and Windows of Opportunity', in Richardson, J. (Ed), *Constructing a Policy-Making State? Policy Dynamics in the EU*, Oxford: Oxford University Press, 147–69.

Falkner, G. (2012) 'Promoting Policy Dynamism: The Pathways Interlinking Neo-functionalism and Intergovernmentalism', in Richardson, J. (Ed), 2012, *Constructing a Policy-Making State? Policy Dynamics in the EU*, Oxford: Oxford University Press, 292–308.

Farrell, H. and Héritier, A. (2005) 'A Rationalist-Institutionalist Explanation of Endogenous Regional Integration', *Journal of European Public Policy* 12(2): 273–90.

Fischer, F. (2003) *Reframing Public Policy: Discursive Politics and Deliberative Practices*, Oxford: Oxford University Press.

Garrett, G. and Weingast, G. (1993) 'Ideas, Interests and Institutions: Constructing the European Community's Internal Market', in Goldstein, J. and Keohane, R. (Eds), *Ideas and Foreign Policy: Beliefs, Institutions and Political Change*, Ithaca, NY: Cornell University Press.

Greer, S. (2012) 'Polity-making without Policy-making: European Union Healthcare Services Policy', in Richardson, J. (Ed), *Constructing a Policy-making State? Policy Dynamics in the EU*, Oxford: Oxford University Press: 270–91.

Haas, E. (1958) *The Uniting of Europe. Political, Social, and Economic Forces 1950–1957*, Stanford, CA: Stanford University Press.

Haas, P. (1992) 'Introduction: Epistemic Communities and International Policy Co-ordination', *International Organization* 46(1): 1–35.

Hechter, M. (1990) 'Comment: On the Inadequacy of Game Theory for the Solution of Real-world Collective Action Problems', in Cook, K. S. and Levi, M. (Eds), *The Limits of Rationality*, Chicago: University of Chicago Press.

Heclo, H. (1978) 'Issue Networks and the Executive Establishment', in King, A. (Ed), *The New American Political System*, Washington, DC: American Enterprise Institute.

Héritier, A. (1999) *Policy-Making and Diversity in Europe: Escape from Deadlock*, Cambridge: Cambridge University Press.

Hix, S. and Høyland, B. (2011) *The Political System of the European Union*, Basingstoke: Palgrave Macmillan.

Hodson, D. (2012) 'The EMU Paradox: Centralization and Decentralization in EU Macroeconomic Policy', in Richardson, J. (Ed), *Constructing a Policy-Making State? Policy Dynamics in the EU*, Oxford: Oxford University Press: 170–88.

Hoffmann, S. (1966) 'Obstinate or Obsolete: The Fate of the Nation-State and the Case of Western Europe', *Daedalus* 95(3): 862–915.

Hood, C. (1999) 'The Garbage Can Model of Organization: Describing a Condition or a Prescriptive Design Principle?' in Egeberg, M. and Laegreed, P. (Eds), *Organizing Political Institutions: Essays for Johan P. Olsen*, Oslo: Scandinavian University Press.

Idema, T. and Kelemen, D. (2006) 'New Modes of Governance, the Open Method of Co-ordination and Other Fashionable Red Herring', *Perspectives on European Integration and Society* 7(1): 108–23.

Jacobsen, K. (1995) 'Much Ado about Ideas: The Cognitive Factor in Economic Policy', *World Politics* 47: 283–310.

Jones, E., Menon, A., and Weatherill, S. (Eds) (2012) *The Oxford Handbook of the European Union*, Oxford: Oxford University Press.

Jordan, J. and Richardson, J. (1982) 'The British Policy Style or the Logic of Negotiation?' in Richardson, J. (Ed.), *Policy Styles in Western Europe*, London: Allen and Unwin: 80–110.

Kagan, R. (2001) *Adversarial Legalism: The American way of Law*, Cambridge, MA: Harvard University Press.

Kingdon, J. (1984) *Agendas, Alternatives, and Public Policies*, New York: HarperCollins.

Laffan, B., O'Donnell, R., and Smith, M. (2000) *Europe's Experimental Union*, London: Routledge.

Lawton, T. (1999) 'Governing the Skies: Conditions for the Europeanization of Airline Policy' *Journal of Public Policy* 19(1): 91–112.

Lindblom, C. (1959) 'The Science of "Muddling Through"', *Public Administration Review* 19(2): 79–88.

Majone, G. (1994) 'The Rise of the Regulatory State in Europe', *West European Politics* 17(3): 77–101.

Majone, G. (1996) *Regulating Europe*, London: Routledge.

Mazey, S. and Richardson, J. (1995) 'Promiscuous Policymaking: The European Policy Style?', in Rhodes, C. and Mazey, S. (Eds), *The State of the European Union. Building a European Polity?*, Boulder, CO: Lynn Rienner: 337–60.

Niemann, A. (2006) *Explaining Decisions in the EU*, Cambridge: Cambridge University Press.

Niemann, A. (2012) 'The Dynamics of EU Migration Policy: From Maastricht to Lisbon', in Richardson, J. (Ed), *Constructing a Policy-Making State? Policy Dynamics in the EU*, Oxford: Oxford University Press: 209–33.

Olsen, J. (2007) *Europe in Search of Political Order*, Oxford: Oxford University Press.

Peters, B. G. (1994) 'Agenda-setting in the European Community', *Journal of European Public Policy* 1(1): 9–26.

Poletti, A. (2011) 'World Trade Organization Judicialization and Preference Convergence in EU Trade Policy: Making the Agent's Life Easier', *Journal of European Public Policy* 18(3): 361–82.

Princen, S. (2007) 'Agenda-setting in the European Union: A Theoretical Exploration and Agenda for Research', *Journal of European Public Policy* 14(1): 21–38.

Princen, S. (2012) 'Agenda-setting and the Formation of an EU Policy-making State', in Richardson, J. (Ed), *Constructing a Policy-making State? Policy Dynamics in the EU*, Oxford: Oxford University Press: 29–45.

Radaelli, C. (2003) 'The Europeanization of Public Policy' in Featherstone, K. and Radaelli, C. (Eds), *The Politics of Europeanization*, Oxford: Oxford University Press: 27–56.

Rein, H. and Schön, D. (1991) 'Frame-Reflective Policy Discourse', in Wagner, P. Weiss, C. Wittrock, B. and Wollman, H. (Eds), *Social Sciences, Modern States: National Experiences and Theoretical Crossroads*, Cambridge: Cambridge University Press.

Rhodes, M. (1995) 'A Regulatory Conundrum: Industrial Relations and the Social Dimension', in Leibfreid, S. and Pierson, P. (Eds), *European Social Policy: Between Fragmentation and Integration*, Washington, DC: Brookings Institution, 78–122.

Rhodes, M. (2010) 'Employment Policy: Between Efficiency and Experimentation', in Wallace, H. Pollack, M. and Young, A. (Eds), *Policy-Making in the European Union*, Oxford: Oxford University Press, 283–306.

Richardson, J. (Ed) (1982) *Policy Styles in Western Europe*, London: Allen and Unwin.

Richardson, J. (1994) 'EU Water Policy-making: Uncertain Agendas, Shifting Networks and Complex Coalitions', *Environmental Politics* 4(4): 139–67.

Richardson, J. (2000) 'Government, Interest Groups and Policy Change', *Political Studies* 48(5): 1006–25.

Richardson, J. (Ed) (2012a) *Constructing a Policy-making State? Policy Dynamics in the EU*, Oxford: Oxford University Press.

Richardson, J. (2012b) 'New Governance or Old Governance? A Policy Style Perspective', in Levi-Faur, D. (Ed), *Oxford Handbook of Governance*, Oxford: Oxford University Press: 311–24.

Richardson, J. and Jordan, G. (1979) *Governing under Pressure: The Policy Process in a Post-Parliamentary Democracy*, Oxford: Martin Robertson.

Rittberger, B. and Richardson, J. (2003) 'Old Wine in New Bottles? The Commission and the Use of Environmental Policy Instruments', *Public Administration* 81(3): 575–606.

Sabatier, P. (1988) 'An Advocacy Coalition Framework of Policy Change and the Role of Policy Orientated Learning Therein', *Policy Sciences* 21: 128–68.

Sabel, C. and Zeitlin, J. (2008) 'Learning from Difference: The New Architecture of Experimentalist Governance in the European Union', *European Law Journal* 14(3): 271–327.

Schattschneider, E. E. (1960) *The Semi-Sovereign People: A Realist's View of Democracy in America*, New York: Holt.

Scharpf, F. (2012) 'Perpetual Momentum: Directed and Unconstrained?', *Journal of European Public Policy* 19(1): 127–39.

Scharpf, F. (2010) *Community and Autonomy. Institutions, Policies and Legitimacy in Multilevel Europe*, Frankfurt/New York: Campus Verlag.

Schön, D.A. and Rein, M. (1994) *Frame Reflection: Toward the Resolution of Intractable Policy Controversies*, New York: Basic Books.

Sebenius, J.K. (1992) 'Challenging Conventional Explanations of International Co-operation: Negotiation Analysis and the Case of Epistemic Communities', *International Organization* 46(1): 323–65.

Selck, T. (2005) 'The Absence of Inertia in EU Legislative Decision-making', *Journal of Common Market Studies* 43(5): 1055–107.

Skocpol, T. (2008) 'Bringing the State Back In: Retrospect and Prospect', *Scandinavian Political Studies* 31(2): 109–24.

Stephenson, P. (2012) 'Image and Venue as Factors Mediating Latent Spillover Pressure for Agenda-setting Change', *Journal of European Public Policy* 19(6): 797–816.

Stone Sweet, A. (2004) *The Judicial Construction of Europe*, Oxford: Oxford University Press.

Thomson, J. (1995) 'Sate Sovereignty in International Relations: Bridging the Gap between Theory and Empirical Research', *International Studies Quarterly* 39(2): 213–33.

Tsebelis, G. (1990) *Nested Games: Rational Choice in Comparative Politics*, Berkeley: University of California Press.

Wildavsky, A. (1979) *The Art and Craft of Policy Analysis*, London: Macmillan.

Zahariadis, N. (2008), 'Ambiguity and Choice in European Public Policy', *Journal of European Public Policy* 15(4): 514–30.

Zweifel, T.D. (2002) '. . . Who is without sin cast the first stone: the EU's Democratic Deficit in Comparison', *Journal of European Public Policy* 9(5): 812–40.

Chapter 2

The EU as a system of differentiated integration

A challenge for theories of European integration?

FRANK SCHIMMELFENNIG AND BERTHOLD RITTBERGER

Introduction

The story of European integration is a story of growth. From its initial specialization in the coal and steel industries, the scope of European integration has broadened to all major policies and acquired an exclusive policy-making competence in some of them (such as external commercial policy or monetary policy). Intergovernmental decision-making has been increasingly replaced by majority voting, co-decision power of the directly elected European Parliament, and delegation to strong agencies such as the European Central Bank. This process whereby competencies are centralized and shared at the EU level is what we call 'vertical integration'. From originally six member states, the EU has expanded to 28. This is 'horizontal integration'. And whereas growth has not been linear but interrupted by drawbacks and periods of stagnation, formal steps backward have not (yet) occurred.

This remarkable expansion of tasks, competencies and membership is, however, only part of the story. From its beginnings, European integration has varied between policies that were strongly integrated and those with only few, if any, competencies of the Community. Whereas the EU has a common currency or a common market, it only has a rudimentary common security and defence policy. This situation, whereby policy areas are characterized by different levels of centralization, is what we call 'vertical differentiation'. Moreover, in the past 20 years, many new integration steps have not applied uniformly to all member states. At the same time, non-member states have come to participate increasingly in the EU's policies. Not all member states belong to the eurozone, but some non-member states participate in the Schengen and the internal market (through the European Economic Area). This is what we call 'horizontal differentiation'. Integration in the EU thus varies across both policies and countries and is vertically and horizontally differentiated, which is why we call the EU a system of differentiated integration.

Integration theories tell us why, when and how integration occurs. The theoretical debate about the dynamics of EU integration has long been dominated by two 'families' of integration theorizing: intergovernmentalism and supranationalism. More recently, a constructivist approach to integration theory has been forming. Rather than offering a history of the development of the theoretical debate, we describe the core assumptions of the theories and specify their main hypotheses. Traditionally, integration theories have focused on explaining the conditions and mechanisms of integration growth. In this chapter, we show that these three perspectives on European integration can also capture the differentiated character of the EU polity. We therefore add hypotheses on differentiation.[1]

In the next section, we introduce the concept of differentiated integration. The ensuing section provides an overview of integration theory, followed by a presentation of the main theories of European integration: intergovernmentalism, supranationalism, and constructivism.

The EU: a system of differentiated integration

Polities can be conceptualized as three-dimensional configurations of authority:

- *Level of centralization*. Polities that monopolize authoritative decisions in the centre have a maximum level of centralization, whereas decision-making authority dispersed equally across a multitude of political actors indicate a low level of centralization.

- *Functional scope* varies between authority over a single issue and authority over the entire range of public policies.
- *Territorial extension*. The authority of a polity can be limited geographically to a single political territory, or it may encompass several territories – up to the entire world.

Figure 2.1 illustrates different types of polities resulting from variation in the configuration of authority. The level of centralization is shown on the y-axis, functional scope on the z-axis, and territorial extension on the horizontal x-axis. Archetypical configurations are the (unitary) state and the international organization. In the unitary state, all policies are decided at the same (central) level and cover the same (limited) territory. In addition, the state traditionally has maximum functional scope: it covers all policy areas. By contrast, international organizations are typically decentralized (i.e. they display low levels of centralization) and task specific (i.e. they have limited functional scope, often encompassing only one particular policy area) but cover more territories.

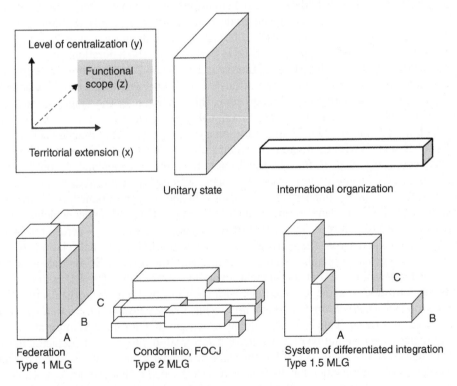

Figure 2.1 A three-dimensional representation of polity types

Source: Dirk Leuffen, Berthold Rittberger, and Frank Schimmelfennig, *Differentiated Integration: Explaining Variation in the European Union*, 2013, Palgrave Macmillan. Reproduced with permission of Palgrave Macmillan.

The lower three shapes in Figure 2.1 represent more complex configurations of authority. The federation differs from the unitary state in that at least one policy area is governed at the subnational (regional) level (sector B) or co-governed by subnational and national authorities (sector C), whereas other sectors are fully centralized (A). The territorial extension and functional scope of the federation, however, is of the same order as that of unitary states. It deals with all policy areas on a closed territory (note, however, that a federation's extension grows with the number of subunits of which it is composed). This is also the basic model of federalist conceptions of European integration, which assume a set of member states that form a Union and allocate the authority over policy sectors to themselves, to the Union or, as mixed competences, to both states and the Union.

The second configuration consists of task-specific jurisdictions with intersecting memberships. In the international domain, the coexistence of hundreds of international organizations, most of them highly specialized, some working in the same policy fields, with variable, overlapping membership and different regional focus, follows this type. The idea of FOCJ (functional, overlapping, competing jurisdictions) as 'competitive governments for Europe' by Frey and Eichenberger (1996) fits here. So does Philippe Schmitter's 'condominio', 'based on variation in both territorial and functional constituencies', which he considered to be the 'most probable trajectory for the EU' (1996: 136). He describes it as 'many Europes', in which 'there would be multiple regional institutions acting autonomously to solve common problems and produce different public goods' (Schmitter 1996: 136). Liesbet Hooghe and Gary Marks (2003) label this configuration 'type-2 multi-level governance' in contrast to 'type-1 multi-level governance', the federation.

In our view, however, the EU is neither type 1 nor type 2, but a hybrid type. In contrast to federal, type 1 governance, the extension of membership varies by policy or task. The EU has varying borders for the eurozone, the Schengen, or the Single Market. On the other hand, categorizing the EU as functional type 2 governance ignores the extent to which the EU has developed an institutional core or centre that reaches across the EU's policy sectors with their variation in centralization and territorial scope. This institutional core is constituted, first, by the Treaty on European Union and, second, by the EU's institutions, namely the European Council, which gives general directions for all policy sectors of the EU and for treaty revisions. In addition, the Council, the European Commission, the European Parliament and the European Court of Justice which are also present – albeit to different degrees and with varying competences – across the board of EU activities and across the territories into which the EU's external relations reach. Finally, a core group of member states – starting with the original EC-6 – takes part in all the activities of the EU at the highest level of centralization. The EU is not 'many Europes' with task-specific jurisdictions, with each having their own organization, but one Europe with *a single organizational and member state core and a territorial outreach that varies by function*. This is how we define a 'system of differentiated integration'.

A graphical representation of a system of differentiated integration is depicted in the lower-right corner of Figure 2.1. It has the same functional scope as the state and the different levels of centralization for the policy areas A through C that characterize a federal state. In addition to variation in the level of centralization, the territorial extension also varies across policy sectors. In this example, the highly centralized sector A is limited to a few territories, resembling a state's authority pattern, whereas sector B is more similar to an international organization. Sector C combines medium-high centralization with extended territorial coverage. Policy sector A is more complex than are sectors B and C because a few territories accept a high level of centralization in this sector but one does not. An example for the latter would be the Economic and Monetary Union (EMU) – with Denmark participating in the Exchange Rate Mechanism but not in the eurozone.

Based on this concept of the EU as a system of differentiated integration, we define European integration as a process whereby (a) competencies are increasingly shared across EU member states or delegated to autonomous supranational institutions ('vertical integration' or 'deepening') and (b) the EU expands territorially by accepting new members and spreading its rules and policies to additional countries ('horizontal integration' or 'widening'). Both processes are differentiated across policies, however. Vertical integration can remain at the level of intergovernmental coordination and cooperation as in the Common Security and Defence Policy (CSDP), or it may be fully centralized as in monetary policy and competition policy where decisions are exclusively in the hands of supranational bodies, the European Central Bank and the European Commission. Horizontal integration can be limited to a sub-group of EU member states as in the eurozone or extend beyond the formal borders of the EU as in the European Economic Area for the internal market.

Figure 2.2 shows the current distribution of major EU policy areas across the vertical and horizontal dimensions of integration. The scale for vertical integration is from 0 for no integration (i.e. policy-making prerogatives remain exclusively at the national level) to 5 for supranational centralization; the scale for horizontal integration reflects the percentage share of European countries covered by EU rules in 20 per cent increments. Whereas most policies cluster in the upper right corner representing EU members (plus a few additional countries) for horizontal and co-decision for vertical integration (the main EU bodies share policy-making competencies), there are a few marked outliers. Monetary policy is supranationally centralized but limited to a subset of EU member states; by contrast, taxation and security policies affect all EU members but at a lower,

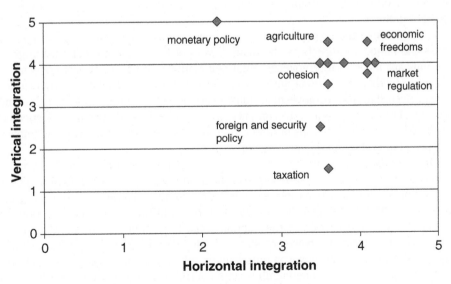

Figure 2.2 EU policies in vertical and horizontal integration[2]

mainly intergovernmental level of vertical integration. Finally, whereas agricultural and cohesion or regional policies only cover full members of the EU, market freedoms and market regulation include the countries of the European Economic Area and, in part, Switzerland and Turkey.

Theories of European integration

Theories of European integration stipulate the conditions, timing and mechanisms under which competencies and boundaries shift in the European multilevel system. They explain the scope and dynamics of integration and allow us to formulate expectations as to when and under what conditions integration will progress (or stall). And they should be able to tell us why some policies are more vertically and/or horizontally integrated than others. Irrespective of the diversity of theories of European integration (see e.g. Caporaso and Keeler 1995; Rosamond 2000; Cram 2001; Wiener and Diez 2009 for overviews), we argue that these approaches can be grouped into three broad 'schools of thought': intergovernmentalism, supranationalism, and constructivism.

Neofunctionalism, belonging to the supranationalist 'school of thought', was the dominant theory of integration in the early periods of integration theorizing, with prominent scholars such as Ernst Haas, Leon Lindberg, Joseph Nye, and Philippe Schmitter defining the neofunctionalist research agenda. The mid-sixties saw the birth of intergovernmentalism to mark a counterpoint to neofunctionalism with Stanley Hoffmann being its most prominent proponent. Since the mid-eighties, both 'schools of thought' have undergone a process of internal diversification. Whereas Andrew Moravcsik's liberal intergovernmentalism was the major new innovation within the intergovernmentalist camp, Wayne Sandholtz's and Alec Stone Sweet's supranational institutionalism marked a major refinement of neofunctionalism. Constructivism has travelled more recently from International Relations to the study of European integration. In this chapter, we concentrate on the basic assumptions and propositions that constitute the core of each school of thought.

As the name of the theory indicates, *intergovernmentalism* regards national governments and national interests as the main drivers of European integration. Integration decisions are made in intergovernmental negotiations in which national governments bargain to further the national interest and in which the most powerful governments prevail. According to intergovernmentalism, the process of integration remains under the control of member state governments, which collectively determine the speed and substance of any further steps of integration. It thus denies a transformative impact of European integration on the state system.

Supranationalism, in turn, considers actors and processes above and beyond the nation-state to be the mainspring of European integration. Supranational actors and transnational interest groups increasingly gain autonomy throughout the integration process and attempt to push the integration process in their preferred direction. Processes of institutionalization at the supranational level support supranational organizations and constrain the power of states. Under certain conditions, the institutions created by member state governments trigger self-reinforcing processes which beget further integration and escape member state control. Integration thus has a transformative impact on the state system and state actors.

Finally, in the *constructivist* perspective, European integration is about community building driven by ideational preferences and processes. The dissemination and distribution of common, 'European' identities, values, norms, and policy beliefs determines the strength of the community and, consequently, the speed, the extent, and the direction of integration. Processes of arguing and persuasion characterize the negotiations. Traditionally, the main actors in the European community-building process have been national and supranational elites but citizens have become more relevant over time – in particular as a result of Euro-sceptic mobilization. We now address these three 'schools of thought' in more detail.

Intergovernmentalism

Intergovernmentalism is a variant of rationalist institutionalism in International Relations (IR) theory specifically tailored to explain European integration. We therefore begin our presentation of intergovernmentalism by explicating its theoretical roots in rationalist IR theory and then move on to concrete propositions on European (differentiated) integration. The presentation is mainly based on Andrew Moravcsik's 'Choice for Europe' (1998, above all, see pp. 3–77), the most complete and theoretically sophisticated treatment of intergovernmentalist integration theory. Table 2.1 provides an overview.

Rationalist institutionalism

It is the first, basic assumption of intergovernmentalism that because European integration is similar enough to international politics, and the EU is sufficiently like other international institutions, it can be profitably studied and explained from an *IR perspective*. Indeed, Moravcsik maintains that the 'EC is best seen as an international regime for

Table 2.1   Intergovernmentalism

General assumptions	Rationalist institutionalism in International Relations: rational states in an interdependent and anarchical international system
Explanatory theory	Bargaining theory Club theory Functional theory of institutions
Factors explaining integration	Extent and distribution of international interdependence Exogenous preferences and relative bargaining power • *LI*: sector-specific societal preferences, issue-area power, and compliance costs • *RI*: geopolitical preferences, overall power of states, and autonomy costs

policy co-ordination' (1993: 480; cf. Hoffmann 1982: 33) and that European integration represents 'a subset of general tendencies among democratic states in modern world politics' (1998: 5). IR theories traditionally assume that states are the central actors in international politics and that they act in a context of anarchy, that is in the absence of a centralized authority making and enforcing political decisions. Policy-making in international politics generally takes place in intergovernmental negotiations, and agreements require the consent of all state participants.

According to the second basic assumption, intergovernmentalism is rooted in a *rationalist framework*, which entails a general explanatory programme and basic action-theoretic assumptions. As for the explanatory programme, rationalism is an individualist or agency theory, which requires an explanation of, first, actor preferences and, second, collective outcomes as a result of aggregated individual actions based on these preferences. The core action-theoretic assumption is 'rational choice': actors calculate the utility of alternative courses of action and choose the one that maximizes their utility under the given circumstances. Rationalist institutionalism in IR theory then seeks to explain the establishment and design of international institutions as a collective outcome of interdependent ('strategic') rational state choices and intergovernmental negotiations in an anarchical context.

In correspondence with IR rational institutionalism, intergovernmentalism generally assumes that governmental preferences are exogenous; that is, they are not formed or changed in the course of international negotiations or by international institutions. Governments enter negotiations with predefined ('national') interests and leave them with the same interests. The international institutional or interaction context has an impact on the costs of pursuing state interests and attaining state goals but does not affect the substance of these interests and goals.

Another commonality is the bargaining theory of international cooperation and the functional theory of institutions that Moravcsik employs to explain integration. Rationalist institutionalism distinguishes several interrelated problems of international collective choice in problematic situations of international interdependence – that is situations in which non-cooperative behaviour is the individually rational choice but, in the end, leaves all states worse off. The basic problem consists in overcoming such collectively suboptimal outcomes and achieving coordination or cooperation for mutual benefit. This efficiency problem, however, is connected to problems of distribution and enforcement. First, how are the mutual gains of cooperation distributed among the states? Second, how are states prevented from defecting from an agreement in order to exploit the cooperation of others?

In this context, rational-institutionalist theory argues that the outcome of international negotiations, that is whether and on which terms cooperation comes about, depends on the relative bargaining power of the actors, on one hand, and on the effects of international institutions on the negotiation process, on the other. First, efficient, welfare-maximizing solutions to problematic situations of international interdependence require reliable information on the state of the world, cause–effect relationships and other actors' preferences and capabilities. International institutions are better at providing this information than governments alone. They furthermore reduce transaction costs by providing a forum for multi-actor negotiations and services for effective and efficient communication.

Second, the solution to the problem of distribution depends on the actors' bargaining power. Bargaining power results from the asymmetrical distribution of (1) information and (2) the benefits of a specific agreement (compared to those of alternative outcomes or 'outside options'). Generally, those actors that have more and better information are able to manipulate the outcome to their advantage (cf. Schneider and Cederman 1994), and those actors that are least in need of a specific agreement are best able to threaten the others with non-cooperation and thereby force them to make concessions.

Finally, compliance with international norms and rules requires effective monitoring and sanctioning. Again, international institutions are established because they fulfil these tasks more effectively and efficiently than individual states. Different institutional designs then reflect the specific problems of cooperation caused by, above all, the severity of distributional conflict and enforcement problems and by uncertainty about the preferences of other actors and the state of the world (Koremenos *et al.* 2001). Bargaining theory thus mainly explains the functional scope of European integration whereas the rationalist theory of international institutions accounts for vertical integration. What about horizontal integration then?

When states integrate their markets and economies, they produce external effects for non-member countries (for instance by diverting trade and investments). However, third countries can also produce externalities for the integrated states. For example lower taxation rates or less demanding social and environmental regulatory rules tend to attract businesses away from the integrated market and thus bring its rules and policies under pressure. In addition, horizontal integration might produce economies of scale and increase the budget of the international organization. Thus, in a rationalist perspective, the question is whether a given integrated area already has optimal size or whether collective welfare may be maximized by admitting additional countries. The rationalist theory that addresses the problem of organizational size is club theory. A club is a voluntary association deriving mutual benefit from producing and sharing collective goods. Membership in clubs can be limited – and needs to be because new members are not only additional contributors to the club goods but also rival consumers who restrict the old members' access to the club goods (causing so-called crowding costs). The core hypothesis of club theory therefore posits that a club will expand (only) until the marginal costs of admitting a new member equals the marginal benefits. Because clubs are voluntary associations, all old and new members must derive a positive utility from expansion lest they use their veto. The states have to find an efficient, welfare-maximizing solution (an optimal size for the integrated area), to distribute the costs and benefits of enlargement among the old and new members, and to secure compliance. Correspondingly, bargaining theory and the functional theory of institutions are used to explain horizontal integration as well.

Intergovernmentalism and European integration

Which specific propositions on European integration does intergovernmentalism derive from these general rational-institutionalist assumptions? The theoretical framework still leaves the relevant actors and preferences as well as their resources and constraints unspecified. It also does not provide concrete hypotheses about the extent of vertical and horizontal integration in European integration or the specific institutional design of the European Union. To rectify this state of affairs, we have to substantiate actors' preferences, their sources of bargaining power and the relevance of international institutions. To do so, we introduce two versions of intergovernmentalism: a realist and a liberal version.

Two main authors represent traditional, realist intergovernmentalism: Stanley Hoffmann (1966, 1982) and Alan Milward (1984, 1994). These are their core tenets:

- Member states are and will remain the dominant actors in the process of European integration: they shape European integration according to national goals and interests.
- The extent of European integration is limited by states' ultimate interest in autonomy, the interest in self-preservation of nation-state bureaucracies, the diversity of national situations and traditions, the dominance of national identities, and by external actors and influences (such as the United States or the North Atlantic Treaty Organization).
- European integration does not undermine the nation-state but has strengthened it in the post–World War II reconstruction, in the global competition with other economic powers and emerging markets, and against domestic societal interests and pressures.
- Integration is limited to the economic sector and related 'low politics'; core functions of the state (the 'high politics' of internal and external security or foreign policy) will be prevented from being integrated by states anxious to preserve their autonomy.
- For the same reason, the supranational organizations of the EU are and will remain weak. They lack the expertise, the resources, or the popular support to expand their power at the expense of the member states.

Thus, the analysis of European integration must start with the preferences of states or governments, as well as their interdependencies and interest constellations, and must focus on negotiations among governments and between governments and the community organizations.

Andrew Moravcsik's liberal intergovernmentalism (LI) shares the intergovernmentalist thrust of these propositions in general but embeds them systematically in a liberal theory of international relations and a rationalist analysis of international institutions. In its most condensed form, it is the general argument of LI that 'EU integration can best be understood as a series of rational choices made by national leaders. These choices responded to constraints and opportunities stemming from the economic interests of powerful domestic constituents, the relative power of each state in the international system, and the role of institutions in bolstering the credibility of interstate commitments' (Moravcsik 1998: 18).

As indicated by the label *liberal* intergovernmentalism, LI follows a liberal theory of foreign policy preference formation: governmental preferences are issue specific and reflect the interests of societal interest groups (intermediated by domestic political institutions). In agricultural policy, for instance they reflect the cost-benefit calculations and the relative power of agricultural producers and consumers, whereas in energy policy, they reflect the interests of the dominant energy producers and consumers, and so on. Insofar as European integration has been predominantly economic, so have state preferences. While the general interest in European integration resulted from the pressure to cooperate for mutual benefit from economic gains in an expanding and 'globalizing' international economy, concrete preferences emerged 'from a process of domestic conflict in which specific sectoral interests, adjustment costs and, sometimes, geopolitical concerns played an important role'. They reflected 'primarily the commercial interests of powerful economic producers' in market integration and 'secondarily the macro-economic preferences of ruling governmental coalitions' – as in monetary integration (Moravcsik 1998: 3). In other words, domestic interests, shaped mainly by the competitiveness of the national economy, acted as a filter between the structural incentives of the international economy and the national preferences in European integration. As a consequence, governments pursue integration as 'a means to secure commercial advantages for producer groups, subject to regulatory and budgetary constraints' (Moravcsik 1998: 38). To the extent that European integration expands into sectoral domains other than economic issue areas, other interests and interest groups become relevant. In contrast, realist intergovernmentalism (RI) assumes that governments have comprehensive ('geopolitical', according to Moravcsik) foreign policy goals that span and dominate specific sectors, and that they are able to define and pursue them independently of societal pressures. These goals are the maximization of state autonomy, security, or influence.

LI describes the most relevant negotiation processes in European integration as processes of *intergovernmental bargaining* concerning the *distribution* of gains from substantive cooperation. More concretely, they consist of *hard* bargaining,

> in which credible threats to veto proposals, to withhold financial side-payments, and to form alternative alliances excluding recalcitrant governments carried the day. The outcomes reflected the relative power of states – more precisely patterns of asymmetrical interdependence. Those who gained the most economically from integration compromised the most on the margin to realize it, whereas those who gained the least or for whom the costs of adaptation were highest imposed conditions.
>
> (Moravcsik 1998: 3)

The difference in the assumptions about state preferences between RI and LI entails differences in the explanation of negotiations and integration outcomes. First, LI assumes that just as states have issue-specific preferences, they also have issue-specific bargaining power. It is the relative intensity of issue-specific preferences that determines the bargaining power of the actors – in contrast with the overall power resources (such as territory, population, armed forces) that realism emphasizes. As a consequence, small states may well stand up to big states in EU negotiations or extract concessions in specific issue areas.

The choice and the design of institutions are also driven by governments and by their concern about each other's future compliance with the substantive deals reached. By transferring sovereignty to international institutions, governments remove issues from the influence of domestic politics, which might build up pressure for non-compliance if costs for powerful domestic actors are high. They also remove them from decentralized intergovernmental control, which may be too weak to secure compliance, in particular if powerful member states violate the rules (Moravcsik 1998: 9, 73). The degree to which governments favour the pooling (voting by procedures other than unanimity) and the delegation of sovereignty to supranational institutions, depends on the value they place on the issues and substantive outcomes in question: The higher the gains of a cooperative agreement for a government, and the higher the risk of non-compliance by other governments, the higher its readiness to cede competences to the EU to prevent potential losers from revising the policy (Moravcsik 1998: 9, 486–487).

In contrast with LI, RI assumes that states are primarily concerned about autonomy and influence when choosing and designing international institutions. They only consent to transferring competencies to the EU if they expect net gains in autonomy and influence. This, for instance, is the essence of Joseph Grieco's (1996) voice-opportunity thesis, which posits that weak states are particularly interested in European integration and willing to sacrifice formal sovereignty because they see it as a way to bind the stronger states and to enhance their influence on international outcomes. Another trade-off is captured by Klaus Dieter Wolf's (1999) 'new raison d'état'. Governments agree to those transfers of national competencies, and thus to external autonomy losses that reduce their domestic vulnerability to societal pressures. Social movements and interest groups cannot organize and influence politics at the European level as effectively as in the domestic context.

The core propositions of intergovernmentalism have three negative corollaries. First, the efficiency problem of international negotiations, the search for welfare-maximizing collective solutions, is far less relevant in European integration than is the distribution problem. Information and ideas are plentiful and symmetrically distributed among states, and transaction costs are generally low so that intergovernmental negotiations reliably produce efficient outcomes (Moravcsik 1998: 479–480). It follows, second, that the bargaining power of supranational actors is low because they are deprived of their main bargaining resource: scarce and asymmetrically distributed information. Finally, if supranational actors obtain competencies nevertheless, it is only because governments need them to monitor and sanction each other. But they continue to act in the interest and under the control of the member states.

Intergovernmentalism and differentiated integration

Under conditions of international treaty making, in which each state has veto power, the extent of vertical and horizontal integration would be decided by the state with the strongest bargaining power. This state would block any further vertical or horizontal integration that is not in its interest. Beyond the lowest common intergovernmental denominator, the EU would be subject to severe trade-offs. If it wanted to engage in further vertical integration, it would lose or have to exclude those states that do not benefit from transferring policy competences to the EU or from strengthening the EU's decision-making and enforcement powers. If, on the other hand, it wanted to increase its membership, it might have to reduce its level of centralization in order to accommodate the least integration-friendly state. This is known and debated as the 'widening-deepening dilemma' of integration.

In an intergovernmentalist perspective, differentiated integration can solve this dilemma by overcoming the rigidities of uniform integration and creating opportunities for policies to be integrated at different levels of centralization and for different groups of countries to cooperate among each other separately at the level of integration that they prefer. It is thus an efficient strategy for accommodating international diversity and avoiding deadlock when intergovernmental consent is required.

For RI, differentiated integration results from different autonomy costs across sectors and countries. In the 1960s, Stanley Hoffmann introduced the distinction between 'high politics' and 'low politics' to explain the limits of integration and spillover. We argue that the distinction between 'high' and 'low' politics is reflected in the degree to which different policy areas are 'politicized', that is how salient a policy is and how much publics and public opinion mobilize around a particular issue. 'High politics' include those policy areas that concern the security and status of a state in the international system. By contrast, in the areas of 'low politics', states can pursue a common good and realize mutual gains without compromising their national sovereignty, security and power status. In general, foreign and internal as well as security policy are the core domains of 'high politics', but taxation, energy and monetary policy can be considered key areas of national sovereignty as well (Hoffmann 1966). In line with this reasoning, we should expect a high level of vertical integration first and foremost in areas of 'low politics', where the potential for politicization is low, whereas highly politicized areas are unlikely to be integrated at all or will be integrated later than the 'low politics' areas. Finally, 'high politics' areas will also be less territorially extended than 'low politics' sectors because more states shy away from integration if autonomy costs are high. In the RI perspective, then, vertical and horizontal differentiation across policies reflects variation in politicization.

LI hypothesizes that the likelihood of integration increases with the homogeneity of national interests. If interests converge, there is no need for differentiation because all countries will be able to agree on the same level of integration. Yet if interests diverge because of unequal exposure to interdependence, the state whose interests are the closest to the status quo has the highest bargaining power and determines the outcome. This outcome, however, leaves many governments dissatisfied that would have preferred a different extent of integration. These governments have an incentive to seek differentiation in order to move closer to their preference.

Differentiated integration as a remedy for deadlock caused by heterogeneous state preferences works under the condition that all participating states regard differentiation as more beneficial than the uniform status quo. Generally, that should be the case: All states can choose a level of integration that is in line with their level of interdependence and their integration preferences, and all states benefit from not having to accommodate states with incompatible interests. Differentiated integration may, however, be undermined by high transaction costs – differentiation makes integration more complex, cumbersome, and time-consuming – and by negative externalities. Negative externalities result from negative interdependence between differentiated policies. The fact that one policy is more integrated than the other may create costs for the more or the less integrated policy. And the fact that two groups of countries cooperate at different levels of integration may affect at least one of the groups negatively. For instance, the (still) weakly integrated fiscal policy of the EU is seen to undermine the more integrated monetary policy and being the root cause of the Euro-crisis. An example for negative externalities in horizontal differentiation would be a common market in which one group of countries was bound by more costly labour or environmental regulation than another.

Intergovernmentalism: basic assumptions about differentiated integration

- International interdependence creates demand for integration. The position of a state in international interdependence explains state preferences. Asymmetrical interdependence produces differential bargaining power.
- States (governments) are the relevant actors who rationally initiate, steer and control the process of integration based on exogenous, predominantly material preferences.
- Integration is negotiated between governments and reflects intergovernmental constellations of preferences and power.
- Differentiated integration results from different levels of international interdependence and the heterogeneity of state preferences.

Intergovernmentalism: hypotheses about differentiated integration

Intergovernmentalist hypotheses about vertical and horizontal integration have a realist and a liberal variant:

- The vertical and horizontal integration of a policy increases with the extent of international interdependence, the homogeneity of state preferences, and the severity of the compliance problems (LI); it decreases as the autonomy costs/ politicization of integration increase (RI).
- Vertical differentiation increases with the variation of interdependence, preference homogeneity, compliance problems (LI), and autonomy costs/politicization (RI) across policies; it decreases as transaction costs and negative externalities increase.
- The horizontal differentiation of a policy increases with the variation of interdependence, preferences (LI) and autonomy costs/politicization (RI) across countries; it decreases as transaction costs and negative externalities increase.

Supranationalism

Like intergovernmentalism, supranationalism has its origins in IR theory. In contrast to intergovernmentalism, supranationalism has a transformative ontology: It holds that the international system is not bound to be anarchical but can be transformed through processes of institutionalization. Furthermore, supranationalism assumes that the process of integration has a transformative and self-reinforcing effect: Even though the beginnings of the integration project may well reflect the interests of the most powerful states, further integration has been largely the result of a self-reinforcing dynamic that was and is beyond the control of the member states. Table 2.2 provides an overview of supranationalism.

Historical institutionalism

To capture self-reinforcing processes conceptually, historical institutionalism constitutes a useful starting point, because it qualifies and criticizes the functional theories of institution-building prominent in LI. Functional theories of institution-building explain

Table 2.2 Supranationalism

General assumptions	*Historical institutionalism*
	Rational national, transnational, and supranational actors
	Unintended consequences and path dependency of institution building
Explanatory theory	Principal–agent theory, incomplete contracting theory, path dependence
Factors explaining integration	Intensity of transnational exchanges, autonomy of supranational actors, rule density

institutional choices by imputing these choices from the effects which states wish these institutions to produce: Hence, institutional choices are explained by their (expected) effects and functional theorists assume that the effects of institutions correspond to what the founders had in mind when they created the institutions in the first place. Historical institutionalists reject this conjecture (Pierson 1996, 2000).

First, historical institutionalists doubt that political actors are as far-sighted as suggested by functional theorists; instead, historical institutionalists assume that political actors have rather short time horizons and do not always take into account the potential long-term consequences of their initial institutional choices. Second, historical institutionalists dispute that actors can foresee the exact consequences of their actions; initial institutional choices can thus have 'unintended consequences': Complex social processes which involve a large number of actors are likely to produce feedback loops and interaction effects which cannot be foreseen or understood by the most farsighted of actors (Pierson 1998: 39). Third, historical institutionalists contend that political actors can only marginally correct certain institutional developments due to institutional path dependence (Pierson 1996). For instance vested interests and prohibitive decision rules (such as the need for unanimity to revise the EU treaties) make policy reversal difficult to obtain.

According to the functional theory of institutions, governments, acting as political 'principals', delegate considerable decision-making authority to 'agents' to fulfil certain collective tasks effectively and efficiently (see Pollack 1997). Yet, several problems come with the delegation of tasks to agents. The first problem is adverse selection: How can principals be sure that they have selected the 'right' agent? The second problem is one of moral hazard: Once an agent is selected, how can principals be sure that the agent does not develop an agenda of his or her own, which contradicts the preferences of the principals? In both instances, the principal faces the problem of asymmetrical information: In the case of adverse selection principals are uncertain about the true motives of the agent *prior* to establishing the contractual relationship. In the case of moral hazard, the principal is uncertain about the activities of the agent once the contractual relationship is in place.

The 'incomplete' nature of contracts, such as international treaties, tends to exacerbate this problem of agency slippage and bureaucratic drift. The notion of an 'incomplete contract' stipulates that the process of contracting is fraught with uncertainties, because it is hard for the contracting parties to anticipate contingencies arising in the future, which could prompt parties subject to the contract to offer conflicting interpretations over the initial contract. Moreover, asymmetric or incomplete information raises the costs of negotiating and may result in a contract or treaty that represents a second-best option for the parties involved. As a result, contractual imperfections tend to force the contracting parties to renegotiate aspects of the initial bargain (Cooley and Spruyt 2009: 26). Moreover, contractual incompleteness tends to increase agents' discretion and hence their autonomy vis-à-vis their principals.

Finally, institutional path dependence (Pierson 1996, 2000) refers to the idea that institutions are difficult to reform once they have been created – even if they develop in unintended ways – become inefficient because of changing circumstances or contradict the preferences of the principals. In order to stabilize institutions, political actors often introduce high thresholds to change them (for instance supermajority or unanimity decision rules), which can block institutional reforms even if they are desired by a majority. Over time, institutional changes may lose their attractiveness due to the existence of *sunk costs*: When new institutions are introduced, actors make personal investments to adapt to the new institutions. These investments are often so high that, as a consequence, actors 'stick' to these institutions even if new and more efficient alternatives appear which – absent these investments or sunk costs – would be more attractive. Unless there are major 'exogenous shocks' (such as wars, revolutions, economic crises) the institutional route once taken becomes increasingly hard to change.

Supranationalism and European integration

Supranationalists have traditionally subsumed mechanisms of transformative change under the label of *spillover*. In spillovers Ernst Haas saw the central mechanism to explain the 'expansive logic' of European integration (see Haas 1968: 283–317). Later works have categorized the factors and conditions producing integration's expansive logic into *functional, political*, and *cultivated* spillover mechanisms (see Schmitter 1969; Tranholm-Mikkelsen 1991: 15–16).

Functional spillover

Functional spillover results from the connectedness of different policy sectors. The functional spillover mechanism postulates that there will be a demand for further integration if the gains resulting from integration in policy sector A remain suboptimal, unless adjacent policy sectors B and C will also be integrated or when integration of A has negative effects on sectors B and C unless they are all being integrated collectively (see Lindberg and Scheingold 1970: 117). Put differently, the externalities of integrating a particular policy sector incite governments to undertake further, previously unplanned, steps of integration in other policy sectors in order to prevent welfare losses. A similar logic is behind what Haas calls 'geographical spillover' as a trigger of horizontal integration (1968: 313–315): States initially reluctant to join the EU will feel pressured to join eventually given the negative externalities of staying outside the Community.

Political spillover

Political spillover occurs as a reaction to initial integrative steps once interest groups, bureaucrats, and other domestic political actors direct their expectations and activities at the new, supranational level of decision-making. To the degree that integration improves the likelihood that the actors will realize their political aims at the supranational level rather than on the national level, we are likely to observe the formation of transnational coalitions and the development of common problem-solving perspectives (Haas 1968: xxxiv). Interest groups, bureaucrats and other domestic actors will – based on these newly acquired identities, attitudes, and coalitions – exercise pressure and influence on governments and press them to advance the process of integration.

Institutional spillover

This third kind of spillover is triggered by the activities of the EU's supranational actors, the Commission, the European Court of Justice, and the European Parliament. On one hand, these actors contribute to the processes of functional and political spillover: They allude to connections between different policy sectors and point to the potential positive externalities of further integration and, conversely, the negative externalities and consequences of potential failures to advance sector integration (Nye 1971: 59). For the same reason, supranational actors support the formation of transnational coalitions. On the other hand, supranational actors – first and foremost the Commission – also help the governments of EU member states to discover their common interests and possibilities for efficient cooperation. Furthermore, they play a crucial role in helping the member states to 'upgrade their common interest' (see Haas 1961) in finding bargaining solutions which are considered optimal from an integration perspective. This argument, however, is founded on the condition that supranational organizations possess an information advantage vis-à-vis the member state governments which they are willing to fully exploit (a condition that runs fundamentally counter to intergovernmentalist assumptions). According to this perspective, the Commission, for instance, seeks to 'cultivate' the ground to advance the integration process through its role as a mediator and provider of ideas, a process also referred to as *cultivated spillover*.

The work of a 'supranationalist' group of researchers around Alec Stone Sweet, Wayne Sandholtz, and Neil Fligstein provides the most prominent example of research in the tradition of Ernst Haas (Stone Sweet and Sandholtz 1997, 1998; Fligstein and Stone Sweet 2001, 2002; Stone Sweet *et al.* 2001). In their works, they have argued that European integration progresses as a result of the interplay of three developments: the expansion of transnational exchange, supranational actors' capacity to pursue an integrative agenda, and the role of European rule-making in solving policy externalities (see Stone Sweet and Sandholtz 1997: 301). Stone Sweet and Sandholtz advance their argument in close correspondence with the concepts of functional and political spillover: As transnational economic exchange expands, the costs of national rule-making increases, as does the demand of transnational actors – interest groups, transnational corporations, and producer and consumer groups – for supranational rules and policy coordination. This demand will be stronger, the more these actors expect to profit from cross-border exchange and hence, the larger the perceived advantage of uniform EU-level rules and policy harmonization is vis-à-vis different national rules. Transnational actors direct their demands for uniform EU-level rules to facilitate cross-border exchange at their respective national governments, yet if these prove reluctant to push the agenda for more uniform EU-level rules, transnational and societal actors will increasingly turn to supranational institutions to voice their demands. In sync with the logic of institutional spillover, the Commission and the European Court of Justice use the powers and information at their disposal to expand the scope of EU-level rules to facilitate cross-border exchange and thus help to increase collective transnational utility (Sandholtz and Stone Sweet 1997: 299, 306; 1998: 4).

Apart from the integrative impetus generated by transnational agents promoting cross-border exchange and uniform EU-level rules, Stone Sweet and Sandholtz advance another factor for explaining further integration. This factor can be captured in what they call the logic of *institutionalization* (1997: 310–312; Fligstein and Stone Sweet 2001: 31; see also Haas 1968: 283). Even though the EU's primary law laid down in the treaties may have been created by member state governments, reflecting their preferences and respective bargaining power, the application of the EU Treaty may develop in directions unforeseen or unintended by member state governments. First, actors who operate under the treaty rules adapt to them and use the opportunities offered by these rules to realize their own preferences. These preferences may, however, not be congruent with those of the member states who enacted the rules in the first place (see Lindner and Rittberger 2003: 451–455). Second, treaty rules never represent a 'complete contract' which caters for every possible contingency. Hence, rules are open to interpretation; actors (obviously) may offer controversial interpretations, and sometimes they may not even offer clear prescriptions or proscriptions for action. In situations such as these, supranational organizations such as the Court and the Commission – which have been endowed by the member states with applying and interpreting these treaty rules – may exploit this 'grey zone' for their own advantage. The process of rule modification and rule interpretation is a continuous process:

> As they interpret and apply the rules, courts, legislators, and administrators necessarily modify them by establishing their effective meaning. The new or changed rules then guide subsequent interactions, as the actors which act under these rules adapt their behaviours to the rules. The disputes that arise thereafter take shape in an altered rule structure and initiate the processes that will again reinterpret and modify the rules. The new rules guide actor behaviour, and so on.
>
> (Stone Sweet and Sandholtz 1997: 310)

In contrast to the expectations of early neofunctionalism, integration is not assumed to progress automatically and in a linear fashion. Yet, supranationalism expects that once a certain level of integration is reached, this will be next to impossible for governments to reverse (Fligstein and Stone Sweet 2001: 38, 55). As stated earlier, supranationalism takes recourse to the mechanisms of high institutional thresholds and sunk costs postulated by historical institutionalism in order to explain the (near) irreversibility of an institutional path once taken (Pierson 1998: 43–47). First, the rules to amend or change the treaties are very restrictive because they demand unanimous agreement among the member state governments plus ratification in each member state; furthermore, policy changes within the treaties require at least a qualified majority. When thus only a minority of states benefits from a particular rule, it will do everything it can to block change. EU policy-making thus possesses a high degree of 'policy stability' (Tsebelis

2002: 281–2). Second, over the course of the past half-century, national political systems have become increasingly penetrated by rules originating at the EU level. The sunk costs of adapting national rules and policy-making processes to the exigencies of EU politics render the mere existence of a state outside the EU increasingly unattractive. In this sense 'exit' is also becoming an ever more unlikely policy option for an EU member state, as is the threat of leaving the EU as a credible bargaining strategy.

Intergovernmentalism and supranationalism converge on several issues. Both approaches are founded on a rationalist model of action. Both see the most fundamental source of integration in societal interests. Supranationalism does also *not* dispute that governments are powerful actors in the integration process and that bargaining constitutes an important mode of interaction among the member states (Stone Sweet and Sandholtz 1997: 314; Pierson 1998: 29). Yet, supranationalism claims that governments are not *the* central actors and that interstate bargaining is not the only mode of interaction through which preferences are aggregated. Obviously, there are also a number of differences. First, supranationalism stipulates that socio-economic pressure for integration, for instance by producer groups, is not only channelled through the state; rather, societal and transnational actors form transnational coalitions and direct their demands to supranational institutions, thus bypassing the state. Second, intergovernmental negotiations are embedded in transnational and supranational contexts: Intergovernmental conferences take place in an environment subject to significant changes in the period between two intergovernmental conferences. In this respect, intergovernmental conferences are convened against the background of new demands by transnational actor coalitions and an institutional context shaped by the self-reinforcing dynamic of the process of institutionalization mentioned earlier. Third, supranational organizations are not only willing but also capable to make extensive use of their powers and promote rules and policies, which member states would not have agreed on during intergovernmental negotiations (see e.g. Lindner and Rittberger 2003; Rittberger and Stacey 2003). In the light of the preceding discussion, the demand for further integration is less the result of 'exogenous shocks' but rather of endogenous, path-dependent processes, and intergovernmental negotiations are less the generators of integration but its product (Caporaso 1998: 350; Stone Sweet and Sandholtz 1998: 12, 26).

Supranationalism and differentiated integration

The same two major forces that drive progress in integration in general also account for differentiated integration. First, differentiation may be caused by variation in the intensity of transnational exchange between different sectors and countries. Second, it may be affected by the capacity and preferences of supranational actors to promote their policy and institutional interests by furthering the integration process.

We start from the assumption that both transnational and supranational actors tend to be interested in unified rather than differentiated integration. First, supranational actors have an institutional interest to achieve high levels of centralization across the board of policies in order to maximize their own turf and competences. They also tend to believe that supranational regulation is more efficient than (diverse) national regulations. For these reasons, they work toward minimizing the vertical differentiation inherent in a gradual integration process in favour of high vertical integration in all policy areas.

Supranational actors also have an institutional interest in avoiding horizontal differentiation. Horizontal differentiation makes European governance more complicated. Decision-making and monitoring become more cumbersome. Internal differentiation comes with exemptions and derogations that need to be managed by the supranational organizations and sometimes requires additional organizational set-ups. For instance, the eurozone countries often meet separately but then there is a need to consult and discuss with the non-eurozone countries on financial and monetary issues as well. Horizontal differentiation with non-EU member states also goes hand in hand with a proliferation of 'association councils' and 'bilateral committees' and does not allow for centralized enforcement. Supranational actors should welcome the fact that horizontal differentiation allows member states to move ahead with supranational integration despite the opposition of others and expands supranational rules to countries that are otherwise unwilling or unable to join the EU. But they are unlikely to accept differentiation as a permanent condition and will work towards overcoming opt-outs and towards membership of associated countries.

Finally, transnational actors can be expected to be comfortable with vertical differentiation but less so with horizontal differentiation. They often have a policy-specific agenda and organization and strive for the level of centralization that corresponds to the level of transnational interactions in their area and that suits their policy-specific interests. But for each policy sector, they will want to ensure that all states participate. For instance, transnational business associations seek to create a level playing field for their members across the EU. The same is true for transnational trade unions trying to prevent a race to the bottom as a consequence of 'social dumping'. Transnational civil society organizations such as environmental or women's rights associations pursue the system-wide improvement of standards. By contrast, initiatives for horizontal differentiation are usually rooted in the special interests or deviant preferences of national governments or societal actors. It then depends on the strength and capacity of transnational and supranational actors whether they can counteract these initiatives and push for more unified integration.

Supranationalism: basic assumptions about differentiated integration

- The process of European integration generates a self-reinforcing dynamic, which begets further integration, which governments did not intend and which they are unable to control or to reverse.
- Transnational societal actors in conjunction with supranational actors are the relevant actors pushing the integration process. Integration develops as a result of complex transnational social and institutional processes and transcends the preferences and power constellations of national governments.
- Differentiated integration results from differences across policies and countries in the scope and intensity of transnational exchanges and the capacity of supranational actors.

Supranationalism: hypotheses about differentiated integration

- Vertical and horizontal integration is likely to progress, if it increases transnational societal actors' expected utility and to the degree to which supranational actors possess and are able to make use of their capacity to further the interests of transnational actors.

- Vertical differentiation increases with differences across policies in the intensity of transnational exchanges and the capacity of supranational actors.
- The horizontal differentiation of a policy decreases with the geographical scope of transnational exchanges and the capacity of supranational actors.

Constructivism

Constructivism is a comparatively recent addition to the portfolio of theoretical approaches to European integration. As in the case of intergovernmentalism and supranationalism, the theory was imported from IR, where constructivism had established itself in the 1990s as the counterpart to the rationalist mainstream. Correspondingly, constructivism is not as consolidated as intergovernmentalism or supranationalism as a theory of European integration. Table 2.3 provides an overview of its theoretical foundations.

Sociological institutionalism

Constructivism takes recourse to an institution theoretic perspective that is different from both rational and historical institutionalism: sociological institutionalism. Sociological institutionalism is founded on an idealist ontology and a logic of action driven by 'appropriateness' and not by 'anticipated consequences'. According to the logic of appropriateness, actors follow what is normatively expected of them in a particular role or situation (March and Olsen 1989: 160–161). From a sociological institutionalist perspective, states interact in a highly institutionalized and culturally dense environment, which is structured by collectively held ideational schemes and rules. In contrast to both intergovernmentalism and supranationalism, constructivism takes preferences not as exogenous; preferences are endogenous, the products of ideational structures and social interaction. Consequently, international institutions are not so much instruments to efficiently solve collective action problems; rather, their goals, designs, and procedures mirror collectively held norms and values and a common identity.

Table 2.3 Constructivism

General assumptions	*Sociological institutionalism*
	Primacy of ideas
	Logic of appropriateness and arguing
Explanatory theory	Community theory of institutions
	Argumentation theory
	Socialization theory
Factors explaining integration	Ideational consensus
	Legitimacy of arguments and institutional settings
	Legitimacy, exposure

Sociological institutionalism offers three substantive theories that specify how ideas affect international negotiations and institutions. The ideational or community theory of institutions specifies under which conditions international institutions are formed, how they work and what they do. According to sociological institutionalism, international organizations are 'community representatives' (Abbott and Snidal 1998: 24). The origins, goals, and procedures of international institutions are shaped by the standards of legitimacy and appropriateness of the international community they represent (and which constitutes their cultural and institutional environment) – rather than by the utilitarian demand for efficient problem solving.

Argumentation theory explains the outcome of international negotiations in which ideas are contested. It is the constructivist counterpart of bargaining theory. Arguing is a negotiation mode based on the use of arguments – in contrast with the use of threats and promises in the bargaining mode. Actors enter into arguing mode when claims are contested and exchange arguments that provide justifications for their claims. The better arguments prevail and produce a new ideational consensus that promotes and advances community and institution building.

Finally, the theory of international socialization tells us how international institutions shape and transform the ideas of international actors. Its purpose is similar to the path dependence mechanism in historical institutionalism. According to sociological institutionalism, international organizations are not only community representatives but also community-building agencies; that is they constitute and change actors' understanding of a situation and problem as well as their interests and identities. Theories of international socialization postulate and analyse different mechanisms und conditions for the transformation of interests and identities of state and non-state actors in international institutions; furthermore, they propose mechanisms for the change of state and societal structures as a consequence of these transformations. In the context of European integration research, the effects of EU-level institutions on domestic institutions and actors are analysed by the research programme on 'Europeanization' (see e.g. Cowles *et al.* 2001; Featherstone and Radaelli 2003). In the constructivist theory of socialization, the central mechanisms capturing transformative processes are social learning mechanisms, processes of imitation, persuasion and social influence. Checkel (2001: 562–563) and Johnston (2001: 498–499) have elaborated a catalogue of conditions under which these mechanisms are likely to be effective (see also Risse 2000: 19). Social learning is most likely when actors face novel situations characterized by high uncertainty; when a socializing agent possesses the authority to act on behalf of a community or a collectivity with which a particular actor identifies or desires to belong to, when the social learning process affects norms and rules which enjoy a high degree of legitimacy in the community or collectivity, when the social learning process takes place in an environment corresponding to an 'ideal speech situation' which encourages deliberation and is characterized by the absence of external and political constraints, and when the domestic or societal resonance of international norms and rules is high (or, at least, when domestic/societal rules and norms do not contradict international rules and norms).

Constructivism and European integration

In the constructivist perspective, European integration is at its core a process of community building. Over time, community building and (institutional) integration mutually influence and potentially reinforce each other. The constructivist research programme in European integration studies has three distinct foci that can be seen in a temporal sequence – roughly equivalent to the three-step explanation of integration in liberal intergovernmentalism. The first focus is on the effects of ideas on integration preferences. The second asks how the intersubjective context of negotiations and decision-making affect integration outcomes. Finally, constructivists are interested in the effects of European integration and institutions on community building. The three foci correspond roughly to the three explanatory approaches. The community theory of institutions explains integration by ideational preferences, the theory of argumentation explains the outcome of negotiations, and socialization theory explains the effect of community institutions on actor beliefs and preferences.

Initially, institutional integration depends on the strength of transnational community: the stronger the collective, 'European' identity, and the larger the pool of common or compatible ideas, the more institutional integration we will see. By contrast, weak European and strong national identities generate resistance to institutional integration, and without shared normative and causal beliefs, common institutions and integrated policies are hard to agree on.

At least in the beginning of the integration process, the ideas that shape integration preferences mostly stem from the national political and cultural environment. National policy paradigms regarding economic and other policies, national constitutional values and norms, and national identities and images of Europe inform preferences on the desirability, form, and substance of European integration. Constructivists assert that these ideas need not necessarily be harmonized but must at least be compatible in order to allow for integration. For instance, empirical research shows that *exclusive* national identities weaken support for the EU (Hooghe and Marks 2005). By contrast, having a national identity is not detrimental to support for European integration if people feel at least somewhat 'European', too. In addition, Ole Wæver argues that the different visions of Europe he finds embedded in national identity discourses do not need to be replaced by a harmonized European vision. For stable integration, it is sufficient if these visions are compatible and include the European project as a part of national identities (Wæver 2009).

Once established, integrated institutions that provide for dense interactions and possess high legitimacy deepen the community through legitimation and socialization processes. Integrated policy-making generates intense and frequent contacts and cooperation and takes place in a distinct environment structured by community norms. This environment facilitates integration-friendly decisions and promotes social learning processes that have the potential to overcome conflicts about integration, restructure discourses, and transform identities.

In the intergovernmentalist perspective, integration outcomes result from constellations of interests and power. If national interests diverge, states with superior bargaining power are able to shape integration according to their interests. By contrast, constructivists claim that actors with conflicting preferences engage in a process of arguing in which the 'better' argument prevails. The quality of an argument is mainly determined by its relative legitimacy in a given community environment. The political systems of the member states and the EU treaties stipulate liberal democracy as a fundamental and uncontested norm of legitimacy. In line with this norm, the EU has made enlargement decisions and decisions to democratize and constitutionalize the EU that have run against intergovernmental constellations of preferences and bargaining power (Schimmelfennig 2001; Rittberger 2005).

Even if arguing fails because standards of legitimacy are too weak or too controversial to adjudicate between claims, negotiations do not necessarily resort to hard, strategic bargaining. Rather, constructivist analyses point to informal norms of deliberation, compromise, and consensus that govern intergovernmental negotiations and decision-making in the EU (see Joerges and Neyer 1997; Lewis 1998, 2003).

Finally, constructivism expects processes of 'European' socialization at the levels of governments, individual officials participating in integrated policy-making, and citizens under two main conditions: high levels of exposure and high degrees of legitimacy. First, European socialization is more likely to be successful if actors are frequently and intensively exposed to the outcomes of European integration, EU institutions, and European ideas. Exposure is facilitated if the actors are willing to engage in contacts with the EU and open to adopting new ideas. Second, European socialization requires that actors find these ideas legitimate. This is more likely to be the case that if actors identify with 'Europe', European ideas will resonate with prior individual or national ideas, and socialization will take place in a deliberative setting.

Constructivism and differentiated integration

The constructivist explanation of differentiated integration is structurally similar to intergovernmentalism but based on legitimacy rather than efficiency considerations. Whereas intergovernmentalism stresses unequal interdependence as the main source of differentiation, constructivism emphasizes imperfect ideational consensus. The 'heterogeneity of preferences' in intergovernmentalism corresponds to 'ideational heterogeneity' in constructivism. Politicization is considered a relevant factor for differentiation in both theories. For (realist) intergovernmentalism, however, politicization results from threats to autonomy and security, whereas constructivism explains politicization by threats to national identity or fundamental national values and norms.

Policies with a strong ideational consensus are likely to be more integrated – and integrated earlier – than those in which policy ideas are contested. Likewise, countries with a Euro-sceptic population and a strong national identity are more likely to reject or delay membership, and opt out from individual policies, than countries with a strong European identity and support for supranational integration. In this context, it also matters to what extent policies are relevant for national identity and rely on ideational support. 'Technical issues' are likely to be more integrated than are 'identity issues' because international ideational consensus is less relevant for such issues and not required for agreement. Even if there is ideational contestation, actors are more likely to compromise on the integration of technical rather than identity-relevant issues.

Constructivism: basic assumptions about differentiated integration

- Integration fundamentally depends on the extent of ideational consensus among the actors participating in the integration process.
- Integration is supported by the institutionalization of common norms, values, and policy ideas in the EU and by argumentative settings at the supranational level.

- Successful integration contributes to the further institutionalization of ideas in the EU and generates socialization processes, which potentially increase the commonality or compatibility of ideas among the participating actors. Both institutionalization and socialization increase the likelihood of future integration.
- Differentiated integration results from differences across policies and countries in the level of ideational consensus.

Constructivism: hypotheses about differentiated integration

- Vertical and horizontal integration is likely to progress, if the actors' ideational consensus on integration increases and integrative efforts enjoy a high degree of legitimacy.
- Vertical differentiation increases with differences across policies in the level of consensus, legitimacy, and politicization.
- The horizontal differentiation of a policy decreases with international ideational heterogeneity, contestation of integration, and politicization.

Conclusion

In this chapter we presented the most important theories, which are currently employed to explain European integration in its vertical and horizontal dimension: intergovernmentalism, supranationalism, and constructivism. Moreover, we argued that the increasingly differentiated character of the European integration project calls for adapting integration theories to capture this development. We took up this challenge and presented the different theories' basic assumptions and hypotheses about differentiated integration. Differentiation is already a hallmark of European integration and it is likely to stay: The eurozone and the Schengen are only the most prominent examples of differentiated integration. Recent moves towards stronger fiscal policy coordination, 'banking union' or financial transaction tax are all characterized by horizontal differentiation. 'Deepening' may thus beget more horizontal differentiation.

Our discussion of the different integration theoretic perspectives also suggests that not one single theory of European integration can claim to possess the explanatory power to account for 'European (differentiated) integration' in its entirety. As existing theory-driven empirical research has amply demonstrated, a combination of the factors and conditions postulated by different theories of integration may be necessary to account for phenomena of vertical and horizontal integration as well as differentiation. We echo others when we claim that intergovernmentalism and supranationalism are not incommensurable, but can in principle engage in a fruitful 'theoretical dialogue' (Jupille *et al.* 2003: 19). For instance, there is no reason why LI should not be generally open to theoretical 'dialogue' with approaches sharing its rationalist foundations and a positivist commitment to theory testing, such as supranationalism. However, given its emphasis on states as key actors in the integration process, LI has been particularly 'strong' in accounting for the main substantive and institutional outcomes of intergovernmental conferences, whereas supranationalism – with its emphasis on the autonomous influence of supranational actors and institutions – has been able to capture processes and outcomes of integration which occur or have their foundation *in-between*

Treaty re-negotiations (Stone Sweet *et al.* 2001; Fligstein and Stone Sweet 2002; Hix 2002; Farrell and Héritier 2003; Rittberger and Stacey 2003; Héritier 2007). We also see that theoretical dialogue can occur between approaches, which do not necessarily share the same theoretical foundations. By identifying a theory's respective 'home turf', by specifying the elements of each theory that do the explaining, and 'by bringing together each home turf in some larger picture' (Jupille *et al.* 2003: 21), we can offer *additive* explanations of integration phenomena which we could otherwise only partially account for. Work on horizontal integration in the EU ('enlargement') has demonstrated that elements from constructivist approaches are a necessary complement to rationalist approaches such as LI in order to account for the decision of EU member states to support Eastern enlargement (Schimmelfennig 2001, 2003). Leuffen *et al.* (2013) have demonstrated, that empirical analyses of horizontal differentiation, especially decisions of EU member states to opt out from common policies, relate to the level of politicization of the particular policy in the domestic political context. Opt-outs from the eurozone, the Schengen, or matters of defence, which publics as well as political elites may deem particularly relevant for national identity, are thus a domain where constructivist hypotheses possess explanatory leverage (Schimmelfennig and Winzen 2014).

In order to reap the benefits of theoretical dialogue, it is, however, unavoidable for students of European integration to specify the elements of their theories, to deduce testable hypotheses and to be aware of the empirical domain in which the theory is expected to do 'best' in explaining integration phenomena. In this chapter we have sought to offer an integration theoretic toolbox which, as we hope, proves to be user-friendly while, at the same, encourages rigorous theory-driven research on European integration.

Notes

1 This chapter builds on the theory chapters of a recent book on differentiated integration in the EU co-authored with Dirk Leuffen (Leuffen *et al.* 2013).
2 For details on the measurement and data, see Leuffen *et al.* (2013).

References

Abbott, K. W. and Snidal, D. (1998) 'Why States Act through Formal International Organizations', *Journal of Conflict Resolution*, 42: 3–32.
Caporaso, J. A. (1998) 'Regional Integration Theory: Understanding Our Past and Anticipating Our Future', in W. Sandholtz and A. Stone Sweet (eds) *European Integration and Supranational Governance*, Oxford: Oxford University Press.
Caporaso, J. A. and Keeler, J.T.S. (1995) 'The European Union and Regional Integration Theory', in C. Rhodes and S. Mazey (eds) *The State of the European Union. Building a European Polity*, Boulder: Lynne Rienner.
Checkel, J. T. (2001) 'Why Comply? Social Learning and European Identity Change', *International Organization*, 55: 553–588.
Cooley, A. and Spruyt, H. (2009) *Contracting States. Sovereign Transfers in International Relations*, Princeton: Princeton University Press.
Cowles, M. G., Caporaso, J. and Risse, T. (eds) (2001) *Transforming Europe. Europeanization and Domestic Change*, Ithaca: Cornell University Press.

Cram, L. (2001) 'Integration Theory and the Study of the European Policy Process: Towards a Synthesis of Approaches', in J. Richardson (ed) *European Union. Power and Policy-Making*, 2nd edn, London: Routledge.

Farrell, H. and Héritier, A. (2003) 'Formal and Informal Institutions under Codecision: Continuous Constitution-Building in Europe', *Governance*, 16: 577–600.

Featherstone, K. and Radaelli, C. (eds) (2003) *The Politics of Europeanisation*, Oxford: Oxford University Press.

Fligstein, N. and Stone Sweet, A. (2001) 'Institutionalizing the Treaty of Rome', in A. Stone Sweet, W. Sandholtz and N. Fligstein (eds) *The Institutionalization of Europe*, Oxford: Oxford University Press.

Fligstein, N. and Stone Sweet, A. (2002) 'Constructing Polities and Markets: An Institutionalist Account of European Integration', *American Journal of Sociology*, 107: 1206–1243.

Frey, B. S. and Eichenberger, R. (1996) 'FOCJ: Competitive Governments for Europe', *International Review of Law and Economics*, 16: 315–327.

Grieco, J. (1996) 'State Interests and Institutional Rule Trajectories: A Neorealist Interpretation of the Maastricht Treaty and European Economic and Monetary Union', *Security Studies*, 5: 261–306.

Haas, E. B. (1961) 'International Integration: The European and the Universal Process', *International Organization*, 15: 366–392.

Haas, E. B. (1968) *The Uniting of Europe. Political, Social, and Economic Forces 1950–1957*, Stanford: Stanford University Press.

Héritier, A. (2007) *Explaining Institutional Change in Europe*, Oxford: Oxford University Press.

Hix, S. (2002) 'Constitutional Agenda-Setting through Discretion in Rule Interpretation: Why the European Parliament Won at Amsterdam', *British Journal of Political Science*, 32: 259–280.

Hoffmann, S. (1966) 'Obstinate or Obsolete? The Fate of the Nation-State and the Case of Western Europe', *Daedalus*, 95: 862–915.

Hoffmann, S. (1982) 'Reflections on the Nation-State in Western Europe Today', *Journal of Common Market Studies*, 21: 21–37.

Hooghe, L. and Marks, G. (2003) 'Unravelling the Central State, but How? Types of Multi-Level Governance', *American Political Science Review*, 97: 233–243.

Hooghe, L. and Marks, G. (2005) 'Calculation, Community and Cues: Public Opinion on European Integration', *European Union Politics*, 6: 419–443.

Joerges, C. and Neyer, J. (1997) 'From Intergovernmental Bargaining to Deliberative Political Process: The Constitutionalization of Comitology', *European Law Journal*, 3: 273–299.

Johnston, A. I. (2001) 'Treating International Institutions as Social Environments', *International Studies Quarterly*, 45: 487–515.

Jupille, J., Caporaso, J. A. and Checkel, J. (2003) 'Integrating Institutions. Rationalism, Constructivism, and the Study of the European Union', *Comparative Political Studies*, 36: 7–40.

Koremenos, B., Lipson, C. and Snidal, D. (2001) 'The Rational Design of International Institutions', *International Organization*, 55: 761–799.

Leuffen, D., Rittberger, B. and Schimmelfennig, F. (2013) *Differentiated Integration. Explaining Variation in the European Union*, Basingstoke: Palgrave Macmillan.

Lewis, J. (1998) 'Is the "Hard Bargaining" Image of The Council Misleading? The Committee of Permanent Representatives and the Local Elections Directive', *Journal of Common Market Studies*, 36: 479–504.

Lewis, J. (2003) 'Institutional Environments and Everyday EU Decision Making. Rationalist or Constructivist?', *Comparative Political Studies*, 36: 97–124.

Lindberg, L. and Scheingold, S. (1970) *Europe's Would-Be Polity*, Englewood Cliffs: Prentice-Hall.

Lindner, J. and Rittberger, B. (2003) 'The Creation, Interpretation and Contestation of Institutions – Revisiting Historical Institutionalism', *Journal of Common Market Studies*, 41: 445–473.

March, J. G. and Olsen, Johan P. (1989) *Rediscovering Institutions. The Organizational Basis of Politics*, New York: Free Press.

Milward, A. S. (1984) *The Reconstruction of Western Europe 1945–51*, London: Methuen.

Milward, A. S. (1994) *The European Rescue of the Nation-State*, London: Routledge.

Moravcsik, A. (1993) 'Preferences and Power in the European Community: A Liberal Intergovernmentalist Approach', *Journal of Common Market Studies*, 31: 473–524.

Moravcsik, A. (1998) *The Choice for Europe: Social Power and State Purpose from Messina to Maastricht*, Ithaca: Cornell University Press.

Nye, J. S. (1971) *Peace in Parts: Integration and Conflict in Regional Organization*, Boston: Little Brown and Company.

Pierson, P. (1996) 'The Path to European Integration: A Historical-Institutionalist Analysis', *Comparative Political Studies*, 29: 123–163.

Pierson, P. (1998) 'The Path to European Integration: A Historical-Institutionalist Analysis', in W. Sandholtz and A. Stone Sweet (eds) *European Integration and Supranational Governance*, Oxford: Oxford University Press.

Pierson, P. (2000) 'Increasing returns, Path Dependence, and the Study of Politics', *American Political Science Review*, 94: 251–267.

Pollack, M. A. (1997) 'Delegation, Agency, and Agenda Setting in the European Community', *International Organization*, 51: 99–134.

Risse, T. (2000) '"Let's Argue!": Communicative Action in World Politics', *International Organization*, 54: 1–39.

Rittberger, B. (2005) *Building Europe's Parliament. Democratic Representation beyond the Nation-State*, Oxford: Oxford University Press.

Rittberger, B. and Stacey, J. (2003) 'Dynamics of Formal and Informal Institutional Change in the EU', special issue of the *Journal of European Public Policy*, 10: 6.

Rosamond, B. (2000) *Theories of European Integration*, Basingstoke: Palgrave Macmillan.

Schimmelfennig, F. (2001) 'The Community Trap: Liberal Norms, Rhetorical Action, and the Eastern Enlargement of the European Union', *International Organization*, 55: 47–80.

Schimmelfennig, F. (2003) *The EU, NATO and the Integration of Europe. Rules and Rhetoric*, Cambridge: Cambridge University Press.

Schimmelfennig, F. and Winzen, T. (2014) 'Instrumental and Constitutional Differentiation in the European Union', *Journal of Common Market Studies* 52: 354–370.

Schmitter, P. C. (1969) 'Three Neofunctional Hypotheses about International Integration', *International Organization*, 23: 161–166.

Schmitter, P. C. (1996) 'Imagining the Future of the Euro-Polity with the Help of New Concepts', in G. Marks, F. W. Scharpf, P. C. Schmitter and W. Streeck (eds) *Governance in the European Union*, London: Sage.

Schneider, G. and Cederman, L. E. (1994) 'The Change of Tide in Political Cooperation: A Limited Information Model of European Integration', *International Organization*, 48: 633–662.

Stone Sweet, A. and Sandholtz, W. (1997) 'European Integration and supranational governance', *Journal of European Public Policy*, 4: 297–317.

Stone Sweet, A. and Sandholtz, W. (1998) 'Integration, Supranational Governance, and the Institutionalization of the European Polity', in W. Sandholtz and A. Stone Sweet (eds) *European Integration and Supranational Governance*, Oxford: Oxford University Press.

Stone Sweet, A., Sandholtz, W. and Fligstein, N. (eds) (2001) *The Institutionalization of Europe*, Oxford: Oxford University Press.

Tranholm-Mikkelsen, J. (1991) 'Neo-functionalism: Obstinate or Obsolete? A Reappraisal in the Light of the New Dynamism of the EC', *Millenium*, 20: 1–22.

Tsebelis, G. (2002) *Veto Players. How Political Institutions Work*, Princeton and New York: Princeton University Press and Russell Sage Foundation.

Wæver, O. (2009) 'Discursive Approaches', in A. Wiener and T. Diez (eds) *European Integration Theory*, 2nd edn, Oxford: Oxford University Press.

Wiener, A. and Diez, T. (2009) *European Integration Theory*, 2nd edn, Oxford: Oxford University Press.

Wolf, K. D. (1999) 'The New Raison d'État as a Problem for Democracy in World Society', *European Journal of International Relations*, 5: 333–363.

Chapter 3

The politics of multispeed integration in the European Union

CHRISTIAN B. JENSEN AND JONATHAN B. SLAPIN

Introduction

Recent European history is replete with examples of member states seeking opt outs from certain areas of decision-making. In late 2011, for example, the British government has debated whether to participate in the process of implementing new European Union (EU) financial regulations. On one hand, the UK clearly opposes new regulations supported by the vast majority of member states, believing the regulations would reduce the City of London's global competitiveness. On the other, it fears that if it does not participate in the European decision-making process, it will be shut out of European financial markets. Meanwhile, other member states have become increasingly fed up with British attempts to, in their view, undermine and water down the new policies.

Laggards have frequently in the past desired a multispeed approach to integration to avoid implementing policies to which they object. The British under Prime Minister John Major for example sought an opt-out from the EU's social policy contained in the Maastricht Treaty. Following their failure to ratify the Maastricht Treaty, the Danes, along with the UK, demanded an opt-out from Economic and Monetary Union (EMU).

Laggards, however, are not alone in calling for a multispeed approach. While laggards talk of opt-outs, Europhiles often speak of 'enhanced' or 'closer' cooperation. Calls for a multispeed approach to European integration that allow some member states desiring deeper integration to pursue ambitious projects without hinderance from laggards have also been common.[1] In the early 1980s, amid Margaret Thatcher's threats to veto all EU activity until she secured a budget rebate for the UK, French president François Mitterrand suggested that other member states leave Britian on the sidelines.[2] Again, while negotiating the 1997 Treaty of Amsterdam, the French and the Germans pressed for an 'enhanced cooperation' clause, to allow for deeper cooperation among a small group of member states, over British protests.[3]

Despite the difference in language, the result is the same – two groups of member states pursuing integration at different speeds. Moreover, multispeed proposals have been at times resisted and at times accepted by both camps. Although, a multispeed approach might allow laggards to avoid swallowing distasteful policies, they may fear being left on the sidelines. States preferring deeper cooperation, on the other hand, relish the thought of moving Europe into new policy areas without pesky laggards holding them back. Nevertheless, they worry that such an approach undermines the goal of a united Europe. This leads us to the puzzle we examine in this chapter. Under what circumstances do laggards (integrationists) support (oppose) a multispeed Europe? To investigate this question, we draw on scholarship on the rational design of international organizations, European Union decision-making, and the role of exit and voice in bargaining.

We begin by reviewing the literature on multispeed integration in the EU and other organizations.We then investigate the institutions and member state preferences that lead both camps to accept and resist multispeed proposals, paying particular attention to how a multispeed approach affects bargaining after states have opted out. Our primary insight is that decisions to implement a multispeed approach alter the identity and location of the pivotal actor in the Council, therefore altering possible policy outcomes. Whether laggards or integrationists prefer a multispeed approach depends on who benefits in terms of policy outcomes from multispeed integration following a change in identity and location of the pivotal actor.

Multispeed integration in the EU and beyond

The major theoretical traditions in European integration literature – supranationalism (e.g. Marks *et al.* 1996), liberal intergovernmentalism (e.g. Moravcsik 1998), and new institutionalism (e.g. Tsebelis and Garrett 2001) – have largely neglected the topic of multispeed integration. Moravcsik (1998: 471), for instance, acknowledges that a "two-track", or "flexible" Europe is a legacy of the Maastricht Treaty, but his liberal intergovernmental theory does not specifically address when and why member states pursue this option. Likewise, Tsebelis and Garrett's (2001) theory of legislative decision-making does not account for a multispeed process. And supranationalists, who tend to place less emphasis on member state governments in theories of integration, do not explore why governments sometimes wish to opt out of decision-making.

Some scholars have suggested that multispeed integration has the potential, albeit unlikely, to lead to a breakdown of the European project as member states pick and chose from the menu of rules they wish to enforce (Kelemen 2007). When considering future paths for European integration, Schmitter (1996) has suggested that a Europe with multiple centers and different memberships advancing with integration at various speeds is a suboptimal, yet likely outcome for the EU. Other scholars are more sanguine about the prospects for multispeed approaches. Literature on international organizations for example finds that flexibililty often increases the likelihood of cooperation. Downs *et al.* (1998) argue that deeper integration is possible if the states preferring more cooperation integrate first, allowing other states to join them later. If laggards are let into the union too soon, they will wield their veto power to block further integration that would have been possible if they had been kept on the sidelines until a later date. Before exploring our model, we examine the various literatures on EU integration, international organizations, and federalism with respect to their implications for multispeed integration in the EU.

Multispeed integration in EU literature

EU research generally discusses three categories of multispeed integration: multispeed, variable geometry and à la carte (see Stubb 1996; 2002; Warleigh 2002). Multispeed integration is characterized by a core of member states moving forward on some dimension of integration with the assumption that those that lag behind will eventually join when they are able and willing to do so. Membership in the eurozone represents a prominent example. The second catagory, variable geometry, refers to the establishment of a permanent division between member states, usually outside the framework of the EU treaties, in which some states pursue deeper cooperation. An example would be the Schengen agreement to remove border controls. In the final category, à la carte membership, member states select the aspects of European integration in which they wish to participate based solely upon their willingness, rather than their ability, to implement policy. The UK opt out of the Social Charter provides a good example. Our analysis is primarily concerned with cases in which states opt out, or pursue deeper cooperation, based upon their policy preferences rather than their ability to implement policy. Thus we are primarily focused on the latter two categories.

Recent work theorizes why member states pursue multispeed integration in some areas, but not in others (Harstad 2006; Kölliker 2006; Labeta 2009). Kölliker (2006) argues that multispeed integration is least likely in policy areas that handle public goods where common pool resource problems are likely to arise. When it is difficult to exclude member states outside of the new core from partaking in benefits produced by those participating in the core, there is little incentive to form a core in the first place. However, when it is possible to prevent outsiders from free-riding, core states desiring deeper integration have a stronger incentive to cooperate. Moreover, member states outside the core have a stronger incentive to eventually join the core.[4] This work represents a great advance in understanding incentives for creating a multispeed Europe; however, it still overlooks the role of member state preferences and EU institutions, such as voting rules, that lie at the heart of our argument.

Flexibility and opt-outs in international organizations

The decision to create a multispeed Europe is, in essence, a decision to create more flexibility in EU decision-making. Recent literature on the rational design of international organizations has argued that flexible institutions, including the presence of escape clauses as well as the ability to renegotiate terms of agreements following a specific period of time, allows for stronger institutional cooperation but also involves costs (Downs and Rocke 1995; Koremenos *et al.* 2001; Rosendorff 2005; Rosendorff and Milner 2001). Some have even suggested that increased legalization may backfire, leading to less cooperation (at least in the form of trade liberalization) because states refuse to participate in highly legalized regimes that go too far (Goldstein and Martin 2000).

Renegotiating treaties is costly as it involves not only coming to new agreements with negotiating partners, but may also involve putting together new domestic political coalitions, whose support may be necessary for ratification (Koremenos 2005). Creating escape clauses may be very costly in the presence of incomplete information. If it is difficult to know when a partner state is reneging on obligations because domestic politics makes it absolutely necessary or whether they are simply trying to avoid costs of compliance, states may use escape clauses in a way that undermines the entire treaty (Rosendorff 2005).

This literature suggests that creating a multispeed Europe may be a double-edged sword. On one hand, as the EU diversifies by adding more states, a multispeed approach may offer flexibility so that all member states can choose a policy option sufficiently close to their ideal. On the other hand, it may increase bargaining costs and limit the degree to which states integrate by offering them an opt-out that would not otherwise exist.

Exit, voice and federal bargaining

Models using Hirschman's (1970) influential exit, voice and loyalty framework (e.g. Bednar 2007; Dowding *et al.* 2000; Dowding and John 2008; Gehlbach 2006; Slapin 2009) offer insights into how the creation of a multispeed Europe is likely to affect bargaining power among member states. When facing a proposal on integration with which they do not agree, member states have the option to voice their discontent, perhaps through vetoing policy change, or to opt out of the given policy, akin to partial exit from the EU. Which of these strategies states choose (and, indeed, are even available to states) depends on the costs associated with allowing the laggard to opt out for both integrationists and the laggards.[5] If integrationist states sincerely desire the participation of laggards, and laggards do not fear being left on the sidelines, laggards can threaten to veto legislation unless their demands for slower and shallower unification are met. Integrationists prefer that laggards block change in a union that encompasses all member states over the creation of a multispeed union where laggards cannot block change and are instead left behind on certain contentious issues.

On the other hand, if laggards pay a high price for being left behind by integrationists on a particular issue and integrationists are more concerned about deeper cooperation among a select few than shallower cooperation among all states, laggards will not be able exercise their veto. If laggards did exercise their veto, integrationists may opt to create a multispeed Europe that leaves the laggards on the sidelines. Fearing this, they choose to go along with the policy of deeper integration. Generally, this literature suggests that both laggards and integrationists must weigh the costs and benefits of deeper integration against the costs and benefits of pursuing integration in smaller groups.

Legal foundations of a multispeed Europe

There are many legal avenues for a multispeed process. Integrationist states could pursue deeper integration outside of the framework of the EU (i.e. variable geometry). Alternatively, member states can pursue different levels of cooperation within the legal framework of the EU (i.e. à la carte). We are interested in situations in which a single, discrete, decision to opt in or opt out on a particular policy has implications for an entire policy area.

There are two primary legal mechanisms for pursuing a multispeed approach within the treaties.[6] The first is Art. 114(4) TFEU, which was first introduced with the Single European Act (SEA) and allows member states, under strict conditions, to apply national rules after they have been outvoted by a qualified majority in the Council (Ehlermann 1998). This clause means that, in certain circumstances, laggards can opt out after a vote has been taken. Of course, knowing this, integrationists may not push for a vote with which they know laggard states will not comply.

The second mechanism is the provison for closer cooperation found in Art. 20 TEU, first introduced with the Treaty of Amsterdam. This provision allows a majority of member states to pursue deeper integration as a last resort when there is no other way to pursue integration within the EU framework. According to Art. 329 TFEU, member states in the Council may unanimously vote to invoke Art. 20 on a proposal from the Commission (requested by those states who wish to pursue enhanced cooperation) with the consent of the European Parliament. Art. 20 TEU addresses how decisions are taken when not all member states participate in the decision-making process. It states that '. . . only members of the Council representing the Member States participating in enhanced cooperation shall take part in the vote'. The qualified majority threshold is recalculated based on the states participating in the policy area. Thus, leaving the laggards on the sidelines effectively changes the identity and location of the pivotal member of the Council.

We present a model which examines decision-making once member states have decided to allow for a multispeed approach. We are interested in exploring the policy consequences of a multispeed approach, and what these consequences mean for future decisions regarding opt-outs. The model holds in any situation in which a laggard member state can opt out after being made worse off than it currently is as a result of the decision-making process. This can occur both when a multispeed approach is pursued outside or within the treaty framework.

The model: how losing votes leads to opt-outs

EU decision-making usually involves a supranational agenda setter, such as the Commission, proposing policy changes to the member states, oftentimes in conjunction with the European Parliament (EP). Our theory of multispeed integration is based on a simplified version of EU decision making that excludes the EP. This simplification is an accurate reflection of the decision-making procedure in many policy areas, including the management of the euro. It is also an innocuous assumption whenever the EP has similar preferences to the Commission or to member states preferring deeper cooperation. At the heart of our model is the notion that governments make cost–benefit calculations about whether to participate in different aspects of European integration. Is a government better off participating in the policymaking process, and presumably having some influence over it, even if it means the government is forced to implement some decisions it would rather not? Or is the government better off opting out and remaining unconstrained by EU policymaking, even if it means not receiving the full benefits of integration? The calculus is not all that different from the decision to join the EU in the first place, except that once a member, a government can only apply its calculus to particular issues. Moreover, our model considers how decision-making rules and member state preferences interact to influence government opt-out decisions. Specifically, we argue that governments are more likely to opt out of policy making in an area when their allies on a particular issue have already opted out of decision-making in that area. This calculus suggests the possibility of "opt-out cascades" in which one state opts out, leading a second state to opt out, even though the second state may have preferred to remain part of the process had the first state remained as well.

Our model applies a spatial logic. We assume that a single dimension can represent a policy area, and that member state governments make decisions about participating based on their rational calculations of the policy outcomes member states are likely to agree to in that policy area. The supranational agenda setter always prefers the most policy change in the direction of deeper cooperation and is able to make a proposal to the member states. Member state governments, in our model, all desire some change in the direction of deeper cooperation, but they vary in the degree of cooperation they wish to pursue. Last, we define the pivotal member state as that member state whose vote will be decisive in passing the proposal from the supranational agenda setter. The identity and location of the pivotal member is determined by configuration of all member state preferences and the voting rule. Under a qualified majority rule, depending upon the alignment of preferences, some set of member state governments could be made worse off than they would under the status quo policy. These governments are the ones with the greatest incentive to opt out of decision-making on this dimension.

By going it alone, they would not need to implement the EU policies with which they do not agree.

Weighing against the decision to opt out are non-policy related costs associated with leaving the decision-making process. For a laggard member state (a state preferring little or no further cooperation in this area under debate), these non-policy costs could include loss of overall influence in the EU that could result. The state's reputation as a reliable European partner may suffer if it opts out of a policy area that most other member states support. Reputational costs may have an impact on the laggard's ability to effectively work with the other member states in other policy areas. These non-policy costs may lead a laggard member state to continue participating despite being on the losing end of the policy debate. However, when these non-policy costs are lower than the policy costs of losing consistently in the new policy area, a laggard will decide to opt out. This calculation leads to laggard induced multispeed integration.

There are non-policy costs associated with a laggard's opt-out for the supranational actor making the initial policy proposal as well. It desires the participation of all member states. While the supranational agenda setter may settle for multispeed integration, it prefers a single approach for the EU. When drafting a proposal, the agenda setter may balance its desire to see every member state participate against the gains it would realize by seeing its ideal proposal pass (the proposal it could muster qualified majority support if no opt outs were possible). If the supranational agenda setter is reluctant to force the laggard state to opt out, it will only make proposals that the laggard would prefer to opting out. In effect, the mere possibility of a member state opt out can lead the supranational agenda setter to moderate its proposals. But moderation will only occur when the potential gains of proposing a more integrationist version of the policy are outweighed by the potential losses associated with accepting a multispeed approach. Conversely, if the policy gains to the agenda setter of a more integrationist proposal are very high relative to the costs of a member state opting out, it may decide to make a proposal it knows will induce a laggard state to seek an opt out.

Once the supranational actor has made a proposal, the laggard must consider the policy benefits/costs and non-policy costs. When the laggard sees the policy as so pernicious that the policy losses associated with living with the new proposal exceed the non-policy costs associated with opting out, the laggard will seek to opt out of the entire policy area. On the other hand, if the laggard member state perceives the non-policy costs associated with opting out as exceeding the policy losses associated with the new policy proposal, it will vote against the proposal but continue to participate in the policy area even if the proposal passes, thus incurring the policy loss.

Our analysis goes beyond examining the costs and benefits for a single decision to opt out. When the EU begins integrating in a new policy area, the result is a series of decisions within the same policy area. A laggard member state could expect to be on the losing end of many related policies. When it decides to opt out, it is not only opting out of a single policy, it is changing the number of member states participating in decisions on related policies down the road. One important additional consequence of a state opting out is that this single opt-out can change the identity of the pivotal member state, thus the outcome, on these future decisions.

When the number of member states participating in decision-making process is reduced through the removal of the most reluctant member state, the position of the pivotal member state often shifts closer to the position of the agenda-setting supranational actor. And, indeed, the identity of the pivot likely shifts as well. In other words, after the laggard opts out, future policies in this area may be significantly more integrationist than they would have been had the opt not taken place. That, in turn, changes the calculation for the most reluctant member state that remains. Suppose there are two laggard member states. When the original integration project is proposed, one of these states decides to opt out and the other decides to stay based on their respective comparisons of the policy losses associated with the new policy and the non-policy costs associated with opting out. However, as soon as the first laggard decides to opt out, the second laggard must recalculate its assessment of these relative costs and benefits. Furthermore, it must do this with the understanding that, because of the other laggard's opt out, the pivotal member state and the policy content of future policies in this area will have shifted towards the ideal point of the agenda setter. If these shifts increase the policy losses for the second laggard enough, it may respond to the first laggard's decision by opting out itself. If we extrapolate this further we could imagine several states opting out, one after another, in response to anticipated shifts in the pivotal member state's position brought about by the initial opt-out. Under the right circumstances, an opt-out by one laggard can lead to a cascade of opt outs.

In the following section, we present a series of cases designed to demonstrate the plausibility of our model. We are not presenting these cases as a definitive test of a hypothesis. However, the cases we examine are among the highest profile examples of a small number of examples that fit the circumstances our model is designed to explain.

Case Studies

Opt-Out Cascades: Swedish Opt-Out from the EMU

Our model has suggested conditions under which an opt-out cascade (states opting out because previous states' decisions to opt out created favorable conditions for subsequent opt outs) is possible. In the case of EMU, the UK and Denmark assumed the role of laggards and opted out right from the start. Their decisions to opt out are straightforward from the point of view of our model. The policy costs to them for participating in EMU were too high, so they were willing to pay the non-policy costs associated with opting out. Integrationist states preferred to see the laggards leave. The integrationist member states were willing to pay their own non-policy costs associated with a multispeed approach rather than to water down or get rid of the monetary union in an effort to maintain a single policy. However, the decision by the UK and Denmark to leave set up an opt-out cascade in which Sweden opted out in part because of the changes to the policy space that resulted from the earlier opt-outs.

A key reason for the Swedish decision to opt out of the EMU, cited by a report by an advisory committee led by Lars Calmfors (Calmfors et al. 1997), was that the UK and Denmark had already opted out (Novack 1999: 7). Although Sweden was not an EU member state at the time that Denmark and the UK opted out of the EMU, we argue that had Denmark and the UK decided to participate in the EMU, Sweden would have been much more likely to participate when it joined the EU. Key to Sweden's decision was the position of the pivotal actor in the decision-making process. In terms of our model, the British and Danish opt-outs shifted the pivotal member state in a direction that enabled outcomes that the Swedes found unacceptable.

The cascade observation predicted by our model requires a particular preference ordering of states. States that opt out second or third should be less Euro-sceptic on the dimension in question than the state that opts out first. As the dimension in question here is monetary integration, we first look at average interest rates from 1990 to 2000 to give a rough idea of what interest rates fiscal authorities in the various member states would have preferred. We rank these averages from lowest to highest. We chose to use the interest rates as the dimension along which to place the member states because the European Central Bank's (ECB) most important policy decision is the setting of interest rate targets for the eurozone countries. We do not argue that this ranking is a direct measure of preferences but rather a heuristic tool for estimating what interest rates governments would be most likely to prefer. We base this on the assumption that governments are more likely to prefer interest rates from the ECB that are most similar to the interest rates they had established at the national level prior to joining the euro.

Regarding EMU policy decisions, there is a supranational agenda setter in the form of the ECB's Executive Board. The Governing Council, the main decision-making body of the ECB, is made up of the six-member Executive Board plus representatives of the central banks of the countries participating in the common currency and votes by simple majority. The Executive Board's membership, which includes the president of the ECB, is appointed by the member state governments of the eurozone. Simon Hix (2005: 331–332) argues that it is reasonable to assume that the six votes from the Executive Board will support higher interest rates as a means to avoid inflation.[7] In terms of our model, the supranational agenda setter will propose a policy that has a higher interest rate than that preferred by the pivotal member state.

When all 15 pre-enlargement member states are included, the winning coalition consists of the Executive Board plus the representatives of the central banks from the five member states with the highest interest rate preferences. When only 12 or 13 of the pre-enlargement member states are included, the winning coalition consists of the Executive Board and the representatives of the central banks from the four member states with the highest interest rate preferences.

Table 3.1 presents member states' average interest rates, 1990–2000, and the ranking of those averages. When we match the voting rules with the rankings of the averages, we find that if all 15 member states had participated in the common currency, the UK would be the pivotal state with Sweden solidly inside the range of the winning coalition. However, with Denmark and the UK outside the EMU, Sweden's position within the winning coalition becomes tenuous. If the Swedish government had much uncertainty about its own interest rate preferences relative to those of the other member states, opting out probably looked like the safest option. This would not have been the case had Sweden been able to rely on the cooperation of the British and Danish representatives on the ECB governing council.

When the UK and Denmark opted out it may have also reduced the costs of other states opting out after them. Under some interpretations of its terms, Sweden's opt-out

Table 3.1   EU15 average annual long-term fixed interest rates, 1990–2000

Country	Average (1990–2000)	Ranking of Average
Spain	9.13	1
Italy	8.70	2
Sweden	8.37	3
Finland	8.33	4
United Kingdom	7.78	5
Portugal	7.44	6
Denmark	7.40	7
Ireland	7.39	8
Belgium	7.02	9
Greece	6.97	10
France	6.87	11
Austria	6.66	12
The Netherlands	6.57	13
Germany	6.50	14
Luxembourg	5.88	15

Source: OECD (http://stats.oecd.org/Index.aspx?DatasetCode=MEI_FIN).

was a technical violation of its accession treaty. But the heaviest sanctions for violating the treaty can only be imposed through Article 7 of the TEU, which allows for the suspension of voting rights for a wayward member state but only if there is a unanimous vote of the other member states. When the UK and Denmark opted out it may have made it impossible for the Council to impose this sanction on any member state that wants to opt out even if its accession treaty requires participation. This may suggest that cascades are a function only of a previous country's opting out. However, this would lead to the conclusion that opt-outs always lead to cascades, which we do not believe is the case. Our argument is that cascades are a function both of the distribution of preferences, the costs and benefits of participation versus the costs and benefits of exit, and voting rules.

Opt-outs without cascades: the Schengen Agreement, the Social Charter and the New Fiscal Pact of 2011

Our model predicts two possible situations of opt out without cascades. In the first, the laggard initiates a multispeed approach, allowing the agenda setter and the integrationist member states to move on without them. In the second, the integrationist agenda setter initiates. While these two scenarios are empirically distinguishable, from the point of view of our model, they are theoretically equivalent. An integrationist agenda setter may recognize that it could realize important policy gains from a multispeed approach that excludes a laggard. To achieve this desirable end, the agenda setter could propose a policy that is so distasteful to the laggard that the laggard has little choice but to opt out. In this section, we discuss both types. The Schengen Agreement is an instance of a multispeed approach initiated by an integrationist agenda setter. The Social Charter and the New Fiscal Pact of 2011 are examples of multispeed approaches initiated by a laggard.

The Schengen Agreement is one of the most prominent examples of a multispeed approach adopted because of the desire of integrationist governments to move forward without laggards. Although initially not formally part of the EU framework, the Schengen Agreement was deeply intertwined with EU policies from its beginning. The free movement of peoples caused complications for immigration policies for the member states. In 1985, France, Germany and the Benelux countries adopted the Schengen Accord outside the normal framework of EU decision-making. By initiating the integration of migration policy outside the EU, these five member states were able to move forward on a dimension of integration without compromising with laggard governments (Guiraudon 2000). The five original Schengen countries wished to move forward on the application of free movement of peoples to non-EU citizens. Denmark, Ireland, Greece and the UK opposed the application of this principle to citizens of non-EU member states (Kölliker 2006: 212; Nanz 1995: 31; Wiener 1999). Of these states the UK has been most persistent in its opposition. Denmark's opposition is based primarily on the legal basis of the Schengen protocols while British governments have opposed the substance of the protocols themselves (Wiener 1999). Ireland's decision to opt out of Schengen, meanwhile, is driven by its desire to retain its common travel area with the UK. This leads to an arrangement of preferences on Schengen that places the UK at the laggard end of the spectrum and Germany at the most integrationist with the rest of the member states arranged between them. This preference distribution is consistent with recent theoretical analyses of EU immigration policy (Givens and Luedtke 2004).

In the early stages of Schengen's development, integrationist governments sought a multispeed approach. In 1985 there were 10 member states, with Spain and Portugal set to join the following year. As the SEA was being negotiated, Denmark, Ireland and the UK opposed the full incorporation of Schengen into the amended treaty. Belgium, France, Germany, Luxembourg and the Netherlands opposed the opening of their borders completely to Greece, Italy, Portugal and Spain. The argument presented in the negotiations was that Mediterranean countries were incapable of enforcing their border regulations (Dinan 2010: 531). In both the original 1985 Schengen Agreement and the SEA negotiations in 1986, the integrationist bloc of governments chose to exclude member states whether or not the excluded governments wanted to participate.

The situation changed in the 1990s when the Schengen protocols were incorporated into the Amsterdam Treaty. By that time, a qualified majority of governments was ready to participate and the laggards – the UK, Ireland and, to a lesser extent, Denmark – sought opt-outs (Wiener 1999). In terms of our model, Schengen was set up so that once it was incorporated into the treaty framework, the laggards were willing to pay the non-policy cost to exit (or, in this case, remain out), and the integrationists were also willing to pay their own non-policy costs to allow them to stay out. The policy benefits for both sides associated with moving forward without the laggards were too great. At the same time, however, the difference in the position of the pivot in the hypothetical scenario where Denmark, the UK and Ireland would have participated, compared with the scenario where they did not, was not great enough to lead other states to opt out.

If the Schengen represents a situation where the integrationist side initiated the multispeed approach, the Social Charter represents a scenario in which the laggard insisted on a multispeed approach. The British government under John Major was opposed to including the Social Charter in the Maastricht Treaty, and threatened to block the new treaty unless the UK was exempted from the Social Protocol sections. In the debates about the inclusion of the Social Charter, only the Major government opposed the basic premise of a common European social policy. This opposition was based on that government's unusual, for Europe, approach to social policy and industrial relations (Towers 1992). The UK was not the only member to resist the implementation of the Social Charter. However, in the end, it was the only member state that could not be brought into the fold (Kölliker 2006: 183). Given that the Social Charter was going to allow for social policy to be passed by qualified majority vote, the UK government's unique opposition to a European social policy would have placed that government on the losing side of the pivotal member state in most if not all social policy votes in the Council of Ministers. The Major government knew that the UK would not be able to block proposals and it feared that the pivot preferred substantially more integration than the UK. This led the UK to seek an opt-out on this issue. Later, under the Blair government, which held a more integrationist position with regard to EU social policy, the decision to opt out was reversed. This supports our hypothesis that laggard states that are far more Euro-sceptic than the pivot will pursue an opt-out, and this will be supported. Given that all other member states generally supported the inclusion of the Social Charter, the UK's opt-out did not greatly shift the position of the pivot, and thus, no cascade occurred.

A final recent example of laggard initiated multispeed integration occurred in December 2011 when the European Council convened in Brussels to address the ongoing debt and banking crisis in the eurozone. The proposed new fiscal compact and stabilization mechanism was designed to both stabilize the crisis and increase the level of integration with regard to fiscal discipline in the eurozone. It also addressed capitalization and liquidity issues in the banking sector. The original proposal was to involve participation of all 27 member states. However, at the last minute, Prime Minister Cameron withdrew from the talks and declared that the UK would not participate. In his statements on the matter to Parliament on 12 December 2011, the prime minister characterized this as a British veto. However, the remaining 26 member states moved forward with a joint statement on the matter without the UK. In effect, what Cameron did in 2011 was not cast a veto, but opt out in line with the kind of multispeed approach to integration discussed in this chapter.

The drama surrounding the negotiations for a new treaty to respond to the Euro crisis in December 2011 provides an example of several of the dynamics we lay out in our model. The British government was unwilling to submit to new financial services regulations. The French government was unwilling to move forward without such regulations. The German government was concerned that if Britain were not included, the German government would be faced with a disadvantageous strategic scenario.

Prime Minister David Cameron was concerned not simply about the particular content of the treaty modifications proposed in 2011 but by the overall context of EU financial regulation. His statement, in response to a question from David Miliband (Labour, South Shield), shortly after the British walked away from the treaty is instructive, "There have been any number of examples of frankly discriminatory legislation against financial services in the European Union that have affected Britain very badly" (House of Commons Debates, 12 December 2011). The prime minister's statement illustrates our premise that when a member state government considers whether to participate in some area of new integration, that government examines its prospects for winning individual votes in the future. In this case, Prime Minister Cameron was defending his decision not to participate in the new EU financial services framework by pointing to a pattern of decisions that he determined were bad for Britain.

A key element of our model is that when one country opts out, it changes the identity of the pivotal member state and therefore changes the possible policy outcomes in that area for those member states that remain. Reports at the time suggested that "[German chancellor Merkel] badly wanted Britain to stay on the inside track of the EU, we learned, fearing that she would find herself alone in the room with France and the Club Med countries" (*The Economist*, "Bagehot", 9 December 2011). With the British government no longer participating, Germany now faced a different strategic situation with different member states likely to be pivotal in the negotiations.

There were also reports at the time that President Sarkozy of France believed moving forward with a smaller set of member states increased French influence (*The Economist*, "Bagehot", 9 December 2011). In this view, the French president was insisting on subjecting British banks to new EU financial services regulations because France was willing to risk a British opt out. In other words, the French government did not believe that the benefits of moving forward with all 27-member states were worth the compromises that the British government was demanding. By refusing to compromise with the British government, the French forced a situation where Cameron felt he had to walk away, possibly shifting the pivot and leaving France in a better strategic position.

Conclusion

Giandomenico Majone has written that European integration is evolving into a "number of, often overlapping, state groupings established for cooperation in a variety of fields" (Majone 2009: 205). Thus, explaining the progress of European integration has to include an examination of when member states will or will not participate. Given the highly institutionalized nature of EU decision-making, such a theory has to account for decision-making institutions. Member states compare policy outcomes that would occur following opt-outs with those that would have occurred if the all states had remained part of the decision-making process. They also weigh the relative benefits of these policy outcomes against the costs of exiting. Our crucial insight is that a decision to opt out by one member state affects the identity and location of the pivotal member state in Council decision-making. This, in turn, affects policy outcomes and may potentially affect other states' preferences with regard to opting out of EU decision-making within a particular policy area.

Our analysis has several policy implications. From the point of view of advocates of a fully harmonized and integrated EU, the most distressing scenario is when a cascade of several opt-outs occurs. When a single member state opts out, it may not undermine the perceived legitimacy of integration in that particular policy area. A threatened opt-out under these circumstances may not be effective in shifting policy in the desired direction. Indeed, it may further empower exactly those member state governments whose policy preferences the state seeking an opt-out sees as problematic. This was the case in the interaction between the UK, Germany and France with regard to the Cameron government's opt-out of the 2011 treaty response to the ongoing crisis in the eurozone that we discussed at the end of the previous section.

However, if first one, then several more member states opt out in succession, it may undermine the legitimacy of the project as whole. The integrationist member state governments would be forced to weigh the value of minimal progress among a unified front against the prospect of more substantial progress among fewer members and damaged legitimacy going into the future. We find that cascades are possible even when all the member states want policy to move in the same direction. An opt-out cascade has the potential to derail unified integration even in policy areas that integrationists may view as the most promising opportunities for broadly increased integration.

Moreover, the passage of the treaties that allow member states to opt out may encourage the most integrationist member states to sacrifice unity in the pursuit of rapid integration. If this pattern were repeated in an increasing number of policy areas, it could unravel the regulatory basis of the harmonized common market.

In particular, our model suggests that the possibility of cascades may pose a particular problem for EU responses to the ongoing eurozone crisis. If Britain's opt-out in 2011 were followed up by further opt-outs by other member state governments, it could unravel the fragile network of policy compromises and bailouts that have so far been keeping the eurozone intact. At the time this chapter was written, no such cascade had developed. However, this does not preclude the possibility in the future.

Acknowledgements

An earlier version of this chapter was published in 'Institutional Hokey-Pokey: The Politics of Multispeed Integration in the European Union', *Journal of European Public Policy*, vol. 19, no. 6 (2012): 779–795 (Taylor & Francis Ltd, www.tandfonline.com), reprinted by permission of the publisher. Earlier versions of this chapter were also presented at the annual meeting of the Midwest Political Science Association, Chicago, 2009; the biannual meeting of the European Union Studies Association, Los Angeles, 2009; and the Dublin European Institute, University College Dublin, October 2009. We are very grateful to Sergio Fabbrini, Dan Kelemen, Will Phelan, Thomas Sattler, Daniel Thomas and several anonymous reviewers for their extensive thoughts and insights on earlier drafts.

Notes

1   There are many different terms used to describe a pattern of integration in which some member states pursue integration at a faster rate than others. These include among others 'multispeed Europe', 'variable geometry', 'Europe à la carte', and 'differentiated integration'. For an explanation of the distinctions between these various terminologies, see Ehlermann (1998), Stubb (1996; 2002), and Warleigh (2002).

2   Michael Dobbs, 'Mitterrand Urges Western Europe To Strengthen Political Integration', *The Washington Post*, May 25, 1984, A25.

3   John Palmer, 'New Routes to Union', *The Guardian*, October 23, 1996, 11.

4   Labeta (2009) expands on this public goods model by exploring which governments benefit from different types of externalities. She argues there are limited circumstances under which both integrationists and laggards support a flexible approach to integration.

5   Several models examine how costs associated with opting out of a particular policy affect bargaining in the EU and other international organizations (e.g. Schneider and Cederman 1994; Slapin 2009; Voeten 2001). Other literature examines how policy differentiation among member states affects the trade-off between widening and deepening within international organizations (Gilligan 2004; Stone *et al.* 2008). Our approach differs from previous studies by focusing on how opting out affects the identity and location of the pivotal decision-maker. No model of which we are aware examines how the opting out interacts with the EU's decision-making rules.

6   Other mechanisms include Article 350 TFEU, which allows for deeper cooperation among the Benelux countries, and Article 184 TFEU, which allows for cooperation among a subset of member states in the areas of research and technological development. These mechanisms focus on either particular regions or policy areas, and are therefore not as encompassing as the mechanisms on which we focus. All treaty article numbers refer to the Lisbon Treaty.

7   For an excellent discussion of the inflation avoidant tendencies of independent central banks see Eijffinger and De Haan (1996: 29–31).

References

Bednar, J. (2007) 'Valuing Exit Options', *Publius: the Journal of Federalism* 37(2): 190–208.

Calmfors, L., H. Flam, N. Gottfries, J. H. Matlary, M. Jerneck, R. Lindahi, C.N. Berntsson, E. Rabinowicz and A. Vredin. (1997) *EMU – A Swedish Perspective*. Boston: Kluwer Academic Publishers.

Dinan, D. (2010) *Ever Closer Union: An Introduction to European Integration*. Boulder, CO: Lynne Reiner Publishers.

Dowding, K. and P. John. (2008) 'The Three Exit, Three Voice and Loyalty Framework: A Test with Survey Data on Local Services', *Political Studies* 56(2): 288–311.

Dowding, K, P. John, T. Mergoupis and M. van Vugt (2000) 'Exit, Voice and Loyalty: Analytic and Empirical Developments', *European Journal of Political Research* 37(4): 469–495.

Downs, G. and D.M. Rocke (1995) *Optimal Imperfection? Domestic Uncertainty and Institutions in International Relations*. Princeton, NJ: Princeton University Press.

Downs, G., D.M. Rocke and P. Barsoom. (1998) 'Managing the Evolution of Cooperation' *International Organization* 52(2): 397.

Ehlermann, C.D. (1998) 'Differentiation, Flexibility, Closer Co-operation: The New Provisions of the Amsterdam Treaty', *European Law Journal* 4(3): 246–270.

Eijffinger, S.C.W. and J. De Haan. (1996) *The Political Economy of Central Bank Independence*, Special Papers in International Economics n. 19. Institutional Finance Section, Department of Economics. Princeton, NJ: Princeton University

Gehlbach, S. (2006) 'A Formal Model of Exit and Voice', *Rationality and Society* 18(4): 395–418.

Gilligan, M. (2004) 'Is There a Broader-Deeper Trade-Off in International Multilateral Agreements?', *International Organization* 58(3): 459–484.

Givens, T. and A. Luedtke. (2004) 'The Politics of European Union Immigration Policy: Institutions, Salience, and Harmonization', *Policy Studies Journal* 32(1): 145–165.

Goldstein, J. L. and L. Martin. (2000) 'Legalization, Trade Liberalization, and Domestic Politics: A Cautionary Note', *International Organziation* 54(3): 603–632.

Guiraudon, V. (2000) 'European Integration and Migration Policy: Vertical Policy-Making as Venue Shopping', *Journal of Common Market Studies* 38(2): 251–271.

Harstad, B. (2006) 'Flexible Integration? Mandatory and Minimum Participation Rules', *Scandinavian Journal of Economics* 108(4): 683–702.

Hirschman, A. O. (1970) *Exit, Voice, and Loyalty*. Cambridge, MA: Harvard University Press.

Hix, S. (2005) *The Political System of the European Union* (2nd ed.). New York: Palgrave Macmillan.

Kelemen, R. D. (2007) 'Built to Last? The Durability of EU Federalism', in S. Meunier and K. McNamara (eds.), *Making History: State of the European Union*, Vol. 8, Oxford: Oxford University Press, pp. 51–66.

Kölliker, A. (2006) *Flexibility and European Unification: The Logic of Differentiated Integration*. New York: Rowman & Littlefield.

Koremenos, B. (2005) 'Contracting around International Uncertainty', *American Political Science Review* 99(4): 549–565.

Koremenos, B., C. Lipson and D. Snidal. (2001) 'Rational Design of International Institutions', *International Organization* 55(4): 761–799.

Labeta, J. (2009) 'Leaders, Laggards, and the Logic of Flexible Integration', Ph.D. dissertation, Department of Politics and International Relations, University of Oxford.

Majone, G. (2009) *Europe as the Would-be World Power: The EU at Fifty*. New York, NY: Cambridge University Press.

Marks, G., L. Hooghe, and K. Blank. (1996) 'European Integration from the 1980's: State-centric v. Multi-level Governance', *Journal of Common Market Studies* 34(3): 341–378.

Moravcsik, A. (1998) *The Choice for Europe*. Ithaca, NY: Cornell University Press.

Nanz, K. (1995) 'The Schengen Agreement: Preparing the Free Movement of Persons in the European Union', in B. Roland and J. Monar (eds.), *Justice and Home Affairs in the European Union: The Development of the Third Pillar*, Brussels: European Interuniversity Press, pp. 29–48.

Novack, J. (1999) *The Different Approaches of Two Neighbors: The Finnish and Swedish Decisions on Participating in the Third Stage of EMU*, paper presented at the Sixth Biennial European Community Studies Association Conference in Pittsburgh, PA, 2–5 June.

Rosendorff, B. P. (2005). 'Stability and Rigidity: Politics and Design of the WTO's Dispute Settlement Procedure', *American Political Science Review* 99(3): 389–400.

Rosendorff, B. P. and H. Milner. (2001) 'The Optimal Design of Internatioanl Trade Institutions: Uncertainty and Escape', *International Organization* 55(4): 829–857.

Schmitter, P. (1996) 'Imagining the Future of the Euro-Polity with the Help of New Concepts', in M. Gary, F. Scharpf, P. Schmitter and W. Streeck (eds.), *Governance in the European Union*, London: Sage Publications, pp 121–150.

Schneider, G. and L. Cederman. (1994) 'The Change of Tide in Political Cooperation: A Limited Information Model of European Integration', *International Organization* 48(4): 633–662.

Slapin, J. B. (2009) 'Exit, Voice, and Cooperation: Bargaining Power in International Organizations and Federal Systems', *Journal of Theoretical Politics* 21(2): 187–211.

Stone, R., B. Slantchev, and T. London. (2008) 'Choosing How to Cooperate: A Repeated Public-Goods Model of International Relations', *International Studies Quarterly* 52(2): 335–362.

Stubb, A. (1996) 'A Categorization of Differentiated Integration', *Journal of Common Market Studies* 34(2): 283–295.

Stubb, A. (2002) *Negotiating Flexibility in the European Union: Amsterdam, Nice and Beyond.* New York: Palgrave Macmillan.

Towers, B. (1992) 'Two Speed Ahead: Social Europe and the UK after Maastricht', *Industrial Relations Journal* 23(2): 83–89.

Tsebelis, G. and G. Garrett. (2000) 'Legislative Politics in the European Union', *European Union Politics* 1(1): 9–36.

Tsebelis, G. and G. Garrett (2001) 'The Institutional Determinants of Intergovernmentalism and Supranationalism in the EU', *International Organization* 55(2): 357–390.

Voeten, E. (2001) 'Outside Options and the Logic of Security Council Actions', *American Political Science Review* 95(4): 845–858.

Warleigh, A. (2002) *Flexible Integration: Which Model for the European Union?* London: Sheffield Academic Press.

Wiener, A. (1999) 'Forging Flexibility – the British 'No' to Schengen', *European Journal of Migration and Law* 1: 441–463.

Part II

INSTITUTIONAL PROCESSING

INSTITUTIONAL
PROCESSING

Chapter 4

The European Commission

ARNDT WONKA

Introduction

The European Commission is one of the most visible institutions of the European Union (EU) and, many would argue, one of the most powerful that, over the last decades, had a strong impact on the course of European integration. Its visibility might be explained by the fact that it resembles a government of the European Union: It occupies a central role in EU policy-making, and its large administrative apparatus is politically headed by experienced politicians who regularly make it to the press with their policy proposals. Quite regularly, however, the Commission's prominent role in EU politics is strongly contested. Governments as well as interest groups tend to blame unpopular EU decisions on the Commission's bureaucratic ignorance. The Commission is then equated with "Brussels" apparently unrestrained striving for an "ever-closer" European Union. In this chapter "the Commission" is analytically disaggregated to highlight its bureaucratic as well as political characteristics. The disaggregated perspective on the Commission sheds light on its bureaucratic and political qualities as well as on the considerable heterogeneity of attitudes and preferences which shape the Commission's work and its behaviour in EU politics.

The chapter is divided in three subsections. The first subsection describes the organizational make-up of the European Commission, its political leadership and administrative staff as well as its competencies in order to characterize the politico-administrative actor qualities of the Commission. This section concludes with a concise description of the institutional and political environment in which the Commission acts in EU policy-making. The second subsection discusses the Commission's behaviour in EU policy-making. It focuses on the diverse resources the Commission draws on to influence EU policies and on the political dynamics that shape decision-making inside the Commission. These intra-institutional dynamics determine the way in which the Commission acts in EU inter-institutional decision-making. Based on the insights gained in the previous sections, the final subsection discusses the goals the Commission pursues in EU policy-making and the power it has in shaping EU politics and EU policies.

The European Commission in EU policy-making

The European Commission: competencies, organizational structure, staff and political leadership

In the academic literature as well as in popular accounts the European Commission is very often portrayed as a unitary actor which is invariantly – over time and across policy areas – striving for the expansion of its own influence in EU policy-making by working towards the extension of the EU's legislative scope. The conceptualization of the European Commission as a unitary actor is, however, an analytical oversimplification which masks diverging perspectives and at times political conflicts inside the Commission. Since these significantly affect the Commission's behaviour in EU policy-making, this chapter conceptualizes the Commission as a collective actor. The collective quality of the Commission is marked by two dimensions: Work inside the Commission is *horizontally* divided among Directorates General (DGs), the Commission's administrative apparatuses responsible for the different policy areas in which the European Union is active. Moreover, a *vertical* dimension separates the administrators in the DGs from the Commission President and European Commissioners who form the Commission's political leadership. Before describing core characteristics of the European Commission along these two dimensions, I present the Commission's competencies in EU policy-making and politics.

Competencies

The European Commission has competencies to become active in three broad areas: EU policy-making, policy implementation and monitoring and, finally, external representation.

Policy-making

In legislative *policy-making* the Commission has the exclusive right to formulate proposals. Formulating legislative proposals is one of the core tasks of the European Commission allowing it to shape the content of EU policies as well as course of European integration. The fact that, over the last 35 years, the Commission has submitted more than 9,000 legislative proposals to the European Parliament and to the Council (Häge 2011: 462–463) shows that it is making extensive use of this right. In addition, the Commission very regularly publishes communications and working papers to indicate that it will become active in a specific area in the near future and to test the political reactions to its policy-making plans.

It should, however, be noted that not all of these proposals and consultation papers result from the Commission's own initiative. Very regularly, the Commission is asked to become active by governments in the Council or the European Parliament. Moreover, the Lisbon Treaty introduced the "European citizens' initiative," which allows at least one million citizens from at least seven member states to ask the Commission to propose legislation in a specific area. The request to become active by a European citizens' initiative, however, is not binding for the Commission.

Policy implementation and monitoring implementation

The Commission also plays a prominent role in the implementation of EU policies. While the actual implementation of EU policies in the EU's member states is being carried out by national and regional administrations, the Commission is often co-responsible for determining specific standards that must be applied. This responsibility is laid down in legislative acts which define the general framework but delegate the setting of specific standards to the Commission. The Commission's implementation activities are very often supported and scrutinized by comitology committees composed of Commission representatives and representatives from each member state. These committees provide the Commission with local and technical expertise. At the same time they check that the Commission is acting within framework defined by the respective legal act. 306 comitology committees were operating in 2012 (December).[1]

Monitoring the compliance with EU treaties and EU legislation is another important field of activity of the European Commission. By delegating these powers to the Commission and to the European Court of Justice, member states show their commitment to comply with the decisions taken at the EU level. The European Commission can initiate infringement proceedings against private actors, for example firms, or against member states themselves if they are considered to breach or fail to implement EU law. If the Court of Justice of the European Union convicts a firm or a member state for non-compliance with EU law, firms and member states can be obliged to pay considerable fines. In 2011 the Court of Justice ruled in 72 cases that a state infringed EU law.

External representation

The European Commission also represents the EU vis-à-vis third countries and in international organizations. Its External Action Service entertains about 130 delegations in countries around the world to be informed about local and regional developments. More consequential for actual policy-making, however, is the fact that the Commission negotiates trade agreements and international treaties on behalf of the EU. These international treaties can in principle cover all policy areas in which the EU treaties provide the EU with competencies, and the negotiations on these treaties are of high political salience, not least given the EU's extensive integration in global trade.

Organizational structure: DGs and political leadership

In this chapter, the Commission is conceptualized not as a unitary but as a collective actor, in which work is *vertically* divided between the political leadership – the Commission president and the Commissioners – and the bureaucratic staff as well as *horizontally* divided between DGs and Services responsible for the different policy areas in which the Commission and the EU are active (Table 4.1).

Table 4.1 Directorates general and services

Name of Directorate General	Employees	Budget (in million €)
Directorates General		
Agriculture and Rural Development	922	56 344
Budget	400	67
Climate Action	140	*
Communications Networks, Content and Technology	801	1 389
Competition	724	92
Economic and Financial Affairs	651	428
Education and Culture	472	2 373
Employment, Social Affairs and Inclusion	583	10 429
Energy	484	814
Enlargement	271	832

Name of Directorate General	Employees	Budget (in million €)
Directorates General		
Enterprise and Industry	756	1 162
Environment	448	391*
EuropeAid Development & Cooperation	1 193	1 207
Health and Consumers	730	593
Home Affairs	260	733
Humanitarian Aid and Civil Protection	208	829
Internal Market and Services	489	100
Justice	311	184
Maritime Affairs and Fisheries	286	680
Mobility and Transport	431	984
Regional Policy	559	37 434
Research and Innovation	1 119	5 220
Secretariat-General	452	
Taxation and Customs Union	433	112
Trade	544	102
Services		
European Anti-Fraud Office (OLAF)	354	69
Internal Audit Service	97	12
Legal Service	382	

Note: Only those Directorates General and Services which can be expected to play a role in policy-making have been listed (for an exhaustive list, see: http://ec.europa.eu/about/ds_en.htm).
* Directorates General for Climate and for Environment share one budget.
Sources: Number of employees (officials and temporary agents; January 2014); Budget (Official Journal L66 of 08/03/2013, Section III Commission; DGs' payments in 2013)

The Commission's administrative apparatus currently consists of 33 DGs and 11 Services. In 1958 the Commission of the European Economic Community started to operate with nine DGs and Services. Since then, and after a couple of treaty changes and territorial enlargements, their number has more than quadrupled. Currently the Commission's DGs and Services employ about 22,600 permanent officials. In addition, another about 10,000 non-permanently employed temporary agents, contract agents and seconded nationals worked for the Commission in 2013.[2] Of the EU's overall budget of 150.9 billion euros for 2013, around 2 per cent were spent on financing the Commission's administrative personnel.[3] The Commission's administrative staff is recruited through a selective entry exam, the "concours," which shall guarantee that hires are based on merit. At the same time, the Commission aims at representing citizens from all member states in the Commission's DGs and Services roughly in line with member states' population size, the number of seats a country has in the European Parliament and its voting weight in the Council (Gravier 2008). Keeping this national balance was particularly challenging after 12 member states entered the EU in 2004 and 2007, which the Commission, however, managed successfully: currently about 25 per cent of all policy relevant positions in the Commission's DGs and Services are held by citizens from the 12 new member states.[4]

The Services mostly deal with general administrative issues, while the DGs are responsible for the different policy areas in which the EU is active. DGs are generally made up of several directorates with each directorate again being subdivided into a number of specialized units. Administrative leadership over DGs is exercised by a director-general who bears responsibility for the administrative activities in these. Besides these commonalities, DGs and Services vary considerably in their size (Table 4.1). With more than 900 staff members and a budget of about 56 billion euros (in 2013), the DG for Agriculture and Rural Affairs is one of the biggest and resource rich, while the DG for Climate Action is one of the smallest DGs in the Commission. Given the fact that the EU is most active in regulatory rather than distributive policy-making, the size of the budget of a DG should, however, not be equated with its influence and power in EU policy-making.

In addition, considerable heterogeneity also exists in the attitudes and political preferences of the Commission's administrative staff. While Commission officials in general are more supportive of European integration than citizens in the member states, their attitudes vary considerably regarding the question of the extent to which political authorities should interfere in economic markets and engage in redistributive welfare politics as well as with regard to the question on the role which governments and the European Commission respectively should play in EU policy-making (Hooghe 2001, 2005). Liesbet Hooghe's work shows that a considerable part of the variation in Commission officials' attitudes can be explained by officials' nationality and prior professional experiences. Officials from federal countries prefer a strong role for EU institutions in EU policy-making, while those from large and unitary member states, which have previously worked in their country's administration, want governments to be in the driver's seat. Officials working in technical DGs, on the other hand, seem to have no general preference for the distribution of power between governments and EU institutions, but express a preference for institutional solutions which are most effective in solving the problem at hand (Hooghe 2012).

Empirical studies on the behaviour of Commission administrators show, however, that the personal attitudes of the Commission staff as well as their national background have at best a limited impact on how they conduct their work in the Commission. The professional interactions of the Commission staff and their personal networks are, as should be expected for a bureaucratic organization, driven by formal responsibilities and the institutionally induced need for co-operation across units and departments in the DGs rather than administrators' partisan identification, their political attitudes or their nationality (Michelmann 1978; Suvarierol 2008; Trondal 2008: 477; Kassim *et al.* 2013: 86, 102, 189). Their reported contact behaviour corresponds with administrators' self-perception as technical problem solvers and representatives of EU interests, who are aware of the political salience of their work and appreciate being part of the political game, yet report not to be strongly driven by (party) political motives themselves (Bauer and Ege 2012: 410, 412, 415). Being sensitive to the political side of their job allows Commission administrators to balance technical and political aspects of their work and, consequently, to act successfully in EU policy-making.

Commission officials' self-reported professionalism also extends to their relationship with the Commission's leadership. The vast majority of Commission officials do think that it is their and their department's responsibility to support the positions which were agreed by the political leadership in the college of Commissioners (Bauer and Ege 2012: 416). If they indeed act accordingly, the Commission would function like a Weberian bureaucracy in which political decisions are taken by the political leadership. The hierarchical orientation of Commission administrators might, however, not only result from supervision and their professional ethos but also because of pragmatic political considerations. The members of the services need to secure their Commissioners' support for a policy to be able to push it up the hierarchical levels of their DG and to get it successfully passed in the College. Their work should thus be strongly shaped by their expectations and perceptions of their Commissioners' political preferences and strategic considerations. The following statement by an official in DG Environment expresses the rationale of this hierarchical orientation:

> No, as I said, there are lots of and lots of ideas. The ideas are all over the place. [. . .] So, no problem, we go and find an idea. [. . .] How are you going to do it [get a policy accepted by your superiors in the DGs; AW]? Well, that's a question of political opportunity [. . .] Does your commissioner want to do it? Does your commissioner have political feel, think she can do that?[5]

It has been shown earlier that, at the administrative level, the European Commission is marked by considerable heterogeneity. This is true for the capacities and competencies of different DGs and with regard to the attitudes and preferences of the Commission staff. Taking into account this heterogeneity at the Commission's administrative level, already points towards a conceptualization of the Commission as a collective rather than a unitary actor which is invariantly and cohesively working towards the realization of a common policy agenda and shared institutional interests. The following discussion of the Commission's political leadership and the discussion of decision-making inside the Commission will further strengthen this point.

The political responsibility for the work in the European Commission lies with the European Commissioners and the president of the European Commission. The Commission's political leadership is selected and appointed in a three-stage process. During the first stage, governments select a Commission president who must be approved by governments in the European Council and by the European Parliament. In the second stage, each member state, except for the country of origin of the Commission president, proposes a candidate Commissioner. In the third stage, governments in the Council and members of the European Parliament vote on the Commission as a whole, which is successfully appointed if it is approved by a simple majority in the European Parliament and a qualified majority in the European Council (Wonka 2007: 171). While the European Parliament's formal powers in the appointment process have been gradually increased, the outcomes are still very much dominated by governments. Governments shall take into account the political majorities in the European Parliament when selecting the Commission president. Selecting the candidate for the presidency as well as their own Commissioner is, however, still the sole responsibility of governments.

The vast majority of Commissioners who have been nominated since 1958 are experienced party politicians who have previously served as members of their country's parliament, ministers or prime ministers in their country. The share of those who had no political post before entering the Commission is, and has especially since the adoption of the Single European Act in 1985 been constantly low. Governments' preference for experienced politicians instead of technocrats with administrative and diplomatic leadership experience also reflects in the small share of Commissioners who were not member of a political party at the time of their appointment (Graph 4.1). Instead, governments usually nominate Commissioners who share their party affiliation which is, again, particularly pronounced since the re-invigoration of the European integration process through the Single European Act. By nominating personalities with extensive experience in other political posts and a shared party affiliation, governments try to secure some influence on politics and policy-making inside the Commission (Döring 2007; Wonka 2007).

At the same time these characteristics of European Commissioners show that governments are not overly concerned about reinforcing the Commission's reputation as an independent actor as prescribed in the treaties. Otherwise, they should show a stronger inclination to nominate individuals with no or at least not an extensive party political career before entering the Commission. Whether and to which extent the party political affiliation of Commissioners as well as their nationalities does play a role in internal decision-making and for the Commission's behaviour in inter-institutional decision-making is discussed in the section on "resources and intra-institutional decision-making dynamics".

Each Commissioner is leading one or more DGs while the Commission president is heading the secretariat general and the Legal Service. Commissioners are, however,

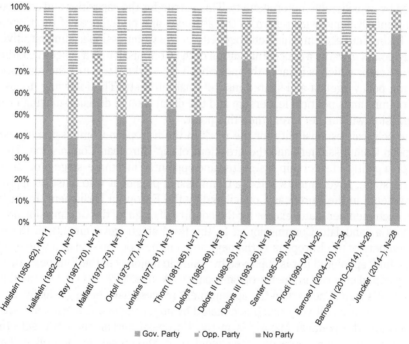

Graph 4.1 Political profile of European Commissioners
Source: Wonka 2007; author's data.

not individually responsible for the work in their DG. Instead, the Commissioners and the Commission president are collectively responsible for the work of the Commission: once a decision is taken, all Commissioners are asked to publicly defend the decision, irrespective of whether they opposed the decision in internal decision-making before. To debate decisions and to negotiate compromises, Commissioners meet weekly in the College of Commissioners. The college is the Commission's leadership body in which the principle of collective responsibility is politically realized and where Commissioners discuss proposals which cause conflict between Commissioners and their DGs.

Meetings in the college are prepared by members of the Commissioners' personal cabinets. In these preparatory meetings issues which are not highly conflictive are being solved and afterwards formally adopted by the Commissioners in the college. Discussions in the weekly meetings of the college are thus restricted to highly conflictive proposals and to the political discussion of future policies and initiatives. During the term of the Prodi Commission (1999–04), only 230 of the 1,324 legislative proposals (17.4 per cent) adopted by the Commissioners made it to the college. And only 101 (7.6 per cent) of these legislative proposals were treated as so-called B-points and thus explicitly discussed and possibly changed during the college meeting.[6] The work of European Commissioners thus seems to be governed by a relatively strong division of labour. Conflict at the decision-taking phase is rare.

The European Commission's inter-institutional and political environment: past and present

The institutional and the political environment in which the European Commission acts in EU policy-making has changed considerably over the past five decades. In order to be able to act successfully, the Commission needs to take these changes into account.

Each proposal drafted by the Commission needs to be adopted by governments in the Council. The Single European Act established the qualified majority quorum for most policy areas related to the common market and successive treaties further extended qualified majority voting to other issue areas. In the early 1990s the EU was transformed into a truly bicameral system made up of the Council and the European Parliament. The Maastricht Treaty in 1993 introduced the co-decision procedure in which the European Parliament has veto power, that is must agree for a legislative act to be successfully adopted. Having only had consultation powers before, this marked a significant change in the EU's institutional landscape. Since the early 2000s, about 50 per cent of all EU legislation is passed in the co-decision procedure (Häge 2011: 13). While the Commission previously only had to take into account the positions of the member states in the Council when formulating proposals that have the chance of being adopted, it now also has to accommodate the positions of the political groups in the European Parliament by offering concessions and compromises.

Another notable development in the EU's institutional landscape is the successive strengthening of the European Council. Having started as an informal forum in 1974 it is now a formally established organ of the European Union mandated to provide the general political direction and the priorities of the European Union. The Treaty of Lisbon (2009) established a permanent Council presidency selected and appointed by governments for 2.5 years. The permanent Council president shall increase the continuity of the European Council's work, and it might increase the institution's political power.

For the European Commission the European Council is a competitor for political attention in setting the European Union's topical agenda. Moreover, governments now have another institution which they can ask to develop policy ideas and first sketches of policy proposals. In the course of the still ongoing Euro and economic crisis, governments relied heavily on the European Council president instead of the European Commission to develop first drafts of future policies and institutional innovations which shall address the current crises.

In its executive activities, the Commission is supported by an increasing number of EU regulatory agencies (see Rittberger and Wonka, in this volume). Since the 1990s their number has grown to the more than 30 agencies operating today. The European Commission regularly relies on agencies' expertise not only for the implementation of EU regulation but also when drafting new legislation. Moreover, given their decentralized structure and their close cooperation with agencies at the national level, EU agencies help the Commission to create and sustain regulatory networks which bring together diverse actors from the national and the supranational level. Egeberg and Trondal (2011) argue that EU agencies and the Commission share interests and that the former increase the Commission's power in EU policy-making by contributing to EU executive capacities. At the same time, however, national administrations are strongly represented in EU agencies (Kelemen 2002; Wonka and Rittberger 2010), and most agencies rely on the expertise and resources of national administrations in their daily work. Agency staff, moreover, is rather sceptic about increasing the powers of the Commission (Wonka and Rittberger 2011: 900). While agencies definitely increase EU executive capacities, their effects on the Commission's power in regulatory policy-making are ambivalent.

Finally, another notable environmental change which can be expected to have an impact on the Commission's behaviour and power in policy-making is the increasing economic and political heterogeneity of the member states as well as the changes in citizens' attitudes on the European Union. Since its establishment in 1958 the membership of the European Union has increased from 6 to 28 states. This increase in numbers resulted in greater heterogeneity of the EU's members regarding their economic and institutional capacities as well as their regulatory and welfare state regimes. The Commission needs to take the increased heterogeneity of domestic situations into account when drafting policy proposals. Otherwise, it risks that its proposals are not accepted in the Council and in the European Parliament and that EU policies are not effectively implemented. Of course, the Commission can fail in the anticipation of possible political opposition. It might be incompletely or incorrectly informed about domestic situations or political opposition might only form once the Commission has published a proposal and domestic interest groups and political parties subsequently began to deal with the substance of a proposal and politically mobilized only afterwards.

Moreover, it has been argued that the European Union has moved from the era of the "permissive consensus" to the era of "constraining dissensus" (Hooghe and Marks 2009; De Wilde and Zürn 2012). The permissive consensus allowed, so the argument, political elites to engage in EU policy-making and move forward with the European integration project, without involving citizens and without having to fear political resistance. The era of the constraining dissensus, on the other hand, is said to be marked by an increased politicization of EU policy-making, which results from the political mobilization of political parties against EU policies and the European integration project and European citizens' greater scepticism vis-à-vis the integration process. Eurobarometer data for the last decade shows that citizens' trust in the Commission strongly correlates (0.8) with their appreciation of the EU as a whole. Given the greater public scepticism and the outright political opposition to the European Union, the Commission might refrain from potentially controversial political initiatives in order to avoid political opposition.

While the Commission will have to take into account the politico-economic heterogeneity of the EU28 and possible phases of politicization in specific policy areas, these factors so far did not lead to a strong decrease in the Commission's level of activity in EU policy-making: While the number of directives proposed has been stable for the last 30 years and decisions actually increased, only the number of regulations has decreased between 1990 and 1995 but remained relatively stable since then (Häge 2011: 466). At the same time, the EU has increasingly relied on non-legislative means of policy-making, such as the Open Method of Coordination (OMC), in areas in which the EU has no legislative competencies and in which governments are hesitant to accept supranational rule, such as economic and social policy-making (Art. 5 AEUV). While the regulatory effectiveness and the legitimacy of OMC measures such as soft law and benchmarking are still debated (Eberlein and Kerwer 2004; Sabel and Zeitlin 2008), these "new modes of governance" provide the Commission with an opportunity to initiate and frame political debates also in politically sensitive areas.

The European Commission in EU policy-making: resources and intra-institutional decision-making dynamics

To be able to act effectively in EU policy-making the Commission relies on diverse resources. In the following I discuss the most important of these: information, networks and formal procedural competencies. Moreover, the dynamics unfolding between DGs and Commissioners in internal decision-making determine not only the content of the policy proposals leaving the Commission but also the way in which the Commission acts in EU policy-making. Three possible drivers of these intra-institutional conflicts are discussed: sectoral and institutional conflicts between DGs, on one hand, and national conflicts, as well as party political conflicts among Commissioners, on the other.

Power resources of the European Commission

Information and expertise

To be able to act effectively, political actors need to have information on the technical feasibility of their political plans as well as information on possible political opposition to these. For various reasons, obtaining this information is a challenge for the European Commission. As I discussed earlier, member states differ considerably in the structure of their political and economic systems, their economic capacities and regulatory regimes and in the conflicts and sensitivities which define domestic political contestation. Moreover, and partly as a result of this, the EU multilevel polity lacks an integrated system of interest intermediation in which strong European political parties and European interest groups would collect information on the situation and preferences at the domestic and regional levels to aggregate them to a European position.

Instead, interest intermediation in the EU is characterized by multilevel activities of national interest groups and political parties as well as European groups, which enter variable multinational or supranational coalitions with other domestic actors and unite behind a common European position only if they have sufficiently similar preferences concerning specific policies. More than 3,500 groups are estimated to be currently active in the EU's multilevel polity, about a half of which are representing domestic interests (Wonka *et al.* 2010). Because of member states' heterogeneity and the lack of an integrated system of interest intermediation, the Commission needs to invest considerable efforts to collect information on the regulatory and political situation in different member states and on the possible reactions to its proposals when drafting its policy proposals. Otherwise, it risks that its policies fail to reach both, the intended regulatory effect as well as sufficient political support in the Council and the European Parliament.

To assess the situation in the different member states, the Commission relies on the experts in its different DGs. At the same time, however, it consults extensively with different European and national actors. One instrument used by the Commission to obtain reactions from national and European political actors to its planned policies is the publication of white and green papers. In these papers, the Commission sketches the content of future policies. Green papers are released at an early stage and only broadly sketch the content of these policies, while white papers are already relatively detailed as regards the exact form and content of future policies. Moreover, during the last decade, the Commission has increasingly relied on formal consultations with interested national and European actors. In these, the Commission invites private and public actors to comment on its draft proposals. In addition to the functional considerations just discussed, the Commission might try to use these consultations to increase the political legitimacy of its proposals and thus its own authority in decision-making procedures on these.

Moreover, the administrators of the different DGs consult extensively with private and public actors, located both in the member states and at the European level. An important institutional forum for these exchanges are the numerous expert groups set up by the Commission (Larsson 2003; Gornitzka and Sverdrup 2008). For national representatives as well as private actors participation in these groups might be attractive as they get information on future political developments at an early stage, thus putting them in a privileged position in trying to exert influence on the policies debated. The scope and the mandate of these experts groups vary. Some deal with questions of implementation, others are meant to assist the formulation of policies and still others are set up to exchange early ideas on the development of future policies. Moreover, expert groups differ regarding their membership. While some have a purely administrative membership, bringing together members of the European Commission and of relevant member state administrations, others are composed more diversely by, in addition, including representatives of firms and interest groups.

At the beginning of 2013, 770 expert committees were operating in the Commission's various DGs.[7] Of these about 80 per cent were exclusively composed of members of competent national administrations, thus contributing to close multilevel linkages between European administrations. The density of these multilevel interactions, however, varies considerably between DGs: Most expert groups – 109 – are affiliated with DG Taxation and Customs Union, followed by the 73 expert groups entertained by DG Health and Consumers, while DG Regional Policy and DG Economic and Financial Affairs on the other hand entertain eight and ten expert groups respectively.

Administrative and political networks

Moreover, the Commission entertains networks with national administrations, national and European agencies as well as private actors. These networks are set up for specific tasks; they exist for longer periods and administrative and organizational support for their work is often financed and provided by the Commission's services. Exchanges in these networks also serve the purpose of exchanging views on policies to be developed. At the same time, these networks are established in policy areas in which the EU does not have competencies to act with the aim of arriving at the informal coordination of policies (Levi-Faur 2011; Maggetti and Gilardi 2011). Its participation in those networks and its central coordinative role in these put the Commission in a privileged position in trying to shape policies in areas reaching beyond the strict confines of the European treaties. Moreover, the Commission can use the ties provided by the networks to politically strengthen its role vis-à-vis other political actors at the national and European level.

It was argued earlier that the Commission needs information and expertise on the regulatory, institutional and politico-economic situation in its member states to be able to act successfully in EU policy-making. Having this information allows the Commission to anticipate political opposition to its proposals not only in the member states themselves but also in the Council and in the European Parliament. Moreover, this information is also needed for functional reasons, since it facilitates the ability of Commissioners and their DGs to draft proposals which are an adequate policy response to possibly different situations in the EU's member states. Since the Commission to a considerable extent relies on external sources to obtain this information, its success in EU policy-making also depends on the successful cooperation with diverse actors in its consultations, working groups and networks.

Institutional resources: agenda setting and monitoring

The previously mentioned resources are soft and complementary: the Commission can employ them to politically and substantively improve the proposals and decisions and to win support for its initiatives. They do not, however, provide the Commission with direct and enforceable means to shape EU policies and decisions. The Commission's direct and authoritative influence on EU policies is guaranteed by its formal competencies in EU policy-making and its central role in monitoring member states' efforts in implementation of EU policies, which have already been discussed in the introductory section of this chapter.

Its monopoly power to draft legislative proposals allows the Commission to formally set the EU policy agenda. The powers arising from this agenda setting competence vary, however, across policy areas and proposals. In policy areas in which the member states decide by unanimity, the Commission's room for manoeuvre is more restricted than in areas in which the Council decides by qualified majority where individual member states can be overruled. Moreover, the attention which individual proposals receive both by political elites and the broader public via media varies significantly, also affecting the Commission's ability to shape the content of EU policies. Once political elites and the broader public have turned their attention to individual proposals, opposition to a proposal might form early on and significantly reduce the Commission's room for manoeuvre. Moreover, its central role in infringement proceedings provides the Commission with additional leverage also in EU policy-making. The Commission can use these to challenge the legal status quo. To prevent this and to be able to secure their political say in the decision, governments might change previously held positions and be willing to agree to policies whose adoption they previously refused (Schmidt 2000).

Intra-institutional conflicts and dynamics

It was argued earlier that the European Commission is marked by a considerable heterogeneity: DGs vary considerably in the size of their personnel, budget and competencies. In addition, at the individual level the attitudes and perceptions of the Commission's administrative staff diverge substantially. Moreover, the Commission's political leadership is mostly made up of experienced politicians with political ties to their home countries. These factors can be expected to shape the dynamics and conflicts in internal Commission decision-making, which again shapes the positions taken and the policies proposed by the Commission in EU policy-making.

Three types of conflicts will be considered in the following: First, sectoral conflicts which reflect diverging institutional interests of DGs and their Commissioners and/or differences in their technical assessments of the effectiveness of policies to address specific problems. Second, the discussions and cooperation of Commissioners in the College might be driven by partisan concerns and result in partisan conflicts. And, finally, Commissioners from different member states might try to get their home country's interests recognized when formulating and taking decisions in the College of Commissioners.

When discussing the dynamics of decision-making inside the Commission, a first crucial observation is that the vast majority of decisions taken in the European Commission lead to little or no controversies between Commissioners. Only a minority of proposals are discussed and adopted in the College, where those proposals are dealt with on which differences of opinion remain after the early stage consultations between DGs and Commissioners. During the term of the Prodi Commission (1999–2004), less than 20 per cent of the more than 1,300 legislative proposals adopted made it to College (Wonka 2008a: 1151). And only about 8 per cent of these issues could not be resolved by the Commissioners' cabinet and were thus discussed by the Commissioners themselves as B-points during their meetings (Wonka 2008b: 150). The vast majority of policy proposals formulated by the Commission thus seem to deal with specific technical issues that are of low political salience and of little interest to other DGs and Commissioners. The large share of uncontroversial technical proposals corresponds with the very large share of DGs' staff perceiving their own role as contributing to technically and substantively sound EU policy-making (Bauer and Ege 2012: 417). It is also in line with the strong loyalty vis-à-vis their own DGs and the weight attributed to the considerations of colleagues from the DG reported by those working in the Commission's apparatus (Trondal 2008: 478).

What, however, are the factors driving conflicts in the minority of policies which are discussed and collectively adopted by the Commission's political leadership? Because of the unavailability of appropriate data, we lack quantitative studies on the political dynamics of decision-making in the Commission. The few qualitative studies investigating conflicts in Commission decision-making find that party political conflicts are rare (Egeberg 2006; Wonka 2008a). Instead, Commissioners whose parties are belonging to different ideological party families seem to cooperate and coalesce also in highly conflictive cases (Wonka 2008a). This, again, is in line with the perception of DGs' staff. Administrators in the DGs report party politics to have a marginal impact on their everyday work (Bauer and Ege 2012: 410), while members of Commissioners' personal cabinets consider it to be more important but still not a dominant political force in their work (Kassim *et al.* 2013: 120).

If conflicts arise between Commissioners and DGs, they rather seem to be motivated by conflicting sectoral and national interests. In both, regulatory policy-making as well as in trade policy-making, it has been observed that conflicts in the Commission arise between DGs that have diverging functional policy and/or institutional interests (Egeberg 2006; Dür and Zimmermann 2007: 774; Wonka 2008a; Hartlapp *et al.* 2013: 425, 438). In regulatory policy-making such conflicts occur, for example, between Commissioners and DGs responsible for industry and economics, on the one hand, and environmental and social affairs Commissioners, on the other. In trade politics the Commissioner responsible for trade regularly faces, amongst others, the opposition of the Commissioner responsible for agriculture. The positions taken by DGs on a particular policy can also change if political responsibilities in the Commission are reshuffled, indicating that the political leadership exercised by Commissioners over their DGs does indeed matter and that the positions taken by DGs in EU policy-making are neither structurally determined nor solely driven by stable bureaucratic interests (Wonka 2008a).

In addition, national interests also do play a role in Commission decision-making: Commissioners also take positions which are in line with their country's governments. Moreover, Commissioners whose DGs have no functional interest in a policy do take positions on proposals which correspond with those of their home countries' governments, further indicating that it is not only competing sectoral interests that lead to clashes between Commissioners and DGs. Given governments' careful selection of Commissioners and taking into account member states' resistance to give up their seat in the Commission, the occurrence of conflicts motivated by Commissioners close political ties to their home countries hardly comes as a big surprise.

The discussion of conflicts in Commission decision-making confirms the usefulness of treating the European Commission as a collective rather than a unitary actor. The limited analytical value of conceptualizing the Commission as a unitary actor already became apparent in the discussion of the heterogeneous attitudes and preferences which characterize the Commission's administrative staff. The discussion of conflicts in the Commission's political leadership added to this. Only by taking into account the collective quality of the European Commission will it be possible to take into account the dynamics shaping its actions in EU politics and the positions it takes in EU policy-making.

The European Commission in EU policy-making: positions and power

In the previous section I discussed the resources the Commission relies on in EU policy-making as well as the intra-institutional dynamics and conflicts that shape its behaviour in EU politics. In the following section I discuss the goals the Commission pursues in inter-institutional decision-making and the positions it takes as well as the power it is said to have in EU policy-making processes.

Commission preferences and positions

The conception of the goals and preferences pursued by the Commission in EU policy-making which dominates in the literature, portrays it as an organization which, whenever the political opportunity arises, is successfully pushing for the transfer of competencies from member states to the European Union and for the EU wide harmonization of regulation (Cram 1994). This expansionist conception of the European Commission is in line with rational theories of bureaucracies which hold that bureaucratic actors in general have incentives and the means to expand their budgets (Niskanen 1971) and competencies (Moe 1990: 143–145; Majone 1996: 34–36, 64–66) in order to increase their power in policy-making. In EU studies, the expansionist conception has its intellectual roots in neo-functionalist and supranationalist theories of European integration (Schimmelfennig and Rittberger, this volume; Haas 1958; Stone Sweet and Sandholtz 1997; Pollack 2003). And it is widely adopted by scholars drawing on the sociological and rationalist variants of neo-institutionalism to analyse EU politics (Aspinwall and Schneider 2000; Tsebelis and Garrett 2000; Hörl *et al.* 2005). Contrary to this pro-integrationist conception of the Commission, intergovernmentalist and realist approaches to European integration argue that the preferences of the European Commission and other supranational institutions neither strongly diverge from those of the member states, nor do they consider the Commission to have an independent influence on the course of European integration and the content of EU policies (Moravcsik 1998: 55, 69).

The factors assumed to lead the Commission to pursue a pro-integrationist agenda are diverse and not always well explicated. This might have to do with the unitary conception of the Commission which dominates the literature. From such a perspective, it is impossible to tell whether the positions the Commission takes in EU policy-making have their origin in the preferences and attitudes of the Commission's administrative staff or whether they reflect the preferences of individual Commissioners or its collective political leadership. Three sources for the Commission's pro-integrationist preferences are more or less explicitly discussed in the literature: a common institutional interest, actors' preferences and organizational norms.

First, it is argued that the Commission has an *institutional interest* in extending its own power and authority in EU politics. Given its limited influence on the EU budget, the Commission might try to increase its power by pushing for the EU-wide harmonization of ever more policies and by working towards the extension of supranational competencies to ever more policy areas which formerly fell under the exclusive authority of member states (Majone 1996). This perspective neglects, however, that, as has been shown above, different DGs might compete for influence on a policy in the internal decision-making process. As a result, there are competing views on what "the Commission's" institutional interest might be, which again might lead to a reduction of the Commission's capacity to strategically act in EU policy-making. Moreover, it is unclear, who exactly defines and expresses this institutional interest inside the Commission.

A second line of reasoning, which is complementing the institutional argument rather than competing with it, argues that *actors* inside the Commission hold specific preferences that lead the Commission to act in a specific way. Two types of actors need to be distinguished: Commission officials in DGs on the one hand and the political leadership made up by Commissioners and the Commission president on the other. Officials in the Commission's DGs might, in line with the institutional argument, have a preference for the further integration of Europe and for harmonization to increase their power in EU policy-making. The pro-integrationist preferences of the Commission's staff might also be explained by a self-selection process in which those who identify with the European integration process seek employment in the Commission in the first place. This latter argument is confirmed by a recent study which finds that the "commitment to Europe" is the reason most often named by Commission staff when asked why they joined the Commission (Kassim *et al.* 2013: 252).

Commissioners might also strive for integration and harmonization to increase their power in shaping EU policies. At the same time, Commissioners are to a large extent experienced national politicians who have been selected and appointed by member states' governments. They might be concerned about their re-nomination for political jobs at the national or European level and thus not act completely independent of the governments and core political interests in their home country. As discussed earlier, the preferences they voice and pursue in their work in the Commission might be much closer to their country's interests than postulated by supranationalists (Döring 2007; Wonka 2007).

A third perspective posits that organizational *norms and role expectations* strongly shape the behaviour both of Commission officials and Commissioners. These norms and roles can be specific for different DGs and might contain norms and expectations specific for the respective policy area in which a DG operates. Such DG specific norms and role expectations might lead to conflicts between different departments. The norms and roles at the same time might consist of behavioural expectations which are shared by the whole institution, thus leading to coherent behaviour across DGs and organizational levels (Egeberg 2006; Trondal 2008). Analytically the structurally induced norm and role induced behaviour differs considerably from the actor centred explanations of preferences discussed in the previous paragraph. Empirically, however, it will be harder to distinguish the two.

When describing the Commission's positions in EU policy-making, the vast majority of qualitative as well as quantitative empirical analyses describe these in opposition to the positions of member states. The fact that the Commission takes positions which differ at least from those taken by some member states is commonly interpreted as a sign of the Commission's entrepreneurial striving for more European integration and harmonization and for its attempts to gain more powers in EU policy-making. This interpretation certainly does have some explanatory power, especially in policy-making processes dealing with institutional and budgetary questions, which have a direct impact on the Commission's future role and power in EU politics. Quite regularly, however, conceptualizing the Commission's as a pro-integrationist activist is substantively and analytically misleading. A considerable share of EU policies are re-regulations and specifications of existing European legislation, which do not touch on the vertical distribution of power between national and European actors or increase the level of harmonization of national policies (Thomson *et al.* 2004: 251–253).

If the Commission's invariant preference for more integration is implausible as a universal explanation for the Commission's behaviour in EU policy-making, additional factors that have a systematic impact on the Commission's positioning in EU politics need to be taken into account. Parts of these factors have already been discussed in the earlier section on intra-institutional dynamics: In case conflicts arise during the formulation of policy proposal in the Commission, these conflicts regularly result from diverging policy preferences of DGs involved and/or affected by a policy. Conflicts between DGs cannot (necessarily) be reduced to rivalries over their future political power, but concern differing concerns about the appropriate regulatory goals – for example free trade versus the protection of farmers and economic competition versus environmental and consumer protection – and the relative distribution of political and economic costs and benefits of a decision.

In addition, the nationality of a Commissioner also reflects in the policies prepared by his or her DG. As Thomson shows, the extent to which a Commissioner can accommodate the position of the government of his home country depends on the decision-making rules: In decisions adopted by unanimity in the Council, nationality does not play a role as Commissioners need to formulate a proposal which can be accepted by all governments. If a proposal, however, needs only the approval of a qualified majority in the Council, Commissioners use the political discretion to propose policies which are relatively close to the position which their country's government takes in the Council (Thomson 2008, 2011: 95–98). In a case study on internal decision-making, Wonka found that Commissioners who are in charge of DGs which have no substantive or sectoral links to a specific policy decision have intervened in internal decision-making on such policies (Wonka 2008a). Since institutional and/or policy-related rivalries between DGs cannot explain such behaviour, these interventions are a further indication that Commissioners at times defend the interests of their country of origin in internal Commission politics.

Observing that the Commission is frequently taking positions that diverge from those of some member states must, finally, not necessarily be explained by diverging political interests. Member states of the European Union vary considerably regarding their economic structure and capacities as well as with regard to their institutional structures, the political and technical and nature of their regulatory regimes and concerning their political cultures and sensitivities. This heterogeneity does affect governments' interests and the positions they take in EU policy-making. Its institutional position in the EU's political system demands the Commission to come up with an EU-wide binding policy proposal. Given its institutional role and its political mandate, it is difficult to see how the Commission could even in principle satisfy all governments when formulating its policy proposals to avoid conflicts in later stages of the policy-making process. Moreover, some governments might not have formed or agreed on a position that the Commission could take into account when it prepares its proposal, amongst others reasons, because of a lack of capacities of national administrations for dealing with EU issues (Panke 2012: 134–140). It is undisputed that quite regularly the Commission clashes with member states in EU policy-making, because they assess situations differently and pursue different political goals. As has been argued in this paragraph, however, not all divergences can be traced back to diverging goals and preferences. Some are structurally built in the EU's political system.

Power

How powerful is the Commission in EU policy-making? That is to what extent and under which conditions is it able to shape EU policies in line with its own preferences and against the preferences of, at least, some member state governments? The power of the Commission in EU policy-making is systematically influenced by its formal powers and the formal rules by which a decision is made, the preferences and positions of governments and the European Parliament. Of course, Commission's power is also shaped by situation specific factors that are harder to theorize.

The Commission's formal power in EU policy-making varies considerably across policy areas and the institutional rules according to which decisions are taken in these policy areas. The Commission's formal power in EU legislative policy-making is highest in areas in which the Council decides by qualified majority. If legislation can be adopted by qualified majority in the Council, the Commission must not necessarily take into account the preferences voiced by all member states when drafting its proposal, but only the positions taken by those governments which are needed to form a sufficiently large majority coalition in the Council. Under unanimity, on the other hand, every government can threaten the Commission to veto its proposal, thus forcing it to make more concessions to secure the agreement of all governments. Given that since the coming into force of the Single European Act, the Council decides by qualified majority in most policy areas related to the establishment of a common European market and that successive European treaties including the Lisbon Treaty, which recently came into force, further extended the qualified majority rule to additional policy areas, the formal conditions for strong influence of the Commission in EU policy-making are given. The unanimity rule is in place in some areas of justice and home affairs as well as tax and social policies in which the EU has no competencies to adopt binding legislation. In these policy areas the Commission shall, according to the treaties, facilitate the coordination of policies amongst member states.

The Commission also has considerable influence on policies in areas in which it does not need the agreement of governments and/or the European Parliament to enact new policies but instead that of the European Court of Justice: monitoring and enforcing member states' compliance with EU primary and secondary law, are the prime examples of these "non-majoritarian" powers. Whether or not the Commission can actually use these powers depends on the compatibility of its goals and ideas with those of the European Court of Justice. Both institutions are not directly accountable to voters and, as discussed previously, are often argued to be natural partners in pursuing shared supranational interests (Scharpf 1999; Pollack 2003). As a consequence, while the Commission's power in these non-majoritarian decisions is conditional on the European Court of Justice's support, this support for the Commission is often taken for granted.

In addition to these institutional factors, the Commission's power in EU policy-making is determined by factors which are situation specific and therefore harder to theorize. The most crucial factor determining the Commission's influence is the opposition it faces by member states in the Council and from members of the European Parliament. The stronger the position of the Commission and those of governments and, in cases in which the it co-decides, the European Parliamentarians diverge, and the more political importance governments and Parliamentarians attach to a proposal, the more compromises the Commission will have to make to get its proposal accepted. A problem the Commission faces is that members of the Council and the European Parliament might only form its political positions or consider it as politically important, once the Commission has submitted its proposal to the legislative institutions.

An important reason for the late formation of positions and political opposition is that governments and Parliamentarians sometimes have difficulties in assessing the political and technical implications of proposals and, as a consequence, also its political importance. This is especially true for technical proposals, which are rather common in EU policy-making. For such an assessment, governments often rely on the input and mobilization of specialized interest groups. If these groups only mobilize once a proposal has entered the inter-institutional decision-making phase, the political situation in the Council and the European Parliament might considerably change and the Commission faces political opposition which it could not anticipate when it formulated its proposal. These "delayed" political dynamics and the resulting difficulties in anticipating political opposition significantly affect the Commission's power in decision-making on a respective policy. To reduce the difficulties resulting from these delayed political dynamics the Commission, as has been described above, consults extensively with private and public stakeholders before proposing new legislation.

Finally, exogenous events whose occurrence cannot be directly influenced by the EU's political actors and institutions, such as the BSE crisis, tanker disasters or the current economic and financial crisis, open windows of opportunities which the Commission can use to become politically active. The Commission might not only use this opportunity to argue for the need for EU regulation and/or institutions to address the respective problem. Governments might also depend on the Commission's expertise and resources to come up with relatively quick policy solutions in such a situation, further strengthening the Commission's possible power in such situations.

Conclusion

It is safe to conclude that over the course of the last more than 50 years, the European Commission has had considerable influence on the content of EU policies and on the course of the European integration project. While supranationalists and neo-functionalists might sometimes overestimate the centrality of the Commission in EU policy-making, intergovernmentalists certainly underestimate its political importance for political developments in the European Union. And both, at times, neglect that this influence is not exercised in complete independence of national governments and administrative elites and fail to systematically explicate the political conditions that put the Commission in a powerful political position.

While there are no reasons to expect changes in the Commission's formal role in EU legislative policy-making, it will be interesting to see how the institutional strengthening of the European Council through the Lisbon Treaty will affect the Commission's informal power as initiator and facilitator of political discussions and projects. During the current political crisis, governments have strongly relied on the European Council and its president Herman van Rompuy to coordinate their political activities and to come up with ideas and initial drafts for future activities at the EU level. This might indicate a shift of power from the Commission to the European Council. Whether this shift is just a momentary result of the crises or whether it marks a more permanent attempt of governments to increase their own weight in the coordination and preparation of EU policies will have to be seen in the future.

Notes

1 http://ec.europa.eu/transparency/regcomitology/index.cfm?do=List.list (accessed on 6 December 2012).
2 http://ec.europa.eu/civil_service/about/figures/index_en.htm (accessed on 11 February 2014).

3   http://ec.europa.eu/budget/figures/2013/2013_en.cfm (accessed on 11 February 2014).
4   http://ec.europa.eu/civil_service/docs/europa_sp2_bs_nat_x_grade_en.pdf (accessed on 11 February 2014).
5   Interview with a former member of the Danish Environment Commissioner Bjerregaard's cabinet in 2000. I am grateful to M. Rainer Lepsius who directed the DFG-funded sociological research project "Regieren in der Europäischen Union" (SPP 1023) and provided me with the interview transcript.
6   Decisions in the Commission can be taken in four different procedures. Only proposals and decisions decided in the so-called oral procedure are dealt with in the college of Commissioners. The application of the oral procedure at the same time is an indicator for conflicts in internal decision-making: "Where differences of opinion remain at the end of interservice consultation, the only way to obtain Commission approval of the document is by oral procedure" (European Commission 2004: 10)
7   http://ec.europa.eu/transparency/regexpert/index.cfm (accessed on 9 January 2013).

References

Aspinwall, M.D. and G. Schneider (2000). "Same Menu, Separate Tables: The Institutionalist Turn in Political Science and the Study of European Integration." *European Journal of Political Research* 38(1): 1–36.

Bauer, M.W. and J. Ege (2012). "Politicization within the European Commission's bureaucracy." *International Review of Administrative Sciences* 78(3): 403–424.

Cram, L. (1994). "The European Commission as a Multi-Organization: Social Policy and IT Policy in the EU." *Journal of European Public Policy* 1(2): 195–217.

De Wilde, P. and M. Zürn (2012). "Can the Politicization of European Integration be Reversed?" *Journal of Common Market Studies* 50(1): 137–153.

Döring, H. (2007). "The Composition of the College of Commissioners: Patterns of Delegation." *European Union Politics* 8(2): 209–230.

Dür, A. and H. Zimmermann (2007). "Introduction: The EU in International Trade Negotiations." *Journal of Common Market Studies* 45(4): 771–787.

Eberlein, B and D. Kerwer (2004). "New Governance in the European Union." *Journal of Common Market Studies* 42(1): 121–142-

Egeberg, M. (2006). "Executive Politics as Usual: Role Behaviour and Conflict Dimensions in the College of European Commissioners." *Journal of European Public Policy* 13(1): 1–15.

Egeberg, M. and J. Trondal (2011). "EU-level Agencies: New Executive Centre Formation or Vehicles for National Control?" *Journal of European Public Policy* 18(6): 868–887.

European Commission (2004). *Manual of Operating Procedures of the Commission*. Brussels: European Commission.

Gornitzka, Å. and U. Sverdrup (2008). "Who Consults? The Configuration of Expert Groups in the European Union." *West European Politics* 31(4): 725–750.

Gravier, M. (2008). "The 2004 Enlargement Staff Policy of the European Commission: The Case for Representative Bureaucracy." *Journal of Common Market Studies* 46(5): 1025–1047.

Haas, P. (1958). *The Uniting of Europe*. Stanford, Stanford University Press.

Häge, F. (2011). "The European Union Policy-making Dataset." *European Union Politics* 12(3): 455–477.

Hartlapp, M., J. Metz and C. Rauh (2013). "Linking Agenda Setting to Coordination Structures: Bureaucratic Politics inside the European Commission." *Journal of European Integration* 35(4): 425–441

Hooghe, L. (2001). *The European Commission and the Integration of Europe. Images of Governance*. Cambridge, Cambridge University Press.

Hooghe, L. (2005). "Several Roads Lead to International Norms, but Few Via International Socialization: A Case Study of the European Commission." *International Organization* 59: 861–898.

Hooghe, L. (2012). "Images of Europe: How Commission Officials Conceive Their Institution's Role." *Journal of Common Market Studies* 50(1): 87–111.

Hooghe, L. and G. Marks (2009). "A Postfunctionalist Theory of European Integration: From Permissive Consensus to Constraining Dissensus." *British Journal of Political Science* 39(1): 1–23.

Hörl, B., A. Warntjen and A. Wonka. (2005). "Built on Quicksand? A Decade of Procedural Spatial Models on EU Legislative Decision-Making." *Journal of European Public Policy* 12(3): 592–606.

Kassim, H., J. Peterson, M. W. Bauer, S. Connolly, R. Dehousse, L. Hooghe and A. Thompson (2013). *The European Commission of the Twenty-First Century*. Oxford, Oxford University Press.

Kelemen, D. R. (2002). "The Politics of 'Eurocratic' Structure and the New European Agencies." *West European Politics* 25(4): 93–118.

Larsson, T. (2003). *Precooking in the European Union – The World of Expert Groups*. Fritzes Offentliga Publikationer: 178. Stockholm, ESO.

Levi-Faur, D. (2011). "Regulatory Networks and Regulatory Agencification: Toward a Single European Regulatory Space." *Journal of European Public Policy* 18(6): 810–829.

Maggetti, M. and F. Gilardi (2011). "The Policy-making Structure of European Regulatory Networks and the Domestic Adoption of Standards." *Journal of European Public Policy* 18(6): 830–847.

Majone, G., Ed. (1996). *Regulating Europe*. London, Routledge.

Michelmann, H. J. (1978). "Multinational Staffing and Organizational Functioning in the Commission of the European Communities." *International Organization* 32(2): 477–496.

Moe, T. (1990). "The Politics of Structural Choice: Toward a Theory of Public Bureaucracy." In *Organization Theory. From Chester Barnard to the Present and Beyond*, O.E. Williamson, ed. Oxford, Oxford University Press: 116–153.

Moravcsik, A. (1998). *The Choice for Europe: Social Purpose and State Power from Messina to Maastricht*. Ithaca, Cornell University Press.

Niskanen, W. A. (1971). *Bureaucracy and Representative Government*. Chicago, Aldine Atherton Inc.

Panke, Diana (2012). "Lobbying Institutional Key Players: How States Seek to Influence the European Commission, the Council Presidency and the European Parliament." *Journal of Common Market Studies* 50(1): 129–150

Pollack, M. A. (2003). *The Engines of Integration. Delegation, Agency and Agenda Setting in the EU*. Oxford, Oxford University Press.

Sabel, C. F. and J. Zeitlin (2008). "Learning from Difference: The New Architecture of Experimentalist Governance in the EU." *European Law Journal* 14(3): 271–327.

Scharpf, F. W. (1999). *Governing in Europe – Democratic and Effective?* Oxford, Oxford University Press.

Schmidt, S. K. (2000). "Only an Agenda Setter? The European Commission's Power over the Council of Ministers." *European Union Politics* 1(1): 37–61.

Stone Sweet, A. and W. Sandholtz (1997). "European Integration and Supranational Governance." *Journal of European Public Policy* 4(3): 297–317.

Suvarierol, S. (2008). "Beyond the Myth of Nationality: Analysing Networks within the European Commission." *West European Politics* 31(4): 701–724.

Thomson, R. (2008). "National Actors in International Organizations. The Case of the European Commission." *Comparative Political Studies* 41(2): 169–192.

Thomson, R. (2011). *Resolving Controversy in the European Union. Legislative Decision-Making Before and After Enlargement*. Cambridge, Cambridge University Press.

Thomson, R., J. Boerefijn and F. Stokman (2004). "Actor alignments in European Union decision making." *European Journal of Political Research* 43: 237–261.

Trondal, J. (2008). "The Anatomy of Autonomy: Reassessing the Autonomy of the European Commission." *European Journal of Political Research* 47: 467–488.

Tsebelis, G. and G. Garrett (2000). "Legislative Politics in the European Union." *European Union Politics* 1(1): 9–36.

Wonka, A. (2007). "Technocratic and Independent? The Appointment of European Commissioners and its Policy Implications." *Journal of European Public Policy* 14(2): 171–191.

Wonka, A. (2008a). "Decision-making Dynamics in the European Commission: Partisan, National or Sectoral?" *Journal of European Public Policy* 15(8): 1145–1163.

Wonka, A. (2008b). *Die Europäische Kommission. Supranationale Bürokratie oder Agent der Mitgliedstaaten?* Baden-Baden, Nomos.

Wonka, A. and B. Rittberger (2010). "Credibility, Complexity and Uncertainty: Determinants of Institutional Independence of 29 EU agencies." *West European Politics* 33(4): 730–752.

Wonka, A. and B. Rittberger (2011). "Perspectives on EU Governance: An Empirical Assessment of the Political Attitudes of EU Agency Professionals." *Journal of European Public Policy* 18(6): 888–908.

Wonka, A., F. R. Baumgartner, C. Mahoney and J. Berkhout. (2010). "Measuring the Size and Scope of the EU Interest Group Population." *European Union Politics* 11(3): 463–476.

Chapter 5

The EU's multilevel parliamentary system

Berthold Rittberger and Thomas Winzen

European integration and parliamentary democracy

During the Euro crisis, parliaments have once again become a focal point in the public debate about the future of the European Union (EU). Many commentators worry that national parliaments are reduced to the status of marginal observers of government attempts to solve the Euro crisis by gradually upgrading fiscal policy integration. In a similar vein, the European Parliament (EP) plays no relevant role in the choices over the future architecture of the Eurozone. Such concerns are hardly surprising because parliaments are the institutions we associate with representative democracy. Yet, these concerns are all the more troublesome, as the marginalization of national parliaments appears to reinforce long-standing criticisms of the EU's democratic deficit.

In this chapter, we take one step back from the contemporary discussions about parliaments and the Euro crisis. In the past decades, scholars have produced a steady stream of research on European integration and parliamentary democracy. One strand of this literature takes issue with the expansion of the powers of the EP and explores the causes of the gradual "parliamentarisation" of the EU. The second strand zooms onto the domestic level and explores the challenge European integration poses for national parliaments. While the powers of the EP have been expanded with every major revision of the founding treaties, many see in national parliaments the main losers of European integration. Proponents of the "de-parliamentarisation" thesis commonly advance several arguments to underwrite this claim: First, national parliaments are considered to be mere "administrative extensions" (Duina and Oliver 2005: 174) of EU decision-making because EU law is either directly applicable or has to be transposed in the shadow of (supranationally enforced) sanctions. Second, the EU's multilevel system of decision-making has led to a strengthening of

> domestic governments as they, and not backbench parliamentarians and people outside the executive branch, participate in decision-making in the various EU institutions . . . The dominant position of domestic governments in both national and European politics . . . reduces the influence of parliaments at all stages of the decision-making process.
>
> (O'Brennan and Raunio 2007a: 4; see also Moravcsik 1994)

European integration is thus said to create a problem of distance (e.g. Dahl 1994). National parliaments, as domestic actors, find it difficult to monitor what governments, diplomats and bureaucrats do at the European level. Decision-making and decision shaping often take place in inaccessible or invisible arenas such as administrative working groups. While this is also the case in other international organisations, the intensity of day-to-day EU decision-making may be said to make this concern particularly important. Third, parliamentary deficits emerge to the extent that European integration threatens to break the chain of democratic accountability from governments to national parliaments (Rittberger 2005; Rittberger and Schimmelfennig 2006; Schimmelfennig 2010): If EU decision-making moves from unanimity to majority voting or when supranational organisations obtain decision-making powers, national governments and parliaments can be overruled, which weakens domestic accountability and puts stress on democratic legitimacy.

According to some scholars, the de-parliamentarisation thesis is exaggerated. First, the proponents of the thesis can be said to have a point to the extent that European integration encroaches on competencies that national parliaments have "lost" because of integration. For instance, the fact that the EU has exclusive competencies in monetary policy-making does not cause a "parliamentary deficit" because national parliaments have deliberately delegated monetary policy to central banks in the domestic sphere prior to integration in monetary policy (Moravcsik 2002). Second, the de-parliamentarisation thesis is not really problematic as long as the EU decides on matters that national parliaments have previously decided on but that are either not very controversial or salient. We may think of technical and regulatory policy questions that tend to generate little controversy or redistributive implications (Majone 1998, 2002). Hence, discussions about the challenge European integration poses to national parliaments become interesting as the EU's competences expand into areas normally subject to parliamentary decision-making and into redistributive, identity and security relevant issues that tend to be highly politicised and cause political controversy. We note, however, that there is now widespread agreement that precisely this has increasingly happened since the mid-1980s (Føllesdal and Hix 2006; Hooghe and Marks 2008; Genschel and Jachtenfuchs 2013).

Arguments about de-parliamentarisation also appear to be exaggerated because European integration goes hand in hand with parliamentarisation processes (Rittberger 2005; Føllesdal and Hix 2006; Rittberger and Schimmelfennig 2006; Schimmelfennig 2010). First, parliamentarisation occurs at the supranational level through the extension of the EP's powers. Second, at the national level, we can witness a growing involvement of national parliaments in matters of EU politics, which also extends transnationally through inter-parliamentary interaction and cooperation. In this context, we could thus speak about a re-parliamentarisation of national parliaments in EU affairs.

The first task for this chapter is thus to chart and explain these two parliamentarisation processes at the supranational as well as on the national level. Yet, parliamentarisation is not a panacea for democratic shortcomings in the EU. First, it may impair the efficiency of EU decision-making. For those who maintain that European integration draws its legitimacy from positive output, parliamentarisation may appear as a threat, rather than an opportunity to increase democratic legitimacy (e.g. Majone 2002). Second, some might think of parliamentarisation as merely "façade democratisation" that ultimately fails to involve citizens and redirect political behaviour and loyalties (Bartolini 2005). The second task of this chapter is thus to take stock of what we have learned about these concerns by asking how parliamentarisation affects the efficiency and legitimacy of European integration.

The evolution of Europe's multilevel parliamentary system

This section shows that the EU has gradually developed a multilevel parliamentary system characterised by a vertical division of labour, weak horizontal integration and cross-national variation (see also Crum and Fossum 2009). First, the EP has evolved into a powerful legislature that participates in decision-making at the European level on equal footing with the national governments in the Council. National parliaments have gradually improved their ability to control their governments' conduct in the EU. Yet, they have only a weakly developed direct role at the European level. Second, there is little evidence of meaningful transnational integration of parliamentary activities across the member states. Yet, there are arenas for information exchange and, since the Lisbon Treaty, procedures that could encourage greater horizontal integration. Third, given that the EU has 27 member states, it is not surprising to find cross-national divergence in national parliamentary adaptation to European integration. To elaborate these points, we now discuss the EP's rise at the European level and then turn to national parliaments' engagement with integration.

The European Parliament: undisputed winner of integration?

The powers of the EP have been gradually extended over the past decades. For the first decades of its existence and even in the aftermath of the first direct elections in 1979, the EP's competencies to affect Community legislation were highly circumscribed, providing it with a mere right to be consulted on legislative matters. This situation was only altered with the adoption of the SEA in 1986. Since then, successive treaty reforms have seen a rapid expansion of the EP's legislative competences, both with regard to the range of policies that require legislative "input" by the EP and with a view to the scope of its influence: The co-operation procedure adopted in the Single European Act (SEA) provided the EP with limited agenda-setting powers (Tsebelis 1994), the co-decision procedure, introduced at Maastricht, and its subsequent reform at Amsterdam, further extended the EP's formal influence over EU legislation, while reducing the influence of the Commission. The Lisbon Treaty declared the co-decision procedure to be the "Ordinary Legislative Procedure" (OLP), and hence the main legislative procedure for the adoption of EU legislation. The OLP thus enshrines the role of the EP as the co-equal legislator alongside the Council not only formally, the Lisbon Treaty also placed a considerable number of policy areas under the OLP, thereby enhancing the EP's reach in two ways (see Tiilikainen 2011). First, the OLP now applies in areas previously covered by another legislative procedure (e.g. Common Agricultural Policy, immigration policy and police cooperation, macroeconomic coordination). Overall, the reach of the OLP was almost doubled, from 45 to 84 specific policy provisions (Maurer and von Ondarza 2012). Second, the OLP also applies to competencies, which were newly conferred on the EU, such as energy policy and the citizens' initiative. Still, the EP is excluded from legislative co-decision in many policy areas, mostly those affecting the welfare state (e.g. measures relating to employment and social policy), taxation (e.g. tax harmonization measures) and (non-EU) third-country nationals.

The Lisbon Treaty not only extended the EP's legislative role; it also bolstered its influence over the annual budget and the investiture of the Commission. The annual budgetary procedure now resembles the OLP, which makes the EP the co-equal arm of the budgetary authority. The procedure for the adoption of the annual budget now resembles the OLP (see Tiilikainen 2011; Maurer and von Ondarza 2012). The EP's role in the adoption of the multiannual financial framework (MFF), which defines the main categories for EU expenditure and sets the maximum levels for expenditure, was also modified: Not only was the procedure for adopting the MFF formalised in the Lisbon Treaty (it was previously based on an Inter-institutional Agreement); the Council now also has to obtain the consent of the EP prior to adopting an agreement, rather than presenting the EP with a "take-it-or-leave-it" offer.

Turning to the EP's elective function, the EP's role in the investiture of the Commission has also been enhanced: When nominating its candidate for Commission president, the Council now has to take into account the results of the EP elections, which effectively implies that the Commission president needs to muster the support of the EP's main party group.

Focussing on treaty reforms is instructive to assess the potential of the EP to affect legislation, the budget and the make-up of the Commission, but it does not tell us how the competencies acquired by the EP over the past decades translate into actual policy influence. There is very broad literature, which examines the relative power of the different EU actors in the legislative process and their ability to affect policy outcomes (see Thomson, in this volume). This literature differentiates between procedural models and bargaining models to assess the actors' relative power over legislation. Procedural models derive the relative influence of EU actors from the *formal* decision-making rules and actors' preferences. The formal rules are considered important, because they define which actor or actors can set the legislative agenda, amend or block proposals, and they state which majority thresholds need to be passed for agreement to ensue. In contrast, bargaining models highlight *informal* bargaining processes, such as the use of strategies based on actors' relative power, logrolling or the search for compromise, in order to predict and explain legislative outcomes (see Thomson *et al.* 2006; Thomson 2011). Comparing different sets of decision-making models, Thomson (2011) finds that the notion of the EP as co-equal legislator under the co-decision procedure (now the OLP) has to be qualified. When it comes to assess the relative influence of the EP vis-à-vis the Council over legislative outcomes, Thomson's (2011) results accord the EP a level of influence, which is equivalent to the power of two or three large member states. While the influence of the EP has grown over time, especially with the adoption and extension of co-decision/OLP, the EP's actual ability to affect legislation is, however, less than some researchers have argued (see Tsebelis and Garrett 2000) or practitioners have hoped for.

National parliaments: domestic adaptation to Europe

Studies of how national parliaments cope with European integration have become widespread since the early 1990s (see Raunio 2009). This literature is mainly interested in the steps parliaments take to affect policy *before* the EU decides and their capacity to bind their respective governments in EU negotiations. The main insights of this literature are that parliaments have adapted institutionally, focussing on new structures and procedures to control what their governments do at the European level. Yet, the literature also highlights discrepancies between institutional adaptation and actual parliamentary behaviour and hardly any transnational parliamentary integration.

To begin with, parliaments have adapted institutionally to European integration (see e.g. Norton 1995; Maurer and Wessels 2001b; Winzen 2012). They have created various formal rules and organisational structures enabling them to better control national governments' conduct in EU decision-making. These rules and structures are commonly referred to as "oversight institutions". Oversight institutions come in different types.

First, there are procedures and rights that secure access to information. For instance, the governments may be compelled to deliver a memorandum about the issue under negotiations in the EU to national parliaments. Second, parliaments commit organisational resources by creating European Affairs Committees or involving sectoral committees in monitoring EU decision-making. Third, some polities also adopt rules that make it difficult for the government to ignore parliament on EU-related issues. For instance, the so-called "scrutiny reserve" envisages that national parliaments need to be given the time to examine an issue before the government can commit its position at the EU level. Mandating rights go even further, as they empower national parliaments to approve or even determine the government's negotiation position. Box 5.1 displays two illustrative examples from Austria and the United Kingdom.

Yet, institutional adaptation has proceeded unevenly. First, the above provisions have gradually evolved over the course of integration. The 1973 Nordic enlargement brought in parliaments and parliamentarians from Denmark and the UK with more pronounced interests in their governments' involvement in EU affairs. Since the mid-1980s, we observe significant reform activities in basically all national parliaments (Winzen 2012). Second, there are cross-national differences with regard to how national parliaments have institutionally responded to European integration. Table 5.1 displays a number of comparisons that exist in the current literature. Northern European parliaments tend

---

Box 5.1 The British scrutiny reserve and Austrian mandating rights

Excerpt from the House of Commons' scrutiny reserve resolution (version of 17 June 1998):

(1)   No Minister of the Crown should give agreement in the Council or in the European Council to any proposal for European Community legislation or for a common strategy, joint action or common position under Title V or a common position, framework decision, decision or convention under Title VI of the Treaty on European Union –
  (a)   which is still subject to scrutiny (that is, on which the European Scrutiny Committee has not completed its scrutiny) or
  (b)   which is awaiting consideration by the House (that is, which has been recommended by the European Scrutiny Committee for consideration pursuant to Standing Order No. 119 (European Standing Committees) but in respect of which the House has not come to a Resolution).

Excerpt from Article 23e(2) of the Austrian Federal Constitutional Law:

Is the competent member of the Federal Government in possession of an opinion by the National Council about a project within the framework of the European Union [. . .], then the member is bound by this opinion during European Union negotiations and voting. Deviation is only admissible for imperative foreign and integrative policy reasons.

---

to have stronger oversight institutions than Southern ones. Moreover, the post-2004 accession countries have particularly strong parliaments. Scholars trace this phenomenon to the adoption (but not necessarily application) of best practices from elsewhere (e.g. O'Brennan and Raunio 2007b).

Institutional adaptation is one dimension to assess national parliaments' responses to European integration; behavioural responses are another dimension. Even a parliament with a European Affairs Committee and mandating rights does not automatically make a very active and assertive parliament vis-à-vis its government. When it comes to mandates, the governing parties normally protect the government from the opposition and tend to resolve conflicts with cabinet members informally (Auel 2007). However, there is also evidence that "in the shadow of the mandate" governments pay attention to the preferences of their own supporters and mainstream opponents (Pollak and Slominski 2009; Christiansen and Pedersen 2011). It is also uncontested that some parliaments, such as the Danish and Finish ones, use their committee structures and information rights actively. Moreover, we should not expect that parliaments look into each and every issue under negotiation in the EU or issue a mandate in every case. The relevant benchmark should be that oversight institutions help national parliamentarians to identify what is relevant to them and to interfere *if* they disagree with the government.

Table 5.1 Assessments of national parliamentary oversight in European Union affairs

Year of measurement	Winzen 2010	Karlas 1 2010	Karlas 2 2010	Winzen 1999	D&A 1999	M&W 1999	Bergman 1999
Scale	0–3	0–12	0–8	0–3	1–3	1–5	1–15
Denmark	2.7	8.0		2.5	3	1	1
Finland	2.5	8.5		2.5	2	2	2
Lithuania	2.5	8.5	7				
Slovakia	2.5	6.5	6				
Romania	2.3	6.0	5				
Estonia	2.2	8.5	6				
Germany	2.2	7.0		2.2	1	3	5
Bulgaria	2.0	4.5	3				
Hungary	2.0	7.0	6				
Latvia	2.0	6.5	4				
Poland	2.0	7.5	5				
Slovenia	2.0	7.5	5				
Austria	1.8	6.5		1.7	2	2	4

(Continued)

Table 5.1 (Continued)

Year of measurement	Winzen	Karlas 1	Karlas 2	Winzen	D&A	M&W	Bergman
	2010	2010	2010	1999	1999	1999	1999
Scale	0–3	0–12	0–8	0–3	1–3	1–5	1–15
Czech Republic	1.8	4.5	4				
Netherlands	1.8	6.5		1.3	1	3	7
Sweden	1.8	7.5		1.8	2	2	3
Italy	1.7	5.5		0.8	2	5	8
United Kingdom	1.7	4.5		1.7	1	4	6
Ireland	1.5	2.0		0.5	1	5	9
Malta	1.5	2.5					
Portugal	1.5	2.0		0.7	1	5	13
France	1.2	5.5		1.0	1	4	10
Greece	0.8	2.0		0.7	1	5	15
Spain	0.8	2.0		0.8	1	5	14
Belgium	0.7	2.0		0.7	1	5	11
Luxembourg	0.7	3.0		0.7	1	5	12
Cyprus	0.3	2.0					

Note: "Year of measurement" identifies the approximate year that the assessment targets. Winzen, Karlas 1 and Karlas 2 measure the strength of parliaments' oversight institutions in EU affairs. Karlas 1 and 2 also employ selected behavioural indicators. D&A draws on a survey asking experts to rank backbench influence on the cabinet in EU affairs as weak, medium or strong. M&W summarises contributions to an edited volume also relying mostly on institutional indicators. Bergman is a ranking of the author.
Sources: Table adapted from Winzen (2012). Winzen: Winzen (2012). Karlas 1: Karlas (2012). Karlas 2: Karlas (2011). D&A: Delegation and Accountability dataset (see Strøm *et al.* 2003). M&W: Maurer and Wessels (2001b). Bergman: Bergman (2000).

The main message that we want to convey here is that there is a need for more comparative information on what parliaments actually do in EU affairs. Otherwise, it remains ambiguous to what extent institutional adaptation increases control over the government, to what extent it is absorbed by party political dynamics, and whether the parliamentary arena is less important than intra-party arenas (on intra-party politics in EU affairs, see Poguntke *et al.* 2007; Carter and Poguntke 2010). Current projects on parliamentary behaviour in EU affairs are likely to yield more conclusive insights in the coming years (for first contributions to this research agenda, see de Ruiter 2013; Finke and Dannwolf 2013). What we can say is that institutional adaptation has not damaged parliamentary control of

EU affairs. Moreover, from a longer-term perspective, it is hard to deny that parliaments have gradually become more active in EU affairs and that reforms, such as the creation of European Affairs Committees, have helped in this regard (Raunio and Hix 2000).

In what ways do national parliaments affect EU policy directly? National parliaments' direct role at the European level is only weakly developed (see Raunio 2009: 322–5). In the 1990s, academics, commentators (and a limited number of decision-makers) discussed the idea of a "congress" or a "second chamber" of national parliaments at the European level (for an overview, see Maurer and Wessels 2001a: 465–75). Such proposals never enjoyed much support among governments and parliaments across the EU (European Parliament 1996). First, they came at a time when the tide turned towards "simplification" and streamlining EU decision-making to prepare for Eastern enlargement. Moreover, parliamentarisation at the European level – by augmenting the EP's power – already constituted a potential threat to efficiency (see the following discussion). Second, the proposals also came at a time when several parliaments had already successfully invested in domestic oversight of the government and saw limited added value in a direct role at the European level (Winzen 2013a: 52–71).

Instead of a direct role at the European level, more modest ways to bring national parliaments into EU decision-making included the institutionalisation of a subsidiarity control procedure (Rittberger 2005: 177–96). On the request of a third of national parliaments, the Commission has to re-consider draft legislation and justify why it withdraws, upholds or amends the draft (this is the so-called "yellow card"). If a majority of national parliaments shares the view that a legislative proposal infringes the subsidiarity principle (the so-called "orange card") and the Commission does not withdraw the proposal, either the EP or the Council may decide that the proposal should not be considered further. National parliaments may also lodge a complaint about a subsidiarity violation before the European Court of Justice, via their national governments. Furthermore, the Commission also entertains a "political dialogue" inviting parliaments to submit observations on policy initiatives.[1] There is some dispute about the potential and actual impact of such reforms (Raunio 2009: 322–5; Cooper 2012). In any case, subsidiarity control or the political dialogue reinforces the status quo of parliaments as domestic actors that may, on occasion, communicate their views to the EU level. This is why recent contributions speak of "individual efforts in the collective interest" (Kiiver 2007) or the "gatekeepers" of European integration (Raunio 2011).

If there is no formal direct role, do parliamentary actors, such as political parties, entertain informal links to the European level with the goal to affect policy? First, there is little evidence that national parties control the voting behaviour of their members of the European Parliament (MEPs; Mühlböck 2012) or, more generally, the behaviour of party members active in EU decision-making arenas (Carter and Poguntke 2010). Second, some other studies nevertheless suggest that parliamentarians use contacts and activities at the European level to obtain information on EU policies. Stripped of opportunities to affect their government's EU-related policy, opposition parties from Germany have more contacts with their fellow party members in the EP than do government parties (Wonka and Rittberger 2013). MEPs whose party is in opposition domestically also make more ample use of the opportunity to pose questions to the Commission than MEPs from national government parties (Proksch and Slapin 2011). A survey shows that a majority of MEPs has at least monthly contacts to national parliamentarians from the same party or to party executives. Systematic coordination on voting in the EP, however, is rare (Miklin and Crum 2011; see also the survey data presented in Scully *et al.* 2012). Although these points indicate some cross-level integration, the impact of domestic strategic incentives (i.e. government or opposition status) suggests that cross-level activities aim at advantages in the national arena. Overall, the results are still tentative and there is clearly a mismatch between quantitative studies and qualitative studies about whether and what kind of links exist across levels (for qualitative studies, see e.g. Poguntke *et al.* 2007).

Finally, transnational inter-parliamentary cooperation does not appear to extend beyond loose information exchanges on general topics (see Raunio 2009: 322–5). There are arenas for inter-parliamentary cooperation such as the Conferences of European Affairs Committees (known by its French acronym COSAC). Yet, parliaments use this forum mainly to discuss how best to organise domestic governmental oversight and pay little attention to policy (Raunio 2011). Moreover, MEPs report that they rarely contact national parliamentarians that are not from the same member states (Miklin and Crum 2011). The aforementioned new procedures of subsidiarity control are a possible incentive for inter-parliamentary cooperation (Cooper 2012). This is because the procedures only have bite if a certain number of parliaments collectively decides to activate the subsidiarity control mechanism. Yet, such incentives are of course only meaningful if national parliaments' political assessments of a legislative initiative converge in the first place. If parliaments disagree they have no reason and incentive to try to coordinate their views on subsidiarity. If parliaments agree, the question becomes whether they can overcome coordination challenges *and* whether they might not prefer the easier option of telling their government to object to the legislative initiative in the Council (see Raunio 2009: 322–5).

Explaining Europe's multilevel parliamentary system

The preceding section offered an overview of the characteristics of the EU's multilevel parliamentary system. We now turn to the question how we got there. What explains the EP's empowerment and what explains national parliaments' domestic institutional adaptation?

The parliamentarisation of EU politics: power politics, legitimacy or efficiency?

Explanations for the EP's gradual and steady empowerment can be categorised by distinguishing between the main actors pushing for the EP's empowerment, on one hand, and by focusing on the institutional constraints, which have an impact on how these actors pursue their preferences, on the other hand (see Table 5.2). With regard to the actor-dimension, some authors argue that the member states are the drivers (or brakemen) of parliamentarisation, while others claim that the EP itself can successfully employ its existing competencies to press for an extension of its powers under certain conditions, which we discuss later. On the second dimension, which captures the institutional constraints under which these actors operate, differences in scholarship amount to the role and nature of institutional constraints and how they affect the EP's

Table 5.2 Logics of parliamentarisation

	Main actors	
Institutional constraints	Member states	European Parliament
Institutional rules and capacities	(1) Governments as policy seekers	(2) EP as power seeker
Norms and standards of legitimacy	(3) Governments as legitimacy seekers	(4) EP as legitimacy seeker

and member states' ability to realise their goals. While some scholars in the rationalist institutionalist tradition argue that institutional constraints reflect prevailing decision rules and power distributions among actors, other scholars, drawing on constructivism and sociological institutionalism, posit that institutional constraints have a normative component, which compels actors to respect particular standards of legitimacy.

1   König (2008) has offered a rationalist explanation for why member states (may) want to empower the EP, which posits that governments compare policy outcomes they expect to obtain under different legislative procedures. He argues that when governments compare policy outcomes under the consultation procedure, which sidesteps the EP, and the co-decision procedure (now the OLP), which formally puts the EP on equal footing with the Council, governments expect to be, on average, better off under the co-decision procedure. Yet, even though the EP is formally on par with the Council, the Council has a bargaining advantage, which results from asymmetrically distributed information in favour of the Council: While the EP's position on a legislative proposal is debated in the open, the EP is not involved in the Council's internal deliberations and therefore does not have full information about the Council's equilibrium policy (see König 2008: 173–4). As a result, the Council can trick the EP and misrepresent its own ideal policy in the bargain with the EP, "which may . . . increase the benefits of the member states against the submission of the first 'true' position" (König 2008: 174). Thus, when faced with a choice between different supranational decision-making rules, the Council tends to opt for a decision rule maximising its policy preferences. In the case at hand, the Council will prefer the co-decision procedure involving the EP over the consultation procedure. Following up on this argument, König claims that member state governments are well aware of this rationale at Intergovernmental Conferences (IGCs), when decision-making procedures are subject to debate and revision. Yet, the argument remains to be tested empirically: When member states have shifted policy areas from consultation to co-decision viz. the OLP, they expected policy outcomes to be more beneficial under co-decision than under consultation.

2   The second set of explanations suggests that the EP does not have to rely on governments to be granted more competencies, but can be a master of its own fate by engaging in bargaining over the interpretation of existing treaty provisions in the context of day-to-day policy-making in the EU. While the member states have

an interest in preserving the treaty-based institutional status quo and hence the existing distribution of decision-making power among the EU's legislative actors, the EP has tended to see its grant of powers, resulting from interstate negotiations at IGCs, as insufficient. The EP, therefore, has an interest in extending its competencies beyond what it is granted in the treaties (see Hix 2002; Farrell and Héritier 2003; Farrell and Héritier 2007; Héritier 2007; 2012). In order to do so, the EP exploits the "incompleteness" of the treaties and interprets its grants of powers expansively, in a way that governments have not foreseen when they negotiated and adopted the treaties. The EP tends to succeed in imposing its interpretation of the treaty rules on the Council because it has a longer time horizon relative to the member states in the Council and the Council presidency and a lower sensitivity to failure. The EP plays a long-term institutional power game while the Council members are geared towards obtaining concrete outcomes on policy. While member state governments are concerned about reaping publicly visible policy gains in the short-run, the second-order nature of EP elections implies that the re-election success of MEPs is much less dependent on their political performance. Consequently, MEPs can focus on the long-term inter-institutional power game, threatening the Council to block legislation unless it grants the EP more say in inter-institutional bargains by accepting to informally alter the decision-making rules to the EP's advantage. For example following the adoption of the Maastricht Treaty, the EP successfully threatened to block legislation under the newly introduced co-decision procedure if the Council adhered to the final stage of the procedure, which gave it the right to present the EP with a take-it-or-leave-it offer. The EP did not like this treaty provision as it rebuffed its aspirations to become co-equal legislator. By threatening to block legislation under co-decisions procedure, it extracted the institutional concession from the Council that it would refrain from presenting the EP with a take-it-or-leave-it proposal following the conciliation stage. This informal change in the application of the Maastricht version of the co-decision procedure was eventually formalised in the Amsterdam Treaty (see Hix 2002).

3   In the preceding explanations, member state governments and the EP were constrained by existing institutional rules and provisions in order to realise the policy- or power-related objectives. The following explanations do not question the assumption that political actors, such as member state governments and the EP, are trying to maximise their utility (however defined) under given institutional constraints. Yet, they follow sociological institutionalists by claiming that actors are embedded in a community environment, which reflects commonly shared norms and standards of (in)appropriate behaviour. According to this perspective, the relevant institutions affecting actors' ability to realise their preferences are the collectively held norms and values that constitute their community environment. Rittberger and Schimmelfennig (2006) argue that European integration is embedded in such an international community environment: The member states of the EU all share an explicit commitment to fundamental liberal-democratic values and norms. This shared normative environment has several implications for the analysis of the expansion of the EP's powers. First, concerns about the EP's powers become a relevant issue when the existing institutional structure of the

EU contradicts the EU's constitutive liberal-democratic values, that is when the existing institutional structure lacks legitimacy. Second, the EU's institutional structure lacks legitimacy if there is a clear gap between the liberal-democratic norms that define the community's identity and hence function as a standard of legitimacy, on one hand, and the performance of the existing institutions in the light of this standard, on the other hand (see Schimmelfennig 2010; Rittberger 2012). The principle of representative democracy or parliamentarism can be subsumed under this standard of legitimacy, which is shared by all EU actors. Parliamentarism is "understood as the principle that assemblies of representatives elected by the people make and/or decide on the state's laws and budget, appoint state officials and hold the executive accountable" (Roederer-Rynning and Schimmelfennig 2012: 954).

The legitimacy gap thus refers to a situation whereby the principle of representative democracy is undermined. When, for example, policy-making competencies are transferred from the national to the EU level, national parliaments are stripped off policy-making prerogatives, while the governments of the member states retain or even enhance their central status of decision-makers in EU policy-making. Yet, as long as unanimity remains the decision-rule, democratic accountability chains remain intact since governments continue to be accountable to their national parliaments. As soon as national governments can be outvoted (under qualified majority), national parliaments lose their ability to control Community legislation and to hold their governments to account for supranational policies the majority does not support (Rittberger 2005: 46–8). When policy-making competencies are transferred to the EU level and the qualified majority rule applies in the Council, political actors can scandalise such instances as highly problematic, since the principle of representative democracy and hence the commonly shared standard of legitimacy is undermined. Potentially successful solutions geared towards closing the legitimacy gap have to be directed at restoring the principle of representative democracy and parliamentarism. These solutions have to pay tribute to upholding the standard of legitimacy, either by empowering the EP or by strengthening national parliaments. This legitimacy-seeking logic has been applied to various instances of the EP's empowerment in the area of legislative and budgetary politics (Rittberger 2005, 2012; Rittberger and Schimmelfennig 2006; Schimmelfennig 2010). For instance, during the negotiations of the SEA, the adoption of qualified majority voting for legislative decision-making in the Council raised concerns about democratic accountability, since the link in the accountability chain between governments and national parliaments was no longer intact since individual governments could be outvoted. Not only MEPs and domestic MPs pointed to this legitimacy gap and scandalised this situation as normatively untenable; also some national governments argued that the legitimacy gap could only be narrowed if the legislative competencies of the EP are increased to compensate for the decline of prerogatives of domestic parliaments (see Rittberger 2005).

4   While governments eventually have to take the decision to expand the EP's power during IGCs, not only governments can successfully exercise normative pressure on their counterparts to narrow the legitimacy gap; as Thomas (2006) has shown, the role of federalist-spirited parliamentarians inside and outside the EP proved

to be vital in defining the constitutional identity of the EEC in its early decades, by promoting the institutionalization of the principle of liberal democracy. When the six founding members of the EEC debated an association agreement and the potential for Spanish accession under General Franco's authoritarian rule, federalist militants, politicians in the EP as well as trade unionists insisted that despite the absence of official membership criteria, contemplating the accession of Spain was not compatible with the principles of democracy, human rights and the rule of law, principles that the EEC should protect and promote. Thomas thus shows that "by publicizing Spain's request and portraying the EEC's choice in terms of existing domestic and international norms, European parliamentarians and trade union activists delegitimated the outcome preferred by Paris and Bonn" (2006: 1206). What is more, the Spanish case established a precedent, a first significant step towards the establishment of a standard of legitimacy defined by parliamentarism and human rights, which was to guide future decisions on accessions.

National parliaments' adaptation to Europe: conditions and mechanisms

National parliaments have gradually and unevenly adapted to European integration. Why and how has this happened? We focus on institutional adaptation here because there still is little systematic comparative research into parliamentary behaviour in EU affairs (but see Auel and Benz 2005; Auel 2007; de Ruiter 2013; Finke and Dannwolf 2013). Specifically, we ask why the strength of parliaments' oversight institutions to control the national government varies over time and across countries. As in the case of the EP's parliamentarisation, we focus on the main theoretical arguments.

Explaining parliamentary adaptation requires us to think at two levels of analysis. At the macro-level, we ask what conditions align with stronger or weaker oversight. For instance, we might find stronger parliaments in countries with high levels of Euroscepticism. We also ask what mechanisms connect macro-level conditions. This requires us to focus on political actors, their dispositions and power at the micro-level. For instance, who are the actors that link popular Euro-scepticism to parliamentary oversight institutions and what motivates their actions? Existing contributions offer a great number of conceivable macro-level conditions and micro-level mechanisms (for an overview, see Goetz and Meyer-Sahling 2008). The sheer number of arguments, however, gives the impression of a fragmented field of research that is not easily accessible for a wider audience. Hence, we try to limit ourselves here to the main conceptual differences at the macro- and micro-level.

It is important to point out that parliaments are not unitary actors. The question of who the relevant actors in parliament are adds complexity to explanatory endeavours. Who plays a major role, and who is sidelined? In most cases, it makes sense to think that the key actors are parliamentary parties. Moreover, most of the explanations below identify the government supporting parties as the key decision-makers on oversight institutions (Saalfeld 2005; Winzen 2013b). They have the votes necessary to make or prevent change in government-sponsored policy. At the same time, they also rely less on oversight institutions than the opposition because they have intra-party ties to the government. Thus, it is particularly puzzling why government supporters might want strong oversight institutions, while it would be less puzzling if the opposition were to press for institutional reform.

Table 5.3 displays four different rationales for why national parliaments want to control the government in EU affairs (see Winzen 2013b). Parliaments encounter pressure for institutional adaptation from the growing salience of European integration, domestic party and electoral politics in EU affairs and the characteristics of their own place in a country's political system. These four major conceptual distinctions subsume several more specific explanations. Moreover, these four rationales contain different ideas of who the main actors are and of what motivates them to ask for oversight institutions.

First, most literature shares the expectation that parliaments adopt stronger oversight institutions as European integration becomes more salient (Norton 1995; Raunio 1999; Martin 2000; Raunio and Hix 2000; Winzen 2013b). Primarily, the salience of European integration for parliaments grows as the EU "deepens"; that is as it acquires more important competences, it becomes more centralised and gives more powers to supranational actors. The deepening of integration challenges parliamentary authority and, at the same time, raises the importance of controlling the government's participation in EU decision-making. These challenges provide parliamentary parties with incentives to strengthen domestic oversight of EU affairs. There are three possibilities why exactly parliamentary parties react to the salience of integration. First, they have a basic interest in participation in important policy decisions. Oversight institutions help parliamentary parties to make sure that the government does not ignore them when it comes to the question what goals and strategies to pursue in EU decision-making. Second, in analogy to the sociological institutionalist explanations of the EP's empowerment, national parliaments may be concerned about the democratic legitimacy of EU decision-making. In particular, they are the main source for democratic legitimacy of the conduct of national governments in EU decision-making (see e.g. Bergman 2000). As integration deepens, parliamentary legitimacy concerns grow and trigger the creation of oversight institutions. Third, some scholars contend that oversight institutions have little to do with parliamentary demands for participation or with democratic legitimacy deficits. Instead, they maintain that governments and their parliamentary supporters seek to maximise the country's bargaining power in EU negotiations to get outcomes

Table 5.3 Explanations of national parliamentary oversight in EU affairs

Concept	Indicators	Parliamentary motivations
Salience of European integration	Depth of EU integration Party perceptions	Policy Legitimacy National interest
Acceptable government policy	Coalition conflict Intra-party conflict Minority government	Policy
Electoral survival	Euroscepticism	Protection Appeasement Collusion
Domestic parliamentary strength	Institutionalisation Prestige	Compensation Appropriateness

close to the perceived national interest (e.g. Pahre 1997). One way how EU-level nego-tiators may try to avoid concessions to other countries or supranational actors is by highlighting domestic constraints: They point out that the national parliament does not allow any deviations from their bargaining position. The actual presence of strong domestic oversight adds credibility to such a claim. Finally, it is worth noting that the EU's "depth" is the most intuitive indicator of how salient parliaments find European integration. Yet, it may also be the case that, at a given "depth", different parliamentary parties perceive the EU to be more or less salient. For instance, survey data show that British parties attribute higher salience to integration than do German parties (Bakker *et al.* 2012). Such subjective party perceptions may also trigger parliamentary concerns over policy participation, democratic legitimacy or the national interest.

A second strand in the literature sets out from the observation that parliaments want the government's policy at the EU level to be aligned to their preferences. Nor-mally, this should not be problematic for the parliamentary majority parties because they choose and maintain the government in the first place. Yet, if they have doubt that the government pursues the preferred policy of the majority factions, they can create stronger oversight institutions (Saalfeld 2005; Winzen 2013b). First, if governing parties have different views on EU policy, each party can use oversight institutions to monitor the other. Second, if there is conflict inside a governing party between the leadership and the parliamentarians, the latter might want guarantees that parliament gets a say on important issues. Third, while the previous arguments depict the parties supporting the government as the central actors, we may also consider the conditions under which opposition parties play a role. Opposition parties obviously have good reason to think that the government's EU policy does not match their policy preferences. Under minor-ity government, they have the chance to create strong oversight institutions to raise their influence on government policy (e.g. Pahre 1997; Bergman 2000).

Third, parliamentary parties have a basic interest in electoral survival. Hence, they want more control if they think that government activity at the EU level could have electoral repercussions. This may be particularly pronounced in Eurosceptic countries (e.g. Raunio 2005) where integration lacks diffuse support and voters are more likely to pay attention to whether EU policies are beneficial to them individually or to their country as a whole (de Vries 2007). The literature suggests various possible reasons why parliamentarians, especially government supporters, want oversight institutions if their electoral survival is endangered. First, they want to have access to mechanisms and institutions that keep them informed and allow them to intervene in the policy process if necessary. Second, strong parliamentary institutions might be a symbolic way to appease voters that are angry over the loss of national sovereignty. For instance, the Irish parliament implemented stronger parliamentary oversight institutions before rerunning a failed referendum on the Treaty of Nice (see the contributions in Barrett 2008). Third, mainstream governing and opposition parties may agree on strong over-sight institutions as a way to avoid conflict on EU topics (e.g. Auel and Raunio 2014), since they are historically implicated in building the EU and often more pro-European than their voters. Hence, they have little appetite for public controversy, especially if their audience is Euro-sceptic (see also the following discussion).

Fourth, several recent contributions argue that we see strong oversight institutions in parliaments that are also "strong" in domestic politics (Dimitrakopoulos 2001; Raunio 2005; Karlas 2012). "Strong" parliaments, for instance, have a well-developed system of committees and control their own timetable and legislative agenda (e.g. Döring 1995; Strøm 1998). Strength also refers to a parliament's prestige and status in the national political system and constitution. For instance, the constitutional law of a country may require decision-makers to protect the parliament's formal authority in the European integration process. The strength of the parliament in domestic politics may lead to strong oversight institutions in EU affairs in two ways. First, following a logic of compensation, in polities with strong parliaments, parliamentarians lose more as a consequence of European integration than MPs in "weak" parliaments. In turn, MPs from "strong" parliaments ask for compensation in the form of strong government oversight. Second, there is a mechanism based on the logic of appropriateness (e.g. Dimitrakopoulos 2001), which posits that domestic parliamentary strength reflects the widely accepted, "appropriate" level of parliamentary involvement in policy-making. Parliamentarians seek to maintain this to the extent possible in EU affairs and, thus, adopt oversight institutions to maintain time-honoured appropriate legislative-executive relations. Moreover, although this point has not been explored much in the literature, one should note that standards of appropriate legislative-executive relations may even have an effect if not all parliamentarians want to follow them in a particular situation. Imagine, for instance, that the opposition demands strong oversight institutions while the government supporters are opposed. In analogy to explanations of the EP's powers, the weak actors may then scandalise the "inappropriate" behaviour of their powerful opponents and possibly even enlist the support of third actors such as constitutional courts.

Legitimacy and efficiency in Europe's multilevel parliamentary system

The democratic quality of the EU continues to be subject of intense debate (see Kröger, in this volume). Unsurprisingly, the EP and national parliaments find themselves at the centre of this debate, since they embody – like no other institution – the principle of representative democracy. What can and do these parliamentary institutions contribute to the democratic quality of the EU? We start by highlighting the main arguments in the debate about the EP's contribution to the democratic legitimacy of the EU, before turning to national parliaments and their potential to address and even redress the often-lamented democratic deficit of the EU.

The empowerment of the EP and the democratic deficit: cure or bitter pill?

Following the so-called standard version (Føllesdal and Hix 2006) of the EU's democratic deficit, the EP is (still) not a parliament "proper". Even though its legislative und budgetary competencies have been enhanced, it is still considered secondary to the Council in the adoption of EU legislation as well as the multiannual financial framework, which sets the key expenditure ceilings. Moreover, its elective function is meagre because governments and not the EP have most say in the election of the Commission and its President. Moreover, increasing the EP's powers even further would not guarantee that elections to the EP would lose their character as "second-order national contests" (Reif and Schmitt 1980). EP elections are neither about EU political parties nor about their policy agendas, but continue to be decided and fought on domestic issues by national parties. Voters use these elections to cast protest votes against domestic parties in government and are hardly influenced by the attitudes that citizens hold towards the EU (Føllesdal and Hix 2006: 535–6). Consequently, the expansion of the EP's powers may not reduce the democratic deficit as long as political debate and contestation revolves around domestic issues, with European issues being sidestepped in electoral contests. While this is only one worry that scholars have voiced, we will now present four arguments in the debate about the EU's democratic deficit and how they relate to the EP and its potential contribution to the democratic quality of the EU (see Rittberger 2010).

A first group of scholars argue that the qualms about a democratic deficit are largely misplaced. Moravcsik (2002) has argued that the EU is neither a "superstate" nor an unaccountable technocracy. When comparing the EU to the practice of democratic governance in most liberal democratic systems, the EU performs quite favourably (see Moravcsik 2002). Turning the "standard version" on its head, Moravcsik argues that "[c]constitutional checks and balances, indirect democratic control via national governments, and the increasing powers of the European Parliament are sufficient to ensure that EU policy-making is ... transparent, effective and politically responsive to the demands of the European citizens" (Moravcsik 2002: 605). The EP plays thus not only an important role in ensuring direct accountability, its involvement in EU legislation adds a procedural constraint to decision-making, which inhibits "bureaucratic despotism" by Brussels (Moravcsik 2002: 606).

Others go even further and argue that it is grossly misleading – a "category mistake" (Majone 2006a: 618) – to evaluate the legitimacy of the EU according to standards of *democratic* legitimacy. The steady empowerment of the EP does not address but potentially even exacerbate the EU's legitimacy deficit, because "More democracy" unduly politicises EU-decision-making. According to Majone, attempts to make the EU more democratic are ill founded because this strategy overlooks the in-built trade-off between the functional, technocratic "Community method" and the principle of democracy and participation. The Community's founders and subsequent political leaders deliberately opted for the Community method to enhance the efficiency and effectiveness of the policy process and to produce welfare-enhancing outcomes. Regulatory policies, such as competition policy, the removal of trade barriers or monetary policy, were designed to address and redress market failures to the benefit of all. For these Pareto-improving policies to be effective, they have to be taken in a "non-majoritarian" fashion. This implies that they must be excluded from the adversarial power play of electoral and parliamentary politics. Otherwise, decisions would be unduly politicised whereby their credibility and Pareto-efficient effects would be undermined and the EU's (output) legitimacy would suffer (Majone 2002). The functional approach to integration thus has an "inherent tendency ... too sacrifice democracy on the altar of integration" (Majone 2006b: 8). Consequently, legitimacy has to be generated by the "outputs" the system produces and not by tampering with the EP's powers.

The third perspective presented here echoes Majone's assessment that the empowerment of the EP does not reduce the EU's legitimacy deficit, but the reasons leading to this assessment differ. While Majone sees the arguments about a *democratic* deficit misplaced, Bartolini (2005) argues that there is a democratic deficit in the EU, which has deep structural causes. The EU's present institutional structure cannot engender the political structuring processes, which produce a system of interest differentiation manifested in the formation of political movements, alliances and parties. European integration, argues Bartolini, leads to a de-structuring of "previous locally rooted political structures and systems of representation" (Bartolini 2005: 386), which is reflected in a weakening of partisan alignments and a "lack of any party thematization of EU issues [leaving, B. R./T. W.] the mass public attitudes towards the EU largely unstructured" (Bartolini 2005: 385). He concludes that the prospects for political restructuring at the EU level are bleak and that institutional, top-down democratization does not work, because political structures representing different interests and identities are absent. Democratic engineering, such as the empowerment of the European Parliament or experimentation with a Philadelphia-style constitutional convention, have to fail eventually as long as possibilities for "exit" and boundary transcendence are pervasive: Under these conditions, the EU will neither be able to "enforce 'positive' costly integration" nor generate "incentives to structure 'voice' at the European level" (Bartolini 2005: 408).

Not all scholars view the contribution of the EP to address or redress the democratic deficit as misplaced (Majone) or futile (Bartolini). While Moravcsik emphasises the positive contribution the EP makes to democratic accountability, Føllesdal and Hix (2006) argue that the EP is likely to play an important role in reducing the democratic deficit as it is the most promising arena for structured (party) political contestation to emerge, grow, and possibly spillover into other institutions. According to their diagnosis, citizen apathy, which is at the heart of the EU's democratic malaise, "is partly endogenous, a consequence of lack of political contestation" (Føllesdal and Hix 2006: 551). Contrary to Majone, they posit that the EU needs more "politics" and political competition on EU issues to spur "political debate, which in turn promotes the formation of public opinion on different policy options" (Føllesdal and Hix 2006: 550). Føllesdal and Hix also purport that the present institutional features of the EU insulate the EU from political competition. In order to link the EU arena and national political arenas as well as publics, they suggest that institutional reforms can help to bring about political contestation and controversies, which would engender EU-wide debates on EU issues and hence lead to political structuring. In order to intensify political debate and contestation about EU politics, they propose, *inter alia*, to allow for an electoral contest for the office of Commission President who could be elected by national parliaments or citizens directly. Less ambitious proposals, which were partially taken up by the Lisbon Treaty, established that the nomination process for the position of Commission president needs to take due notice of the result of the previous EP elections, thereby establishing a link between the party-political majority in the EP and the candidate for Commission president. This practice has been tested in the context of the 2014 EP elections, with the major transnational party groups nominating a candidate for the post of Commission president in the run-up to the elections. Whether this practice carries the expected positive implications for political competition "with candidates declaring themselves before the European elections, issuing manifestos for their term in office, and the transnational parties and the governments than declaring their support for one or the other of the candidates" (Føllesdal and Hix 2006: 554), remains an interesting question to be further explored.

National parliaments and EU decision-making

The Lisbon Treaty (in particular Articles 10 and 12) lists national parliamentary oversight of governments as one of the practices that makes the EU democratic. Moreover, some of the explanations surveyed earlier even suggest that parliaments create stronger oversight institutions because they have concerns about the EU's democratic legitimacy. One may, thus, ask whether stronger parliamentary control of their governments actually lends the EU more legitimacy. Writing at the time of the Euro crisis, this question has come to the fore in an almost dramatic fashion, because for many observers the EU's legitimacy also depends on its ability to act swiftly and decisively. While noting such concerns, the German Constitutional Court nonetheless recently argued that national parliaments not only have a right, but also a duty, to make themselves heard and be informed on decisions effectively bailing out debt-ridden Euro countries.

There are various reasons why strong national parliamentary oversight of the government could handicap the efficiency of EU decision-making. Studies show that these concerns are actually on the minds of parliamentarians (Auel 2005, 2007; Benz 2004). Under conditions of strong parliamentary oversight, parliamentarians might demand detailed information from the government on EU negotiations and on the government's position. They might even pass a resolution with negotiation instructions that, in some instances, bind the government formally. There are thus three efficiency-related problems. First, such strong constraints limit the government's ability to negotiate flexibly and to adjust quickly to changing EU-level developments. Second, parliamentary interference could unravel a position that the government put together in laborious inter-departmental coordination. Third, domestic parliamentary oversight could deadlock Council negotiations if many governments are unable to make any commitments before the domestic parliament has expressed its viewpoint and, conversely, are unable to offer any concessions afterwards. The first argument, for instance, featured prominently among German parliamentarians and government members when the Constitutional Court decided in favour of parliamentary oversight in the case of the government's dispersion of bailout funds. Yet, we should not be led to believe that such concerns only matter in times of crisis or in Germany with its strong Constitutional Court. As illustrated in Box 5.2, the Dutch government expressed reservations about parliamentary oversight being too strong throughout the 1990s.

There are also signs that governments and parliaments might use informal practices and rules to avoid the detrimental effects of parliamentary oversight on negotiation efficiency. Governments can enter into contacts with parliamentarians early to build consensus on the "national interest" to be defended at the European level. This might require the government to accommodate the concerns of its own parliamentary supporters but also of mainstream opposition parties that might otherwise be tempted to use all their information and opportunities obstruct the government's EU policy (Auel 2007). Mainstream opposition parties are likely to be open to cooperation with the government for several reasons (Auel and Raunio 2014). In terms of EU support, they tend to be closer to other mainstream (governing) parties than to their voters. Consequently, it is difficult for them to win votes with European topics. Instead, they may be inclined to prefer influence on the government's EU policy.

There is no hard and fast empirical evidence for or against the view that parliamentary oversight creates efficiency problems. Similarly, we do not possess conclusive evidence

---

Box 5.2 **The Dutch debate parliamentary oversight and decision-making efficiency in the EU in the 1990s**

Excerpts from the Dutch government report on "Parliament and European Union" (Original: "Parlement en Europese Unie", Kamerstuk 25181, No. 2, 1996, pages 3–6, authors' translation)

Further, it is important that European decision-making is not only character-ised by legislative elements – certainly in comparison to "classical" interna-tional organisations – but also by a particular dynamic and by a complex negotiation situation; there are fifteen member states that, amongst each other and, depending on the type of decision, with a smaller or larger role of the European Commission and the European Parliament, have to deal with a large number of (often complex and at the same time very concrete) dossiers in a short period. In this complex negotiation process, the government has to be able to formulate and take positions on short, sometimes very short, notice.

The question that repeatedly comes up regarding European decision-mak-ing and on which this note attempts to provide an answer is: how can the Dutch parliament be given the opportunity to exercise its control and leg-islative tasks optimally without compromising the flexibility and effective-ness the government needs to participate effectively in EU negotiations?
[. . .]

Further, the effectiveness of the Council requires that the fifteen member states (and even more in the future) are not all bound to as many parliamentary mandates.

---

for the view that government and parliament use informal practices to avoid such prob-lems. Yet, some observers suggest that the Danish government interacts early with the European Affairs Committee to avoid unexpected mandates and controversy (Riis 2007). Other indications include consensual parliamentary behaviour across governing and opposition parties (Pollak and Slominski 2009; Christiansen and Pedersen 2011) or the observation that debates on the EU budget are limited – that is participants make few claims – if the government involves parliament early (de Wilde 2011a).

Does parliamentary oversight make the EU more legitimate? It does in the sense that it strengthens the chain of delegation between parliament and government (Bergman 2000). Parliamentarians from government and opposition parties receive more infor-mation on what happens in EU policy-making and, in some countries, have means to interfere if they think that the government's position does not represent their views. Does parliamentary oversight also bring the EU closer to the voters, or – as necessary first step – does it make EU policies more visible to voters (Auel and Raunio 2014)? There are three reasons why parliamentary oversight could improve the visibility of EU affairs for voters. First, opposition parties obtain information that they can use to iden-tify whether the government made controversial choices that can be exploited in public or parliamentary debate (for a study of EU-related parliamentary debates, see Wendler 2014). Second, parliamentary oversight provides the opposition with opportunities to criticise the government and governing parties in the parliamentary arena. Third, if the opposition criticises the government publicly or in the parliamentary arena, government supporters may feel the need to defend the government, creating a larger and more visible debate and audience. Yet, one might also argue that parliamentary oversight is more likely to depoliticise EU affairs and make it even less visible to voters than is already the case (Auel and Raunio 2014). For reasons outlined earlier, mainstream government and opposition parties do not have too strong an interest to fight publicly over European issues. Thus, they prefer to resolve conflict consensually. Oversight institutions such as information rights and parliamentary committees help the government, governing and opposition parties to identify controversy and resolve it before it erupts publicly. Besides the tentative evidence mentioned earlier, the depoliticisation argument is also in line with the fact that there are very few plenary debates on EU topics (Raunio 2009). If anything, the evidence suggests that parliaments react to, rather than generate, widespread public attention to the EU as occasionally occurs on major issues such as the Services Directive (Miklin 2009) or in Euro-sceptic countries (see also de Wilde 2011b).

Conclusion

This chapter has taken issue with the role of the EP and national parliaments in the EU's multilevel system. We started by exploring the consequences of the ongoing process of European integration for the prerogatives of the EP as well as for national parliaments. Both sets of institutions underwent significant adaptations: the EP's powers were gradually extended, while national parliaments primarily bolstered their oversight role, albeit unevenly across the EU-27. We also evaluated these changes, asking if they help to redress the often-lamented democratic deficit of the EU. But, most importantly, this chapter aimed at explaining the development of the EU's multilevel parliamentary system. We have assumed previously that the EP and national parliaments evolve in parallel. According to this perspective, European and national arenas of parliamentarisation are independent. Recent research, however, questions this assumption, and hypothesises that the institutional changes affecting the EP and national parliaments are interrelated and co-evolve (Winzen et al. 2015). The EP and national parliaments are representative institutions in the EU's multilevel system, act in a shared decision-making environment, confront overlapping electorates and contain members from the same political parties. Moreover, national parliaments have to ratify the constitutional changes giving powers to the EP. Hence, it is promising and necessary to explore the interdependencies in the multilevel parliamentary system (Crum and Fossum 2009). Initial evidence indicates that national parliaments create stronger oversight institutions if they oppose parliamentarisation at the European level (Winzen et al. 2015).

While this line of research promises to provide us with a better understanding of how processes of parliamentarisation at the domestic and EU level are interlinked, explanations for domestic parliamentary adaptation also suffer from a number of shortcomings, which future research should address. While we know a lot about processes of institutional adaptation, research on parliamentary behaviour in EU affairs is still in its infancy. It is also weakly understood to what extent the government can and tries to suppress parliamentary demands for stronger oversight institutions. Moreover, the question about institutional diffusion is a critical one: Do parliaments learn from each other about the best way to organise oversight? Anecdotal evidence suggests that this has happened, especially after Eastern Enlargement (e.g. O'Brennan and Raunio 2007b; Buzogány 2013). Another largely neglected issue is the role of Constitutional Courts and referendums. These institutions and events might push parliamentarians towards legislative reforms. Finally, this review has focussed on parliamentary oversight of the national government. Oversight is still the main EU-related activity for national parliaments. Yet, we may ask why a strong direct role at the EU level has not materialised and why do we fail to observe stronger ties between parliaments in more institutionalised forms of transnational cooperation? Answering these questions would provide a more comprehensive picture of parliamentary adaptation to European integration.

Note

1   The European Commission provides information on the political dialogue on a website: http://ec.europa.eu/dgs/secretariat_general/relations/relations_other/npo/index_en.htm (accessed 15 February 2014). This website also links to the Inter-parliamentary Information Exchange (IPEX) with information on subsidiarity control. Note that the quality and cross-national comparability of the information on IPEX is not clear.

References

Auel, Katrin. 2005. "Introduction: The Europeanisation of Parliamentary Democracy." *The Journal of Legislative Studies* 11 (3):303–18.
———. 2007. "Democratic Accountability and National Parliaments: Redefining the Impact of Parliamentary Scrutiny in EU Affairs." *European Law Journal* 13:487–504.
Auel, Katrin, and Arthur Benz. 2005. "The Politics of Adaptation: The Europeanisation of National Parliamentary Systems." *The Journal of Legislative Studies* 11 (3):372–93.
Auel, Katrin, and Tapio Raunio, eds. 2014. "Connecting with the Electorate? Parliamentary Communication in EU Affairs." *Journal of Legislative Studies* 20:1.
Bakker, Ryan, Catherine De Vries, Erica Edwards, Liesbet Hooghe, Seth K. Jolly, Gary Marks, Jonathan Polk, Jan Rovny, Marco Steenbergen, and Milada Vachudova. 2012. "Measuring Party Positions in Europe: The Chapel Hill Expert Survey Trend File, 1999–2010." *Party Politics*. Published electronically 29 April 2012. doi:10.1177/1354068812462931
Barrett, Gavin, ed. 2008. *National Parliaments and the European Union: The Constitutional Challenge for the Oireachtas and Other Member State Legislatures*. Dublin: Clarus Press.
Bartolini, Stefano. 2005. *Restructuring Europe. Centre Formation, System Building, and Political Structuring Between the Nation State and the European Union*. Oxford: Oxford University Press.
Benz, Arthur. 2004. "Path-Dependent Institutions and Strategic Veto Players: National Parliaments in the European Union." *West European Politics* 27 (5):875–900.
Bergman, Torbjörn. 2000. "The European Union as the Next Step of Delegation and Accountability." *European Journal of Political Research* 37 (3):415–29.
Buzogány, Aron. 2013. "Learning from the Best? Interparliamentary Networks and the Parliamentary Scrutiny of EU Decision-Making." In *Practices of Inter-Parliamentary Coordination in International Politics*, ed. B. Crum and J. E. Fossum. Colchester: ECPR Press, 17–32.

Carter, Elisabeth, and Thomas Poguntke. 2010. "How European Integration Changes National Parties: Evidence from a 15-Country Study." *West European Politics* 33 (2):297–324.

Christiansen, Flemming J., and Rasmus B. Pedersen. 2011. "'Europeanization' and Coalition Patterns in Minority Parliamentary Systems." In *Parliamentary Government in the Nordic Countries at a Crossroads*, ed. T. Persson and M. Wiberg. Stockholm: Santérus, 63–84.

Cooper, Ian. 2012. "A 'Virtual Third Chamber' for the European Union? National Parliaments after the Treaty of Lisbon." *West European Politics* 35 (3):441–65.

Crum, Ben, and John E. Fossum. 2009. "The Multilevel Parliamentary Field: A Framework for Theorizing Representative Democracy in the EU." *European Political Science Review* 1 (2):249–71.

Dahl, Robert A. 1994. "A Democratic Dilemma: System Effectiveness versus Citizen Participation." *Political Science Quarterly* 109 (1):23–34.

de Ruiter, Rik. 2013. "Under the Radar? National Parliaments and the Ordinary Legislative Procedure in the European Union." *Journal of European Public Policy* 20 (8):1196–212.

de Vries, Catherine E. 2007. "Sleeping Giant: Fact or Fairytale?: How European Integration Affects National Elections." *European Union Politics* 8 (3):363–85.

de Wilde, Pieter. 2011a. "Ex Ante vs. Ex Post: The Trade-off between Partisan Conflict and Visibility in Debating EU Policy-formulation in National Parliaments." *Journal of European Public Policy* 18 (5):672–89.

———. 2011b. "No Effect, Weapon of the Weak or Reinforcing Executive Dominance? How Media Coverage Affects National Parliaments' Involvement in EU Policy-formulation." *Comparative European Politics* 9 (2):123–44.

Dimitrakopoulos, Dionyssis G. 2001. "Incrementalism and Path Dependence: European Integration and Institutional Change in National Parliaments." *Journal of Common Market Studies* 39:405–22.

Döring, Herbert. 1995. *Parliaments and Majority Rule in Western Europe*. Frankfurt: Campus.

Duina, Francesco, and Michael J. Oliver. 2005. "National Parliaments in the European Union: Are There Any Benefits to Integration?" *European Law Journal* 11:173–95.

European Parliament. 1996. Intergovernmental *Conference Briefing No. 6 (Third update 25th March 1996): Role of the National Parliaments*. Available from http://www.europarl.europa.eu/igc1996/fiches/fiche6_en.htm.

Farrell, Henry, and Adrienne Héritier. 2003. "Formal and Informal Institutions Under Codecision: Continuous Constitution-Building in Europe." *Governance* 16:577–600.

———. 2007. "Codecision and institutional change." *West European Politics* 30 (2):285–300.

Finke, Daniel, and Tanja Dannwolf. 2013. "Domestic Scrutiny of European Union Politics: Between Whistle Blowing and Opposition Control." *European Journal of Political Research* 52 (6):715–46.

Føllesdal, Andreas, and Simon Hix. 2006. "Why There Is a Democratic Deficit in the EU: A Response to Majone and Moravcsik." *Journal of Common Market Studies* 44 (3):533–62.

Genschel, Philipp, and Markus Jachtenfuchs, eds. 2013. *Regulatory or Federal? The European Integration of Core State Powers*. Oxford: Oxford University Press.

Goetz, Klaus H., and Jan-Hinrik Meyer-Sahling. 2008. "The Europeanisation of national political systems: Parliaments and executives." *Living Reviews in European Governance* 3 (2).

Héritier, Adrienne. 2007. *Explaining Institutional Change in Europe*. Oxford: Oxford University Press.

———. 2012. "Institutional Change in Europe: Co-decision and Comitology Transformed." *Journal of Common Market Studies* 50:38–54.

Hix, Simon. 2002. "Constitutional Agenda-Setting through Discretion in Rule Interpretation: Why the European Parliament Won at Amsterdam." *British Journal of Political Science* 32 (02):259–80.

Hooghe, Liesbet, and Gary Marks. 2008. "A Postfunctionalist Theory of European Integration: From Permissive Consensus to Constraining Dissensus." *British Journal of Political Science* 39 (01):1–23.

Karlas, Jan. 2011. "Parliamentary Control of EU affairs in Central and Eastern Europe: Explaining the Variation." *Journal of European Public Policy* 18 (2):258–73.

———. 2012. "National Parliamentary Control of EU Affairs: Institutional Design after Enlargement." *West European Politics* 35 (5):1095–113.

Kiiver, Philipp. 2007. "European Scrutiny in National Parliaments: Individual Efforts in the Collective Interest?" In *National Parliaments within the Enlarged European Union*, ed. J. O'Brennan and T. Raunio. London: Routledge, 66–78.

König, Thomas. 2008. "Why Do Member States Empower the European Parliament?" *Journal of European Public Policy* 15 (2):167–88.

Majone, Giandomenico. 1998. "Europe's 'Democratic Deficit': The Question of Standards." *European Law Journal* 4 (1):5–28.

———. 2002. "The European Commission: The Limits of Centralization and the Perils of Parliamentarization." *Governance* 15 (3):375–92.

———. 2006a. "The Common Sense of European Integration." *Journal of European Public Policy* 13:607–26.

———. 2006b. "Is the European Constitutional Settlement Really Successful and Stable." Notre Europe Etudes & Recherches, Paris.

Martin, Lisa L. 2000. *Democratic Commitments*. Princeton: Princeton University Press.

Maurer, Andreas, and Nicolai von Ondarza, eds. 2012. *Der Vertrag von Lissabon: Umsetzung und Reformen. Onlinedossiers der Stiftung Wissenschaft und Politik*. Berlin: Stiftung Wissenschaft und Politik.

Maurer, Andreas, and Wolfgang Wessels. 2001a. "National Parliaments after Amsterdam: From Slow Adapters to National Players?" In *National Parliaments on their Ways to Europe: Losers or Latecomers?*, ed. A. Maurer and W. Wessels. Baden-Baden: Nomos, 425–76.

———, eds. 2001b. *National Parliaments on their Ways to Europe: Losers or Latecomers*. Baden-Baden: Nomos.

Miklin, Eric. 2009. "Government Positions on the EU Services Directive in the Council: National Interests or Individual Ideological Preferences?" *West European Politics* 32 (5):943–62.

Miklin, Eric, and Ben Crum. 2011. "Inter-Parliamentary Contacts of Members of the European Parliament: Report of a Survey." RECON Online Working Paper 2011/08, Reconstituting Democracy in Europe, ARENA Centre for European Statistics, University of Oslo.

Moravcsik, Andrew. 1994. "Why the European Union Strengthens the State: Domestic Politics and International Cooperation." Center for European Studies Working Paper Series 52, Harvard Univeristy, Cambridge, MA.

———. 2002. "In Defence of the 'Democratic Deficit': Reassessing Legitimacy in the European Union." *Journal of Common Market Studies* 40 (4):603–24.

Mühlböck, Monika. 2012. "National versus European: Party Control over Members of the European Parliament." *West European Politics* 35 (3):607–31.

Norton, Philip. 1995. "Conclusion: Addressing the Democratic Deficit." *The Journal of Legislative Studies* 1 (3):177–93.

O'Brennan, John, and Tapio Raunio. 2007a. "Introduction: Deparliamentarization and European Integration." In *National Parliaments within the Enlarged European Union: From 'Victims' of Integration to Competitive Actors*, ed. J. O'Brennan and T. Raunio. London: Routledge, 1–26.

———, eds. 2007b. *National Parliaments within the Enlarged European Union: From 'Victims' of Integration to Competitive Actors*. New York: Routledge.

Pahre, Robert. 1997. "Endogenous Domestic Institutions in Two-level Games and Parliamentary Oversight of the European Union." *Journal of Conflict Resolution* 41 (1):147–74.

Poguntke, Thomas, Nicholas Aylott, Elisabeth Carter, Robert Ladrech, and Kurt Richard Luther, eds. 2007. *The Europeanization of National Political Parties: Power and organizational adaptation*. New York: Routledge.

Pollak, Johannes, and Peter Slominski. 2009. "Zwischen De-und Reparlamentarisierung: Der österreichische Nationalrat und seine Mitwirkungsrechte in EU Angelegenheiten." *Österreichische Zeitschrift für Politikwissenschaften* 2:193–212.

Proksch, Sven-Oliver, and Jonathan B. Slapin. 2011. "Parliamentary Questions and Oversight in the European Union." *European Journal of Political Research* 50 (1):53–79.

Raunio, Tapio. 1999. "Always One Step Behind? National Legislatures and the European Union." *Government and Opposition* 34 (2):180–202.

———. 2005. "Holding Governments Accountable in European Affairs: Explaining Cross-national Variation." *The Journal of Legislative Studies* 11 (3–4):319–42.

———. 2009. "National Parliaments and European Integration: What We Know and Agenda for Future Research." *The Journal of Legislative Studies* 15 (4):317–34.

———. 2011. "The Gatekeepers of European Integration? The Functions of National Parliaments in the EU Political System." *Journal of European Integration* 33 (3):303–21.

Raunio, Tapio, and Simon Hix. 2000. "Backbenchers Learn to Fight Back: European Integration and Parliamentary Government." *West European Politics* 23 (4):142–68.

Reif, Karlheinz, and Hermann Schmitt. 1980. "Nine Second-Order National Elections: A Conceptual Framework for the Analysis of European Election Results." *European Journal of Political Research* 8 (1):3–44.

Riis, Peter. 2007. "National Parliamentary Control of EU Decision-making in Denmark." In *National Parliaments and European Democracy*, ed. O. Tans, C. Zoethout and J. Peters. Groningen: Europa Law Publishing, 185–204.

Rittberger, Berthold. 2005. *Building Europe's Parliament: Democratic Representation beyond the Nation-State*. Oxford: Oxford University Press.

———. 2010. "Democracy and European Union Governance." In *Research Agendas in EU Studies. Stalking the Elephant*, ed. M. Egan, N. Nugent and W.E. Paterson. Basingstoke: Palgrave Macmillan, 134–67.

———. 2012. "Institutionalizing Representative Democracy in the European Union: The Case of the European Parliament." *JCMS: Journal of Common Market Studies* 50:18–37.

Rittberger, Berthold, and Frank Schimmelfennig. 2006. "Explaining the constitutionalization of the European Union." *Journal of European Public Policy* 13 (8):1148–67.

Roederer-Rynning, Christilla, and Frank Schimmelfennig. 2012. "Bringing Codecision to Agriculture: A Hard Case of Parliamentarization." *Journal of European Public Policy* 19 (7):951–68.

Saalfeld, Thomas. 2005. "Deliberate Delegation or Abdication? Government Backbenchers, Ministers and European Union Legislation." *Journal of Legislative Studies* 11:343–71.

Schimmelfennig, Frank. 2010. "The Normative Origins of Democracy in the European Union: Toward a Transformationalist Theory of Democratization." *European Political Science Review* 2 (2):211–33.

Scully, Roger, Simon Hix, and David M. Farrell. 2012. "National or European Parliamentarians? Evidence from a New Survey of the Members of the European Parliament." *Journal of Common Market Studies* 50 (4):670–83.

Strøm, Kaare. 1998. "Parliamentary Committees in European Democracies." *The Journal of Legislative Studies* 4 (1):21–59.

Strøm, Kaare, Wolfgang C. Müller, and Torbjörn Bergman, eds. 2003. *Delegation and Accountability in Parliamentary Democracies*. Oxford: Oxford University Press.

Thomas, Daniel C. 2006. "Constitutionalization through Enlargement: The Contested Origins of the EU's Democratic Identity." *Journal of European Public Policy* 13 (8):1190–210.

Thomson, Robert. 2011. *Resolving Controversy in the European Union*. Cambridge: Cambridge University Press.

Thomson, Robert, Frans N. Stokman, Christopher H. Achen, and Thomas König, eds. 2006. *The European Union Decides*. Cambridge: Cambridge University Press.

Tiilikainen, Teja. 2011. "The Empowered European Parliament. Accommodation to the New Functions Provided by the Lisbon Treaty." Finnish Institute of International Affairs Briefing Paper 91, Finnish Institute of International Affairs, Helsinki.

Tsebelis, George. 1994. "The Power of the European Parliament as a Conditional Agenda Setter." *The American Political Science Review* 88 (1):128–42.

Tsebelis, George, and Geoffrey Garrett. 2000. "Legislative Politics in the European Union." *European Union Politics* 1 (1):9–36.

Wendler, Frank. 2014. "Justification and Political Polarization in national parliamentary debates on EU treaty reform." *Journal of European Public Policy* 21 (4):549–67.

Winzen, Thomas. 2012. "National Parliamentary Control of European Union Affairs: A Cross-national and Longitudinal Comparison." *West European Politics* 35 (3):657–72.

———. 2013a. *Beyond the Decline of Parliament: European Integration and National Representative Democracy*. Doctoral dissertation, ETH Zurich.

———. 2013b. "European Integration and National Parliamentary Oversight Institutions." *European Union Politics* 14 (2):297–323.

Winzen, Thomas, Christilla Roederer-Rynning, and Frank Schimmelfennig. 2015. Parliamentary Co-Evolution: National Parliamentary Reactions to the Empowerment of the European Parliament. *Journal of European Public Policy* 22 (1):75–93.

Wonka, Arndt, and Berthold Rittberger. 2013. "The Ties that Bind? Intra-party Information Exchanges of German MPs in EU Multi-level Politics." *West European Politics* 37 (3): 624–43.

Chapter 6

The councils of the EU

Intergovernmental bargaining in a supranational polity

Daniel Naurin

Introduction: the councils of the EU

The councils of the European Union are the main strongholds of the most powerful actors in the EU system – the member states' governments. The European Council, comprised of the heads of state and governments, has gradually developed into the main agenda setter of the larger developments of the EU, in spite of the Commissions monopoly of legislative initiative. According to the treaties, the European Council "shall provide the Union with the necessary impetus for its development and shall define the general political directions and priorities thereof" (TEU 15.1). In practice, the European Council has become the default crisis manager of the EU, handling events such as the constitutional crisis of 2005 and the economic crisis of 2008 and onwards. Having that role in a political system, which tends to find itself in a more or less perpetual crisis, makes for a strong executive power.

The Council of Ministers (or simply the Council, as it is formally referred to in the treaties) is where ministers and national officials meet to negotiate and decide on the bulk of the EU's day-to-day businesses. The Council of Ministers holds both legislative and executive functions, although it has seen the latter increasingly sliding upwards towards the European Council in the last years. It is still the prime legislative institution of the EU – no legislation is passed without the consent of the Council – but it has had to get used to sharing legislative power with the European Parliament on most issues.

Just like the European Union itself, the Council of Ministers is not easily classified into any pre-existing political science category, not because it performs unfamiliar tasks, or does so in unfamiliar ways but because the combination of tasks and procedures is rare. The Council is a "complex and chameleon-like beast" (Wallace 2002: 342). It is both–and, and depending-on: Both executive and legislative in its functions, both national and European in its interests and incentives, both intergovernmental and supranational in its procedures, much depending on the policy area and the policy agenda of the day.

The two Councils differ both in functions and in working methods. The European Council is more clearly intergovernmental, although the new presidency introduced by the Lisbon Treaty has implied more of supranational coordination. The Council of Ministers is, literally, intergovernmental but is also closely attached to and dependent on the supranational institutions of the EU, in particular in its legislative capacity. The Council of Ministers is a forum for intergovernmental negotiations but one that is deeply embedded into a political system with polity-like ambitions. The output is much more than intergovernmental agreements – it is legislation with direct effect and supremacy over national law. The commitments made are binding, monitored by the Commission and the Court of Justice, and are usually complied with.

The meeting frequency of the Councils in all their different configurations is intense. It is a permanently operating negotiation machine, with hundreds of officials meeting every day. Formal and informal rules of procedure have developed to oil the machinery, including more or less supranational functions, such as the general secretariat, the presidency and the high representative for foreign affairs and security policy. Inter-institutional meetings with the European Parliament and the Commission also add to the agenda, in particular within the ordinary legislative procedure.

All this leads to interactions being influenced both by social experiences and by a long shadow of the future. The member states' representatives recognise that they are in the same boat, and are likely to remain so for the foreseeable future. This insight has contributed to the development of a cooperative-bargaining style and a sometimes relaxed attitude towards formal rules. Consensus behaviour – being prepared to compromise more than you have to – is an important norm (at least among some member states, as we shall see). The main mission of the chief ambassadors of the member states' permanent representations (the COREPER, or Committee of Permanent Representatives) is to reach agreement, rather than stubbornly defend their national positions at all costs.

In many respects, therefore, the Councils are more than arenas for intergovernmental negotiations. They are institutions, with institutional memories and institutional preferences. Compared to other intergovernmental organisations the Councils also deal with policy issues normally handled in national rather than in international politics, including distributive and regulative policies with sometimes high domestic salience. On the other hand, the Council lacks the political-ideological coordination that political parties perform in national political systems. The dominant conflict dimensions tend to remain intergovernmental and sector based rather than ideological.

The procedures developed in the Council for reaching agreement, both between the 28 member states and in the inter-institutional negotiations with the European Parliament and the Commission, have a rather impressive track record. About 90 per cent of the Commission proposals eventually see their way through the committee system in some form or the other. The underlying perception among the member states that European integration – on balance – is worthwhile constitutes an important permanent incentive for upholding the cooperative attitude in the negotiations.

The backside of the Councils' mode of decision-making is the lack of transparency and accountability. Although the Council of Minsters has implemented a range of transparency reforms in the last decades negotiations are still held behind closed doors. The lack of public political debate in "normal" ideological terms has also contributed to the image of the Councils as unusually non-transparent institutions.

This chapter first describes the organisational components of the Council structure and the formal and informal division of labour between different levels and units that has developed. Thereafter the prevalent decision-making mode of the Councils is discussed, including the use of voting, negotiations and coalition building. Throughout the chapter close attention is kept to the relative power between member states, institutional actors and bureaucrats. The last section concludes by reflecting over the effectiveness, transparency and legitimacy of the Councils.

The European Council

The European Council met for the first time in 1975 but achieved treaty status as an EU institution only in the Lisbon Treaty, which came into force in December 2009. It consists of the 28 heads of state or government, that is the leaders of the EU member states. Also present at its meetings are the president of the European Council, the president of the Commission and the high representative of the Union for Foreign Affairs and Security Policy. The presidents of the European Parliament and the European Central Bank may also be invited depending on the agenda.

The Lisbon Treaty made the distinction between the two Councils clearer also by introducing an elected Presidency of the European Council, while the Council of Ministers retains the six-month rotation between member states on the presidency post.

Still, the two Councils are connected in many ways. The General Affairs Council contributes to the preparation of European Council meetings, and the COREPER ambassadors assist the heads of government during the meetings. The cabinet of the president of the European Council is relatively small and relies on the general secretariat of the Council – a backbone for both Councils – both for administrative and legal advice.

The European Council has four regular meetings per year, but can meet more often if circumstances so require. That has indeed been the case in the last years, in particular due to the economic crisis. During 2011–2012 the European Council met 13 times (with an additional four meetings of the heads of state or government of the euro area). The many meetings recently mirror the increasing importance of the European Council's role of crisis manager of last resort. When the EU needs to respond to some important event, the call is usually the European Council's. The fact that the Commission president is also present, although without a formal vote, makes these meetings a concentration of executive power in the EU.

The European Council handles the big questions: long-term agenda setting, treaty reform, foreign and security policy making, enlargements, coordination of macroeconomic policy and the multi-annual financial framework. The heads of government also often delegate tasks to other institutions. They may ask the Commission to draw up a report, or encourage the Council of Ministers to speed up the coordination of its position in a certain field. In Laeken 2001 the European Council decided that the next treaty revision would be preceded by a convention, and in later meetings it subsequently revised the Convention's suggested "Constitution" into the Treaty of Lisbon. The European Council also makes key appointments, such as the president of the Commission (the nominee shall be approved by the European Parliament), the European Central Bank and the high representative.

Although its meetings are often closely monitored from outside by the media, especially when there is a new "crisis" to be addressed, the negotiations are strictly held behind closed doors. Some of the heads of government like to make a few statements to the cameras before they proceed into the building, but after that it is difficult to follow what happens. Leakages to the press occur and are sometimes part of the bargaining strategy, but they can hardly compensate for the lack of transparency. In some member states the EU Committee of the Parliament has a direct line open with its prime minister during the meeting for real time anchoring of positions at the national level. How tightly connected to the domestic level the ministers are varies a lot between the member states.

The most visible output of the European Council are the "Conclusions of the Presidency", which are issued after each formal meeting. Looking at these documents over time one can see that three broad themes have dominated the agenda of the European Council over the years. Foreign and Security policy is the most frequent agenda item, with about 30 per cent of the statements made in the 1975–2010 period. Second and third are macroeconomic issues (15 per cent) and institutional governance issues (11 per cent). These three themes have accounted for about 50 per cent of the agenda relatively consistently over the whole period (Alexandrova *et al.* 2012: 75).

The European Council was initially created as an informal discussion club for the EU leaders, who numbered only nine at its first meeting. Subsequent enlargements of its membership, and increasing institutionalisation of its proceedings, have transformed the mode of interaction in the group. The negotiations now start long before the heads of government meet in Brussels, with coordination in COREPER, by foreign (or recently often finance) ministers, and in bilateral contacts between capitals.

During the meetings discussions are increasingly taking place bilaterally or in groups of states, rather than in plenum. The informality of the procedures gives the larger member states a lot of room for manoeuvre. The Franco-German coordination during the euro crises often presented both the presidency and the other member states with more or less ready-made solutions. However, smaller states may still have a say on issues to which they attach high salience (Tallberg 2008).

Ministers, committees and working groups

The Council of Ministers deals with a broad range of legislative and non-legislative issues. This includes the ordinary legislative procedure, but also macro-economic coordination and decision making within the Common Foreign and Security Policy (CFSP). It meets in 10 configurations, with different ministers attending depending on the items on the agenda. The meeting frequency of the different configurations varies, and reflects the weight of different policy areas on the EU agenda (Table 6.1). Most busy are the foreign ministers (13 meetings in 2012), the finance ministers (12 meetings) and the agriculture and fisheries ministers (11 meetings). The General Affairs Council (consisting of ministers of foreign and/or European affairs), which has a horizontal and coordinating role, also meets frequently (11 meetings in 2012). The Council configuration on education, youth, culture and sport, on the other hand, only had three meetings in 2012 due to the relatively low level of EU activity in these areas.

Table 6.1   Ministers meetings

Council configuration	No of meetings in 2012
Foreign Affairs	13
Economic and Financial affairs	12
Agriculture and Fisheries	11
General Affairs	11
Transport, Telecommunications and Energy	7
Justice and Home Affairs	5
Competitiveness (Internal market, Industry, Research and Space)	4
Employment, Social Policy, Health and Consumer Affairs	4
Environment	4
Education, Youth, Culture and Sport	3
Sum 2012	**74**

The 74 meetings of ministers in 2012 was only the tip of the Council iceberg, however. Responsible for the preparation of the meetings is COREPER, made up of the chief ambassadors of the member states' representations. Its meetings in turn are prepared by some 150 to 200 working groups and committees consisting of member state representatives and are attended by the Commission officials responsible for the particular dossiers under discussion.

Under the ordinary legislative procedure, after the Commission has forwarded its proposal to the Council this is normally first addressed by a lower-level working group. If agreement (which may be based on a qualified majority) is found already at this stage, the proposal is passed up through the Council hierarchy to formal adoption by the minsters without further ado. On other occasions a proposal may travel up and down the Council system. After a COREPER or a ministerial discussion the proposal may come back to the working group for final polishing before it returns to the minsters for formal adoption.

Agendas are prepared and meetings are chaired by the rotating presidency, with the assistance of the general secretariat. The Commission also has an active role in the meetings explaining and defending its proposals. The presidency usually gives the word to the representative of the Commission first for presentation and clarification of its proposal. Before the Eastern enlargements there used to be a more or less systematic *tour de table*, with member state representatives outlining their positions. With 28 members around the table this procedure has become untenable. The norm now is that representatives only speak at the meeting if they have a serious problem with the proposal.

When the Council meets in public, which it is required to on legislative acts since the Lisbon Treaty, a *tour de table* is sometimes organised around some specific question posed by the Presidency. The ministers then get to speak to the cameras for a minute or two to state their response, with the Presidency carefully keeping track of the time. Just as for the European Council much of the important discussions take place bilaterally, or in smaller groups of state representatives, rather than in plenary.

The agendas of the ministers' meetings consist of two types of items, A-points and B-points. The A-points concern proposals that have already been concluded at a previous meeting, and the ministers' role is only to formally adopt them. The B-points, on the other hand, are items that are open for discussion by the ministers. What should become an A- or a B-point is decided at lower levels in the Council hierarchy, and in particular in the COREPER. That decision needs to balance the risk for overcrowded and ineffective meetings of ministers with the possibility that politically sensitive decisions are taken at the civil service level.

Delegation of decision-making power to bureaucrats is inevitable in all political systems, but the EU is an outlier in this respect. Not only is the power to propose legislation delegated to an independent agency (the Commission); a large part of the actual decision-making – the negotiations in the Council – is also conducted by unelected officials.

The exact degree of bureaucratic power in the Council is difficult to measure, however. Just counting the proportion of A- and B-points on the agendas does not give a reliable indicator. Many A-points, that is formal adoptions of ministers without discussion, have previously appeared on other Council meetings as B-points. In fact, the Council very rarely adopts a proposal as a B-point. Normally, when the ministers come to an agreement on a B-point the item is sent back to COREPER or some other committee or working group for final legal and linguistic checks and is returned as an A-point at the next meeting.

The most thorough attempt so far to answer the question: "Who decides in the Council?" found that the ministers were seriously involved in somewhere between 35 to 48 per cent of all dossiers. The COREPER and other higher-level committees were decisive in about 22 per cent of the proposals, while the lower-level working parties were the primary decision-makers in 31 to 43 per cent. This study (Häge 2008) was based on 180 legislative proposals adopted in 2003, and it avoids the pitfall of counting the same proposal several times.

One caveat with respect to these figures is that while the ministers seem to be involved in relatively many proposals they are most likely to focus only on some details of each proposal. The total share of legislative text being discussed by ministers is clearly much lower than 48 per cent. On the other hand, those details are likely to be the politically sensitive parts of the proposal (however that is defined).

A further complicating factor for anyone trying to gauge the degree of bureaucratic power in the Council is the fact that the negotiations in the committees and working groups are (or at least should be) based on the instructions given to the officials by the ministries. A well-organised ministry will make sure that the political values and preferences of the minister are transformed into clear and timely instructions to the permanent representation in Brussels. How well this works varies among ministries and member states. Having clear instructions is an advantage in the negotiations as it gives a platform for making arguments and building alliances.

The presidency and the general secretariat

The presidency and the general secretariat are two institutional actors with important roles in oiling the Council negotiation machinery. The general secretariat is the Council's own administrative support structure, with a permanent staff of about 2800 (February 2013). The presidency of the Council of Ministers rotates among the member states every six months according to a given schedule, while the European Council elects a president for two-and-a-half years (renewable once). Since the Treaty of Lisbon came into force one Council configuration – the Foreign Affairs Council – is not chaired by the six-month presidency, but by the high representative of the Union for Foreign Affairs and Security Policy. Consequently, a number of working parties in the foreign affairs field have a permanent chairperson appointed by the high representative.

The most important task of both the presidency and the general secretariat is to facilitate agreements between member states. Presidencies are often evaluated based on whether the Council managed to deliver decisions or not during its term. The president, assisted by the general secretariat, is responsible for the concrete organisation of the meetings, the preparation of agendas and the chairing of the meeting. The general secretariat provides not only administrative support and legal advice to the presidency and the member states but also an institutional memory for the Council. Ministers come and go, whereas the general secretariat remains, keeping an eye on the institutional interests of the Council. The general secretariat has also successfully developed the trust of the member states as an unbiased third party to which it is possible to turn for information on the substance of proposals and the status of the negotiation process (Beach 2008).

Over the years EU scholars have debated the ability of member states to make use of their turn as presidents for promoting their own national interests. Earlier accounts often described the presidency as a responsibility without power, pointing at the limited ability of presidents in setting the agenda during such a short term and the powerful norms requiring presidencies to act as honest brokers. Latter research, both case study based and quantitative studies, have concluded that being the president does give an opportunity to promote one's own interests and that the member states are not too shy to make use of that (Tallberg 2004, 2010; Thomson 2008; Warntjen 2008).

The crucial resource that the presidency has, and which can be used both for "creating" and "claiming value" – that is reaching agreements that benefit not only the group generally but also the presidency specifically – is information. The presidency's brokerage role includes having bilateral talks ("confessionals") with those member states that have a special concern in relation to a proposal. The general secretariat also helps the presidency in keeping track of the member states positions during the negotiations, monitoring whether a qualified majority seems to be within reach or not.

This means that the presidency gets a unique overview of how the negotiations are proceeding and what are the preferences and positions of the member states. That information, in combination with the presidency's prerogative of suggesting compromise solutions, gives it an opportunity to steer the process towards an outcome that it prefers, within the range of possible agreements.

The presidency also has an important role in representing the Council vis-à-vis other institutions, in particular the EP under the ordinary legislative procedure. An important trend in the policy making process of the EU in the last years has been a strong increase in the number of early agreements based on informal trilogues among the Commission, the EP and the Council. The institutions have found that an effective way of processing legislative proposals is to organise informal meetings with key actors from the three institutions. From the Council's side, the presidency is the main actor in this process, while the rapporteur plays a similar role for the EP.

The trilogues have been criticised for the informality and lack of transparency. It has also led to discussions on whether they may lead to unwanted power redistributions within the institutions, to the advantage of the "relais" actors representing their institutions in the discussions and thereby getting privileged information on the progress (Farrell and Héritier 2004). While some research supports the proposition that the rapporteurs in the EP have been strengthened because of the practice with informal trilogues, so far no such evidence exists for the Council (Häge and Naurin 2013).

Voting and decision-making

The extensive applicability of qualified majority voting (QMV) in the Council of Ministers is a symptom of its status as both intergovernmental and supranational. The main rationale for "pooling sovereignty" by allowing for QMV is to increase the decision-making effectiveness. The backside for the member states is that they expose themselves to the risk of being outvoted on important policy issues. The evolution of the voting rules – formal and informal – over the years has to a large extent concerned the balancing of these two factors.

The general trend historically has been a continuous extension of the application of the QMV rule in treaty revisions. The Lisbon Treaty, which made QMV the default rule, includes 113 articles where QMV applies. During 2010–2011 about 90 per cent of the legislative decisions were formally adopted under the ordinary legislative procedure, i.e. with qualified majority as the rule in the Council (and co-decision by the European Parliament).[1] Broadly, unanimity is kept for "constitutional" issues (such as treaty reform), decision-making within particularly sensitive areas (such as the CFSP, budgetary issues and taxation) and systemic agreements with third countries.

The question of how to define the rules for what should constitute a qualified majority in the Council has been increasingly contentious, in particular as a consequence of the enlargements from the 1990s and onwards. Since the 1950s a system of weighted votes has been in place, where each member state has a given number of votes roughly in proportion to their population. Smaller and medium-sized countries have had more votes per capita, however, reflecting the EUs hybrid character of a union of both states and people. Approximately 74 per cent of the votes have been necessary for a qualified majority, which is a fairly high threshold.

The relative voting weights were one of the toughest issues in the discussions leading up to the Lisbon Treaty. In particular the Polish and Spanish governments, who had previously negotiated favourable weights, tried to fight proposals with the effect that the population criteria should be allowed to weigh heavier. The compromise eventually moved away from the old weighted-votes formula and established a new "double majority" system, whereby a qualified majority has to include at least 55 per cent of the members of the Council, representing at least 65 per cent of the population of the Union. A blocking minority has to include at least four Council members (Article 16.4 TEU). The new rules took effect from 1 November 2014.

Historically, the member states have only gradually and cautiously accepted the idea of being outvoted, and have been much creative in finding ways of avoiding, or softening the fall for, outvoted minorities. The Treaty of Rome anticipated a phase-in of QMV in a number of areas, including the internal market and agriculture. This was slowed by the "empty chair crisis" and the Luxembourg compromise, following from the clash between the Commission and France in 1965–1966 over the funding of the common agriculture policy. The compromise, which brought the French ministers back to Brussels, was only a footnote to the minutes of a Council session but was given informal status as a procedural norm preventing agreements by QMV that challenged "very important interests" of a member state.

Similar language has subsequently found its way into the treaties, in the form of so-called emergency breaks. The first of this sort appeared in the Treaty of Amsterdam in 1996, when QMV was extended to the fields of justice and home affairs and to the CFSP. These provisions were retained in a somewhat revised form in the Lisbon Treaty and were extended to the area of social security measures for migrant workers on the request of the UK. The provision for CFSP states that "[i]f a member of the Council declares that, for vital and stated reasons of national policy, it intends to oppose the adoption of a decision to be taken by qualified majority, a vote shall not be taken" (Article 31.2 TEU). The search for a consensus outcome shall than continue.

Voting rules are important, as evident by the tough negotiations preceding any revisions of the rules. They are controversial because they define the formal powers of the member states in the decision making process. They also influence negotiation behaviour and, ultimately, decision outcomes. But formal rules are only part of the story of voting and decision-making in the Council. Legal texts and rules of procedure alone give a misleading picture of how voting is practiced and decisions are taken. More important than the highly visible conflicts concerning the application of QMV, and the installation of formal "airbags" for minorities, has been the more silent development of an informal practice of consensus behaviour.

In fact, although the shadow of the voting rules looms over the parties in every negotiation the Council almost never "votes", in the simple sense of letting the decision be determined by explicit statements of positions, for example in the form of raising hands. The voting records that are published by the Council are produced after the real decision has been taken, and by a different decision-making technique. The records therefore are questionable as indicators of member states' preferences or of winners and losers in the negotiations. Furthermore, a large majority of decisions are not explicitly contested at all.

According to the Council Rules of Procedure, the presidency has a key role in deciding whether to call a vote (although it may also be required to do so by a majority of member states). In practice, however, roll calls are very rare. Instead, what normally happens is that the Council uses a decision-making technique that is called apparent consensus (Novak 2012; Urfalino 2006). This is a method for taking collective decisions, that is distinct from unanimity and an alternative to roll-call voting.

Typically, what happens when a decision is taken in the Council is that the Presidency, after having listened to the discussions, having had bilateral talks with the most concerned member states, and having "taken a sense of the meeting", *declares* that the threshold has been reached and notes if there are any objections to this view. Such a statement may take different forms, such as "Ok, so, everybody can live with the text?" or "Can we consider this text as adopted then?" (Novak 2007: 5). A member state that is against the proposal only speaks up at this stage if it disagrees with the presidency's judgement that the threshold has been reached. This is rare and would indicate that the presidency has not done its job properly, because it should not take this step if a blocking minority still existed.

A member state that is unhappy with the proposal but accepts the defeat remains silent. The formal adoption of the decision usually comes as an A-point at a Council meeting a few weeks later, and may be performed by a different Council configuration. It is only at this later stage that votes are registered. This is why, according to the records, fisheries ministers may have voted on legislation concerning emissions from cars, working time regulations or other issues they have not been involved in and know nothing about. In the period between the apparent consensus decision by the responsible Council configuration, or the COREPER, and the formal adoption of the text at a following Council meeting, member states inform the general secretariat on whether they intend to register a no vote, or an abstention, or if they wish to add a formal statement in the records. The general secretariat then prepares a colourful voting board for public display as the presidency declares the measure adopted, with green, red and yellow arrows for member states in favour, against or abstaining.

This routine means that a member state's choice of whether to publicly signal discontent is distinct from its choice on whether to support the proposal during the negotiations. Since indicative votes are normally not carried out, the situation surrounding the apparent consensus decision is relatively non-transparent also to the parties involved.

The presidency, assisted by the general secretariat, has a key role in determining whether the threshold has been met. As discussed before, the information asymmetry to the presidency's advantage, in combination with its procedural privilege to choose when it is time to go to a decision, gives it a powerful position in this process.

Why has the Council settled for this relatively non-transparent decision-making technique, vulnerable to manipulation, instead of following the roll call procedure set out in the Rules of Procedure? Apparent consensus is related to the international organisation side of the Council. In fact, this decision-making technique is common in international organisations. For example, in the World Trade Organization (WTO) roll-call voting is formally possible, but in practise decisions are taken by consensus. If no one objects to the chairperson's proposition that an agreement exists the deal is done.

The rationale for apparent consensus lies in its ability to secure the basic interests of both more powerful and less powerful actors. Smaller states normally have a less valuable BATNA (Best Alternative To a Negotiated Agreement) than larger states, which makes them more willing to compromise on relative gains in order to secure an absolute gain. At the same time, the international norm of state sovereignty says that states officially should be treated as equals. The apparent consensus procedure makes it possible for the smaller states to give concessions to the larger ones without losing face. The method has been described as organised hypocrisy (Steinberg 2002). The fact that some are more equal than others is covered up by consensus. The informality of the procedure makes it possible for the more powerful actors to take advantage of their power resources and push for concessions.

The particular version of apparent consensus decision-making applied in the Council also maximises the flexibility for the governments when it comes to the difficult task of communicating defeats. Registered votes in the Council are signalling devices, primarily to domestic constituencies, rather than revealed preferences. There may be both costs in terms of embarrassment and benefits in terms of constituency support involved in signalling. The present procedure lets the member states decide whether they want to signal discontent.

It follows that the voting records should be treated with care when it comes to drawing conclusions on how decisions are made in the Council. If wrongly used, the data will underestimate the level of conflict surrounding the proposals. The practice of using apparent consensus as the decision-making technique gives the member states a chance to gloss over conflicts and avoid pointing out losers in the negotiations. Being in favour on paper afterwards does not necessarily mean that one supported the winning proposal during the negotiations.

Furthermore, proposals that are too conflict-ridden to be able to reach the qualified majority threshold will not turn up in the voting records at all, because these only contain information on successfully adopted acts. There is also a strategic incentive for the Commission to avoid failure in the Council. The Commission will refrain from tabling a proposal in the first place if it does not anticipate that it will gain enough support among the member states and the European Parliament.

For all these reasons – and due to the fact that real consensus behaviour is also practised in the Council – the level of consensus displayed in the voting records is extremely high. The number of votes in favour (i.e. neither against or abstention) on legislative acts is around 98 per cent in the last years. Interestingly, the "Big 3" stand out with respect to their behaviour in the voting records. While the UK and Germany have abstained or voted against legislative proposals most often of all 27 member states between 2007 and 2012, France is the only member state that has registered as being in favour of *all* 630 legislative decisions in this period (Naurin *et al.* forthcoming).

The policy areas that have generated the most explicit contestation in recent years are those with financial implications – in particular agriculture, regional development and budgetary issues. Environment and public health also spurs more activity than average in the voting records, in particular when also statements for the minutes are counted (which is a milder form of protest than is voting against or abstaining; Naurin *et al.* forthcoming).

Conflict dimensions and coalition building

More opportunities for qualified majority voting through treaty reforms, and a drastic increase in the number of actors involved in the negotiations as a consequence of the enlargements of the EU, have made coalition building increasingly important in the Council. Coalitions may reduce complexity by narrowing down the number of alternatives and parties involved. Successful coalition building may also crucially affect how much particular actors are able to gain from the negotiations. They also have dysfunctional effects if they reach a certain degree of stability, such as preventing information flows and opportunities for issue linkages within the larger group and thereby making cooperative bargaining across coalitions more difficult (Raiffa 1982).

Earlier accounts of the Council have often asserted that coalitions are fluid and tend to shift from issue to issue (Spence 1995: 380; cf. Nugent 1999: 474). No overarching structure in the member states' preferences has contributed to building long-term and cross-cutting coalitions, according to this view. Two countries that were on the same side with respect to farm subsidies may just as well be on different sides when it came to working time regulations. This view also fits a picture of the Council as being consensual and inclusive. Fixed minorities on certain conflict dimensions could be a threat to the legitimacy of the system.

A somewhat contrary claim that exists in the literature is that the EU in general, including the Council, is approaching "normal" politics, meaning in particular left-right politics, as at the national level (Hix 2008; cf. Lindberg *et al.* 2008). As the EU becomes increasingly state-like in its tasks, so does its politics, it is argued. Furthermore, the "normal-politics" thesis is not only proposed as an empirical claim but also as a normative goal. Connecting the politics of the EU to the dominating conflict dimensions of national party politics and election campaigns would anchor the European Union more firmly in the normal democratic lives of European societies. If policy alternatives and actor alignments were formed along well-known dimensions EU politics could become more accessible also to a broader public (Follesdal and Hix 2006; Hix 2008). The alternative is conceived as nation-state diplomacy – governments engaged in foreign policy – which has always been remote to political parties, social movements and public opinion.

However, the empirical research gives little support to the normal-politics thesis. While some early research before the Eastern enlargements based on voting records found traces of left–right alignments in the Council (Mattila 2004), latter research has concluded that alliances in the Council are more or less unrelated to party ideology. This applies both to studies of bargaining positions and cooperation behaviour (Naurin 2008; Thomson 2009; cf. Tallberg and Johansson 2008 for the European Council). Instead, geographical proximity – coalitions of neighbouring states – is the dominating pattern, regardless of which party that is in government.

Figure 6.1 shows an image of the cooperation patterns in the Council working groups and committees based on Naurin and Lindahl's survey of 2014, including interviews with 249 member state representatives within a broad range of policy areas. The picture may be read as a distance map, where member states closer to each other cooperate more often. The figure shows clearly the tendency for northern, southern and eastern member states to cluster together in their choices of cooperation partners.

Figure 6.1 tells us what the most common alliances look like at an aggregate level, but how stable are these patterns? The respondents to the survey were asked how common the alliances were "[f]or the countries that you have mentioned as your most common cooperation partners; on how many issues would you estimate that you cooperate on average (as a share of all the issues you are involved in)". The average answer for all respondents was 46 per cent. The most common alliances would thus exist in about half of the issues, according to the subjective judgements of the actors involved.

This may be compared to Thomson's study of bargaining positions where he finds that the geographical patterns are the most common, but that they show up significantly only in about a quarter to a third of all issues (Thomson 2011: 76). It is clearly the case that although coalition building has become more important and that geographical patterns based on national sector interests, rather than political ideologies, are the most

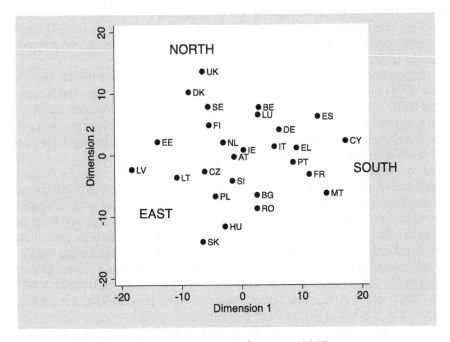

Figure 6.1 Cooperation patterns in the council of ministers 2012

Note: Based on the question, "Which member states do you most often cooperate with within your working group, in order to develop a common position?" Non-metric multidimensional scaling, Stress 0.16.

common, there is still quite a lot of fluidity in the existing alliances. The fact that different blocs are not permanently depicted against each other is important for the stability and legitimacy of the EU as a political system.

Negotiations

The Councils are first and foremost forums for negotiation between representatives of the member states' governments. Sometimes these negotiations are characterised by hard bargaining tactics, threats of veto and exits, such as at the infamous European Council meeting in December 2011, during which David Cameron refused to allow the euro states to move on towards fiscal union within the treaties if the UK was not given concessions in other areas. Often, however, and in particular in the Council of Ministers, the negotiations are conducted in a cooperative mode. A cooperative attitude – searching for common solutions, considering each other's preferences, sharing information and being prepared to compromise – increases the chances for finding agreements that all or most parties can accept. In negotiation theory such negotiations are called integrative (Walton and McKersie 1965) or problem-solving (Fisher, Ury and Patton 1997).

Negotiations in the Council are even claimed to go beyond cooperative in some respects. For example there has been quite a lot of attention given to the idea of deliberation as a mode of interaction. According to the normative story of deliberative democracy politics should be more about giving good reasons than forcing or striking deals. "Arguing", rather than bargaining or voting, is said to be at the heart of democracy. Also within international relations arguing has been upheld as a possible and normatively compelling alternative to unmasked power politics (Risse 2000). In the EU "deliberative supranationalism" has been promoted as a solution to the problems of democratic legitimacy (Eriksen and Fossum 2000).

An impressive number of studies of deliberation in the EU have tried to test the relevance of this theory to the empirical realities on the ground (Joerges and Neyer 1997; Naurin 2007, 2010; Niemann 2004; Pollack and Shaffer 2008; Warntjen 2010). Differences in how the key concepts of deliberation, arguing and bargaining have been conceptualised and measured contributions to variations in findings in the field. One general pattern nevertheless is that deliberation seems to be present during less politically heated conditions (non-politicised and technical issues, soft law, advisory committees, pre-negotiation phases), but absent under more demanding political circumstances. This condition clearly limits the overall significance of deliberation in the Council.

Another common claim is that Council negotiations are characterised by generous consensus behaviour on the part of the member states' representatives. Council negotiators are not only willing to compromise on their ideal positions; according to this view, they are even prepared to do so more than what would be optimal for them in the short run, given the formal rules and the preference distribution in the issue at hand. Consensus behaviour means giving something extra while possibly (but not necessarily) expecting that this will generate other gains later.

The clearest expression of consensus behaviour is when it is practised by a winning majority or a blocking minority. When the voting rule is qualified majority consensus behaviour means that an existing majority gives something extra to the states in the non-blocking minority, even if they could rely on their votes to get all of what they want.

If a blocking minority exists, or if the rule is unanimity, consensus behaviour is practised by states that refrain from blocking the decision in order to achieve a compromise solution, even if they would prefer the status quo. In more technical terms it means that the agreement does not have to be Pareto optimal.

Consensus behaviour thus implies refraining from taking advantage of the formal rules and the distribution of preferences to optimise one's short-term gains. The opposite of consensus behaviour therefore is to push for one's own interests in the issue at hand, without considering the preferences of others beyond what is necessary for achieving one's goal. It means building minimum winning coalitions, blocking non-optimal proposals and using formal rules to achieve as much as possible in the short run.

Consensus behaviour in the Council is often assumed to come in the form of diffuse reciprocity. Specific and diffuse reciprocity are two alternative cooperative exchange models in international negotiations (Keohane 1986). Specific reciprocity refers to a direct or strictly delimited sequential exchange of equivalent goods between specified partners: "If I give you X, you give me Y, and X and Y should be defined as follows." Diffuse reciprocity, on the other hand, is less precise about the specificities of the exchange: "If I give X, I assume that I will be compensated in some way in the future."

Diffuse reciprocity implies an expectation that favours will be returned, but allows for some vagueness in timing and scope. Refraining from demanding an exact compensation is what makes diffuse reciprocity – but not specific reciprocity – a form of consensus behaviour. The "extra" that is given is the flexibility allowed to the other party with respect to returning the favour.

Specific reciprocity, on the other hand, relies on more narrow market logic, through which the parties get in return only the equivalent of what they bring to the deal. This is still cooperative behaviour, but it is not consensus behaviour as defined here. In fact, if the trading is successful enough to produce a satisfactory solution for all consensus behaviour will not be necessary anymore as no minorities or special concerns will have to be considered.

Not all observers agree that consensus behaviour is particularly widespread in the Council. Häge (2012) for example argues that the main motivation of the member states is to build coalitions to form a non-blocking minority in order to avoid being outvoted (see also Novak 2010). Still, there is quite convincing evidence that not only cooperative negotiation behaviour in general, but consensus behaviour as defined here, is practised in the Council.

The evidence is found both among insiders' accounts of the procedures and in systematic qualitative and quantitative research. The picture drawn by Lewis from qualitative interviews with more than a hundred officials from the permanent representations is that appropriate behaviour in Council negotiations includes refraining from pushing for a qualified majority and practicing "mutual responsiveness" (Lewis 2005: 939). The research by Thomson and colleagues, including 331 controversial issues that were negotiated between 1999 and 2008, also contains evidence of consensus behaviour (Thomson 2011; Thomson *et al.* 2006; see also König and Junge 2009). Thomson evaluates the predictive accuracy of a range of different bargaining models, some of which emphasise the formal procedures and some which are based on informal bargaining. Interestingly, none of the more sophisticated models, which include information on relative power, salience, reference points and procedural rules, is able to outperform the simplest compromise model. The latter baseline model predicts that the outcome will be the mean position of all member states, the European Commission and the European Parliament (for a critical discussion of these results, see Leinaweaver and Thomson [2014] and Slapin [2014]).

The survey data collected by Naurin and Lindahl also contains evidence of consensus behaviour. They interviewed 257 member state representatives in Council working groups and committees in 2009 and asked them to respond to different scenarios relating to consensus behaviour. The conflictual veto-playing alternative was the least likely of the four. On average, the respondents estimated the likeliness of blocking a decision that they do not like, and which they have the power to block, to 2.0 on the scale from 1 (very unlikely) to 5 (very likely). The most likely response corresponded to the diffuse reciprocity model (3.3), while the specific reciprocity alternative was marginally more likely than a "communal sharing" alternative, in which the respondent is prepared to give a favour without expecting any compensation (2.8 and 2.6, respectively).

These findings clearly provide evidence of consensus behaviour in the Council. However, the study by Naurin and Lindahl also indicates an important and somewhat disturbing difference between member states. The "Big 3" in the Council – France, Germany and the UK – act significantly different compared to all the other member states with respect to consensus behaviour. For them, veto-playing and specific demands were the most likely responses (Naurin 2013).

What explains consensus behaviour? Why would member states give favours, rather than try to get the most out for themselves of every single proposal? Often this type of behaviour is assumed to be norm driven, which means that there is a commonly recognised informal rule that guides actors. Adhering to this norm implies respecting the equality (or legitimate ranking) of the actors involved, while trying to find solutions that are as inclusive as possible. If the norm is internalised the actors genuinely believe that consensus behaviour is the morally right way to act. Actors who have not reached such an elevated moral standard may follow the norm anyway in order to avoid reputational costs.

Norm following may also be less immediately rational and more habitual. References in the literature to a "consensus-reflex" alludes to the existence of a logic of appropriateness, in which actors behave according to their gut feeling, which points them towards what they should do "in a situation like this", rather than calculate on the moral or self-interested costs and benefits.

There may be both economic and sociological sources of a consensus norm. From a rational self-interested point of view, paying a little extra today may generate larger gains tomorrow. A general belief in European integration as overall beneficial, although sometimes costly in the short run, provides a powerful underlying rationale in favour of cooperation. Given such a rationale, actors involved in repeated games may solve collective-action problems by learning over time that a cooperative strategy is more beneficial in the long run. Few, if any, other international organisations have so many repeated games, and such a long shadow of the future, as the EU.

Furthermore, while pooling sovereignty by allowing for qualified majority decisions increases the collective decision-making efficiency it also implies risks for member states that they will be outvoted on important issues. Nurturing a consensus norm – an informal procedure that allows for some flexibility vis-à-vis the formal rules – may function as an insurance against that risk. Compromising more than you have to when others are in trouble can be seen as the premium you pay for that insurance.

There are other functional factors also speaking in favour of consensus behaviour. For example a consensus norm strengthens the Council's inter-institutional position vis-à-vis the Commission and the European Parliament. Transaction costs arguments may also be made. When handling a large number and a broad range of issues as the Council does diffuse reciprocity is a more efficient relational model than specific reciprocity.

Relative power

The consensus norm is hardly strong enough, however, to transcend basic power imbalances in the Council. France, Germany and the UK behave differently than the other member states, both in terms of voting and consensus behaviour. With respect to the latter, it is reasonable to assume that they face different incentives than the rest. As representatives of the major economies and political powers of Europe they are less dependent on European solutions to economic and political problems generally, which gives them a more valuable BATNA in negotiation theory terms.

Furthermore, their power resources make them less vulnerable to reputational costs among negotiating peers in Brussels. Put bluntly, they can break norms and still count on having a strong voice and being valued as coalition partners. Their powers and ability to build coalitions also make it less likely that they will end up in non-blocking minorities on salient issues, moderating the insurance rationale for paying tribute to the consensus norm.

Formally, the Big 3 is not a special category. In terms of voting power – in particular after the Lisbon Treaty – Germany is clearly bigger than the rest, while Italy is on par with France and the UK. Informally, however, Italy is not "big" in the same sense as the other three (cf. Tallberg 2008: 690). Figure 6.2 compares formal voting power with informal reputational power. The left part of the figure displays the Normalised Banzhaf Index (NBI) before and after the last treaty revision. This is a voting power measure based on the relative frequency with which a member state will be in a pivotal position, that is in a position of turning a losing coalition into a winning one. The power score is simply a function of the voting weights and the majority threshold and does not take into account the policy positions of the member states.

The left panel shows the distribution of formal voting power as measured by NBI based on the Nice Treaty rules that apply until November 2014, and the new double-majority rule that will be in operation after that (Barr and Passarelli 2009). The scale can be interpreted as the share of total voting power in the Council that each member state has. The pattern is rather striking, in particular with respect to Germany whose voting power increased from 8 to 12 per cent of the total voting power in the Council. It is also clear from the figure why Poland and Spain (unsuccessfully) resisted the change. Overall, the medium-size countries are the losers from the new rules, while the smallest countries also win from the change.

The right panel, on the other hand, displays an index of purportedly influential actors, based on the subjective evaluation of Council negotiators themselves. The following question was asked in Naurin and Lindahl's survey of 249 member state representatives to the Council working groups and committees in 2012: "Please think about the influence that other member states have on your member state during the discussions and negotiations in your working group/committee. In general which other member states have the greatest potential to influence the positions you take during the discussions?"

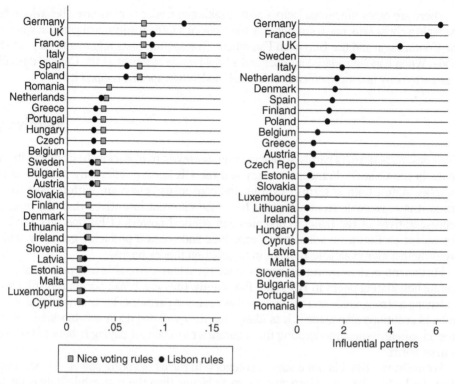

Figure 6.2 Formal and informal relative power

In this picture the Big 3 do stand out, although with the UK slightly behind France and Germany (the difference between the latter two is not statistically significant). The other three larger states in terms of population – Italy, Spain and Poland – constitute a second tier together with the Nordic countries and the Netherlands.

To what extent is formal and informal power translated into power over outcomes, that is an ability to get what one wants from the Council? Given the unequal abilities of the member states to influence each other's positions you would expect that countries such as Romania, Portugal and Bulgaria at the bottom of the influential partners index would be significantly less successful in achieving the outcomes they prefer.

However, interestingly, Thomson finds that this is not the case. In fact, when he compares the initial preferences of the member states with the final outcome in the 331 issues included in the study no member state is significantly more successful than any other (Thomson 2011). This counterintuitive result may be partly explained by shifting alliances, as discussed before, and the fact that the more influential actors often find themselves on different sides. Whether you get what you want from the Council negotiations is more dependent on whether you have a centrist position, which means that you are likely to be close to the final compromise, than your ability to persuade others in the process. Not only power but also "luck" in terms of a favourable preference distribution determines who walks away from the Council negotiations with a smile on their face.

Effectiveness, transparency and legitimacy

The Council of Ministers has an impressive track record with respect to producing agreements among governments with heterogeneous preferences. Only about 10 per cent of the Commission's proposals never see the end of the tunnel as adopted legislation. This is partly because the Commission anticipates the reactions of the member states, and refrains from making proposals in areas where common ground is lacking. But it is also indicative of the effectiveness of the Council machinery. Its norms and institutions are set on getting to yes.

Effectiveness is not the only important value of political institutions, however. A backside of the Council's mode of decision-making is a lack of transparency and links with political debates that are familiar and comprehensible to citizens. The Eurobarometer surveys indicate that the Council is the least trusted of the EU institutions involved in legislation. In the last years, about 35 to 40 per cent of the Europeans say they trust the Council, which is about 5 percentage points lower than the Commission and 10 percentage points lower than the European Parliament.

According to Hix, the Council of Ministers is "probably the most secretive legislative chamber in the world", including "the Chinese National People's Congress" (2008: 152). The European Council, which does not have a legislative role, is even less transparent. More transparency of the Councils is a commonly suggested recipe for enhancing the democratic legitimacy of the EU. However, for the foreseeable future at least, the Council of Ministers is unlikely to become as transparent as normal (read: national democratic) legislatures. The reason is in one sense simple; it is not a normal legislature.

Over the last two decades the Council of Ministers has implemented a range of transparency reforms, some of which are in fact more radical than in many national parliaments. Thousands of documents have been released, and legislative deliberations are regularly broadcasted live on the Internet. The Council is surprisingly transparent in some ways but not in those ways that make people perceive it as transparent and, therefore, find it legitimate.

A few conceptual distinctions may shed light over the paradox of why transparency reforms in the Council do not seem to lead to more perceived transparency. First, one needs to distinguish between transparency and publicity. While transparency means that there is information available about actions and processes within an institution for those who are willing and able to seek it, publicity means that the information is actually spread to and taken in by people outside the institution. There will be no publicity, that is no actual exposure of behaviour to a public audience, no matter how transparent the process or the institution in question is, if the available information about these actions is left unattended (Lindstedt and Naurin 2010).

A second important distinction is that between transparency in process and transparency in rationale (Mansbridge 2009, De Fine Licht *et al.* 2014). Transparency in process refers to information on actions, such as deliberations, negotiations and votes, that took place during the decision-making process and were thus directly fed into the decision. Transparency in rationale, on the other hand, refers to information on the substance of the decisions and of the facts and reasons on which they were based. Conclusions, declarations, press conferences after meetings and, crucially, public debates are measures for achieving transparency in rationale.

The third distinction that needs to be taken into account here is that between the two faces of "normal" legislatures – committees and plenary debates. In the parliaments, there is a clear division of labour between the two. The committees perform the deliberations and negotiations in the lawmaking process, while the plenary takes care of the vote and the public debate. The behavioural logic that applies in committees prescribes focus on common ground, compromise and agreement. The logic of plenary debates is the opposite – to clarify differences between parties and positions. Committee meetings focus on problem solving and concrete technical details; plenary debates, on principles and ideologies.

A national democratic legislator normally has all of these components to some extent. It has committees and plenary debates. The plenary debates, in which majority and minority parties defend their positions and emphasise weaknesses of the other side, when they work well, produce both transparency in rationale and publicity. They make the technical details of the committee meetings understandable to a broader audience by highlighting the political content of these, the ideologies that support different alternatives and the principles raised.

The Council of Ministers, however, only has two components. It has committee meetings in abundance. Committee decision-making is what the Council does all the time, on all levels. The search for common ground among diverse interests is part of the Council's DNA. It also has considerable transparency in process after the last year's reforms. Agendas and minutes of preparatory meetings are published, although the minutes may, on request, exclude the names of the member states that raised objections in the process. Position taking in ongoing negotiations is broadcasted live (although under strict forms), something which hardly happens in parliamentary committees.

But the Council does not have the three interrelated components of clarifying plenary debates, publicity and transparency in rationale. When the Council is done, and the legislation is adopted as an A-point, the ministers go home to their capitals. The winning majority never needs to justify its position and sharpen its arguments in public debate with the minority.

The Council is transparent in one way (process) but not in the way that makes people beyond a small circle of EU experts understand why the decision-makers decided the way they did (rationale). To explain why the Council is lacking transparency in rationale one has to take into account that it is in many respects more similar to an international organization than a legislative chamber of a democratic polity. The members of the Council are representatives of states rather than of parties. The conflicts played out in the Council concern national interests at the sector level, rather than general political ideas. The problem in this context is that it becomes difficult to have the type of public plenary debates that parliaments have that create transparency in rationale and publicity. Real post-decision debates in the Council would not show left versus right or liberals versus conservatives but Germans versus Greeks and Poles versus Italians. The reason why we do not have these debates is the fear among the members of the Council that the Europeans are not European enough to handle that (cf. Bartolini 2005).

Therefore, the common proposition that a more transparent Council will be an important step towards resolving the democratic deficit of the EU probably misconceives the problem. It is the other way around; the lack of a democratic infrastructure in the EU is the main cause of the lack of transparency in the Council. The absence of (or at least the perceived absence of) a European demos that accepts defeats across borders, or, if you wish, European party politics with the potential of forming such a demos, has led the Council to refrain from the debates that may give transparency in rationale – the type of transparency that may produce publicity and legitimacy.

Note

1 Calculated from the EUPOL data set (Häge 2011).

References

Alexandrova, Petya, Carammia, Marcello, and Timmermans, Arco. (2012). Policy Punctuations and Issue Diversity on the European Council Agenda. *Policy Studies Journal*, 40(1), 69–88.

Barr, Jason, and Passarelli, Francesco. (2009). Who Has the Power in the EU? *Mathematical Social Sciences*, 57(3), 339–366.

Bartolini, Stefano. (2005). *Restructuring Europe*. Oxford: Oxford University Press.

Beach, Derek. (2008). The Facilitator of Efficient Negotiations in the Council: The Impact of the Council Secretariat. In D. Naurin and H. Wallace (Eds.), *Games Governments Play In Brussels: Unveiling the Council of the European Union* (pp. 219–237). Basingstoke: Palgrave Macmillan.

De Fine Licht, Jenny, Naurin, Daniel, Esaiasson, Peter, and Gilljam, Mikael. (2014). When Does Transparency Generate Legitimacy? Experimenting on a Context-Bound Relationship. *Governance*, 27(1), 111–134.

Eriksen, Erik Oddvar, and Fossum, John Erik. (2000). *Democracy in the European Union: Integration through Deliberation?* London: Routledge.

Farrell, Henry, and Héritier, Adrienne. (2004). Interorganizational Negotiation and Intraorganizational Power in Shared Decision Making: Early Agreements Under Codecision and Their Impact on the European Parliament and Council. *Comparative Political Studies*, 37(10), 1184–1212.

Fisher, Roger, Ury, William, and Patton, Bruce. (1997). *Getting to Yes: Negotiating an Agreement without Giving In* (2nd ed.). London: Arrow Business Books.

Follesdal, Andreas, and Hix, Simon. (2006). Why There Is a Democratic Deficit in the EU: A Response to Majone and Moravcsik. *Journal of Common Market Studies*, 44(3), 533–562.

Häge, Frank M. (2008). Who Decides in the Council of the European Union? *Journal of Common Market Studies*, 46(3), 533–558.

Häge, Frank M. (2011). The European Union policy-making dataset. *European Union Politics*, 12(3), 455–477.

Häge, Frank M. (2012). Coalition Building and Consensus in the Council of the European Union. *British Journal of Political Science*, 1(1), 1–24.

Häge, Frank M, and Naurin, Daniel. (2013). The Effect of Codecision on Council Decision-making: Informalization, Politicization and Power. *Journal of European Public Policy*, 20(7), 953–971.

Hix, Simon. (2008). *What's Wrong with the European Union and How to Fix It*. Cambridge: Polity.

Joerges, Christian, and Neyer, Jurgen. (1997). Transforming Strategic Interaction into Deliberative Problem-solving: European Comitology in the Foodstuffs Sector. *Journal of European Public Policy*, 4(4), 609–625.

Keohane, Robert O. (1986). Reciprocity in International Relations. *International Organization*, 40(1), 1–27.

König, Thomas, and Junge, Dirk. (2009). Why Don't Veto Players Use Their Power? *European Union Politics*, 10, 507–534.

Leinaweaver, Justin, and Thomson, Robert. (2014). Testing Models of Legislative Decision-making with Measurement Error: The Robust Predictive Power of Bargaining Models over Procedural Models. *European Union Politics*, 15(1), 43–58.

Lewis, Jeffrey. (2005). The Janus Face of Brussels: Socialization and Everyday Decision Making in the European Union. *International Organization*, 59(4), 937–971.

Lindberg, Björn, Rasmussen, Anne, and Warntjen, Andreas. (2008). Party Politics as Usual? The Role of Political Parties in EU Legislative Decision-making. *Journal of European Public Policy*, 15(8), 1107–1126.

Lindstedt, Catharina, and Naurin, Daniel. (2010). Transparency Is not Enough: Making Transparency Effective in Reducing Corruption. *International Political Science Review*, 31(3), 301–322.

Mansbridge, Jane. (2009). A "Selection Model" of Political Representation. *Journal of Political Philosophy*, 17, 369–398.

Mattila, Mikko. (2004). Contested Decisions: Empirical Analysis of Voting in the European Union Council of Ministers. *European Journal of Political Research*, 43(1), 29–50.

Naurin, Daniel. (2007). *Deliberation Behind Closed Doors. Transparency and Lobbying in the European Union*. Colchester: ECPR Press.

Naurin, Daniel. (2008). *Choosing Partners. Coalition-building in the Council of the EU*. Paper presented at the American Political Science Association Annual Meeting, Boston, August 28–31.

Naurin, Daniel. (2010). Most Common When Least Important: Deliberation in the European Union Council of Ministers. *British Journal of Political Science*, 40(1), 31–50.

Naurin, Daniel. (2013). *Generous Concessions in Intergovernmental Negotiations: The Impact of State Power, Decision-making Rules and Gender*. Paper presented at the European Union Studies Association International Biannual Conference, Baltimore, May 9–11.

Naurin, Daniel, Hayes-Renshaw, Fiona, and Wallace, Helen. (forthcoming). *The Council of Ministers* (3rd ed.). Basingstoke: Palgrave Macmillan.

Naurin, Daniel and Lindahl, Rutger (2014). Nätverkskapital och inflytande iEUs ministerråd. In Göran von Sydow (Ed.), *EU Efter Krisen*, SIEPS, 2014(1op), 60–73.

Niemann, Arne. (2004). Between Communicative Action and Strategic Action: The Article 113 Committee and the Negotiations on the WTO Basic Telecommunications Services Agreement. *Journal of European Public Policy*, 11(3), 379–407.

Novak, Stéphanie. (2007). *The Mystery of Consensus in the EU Council of Ministers*. Paper presented at the Midwest Political Science Association, Chicago, April 12–15.

Novak, Stéphanie. (2010). Decision Rules, Social Norms and the Expression of Disagreement: The Case of Qualified-Majority Voting in the Council of the European Union. *Social Science Information*, 49(1), 83–97.

Novak, Stéphanie. (2012). *Transparency versus Accountability? The Case of the EU Council of Ministers*. Paper presented at the Transatlantic Conference on Transparency Research, Utrecht, June 8–9.

Nugent, Neill. (1999). *The Government and Politics of the European Union* (4th ed.). Basingstoke: Palgrave Macmillan.

Pollack, Mark A., and Shaffer, Gregory. (2008). Risk Regulation, Genetically Modified Foods, and the Failure of Deliberation in the Council of Ministers. In D. Naurin and H. Wallace (Eds.), *Unveiling the Council of the EU: Games Governments Play in Brussels* (pp. 144–164). Basingstoke: Palgrave Macmillan.

Raiffa, Howard. (1982). *The Art and Science of Negotiation*. Cambridge, MA: Harvard University Press.

Risse, Thomas. (2000). "Let's Argue!": Communicative Action in World Politics. *International Organization*, 54(1), 1–39.

Slapin, Jonathan B. (2014). Measurement, Model Testing, and Legislative Influence in the European Union. *European Union Politics*, 15(1), 24–42.

Spence, D. (1995). Negotiations, Coalitions and the Resolution of Inter-state Conflicts. In M. Westlake (Ed.), *The Council of the European Union* (pp. 256–276). London: Cartermill.

Steinberg, Richard H. (2002). In the Shadow of Law or Power? Consensus-based Bargaining and Outcomes in the GATT/WTO. *International Organization*, 56(2), 339–374.

Tallberg, Jonas. (2004). The Power of the Presidency: Brokerage, efficiency and distribution in EU negotiations. *Journal of Common Market Studies*, 42(5), 999–1022.

Tallberg, Jonas. (2008). Bargaining Power in the European Council. *Journal of Common Market Studies*, 46(3), 685–708.

Tallberg, Jonas. (2010). Explaining the Institutional Foundations of European Union Negotiations. *Journal of European Public Policy*, 17(5), 633–647.

Tallberg, Jonas, and Johansson, Karl Magnus. (2008). Party Politics in the European Council. *Journal of European Public Policy*, 15(8), 1222–1242.

Thomson, Robert. (2008). The Council Presidency in the European Union: Responsibility with Power. *Journal of Common Market Studies*, 46(3), 593–617.

Thomson, Robert. (2009). Actor Alignments in the European Union before and after Enlargement. *European Journal of Political Research*, 48(6), 756–781.

Thomson, Robert. (2011). *Resolving Controversy in the European Union*. Cambridge: Cambridge University Press.

Thomson, Robert, Stokman, Frans N., Achen, Christopher H., and König, Thomas. (2006). *The European Union Decides*. Cambridge: Cambridge University Press.

Urfalino, Philippe. (2006). *Apparent Consensus and Vote. Two Modes of Collective Decision-making*. Paper presented at the workshop on "The Mechanisms of Collective Decision-Making", Adriano Olivetti Foundation, Rome, April 29.

Wallace, Helen. (2002). The Council: An Institutional Chameleon. *Governance*, 15(3), 325–344.

Walton, Richard E., and McKersie, Robert B. (1965). *A Behavioral Theory of Labor Negotiations: An analysis of a Social Interaction System*. New York: McGraw-Hill.

Warntjen, Andreas. (2008). The Council Presidency – Power Broker or Burden? An Empirical Analysis. *European Union Politics*, 9(3), 315–338.

Warntjen, Andreas. (2010). Between Bargaining and Deliberation: Decision-making in the Council of the European Union. *Journal of European Public Policy*, 17(5), 665–679.

Chapter 7

The shadow of case law

The Court of Justice of the European Union and the policy process

Susanne K. Schmidt

Introduction

The European Court of Justice (ECJ) is generally recognized as being an important "motor" of European integration. By constitutionalizing the Treaty of Rome through path-breaking judgements in the 1960s, it set the European Community apart from ordinary international regimes, transforming it into a political system of a new kind. The implications of this development can hardly be overestimated: Not only did agreements of secondary law receive an unprecedented commitment. By being directly effective and supreme, the Treaty now included direct policy implications that did not require additional decisions by the member states. Most notably this changed the completion of the single market, which could rely on the direct force of the treaty once the Court had started to interpret broadly the free movement provisions for goods, services, persons, and later capital. Next to the single market, the case law on equal payment for women led to a far-reaching non-discrimination policy of the EU.

It is in particular with regard to such policy implications that the role of the ECJ in the European policy process is mainly discussed in the literature. Given the extent to which intergovernmentalism has shaped the integration debate, much of the literature on the ECJ has focused on the question of to what extent rulings of the ECJ have contradicted or followed preferences of the large member states. This has overshadowed attention to the question of how existing case law constrains European policy-making given that judicial policy-making is a possible substitute to legislative policy-making. How does the Council and the Parliament deal with the fact that once case law exists, previous legislative options are being foreclosed? Comparatively few authors have dealt with the interaction of judicial and legislative policy-making in the EU. It is in this sense that I would like to argue that the importance of the ECJ in EU policy-making is both well recognized and misconceived.

In the following, I begin with a central result of political science research on courts: courts are powerful and essentially weak actors at the same time. They are powerful, because they may be a veto player in the policy process. However, they are weak, being passive actors, relying both on cases that are being brought to them and on compliance with their rulings. It is therefore crucial to analyse the institutional conditions of the ECJ's strength as well as the support structure in which it operates. On this basis, the chapter discusses the constitutionalization of the Treaty through the case law of the ECJ. The chapter's main focus – the ECJ's role in the policy process – is structured in the following way: it begins with a discussion of the role of the Court in the implementation of European policies; after this, the ECJ's well-known importance in the fields of the single market and in anti-discrimination is turned to. Major attention will then be paid to the interplay of judicial and legislative policy-making as an often overlooked aspect of the integration process. Several examples from different policy fields show that this is not an isolated phenomenon as there is far-reaching importance of case law for the integration process. I conclude by pointing out that the benefits of supranational or international courts in terms of a strengthened obligation attached to agreements come at the significant cost of a weak legislature being unable to counter unwanted case law developments. Courts beyond the nation-state, the example of the ECJ shows, can surpass national constitutional courts in political significance.

Determinants of the ECJ's strength: institutional position and support structure

The everyday assessment of the political role of courts is much influenced by the standard assumption of the separation of powers where courts adjudicate conflicts based on laws being legitimated by the legislature. The role of adjudicator, guided by texts that are decided elsewhere, at first sight does not allow for greater political significance. It is only when taking into account that laws are generally incomplete contracts, not being able to regulate each everyday situation in full detail but requiring interpretation, that the independent impact of courts becomes apparent. In this way case law develops, complementing the legal texts of the legislature. It guides the future behaviour of courts, and thereby those actors being subject to the rules. The influential theory of Stone Sweet on judicialization explains this development of an increasing importance of the judiciary compared to the legislature in the determination of collectively binding decisions (Stone Sweet 1999). There needs to be a sufficient case load to develop case law, precedent needs to be honoured, and reasons given, allowing litigants to draw on case law to further their interests. Case law plays a particular role in common law systems, where it is one source of law, next to the legislative text. However, civil law systems, which emphasize the guidance by legislative statutes, also have to honour precedent. It is only by adjudicating like cases consistently that justice can be established. If precedent is not taken into account, and like cases are decided differently, it would appear that legal texts have no guiding function and that courts decide arbitrarily. The European Union counts as a mixture of a civil law system and a common law system, given that case law plays a pronounced role (Constantinesco 2000: 74).

If the need for interpretation of legal texts as incomplete contracts necessarily leads to case law, this is only one part of the explanation for the independent political role of courts. Were legislatures always capable of acting unequivocally, it would be easy enough to make sure that courts' interpretation follows the will of the legislature, as otherwise there would be legislative override. However, laws are normally compromises among political actors, and these actors may interpret these compromises differently. Once courts establish their own interpretation, this is likely to favour one party over the other, implying that it is difficult to muster the necessary majority to intervene against the case law.

Yet, courts are politically weak as they rely on being called on to decide cases and on being followed in their judgements. If their judgements become politically too contentious, they also risk changes in their institutional foundations. It is in view of this dependence of courts – and in view of the role that intergovernmentalism has played in European integration studies in general – that the political science discussion of the ECJ has focused heavily on the question whether judgements of the court reflect the interests of large member states (Garrett 1995). This is the starting point of the main other theoretical approach to be introduced here, rational choice institutionalism.

Much of the theoretical discussion of the ECJ has focused on the question of whether the importance of the ECJ implies that its power is used against the interests of the member states. There seems to be a clear answer as analyses of member states' submitted opinions to the court, which were published by the court until the early 1990s, show that it often rules against opinions submitted by a large number of (including big) member states (Granger 2004). The institutional setting and the empirical development where many rulings contradict observations and policies of a high number of member states suggests a large leeway for the Court and little control for the member states (Cichowski 2006: 496). But why would rational member states not curtail a court that is "running wild" (Cappelletti 1987)?

"It is more than plausible that the ECJ's decisions actually reflect the opinion of a majority of judges and, by imperfect proxy a majority of member state governments that appointed them. Thus, an alternative claim is that the Court is acting within its discretion and has not been curtailed because the preferences of the judges are not at odds with those of the member states" (Malecki 2012: 62).

It appears that the powerful political position of courts, resulting from the need for interpretation, and the difficulty of legislative override are the prices member states have to pay for the benefits of an independent judiciary. This is particularly true for the European Union. Here, the detailed provisions of the underlying treaty[1] – when compared to national constitutions – imply that many aspects of integration are guided by treaty provisions, whether secondary law in the form of regulations or directives exists. It is not uncommon for the Court to interpret secondary law in the light of treaty provisions, thereby coming to interpretations that deviate from the express meaning of the legislation,[2] or to read precise obligations out of the treaty, so that member states have to enact steps also when there is no agreement on secondary law (see the later section on constitutionalization). The fact that case law often merely works to favour one legislative actor over another may be taken to deny its independent relevance, as argued by Malecki. However, it has to be recognized that there would not have been a political agreement on this precise judicial interpretation, which favours one interpretation at the costs of others.

As this ongoing academic discussion shows that courts as such, and the ECJ is not composed of unambiguously strong political actors, it is therefore useful to further analyse the ECJ's institutional position and support structure.

The ECJ's institutional position

Several institutional provisions strengthen the independence of the ECJ. A most notable and general one has already been mentioned: the ECJ profits from the fact that the treaty is very difficult to change, requiring the unanimous agreement of member states. The ECJ's leeway is therefore significant and much larger than for courts at the domestic level. The Court is protected by the joint-decision trap. This characterizes situations where the status quo prevails because demanding decisions rules give a minority the power to block changes (Scharpf 2006). This explains why member states counteract rulings only in exceptional circumstances such as the *Barber* judgement (Pierson 1996), where the retroactive application of the case law on company pensions for women was ruled out. Such rare opposition should not, however, be mistaken for general consent, given the large institutional hurdles hampering effective opposition.

ECJ judges, one per member state, are appointed by common accord of the member states for a renewable term of six years (Art. 253 TFEU). With the Treaty of Lisbon, a general hearing procedure was introduced (Art. 255 TFEU) in order to screen candidates for their suitability. Though renewable terms in general make judges susceptible to political pressure, the fact that no dissenting opinions are published shields the judges at the ECJ. The case is different for the advocates general (AGs), who give detailed advisory legal opinions on the cases to the Court, which are published. Nevertheless, a possible fear for no reappointment of the five advocates general of the large member states (the four other positions rotate among the smaller member states anyhow) has not resulted in a situation where these AGs seemingly aim to avoid controversy in stating their opinions.

Based on the US experience, Dan Kelemen (2012) has discussed whether member states can successfully use well-known 'court-curbing' mechanisms against the ECJ. Any measures stripping the court of competences, changing its mandate or reducing its resources faces the problem of the joint-decision trap, explained above. Given this difficulty, jurisdiction stripping has never occurred retroactively – however, by keeping policy areas such as immigration and asylum outside of the ECJ's jurisdiction in the Maastricht Treaty (Kelemen 2012: 46), member states could at least signal their criticism. The question is, whether member states can influence the case law of the Court by appointing Eurosceptic judges. Only the Eurosceptic countries are likely to do so, and Kelemen asks whether such judges could make a difference. For this, they would have to be the median judge in decision-making, which is by simple majority. Depending on the relevance of the issue, the Court sits in chambers of three or five judges, with important decisions being reserved for the Grand Chamber of 13 judges. The plenum of all 27 judges very rarely decides a case, an example being the *Pringle* case (C-370/12) on the ESM (European Stability Mechanism), with another case in 2010, and no cases in 2008–09 and 2011 (Court of Justice of the European Union 2013: 106). In 2012, chambers of five judges decided 54.11 per cent of all cases, chambers of three judges 34.42 per cent and the Grand Chamber decided 8.99 per cent (Court of Justice of the European Union 2013: 96). Looking at the composition of the chambers at the ECJ, Kelemen concludes it to be very unlikely that Eurosceptic member states could make their influence felt by having the median judge (2012: 53f).

The institutional position of the court thus leads to significant independence. To make use of it, the court needs what one may term a support structure. This is also determined by the underlying institutional rules.

The ECJ's support structure

To make use of its independence, the Court is dependent on support regarding the caseload being brought to it and its rulings being implemented by the member states. In this respect, it is first of all necessary to discuss how cases reach the court. Of the different legal procedures, two are of particular relevance: infringement procedures that are handed by the Commission to the Court when member states fail to meet their obligations under European law (Art. 258 TFEU) and the preliminary-ruling procedure, in which national courts ask the ECJ for advice in the interpretation of European law. Since 1994, preliminary rulings have been the most important kind of procedure in most of the years – 2003 being a year when direct actions against member states for failure to fulfil obligations had a higher number (Court of Justice of the European Union 2013: 110). In recent years, preliminary rulings have by far outnumbered all others with 404 (2012) and 423 (2011) against direct actions 73 (2012) and 81 (2011) (Court of Justice of the European Union 2013: 90).

The preliminary ruling procedure has high institutional significance because it establishes a direct link between the ECJ and the member states' courts. Originally, the intention had been to allow for easy access to the interpretation of European law also for lower courts. The establishment of the doctrines of direct effect and supremacy transformed the procedure into one allowing private actors to challenge national law as to its conformance with EU law (Alter 1998: 133–5; Mancini 1989: 606). Whenever lower courts in the member states are in doubt about the relevance of European law for a case they are deciding, they can call on the ECJ for a preliminary ruling, posing specific questions about the implications of European law for this case. This gives private parties indirect access to the court. Moreover, as the ECJ only answers the questions posed by the domestic court, but the latter issues the ruling, member states can hardly ignore European law. By openly opposing it, they would not only question the independence of the judiciary so central to the rule of law, but also their domestic court system. The institutional provision of preliminary rulings, as Weiler argues, leads to a unitary system of judicial decision making (1981: 300).

But why do member state courts address the ECJ? In fact, initially it took a few years until the courts started taking up this opportunity, with the first case being handed in 1961 (Court of Justice of the European Union 2013: 109; Mancini 1989: 605). Why should domestic courts be interested in overturning the domestic legal system with the help of European law? It is generally argued that the preliminary procedure is in fact quite attractive for lower courts. Although always facing the risk of being overturned by the next higher court in their domestic court hierarchy, basing their decision on supreme European law shields them from this risk (Weiler 1994: 518–20). Moreover, lower courts are less concerned with the coherence of the national legal system (Alter 2001: 49). Yet, such an interpretation does not explain why there are significant differences in the use of the reference system in the member states. Focusing on the British experience, Golub argued that there are also disincentives to refer, as this allows keeping control over policy outcomes and to slow down the integration process (1996: 381). Analysing the experience of Danish and Swedish courts, which refer rarely, Marlene Wind has argued that explanations of patterns of referrals have to take into account political culture and the kind of democratic system, as courts from majoritarian democracies are less likely to refer than courts from constitutional democracies. Given that Nordic countries have no tradition of judicial review, there is the assumption that only the highest courts should request preliminary rulings, and in general it is preferred that domestic courts interpret EU law by themselves, based on the *acte clair*[3] doctrine (Wind 2010: 1046, 48, 53, 55).

Supreme and constitutional courts, in contrast, lose power by having the ECJ at the apex of the judicial hierarchy. Consequently, there have been many conflicts between the ECJ and the highest national courts, historically and ongoing as the Lisbon ruling of the German Constitutional Court (GCC) in 2009 shows. In this ruling, the GCC held that the integration process may not undermine the identity of the German Federal Republic, reserving for itself the right to judge whether this was the case next to the right of determining whether acts of European Union organs overstep their mandate and act *ultra vires*. In fact, the GCC posed its first preliminary ruling in 2014 concerning the decision of the European Central Bank to engage in outright monetary transactions in the euro crisis, which the GCC believes to be *ultra vires*. The critical stance of the highest member state courts has been important for the development of the ECJ's case law. Notably its development of an own human rights' jurisdiction is interpreted as an answer to the announcements of the Italian and German constitutional courts in the 1960s and 1970s that they would subject EC law and court rulings to judicial review as long as there was no sufficient fundamental rights protection on this level (Weiler 1986: 1119).

The relationship to lower courts has been less complicated for the ECJ. As Nyikos has shown, domestic courts generally frame the questions of the preliminary procedure in a way that gives clear indications of the sort of answer that is welcome (Nyikos 2006). Often the ECJ follows this lead. It has an incentive to do so as this is an assurance that its verdict will be taken up rather than ignored by the lower court, which would pose the danger of undermining the ECJ's authority. Given this behaviour of lower courts actively asking for certain rulings, Gareth Davies has argued that the ECJ should not be blamed for its activism (G. Davies 2012). On the basis of a case study on the contentious *Mangold* ruling on age discrimination, Stone Sweet and Stranz (2012) show in great detail how litigators may strategically address courts so as to undermine domestic policies with the help of European law, thereby relying on the explicit framing of the issue by the lower court judge (Stone Sweet and Stranz 2012).

Nevertheless, the relationship to lower courts is not necessarily an easy one for the ECJ. After all, it depends on their cooperation. And lower courts may not only address the court in the interest of furthering the relevance of European law. Beach (2001) cites the example of the Irish abortion case (C-159/90) in this respect. At issue was the question whether the freedom of services could undermine the Irish prohibition of abortion. Student associations, who had published information about abortion clinics in the UK, which was illegal under Irish law, had "based their defence upon the right to disseminate information under EC law about services in other Member States" (Beach 2001: 20; see also Nyikos 2006: 528f). The Irish High Court had addressed the ECJ in order to ask about the European law dimension of the case; at the same time it was illusionary that it would have followed a ruling undermining the Irish abortion prohibition. This was made clear by the Irish Supreme Court, who had threatened non-compliance in this case (Beach 2001: 21). The Court therefore ruled, rather wisely, establishing, in principle, the relevance of the services freedom for abortion, but denying its relevance in the case at hand. This gave Ireland the opportunity to include a protocol on abortion at the ongoing negotiation of the Maastricht Treaty.[4]

Concerning the power of the ECJ, the collaboration with lower courts often pursuing distinct policy agendas is thus a central element. A further important group of actors in this context are litigants (Burley and Mattli 1993; Kelemen 2011). The supreme and directly effective legal order grants them a set of legal positions which may be more favourable than those of the domestic legal setting. Given the far-reaching, directly effective economic freedoms of the treaty – covering the freedom of goods, services, persons (establishment and workers' movement) as well as capital (since Maastricht) – economic actors may find here arguments allowing the abolition of domestic restrictions. This is the root of the often criticized "liberal" bias of European law, strengthening individual rights against collective obligations (Scharpf 2010). Another source of European legal positions concerns anti-discrimination. The original provision of equal pay for women in Art. 117 EEC has led to far-reaching case law on anti-discrimination, which – backed by secondary law provisions in different anti-discrimination directives – implies that any kind of discriminatory practice at the national level stands good chances of being overruled by reference to European law (Alter and Vargas 2000; Cichowski 2004; Mazey 2012).

Litigants that are empowered by European law are thus not only (large) economic actors but also non-governmental organizations (NGOs), partly helped by *pro bono* activities of law firms. In the EU, to an extent more known from the US than from European countries, litigation has thus become an alternative to lobbying as legal changes can be realized via case law or via secondary law (Bouwen and McCown 2007; Kelemen 2011). There is some dispute in the literature, whether such "positive" results from case law need not recast the critical assessment of the Court (Caporaso and Tarrow 2009). However, anti-discrimination rights are also individual rights, and cannot weaken the argument that only liberal and not republican values are furthered (Höpner and Schäfer 2012; Scharpf 2009).

Next to lower courts and litigants, the Commission is another important ally of the ECJ. It normally joins all cases with observations at the ECJ, where it is not party to the proceeding (Hofmann 2013: 78). Its policy position is a good predictor of the case outcome as it is normally on the winning side (Cichowski 2006: 499). And the Commission is itself an important actor at the court. As guardian of the treaty, the Commission has to monitor the implementation of European law in the member states and can address infringement procedures to them, if member states fail to comply with primary or secondary law. Often, the Commission acts on complaints of private actors who shy away from taking the initiative for legal proceedings themselves. By being able to initiate cases, the Commission is also well poised to strategically influence the development of case law, which may be a helpful pressure on the legislative process, as discussed in the following.

As the discussion has shown, the institutional characteristics and the support structure of the ECJ put it in a powerful position. Nevertheless, as I noted at the beginning of this chapter, the question whether the court diverges from the interests of "rational" member states is still disputed in the literature. Most likely, this dispute cannot be settled as all depends on how discretion and member states' preferences are being delineated. I will return to this point in the Conclusion, arguing that the ambiguous power and weakness of the court shows very well how much the EU has developed into a multilevel system, where few national preferences are as clear cut, such as has happened in the Irish abortion case (and even that was followed soon after by a referendum). Member states are no longer the gatekeepers, channelling input into the supranational system. Rather, different actors have access to different venues, leading to shifting coalitions. If governments in most cases can live with the outcome of the case law (if only for the moment, compared to the cost of intervention against an independent court) does this mean that this is the discretion they gave to the court? Courts and governments have fundamentally different time horizons, as Alter emphasizes (1998: 130f). Moreover, another shortcoming of rational choice approaches should be pointed out: they often assume a perfect malleability of law, which judges can interpret according to political need. In fact, attitudinal approaches, which assume that political preferences of judges determine the outcome of cases, face similar problems (Dyevre 2010: 311). Although legal texts provide for interpretative scope, if laws were setting no limits and all would depend on the preferences of judges or of concerned member states, there would be little reason why political and private actors should try to influence the policy process, and with it the law as its output in the first place.

In this respect, Kelemen (2001) makes an interesting argument. Analysing decisions at the European and the WTO level, he argues that courts are susceptive to political pressure, whenever laws allow for it. Only when legal texts are open enough, and there has not been case law pointing in another direction, are courts free to follow political pressure. But this is much more difficult if precedent and legal texts are more determinate. In this respect the often-noted strategy of the Court becomes relevant to develop case law incrementally, often initiating new developments in cases of little relevance, so as to avoid immediate member states' opposition (Alter 1998: 131). Such incrementalism allows actors to "test the waters" and to assess the reactions of the legal profession to case law development. Once politically more contentious cases arise, the case law is already more settled, constraining political influence.

Yet, another point of Malecki's remains, concerning the preferences of the judges: Why would these diverge from those of the nominating member states to a noticeable extent? Why would the ECJ, being dependent on compliance, risk taking contentious judgements, often against the explicit opinions of many member states? Being called on, the court has to decide, even if the concrete directions given in legal texts are slim. In such a situation, when possibly due to political compromises the law is equivocal, the "ever closer union" provides guidance, resulting often in a teleological approach to the interpretation of EU law (Pescatore 1983). Even if this disregards wishes of member states, granting individuals legal positions grounded in EU law helps the ECJ foster its own legitimation. It is the ECJ that grants these rights, and by demanding them, individuals indirectly legitimate the ECJ's decisions. Another point has to be mentioned: member states very unevenly submit opinions on ongoing cases (Granger 2004). Given the heterogeneous institutional setting in which the Court operates, it cannot foresee all implications of its rulings (Schmidt 2008). And as we have seen, the Court not only has to watch the member states, but also has to care about the cooperation of the national courts in preliminary procedures. Dyevre (2010: 323) argues that the Court has to take greater care to continuously build on the cooperation of domestic courts than that it has to fear legislative overrides by the member states. Moreover, the Court cannot draw on discussions of a European public sphere which could give indications about likely political reactions to incipient rulings. It is therefore hard to avoid contentious judgements. Considering the complex setting in which the Court operates, it is important to emphasize that the outcome of activist case law does not require an activist court. Even when it should be called entrepreneurial rather than activist (Solanke 2011), the case law can have an activist impact.

To summarize, in the EU, we find a situation where institutional conditions allow for broad access to the Court through the preliminary procedure. As European law is applied directly by domestic courts, member states have difficulty in opposing legal development. Moreover, the unanimous-decision rule to rein in the Court gives the latter very significant independence. The institutional conditions not only further compliance with EU law but also provide an opportunity structure to different actors to invoke domestic reforms via EU law that could not be pushed along otherwise. Next to litigants, lower courts can also further their interests via the ECJ. Another important actor supporting the extensive development of European law is the Commission.

Constitutionalization

Any assessment of the importance of the ECJ for European integration has to start with the seminal rulings of the 1960s, which constitutionalized the Treaty. Without this bold move, the Court could have never played this major role, and European integration would have taken another course, being less able to rely on member states' legal obligations. Being based on an international treaty, the European Economic Community started out with the characteristic weaknesses: a continued dependence on the goodwill of the participating member states, whose acceptance was necessary for advancing any policy decisions, as well as for implementing the agreements. But with two rulings in the 1960s, the ECJ gave the Community a distinct legal character, making it less dependent on the specific agreement to each decision by every member state.

In *Van Gend en Loos* (26/62, 1963) the Court decided that the articles of the treaty take direct effect, if they are sufficiently clear. Individuals could therefore directly invoke these rights in courts. This Dutch case involving customs duties is a good example of the "careful treading" of the Court. As the Netherlands has a monist legal tradition, where international treaty obligations are treated directly as part of the domestic legal system without the adaptation that dualist systems require, the case was well chosen (Bignami 2013: 1320f). To have established the direct effect of the Treaty in a dualist country would have aroused much more opposition. In any case, the direct effect as such did not have such far-reaching implications. These only arose with the second principle, the supremacy of European law, proclaimed a year later in *Costa v ENEL* (6/64; 1964). At issue was an Italian law, enacted subsequent to the Treaty of Rome, with the question of whether this would take precedent being the more recent legal rule. The Court established the supremacy of European law, however denying in this case its relevance as the rule lacked direct effect. Direct effect and the supremacy of the Court effectively constitutionalized the Treaty of Rome (Mancini 1989; Stein 1981; Weiler 1991: 2403). A third constitutional principle noted less prominently but relevant nevertheless is the principle of pre-emption, typical of federal systems. It requires that the lower levels give up their competence of regulation once an issue has been regulated at the higher level. It has been much slower to develop, although it is inherently linked to supremacy. If the rules of the higher level are supreme, the question is what happens to the competences of the lower level, whether they are pre-empted in total or remain relevant just for certain situations (Schütze 2006).

Recent historical studies show the purposeful fabrication of cases from early onwards (Alter 2009: chap. 4; Vauchez 2010). Not only did a group of lawyers working at the Commission's legal service, the Court, or being members of the Euro-Law Associations, discuss possibilities of strengthening the ambit of EU law before *van Gend*, but the group members also publicized the decision broadly, emphasizing its transformative character. In particular, they also pointed to the new role that the Court should assume, given the conflict among the member states about the course of integration. The decision in the case of *Costa* was thus clearly awaited. As Schepel and Wesseling (1997: 172f) show, lawyers working for the European institutions have been unusually active in publishing in the major European law journals, using these venues to influence the debate on European law. As Vauchez (2012: 53) shows, moreover, a transnational "esprit de corps" could be developed through conferences, *Festschriften* and eulogies that have instilled consistency into the operation of the Court, although the Court itself has no influence on the appointment of its judges and has to socialize judges from very heterogeneous environments.

Subsequent to the establishment of both principles, further case law consolidated the reach of the Court. With a view to the supremacy of the European order, it was problematic that this supreme order lacked any human rights provisions. In *Stauder* (29/69) the referring German court specifically asked what happens if a Community act deprives a citizen of a fundamental right protected by a country's constitution? The Court held that the protection of individual fundamental rights was part of "general principles" of Community law (Stein 1981: 14). In the case *Internationale Handelsgesellschaft* (11/70), again a German referral, the Court was even more explicit, seeing the protection of fundamental rights as integral part of these principles and being assured by the Community (Stein 1981: 15). New historic work shows in great detail how this development of a supranational legal principle depended on intensive interactions with member state actors (B. Davies 2012; Pollack 2013). Another major step was the *Simmenthal* case (106/77), a reference from an Italian court. At issue was the question, what to do when national laws, enacted after the Treaty, contradicted the Community order? The Italian constitutional court held that it had to be involved to declare the law invalid. However, the ECJ saw incompatible national law "automatically inapplicable," so that lower courts could directly decide against application (Stein 1981: 13).

With a view to direct effect, several extensions took place. The original *van Gend* case had only referred to the "negative" obligation not to enact further barriers. In *Lütticke* (57/65), the issue was the "positive" obligation to remove discriminatory taxes. The Court confirmed the direct effect of the rule once the specified deadline had passed. On this basis, it was possible to abolish countless discriminatory restrictions after the deadline for building the common market by the end of 1969 had lapsed (Stein 1981: 17). Another extension concerned the inclusion of secondary law into direct effect. As regulations are directly applicable, this was not so problematic. But in *van Dyn* (41/74), the question arose whether individuals could base claims directly on directives, even though directives only prescribe the result to be realized in the member state, not the means of achieving it. Nevertheless, the Court agreed to the direct effect of directives (Stein 1981: 20f). As Stein (1981: 22) mentions, this resulted in the first open opposition of a high national court to the case law, when "the French Conseil d'Etat refused in 1978 to allow a German national, Daniel Cohn-Bendit, of May 1968 fame, to rely on the same Council directive against an order by French authorities expelling him from France. The Conseil justified the refusal on the ground that according to Article 189, in principle, no directive could have direct effect in a national legal order." The Bundesfinanzhof also rejected the doctrine but was rebuked for it by the GCC (Mancini 1989: 603).

The question of whether directives have direct effect is not just a technical matter, to be mentioned for the sake of juridical completeness. Rather, it is fundamentally important as it makes it more difficult for member states to simply opt against compliance with non-implementation. Whereas before, member states could only be targeted if the Commission initiated infringement procedures, with direct effect of directives, litigants can enforce their rights at their domestic courts, using "fire alarm control" of insufficient implementation (Mancini 1989: 602).

A final important development concerns horizontal direct effect, where rights are invoked not vertically against the state or public bodies but against individuals. It was first established in the ruling *Walrave* (36/74), a case about discrimination based on nationality by a private bicycle association. More widely noted was however the *Defrenne II* ruling (43/75) shortly afterwards. It involved a stewardess who sued the private airline Sabena on the basis of Art. 119 EEC Treaty requiring equal pay for equal work, as she was being paid less than her male colleague. This was the first in a series of non-discrimination cases (to be discussed further later). An interesting aspect of the case was that Art. 119 explicitly addressed governments, but the Court nevertheless affirmed its direct effect horizontally (Stein 1981: 18–20). The Court has however consistently denied horizontal direct effect of directives (*Marshall*) (Hargreaves 2011: 22). Otherwise the direct effect of Community law is established as long as the criteria for direct effect are met: rules need to be clear and unambiguous; unconditional; and not requiring further action (Hartley 2010: 210).

The ECJ's role in EU policy-making

By strengthening the European rule of law, the Court plays an important role in policy-making in the EU. It is thanks to the rule of law that actors can trust that agreements are kept and policies implemented, despite incentives to defect. This is the traditional role of courts in policy-making, a passive, enabling role, fostering compliance. However, there is also a more hidden role for the Court in EU policy-making, due to its autonomous development of case law. As case law takes effect as precedent for subsequent cases, ongoing legislation takes place "in the shadow of judicial politics" (Schmidt 2011a). In particular, when the Court has been interpreting the Treaty, the Council and the Parliament have to take note of the case law, as secondary law cannot contradict the treaty. I discuss this impact first in the light of the better-known examples of the single market and gender discrimination and then in the light of several more recent policy processes.

Making policies matter: the ECJ's role in fostering compliance

The EU has a good record of compliance with its agreed policies (Hix and Høyland 2011: 100; Zürn and Wolf 2000). Yet it is interesting to ask why member states would agree to partly far-reaching measures of integration, which they find later on difficult to implement? An important early explanation is that member states were simply not aware of the legal obligations thus entered. This, in turn, indirectly points to the unexpected development of judicial enforcement, which is behind the good compliance record (Eichener 1997). This is furthered by the extension of the direct effect, and the broad indirect access to the Court via the preliminary procedure. Infringement procedures and preliminary rulings have, over the years, acquired more teeth, as will be shown later. Moreover, while secondary law such as directives is often equivocal and loosely worded, giving governments most likely the impression that it is not difficult to comply with the agreement, the Court has understood its role as determining "the one and only correct interpretation."

> The above cases illustrate the Court's approach generally to matters of interpretation of Community legislation, and directives in particular. Even where a directive is ambiguously formulated, the Court will not take the view that what one might call different interpretations may coexist. Instead the Court will determine the one and only correct interpretation, leaving little or no discretion to the national legislature. . . . It must none the less be emphasized that this non-deferential approach puts a considerable burden on the Court, and may indeed lead it to fill in significant gaps in the text of the Community legislation which, as was mentioned, is often the result of compromise and may therefore be unclear on crucial policy issues. (Eeckhout 1998: 8)

Eeckhout (1998: 17) also asks whether this implies "judicial activism," "usurping the role of the legislature?" He rejects this idea, as the Court "does not depart from the wording of the directive, and the interpretation which it prescribes is not contrary to the intentions of the legislature. Those intentions are in any event most difficult to determine in Community law." Precise rules, granting clear legal rights, favour what Kelemen calls "Eurolegalism," a variant of the adversarial legalism prominent in the US regulatory approach, as litigants find it then easier to push for implementation in their domestic courts (Kelemen 2011). With its small administrative capacities, the Commission relies on such "fire alarm" control by private actors to foster implementation (Pollack 1996: 445). With European law granting a partly alternative set of rights, private litigants have an incentive to further their position by drawing on these rights in domestic courts. However, this is particularly the case for individual interests. Public interests, like those protected by environmental directives are much more difficult to enforce via infringement procedures as Slepcevic (2009) shows. Kelemen (2011: 44) argues that next to the Court, the European Parliament has also pushed for more precise directives, with little discretion for national authorities and easier judicial enforcement through private litigation.

Nevertheless, preliminary rulings as well as infringement procedures could, for a long time, only establish that certain European rules were not transposed and rights to individuals not granted. If member states did not react, not much would happen, as there were no financial penalties involved. Different to the ECSC (European Coal and Steel Community) Treaty that knew penalties for persistent infringements, the EC Treaty only had the possibility in Art. 260 that the Court would reassert the failure of the member state to fulfil its obligation. With the new surge in integration measures accompanying the completion of the single market in 1992, this issue became subject of the negotiations of the Maastricht Treaty. It was embedded in an overall discussion of the mandate of the Court, as the UK brought in far-reaching reform proposals, attempting to curtail the activism of the Court. However, this only received some support by Germany and France, but not the necessary backing of all member states (Tallberg 2000: 114f). One outcome of the Maastricht reforms was, however, a revised Art. 260 allowing the Commission in cases of perpetuated non-compliance to turn to the Court suggesting the payment of a lump sum or of a penalty alongside the renewed judgement. After a long period of discussion since the 1970s, there was thus finally the possibility to give member states' legal obligations more teeth. At the same time, member states explicitly decided against proposals to introduce member states' liability for failure to fulfil legal obligations, which would have given individuals the possibility to be compensated for breaches of European rights in preliminary rulings.

Based on the new possibilities of Art. 260, the Commission published communications in 1996 and 1997 on its application, to be followed by further notices in the 2000s.[5] But it took until 2000 for the first penalty payment to be imposed, in the case C-387/97 *Commission v Greece*. In late 2003, the Court then confirmed the criteria of the Commission on the determination and application of penalty payments (C-278/01, *Commission v Spain*). These depend on the duration and seriousness of the infringement as well as on the capacity of the country to pay. The next major development was the case C-304/02 *Commission v Spain* (2005) where the Court established that despite the wording of the treaty (penalty *or* lump sum) and irrespective of the proposal of the Commission, the Court could impose a lump sum in addition to the penalty. The Court thus does not feel bound by the proposal of the Commission. This changed the procedure again as both measures differ in their implications: penalties give incentives to stop the infringement right away once imposed. They had led to a practice where member states comply at the last moment – and where the Commission withdraws the Art. 260 procedure once the member state complied. However, lump sums are a clear punishment that needs to be paid even when the member state has complied in the meantime. The Commission therefore no longer withdraws the case after compliance, and there should be a greater dissuasive function now of the combined demand for penalties and lump sums.

A further change was introduced with the Treaty of Lisbon. Art. 260 II simplifies and shortens the procedure. Moreover, the new Art. 260 III introduces the possibility of imposing sanctions at the first procedure. In a communication (SEC(2010)1371fin), the Commission has laid down how it wants to apply this possibility, very much in parallel to the established practice of Art. 260 II.

Sanctions imposed in infringement procedures help to foster compliance, but they offer no remedies in all those areas that are not as closely monitored by the Commission. As mentioned, in the Maastricht negotiations, member states explicitly denied granting the Court the right to order member states to compensate private actors in preliminary rulings. Nevertheless, and despite the criticism that was voiced against the Court at the time, shortly afterwards the Court ruled in *Francovich* (C-6/90 und C-9/90) in 1991 that member states have to compensate individuals for failure to transpose, thereby establishing the principle of state liability which the member states explicitly refused to grant. Despite strong member state opposition, the Court further elucidated the principle in a series of cases in 1996 (*Brasserie du Pêcheur, Factortame III, British Telecommunications, Hedley Lomas, Dillenkofer*). Following this, conditions are that the European law has to confer rights on individuals, the breach must be sufficiently serious, and there must be a causal link between the failure to comply and the loss suffered. The principle is relevant for all violations of European law, not only the non-transposition of directives but also irrespective of the fact whether the law has direct effect (Tallberg 2000: 110). This case law is, of course, very interesting with regard to the continued assumption that the Court only does what the member states would like it to do. If individual litigants can expect compensation from courts, they have stronger incentives to try to enforce European law and "fire alarm control" of European law becomes very effective (Pollack 1996: 455). However, as Tallberg (2000: 166f) shows, most member states did not have provisions in their domestic legal systems where courts could enforce state liability, so that even some litigants of the prominent ECJ cases were not rewarded compensation in domestic courts.

Shaping integration: the single market and anti-discrimination

The promotion of the single market in the 1992 project is one of the most well-known examples for the relevance of the Court for the development of European policies. The direct effect of positive obligations of the Treaty implied that member states had to remove barriers to the single market without relying on further agreement by the Council. Another important step was the interpretation of the freedom of goods as a prohibition of restriction in the cases of *Dassonville* (1974) and *Cassis de Dijon* (1979), instead of a mere prohibition of discrimination. This broad interpretation of the freedom of goods was later transferred to all other freedoms (Oliver and Roth 2004). What does this move imply? If the freedoms are interpreted narrowly as a rule of non-discrimination, traded goods and services from other member states (or firms, willing to establish themselves, etc.) have to comply with the rules of the member state in which they become active. Only, they may not be discriminated against. But if freedoms are interpreted broadly as a prohibition of restriction, traded goods and services from other member states can take the regulation of their home state along. The host country recognizes that they are already regulated in their home country. It would be a restriction of the freedom not to accept the regulation of other member states as equivalent to their own, for which the host state would need good reasons (Schmidt 2007).

The *Cassis de Dijon* case is a good illustration of this change in approach. This French liqueur (Cassis) had lower levels of alcohol content than required in the German regulation of liqueurs and therefore was not allowed to be marketed in Germany. In its observation to the case, the German government tried to argue that such higher alcohol content was justified as a measure to protect health, but it could not convince the Court. As Alter and Meunier have shown in their path-breaking article, the Cassis-ruling would never have had such impact and fame, had it not been for the Commission utilizing it to pushing for the completion of the single market (Alter and Meunier-Aitsahalia 1994). The term *mutual recognition* had not been mentioned as such in the ruling. However, the Commission used this catchword to market its changed approach to the single market. Before, member states had had to agree on common rules for products, services or qualifications in order to build a market. Or actors engaging in trade had to adapt to the different rules of the member states. The approach of mutual recognition changed this. Now, the Commission could argue that the different regulations of member states were in principle equivalent so that they had to mutually recognize each other's goods and services. Common regulation was only necessary, where member states could claim exceptions to the need to recognize each other's rules. Given this presumption that they could no longer enforce their rules on market actors from other member states, governments had clear incentives to agree on common rules in the Council (Majone 1992).

Case law of the Court thus gave an important impetus to the single market programme. The same can be said for the equality of treatment of women and anti-discrimination policy in general. The *Defrenne* case on equal pay, mentioned earlier as an early example of horizontal direct effect, was the beginning to a series of judgements that fundamentally strengthened the position of women in the member states. For the period from 1971 to 2003, Cichowski (2007: 90) counts 86 cases regarding the equality legislation and 61 cases involving Article 141 EC (former Art. 119 EEC, now Art. 157 TFEU) just for preliminary references (Art. 267 TFEU). With such numbers, it is not possible here to summarize the gist of the case law that has dealt with issues of equal pay, pension rights (Stone Sweet and Cichowski 2004), pregnancy and maternity rights (Cichowski 2007: 94–108). The literature in this field has focused mostly on the striking role of private litigation, clearly influenced by the strategies of lawyers and women's groups. For example, the early *Defrenne* cases owed much to the initiative of a Belgian lawyer, Eliane Vogel-Polsky, who had already written on a possible direct effect of Art. 119 in 1967, and had actively looked for appropriate cases to bring to the ECJ (Hoskyns 1996: 68–71). As Cichowski (2007: 74–93) shows, references from the different member states about Art. 141 have been very uneven, much depending on whether trade unions or equal opportunity commissions such as in the UK have supported such action (see also Alter and Vargas 2000). Also national courts have responded very differently to incorporating European sex equality law into the domestic legal system, and this has been another pronounced area of research (Stone Sweet and Cichowski 2004: 180).

The far-reaching case law on sex equality has given an impetus for several directives, which partly codified the case law (Cichowski 2007: 73; Mazey 2012; Stone Sweet and Cichowski 2004: 149). They have been consolidated in the Recast Directive 2006/54 that contains the "main provisions regarding access to employment, including promotion, and to vocational training, as well as working conditions, including pay and occupational social security schemes" (Burri and Prechal 2010: 7). While there is an abundance of literature in the important field of anti-discrimination, reaching from sex equality to, for instance, age-discrimination (Stone Sweet and Stranz 2012), there are, to my knowledge, no detailed analyses of how case law has had an impact on legislative decision-making or on how member states and the European Parliament have dealt with the fact that case law sets important constraints on legislative options. However, if European judicial politics is special because the joint-decision trap proves such a protection, then it is interesting to analyse how the legislature deals with these constraints. It is interesting for (at least) two reasons. First, we do not see these same constraints at the national level. Thus, national constitutions are more easily changed than the treaty, and national constitutional case law is less likely to suddenly invoke major changes and contention, as the courts operate within a political debate, know their domestic institutional setting and can much better assess the implications of case law. Second, the legislature, in this case the governments in the Council and the European Parliament, has greater legitimacy to decide on legal rules than does a court , and thus in the end has to abide by decisions of a much more weakly legitimated institution.

The interaction of judicial and legislative policy-making

If case law is an alternative to secondary law, it is an important constraint in legislative decision-making. This implies that next to the preferences of member states, the EP, and the Commission, existing or pending case law has to be taken into account when analysing decisions, as the default condition of decision-making is shaped judicially (Schmidt 2000). Interestingly, in the many analyses of member states decision-making in the Council, case law is often totally neglected. For example Thomson's (2011) study makes no reference to case law or to the ECJ, even though it analyses cases such as the working time directive that were partly motivated by case law (see below).

In the following, I summarize the main thrust of the literature which analyses the impact of case law on European policy-making. An important distinction has to be emphasized in the beginning: for the legislature operating in the "shadow" of case law, it makes a great difference whether case law relates to the treaty, that is primary law, or to secondary law, as the latter can much more easily be changed and poses less of a constraint. Case law relating to the treaty will therefore be my focus. Generally, the impact of case law can take several forms. In the extremes, it can replace legislation, in the sense of making it superfluous or overruling it. Or case law may not have any influence – the situation assumed by standard rational-choice analyses of the Council – which is discussed further here. Between those poles, I distinguish two different types of cases. Case law may simply motivate legislation. Member states may aim to codify existing case law as this brings it into a general form being more accessible for all market participants. However, case law may also play a more proactive role in the legislative process. This is so when in a policy field case law based on the treaty develops, but member states disagree with its thrust, and want to pre-empt it. Legislation, which normally might not have been a political priority, then presents itself as a "lesser evil" (Schmidt 2000). This pressure may not be only driven by the interest to determine the material policy but also by normative considerations, not to have the court play the role of the legislator. Needless to say, these are analytical differentiations, which actual cases may not fit perfectly.

Replacing or overruling the legislator

In the extreme, case law may make it unnecessary to enact secondary law (Pescatore 1983: 568). An early example was given by Stein. After the ruling 293/83, the Commission excluded from a proposal for a directive on the freedom of movement rules on residence for students, as these had been covered by the case law (Stein 1986: 638). Another example concerns the regulation of part-time work for women, which the Commission withdrew after the *Kowalska* ruling (More 1991: 63f).

Member states do not always accept the way the court shapes policy for them. An interesting, repeated, example is Regulation 1408/71 (now 883/2004), coordinating national social security legislation. The regulation draws a distinction between transportable social security, and territorially bound social assistance measures, which were excluded from it. An annex details the contributory and exportable as well as the non-contributory and non-exportable social policies of member states. Repeatedly, there have been cases where the court has questioned the territoriality of benefits as decided by the Council. And repeatedly, the Council has reaffirmed its position, not necessarily resulting in the court following its lead.

In cases concerning Italy and France (*Piscitello*, C-139/82 (1983) *Giletti et al.*, C-381/85 (1987)), the Court ruled that social measures the member states regarded as territorial were exportable. As France did not comply, the Commission followed up the case with an infringement procedure (C-236/88). As the Court re-emphasized its interpretation, the Council unanimously amended Regulation 1408/71 with Regulation 1247/92, in order to re-establish the territorial nature of non-contributory benefits. In the subsequent cases of C-20/96 *Snares* and C-297/97 *Partridge*, the Court accepted this. But in 2001, in C-215/99 *Jauch* and C-43/99 *Leclere* the Court again overruled the will of the Council as laid down in the regulation (Martinsen 2005a: 100–2; Wasserfallen 2010: 1130). The conflict over the possibility of member states to keep certain kinds of social assistance territorially bound continues (Martinsen and Falkner 2011). For example in 2007 the court reclassified certain sickness cash benefits from the UK in an infringement procedure (C-299/05 *Commission v Parliament and Council*) allowing the exportability of rights, despite the fact that the annex of the regulation excluded this.

Codifying case law

In the wider context of the single market there are several examples of secondary law being decided under the impact of existing or pending case law. Case law narrows the range of feasible policy options. To codify case law in secondary law has the advantage of making the legal setting more transparent and accessible to all actors concerned, furthering legal certainty and equality before the law. In the following, I briefly discuss the Citizenship Directive of 2004, the Services Directive, the 2008 Regulation for Mutual Recognition in Goods, and the failed Working Time Directive.

The citizenship directive

In one of the few articles focusing on the impact of case law on European policy-making, Fabio Wasserfallen (2010) discussed the citizenship directive 2004/38 relating to its rules concerning the rights of students. After the Commission had made its proposal for this Directive, the Court delivered its ruling in the case *Grzelczyk* (C-184/99) in 2001. In this case a French student applied for Minimex support for his last year of study in Belgium, and the Court established a right of residence including economically inactive Union citizens requiring assistance. In doing so, the Court ruled against the requirement of Directive 93/96 that students from other member states need to have sufficient resources to avoid social assistance, as well as its own case law in *Brown* (C-197/ 86; Schmidt 2012: 18; Wind 2009: 258). After the *Grzelczyk* ruling, the Commission changed its proposal for the directive to be in conformity with the case law. Students' residence still depends on them having sufficient resources and medical coverage. However, now the directive allows them to claim assistance, once there is a link to the host country and the need is only temporary (Wasserfallen 2010: 1140f). The Citizenship Directive is thus an example where secondary law included more far-reaching provisions than originally planned in reaction to case law.

The services directive

The proposal for a services directive, published by the Commission in early 2004, resulted in the first highly politically contentious discussion of a single-market directive in the history of integration. The Commission originally proposed a horizontal Directive aiming at all sectors, with the small exemption of lotteries and public, not-for-profit social services like education or culture. Health and general-interest services were originally included. As is well known, the plan to subject the service delivery in this broad area to home-country control met with fierce resistance, particularly from unions, leading to the European Parliament playing a major role in the final compromise of the Services Directive. In it, the scope was narrowed, excluding for instance health. The obligation of member states to enable the services freedom replaced home-country regulation. However, the central Art. 16 of the directive includes a list of regulatory areas for which member states may not impose their host-country rules. Through the backdoor, this re-introduces the contentious home-country control (Schmidt 2009; 2011b). By narrowing down the exceptions of the services freedom for member states, the directive is even more liberal than the previous case law of the Court, as lawyers have shown (Davies 2007: 18; Witte 2007: 12). Comparable to the case of mutual recognition in goods, discussed below, it was only in this way that legal certainty could be re-established. However, in the broad literature on the Services Directive the impact of case law is hardly discussed (Crespy 2010; Crespy and Gajewska 2010; Miklin 2009), which emphasizes the main argument of this article of a surprising neglect of the importance of case law in the analysis of EU policy-making. That case law was, in fact, important for the Services Directive is demonstrated very clearly in the Commission's *Handbook on Implementation of the Services Directive* (European Commission 2007). It interprets Art. 16 with extensive reference to the existing case law, demonstrating that secondary law cannot lag behind the interpretation of primary law through the rulings of the ECJ (Schmidt 2011b: 45).

The regulation for mutual recognition in goods

Similar to the Services Directive, this is also a major piece of recent single-market legislation that, however, received little public attention. Ever since the *Cassis* judgement and the Commission's communication following it, those parts of the single market for goods that were not subject to sector specific regulation were governed by mutual recognition or home-country control. This implies that there is a basic assumption of an equivalent regulation of products across the member states, so that a product "lawfully marketed" (this being the standard formulation) in one member state may be marketed in another one on the basis of the freedom of goods (Art. 34 TFEU). Only in exceptional cases can the exemption of Art. 36 TFEU for public security reasons or of mandatory requirements as developed in the Court's case law be invoked. Despite several communications and other efforts of the Commission to further the working of mutual recognition in the 1990s, there were, for example, 123 cases of alleged infringements of the principle in the realm of products in the 1996–8 period (see COM(1999) 299 final, p. 13). This situation led the Commission to propose a new package for the internal goods market in February 2007, of which the regulation 764/2008 on mutual recognition for goods was a part. Decision-making was swift with the Council agreeing in June 2008. The regulation is interesting in our context as it shows that if case law is codified with the intention of providing legal certainty, this may imply that secondary law needs to go to the extremes of case law, being even more restrictive on the capacity of member states to regulate (Schmidt 2011b: 45–49).

The main point of the Regulation was to clarify the burden of proof (Art. 6 Regulation (EC) No 764/2008), laying down clear obligations and time limits on the member states when refusing a product to be marketed in their territory. The Council here spoke of a reversal of the burden of proof,[6] while the Commission merely admitted to a clarification in view of legal uncertainty (e.g. SEC(2007) 112: 18). In fact, the case law is ambiguous in this respect, laying the onus sometimes on the manufacturer to prove the equivalence of his products (case 188/84), and sometimes on the member states inhibiting the products (case 178/84). In fact, according to general theories of burden of proof, each party has to prove the facts of his or her claims (Lenaerts *et al.* 2006: 24–73). However, as one party relies on the freedom of goods, and the other party on the possibility to restrict it, this cannot settle the issue. The case thus shows that in order to establish legal certainty, and to pre-empt further litigation, secondary law may have to narrow down the available options that are left, given the case law. Had the legislature agreed on imposing the burden of proof on companies, those rulings where the Court had seen the onus on member states would have been an incentive for further litigation. Case law not only constrains legislative options but may even set incentives to agree on legislative rules at the extremes of case law.

Working time directive

The (failed) revision of the Working Time Directive (WTD) (2003/88/EC) is an example where case law concerned secondary law – the earlier WTD. In a series of cases, the ECJ had put national health systems under pressure by ruling that rest times, in particular the on-call time of hospital doctors, has to be counted as working time (SIMAP, C-303/98 and Jaeger, C-151/02). This new legal situation resulted in very costly changes particularly in the health systems of member states.[7] The legislative process to review the Directive started in 2004 (COM(2004) 607). However, it faced the problem of a significant cleavage among member states concerning the UK opt-out that had been granted in the original directive. The southern member states and the European Parliament were firmly against prolonging the opt-out, which the UK insisted on keeping. After protracted negotiations under several Presidencies (Kloka 2013; Nowak 2008), member states finally agreed on a compromise. However, the EP voted against it, and the conciliation procedure failed. In November 2011, the negotiation of the WTD was handed to the social partners, but until the spring of 2014, the Commission had not published a new proposal.[8]

Why would case law and the resulting lack of legal certainty not pressure the EU legislature into agreement so that the reform of the Working Time Directive failed in spring 2009? On one hand, member states that bear the cost of regulation based on case law agreed, while the EP feeling less pressure let the reform fail. On the other hand, member states could have been more compromising towards the European Parliament. A crucial factor seems to be that the case law of the Court relates to secondary law. While the situation of legal uncertainty is problematic, member states need not fear further case law of the Court that they cannot alter eventually through a new directive.[9] Member states may therefore prefer a failed reform in the hope that with another majority in the European Parliament and in the Council, a more favourable compromise may be possible at a later date.

Lesser evil

Lesser evil refers to a situation where the agreement on secondary law becomes a "lesser evil" for the member states, as otherwise a regulation through the courts is feared. I originally illustrated this strategy in a study of electricity liberalization in the 1990s, where the Commission – according to my interpretation[10] – put pressure on member states to agree on a directive by threatening case law with infringement procedures. Had the Council not agreed on the directive, the sector would have been liberalized in a piecemeal fashion through case law, leading to significant legal uncertainty, which was particularly unacceptable in this sector requiring long-term investment decisions (Schmidt 2000).

In the following, I give two more examples where existing or pending case law effectively pushed the Council into agreement on secondary law: the Patient Mobility Directive and the Directive on Military Procurement. The patient mobility case is interesting as the existing case law here came about through preliminary rulings, without open activities and pressure by the Commission. Military procurement, in contrast, comparable to electricity liberalization, draws heavily on the strategy of the Commission. I also briefly summarize some older cases that can be regarded as examples of "lesser evil."

Patient mobility

Patient mobility as a complement to the free movement of workers had been realized through Regulation No 1408/71 in which member states agreed unanimously the modalities of providing health services to each other's citizens. Reimbursement was granted after an ex ante authorization that the patient had to seek (E112 system; Ackermann *et al.* 2008: 1326). As Martinsen has shown, the Court laid down its very different opinion in the *Pierik* cases (C-117/77 & C-182/78) in the late 1970s, by arguing that member states not only had to authorize but also to refund treatment abroad even if this was not refundable within the domestic health services, under the condition that this treatment was internationally recognized as necessary and effective. The Council unanimously overruled the Court (Martinsen 2005b: 1037f). Then, in 1998, a series of cases, based on references from member states' courts, started, in which the ECJ applied the freedom of goods and the freedom to provide services to health, notwithstanding the regulation. In the *Decker* and *Kohll* cases (C-120/95 and C-158/96), the ECJ saw the requirement of an ex ante authorization for buying spectacles abroad and for seeking ambulatory treatment as a disproportionate restriction on these freedoms (Greer 2012). Without summarizing here the whole case law development, it is important to note that in 2001 in *Geraets-Smits/Peerbooms* (C-157/99) the Court argued that in the case of hospital treatment a prior authorization requirement was a restriction to the services freedom, which could be justified. However, the procedure needed to be transparent, timely, and non-discriminatory (Martinsen 2005b: 1042). A further case should be mentioned. In *Watts* (C-372/04), Ms Watts had received a hip replacement in France in order to avoid the waiting times in the National Health Service (NHS), and claimed reimbursement. The case is important, because the Court engaged with the issue of waiting times, going as far as providing criteria for undue delay (Krajewski 2010: 170). Also, the Court made clear that the fundamental freedoms even applied to public health systems providing benefits in kind, such as the British NHS, forcing member states to come up with transparent cost calculations of their hospital services (van de Gronden 2009: 720). Needless to say, this case law development took place, even though many member states submitted written or oral opinions, pointing out the difficulty of integrating the fundamental freedoms into the operation of their health services (Obermaier 2009).

After the original Commission plan failed to integrate health services into the Services Directive, the Commission proposed the Patient Mobility Directive in 2008. In particular the UK, Germany, France, Sweden, and the Netherlands supported the directive, based on their interest in regaining legal certainty by codifying the case law, and – hopefully – putting an end to the string of cases reaching the ECJ, requiring continuous changes to domestic health policy. For the UK it was crucial to protect the central role of the general practitioner in the NHS through a directive. Poland, Slovakia, Portugal, and Romania opposed the directive to the bitter end out of the fear that they would have to reimburse providers of health services with no contract to the health system also in the domestic context, once they had to recognize them for the provision of trans-border services (Kloka 2013). However, these non-contracted providers could not be excluded from the directive as the Commission's legal service argued that existing case law already required this and secondary law could not lag behind this treaty interpretation. Interestingly, in this case, member states were not only motivated by re-establishing legal certainty and pre-empting further case law, but also by the normative argument that the shaping of this policy field should not be left to the courts.

In summary, the ongoing case law development fueled by preliminary procedures made it preferable for member states to agree on a directive as a "lesser evil" to leaving the shaping of this policy field in the hands of the Court. As indicated above, several of the Southern and Central and Eastern European member states opposed the directive. They saw the inclusion of non-contracted providers as interfering with the organization of their health system, contradicting the safeguard of Art. 168 VII TFEU that member states remain responsible for the organization of their health care systems.

Military procurement

Blauberger and Weiss (2013) have analysed the adoption of the Military Procurement Directive 2009. Its agreement poses a puzzle as member states had for long (and as recently as 2005) resisted any moves of the Commission to bring military procurement under single market rules. Instead they had referred to the exemption of Art. 346 TFEU for essential security interests. However, in an infringement procedure only marginally regarding military procurement, the ECJ had argued in 1999 that this exemption from the treaty had to be interpreted narrowly (C-414/97). On this basis, the Commission pursued an infringement procedure against Italy in 2005, regarding the procurement of helicopters for civilian use in a non-competitive tender. In April 2008, the Court argued that procurement law had been violated – even though there might be a potential military usage of the helicopters (C-337/05). This put the member states under the threat of further case law – and of military procurement being subsumed under the general public procurement rules. In the light of this threat, the adoption of the Military Procurement Directive appeared as a "lesser evil," as Blauberger and Weiss argue. They also point out that the beginning of case law development in this field has already led to a first preliminary reference by a Finnish court based on a request of a competitor (C-615/10), so that member states were right to give in to the threat and agree on sector-specific rules, which can give some guidance for the Court.

Older examples

Other researchers have put forward examples demonstrating the "lesser-evil" phenomenon. Thus, member states agreed on the Merger Control Regulation 40/64/89, and therefore on the delegation of these competences to the Commission, after the Court had ruled in the *Philip Morris* case that mergers could fall under the treaty's cartel control competence of Art. 81. With the agreement on a new secondary law, member states could re-establish legal certainty (Bulmer 1994). Similarly, the agreement on road-haulage liberalization was achieved under such pressure. After a Court ruling initiated by the Parliament against the Council for failure to act, the concerned actors feared that liberalization would be achieved through the courts, making it preferable to agree on secondary law (Young 1994). Also the liberalization of air transport followed after the *Nouvelles Frontières* judgement of the Court in 1986, where it had argued that competition rules were also applicable to air transport. This gave the Commission the basis to threaten the airlines with fines, leading to the Council's agreement on two liberalization regulations in late 1987 (Argyris 1989: 10; Button 1992: 155). Finally, Hubschmid and Moser give an interesting example how "lesser evil" may work favouring re-regulation. For the agreement on automobile emission standards, it was crucial that the European Court of Justice had allowed member states stricter environmental standards in its

Danish Bottle case (C-302/86). This allowed those member states favouring stricter environmental standards like the Netherlands, Denmark, and Germany to pursue these unilaterally. But as this disintegrated the internal market, opposing member states such as France and Italy were willing to agree on stricter environmental standards (Hubschmid and Moser 1997: 238), which unified the market again.

Conclusion

In this chapter, I have traced how case law of the ECJ influences EU policy-making. The important role of the ECJ as a motor of integration is broadly recognized in the literature. But surprisingly, attention is largely limited to the cases that mark milestones of the integration process – supremacy, direct effect, state liability. However, if the Court is a motor, this must leave its mark in the multiple policy-processes that drive European integration along.

The case law on the four freedoms of goods, services, persons, and capital with its recent addition of citizenship rights is an important base, next to the provisions of competition law and non-discrimination. Member states may not discriminate against EU citizens based on nationality (or any other reasons, such as age), they also need overriding reasons to restrict their economic activities. And member states may not distort competition by granting special rights or subsidies, or by allowing collusion. By undermining national regulations, this negative integration of the Court sets incentives to member states to agree on secondary law in the Council, to achieve positive integration. Member states have difficulties to take back rulings of the Court. Moreover, in several examples where they have done so, and succeeded in agreeing on secondary law to rein in the Court, the latter has not heeded these rules. The Court is thus an important independent force in EU policy-making.

How relevant is this force? I have given several examples of policies that would not exist in this shape had there not been existing case law prefiguring choices and foreclosing policy options. The Court and its case law were important for the different policies building the single market, notably the liberalization policies. But is this important when regarding all EU policy-making? I would argue that this is a very important part of European integration, with repercussions on other policy fields due to the pervasive nature of the single market. As I have shown, defence procurement is now part of it, as are member states' welfare service to which EU citizens receive access, or their health systems that have to undergo far-reaching reforms because of the judicially enforced rights of patient mobility. And case law development continues, leading to further encroaches on member states' regulatory autonomy.

Thus, not only the single market but also social Europe is built with the help of the Court. Albeit, it is a peculiar social Europe, consisting of liberal, individual rights, of privileges for those being mobile, and of supranationally enforced duties of solidarity that lack the necessary underpinning of republican duties, shared identity and trust (Bellamy 2008; Menéndez 2009; Scharpf 2009).

Though the impact of the Court is broad, it is surprisingly absent from general analyses of EU policy-making and of the functioning of the EU legislature. Interest in the Court is focused on the Court and all too often clinging to the old controversy of whether member states can influence its rulings (Carrubba *et al.* 2008). Yet, as a multilevel polity the EU does not grant its member states exclusive access. The power of the Court relies on the system of preliminary references allowing private litigants indirect access to the Court, and building on the fact that many lower courts pursue policy interests via the EU level. Also policy positions of member states are compromises of conflicting interests – and some of these actors may forward their cause via European law. As case law of the Court, once it exists, becomes part of the *acquis communnautaire* and can hardly be altered, the ECJ is a much more important ally in policy-making than domestic courts can be on the national level. Rather than recognizing that the ECJ plays an important role comparable to constitutional courts in domestic systems, as concluded from the chapter on the ECJ in the last edition of this book (McCown 2006), I would conclude that it is pertinent to recognize that the balance of powers in a supranational polity is skewed, allowing courts to play a much more powerful role than in a domestic setting.

Notes

Research funding of the German Science Foundation through the CRC 597 Transformations of the State is gratefully acknowledged. I would like to thank Sascha Göbel for very able research assistance.
1   In fact, there are two treaties: the Treaty on European Union, dating from Maastricht, and the previous Treaty of Rome, now renamed into Treaty on the Functioning of the European Union (TFEU).
2   An example, discussed further later, is the cross-border provision of health care. The regulation here required an ex ante approval of the home state authorities for a reimbursement. The Court, in contrast, ruled that such a requirement contravenes the services freedom of the treaty in the case of ambulatory services.
3   This implies that references are not necessary when the interpretation of EU law is sufficiently clear and can be expected to be homogeneously applied across member states.
4   Interestingly, shortly afterwards in a referendum in November 1992, Irish voters passed amendments to the constitution, allowing to travel for an abortion and informing about this possibility. See Sterling (1997).
5   See http://ec.europa.eu/eu_law/docs/docs_infringements/sec_2005_1658_en.pdf. And for links to the relevant current documents, see http://ec.europa.eu/eu_law/infringements/infringements_260_en.htm.
6   Luxembourg 23.6.2008, 11062/08 (Presse 186): 'Council approves rules to improve free movement of goods in the EU', p. 2.
7   For the British system see http://www.rcseng.ac.uk/news/surgeons-call-for-solution-on-patient-safety-and-future-training-as-doctors-hours-are-slashed.
8   http://ec.europa.eu/social/main.jsp?catId=706&langId=en&intPageId=205.
9   Nowak criticizes that member states do not follow the interpretations of the Court but aim at modifications. But it is unclear why the rulings of the Court should be sacrosanct.
10   See Eising (2002) for an interpretation that discards such pressure and rather emphasizes learning processes in the Council leading France to give up its opposition.

References

Ackermann, T., Dougan, M., de la Rochère, J. D., Hillion, C., Jacqué, J.-P., Kuijper, P. J., Prechal, S., Roth, W.-H., Slot, P.J. and Winter, J.A. (2008) 'Editoral Comments. Towards an Improved Framework for Cross-border Healthcare', *Common Market Law Review* 45(5): 1325–33.

Alter, K. J. (1998) 'Who are the "Masters of the Treaty"?: European Governments and the European Court of Justice', *International Organization* 52(1): 121–47.

Alter, K. J. (2001) *Establishing the Supremacy of European Law – The Making of an International Rule of Law in Europe*, Oxford: Oxford University Press.

Alter, K. J. (2009) *The European Court's Political Power. Selected Essays*, Oxford: Oxford University Press.

Alter, K. J. and Meunier-Aitsahalia, S. (1994) 'Judicial Politics in the European Community. European Integration and the Pathbreaking Cassis de Dijon Decision', *Comparative Political Studies* 26(4): 535–61.

Alter, K. J. and Vargas, J. (2000) 'Explaining Variation in the Use of European Litigation Strategies. European Community Law and British Gender Equality Policy', *Comparative Political Studies* 33(4): 452–82.

Argyris, N. (1989) 'The EEC Rules of Competition and the Air Transport Sector', *Common Market Law Review* 26(5): 3–32.

Beach, D. (2001) 'Between Law and Politics: Taking the Law Seriously in Rationalist Models of Judicial Autonomy in the EU', paper presented at the ECSA Seventh Biennial International Conference, Madison, 31 May–2 June.

Bellamy, R. (2008) 'Evaluating Union Citizenship: Belongings, Rights and Participation within the EU', *Citizenship Studies* 12(6): 597–611.

Bignami, F. (2013) 'Rethinking the Legal Foundations of the European Constitutional Order: The Lessons of the New Historical Research', *American University International Law Review* 28(5): 1311–35.

Blauberger, M. and Weiss, M. (2013) '"If You Can't Beat Me, Join Me!" How the Commission Pushed and Pulled Member States into Legislating Defence Procurement', *Journal of European Public Policy* 20(8): 1120–38.

Bouwen, P. and McCown, M. (2007) 'Lobbying versus Litigation: Political and Legal Strategies of Interest Representation in the European Union', *Journal of European Public Policy* 14(3): 422–43.

Bulmer, S.J. (1994) 'Institutions and Policy Change in the European Communities: The Case of Merger Control', *Public Administration* 72(3): 423–44.

Burley, A.-M. and Mattli, W. (1993) 'Europe Before the Court: A Political Theory of Legal Integration', *International Organization* 47: 41–76.

Burri, S. and Prechal, S. (2010) *EU Gender Equality Law. Update 2010*, Brussels: European Commission.

Button, K. (1992) 'The Liberalization of Transport Services', in D. Swann (ed.), *The Single European Market and Beyond*, London: Routledge, pp. 146–61.

Caporaso, J.A. and Tarrow, S. (2009) 'Polanyi in Brussels: Supranational Institutions and the Transnational Embedding of Markets', *International Organization* 63(4): 593–620.

Cappelletti, M. (1987) 'Is the European Court of Justice "Running Wild"?', *European Law Review* 12: 3–17.

Carrubba, C. J., Gabel, M. and Hankla, C. (2008) 'Judicial Behavior under Political Constraints: Evidence from the European Court of Justice', *American Political Science Review* 102(4): 435–52.

Cichowski, R. A. (2004) 'Women's Rights, the European Court, and Supranational Constitutionalism', *Law & Society Review* 38(3): 489–512.

Cichowski, R. A. (2006) 'Courts, Rights, and Democratic Participation', *Comparative Political Studies* 39(1): 50–75.

Cichowski, R. A. (2007) *The European Court and Civil Society: Litigation, Mobilization and Governance*, Cambridge: Cambridge University Press.

Constantinesco, V. (2000) 'The ECJ as a Law-Maker: Praeter aut Contra Legem?', in D. O'Keeffe and A. Bavasso (eds.), *Judicial Review in European Union Law*, Vol. 1, The Hague: Kluwer Law International, pp. 73–80.

Court of Justice of the European Union (2013) 'Annual Report 2012', Luxembourg: Publications Office of the European Union, available at http://curia.europa.eu/jcms/upload/docs/applica tion/pdf/2013-04/192685_2012_6020_cdj_ra_2012_en_proof_01.pdf (accessed March 2013).

Crespy, A. (2010) 'When "Bolkestein" is trapped by the French Anti-Liberal Discourse: A Discursive-Institutionalist Account of Preference Formation in the Realm of European Union Multi-Level Politics', *Journal of European Public Policy* 17(8): 1253–70.

Crespy, A. and Gajewska, K. (2010) 'New Parliament, New Cleavages after the Eastern Enlargement? The Conflict over the Services Directive as an Opposition between the Liberals and the Regulators', *Journal of Common Market Studies* 48(5): 1185–208.

Davies, B. (2012) *Resisting the European Court of Justice. West Germany's Confrontation with European Law, 1949–1979*, Cambridge: Cambridge University Press.

Davies, G. (2007) *Services, Citizenship, and the Country of Origin Principle*, Edinburgh: Edinburgh Europa Institute.

Davies, G. (2012) 'Activism Relocated. The Self-Restraint of the European Court of Justice in Its National Context', *Journal of European Public Policy* 19(1): 76–91.

Dyevre, A. (2010) 'Unifying the Field of Comparative Judicial Politics: Towards a General Theory of Judicial Behaviour', *European Political Science Review* 2(2): 297–327.

Eeckhout, P. (1998) 'The European Court of Justice and the Legislature', in P. Eeckhout and T. Tridimas (eds), *Yearbook of the European Law*, Oxford: Oxford University Press, pp. 1–28.

Eichener, V. (1997) 'Effective European Problem-solving: Lessons from the Regulation of Occupational Safety and Environmental Protection', *Journal of European Public Policy* 4(4): 591–608.

Eising, R. (2002) 'Policy Learning in Embedded Negotiations: Explaining EU Electricity Liberalization', *International Organization* 56(1): 85–120.

European Commission (2007) *Handbook on the Implementation of the Services Directive*, Luxembourg: Office for Official Publications of the European Communities, available at http://ec.europa.eu/internal_market/services/docs/services-dir/guides/handbook_en.pdf (accessed 8 March 2013).

Garrett, G. (1995) 'The Politics of Legal Integration in the European Union', *International Organization* 49(1): 171–81.

Golub, J. (1996) 'The Politics of Judicial Discretion: Rethinking the Interaction between National Courts and the European Court of Justice', *West European Politics* 19(2): 360–85.

Granger, M.-P. (2004) 'When Governments Go to Luxembourg . . . : The Influence of Governments on the Court of Justice', *European Law Review* 29(1): 3–31.

Greer, S. (2012) 'Polity-making without Policy-making: European Union Healthcare Services Policy', in J. Richardson (ed.), *Constructing a Policy-Making State? Policy Dynamics in the EU*, Oxford: Oxford University Press, pp. 271–91.

Hargreaves, S. (2011) *EU Law Concentrate. Law Revision and Study Guide*, Oxford: Oxford University Press.

Hartley, T. (2010) *The Foundations of European Union Law*, Oxford: Oxford University Press.

Hix, S. and Høyland, B. (2011) *The Political System of the European Union*, Basingstoke: Palgrave Macmillan.

Hofmann, A. (2013) *Strategies of the Repeat Player – The European Commission between Courtroom and Legislature*, Berlin: epubli GmbH.

Höpner, M. and Schäfer, A. (2012) 'Embeddedness and Regional Integration. Waiting for Polanyi in a Hayekian Setting', *International Organization* 66(3): 429–55.

Hoskyns, C. (1996) *Integrating Gender. Women, Law and Politics in the European Union*, London/New York: Verso.

Hubschmid, C. and Moser, P. (1997) 'The Co-operation Procedure in the EU: Why was the European Parliament Influential in the Decision on Car Emission Standards?', *Journal of Common Market Studies* 35(2): 225–42.

Kelemen, R. D. (2001) 'The Limits of Judicial Power: Trade-Environment Disputes in the GATT/WTO and the EU', *Comparative Political Studies* 34(6): 622–50.

Kelemen, R. D. (2011) *Eurolegalism. The Transformation of Law and Regulation in the European Union*, Cambridge: Harvard University Press.

Kelemen, R. D. (2012) 'The Political Foundations of Judicial Independence in the European Union', *Journal of European Public Policy* 19(1): 43–58.

Kloka, M. (2013) 'Business as usual? Negotiation Dynamics and Legislative Performance in the Council of the European Union after the Eastern Enlargement', unpublished Ph.D. dissertation, Bremen International Graduate School of Social Sciences.

Krajewski, M. (2010) 'Grenzüberschreitende Patientenmobilität in Europa zwischen negativer und positiver Integration der Gesundheitssysteme', *Europarecht* 45(2): 165–87.

Lenaerts, K., Arts, D., Maselis, I. and Bray, R. (2006) *Procedural Law of the European Union*, London: Sweet & Maxwell.

Majone, G. (1992) 'Market Integration and Regulation: Europe after 1992', *Metroeconomica* 43: 131–56.

Malecki, M. (2012) 'Do ECJ Judges All Speak with the Same Voice? Evidence of Divergent Preferences from the Judgements of Chambers', *Journal of European Public Policy* 19(1): 59–75.

Mancini, G. F. (1989) 'The Making of a Constitution for Europe', *Common Market Law Review* 26: 595–614.

Martinsen, D. S. (2005a) 'Social Security Regulation in the EU. The De-Territorialization of Welfare?', in G. De Búrca (ed.), *EU Law and the Welfare State. In Search of Solidarity*, New York: Oxford University Press, pp. 89–110.

Martinsen, D. S. (2005b) 'Towards an Internal Health Market with the European Court', *West European Politics* 28(5): 1035–56.

Martinsen, D. S. and Falkner, G. (2011) 'Social Policy: Problem-Solving Gaps, Partial Exits, and Court-Decision Traps', in G. Falkner (ed.), *The EU's Decision Traps*, New York: Oxford University Press, pp. 128–44.

Mazey, S. (2012) 'Policy Entrepreneurship, Group Mobilization, and the Creation of a New Policy Domain: Women's Rights and the European Union', in J. Richardson (ed.), *Constructing a Policy-Making State? Policy Dynamics in the EU*, Oxford: Oxford University Press, pp. 126–43.

McCown, M. (2006) 'Judicial Law-making and European Integration: the European Court of Justice', in J. Richardson (ed.), *European Union: Power and Policy-making*, Abingdon: Routledge, pp. 171–85.

Menéndez, A. J. (2009) *European Citizenship after Martínez Sala and Baumbast. Has European Law Become More Human but Less Social?*, Oslo: Arena Centre for European Studies University of Oslo.

Miklin, E. (2009) 'Government Positions on the EU Services Directive in the Council: National Interests or Individual Ideological Preferences?', *West European Politics* 32(5): 943–62.

More, G. (1991) 'Severance Pay for Part-Time Workers', *European Law Review* 16: 58–64.

Nowak, T. (2008) 'The Working Time Directive and the European Court of Justice', *Maastricht Journal of European and Comparative Law* 15(4): 447–71.

Nyikos, S. A. (2006) 'Strategic Interaction among Courts within the Preliminary Reference Process – Stage 1: National Court Preemptive Opinions', *European Journal of Political Research* 45(4): 527–50.

Obermaier, A. J. (2009) *The End of Territoriality?: The Impact of ECJ Rulings on British, German and French Social Policy*, Surrey: Ashgate Publishing.

Oliver, P. and Roth, W.-H. (2004) 'The Internal Market and the Four Freedoms', *Common Market Law Review* 41(2): 407–41.

Pescatore, P. (1983) 'La carence du législateur communautaire et le devoir du juge', in G. Lüke, G. Ress and M. R. Will (eds), *Rechtsvergleichung – Gedächtnisschrift für Léontin-Jean Constantinesco*, Köln/Berlin/Bonn/München: Heymanns, pp. 559–80.

Pierson, P. (1996) 'The Path to European Integration: A Historical Institutionalist Perspective', *Comparative Political Studies* 29(2): 123–63.

Pollack, M. A. (1996) 'The New Institutionalism and EC Governance: The Promise and Limits of Institutional Analysis', *Governance* 9(4): 429–85.

Pollack, M. A. (2013) 'The New EU Legal History: What's New, What's Missing?', *American University International Law Review* 28(5): 1257–310.

Scharpf, F. W. (2006) 'The Joint-Decision Trap Revisited', *Journal of Common Market Studies* 44(4): 845–64.

Scharpf, F. W. (2009) 'Legitimacy in the Multilevel European Polity', *European Political Science Review* 1(2): 173–204.

Scharpf, F. W. (2010) 'The asymmetry of European Integration, or Why the EU Cannot be a 'Social Market Economy'', *Socio-Economic Review* 8(2): 211–50.

Schepel, H. and Wesseling, R. (1997) 'The Legal Community: Judges, Lawyers, Officials, and Clerks in the Writing of Europe', *European Law Journal* 3(2): 165–88.

Schmidt, S. K. (2000) 'Only an Agenda Setter? The European Commission's Power over the Council of Ministers', *European Union Politics* 1(1): 37–61.

Schmidt, S. K. (2007) 'Mutual Recognition as a New Mode of Governance', *Journal of European Public Policy* 14(5): 667–81.

Schmidt, S. K. (2008) 'Research Note: Beyond Compliance. The Europeanization of Member States through Negative Integration and Legal Uncertainty', *Journal of Comparative Policy Analysis* 10(3): 299–308.

Schmidt, S. K. (2009) 'When Efficiency Results in Redistribution. The Conflict over the Single Services Market', *West European Politics* 32(4): 847–65.

Schmidt, S. K. (2011a) 'Law-Making in the Shadow of Judicial Politics', in R. Dehousse (ed.), *The "Community Method": Obstinate or Obsolete?*, Basingstoke: Palgrave Macmillan, pp. 43–59.

Schmidt, S. K. (2011b) 'Overcoming the Joint-Decision Trap in Single-Market Legislation: The Interplay between Judicial and Legislative Politics', in G. Falkner (ed.), *The EU's Decision Traps*, New York: Oxford University Press, pp. 38–53.

Schmidt, S. K. (2012) 'Who cares about Nationality? The Path-Dependent Case Law of the ECJ from Goods to Citizens', *Journal of European Public Policy* 19(1): 8–24.

Schütze, R. (2006) 'Supremacy without Pre-emption? The Very Slowly Emergent Doctrine of Community Pre-emption', *Common Market Law Review* 43(4): 1023–48.

Slepcevic, R. (2009) 'The Judicial Enforcement of EU Law through National Courts: Possibilities and Limits', *Journal of European Public Policy* 16(3): 378–94.

Solanke, I. (2011) ''Stop the ECJ'?: An Empirical Analysis of Activism at the Court', *European Law Journal* 17(6): 764–84.

Stein, E. (1981) 'Lawyers, Judges, and the Making of a Transnational Constitution', *American Journal of International Law* 75(1): 1–27.

Stein, T. (1986) 'Richterrecht wie anderswo auch? Der Gerichtshof der Europäischen Gemeinschaften als "Integrationsmotor"', in Hochschullehrer der Juristischen Fakultät der Universität Heidelberg (ed.), *Richterliche Fortbildung. Erscheinungsformen Auftrag und Grenzen, Festschrift zur 600-Jahr-Feier der Ruprechts-Karls-Universität Heidelberg*, Heidelberg: Müller Juristischer Verlag, pp. 619–41.

Sterling, A.-M.E.W. (1997) 'The European Union and Abortion Tourism: Liberalizing Ireland's Abortion Law', *Boston College International and Comparative Law Review* 20(2): 385–406.

Stone Sweet, A. (1999) 'Judicialization and the Construction of Governance', *Comparative Political Studies* 32(2): 147–84.

Stone Sweet, A. and Cichowski, R. (2004) 'Sex Equality', in A. Stone Sweet (ed.), *The Judicial Construction of Europe*, Oxford: Oxford University Press, pp. 147–98.

Stone Sweet, A. and Stranz, K. (2012) 'Rights Adjudication and Constitutional Pluralism in Germany and Europe', *Journal of European Public Policy* 19(1): 92–108.

Tallberg, J. (2000) 'Supranational Influence in EU Enforcement: The ECJ and the Principle of State Liability', *Journal of European Public Policy* 7(1): 104–21.

Thomson, R. (2011) *Resolving Controversy in the European Union. Legislative Decision-Making before and after Enlargement*, Cambridge: Cambridge University Press.

van de Gronden, J. W. (2009) 'Cross-border Health Care in the EU and the Organization of the National Health Care Systems of the Member States: The Dynamics Resulting from the European Court of Justice's Decisions on Free Movement and Competition Law', *Wisconsin International Law Journal* 26(3): 705–60.

Vauchez, A. (2010) 'The Transnational Politics of Judicialization. Van Gend en Loos and the Making of EU Polity', *European Law Journal* 16(1): 1–28.

Vauchez, A. (2012) 'Keeping the Dream Alive: The European Court of Justice and the Transnational Fabric of Integrationist Jurisprudence', *European Political Science Review* 4(1): 51–71.

Wasserfallen, F. (2010) 'The Judiciary as Legislator? How the European Court of Justice Shapes Policy-making in the European Union', *Journal of European Public Policy* 17(8): 1128–46.

Weiler, J.H.H. (1981) 'The Community System: The Dual Character of Supranationalism', *Yearbook of European Law* 1: 267–306.

Weiler, J.H.H. (1986) 'Eurocracy and Distrust: Some Questions Concerning the Role of the European Court of Justice in the Protection of Fundamental Human Rights within the Legal Order of the European Communities', *Washington Law Review* 61: 1103–42.

Weiler, J.H.H. (1991) 'The Transformation of Europe', *The Yale Law Journal* 100(1): 2402–83.

Weiler, J.H.H. (1994) 'A Quiet Revolution. The European Court of Justice and Its Interlocutors', *Comparative Political Studies* 26(4): 510–34.

Wind, M. (2009) 'Post-National Citizenship in Europe: The EU as a "Welfare Rights Generator"?', *The Columbia Journal of European Law* 15(2): 239–64.

Wind, M. (2010) 'The Nordics, the EU and the Reluctance Towards Supranational Judicial Review', *Journal of Common Market Studies* 48(4): 1039–63.

Witte, B. de (2007) *Setting the Scene: How Did Services Get to Bolkestein*, Edinburgh: Edinburgh Europa Institute.

Young, A.R. (1994) *Interests and Institutions: The Politics of Liberalisation in the EC's Road Haulage Industry*, Brighton: University of Sussex.

Zürn, M. and Wolf, D. (2000) 'Europarecht und internationale Regime: zu den Merkmalen von Recht jenseits des Nationalstaates', in E. Grande and M. Jachtenfuchs (eds), *Wie problemlösungsfähig ist die EU? Regieren im europäischen Mehrebenensysten*, Baden-Baden: Nomos, pp. 113–40.

Chapter 8

The distribution of power among the institutions

ROBERT THOMSON

What is power?

Political science is largely devoted to studying power. What is power, of what is it composed, and what are its causes and effects? These are some of the central questions political scientists try to answer for the political systems on which they focus. The most frequently cited definitions of politics highlight the centrality of power. For David Easton, politics is the 'authoritative allocation of values' (1953: 129). In other words, politics involves some 'authority' wielding the power to hand out things that others value. These allocations include the allocation of tangible resources, such as public funds, as well as decisions on a range of other things, such as the contents of legal acts, which may be more or less congruent with various stakeholders' preferences. In another classic definition, Harold Laswell (1936) defined politics as 'who gets what, when, and how'. Laswell's definition also focuses on the distribution of benefits and costs among the members of a society or political system. The distribution of benefits and costs often involve competition and conflict, which means that the relative power of relevant stakeholders and decision-makers is crucial in determining who gets what.

While power has been the object of systematic inquiry for over a century, it remains a contested and oftentimes poorly understood concept, and debates frequently occur on who wields power in any given political system. The European Union (EU) is no exception, because political analysts hold a range of views on the distribution of power among the main institutional actors involved in political decision-making: the European Commission, the European Parliament and the Council. Who has power in the EU matters a great deal. As the farthest-reaching form of international cooperation that presently exists in the world, it is important to understand how this political system works, and no understanding of a political system can neglect the question of who has power. Who has power in the EU matters to citizens, because EU laws affect a broad range of policies. EU laws consist of thousands of common rules regarding standards for products and services, including food, telecommunications and banking. EU laws protect workers' rights, including maternity leave, health and safety conditions and anti-discrimination. The EU also allocates significant amounts of public funds to agriculture, research and regional development. The contents of these common rules and decisions are affected by the distribution of power in the EU. Therefore, to explain how these common rules came about, and to influence future decisions, citizens and stakeholders need an informed answer to the question of who has power.

Uncertainty regarding the distribution of power in the EU is partly because the balance of power among EU institutions has been changing over time and partly because some analyses are not based on a clear understanding of how to conceptualize and assess power appropriately. Journalists and practitioners naturally focus on specific and prominent examples when making their assessments of who has power, but this approach is of limited use in providing a well-founded assessment. For instance, in February 2010 the EP rejected an agreement between the EU and the United States on the transfer of banking information on people living in the EU to the US authorities in the so-called SWIFT case. The EP argued that the agreement did not contain adequate data protection requirements. This was the first time the EP used a new power it had been given in the Lisbon Treaty, which came into effect in December 2009, to block such agreements. The former Belgian prime minister Guy Verhofstadt, an MEP in the liberal ALDE group, described the EP's rejection as 'historic' and said that 'the main reason for the rejection was the fact that the European Council did not meet the guarantees that [EP] President Buzek asked for in his letters to the Presidency of the Council' (*Agence Europe*, 12 February 2010). The agreement was subsequently renegotiated taking into account the EP's concerns. Proponents of the view that the EP carries considerable clout often hold up the SWIFT case and cases like it, in which the EP appears to have influenced decision outcomes decisively. But to what extent do such cases reflect the general balance of power among EU institutions? Perhaps the emphasis placed on such cases is a reflection of some MEPs' desire to appear more important than they actually are, of the Commission and Council's desire to make the EP appear more powerful than it actually is thereby diminishing demands for real power for the EP, or even of researchers' unconscious desire to make the object of their study appear more powerful than it actually is. For every apparent success story that suggests a powerful EP we can also identify an apparent failure. For instance, in a case related thematically to the SWIFT case, in April 2012 the EP approved an agreement between the EU and the United States on sharing airline passengers' data with US authorities. Commenting on this approval, Guy Verhofstadt said, 'Liberals and Democrats strongly believe that this new agreement does not meet the minimum criteria outlined by the Parliament in 2011 and that it is not in line with EU legislation on data privacy' (*EurActiv*, 19 April 2012). Some pundits consider the EP to be ineffective; a respected weekly newspaper even refers dismissively to 'the useless European Parliament' (*The Economist*, 17 September 2011).

Given that anecdotes and observers' impressions are unable to provide a satisfactory analysis of the relative power of the Commission, Council and EP, a different approach is required. The approach applied in this chapter has distinct conceptual and empirical parts to it. The conceptual part reviews the main relevant definitions of power that can inform our assessment of the relative power of the institutions in the EU. The empirical part reviews the results of some relevant systematic qualitative and quantitative evidence on the relative power of the institutions. Specific cases are used to illustrate points but not to draw conclusions about the balance of power among the institutions. In this chapter legislative decision-making is discussed, because legislation has a marked effect on citizens' lives by regulating a range of policy areas, but non-legislative decision-making is also considered because this is of particular relevance in the context of the recent financial crisis. We consider both the decision-making stage in which decision makers discuss proposals that are on the agenda and the preparatory or agenda-setting stage in which issues are framed and placed on the agenda.

Definitions of power

Almost 100 years ago Max Weber, the famous German social scientist and founder of modern sociology, defined power as the potential a person or group has 'to realize their own will in a social action even against the resistance of others' (1914/2007: 247). This simple definition holds a number of insights that are highlighted by later definitions and discussions of power. First, Weber's definition implies that the focus of power is on influencing 'social' or collective actions. In the context of the policy-making in the EU, this implies that the focus of power is on influencing the contents of EU policies, including the contents of legislative acts. Influencing other actors may be an important means to the end of influencing EU policies, but this is not always necessary. By contrast, Dahl's frequently cited definition of power focuses on interactions between actors, rather than outcomes: actor 'A has power over [actor] B to the extent that he can get B to do something that B would not otherwise do' (1957: 203). Depending on the decision rule, it is not always necessary for actor A to convince B to change its behaviour for A to influence decision outcomes. For instance, under the ordinary legislative procedure (called co-decision before the Lisbon Treaty), the Commission formally introduces a legislative proposal, but the Council and EP could in principle change the legislative proposal and adopt an act that the Commission does not support. Therefore, it is not necessary for the Council and EP to change the Commission's behaviour to influence the decision outcome. Despite this important distinction between the definitions of power offered by Weber and Dahl, they share a 'kind of forward-looking intentionality' (Mansbridge 2003: 516). For both Weber and Dahl, people act purposefully when they exercise power with a view to influencing future events.

The important distinction between power and luck is also implicit in Weber's classic definition. The clause 'even against the resistance of others' implies that sometimes actors may realize their preferences without having power. A decision outcome might be the same as the policy position of an actor with little or no power, simply because other powerful actors also took that position, or because that position was an obvious compromise among the positions of other powerful actors. Likewise, the decision outcome might differ from a powerful actor's policy position; perhaps the powerful actor did not care much about the issue; perhaps the decision outcome would have been even farther from the powerful actor's position if that actor had not exercised its power. Barry's famous discussion of power distinguishes between power and luck when examining the agreement between actors' preferences and outcomes:

> If an individual's power is defined as his ability to change outcomes from what they would otherwise have been in the direction he desires, the likelihood of outcomes corresponding to his desires does not depend solely on his power. In addition to his power, it depends on what the outcomes would have been in the absence of his intervention. This is what I shall call luck.
>
> (Barry 1980: 184)

To assess what the decision outcome would have been without the intervention of the political actors we are interested in, we require information on the policy demands of other relevant actors and on how hard they pushed these demands. This is why much of the anecdotal evidence on the power of EU institutions, particularly the EP, is unsatisfactory. The fact that the EP 'got its way' in a particular case does not in itself imply that the EP was powerful in that case. To make such an inference we would also require information on whether competing policy demands were made by other institutions.

By defining power as the 'chance' or probability an actor has to influence outcomes, Weber suggests that power is an attribute, rather than something that is always put into effect, and even when it is put into effect, it does not necessarily achieve the desired result. Whether an actor's power is put into effect or lies dormant depends on the actor's decision on whether to use its power. Some rational choice models of collective decision-making formalize this idea as the distinction between power and influence (Bueno de Mesquita and Stokman 1994; Thomson *et al.* 2006). Power is the potential or capability an actor has to influence other actors and decision outcomes. Influence is the proportion of that potential an actor puts into effect on a given controversial issue. The proportion it will use depends on the salience the actor attaches to the issue.

Weber's definition does not list the factors that contribute to power. However, his discussion of power distinguished itself from Marxist approaches of his day that equated economic power with political power. For Weber, a broad range of resources, not only economic ones, contribute to an actor's power. The relevance of a resource depends on the context in which the controversy occurs. Relevant resources in everyday EU negotiations include the rights an actor receives from the formal decision-making procedures. For example, the EP clearly has more power under the ordinary legislative procedure than under the consultation procedure. In the Council, large member states hold more votes than do small member states, which may give their policy positions more weight in the decision-making process. Timely access to policy relevant information and expertise is also a relevant resource, since it allows actors to make a more convincing case for the policy demands they express. Actors with strong relationships with other actors, so-called network capital (Naurin and Lindhal 2008), also hold a valuable resource, since this allows them to access others through informal channels. If power is conceived of as a set of resources, then different actors may have a similar level of power based on different kinds of resources.

Notwithstanding the conceptual clarity Weber offers us, his definition of power is of limited relevance to analysing the formative or agenda-setting stage of the policy-making process. Defining power as 'realizing one's will even against the resistance from others' focuses our attention on the ways in which explicit controversies are resolved. This obviously implies that there are certain issues on the agenda to be resolved in the first place. Power is also exercised in selecting issues for inclusion on the agenda. Bachrach and Baratz (1970) were among the first political scientists to focus systematically on the agenda-setting stage and to note that non-decisions are at least as important as manifestations of power as decisions. Lukes's (1974) definition of power is also broader than the Weberian definition; it too encompasses agenda-setting power and adds power to the ability to shape other actors' preferences or their perceptions of their own interests. In the EU, most of the agenda-setting stage in legislative politics takes place before the legislative proposal is formulated (Princen 2009). While it may be possible to add relevant issues to the agenda after a legislative proposal has been tabled, the issues included in that proposal must be addressed. The general view is that the European Commission and European Council, composed of heads of state and government, play the most prominent roles during this agenda-setting stage.

In contrast to our focus on how the contemporary system of decision-making works, theories of European integration focus on the development of the system over time. This is a distinct focus but one that is somewhat relevant to the present chapter in that these theories also touch upon the relative power of supranational and governmental actors. One of the earliest theories of European integration, neofunctionalism (Haas 1958; Lindberg 1963; Schmitter 1969), gives an account in which cooperation in one area creates demands for cooperation in other related areas. Integration, therefore, occurs though a process of 'spillover' from one area to another. Neofunctionalism attributes important roles to non-state actors, including the supranational Commission, in realizing demands for integration. This theory is still a reference point for contemporary integration theorists, particularly for those who stress the impact of supranational institutions on the integration process (e.g. Sandholtz and Stone Sweet 1998). However, neofunctionalism has largely been discarded, even by its original proponents (Haas 1975), mainly because it failed to account for the stalling of the European integration process in the 1970s. Regarding the analysis of the current decision-making system, neofunctionalism emphasizes the distinct role and power of the Commission.

Various strands of intergovernmentalism are the main alternatives to neofunctionalism in explaining the course of European integration. Hoffmann (1966) interpreted European integration as a process driven by member states' interests in cooperation, rather than by supranational or non-state actors' interests. Milward's (1992) historical research on the early stages of European integration confirmed the paramount importance of hard bargaining among national governments that were motivated by the pursuit of self-interest, not the supranational actors and ideals emphasized by neofunctionalists. Moravcsik's (1998) liberal intergovernmental theory of integration builds on this intergovernmental tradition. Liberal intergovernmentalism links a theory of national preference formation with a theory of interstate bargaining. The intergovernmental perspective has implications for some aspects of contemporary decision-making. For instance, it leads us to expect that national interests pervade what are supposedly supranational institutions, that member states' policy demands are motivated by domestic interests rather than lofty European ideals and that member states dominate the decision-making process. However, like other integration theorists, intergovernmental theorists are more concerned with explaining the milestones that mark changes to the system, rather than how the present policy-making system works.

These alternative definitions of power make clear that we must consider both the formal and informal sources of power. Therefore, the following section begins this analysis by describing the relative power of the Commission, EP and Council in legislative decision-making based on the treaty rules that set out the main decision-making procedures. While acknowledging the effects of procedural rules on these institutional actors' relative power, the subsequent sections explore other perspectives on the relative power of the institutions. These other perspectives include a consideration of the agenda-setting stage, as well as the possibility that the actual distribution of power differs significantly from the distribution of power suggested by procedural rules. The closing sections of this chapter examine variation in the relative power of the institutions depending on the individuals involved, policy areas and types of issues being dealt with, and the broader context in which policy-making takes place.

Treaty rules and inter-institutional power

Institutions both constrain and empower policymakers, whether the policymakers concerned are Commissioners, MEPs, representatives of member states, or judges. EU practitioners think of institutions as being the main EU bodies, such as the Commission, EP and Council. By contrast, political scientists generally think of institutions more broadly as 'humanly devised constraints that structure political, economic and social interaction' (North 1991: 97). These humanly devised constraints include formal institutions, such as the treaty rules governing the ordinary legislative procedure and voting rules in the Council. They also consist of informal institutions, such as informal norms of behaviour that guide politicians' conduct in early agreements between the EP and

Council. Institutional power therefore depends on how such formal and informal institutional constraints affect political actors' ability to set the agenda and realize their own policy preferences in the face of competing preferences.

The fact that institutions are humanly devised means that they reflect the relative power and preferences of those who designed them; in other words, institutions are 'best seen as congealed tastes' (Riker 1980: 445). The formal rules that govern the EU's policymaking process, including the roles of the supranational Commission and EP relative to the intergovernmental Council, are set out in the treaties. Since member states were the main actors in negotiating these treaties in the intergovernmental conferences in which they were agreed, the formal rules set out in the treaties reflect member states' power and preferences. The level of formal institutional power given to the supranational Commission and EP in the treaties varies by policy area. A large role is given to the supranational Commission and EP in an increasing number of policy areas under the EU's jurisdiction. This is the case for most areas of regulatory policy-making, which includes managing the single market and competition, agriculture and even sensitive areas such as asylum and immigration. This means that the Commission has the right to initiate detailed proposals and the EP and the Council have equal potential to amend and must both approve these proposals in a bicameral procedure (the ordinary legislative procedure). The supranational ECJ also has full powers of judicial review in these areas. In other areas, the intergovernmental Council remains the main policy-making body. This is the case for most macroeconomic policies, which are particularly relevant for eurozone countries, much of external affairs, long-term expenditure policies (in the form of the multiannual financial frameworks), as well as police and judicial cooperation. In these policy areas the Commission plays a less prominent role in initiating new policies, the EP is only consulted, and the ECJ's powers are limited.

The theorists of European integration referred to above have debated why member states would give such a prominent role to the supranational institutions in an increasing number of policy areas under the EU's jurisdiction. Liberal international relations theorists attribute this expansion to a convergence among national governments' policy preferences and the outcomes of political agreements reached among different governments (Moravcsik 1998). In short, national governments agree to give more institutional power to supranational actors when their policy preferences converge. A related explanation refers to the delegation of power as a way of making credible commitments (Majone 2001; Pollack 2003); national governments may wish to commit themselves to a particular principle or goal in the long run, in the knowledge that their own or future governments' short-run incentives may lead them to adopt policies that are not in line with such a commitment. A solution to this problem is to delegate authority to an independent agent. For instance, governments may wish to commit themselves to the principle of a fair and free market, while they are aware that they may come under pressure in the future to pursue parochial protectionist policies that favour national industries. One way of committing credibly in this situation is to grant the Commission considerable formal institutional power to govern the internal market. From these perspectives, although supranational institutions have power, member states are the source of this power. By contrast, historical institutionalists argue that such power relations develop over time through a process of path dependency and are not an intentional choice on the part of national governments (for a review of different institutionalist approaches to European integration, see Aspinwall and Schneider 2000).

There is an additional argument for granting formal power to the EP. As the only institution in the EU with members directly elected by citizens, a powerful EP is an important part of the EU's democratic infrastructure of checks and balances. Part of the argument for having a powerful EP is that the EU has been given competency over policy areas that were previously controlled by national political systems (Lodge 1994: 82–3). In national political systems, parliamentarians check the power of their national governments. Without a strong EP, the transfer of policy competencies to the EU level would mean that governing executives are subject to less control than they previously were in national arenas.

Although national governments supported EU treaties that gave more formal powers to the EU's supranational institutions, the future effects of such treaty rules are not always clear at the time they are granted. This is particularly true when national governments do not know what issues will be on the agenda in a few years' time and what their and their European partners' policy preferences will be on these issues. Some political scientists have specified models of the EU's legislative procedures to examine the effects of successive changes to the EU's decision-making rules on the balance of power among the institutions (e.g. Steunenberg 1994; Tsebelis 1994; Crombez 1996). Formal rules stipulate which actors can introduce proposals, which actors can amend proposals, and the levels of support required for proposals and amendments to be accepted. When one of the institutions is given power to introduce policy proposals, referred to as 'the agenda setter', procedural models assume that the agenda setter will use the formal rules to ensure that decision outcomes are as close as possible to its policy preferences. Procedural models are a useful point of reference for studying the extent to which the practice of politics in the EU differs from the formal rules laid down in the EU treaties and are introduced next.

The value of the disagreement outcome to the decision makers is a key concept in all procedural models. The value that an actor attaches to the disagreement outcome is the value or utility that the actor receives in the event of the failure to adopt a policy proposal, for instance a legislative proposal introduced by the Commission. The disagreement outcome is the scenario in which the proposal is not passed, which often means that the status quo continues. The value actors attach to the disagreement outcome is affected not only by value they attach to the proposal under consideration but also by the effect failure to agree has on the long-term relationships among political actors. For procedural models, the disagreement outcome is a key concept, because it determines whether actors will be willing to reject a proposed outcome.

Consider first the simplest of the EU's legislative procedures, the consultation procedure combined with unanimity voting in the Council of Ministers. Here, the Commission introduces a proposal and the member states must approve it unanimously. The member states may also amend the Commission's proposal by unanimity. The formal rules of decision-making in relation to the consultation procedure are relatively simple, and there is little room for different interpretations of this procedure (Crombez 1996). Since the EP gives only a non-binding opinion in the consultation procedure, the game is reduced to an interaction between the Commission and member states.

The top part of Figure 8.1 gives a stylized illustration of the procedural model's prediction of the decision outcome on an issue subject to consultation and unanimity voting in the Council. The policy space is represented as a unidimensional scale of policy alternatives with actors placed on these alternatives to indicate their policy preferences.

Each actor has a single-peaked preference function, which means that it derives less utility from decision outcomes further away from its preference. Figure 8.1 considers a policy scale, ranging from 0 to 100, on which the Commission takes an extreme policy position, at position 100. One might think of this as a range of policy alternatives from less to more harmonization of a particular policy area. The disagreement outcome is located at position 0 on the scale. Suppose that the member states' policy preferences are distributed between positions 10 and 100 of the policy scale. The alignment of actors in Figure 8.1 is not part of the model; it is for illustrative purposes only, and the model could generate a prediction of the decision outcome for any alignment of actors' policy preferences.

The concept of pivotal positions is central to all procedural models. Which position is pivotal depends on the decision-making rule that applies and the distribution of actors' policy preferences relative to the disagreement outcome. In Figure 8.1, the actor whose position is farthest from the Commission and closest to the disagreement outcome is located at position 10. Therefore, position 10 is referred to as the unanimity pivot, denoted P_U in Figure 8.1. The location of the unanimity pivot defines the range of potential decision outcomes that all member states prefer to the disagreement outcome. This range of outcomes is referred to as the unanimity winset. If the disagreement outcome is located at position 0 and the unanimity pivot is at position 10, then the unanimity winset is the range between positions 0 and 20. If the Commission were to introduce a policy proposal anywhere in this range, all member states would prefer it to the disagreement outcome. Since the Commission aims to realize decision outcomes that are as close as possible to its own policy preference, it will select the policy proposal in this range that is closest to its preference. Therefore, the procedural model's prediction of the decision outcome is 20. Stated more generally, when the consultation procedure is combined with unanimity voting in the Council, the decision outcome will be the policy position within the unanimity winset that is closest to the Commission's preference.

The procedural model of the consultation procedure combined with qualified majority voting (QMV) in the Council is a little more complex. Again, the Commission introduces the legislative proposal, but now the Council must either approve the proposal with a qualified majority of member states or amend it with the support of all member states. The rules for qualified majority voting differ between the EU-15 and the post-2004 peri-

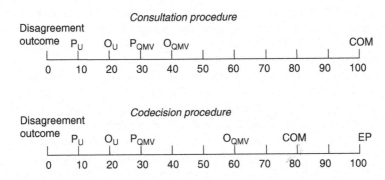

Figure 8.1 Predictions of a procedural model

Source: Adapted from Tsebelis and Garrett (2000) and König and Proksch (2006).

ods, and the Lisbon Treaty introduced a new version of QMV. From 2014, decisions taken by QMV need the approval of 55 per cent of member states, currently 16 of 28 EU members, which make up 65 per cent of the combined total of EU states' populations. To prevent a small number of large states from blocking a decision, the population criterion only applies if at least four member states are against adoption. If only three or fewer states oppose the adoption of a bill, the population criterion will not apply, even if these states have more than 35 per cent of the EU's population. The new system will come into effect gradually. In the first three years after its introduction in 2014, any member state can request that a decision be taken according to the Nice triple-majority rules. The QMV pivot refers to the location of the preference of the member state or states that turn a losing minority into a blocking minority, when counting votes from the state furthest from the agenda setter. Suppose that the member states to the left of position 30 in Figure 8.1 do not control enough votes to block a decision. Furthermore, suppose that with the addition of the votes of the country or countries located at position 30, the states to the left of position 30 control a blocking minority. This makes position 30 the QMV pivot, labelled P_{QMV} in Figure 8.1. If position 30 is the QMVpivot, then the range of positions between position 0 and position 60 is the QMV winset. All the potential outcomes in this range are preferred to the disagreement outcome by a group of member states that controls at least a qualified majority.

When formulating the content of its legislative proposal, the Commission attempts to introduce a proposal that will not be amended by the Council. Since the Council can amend a proposal unanimously, this means that the Commission must also consider the location of the unanimity winset, even when the QMV rule applies. The Commission can secure a decision outcome by introducing a proposal such that the actor (or actors) located at the QMV pivot is indifferent between the Commission's proposal and the possible unanimously supported amendment by the Council. This is position 40 on the top of Figure 8.1. Note that this point is as far from the QMV pivot as the predicted decision outcome under unanimity. This is how the agenda setter is given power by the formal procedural rules.

In contrast to the consultation procedure, procedural modellers have offered competing interpretations of the ordinary legislative procedure (the co-decision procedure before the Lisbon Treaty). In this procedure the Commission introduces a proposal that must be approved by both the Council and the EP, and the Council and the EP formally have equal power as co-legislators. After two readings of a proposal in both the Council and EP, in which neither institution fully accepts the amendments proposed by the other, a conciliation committee composed of representatives of the Council and the EP is formed. This committee then works on a text that must be approved by both if the legislative proposal is to be passed.

Disagreements on how to best model the ordinary legislative procedure focus mainly on the questions of whether the Commission is involved and which actor, if any, has a first-mover advantage in the conciliation committee. Some analysts have argued that the Commission is still an important actor and that its preferences should be taken into account (e.g. Crombez 2003). However, given that the formal rules allow the Council and the EP to amend the Commission's proposal in the conciliation committee without the Commission's approval, most analysts view this procedure as a game between the Council and the EP only. There are also different views on whether the Council, the EP or neither of the two has a first-mover advantage in the ordinary legislative procedure.

Steunenberg (1997) proposes that the EP takes the lead in making a proposal that a qualified majority in the Council prefers to the disagreement outcome. By contrast, Tsebelis and Garrett (1997) suggest that the Council takes the lead in making the proposal. It has also been suggested that neither institution has a first-mover advantage in the negotiations that take place between the Council and EP. In line with this view, Tsebelis and Garrett (2000: 24–5) argue that a reasonable expectation of the decision outcome under co-decision is a Nash 'split the difference' outcome between the Council and the EP. Specifically, the codecision procedure is a bargaining game between the pivotal member state in the Council and the EP. This does not, however, necessarily mean that the outcome is exactly halfway between the position of the Council pivot and the EP. The bargaining space ends when either the Council pivots or the EP is indifferent between the possible decision outcome and the disagreement outcome. Therefore, under QMV, the outcome predicted based on the configuration at the bottom of Figure 8.1 is 60. Note that this is not half way between the position of the QMV pivot (position 30) and the EP (position 100).

How practice differs from formal rules

The practice of politics differs in several salient ways from formal analyses of legislative procedures. First, there is a great deal of informal negotiation between the Council and EP, in which most of the differences between these institutions are resolved and in which the individuals involved make a difference. Second, the Commission is involved in this process even when the formal rules do not give it decision power. Third, external events and contextual factors influence the outcome of negotiations as much as the formal rules of the game. Fourth, the EP oftentimes does not or cannot make full use of the power granted to it in the rules of procedure.

An example that illustrates the difference between the formal procedures and the informal practice is the data retention directive. The proposal, which was introduced in 2005, aimed to align member states' policies regarding the retention of telecommunications data (i.e. phone calls and internet communications) for the purposes of fighting terrorism and crime. One of the controversies raised is depicted in Figure 8.2, and this

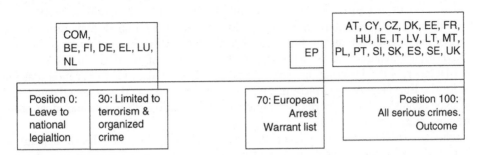

Figure 8.2 A controversy raised by the proposed directive on data retention

Source: Thomson (2011: 199).

Note: Proposal COD/2005/182.

stylized depiction is based on several interviews with key informants who were involved in the decision-making process. This controversy concerned the types of crimes against which retained data could be used. Some actors favoured a text stating that the data could be used against a narrow list of very serious crimes, namely terrorism and organized crime. Member states would be free to allow their law enforcement agencies to use the data against a wider range of crimes if they decided to do so. This policy position, favoured by the Commission, Germany and several other states, is located at position 30 on the first issue. Most of the other member states, including the UK and France, favoured the use of the data against all serious crimes in all member states. This policy position is position 100 on the issue. Note that member states such as the UK and France wanted to ensure that other European countries allowed their law enforcement agencies to use the retained data to fight a broad range of crimes. They were not content to leave this to the discretion of those other states. This was particularly relevant to neighbouring countries that had cross-border crime problems. For instance, the Danish government favoured a system that would allow German law enforcement to use the data retained by German telecommunications operators.

Despite differences of opinion between the Council and the EP, this legislative proposal was adopted after a single reading in the EP. This is not unusual; according to Reh *et al.* (2013) such 'early agreements' occurred in 309 of the 797 politically important legislative acts adopted between 1999 and 2009. In these early agreements informal negotiations are held between representatives of the Council and the EP, and representatives of the Commission are also present. The member state holding the six-month presidency of the Council, as well as the EP rapporteurs and key committee members, play important roles in these informal negotiations. As in many of these cases, the negotiations on the data retention case took place between MEPs and Council members prior to the full EP plenary vote that formally approved the agreement reached between the EP and Council. The EP entered into negotiations with the Council favouring the use of the data against crimes that fall under the European Arrest Warrant, a policy demand that our key informants placed at position 70 on the scale. This was the position of the relevant EP committee and was a compromise among a diverse range of views in the parliament, which are not depicted in the figure. MEPs from the Green and European United Left (GUE) party groups favoured leaving this entirely up to national discretion (position 0). Most of the MEPs from the European People's Party (EPP) group favoured the same position as the UK (position 100), while most of the Swedish, Belgian and Dutch EPP MEPs favoured a more limited list of crimes. Most of the MEPs from the Alliance of Liberals and Democrats for Europe (ALDE) group also favoured a more limited list of crimes than the European Arrest Warrant, while the French and Italian ALDE MEPs favoured the same position as the UK. Most of the MEPs in the Socialists and Democrats (S&D) group favoured using the retained data for the crimes that fell under the European Arrest Warrant. The decision outcome was that retained data could be used against all serious crimes, in line with the position of the UK and most other member states (position 100).

The data retention directive is a clear example of a case in which the EP appears to have had a relatively modest amount of influence on the decision outcomes, despite the fact that this was a co-decision procedure. The decision outcomes appear to be compromises among the diverse positions taken by member states. There are a number of reasons why the EP was particularly weak in this case. First, law and order is a policy area that member states' governments generally consider should be dealt with at the national level. There was some dispute regarding the appropriate legal basis for this legislative proposal. The Commission introduced the proposal based on Article 95, which usually applies to internal market directives. However, the content of the directive clearly raises issues that are central to law and order. Second, the Council had done a considerable amount of policy work on the issue of data retention prior to the introduction of the legislative proposal. Prior to the introduction of the proposal there was another similar proposal on the agenda in the Council. This similar proposal was based on a different treaty article, one that would have allowed the Council to take a decision without involving the EP in a co-decision procedure. The Council had almost reached an agreement on this similar proposal when it was replaced by the Commission's new legislative proposal. This may also have increased the Council's bargaining power. MEPs could have reasoned that the Council may have reverted back to the earlier proposal, which would not have required co-decision, if they attempted to alter the outcome of the Council's negotiations significantly. Third, and perhaps most important, terrorist attacks were carried out in London during this period. In this context, MEPs would not wish to be seen preventing measures that assist anti-terrorism operations. This one example cannot reveal which of these factors was decisive in reducing the EP's influence over the outcome in this case. However, it does illustrate that the practice of politics diverges considerably from the formal rules.

Agenda-setting power

Assessments of the relative power of EU institutions based on the formal procedures do not adequately capture the importance of agenda-setting power. The previously mentioned procedural models reduce an actor's agenda-setting power to its formal right to formulate and introduce policy proposals. Seen in these narrow terms, the Commission has enormous power. However, the concept of agenda-setting power is broader, and includes the exercise of power before legislative proposals are tabled. Seen in these broader terms, other actors, including member states and a range of stakeholders, must be considered too. Research shows that the Commission can be compelled to introduce a proposal by the member states or EP (Rasmussen 2007). In this respect while the Commission is an 'agenda setter' in the language of procedural models, it is not a gatekeeper, in that it cannot keep issues off the agenda (Crombez *et al.* 2006: 324–5).

The European Council, where member states' heads of state and government meet, is the source of many policy initiatives and specific proposals that the Commission must subsequently turn into specific legislative proposals (Tallberg 2008). The previously mentioned data retention directive is an example of a case in which negotiations among member states' representatives took place prior to the introduction of the legislative proposal by the Commission, and these negotiations had a marked effect on the contents of the proposal and the final outcome. Policymaking processes in relation to the Euro-crisis that began in 2008 also illustrate the leading role taken by the European Council, even by a core group of member states led by the German chancellor, Angela Merkel. In addition to member states' heads of state and government, the president of the European Council, currently Herman Van Rompuy, plays a significant role in formulating proposals. At the level of the Council of the EU, where sectoral configurations of national ministers meet, the member state that holds the rotating six-month presidency also affects the selection of issues for consideration. Therefore, procedural models are misleading in that they imply the Commission generally takes initiatives on its own volition.

This broader conception of agenda-setting power also leads us to consider how the Commission and other actors' policy preferences are constructed, particularly in the early formative stages of the policymaking process. Interest groups are important in this respect, and include business groups, sectoral interests such as agricultural organizations, public interest groups such as environmental lobbies, as well as public bodies such as regional representations. The Commission is highly consultative, which means that it often seeks out the opinions of a range of such relevant stakeholders before it formulates policy proposals. For complex and important proposals, such consultations can be extensive and involve the input of hundreds of stakeholders. Researchers have examined these consultation processes systematically (e.g. Beyers and Kerremans 2004; Coen and Richardson 2009; Klüver 2011; Bunea 2013). Bunea's research, for instance, focuses on the detail of consultations in five carefully selected environmental issues, including a proposal to limit CO_2 emissions in passenger cars. A broad range of stakeholders, including car manufacturers and environmental groups, expressed views on the detail of these proposals, and some of these views were translated into the contents of the legislative proposals, and eventually into EU laws. There is no consensus on the relative power of different types of interest groups on the Commission, although some argue that 'concentrated interests', such as business groups, generally exert more influence than 'diffuse interests', such as environmental groups. Perhaps one reason for this is that the Commission often seeks specific expertise when formulating its policy proposals, and concentrated interests are more likely to offer this. What is clear from these consultations is that the Commission seeks to formulate proposals that have broad support among a range of stakeholders in the relevant policy area. In this respect, the legislative proposals are defined both by its responses to demands expressed by stakeholders during the consultation state and by its anticipation of the positions that member states and the EP will take after the introduction of the proposal. In contrast, procedural models focus solely on the Commission's anticipation of the positions taken by the EU's formal legislative actors, such as member states' representatives in the Council.

The Commission's policy preferences are also affected by politics and institutional structures inside its organization. These factors mean that the Commission's policy preferences are more intertwined with member states and other actors' policy preferences than implied by procedural models. This stands to reason from the fact that most Commissioners are experienced politicians at the national level, which leads Wonka (2007) to question whether the Commission is really a 'technocratic' and 'independent' organization. Egeberg (2006) identifies a number of behavioural roles that Commissioners typically play in the policymaking process. These include a role in which Commissioners follow the interests of their home member state, and another role in which their behaviour is informed by their party-political affiliations. Other research demonstrates that while the Commission's policy positions are distinct from member states, under certain conditions there are biases in the Commission's legislative initiatives toward the interests of the home member states of the Commissioners who are primarily responsible for those initiatives (Thomson 2011: chap. 5). This suggests that the Commission's real agenda-setting power, while substantial, is less pronounced than procedural models imply.

Measuring power in the legislative arena

Different approaches have been applied to measure the relative power of the Commission, the EP and the Council. Here, we review three lines of research on relative power in the legislative decision-making process. Each has strengths and limitations. The first approach is essentially reputational; it is based on the assessments of experienced practitioners of EU politics in these institutions. The second approach examines the extent to which the EP amendments are accepted and eventually incorporated into the contents of EU laws. The third approach is a modelling approach; it focuses on the extent to which models with different assumptions about the distribution of power make accurate forecasts of decision outcomes.

In the reputational approach, researchers elicit the views of key informants who are knowledgeable about the practice of inter-institutional politics in the EU. In one application of this approach, a series of semi-structured interviews were held with 21 EU practitioners to obtain their views on the power of the Commission and EP relative to the Council in the legislative decision-making process examined here (see Thomson and Hosli 2006 for a more detailed report). These individuals included policymakers from the Commission, the EP, the Council secretariat and permanent representations of several member states. The selection consisted of people who had considerable experience and positions of responsibility, including two former heads of the Commission's civil service. During the face-to-face semi-structured interviews, respondents were asked for numerical estimates of the power distribution as well as the reasons for the estimates they gave. Their views varied enormously from each other. A majority held a supranational view, in which the Commission and EP held at least as much power as the Council. A substantial minority held an intergovernmental view, in which the Council held most power. There was no clear association between the institutional affiliation of the interviewees and their views; several of those working in the Council held a supranational view. Practitioners working in the same policy area also held different views. Although the practitioners disagreed on the relative power of the Commission, the EP and the Council, they often mentioned similar power resources in relation to each of the institutions. Therefore, they appear to disagree on how these resources should be weighted. Regarding the Commission, the Commission's right to initiate a proposal was often mentioned, as well as its expertise in facilitating agreements between other actors. Regarding the Council's power, respondents referred to the expertise and authority provided by national bureaucracies. Respondents referred to the formal rules in the co-decision procedure as a reason for the EP's power when this decision rule applied. While this approach yields interesting qualitative results, it is limited in at least two respects. First, it shows that there is substantial variation among key informants' judgements and that this variation is partly due to uncertainty regarding how different sources of power should be weighted. Second, although interviewers suggest a definition of power to interviewees, we cannot be sure on which definition of power, if any, they are basing their judgements.

The second approach refers to information on the extent to which EP amendments are incorporated into laws (e.g. Kreppel 2002; Tsebelis *et al.* 2001). A considerable proportion of the EP's amendments are incorporated into laws, particularly when the ordinary legislative procedure applies. Kreppel (2002) finds that in almost half of the EP's substantive amendments, which are distinct from semantic or technical amendments. This type of evidence is highly relevant to questions about variation in the EP's power, for instance the effect of changes in formal rules on the EP's power, notably the change from the old cooperation procedure to the co-decision procedure. However, assessments of the EP's power based on the success of amendments are of limited use for gauging the EP's power relative to other institutions. If we are interested in the extent to which the EP offers an effective check on the power of the other institutions, we are interested in the EP's relative power. To assess the EP's relative power, we need information on opposition to the EP's policy positions by other actors. Research on EP amendments does not fully take into account the extent to which each of the member states supported, opposed or was entirely indifferent to the EP's substantive amendments.

The modelling approach begins with a spatial representation of the policy positions taken by the EU-level actors, such as the one in Figure 8.2 (Thomson and Hosli 2006; Thomson 2011: chap. 8; Costello and Thomson 2013). It then asks what assumptions regarding the distribution of power among the institutions allow a simple bargaining model to make the most accurate predictions of decision outcomes. The simple bargaining model used is a variant of the Nash Bargaining Solution (NBS; Achen 2006). The NBS has a long and distinguished pedigree in decision analysis and has a revered place in the field of game theory. It is a cooperative model, which means that it assumes actors are able to make binding commitments to each other. The variant of the NBS used in this approach assumes that all actors strive to reach a decision outcome, and that failure to agree is highly undesirable. This variant of the NBS is very simple; as a formula it can be reduced to a weighted average of actors' policy positions. The formula also incorporates the level of importance or salience that each actor attaches to the issue at stake. In a comparative test of the predictive power of alternative models, including the procedural models referred to earlier, this variant of the NBS outperformed all other models (Thomson *et al.* 2006).

If it is assumed that the Council holds most of the power in the EU and that the Commission and EP hold only modest amounts of power relative to the Council, the model generates relatively accurate predictions of decision outcomes. By contrast, if it is assumed that the EP holds as much power as the Council, which is the case according to the formalities of the ordinary legislative procedure, or that the Commission wields substantial power, then the model does not predict decision outcomes accurately. For example, with respect to the controversy regarding the data retention directive depicted in Figure 8.2, the model's prediction of the actual decision outcome is most accurate when it is assumed that all of the power is held by the member states in the Council. Attributing any weight or power at all to the Commission or the EP only reduces the accuracy of the model's prediction. This particular controversy in the data retention directive is only one case of course; taken alone, it is no more than an anecdote. However, this approach has been applied to hundreds of cases in the work cited earlier. Depending on the details of the modelling choices made, the EP has between 10 and 20 per cent of the Council's total power in the best-predicting model of decision outcomes under what is now the ordinary legislative procedure, while the Commission has a smaller proportion. We might take the exact percentages with a grain of salt, but the overall conclusion is clear. In practice, the Council dominates EU decision-making when it comes to resolving controversial issues in the legislative process.

There are criticisms of this modelling approach too. This variant of the NBS has been criticized for being too computationally simple, since it can be reduced to a weighted average of actors' policy positions. This is not a serious criticism, since even the most complex models in political science are mathematically trivial. What is relevant is whether it captures the essential elements of the EU's decision-making process that is characterized by cooperative behaviour, inclusiveness, a commitment to reaching some form of agreement, and compromise. Moreover, complexity does not always increase predictive power, since the NBS outperformed many more complex models in this respect. A more relevant criticism of this modelling approach, at least the way in which it has been applied in existing research, is that it focuses on the stage of decision-making between the introduction of the legislative proposal by the European Commission and the adoption of the proposal by the Council and EP. This means that it may not be giving adequate attention to the power of the Commission in the entire policymaking process, particularly in the early agenda-setting stage referred to earlier.

Each of these approaches has its own strengths and weaknesses, but each sheds some light on the distribution of power among the institutions. The reputational approach aggregates the impressions and insights of knowledgeable practitioners, but we cannot be sure that their judgements refer to power as defined by political scientists. The amendment approach is based on information that is readily available and gives insights into how well the EP does under different procedures, but it is limited in gauging the relative power of the institutions, including the Council and the Commission. The modelling approach is based on a method that closely approximates Weber's classic definition of power but is limited in that it has only to be applied to the decision-making stage and ignores the important agenda-setting stage. Despite their differences, most analysts would agree that the Council is the centre of power in the EU, that the Commission has considerable power particularly during the formative stages of the policymaking process and that the EP punches at least somewhat below the weight it is ascribed in the formal procedures.

Variation in the relative power of the institutions

Our ability to generalize about the relative power of the institutions is limited by the fact that power varies considerably depending on the context in question and the individuals involved. Individuals matter in politics, and the people who hold key positions in each of the institutions affect the power of the institution. At the highest levels, the presidents of the Commission, the European Council and the EP have some impact on the standing of the institution they represent. Jacques Delors, who held the Commission presidency between 1985 and 1994 is regarded as the towering figure in the history of this office (Drake 2000). Delors oversaw important advances in the single market announced in the Single European Act of 1985. As well as being a dynamic figure, he was also in the fortunate position of being in office at a time when member states' interests aligned around this important policy programme. Herman Van Rompuy, the former Belgian prime minister, became the first president of the European Council according to the arrangements set out in the Lisbon Treaty. Critics were initially sceptical of whether he would be a strong enough leader, but he has proved to be an effective president during the economic crisis that has plagued the EU since he took office.

At one level down from the apex of each of the institutions, the key actors who affect the power of their institutions differ according to the policy proposal in question. They include the Commissioners who are primarily responsible for particular proposals, the representatives of member states that hold the six-month rotating presidency of the Council and the MEPs with special responsibilities for handling particular policy proposals. These MEPs include the chairs of the relevant parliamentary committees and the rapporteurs and shadow rapporteurs who have the task of drafting the EP's report on particular proposals. Research on the rotating presidency of the Council shows that it confers a modest advantage to the incumbent member state, in the sense that decision outcomes are somewhat closer to the presidential member state's policy positions (e.g. Warntjen 2008). Balanced against this modest advantage is the responsibility the presidency imposes on member states to be a neutral broker and to achieve progress on difficult dossiers. This sometimes means putting aside the national interest.

Perhaps counterintuitively it is not always the most prominent and powerful individuals who confer the most power on their institutions. Schelling (1960: 22) describes the paradoxical sense in which 'the power to constrain an adversary may depend on the power to bind oneself'. In turn, the power to bind oneself may depend on the ability to appear weak in relation to the individuals one represents. Research has found some support for this proposition in relation to the characteristics of EP rapporteurs who represent the EP in negotiations with the Council in the ordinary legislative procedure. Rapporteurs with senior leadership positions in the EP, such as committee chairs, hold a powerful position within the EP. It would not be credible for such senior MEPs to claim to their negotiation partners in the Council that they have no room for manoeuvre and therefore cannot make concessions to the Council since they could not convince their fellow MEPs to accept these. In line with this conjecture, research shows that the EP does worse in negotiations with the Council when rapporteurs are senior MEPs (Costello and Thomson 2011). Other characteristics of rapporteurs matter for the EP's bargaining success too; the EP is more successful in its negotiations with the Council when its rapporteurs are close to the ideological centre in the EP and when they are affiliated with parties that are in government in their home member states.

The prevalence of early agreements in the ordinary legislative procedure raises the question of how the stage at which a legislative proposal is resolved might affect the relative power of the institutions. Early agreements may empower the individuals involved in the negotiations between the Council and the EP, in particular representatives of the member state in the rotating presidency and the EP rapporteurs and relevant committee chairs. These are referred to as relais actors since they are the links between institutions (Farrell and Héritier 2004). It is not clear, however, that this necessarily disadvantages either the Council or the EP. Recent research suggests that it does not; in other words that the EP does just as well, other things being equal, in early agreements than in proposals that are agreed after a second reading or conciliation committee (Rasmussen and Reh 2013). There may, however, be certain types of issues on which MEPs are willing to engage in more protracted conflict with the Council that leads to conciliation committees. These include issues that involve citizens directly, such as the working time directive, which limits the number of hours Europeans can work every week. In 2009, the EP rejected a compromise proposal to amend this directive in the conciliation committee. According to most MEPs, the compromise did not limit the UK's opt-out of the Working Time Directive enough. This was not exactly a victory for the EP, since it in fact wanted to eliminate the optout, but it certainly had an effect on the decision outcome in this case.

Over time, the general trend is that the EP has gained in power relative to the other institutions. What began as an unelected consultative body has developed into a directly elected parliament in a bicameral system, at least according to the formal procedures. The first direct elections to the EP in 1979 increased the EP's legitimacy since the MEPs could then claim to represent citizens. An important ECJ ruling in 1980, the isoglucose case, confirmed that the EP had the right to be consulted before the Council could take a decision. The EP's powers were expanded beyond the right to be consulted in subsequent treaties. The most significant of these expansions was the introduction of the co-decision procedure in the Maastricht Treaty in 1993 that was amended and broadened in scope by the Amsterdam Treaty in 1999. The Lisbon Treaty was the latest round of this process, in which the co-decision procedure was renamed the ordinary legislative procedure and extended to almost all areas of EU law. This was a noteworthy rhetorical change, since it signified that it is now common practice for the EP to be involved in the decision-making process as an equal partner with the Council.

While the EP's formal power has been codified in the procedural rules, its effective power is malleable and can be changed by policy decisions concerning how institutions are run, by events and by individuals. Institutions require resources to give meaning to formal powers. Despite the grandeur of its buildings and expertise of EP officials, MEPs are modestly resourced by comparative standards. Most MEPs have two or three assistants, often at quite junior levels. In addition, MEPs draw on support from staff in their party groups and relevant parliamentary committees, but these staff must also support other MEPs. In contrast, representatives of member states in the Council draw on the resources of large national ministries. Moves are underway to allocate more resources to EP personnel rather than buildings, although these have not yet allowed the EP to make full use of its formally defined potential. Moving all EP operations from Brussels to Strasbourg once a month, to hold meetings in a building that remains empty the rest of the time, is arguably also a distraction from checking the other institutions' power. So there are practical measures available that could change the real inter-institutional balance of power in the future.

Outside events also expose and affect the relative power of EU institutions. The economic crisis that began in 2008 made clear that the European Council is the most powerful of the institutions in shaping the EU's responses in this area. Some observers argue that power in the European Council is highly concentrated in the hands of a few key member states, and even in the person of German chancellor Merkel. When it came to setting the contours of bailout packages and the Fiscal Compact, member states were in the driving seat. The EP played a marginal role in the formative stages of these developments. This is perhaps due to the nature of the events themselves, which are crisis-ridden and require timely responses, which has been difficult to achieve even when decision-making has been concentrated in the European Council. Nonetheless, the EP was able to exert some influence on decision outcomes, not least because the responses to the financial crisis had to be implemented in the form of legislation (the famous six and two packs of financial and fiscal regulation) on which the EP had a say. If the EU is to be as democratic as it possibly can be, which means that citizens' demands and concerns are adequately considered in the decision-making process, then it is vital that the EP is able to use the formal power it has been given effectively.

References

Achen, Christopher H. 2006. Institutional Realism and Bargaining Models, in Robert Thomson, Frans N. Stokman, Christopher H. Achen and Thomas König (eds.) *The European Union Decides*. Cambridge: Cambridge University Press, pp. 86–123.

Aspinwall, M. and Schneider, Gerald. 2000. Same Menu, Separate Tables: The Institutionalist Turn in Political Science and the Study of European Integration. *European Journal of Political Research* 38: 1–36.

Bachrach, Peter and Baratz, Morton S. 1970. *Power and Poverty: Theory and Practice*. New York: Oxford University Press.

Barry, Brian. 1980. Is it Better to be Powerful or Lucky? Part 1. *Political Studies* 28: 183–94.

Beyers, Jan and Kerremans, Bart. 2004. Bureaucrats, Politicians, and Societal Interests: How Is European Policy Making Politicized? *Comparative Political Studies* 37(10): 1119–50.

Bueno de Mesquita, Bruce and Stokman, Frans N. (eds.) 1994. *European Community Decision Making: Models, Applications and Comparisons*. New Haven, CT: Yale University Press.

Bunea, Adriana. 2013. Issues, Preferences and Ties: Determinants of Interest Groups' Preference Attainment in EU Environmental Policy. *Journal of European Public Policy* 20(4): 552–70.

Coen, David and Richardson, Jeremy. (eds.) 2009. *Lobbying the European Union: Institutions, Actors, and Issues*. Oxford: Oxford University Press.

Costello, Rory and Thomson, Robert. 2011. The Nexus of Bicameralism: Rapporteurs' Impact on Decision Outcomes in the European Union. *European Union Politics* 12: 337–57.

Costello, Rory and Thomson, Robert. 2013. The Distribution of Power among EU Institutions: Who Wins under Codecision and Why? *Journal of European Public Policy* 20(7): 1025–39.

Crombez, Christophe. 1996. Legislative Procedures in the European Community. *British Journal of Political Science* 26: 199–228.

Crombez, Christophe. 2003. The Democratic Deficit in the European Union. *European Union Politics* 1: 365–85.

Crombez, Christophe, Groseclose, Tim and Krehbiel, Keith. 2006. Gatekeeping. *Journal of Politics* 68(2): 322–34.

Dahl, Robert. A. 1957. The Concept of Power. *Behavioral Science* 2: 201–15.

Drake, Helen, 2000. *Jacques Delors: Perspectives on a European Leader*. London: Routledge.

Easton, David. 1953. *The Political System: An Inquiry into the Sate of Political Science*. New York: Alfred Knopf.

Egeberg, Morten. 2006. Executive Politics as Usual: Role Behaviour and Conflict Dimensions in the College of European Commissioners. *Journal of European Public Policy* 13(1): 1–15.

Farrell, Henry and Héritier, Adrienne. 2004. Interorganizational Negotiation and Intraorganizational Power in Shared Decision Making. *Comparative Political Studies* 37(10): 1184–1212.

Haas, Ernst. 1958. *The Uniting of Europe*. Stanford, CA: Stanford University Press.

Haas, Ernst. 1975. *The Obsolescence of Regional Integration Theory*. Berkeley, CA: Institute of International Studies.

Hoffmann, Stanley. 1966. Obstinate or Obsolete: The Fate of the Nation-State and the Core of Western Europe. *Daedalus* 95: 862–915.

Klüver, Heike. 2011. The Contextual Nature of Lobbying: Explaining Lobbying Success in the European Union. *European Union Politics* 12(4): 483–506.

König, Thomas and Proksch, Sven-Oliver. 2006. A Procedural Exchange Model of EU Legislative Politics, in Robert Thomson, Frans. N. Stokman, Christopher H. Achen and Thomas König (eds.) *The European Union Decides*. Cambridge: Cambridge University Press, pp. 211–238.

Kreppel, Amie. 2002. *The European Parliament and Supranational Party System: A Study in Institutional Development*. Cambridge: Cambridge University Press.

Laswell, Harold. 1936. *Politics: Who Gets What, When and How*. New York: McGraw-Hill.

Lindberg, Leon N. 1963. *The Political Dynamics of European Economic Integration*. Stanford, CA: Stanford University Press.

Lodge, Juliet. 1994. The European Parliament and the Authority-Legitimacy Crises. *Annals of the American Academy of Political and Social Science* 531: 69–83.

Lukes, Steven. 1974. *Power: A Radical View*. London: Macmillan.

Majone, Giandomenico. 2001. Two Logics of Delegation: Agency and Fiduciary Relations in EU Governance. *European Union Politics* 2: 103–22.

Mansbridge, Jane. 2003. Rethinking Representation. *American Political Science Review* 97: 515–28.

Milward, Alan S. 1992. *The European Rescue of the Nation-State*. London: Routledge.

Moravcsik, Andrew. 1998. *The Choice for Europe*. Ithaca, NY: Cornell University Press.

Naurin, Daniel and Lindahl, Rutger. 2008. East-North-South: Coalition-Building in the Council before and after Enlargement, in Daniel Naurin and Helen Wallace (eds.) *Unveiling the Council of the European Union: Games Governments Play in Brussels*. London: Palgrave Macmillan, pp. 64–80.

North, Douglas C. 1991. Institutions. *Journal of Economic Perspectives* 5(1): 97–112.

Pollack, Mark A. 2003. *The Engines of European Integration: Delegation, Agency and Agenda Setting in the EU*. Oxford: Oxford University Press.

Princen, Sebastiaan. 2009. *Agenda-Setting in the European Union*. Basingstoke: Palgrave.

Rasmussen, Anne. 2007. Challenging the Commission's Right of Initiative? Conditions for Institutional Change and Stability. *West European Politics* 30(2): 244–264.

Rasmussen Anne and Reh, Christine. 2013. The Consequences of Concluding Codecision Early: Trilogues and Intrainstitutional Bargaining Success. *Journal of European Public Policy* 20(7): 1006–1023.

Reh, Christine, Héritier, Adrienne, Bressanelli, Edoardo and Koop, Christel. 2013. The Informal Politics of Legislation: Explaining Secluded Decision Making in the European Union. *Comparative Political Studies* 46(9): 1112–1142.

Riker, William H. 1980. Implications from the Disequilibrium of Majority Rule for the Study of Institutions. *American Political Science Review* 74: 432–446.

Sandholtz, Wayne and Stone Sweet, Alec. 1998. *European Integration and Supranational Governance*. Oxford: Oxford University Press.

Schelling, Thomas, C. 1960. *The Strategy of Conflict*. Cambridge, MA: Harvard University Press.

Schmitter, Philippe C. 1969. Three Neofunctional Hypotheses about European Integration. *International Organization* 23: 161–166.

Steunenberg, Bernard. 1994. Decision-Making under different Institutional Arrangements: Legislation by the European Community. *Journal of Theoretical and Institutional Economics* 150: 642–669.

Steunenberg, Bernard. 1997. Codecision and its Reform: A Comparative Analysis of Decision Making Rules in the European Union, in Bernard Steunenberg and Frans A. van Vught (eds.) *Political Institutions and Public Policy: Perspectives on European Decision Making*. Dordrecht: Kluwer, pp. 205–229.

Tallberg, Jonas. 2008. Bargaining Power in the European Council. *Journal of Common Market Studies* 46(3): 685–708.

Thomson, Robert. 2011. *Resolving Controversy in the European Union: Legislative Decision-making before and after Enlargement*. Cambridge: Cambridge University Press.

Thomson, Robert and Hosli, Madeleine. 2006. Who Has Power in the EU? *Journal of Common Market Studies* 44(2): 391–417.

Thomson, Robert, Stokman, Frans N., Achen, Christopher H. and König, Thomas (eds.) 2006. *The European Union Decides*. Cambridge: Cambridge University Press.

Tsebelis, George. 1994. The Power of the European Parliament as a Conditional Agenda Setter. *American Political Science Review* 88: 128–142.

Tsebelis, George and Garrett, Geoffrey. 1997. Agenda Setting, Vetoes and the European Union's Co-decision Procedure. *Journal of Legislative Studies* 3: 74–92.

Tsebelis, George and Garrett, Geoffrey. 2000. Legislative Politics in the EU. *European Union Politics* 1: 9–36.

Tsebelis, George, Jensen, Christian B., Kalandrakis, Anastassios and Kreppel, Amie. 2001. Legislative Procedures in the European Union: An Empirical Analysis. *British Journal of Political Science* 31: 573–599.

Warntjen, Andreas. 2008. The Council Presidency: Power Broker or Burden? An Empirical Analysis. *European Union Politics* 9: 315–338.

Weber, Max. 2007 [1914]. The Distribution of Power within the Political Community: Class, Status, Party, in Craig Calhoun, Joseph Gerteis, James Moody, Steven Pfaff and Indermohan Virk (eds.) *Classical Sociological Theory*, 2nd edition. Malden MA: Blackwell, pp. 247–254.

Wonka, Arndt. 2007. Technocratic and Independent? The Appointment of European Commissioners and its Policy Implications. *Journal of European Public Policy* 14(2): 169–189.

Chapter 9

The EU budget

Which fiscal capacity at the European level?

HENRIK ENDERLEIN, OLE FUNKE,
AND JOHANNES LINDNER

Introduction

The budget of the European Union (EU) is paradoxical, both in its political salience as well as in its macroeconomic functions. From a perspective of fiscal federalism one could well look at the EU as the "highest" layer of economic governance and thus compare the size and role of the EU budget to that of the US federal government or that of the German federal government. The numbers would then look deceptively small: at roughly 1 per cent of EU gross domestic product (GDP), the EU budget is simply not comparable to the US, where federal spending amounts to around 25 per cent of GDP. On the other hand, by looking at absolute numbers and the policy debates surrounding the EU budget, it becomes clear that this is not a negligible field. The annual spending of the EU budget amounts to around 140 billion euros. And when the trilateral negotiation between EU national governments, the European Commission, and the European Parliament on the EU's multi-annual financial framework take place every seven years, the sum on the bargaining table is more than 1 trillion euro. The political debates surrounding the latest round of negotiation of this kind in the fall of 2012 and spring of 2013 are indicative in this respect: in the UK, the House of Commons took a decision to reject a further nominal increase of the EU budget even before the final round of negotiations at the highest EU level had started, thus triggering debates on whether the UK should leave the EU.[1] A special EU summit on the matter collapsed in November 2012, and the final decision was delayed until the summer of 2013. At the same time, there is hardly any public debate on a year-to-year basis on the spending of the EU. By contrast to national politics, the adoption of the annual EU budget rarely sparks widespread media coverage (even though there can be substantive disagreement between the actors involved in the annual procedure, see the later discussion). So the EU budget might be small in relative terms, but it is large in absolute numbers and from time to time of considerable political importance.

During the euro-area crisis of 2010–2013, the rather paradoxical role of the EU budget became even more apparent. While the crisis gave rise to large rescue schemes worth hundreds of billions of euros and triggered a debate on a fiscal union in the euro area, the question of the size and scope of the EU budget remained largely outside the rescue efforts and the broader policy debate. Rescue measures were undertaken mainly on the basis of instruments completely detached from the EU budget, namely the European Financial Stability Facility (EFSF) and its successor, the European Stability Mechanism (ESM; see also Jones and Fuller, in this volume). In 2012, the Presidents of the four main economic decision-making bodies in the EU (the European Council, the European Commission, the European Central Bank, and the Eurogroup) presented a series of three successive reports with plans for a "Genuine Economic and Monetary Union", which referred in some detail to an "integrated budgetary framework" for the euro area, yet the actual budget of the European Union was not mentioned (despite the fact that the report was published in parallel to the start of the negotiations on the EU's financial framework for 2014 through 2020).

This chapter seeks to cast light on this apparently paradoxical and contradictory position of the EU budget within the general framework of European integration. It presents a two-step institutionalist argument: first, the content and structure of the EU budget is the result of the procedural set-up that governs budgetary decision-making at the EU level, and second, the EU budgetary procedure corresponds by and large to an equilibrium among all actors involved. Altering that equilibrium would require a significant shift in integration, notably towards more fiscal federalism. Such a shift looks currently unlikely, despite the challenges raised in the context of the euro area crisis. At the same time, however, discussions on the scope and size of the EU budget or a parallel "fiscal capacity" at the European level, and in particular at the level of euro area countries, may gain importance in the upcoming years as the question on whether a single currency will need to be complemented with a single fiscal framework remains on the agenda.

The chapter proceeds as follows: Section 2 describes the political and institutional equilibrium on which the current EU budget is based. Section 3 then outlines the actual functioning of the EU budget in its annual and multi-annual procedures. Section 4 discusses possible future adjustments of the EU budget in the context of the aftermath of the sovereign debt crisis, and in particular the possible need for a fiscal capacity at the euro-area level. Section 5 presents the conclusions.

Putting the EU budget into a wider theoretical framework

Integration, delegation, and legitimacy

Analysing the institutional underpinnings of the EU budget and trying to assess them in terms of their level of political integration requires a focus on two different types of approaches that are intimately related. Just like national budgets, the EU budget is rooted in a principal–agent framework. Given the specific set-up of the EU, however, this framework yields quite specific implications deriving from the two sources of EU legitimacy, which are supranational and inter-governmental decision-making. From the perspective of budgetary issues, a focus on the legitimacy resources of the budget as an instrument of redistribution is warranted. This is best achieved in the perspective of the fiscal federalism literature.

Procedures on public finances have to be put into the context of the underlying principal-agent framework (e.g. Buchanan and Tullock 1962). The origins of constitutional orders and their legitimacy and efficiency are grounded in the pooling of individual citizens' sovereignty and the delegation of functions and powers to elected representatives. Citizens, as principals, allow elected representatives, as their agents, to be in charge of public institutions and to take political decisions.

While the principal–agent analogy allows the constitutional choice literature to explain the rationale behind the existence of states, the analogy is also used to analyse institution building at the international level and, in the specific European context, at the supranational level (Pollack 2003, see also the fundamental theoretical text by Riker, 1964). Here, states are regarded as the principals. Under certain circumstances, cooperation among states is beneficial, and states may decide to pool their political sovereignty in selected areas. In the context of pooled sovereignties at the supranational level, there are, however, two types of decision-making procedures:

Intergovernmental cooperation. States agree to take decisions in the relevant policy area by unanimity, thus preserving a considerable degree of "ultimate" sovereignty, deriving from the power of each individual member state to veto decisions. These decisions are legitimised by the direct link between citizens and their national governments and the fact that these governments cannot be outvoted. At the same time, the unanimity rule renders negotiations difficult, as decision-making is clearly hampered by national vetoes.

Supranational governance. States might realise that it is beneficial to take some decisions by qualified majority and to delegate, as principals, certain functions to an (independent) agent helping them to overcome collective action problems. This move towards qualified majority voting and delegation is motivated by an interest in increasing the efficiency of international decision-making. The states sacrifice their veto power and assign political tasks, such as the oversight of the implementation and the role of mediating between states, to a supra-national agent. Yet, supranational governance may, in the view of citizens, be regarded as less legitimate than intergovernmental cooperation, because national governments can be outvoted and supra-national agents exercise power without a direct mandate from the citizens.[2] In order to counteract this lack of legitimisation, supranational actors may be directly (or indirectly) elected by the citizens, thus circumventing national governments as the sole source of legitimacy. However, this increase in legitimacy comes again at the cost of efficiency. The involvement of an additional directly elected agent might increase the complexity of decision-making.

Pooled sovereignty and delegation to supranational agents constitute two main dimensions of *political integration*. A political system of inter-state cooperation is highly integrated when national governments have pooled large parts of their national competences at the supranational level and created strong supranational bodies that can overturn national vetoes.

However, there is also a third dimension of integration. This is the degree of political identification with, and acceptance of, inter-state cooperation. Integration is well advanced when the citizens of the different states are united by a sense of belonging to the same community, when they share common values and goals, and – most relevant from the perspective of this chapter – when they are willing to enter a system of national redistribution.[3]

Income redistribution within a nation-state is a key ingredient in considerations on the optimal scale of government. As the large body of literature on "fiscal federalism" in political science convincingly demonstrates, there is an obvious trade-off between the greater effectiveness of large units and the greater legitimacy of small units (e.g. Oates 1972, 1999; Scharpf 1988; Inman and Rubinfeld 1997). Research in economics has tried to gain objective insights on the appropriate size of nations and has developed positive theories of integration and decentralisation (Alesina and Spolaore 1997; Bolton and Roland 2000). Research in political science has tried to gain insights on the original bargain that establishes a federation (e.g. Riker 1964; Stepan 1999).

The EU, its budget, and the procedural underpinnings

What is relevant from this literature on the redistributive functions of federalism for the understanding of the EU budget and the rules that govern the decision-making process around it is the focus on the importance of appropriate sources of legitimacy and appropriate protections against future exploitation either by the centre or by other states in the bargain over distributive federations. The first two dimensions and the third dimension of integration are obviously interlinked. Political identification and willingness to enter a redistributive framework may evolve as a result of successful pooling and delegation. They are therefore also important preconditions for further pooling and delegation.

Applying these considerations to the European Union, it becomes apparent that any significant reform of the EU budget has to be preceded by a reform of the way the EU budget is adopted. The EU budgetary procedure has gained a very strong degree of "institutional depth" in terms of determining the distributive outcome and preserving the status quo. At the same time, far-reaching changes in the EU budgetary procedure would require a parallel move towards further integration in terms of institutional efficiency and legitimacy, on one hand, and willingness to redistribute income across Europe, on the other. As is argued in this section, the present set-up of the EU budgetary procedure appears to be fully in line with the overall balance between legitimacy and efficiency in the EU institutional framework and corresponds to EU citizens' willingness to allocate and redistribute income across Europe.

With regard to the institutional set-up, the EU level is governed by a combination of supranational and intergovernmental forms of decision-making. In the intergovernmental realm, heads of state or government set the grand lines in the European Council by consensus. Moreover, the European Council adopts treaty changes, which are subsequently ratified according to national domestic procedures. In the Council of Ministers, representatives of national governments take detailed policy decisions upon legislative initiatives from the supranational Commission. Voting rules vary across policy fields. Where unanimity voting still applies, the Council acts as an intergovernmental body, while in the case of qualified majority voting ministers move into the supranational realm. The directly elected European Parliament introduces a link between the supranational decision-making process and the citizens. Its involvement as a strong veto player is largely connected to qualified majority voting in the Council where, in terms of legitimacy, it compensates the loss of member states' veto power. Moreover, it fulfils control functions vis-à-vis the Commission, which, as an independent supranational agent, is not directly legitimated (through elections). The present institutional set-up of the European Union thus combines elements of intergovernmental cooperation and supranational governance and strikes a balance between legitimacy and efficiency concerns.

This overall balance lays the foundation for the specific rules and procedures in the different policy fields of the EU. The involvement of the Commission, the European Parliament, and the Council is a common feature to most policy domains. It caters for similar legitimacy and efficiency concerns regardless of the particular characteristics of the specific policy field.[4]

This meta-level not only overarches but also determines decision-making in the different policy fields of the EU. The complexity or alleged inefficiency of a decision-making procedure can therefore not be exclusively attributed to the institutional provisions governing the specific policy field but they need to be linked to the characteristics of the meta-level. Moreover, the embeddedness in the meta-level constrains the scope of institutional reform in a policy field. Reform proposals that seem appropriate to increase efficiency and legitimacy of the procedure are actually incompatible with the current state of integration.

In the budgetary field, the embeddedness in the meta-level is particularly strong as budgetary decision-making cuts across the different policy fields. The EU budget reflects the range of areas in which sovereignty is pooled at the EU level. Moreover, budgetary decision-making is intertwined with the different legislative procedures, because policy decisions often have a legislative and a budgetary component. Both components need to be coordinated. The legislative and the budgetary realm cannot be viewed as separate policy fields.

Institutional reform in the budgetary area is further complicated by the difficult relationship between efficiency and legitimacy concerns in that domain. Taking into account the limited degree of European citizens' political identification with supranational decision-making at the EU level, it can generally be argued that legitimacy concerns are mainly catered for by a strong involvement of member states' representatives. Such intergovernmental elements, however, necessarily allow for extensive bargaining thus coming at the expense of efficiency concerns, especially with a significantly grown number of EU member states. Budgetary decisions are usually regarded as an issue close to national sovereignty and at the heart of governments' powers. Hence, member states may be reluctant to give up their authority over spending and raising taxes to the supranational level. Moreover, winners and losers of budgetary decisions are more clearly identifiable than in legislative decision-making because costs and benefits are specified in monetary terms. Therefore, the potential for conflict is probably high. At the same time, transparency of costs and losses also lends itself to judgements on the efficiency of the decision-making procedure and the resulting policy outcomes. In contrast to legislative decision-making, complaints about wasted resources and inefficient use of taxpayers' money are widespread in the budgetary field.

In the particular context of European decision-making in the budgetary domain, we would argue that it is possible to simplify the relationship between efficiency and legitimacy concerns as a trade-off (see also Enderlein *et al.* 2005). Using a metaphor, possible solutions to this trade-off are limited by a "Pareto frontier" that is determined by the state of integration (see Figure 9.1). Similarly, the quality and nature of a policy field can be assessed in terms of their Pareto optimality and their location on the Pareto frontier. Shifts to the Pareto frontier itself are triggered by increases or decreases in political integration, for example an increase of citizens' willingness to enter into cross-European redistribution.

As illustrated in Figure 9.1, proponents of reform assume that the budgetary procedure is currently situated at point A, while we assume that the point B is probably a more accurate description of the current procedure. This means, that while the proponents of reform believe that reforms are possible that significantly increase efficiency and legitimacy we contend that improvements could only be marginal and would have to concentrate either on efficiency (leading to B') or legitimacy (leading to B").

We believe this metaphor can contribute to explaining why there has been rather little fundamental change in the realm of the EU budget in recent years (on the long-term perspective see Lindner 2005). One can argue that the main reason for institutional inertia is the lack of suitable (i.e. Pareto superior) procedural alternatives, taking into account the exogenously given state of political integration (i.e. the Pareto frontier). In line with this hypothesis, proponents of far-reaching reforms in the budgetary field would seem to have underestimated, first, the constraints that are set by the general state of integration and, second, the high degree to which the current procedure is

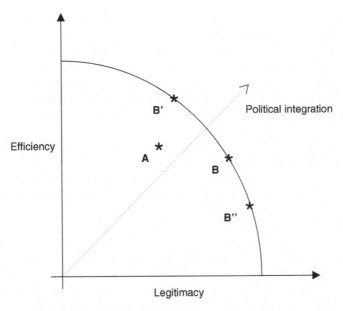

Figure 9.1 The efficiency–legitimacy trade-off

already in tune with these constraints. In the context of the crisis in the euro area, the question has been raised whether the state of political integration will change, thus also allowing for a more fundamental change in political integration (see Section 4).

The EU budgetary procedure: annual and multi-annual framework

The following section assesses the current framework of the EU budget (content and procedures) within the wider context of EU integration. It starts out by focusing on the multi-annual framework before focusing on the procedures and content at the annual level.[5]

The Multi-annual Financial Framework

The Multi-annual Financial Framework (MFF) was a welcome development when it was first introduced in 1988. In the late 1970s and early 1980s, EU budgetary negotiations had been characterised by confrontations between the European Parliament and the Council that eventually led the European Parliament to reject entire draft budgets (Lindner and Rittberger 2003). The early 1980s also saw vigorous complaints from the UK and a lack of sufficient resources, which was prompted by the ballooning of Common Agriculture Policy spending and aggravated when the UK rebate was agreed to. In this context, a framework was intended to significantly restrict the scope for political choice during the actual annual budgetary procedure. By linking revenue and expenditure sides, it ensured that expenditure-led budgets would no longer exceed existing resources (Shackleton 1990).

The MFF combines intergovernmental with supranational elements. It is discussed, on a proposal by the Commission, in the European Council, where it requires unanimous agreement among member states. The involvement of heads of state or government ensures overcoming differences and stalemate among EU ministers. The previously voluntary arrangement, which became known as the "Financial Perspective", is now enshrined in the treaties as the MFF.

Often misjudged as a mere compilation of expenditure ceilings the MFF has in fact evolved as the main instrument shaping not only the overall level but the content of EU expenditure for several years as well. This fact is of even higher importance regarding that the MFF is being decided by unanimity in the Council while needing a simple majority in the European Parliament.

This setting favours a strong status quo bias of the MFF. In the negotiations, national governments use their veto power in order to maximise budgetary gains. Although the MFF is not automatically renewed at the end of the seven-year period, the use of veto power and the bargaining dynamics resulting from it lead to a largely incremental update of the ceilings, thus respecting the key spending interests of member states, such as the rebate for the UK, regional spending for the Union's Cohesion Funds, and unaltered Common Agricultural Policy (CAP) for France.[6] In such a setting, major changes and far-reaching reforms are very unlikely to occur (Begg 1999).[7]

On 8 February 2013, the European Council reached political agreement on the MFF for the period 2014–2020 (see Table 9.1). On 27 June after a hefty power play the Council presidency reached agreement with the Parliament, leaving the Council's figures untouched, while granting more flexibility on the annual rollover of unused funds.

As previous frameworks, EU expenditure up to 2020 will focus largely on two specific policy fields with a strong redistributive bent, namely agricultural and regional polices which alone account for more than 70 per cent of expenditure. While agricultural spending provides European farmers with subsidies, regional spending redistributes funds from richer to poorer Member States. Although often presented as such in official communications (see Leonardi 1999), these policies cannot be regarded as financing genuine European public goods, which one would assume as the rationale for having a EU budget in the first place. This is well reflected in the extensive negotiating process leading to a final compromise, which not only determines the previously mentioned ceilings, but the distribution of more than 70 per cent of EU expenditure among member states and even regions is being set in stone for seven years in advance. After subtracting administration expenditure, this leaves roughly 20 per cent of the overall amount theoretically available for the Commission to finance projects providing genuine European public goods. In contrast, by the mere decision-making process member states are particularly pressed to demand a *juste retour*. In addition, given that welfare state policies still remain national competences, the EU budget is not the key player of budgetary activities in the EU.

Amounting to less than 1 per cent of EU gross national income (GNI),[8] the economic function of the EU budget looks disproportionate in comparison to the legislative functions of the EU (directly determining more than 50 per cent of domestic legislation in EU member states).[9] Thus, while important areas of national sovereignty are pooled at the EU level and a certain degree of political identification and acceptance has been

Table 9.1   The Multi-annual Financial Framework 2014–2020

Commitment appropriations	MFF 2014–20	MFF 2007–13	Comparison 2014–20 v. 2007–13	
	€mn	€mn	€	%
1. Smart and Inclusive Growth	450.763	446.310	+4.5 bn	+1.0
1a. Competitiveness for Growth and Jobs	125.614	91.495	+34.1 bn	+37.3
1b. Economic, social and territorial cohesion	325.149	354.815	–29.7 bn	–8.4
2. Sustainable growth: Natural Resources	373.179	420.682	–47.5 bn	–11.3
3. Security and Citizenship	15.686	12.366	+3.3 bn	+26.8
4. Global Europe	58.704	56.815	+1.9 bn	+3.3
5. Administration	61.629	57.082	+4.5 bn	+8
6. Compensations	27	n/a	+0.027 bn	n/a
Total commitment appropriations	959.988	994.176	–35.2 bn	–3.5
as a percentage of GNI	1,00%	1,12%		
Total payment appropriations	908.400	942.778	-34.4 bn	–3.7
as a percentage of GNI	0,95%	1,06%		

Note: GNI = gross national income.

achieved, as far as redistributive functions are concerned, the nation-state still provides the most important reference point.

The EU budget is expenditure led, so that, within a limit set by agreed spending and revenue ceilings, resources are raised to match the needs to carry out the EU policies. This creates very different incentives for the EP and the Council as the two arms of the budgetary authority. For member states, efforts to reduce expenditure would imply a reduction in their direct contributions, while for the EP it may provide an incentive to suggest expenditure programmes, since the matching financing would be automatically furnished by the member states up to the overall ceiling. The members of the EP (MEPs) thus enjoy a unique position: they gain credit for expenditures agreed by the EP but are not associated with the related costs. In practice, however, differences in the incentives for member states and MEPs have been blurred, on one hand, by a growing acceptance among MEPs of an austerity approach towards budgetary decisions and, on the other hand, by individual member states' interests in those expenditure policies, where they gain more from the budget than they contribute. Consequently the influence of the EP on the MFF has been effectively almost negligible: For the MFF 07–13 the EP managed to top up the Council's compromise by 4 billion euros (+0.5 per cent), in the negotiations on the MFF 14–20 the EP basically gave in to Council's figures before negotiations even started.

The *juste retour* logic is aggravated by the revenue side as of today the budget is mainly financed by inter-governmental direct transfers rather than "genuine" own resources, for example taxes, which facilitates computation of net positions.

The system of own resources has become increasingly less autonomous since its creation in the 1970s when it aimed to give resources to the Community (customs duties, agricultural levies and value-added-tax contributions) that would "belong" to it and would not depend on decisions by national finance ministers. This, together with the granting of the "power of the purse" to the EP in the 1970s, was a development of a *federal* nature, aimed at enhancing the supranational element of the union.

However, as EU expenditure increased the traditional own resources proved insufficient and a fourth resource was established as part of the Delors-I package in 1988. This fourth resource, which now accounts for approximately half of total EU budget revenues, can be regarded as similar to the pre-1970 period in which the Community was financed by contributions from the member states (Begg and Grimwade 1998). The EP has repeatedly and unsuccessfully demanded a reform of the system of own-resources, (re-)establishing an autonomous income base for the EU, underlying its lack of influence in the context of the MFF.

The annual budgetary procedure

The annual budgetary procedure for the EU budget, set out in detail in Article 314 of the treaty, appears to conform with the division of labour between an executive branch that proposes the budget and a legislative branch that adopts it (see Figure 9.2) and which consists of two arms, the Council and the EP. The Commission prepares a draft budget for the subsequent year by September at the latest. The Council then adopts its position and potential amending letters to the draft and sends it to the EP before 1 October. Thereupon, the EP is obliged to present its amendments to the council's position within 42 days. The Council then may accept or reject the EP's amendments within 10 days. In the case of rejection a Conciliation Committee consisting of an equal number of representatives of the Council and the EP is set up. If the Committee fails to agree on a common proposal within 21 days the Commission has to table a new proposal. In case of non-agreement between the Council and the EP by January 1 the Commission is automatically empowered to spend a monthly sum not acceding 1/12 of the previous year's budget appropriations.

The Lisbon Treaty aimed at both simplifying the annual budgetary procedure as well as raising the power of the EP vis-à-vis the Council. In this context the former distinction between "compulsory" and "non-compulsory" expenditure was abolished and the Conciliation Committee was introduced making the budgetary procedure more similar to the ordinary legislative procedure of co-decision (Crombez and Høyland 2015).

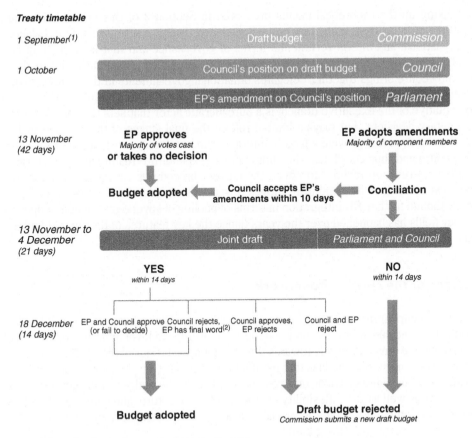

Figure 9.2 The budgetary procedure in the EU

Source: Adapted from European Commission (2012).

Notes: (1) In practice, the Commission endeavours to present the draft budget before the end of April or beginning of May. (2) That means that the EP approves the joint text and then, within 14 days of the Council's rejection, decides (by majority of its component member and 3/5 of the votes cast) to confirm all or some of its amendments.

However, recent research questions this view stressing the importance of persistent strong coalitions in the Council among net-recipients and net-payers, which overrule those minor changes introduced by the Lisbon Treaty. The annual budget struggles for 2011 through 2013 seem to underpin these insights as net payers clearly dominated the negotiations pushing through budgets that saw historically low rates of expenditures increases undercutting the MFF ceilings by several billions.

Although very restrained by the predeterminations of the MFF, the annual budgetary procedure displays a much more supranational setting than the former: The Council votes by qualified majority and often the EP manages to form coalitions with like-minded member states, raising its influence and making it a player on eye level with the member states.

Taking up the theoretical claims presented in Section 2 of this chapter, the main features of the current budgetary procedure clearly display a set-up that, first, balances supranational and intergovernmental forms of governance and that is, second, in line with the overall state of integration in the EU. The largely supranational annual budgetary procedure brings together delegates of national governments in the Council taking decisions by qualified majority and directly elected MEPs. The Commission, as a representative of the executive branch, is a bureaucratic actor that sets the agenda for the budgetary decisions, but plays a limited role in the final stages of the procedure. The ceilings of the MFF provide a largely intergovernmental framework around the annual procedure and thus coordinate the supranational expenditure realm with the intergovernmental revenue realm. Moreover, the current procedures reflect the fact that the political acceptance for significant moves towards fiscal federalism has not emerged – even though further EU integration in terms of pooling of sovereignty in non-budgetary policy fields has happened over the years (since the key features of the current budgetary procedures were introduced).

Implications of the current framework

While the current institutional set-up has enabled the EU to keep the overall level of conflict around budgetary decision-making at the European level limited and to channel redistributive tensions largely towards the renegotiation rounds of the MFF every seven year, the strong status-quo bias that results from such a set-up is widely criticised. Such criticism focuses in particular on two aspects, namely the budget's intergovernmental character as well as the inflexibility of the spending structure, and concludes that "the European Community budget is, arguably, among the least satisfactory elements of EU economic governance" (Begg 2007).

Given the continuous dominance of agricultural and regional spending, it can be debated whether the EU budget was ever meant to serve as a means of EU economic governance. Rather, it can be argued that when established it was first a tool to finance the first (and so far, one of the few) completely integrated former national policies, the CAP. With a monetary union looming on the horizon funds were used to increase the attractiveness to join the single currency for peripheral member states. A similar pattern was used when EU funds were being pledged to promote EU enlargement and, with it, inner reforms of former states behind the Iron Curtain (cf. Neheider and Santos 2011). Hence, the fact that the EU budget overwhelmingly serves transfer purposes rather than investing in EU public goods seems in fact to be owed to the status quo bias stemming from the MFF's decision making procedures. Therefore, demands for the EU budget to be refocused towards investment in EU public goods would need to go hand in hand with proposals for a more supranational decision-making process when negotiating the MFF, that is surrendering of national sovereignty over taxpayers' money or even taxing authority itself. The same holds true for a second striking feature of the EU's finances: its inflexibility. In fact, fixing the distribution of an amount of some 1,000 billion euros for seven years seems to challenge the most advanced centrally planned economies and their five-year plans. Certainly, in recent history partly due to budgetary inflexibility the EU has struggled to act as a strong bloc, in particular when it comes to international crises (e.g. the 2007–2008 world food-price crisis). However, inflexibility may equally be interpreted as a symptom of discord on further integration of policies, such as the Common Foreign and Security Policy (CFSP). Hence, one could easily argue that as long as CFSP is subject to unanimity, its budgetary inflexibility only perfectly mirrors its state of integration.

While the intergovernmental character, as well as the inflexibility of EU spending can be explained with the current state of European integration, there is a third feature of the EU budget, namely the actual economic effects of EU spending, that is less evident. It seems that some of the side effects of the current set-up are often overlooked: Why can the largest beneficiaries of EU regional spending in the past currently be found under the umbrella of financial rescue mechanisms? In contrast, the Commission has repeatedly presented cohesion spending as the main tool to help these countries out of the crisis, despite mixed academic evidence (e.g. Mohl and Hagen 2011; Heinemann *et al.* 2010). Apart from ongoing discussions on the misuse of EU funding, a striking feature of the structural funds is in fact their high degree of pro-cyclicality. For example, as Table 9.2 shows, between 2000 and 2009 Portugal received an annual financial envelope of net 1.6 per cent of GDP, Greece 1.4 per cent and Spain 0.6 per cent.

In assessing these figures one should have in mind, that the average discretional fiscal stimulus in the unprecedented economic downturn of 2009–2010 added up to only 1.1 per cent of member states' GDP in 2009 and 0.8 per cent in 2010. Consequently, for more than 10 years several member states enjoyed a significant fiscal stimulus programme, while already growing well above their potential. Even if properly used, there

Table 9.2 Implicit inner-euro-area-net transfers via structural and cohesion funds 2000–2009

	Annual net transfer		Output gap (% of potential output)
	Per capita	%/GDP	
Belgium	−46 €	−0.2	0.7
Germany	−17 €	−0.1	−0.1
Ireland	+67 €	+0.2	1.1
Greece	+241 €	+1.4	0.5
Spain	+108 €	+0.6	0.9
France	−37 €	−0.1	1.7
Italy	+6 €	+0.0	1.2
Luxembourg	−100 €	−0.2	1.2
Netherlands	−54 €	−0.2	−0.2
Austria	−25 €	−0.1	0.1
Portugal	+238 €	+1.6	0.2
Finland	−10 €	0.0	0.9

Source: Own calculations based on EU-COM Financial Reports 2000–2009, AMECO, Structural and Cohesion Funds including EAFRD, net transfers are corrected for national contributions to the EU budget.

is reason to assume that EU funding fuelled rather than curbed the emergence of macroeconomic imbalances in the euro area.

Up to now it seems as the clearly pro-cyclical features of the EU's structural funds have not properly been scrutinized.

Figure 9.3 ranks member states according to their economic performance in the period 2007–2013. Following the Commission's initial MFF proposal from 2011 one would have found those countries suffering the highest GDP losses under the biggest losers of EU funds for MFF 14–20, whereas those relatively well off were to be granted additional funding: As an extreme case Greece would have lost 42 per cent of its cohesion funding for the period 14–20 compared to 07–13. Spain (−32 per cent), Hungary (−29 per cent), and Slovenia (−39 per cent) were to be found under the biggest losers as well, whereas the biggest winner in nominal terms was Poland – already the largest recipient of regional funding – with an additional 8 billion euros. Various side payments agreed by the European Council partly corrected the initial proposal, yet the overall picture still is clearly pro-cyclical. This feature of EU spending may well be an unintended side product and may be explained by the intergovernmental character of the spending programmes which (once adopted) are often regarded as distributive claims or rights by Member States rather than an instrument of active economic policy-making at the EU level. Yet, by lowering the co-financing rate for EU projects in programme countries hit by the crisis, the EU introduced an element of counter-cyclicality. Moreover, a sign for establishing a stronger link between the EU budget and economic policy-making at the EU level has been the use of the EU budget as a means to provide teeth to the EU's new economic governance framework: It took the Community more than a decade and countless breaches of its Stability and Growth pact before the Council, in March 2012, for the first time ever, decided to freeze EU funding for Hungary because of violations of EU budgetary rules, leading to a swift turnaround of policies in Budapest only weeks later. Macroeconomic conditionality has been enshrined in the new MFF, including the possibility to freeze and withdraw EU funding in cases of

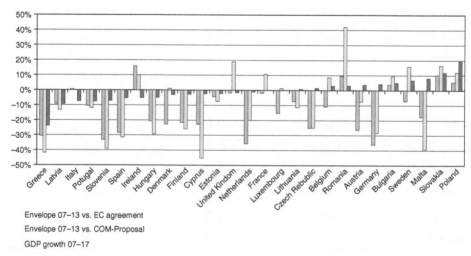

Envelope 07–13 vs. EC agreement

Envelope 07–13 vs. COM-Proposal

GDP growth 07–17

Figure 9.3 GDP growth between 07–13 vs. losses and gains in EU structural funds

Source: Author's calculations, AMECO

breaches of obligations stemming from the Excessive Deficit Procedure (EDP), the Macroeconomic Imbalance Procedure (MIP), or financial assistance programmes. Sanctions kick in early and are subjected to reversed majority voting in the Council (i.e. a majority is needed to prevent sanctions). Whereas the new framework has already been criticized due to the ceilings it provides for potential sanctions and whereas its finally adopted set-up has been less strong than originally envisaged, it provides the Commission with an additional tool for enforcing the new economic governance framework. Moreover and beyond the threat of sanctions, it is also planned (in the form of so-called Partnership Contracts) to connect EU regional spending priorities in the member states more closely and possibly in a more flexible manner with the respective country-specific recommendations resulting from the European Semester.

Which future direction for the EU budget?

In parallel to the negotiations on a new MFF but largely within the institutional and political remit of the euro area rather than the EU, the sovereign debt crisis in the euro area pushed budgetary questions on the top of the European agenda. As described in the chapter on EMU (see Jones and Fuller, in this volume), member states took a number of unprecedented decisions: They created large rescue schemes for euro-area member states facing refinancing difficulties and at the same time tightened the fiscal framework for national budgetary decisions (Fiscal Compact, two pack and six pack). Moreover, under the header of "Genuine EMU" a debate was initiated on how much further integration in the realm of budgetary, economic, and financial policy-making was necessary for creating a stable and durable EMU and how such integration steps would be fully legitimised democratically. A series of three reports under the leadership of the President of the European Council, Herman van Rompuy, in close cooperation with the presidents of the Eurogroup, the European Commission, and the European Central Bank, was published in 2012. Moreover, the European Commission presented in a Communication in December 2012 a "blueprint" for a genuine EMU.

While contributing mainly to further integration in the banking field, these processes have not yet gone far beyond a simple stock-taking exercise in the fiscal realm and the enthusiasm among member states to strengthen the fiscal capacity of the European level (be it at the level of the EU-28 or the EU-18) has been rather limited. And there are indeed good reasons to argue that a scheme comparable to a nation-state budget is not even required for the proper functioning of the EU or of the euro area. Structural economic differences across countries are very high, yet the whole idea of the European project of economic integration has not been based on equalising living conditions through redistribution, but rather on the goal to increase general welfare (see Enderlein and Verdun [2009] for a discussion). The clear political rejection of a "transfer union" in some EU countries (in particular Germany) is indicative in that respect.

On the other hand, there are areas in which further reform steps with fiscal implications could derive more directly from the need to improve or "complete" the euro area against the backdrop of lessons learned from the crisis.

The first such area is *banking union*. Integration in the field of banking supervision and even more importantly resolution (and in the long-term potentially also deposit guarantee schemes) may in fact have also a fiscal dimension. The basic decision by the

European Council in June 2012 to integrate supervision at the European level for the euro area and those member states willing to participate resulted from the need to break the bank–sovereign nexus. It was argued that any European instrument that would provide capital directly to undercapitalised banks and not via the national budget of the respective member state would be acceptable only if the existing national supervisory structures were replaced by a strong European supervisor. Moreover, it had also become clear that a harmonised framework for banking resolution was needed across the EU which would restrict the role of bailouts by national governments and would require – via a new bail-in regime – large parts of resolution costs to be covered by the shareholders and creditors of the banks themselves. Based on this logic, banking union was implemented in 2013–2014 through various decisions by the Council and the Parliament (and an intergovernmental agreement) leading up to the creation of the "Single Supervisory Mechanism" and the "Single Resolution Mechanism", with a "Single Resolution Fund" to finance resolution. This fund will be financed by bank levies in each member state. These will be pooled at the EU level, and national compartments will be progressively mutualised during a transitional period of eight years. Furthermore, the legislation provides a commitment to enhance the borrowing capacity of the SRF, including where possible from public financial arrangements (work is ongoing on the fulfilment of this commitment). It is important to note that this scheme is placed outside the EU budget. Two further areas relate to *fiscal union*. The term *fiscal union* can refer to a multitude of different aspects. While the strengthening of European rules and discretionary powers for the centre in controlling national budgets is very relevant for the fiscal architecture of EMU, the two aspects discussed here relate to (1) creating a "lender of last resort" capable of rescuing member states facing a difficulty of raising capital in the market to roll-over their existing debts or finance new debt and (2) to a macroeconomic stabilisation function that a central budget at the European level could play for the euro area.

With regard to the *lender-of-last-resort function*, the crisis in the euro area gave rise to the creation of two instruments that are not formally part of the EU budget but pool resources at the European level in the euro-area context (as is described in more detail in Chapter 14, in this volume).

The debates around the creation of the EFSF and especially the ESM underline the fact that the EU budget has not been regarded as a means of EU economic governance but a clear distinction was made between euro area and EU context. Theoretically, the budget could have provided all necessary means to underpin an emergency fiscal capacity founded on the community method, as it has been the case in the context of the temporary EFSM, which allowed the Commission to raise debt of up to 60 billion euros, euros guaranteed via the budget. A similar instrument was introduced already in 1972, which granted the Commission the right to issue common bonds in order to provide balance of payments assistance and which had been used during the financial crisis in 2009 and 2010 for non-euro-area member states. In contrast, two of the most powerful fiscal capacities – the EFSF and the ESM – were created as intergovernmental instruments based on multilateral treaties. Hence, they are neither subject to the treaty's budgetary procedure nor to any formal control of the European Parliament as one arm of the budgetary authority. Although key elements were brought into the EU framework (through the so-called two-pack regulations), member states were not ready to bring the budgetary dimension of this instrument of euro area financial assistance under the umbrella of the Community and the EU budgetary framework.

Regarding *macroeconomic stabilisation*, in particular for euro area countries, this aspect was prominently addressed in the report of the "Four Presidents", and it dates back to the time of the first discussions on a single currency in the late 1970s, when one of the main contributions on creating a single currency pointed out: "a Community fiscal stabilisation policy is a key element in any programme for European monetary integration" (MacDougall Report 1977, p. 57). The reason mainly derives from the potentially pro-cyclical effect if inflation differentials persist due to lack of market integration and labour mobility in a monetary union: real interest rates are systematically too high for those countries that are already in downturn while being too low for those economies in a boom or already overheating (Enderlein, 2006; Enderlein *et al.* 2012). Thus, it has been argued that some kind of stabilisation mechanism is necessary in a monetary union to counter this effect and to achieve some degree of convergence across individual member states' business cycles – at least as long as market-based adjustment channels do not work properly (cf. Mundell 1961). Additionally, there is evidence that in integrated economies, dealing with asymmetric regional shocks is most effective on the aggregate, not on the regional level itself (Bayoumi and Masson 1998; Von Hagen 2007). When the euro was conceived in the early 1990s, there was an extensive debate on how such a stabilisation scheme could look like (e.g. Italianer and Pisani-Ferry 1992; Goodhart and Smith 1993; Italianer and Vanheukelen 1993; Von Hagen and Hammond 1998). The need for some form of stabilisation at the European level was shared by many academics and was featured in both the Delors Report and the "One Market, One Money" reports that led up to the creation of the euro. Nevertheless, EMU started without any such scheme in place.

The initial alternative plan that discretionary economic policy coordination under the Broad Economic Guidelines and the set of incentives for member states to keep their own house in order (in terms of building up fiscal buffer in good times and enhancing the flexibility through structural reforms) would substitute for the lack of euro area–wide automatic stabilisers did not show the desired effects. During the first 13 years of EMU, persisting inflation differentials and the lack of enforceable rules at the European level led to substantial current account deficits in some member states while low real interest rates fed asset bubbles in the very same countries. Adjustment channels did not work as properly as they were expected (De Haan 2010; Enderlein *et al.* 2012). This brought the question of macroeconomic stabilisation back into academic discussions (Dullien and Schwarzer 2009). As the main focus was put on strengthening the economic governance framework, policy-makers took up the issue only in 2012 and reopened the debate about a euro area–wide shock absorption mechanism. The Report of the "Four Presidents" of 5 December 2012 called for further analysis on how such a scheme could potentially look like and outlined certain guiding principles to be met. It argued the scheme (1) should not lead to unidirectional or permanent transfers; (2) should not undermine incentives for structural reforms; (3) should be implementable within the framework and the institutions of the Union; (4) should not be an additional crisis-solution mechanism, but rather complement the ESM; and (5) should not lead to an overall increase in tax and expenditure levels (for detailed proposals see Enderlein *et al.* [2013] and Wolff [2012]). The proposals presented in the report were however not taken up by the European Council in December 2012.

Finally, as an additional area with fiscal implications, the debate about "Genuine EMU" brought up – as part of *economic union* – the idea of "reform contracts" that would be coupled with a "solidarity mechanism". In addition to the national ownership that such contracts is meant to stipulate (by being an official commitment of the government), the rationale behind the link to the solidarity mechanism is the creation of positive incentives for member states to implement necessary structural reforms by offsetting in parts and at a case by case basis the political and economic costs associated with these reforms (through budgetary support from the centre). Yet, the scope of such positive incentives (which is still under discussion among member states) would most likely be limited.

Conclusion

Although recent years have seen significant steps in European economic integration, the EU budget, its composition, and its procedures has remained rather unaffected. Looking at the roots and the decision-making procedures one should not be surprised: In its current form, the EU budgetary framework is not prepared to serve as a means to underpin a new framework of economic governance and banking union that is of relevance in particular in the euro-area context. Its procedures were designed around its purpose to serve as a means first to finance the Common Agricultural Policy and later in addition to promote EU enlargement and the integration of new member states. In that respect, the EU budget has retained its intergovernmental nature both in the composition of expenditure, which has remained largely redistributional, as well as in procedures. They are largely in line with the state of political integration for the EU as a whole, in particular the limited acceptance for further steps towards fiscal federalism. Amidst its deepest financial crisis the Community so far has not shown any attempt to redesign its framework of common expenditure but rather has found ways to circumvent any reform by setting up alternative arrangements within the institutional context of the euro area where the direct interdependencies created through monetary integration have established a bargaining space of different sets of economic necessities and political constraints.

Notes

The opinions expressed in this chapter are those of the authors and do not necessarily reflect those of the European Central Bank or the German Ministry of Foreign Affairs.

1   Wolfgang Münchau, "Britain's Bluster Serves the Eurozone Well", *Financial Times*, November 25, 2012. In this article, Münchau talks about the "appalling spectacle of the EU's budget negotiations".

2   However, it is also argued that efficient decision-making procedures yielding effective policy outcomes can also create a high degree of legitimacy (see the distinction between input-and output-legitimacy in Scharpf 1999).

3   This third dimension may also be linked to the idea that a fully integrated political system (at least in its democratic variant) would need a common public sphere that allows for discourse among citizens and the creation of a supra-national demos (e.g. Habermas 2011).

4   This does not mean that there is no variation in the degree to which political authority is delegated to supranational agents in the different domains. Indeed, in certain policy fields, such as competition policy, the Commission is very powerful, while in others, such as the Common Foreign and Security Policy, decisions are taken by unanimity in the Council. However,

policy fields evolve as part of the overall institutional setting. Moreover, they reflect the general scope of pooled sovereignty and degree of political integration and acceptance.

5   The description draws on Laffan (1997), European Commission (2002), Laffan and Lindner (2010) and Lindner (2005).

6   Renegotiations in the European Council take place in conjunction with other political issues. Hence, bargaining (and horse-trading) among Member States combines budgetary issues with non-budgetary issues. In this context, it has been argued that the EU budget fulfils an important "compensation function". It compensates those member states that might incur costs from the integration process and thus, facilitates a consensus for further integration among member states (Folkers 1997).

7   Although the Commission and the EP have, as signatories of the International Agreement, a veto power over the ceilings of the Financial Perspective, they rarely exercise it. Usually, the EP is compensated for its consent to the ceilings through informal extensions of its budgetary powers.

8   GNI is the basis for all EU budgetary calculations. It is broadly comparable to GDP.

9   Although there are no comprehensive studies on the matter, most analyses converge around that level (*The Economist 2003*).

References

Alesina A. and E. Spolaore (1997): "On the Number and Size of Nations", *Quarterly Journal of Economics*, Vol. 107, no. 4 (November), pp. 1027–1056.

Bayoumi, T. and P. Masson (1998): "Liability-Creating versus Non-Liability-Creating Fiscal Stabilization Policies: Ricardian Equivalence, Fiscal Stabilization, and EMU", *Economic Journal*, Vol. 107, no. 449, pp. 1026–1045.

Begg, I. (1999): "Reshaping the EU Budget: Yet another missed opportunity?", South Bank European Paper 5/99, South Bank University.

Begg, I. (2007) "The 2008/2009 review of the EU budget: real or cosmetic?", *CESifo Forum*, Vol. 8, no. 1, 45–50. ISSN 1615-245X, 45.

Begg, I. and N. Grimwade (1998): *Paying for Europe*, Sheffield: Sheffield Academic Press.

Bolton, P and G. Roland (2000): "The Breakup of Nations: A Political Economy Analysis", *The Quarterly Journal of Economics*, Vol. 112, no. 4 (November), pp. 1057–1090.

Buchanan, J.M. and G. Tullock (1962): *The Calculus of Consent*, Ann Arbor: University of Michigan Press.

Crombez, C. and B. Høyland (2015) "The Budgetary Procedure of the European Union and the Implications of the Lisbon Treaty", *European Union Politics*, Vol. 16, no. 1.

De Haan, J. (2010): "Inflation Differentials in the Euro Area: A Survey". In De Haan, J. and H. Berger: *The European Central Bank at Ten*. Heidelberg: Springer, pp. 11–32.

Dullien, S. and D. Schwarzer (2009): "Bringing Macroeconomics into the EU Budget Debate: Why and How?", *Journal of Common Market Studies*, Vol. 47, no. 1, pp. 153–174.

The Economist (2003): "Snoring while a Superstate Emerges?", May 8.

Enderlein, H. (2006): "Adjusting to EMU: The Impact of Monetary Union on Domestic Fiscal and Wage-setting Institutions", *European Union Politics*, Vol. 7, no. 1 (March), pp. 113–140.

Enderlein, H. and A. Verdun (2009): "EMU's Teenage Challenge: what have we learned and can we predict from Political Science?", *Journal of European Public Policy*, Vol. 14, no. 4 (June), 490–507.

Enderlein, H., J. Lindner, O. Calvo-Gonzalez, R. Ritter (2005): "The EU Budget – How Much Scope for Institutional Reform", ECB Occasional Paper Series No. 27. (Also forthcoming in Helge Berger and Thomas Moutos: *Designing the New EU*, Boston: MIT-Press, 2005).

Enderlein, H., P. Bofinger, J.-C. Piris, P. de Grauwe, M. Joao Rodrigues, J. Pisani-Ferry, A. Sapir, and A. Vitorino (2012): "Completing the Euro – A Road Map towards Fiscal Union in Europe". Notre Europe Study No. 92, Notre Europe, Paris.

Enderlein, H., L. Guttenberg, and J. Spiess (2013): "Blueprint for a Cyclical Shock Insurance in the Eurozone". Notre Europe Policy Paper No. 99, Notre Europe, Paris.

European Commission (1977): *Report of the study group on the role of public finance in European integration* ("The MacDougall Report").

European Commission (2002): *European Union Public Finance*, Office for Official Publications of the European Communities, Luxembourg.

European Commission (2012): *EU Budget 2011: Financial Report*, Luxembourg: Publications Office of the European Union.

Folkers, C. (1997): Finanz- und Haushaltspolitik, P. Klemmer: *Handbuch der Europäischen Wirtschaftspolitik*, München: Verlag Franz Vahlen, pp. 561–663.

Goodhart, C. and S. Smith (1993): "Stabilization", *European Economy*, Reports and Studies 5, pp. 417–455.

Habermas, J. (2011): *Zur Verfassung Europas*, Edition Suhrkamp.

Heinemann, F., P. Mohl, and S. Osterloh (2010): "Reforming the EU Budget: Reconciling Needs with Political-Economic Constraints", *Journal of European Integration*, Vol. 32, no. 1, 59–76.

Inman, R.P. and D.L. Rubinfeld (1997): "Rethinking Federalism", *Journal of Economic Perspectives*, Vol. 11, no. 4, pp. 43–64.

Italianer, A. and J. Pisani-Ferry (1992): "Systèmes budgétaires et amortissement des chocs régionaux: implications pour l'Union économique et monétaire", *Economie Prospective Internationale*, Vol. 51, no. 3, pp. 49–69.

Italianer, A. and M. Vanheukelen (1993): "Proposals for Community Stabilization Mechanisms. Some Historical Applications", *European Economy*, Reports and Studies 5, pp. 493–510.

Laffan, B. and J. Lindner (2010): "The EU Budget". In Mark Pollack, Helen Wallace and William Wallace (eds.): *Policy-Making in the European Union*, 6th edition, Oxford: Oxford University Press, pp. 191–212.

Leonardi, R. (1999): *The Socio-economic Impact of Projects Financed by the Cohesion Fund: A Modelling Approach* (3 volumes), Luxembourg: Office of Official Publications of the European Communities.

Lindner, J. (2005): *Conflict in EU Budgetary Politics*, London: Routledge.

Lindner, J. and B. Rittberger (2003): "The Creation, Interpretation and Contestation of Institutions – Revisiting Historical Institutionalism", *Journal of Common Market Studies*, Vol. 41, no. 3, pp. 445–473.

Mohl, P. and T. Hagen (2011): "Do EU Structural Funds Promote regional Employment? Evidence from Dynamic Panel Data Models", Working Paper Series 1403, European Central Bank, Frankfurt.

Mundell, R., 1961. A theory of optimum currency areas. *The American Economic Review*, Vol. 51, no. 4, pp. 657–665.

Neheider, S. and I. Santos (2011): "Reframing the EU Budget Decision-Making Process", *Journal of Common Market Studies*, Vol. 49, no. 3, pp. 631–651.

Oates, W.E. (1972): *Fiscal Federalism*, New York: Harcourt Brace Jovanovich.

Oates, W.E. (1999): "An Essay on Fiscal Federalism", *Journal of Economic Literature*, Vol. XXXVII (September), pp. 1120–1149.

Pollack, M.A. (2003): *The Engine of European Integration – Delegation, Agency, and Agenda Setting in the EU*, Oxford: Oxford University Press.

Riker, W.H. (1964): *Federalism: Origin, Operation, Significance*, Boston: Little, Brown & Co.

Scharpf, F.W. (1988): "The Joint-Decision Trap: Lessons from German Federalism and European Integration", *Public Administration*, Vol. 66, pp. 239–278.

Scharpf, F.W. (1999): *Governing Europe. Effective and Democratic?*, Oxford: Oxford University Press.

Shackleton, M. (1990): *Financing the European Community, The Royal Institute of International Affairs*, London: Pinter Publishers.

Stepan, A. (1999): "Federalism and Democracy: Beyond the U.S. Model", *Journal of Democracy* Vol. 10, no. 4, pp. 19–33.

Von Hagen, J. (2007): Achieving Economic Stabilization by Sharing Risk within Countries. In R. Boadway and A. Shah (eds.): *Intergovernmental Fiscal Transfers*. Washington, DC: World Bank.

Von Hagen, J. and G. Hammond (1998): "Regional Insurance against Asymmetric Shocks: An Empirical Study for the European Community", *The Manchester School*, Vol. 66, no. 3, pp. 331–353.

Wolff, G.B., 2012. *A budget for Europe's monetary union*. Bruegel Policy Contribution 2012/22.

Chapter 10

EU agencies

BERTHOLD RITTBERGER AND ARNDT WONKA

Introducing EU agencies

Agencies are by now an established institutional feature of the EU's multilevel polity. Together with the European Commission, comitology committees and European regulatory networks (ERN), agencies are part and parcel of the EU's executive structure. Today more than 30 agencies partake in the EU's regulatory processes (see Table 10.1). Their tasks and competencies, however, differ considerably. Most EU agencies' competencies are restricted to collecting and disseminating information, tasks often seen to enhance the EU's supranational monitoring capacities and to facilitate the coherence and effectiveness of implementation of EU policies in the member states. From a legal point of view, EU agencies do not possess legislative or discretionary powers vis-à-vis the Commission or other EU bodies. In its *Meroni* ruling, the European Court of Justice (ECJ) declared in 1958 that – unless specified in the EU's primary law – discretionary powers cannot be delegated to other bodies, public or private. For EU agencies, this implies that they are only allowed to take binding decisions if the Commission, the European Parliament and the Council have specified the rules and criteria for taking these (non-legislative) decisions in EU legislation. As a consequence, agencies do not – in a legal sense – exert discretionary powers when taking such decisions. EU agencies are, however, involved in preparing regulatory decisions by providing expertise (Hofmann and Morini 2012; Chiti 2013). The European Medicines Agency (EMA), for instance, plays a crucial role in the preparation of regulatory decisions which are subsequently adopted, usually without any modifications, by the Commission in a comitology committee (Gehring and Krapohl 2007). At the same time, the information provided by agencies with a purely informational mandate can and often does lead to the adoption and development of new EU policies (Martens 2010). In addition, EU agencies are also directly involved in the implementation of EU policies. For instance, the Office for Harmonisation in the Internal Market (Trade Marks and Designs; OHIM) registers the Community trademark, which protects the owner's rights across all member states.

Despite differences in their formal competencies, mandates and organizational resources, all EU regulatory agencies share some central institutional characteristics: They are established by an act of EU secondary legislation and possess legal personality. This allows agencies to enter into contracts with third parties and independently manage their internal affairs. Their status as legal personality also renders agencies and their decisions subject to judicial review. Their legal status thus provides agencies with a certain degree of formal independence from EU and member state institutions in their everyday activities. Governments, the European Commission and, in recent years, the European Parliament can and do, however, influence and control agencies' conduct by employing various ex ante and ex post control mechanisms (see the following section).

Although the EU lacks a template for agencies' design, they show considerable similarities regarding their internal organizational structures. Every EU agency is headed by a director responsible for the management of the agency's tasks and with a duty to report to the agency's management board. In turn, the members of the management board can hold the director and the agency's staff to account and have a decisive influence on agencies' medium term agendas as they formulate yearly work plans. Given their central role in steering the agency, it seems hardly surprising that (with the exception of four agencies),[1] each member state is represented and has a vote on the management board of EU agencies. In addition, while the European Parliament can only nominate representatives for very few agencies, the Commission has up to six representatives and can vote on the management boards of all agencies dealing with internal market policies. The agencies in which the Commission usually lacks representation are those policy areas, where an intergovernmental decision mode tends to dominate. This applies not only to agencies in the former *second* and *third* pillar addressing questions on external security, justice and home affairs but also to the newly established financial supervisory bodies. Finally, some agencies' management boards also allow for the participation of representatives of industry and consumer groups and for observers from non EU-member states.

Since decisions in management boards are taken by (qualified) majority vote, member state representatives are always in the majority and hence – at least formally – in the position to determine the course of the agency and exercise control. In her empirical analysis of the work of management boards in a number of agencies, Busuioc finds, however, that national delegates, generally senior staff from national ministries and agencies, tend to be insufficiently prepared and hence lack steering ability. Moreover, debates in management boards tend to focus on the micromanagement of agencies and on national idiosyncrasies and interests, while the broader regulatory strategy to be pursued by agencies seems to play a secondary role (Busuioc 2012: 725–726, 732; see also section 3.1). At the same time, there is also evidence that the staff members of EU agencies think that the management boards do exercise considerable influence on their work. In a survey we conducted with the staff of nine EU agencies, 43 per cent of the respondents answered that members of the board had at least *some* influence on their work, while 23 per cent perceive this influence to be *great* ($N = 194$). Despite some member state delegates' ineffectiveness in representing the positions of their institutions and countries in the management boards, these boards are perceived to be important venues for directing the work of EU agencies.

Agencies' capacities to act autonomously also tend to be restricted as result of a lack of technical infrastructure and staff to provide the expertise and information needed for their own work. Hence, EU agencies often rely on the infrastructure, expertise and information provided by domestic regulatory bodies as well as by academics and industry. In order to acquire the information needed to carry out their tasks, some agencies or hubs of networks that establish links between national partner agencies and provide ties between these and EU agencies (Levi-Faur 2011). The European Environmental Agency (EEA), for example, plays a central role in coordinating the European Environment Information and Observation Network (EIONET), which facilitates the data collection and processing of several hundred experts and national institutions. Moreover, some agencies established an extensive system of working groups in which members of national regulatory institutions and academics do a substantial part of agencies' regulatory work. The European Food Safety Authority (EFSA), for example, has set up more than ten thematic panels, each subdivided in several issue-specific working groups, which prepare opinions and advice.

The reliance on the resources and information provided by national regulatory bodies corresponds with most agencies' coordinative function in EU policy-making: EU agencies collect information on the domestic regulatory situation from member states' institutions. The analyses provided as well as the exchange between domestic regulators organized by EU agencies aim at improving the communication and cooperation between domestic regulators and shall contribute to the effective implementation of EU policies. By granting only limited powers to EU agencies and by making them dependent on resources provided by national regulators, governments also prevent agencies from taking actions that might impose regulatory burdens on their constituencies. To be able to act effectively EU agencies thus need to find ways to secure the cooperation of their national and European partner institutions.

Finally, EU agencies differ considerably in their size (Table 10.1) and their formal institutional independence (Wonka and Rittberger 2010). The European Asylum Support Office ranges among the smallest agencies with a staff of about 40 and a budget of 10 million euros, while the EMA with a staff of almost 750 and a budget of about 220 million euros ranges at the other end of the scale. As can also be seen from Table 10.1, some agencies have their own sources of revenue which sometimes exceed the funding agencies receive from the EU budget. Consequently, financial independence might increase agencies' political independence and clout in regulatory policy-making.

The evolution of the agency phenomenon over time and across issue areas

Since the early 1990s, the number of EU agencies has grown steadily (see Table 10.1). This growth reflects a general trend in industrialized countries of delegating regulatory tasks to non-majoritarian regulatory organizations, such as agencies and other independent regulatory bodies, which operate outside the institutions of the political arm of the executive (e.g. ministries) and are therefore not directly controlled by elected politicians (Gilardi 2005: 86; Jordana et al. 2011: 1345, 1347). While we discuss the reasons and rationales for agency creation more systematically in the ensuing sections, the Single European Act (SEA) and the associated objective to complete the internal market is an important milestone in this regard, as it increased the demand for regulatory expertise significantly. The SEA and the Commission's White Paper on "Completing the Single Market", adopted in 1985, envisaged entailed the adoption of a vast number of regulatory measures to accompany the internal market programme; it also implied that the domestic implementation of these measures necessitated coordination and monitoring, tasks that have increasingly been delegated to EU agencies.

To master the growing regulatory burden resulting from the SEA and the internal market program, the EU had to step up its bureaucratic capacities. Over the past decades, policy-makers and political observers have increasingly questioned the European Commission's ability to address technical and complex problems effectively and efficiently, because of the political interference of member state governments and the European Parliament with Commission decisions, which threaten to undermine the Commission's impartiality and its credibility to commit to efficiency-oriented, long-term regulatory policy goals (see Majone 2001; Gilardi 2002). According to Majone, EU agencies are thus a functionally adequate institutional response to the Commission's 'credibility crisis' (2000: 284–290). Moreover, in areas where the Commission lacks the competencies for legislative harmonization of regulatory rules, EU agencies with their close ties to national (and international) regulators might be a politically acceptable and functionally appropriate institutional devise to coordinate the regulatory activities of EU member states.

While EU agencies were created to address these regulatory challenges, they are also the product of a political compromise (see Kelemen 2002; Dehousse 2008). While the Commission was quick to volunteer for an extension of its own bureaucratic capacities

Table 10.1 EU Regulatory Agencies

Name of Agency	Year of creation	Task of agency	Location	Staff	Budget (in million €)
European Centre for the Development of Vocational Training (Cedefop)	1975	Supports the development of European vocational and educational training (VET) policies in order to strengthen European cooperation and implementing policies for an attractive VET.	Thessaloniki, Greece	130	17
European Foundation for the Improvement of Living and Working Conditions (Eurofound)	1975	Provides information, advice and expertise on living and working conditions, industrial relations and managing change in Europe.	Dublin, Ireland	116	20
European Environment Agency (EEA)	1990	Provides information on the environment for those involved in developing, adopting, implementing and evaluating environmental policy and the public.	Copenhagen, Denmark	234	35
European Training Foundation (ETF)	1990	Helps developing countries to harness the potential of their human capital through the reform of education, training and labour market systems.	Turin, Italy	136	20
European Monitoring Centre for Drugs and Drug Addiction (EMCDDA)	1993	Gathers and analyses information on drugs and drug addiction.	Lisbon, Portugal	112	14
Translation Centre for the Bodies of the European Union (CdT)	1994	Provides the translation services required by the agencies of the EU.	Luxembourg, Luxembourg	230	50
Community Plant Variety Office (CPVO)	1994	Implements and applies the protection of plant variety rights which allows intellectual property rights to be granted.	Angers, France	46	13

(Continued)

Table 10.1 (Continued)

Name of Agency	Year of creation	Task of agency	Location	Staff	Budget (in million €)
European Agency for Safety and Health at Work (EU-OSHA)	1994	Supports improvement of working conditions in Europe.	Bilbao, Spain	71	14
Office for Harmonisation in the Internal Market (Trade Marks and Designs) (OHIM)	1993	EU's official trade mark and designs office; registers the Community trademark and registers Community design.	Alicante, Spain	775	178
European Medicines Agency (EMA)	1993	Protects and promotes public and animal health; provides scientific evaluations of applications for European marketing authorization for medical products.	London, United Kingdom	737	29 183
European Police Office (EU-ROPOL)	1995	Handles the exchange and analysis of criminal intelligence to improve the effectiveness and cooperation between national law enforcement authorities.	The Hague, Netherlands	592	82
European Union Institute for Security Studies (EUISS)	2001	Researches security issues for the EU and provides a forum for debate; offers analyses and forecasts to the High Representative for Foreign Affairs.	Paris, France	/	/
European Union Satellite Centre (EUSC)	2001	Analyzes earth observation space imagery to support EU's decision-making in the field of Common Foreign and Security Policy.	Torrejón de Ardoz, Spain	105	17
European Food Safety Authority (EFSA)	2002	Responsible for the EU risk assessment regarding food safety; provides independent scientific advice and clear communication on risks.	Parma, Italia	494	75
European Maritime Safety Agency (EMSA)	2002	Helps developing and implementing EU laws on maritime safety, pollution from shipping and maritime security; has responsibilities in areas of preventing and responding to oil spills, vessel monitoring and identification and tracking of vessels.	Lisbon, Portugal	257	53

Agency	Year	Description	Location		
The European Union's Judicial Cooperation Unit (EUROJUST)	2002	Deals with judicial cooperation in criminal matters to improve the coordination of investigations and prosecutions among the judicial authorities of the Member States when dealing with serious cross-border and organized crime.	The Hague, the Netherlands	258	31
European Aviation Safety Agency (EASA)	2002	Promotes the highest common standards of safety and environmental protection in civil aviation and develops common safety and environmental rules at EU level.	Cologne, Germany	701	33 177
European Agency for the Management of Operational Cooperation at the External Borders (FRONTEX)	2004	Promotes, coordinates and develops European border management.	Warsaw, Poland	306	88
European GNSS Agency (GSA)	2004	Supports the Commission in matters relating to satellite radio navigation.	Prague, Czech Republic	61	11
European Railway Agency – promoting safe and compatible rail systems (ERA)	2004	Aims to create an integrated railway area by reinforcing safety and interoperability.	Valenciennes and Lille, France	165	24
European Defence Agency (EDA)	2004	Supports the member states and the Council in their effort to improve European defence capabilities in the field of crisis management.	Brussels, Belgium	116	30
European Centre for Disease Prevention and Control (ECDC)	2004	Identifies, assesses and communicates threats to human health posed by infectious diseases.	Stockholm, Sweden	305	56

(Continued)

Table 10.1 (Continued)

Name of Agency	Year of creation	Task of agency	Location	Staff	Budget (in million €)
European Network and Information Security Agency (ENISA)	2004	Promotes the capability of the European Union, the EU member states and the business community to prevent, address and respond to network and information security problems.	Heraklion, Greece	66	8
European Police College (CEPOL)	2005	Brings together senior police officers with the aim to encourage cross-border cooperation in the fight against crime	Bramshill, United Kingdom	42	8
European Fisheries Control Agency (EFCA)	2005	Promotes common standards for control, inspection and surveillance under the Common Fisheries Policy.	Vigo, Spain	62	9
European Institute for Gender Equality (EIGE)	2006	Supports EU institutions and Member States in promoting equality between women and men and combating sex discrimination.	Vilnius, Lithuania	45	6
European Chemicals Agency (ECHA)	2006	Implements the EU's chemicals legislation and advances safe use of chemicals.	Helsinki, Finland	550	249
European Union Agency for Fundamental Rights (FRA)	2007	Collects and analyses data on fundamental rights.	Vienna, Austria	112	17
Agency for the Cooperation of Energy Regulators (ACER)	2009	Coordinates the work of national energy regulators and works towards a single energy market	Ljubljana, Slovenia	57	20
European Banking Authority (EBA)	2010	Coordinates the work of EU and national bodies safeguarding the stability of the financial system, the transparency of markets and financial products and the protection of depositors and investors.	London, United Kingdom	95	7

Agency	Year	Description	Location			
European Securities and Markets Authority (ESMA)	2010	Works towards enhanced protection of investors and reinforcement of stable and well functioning financial markets in the European Union.	Paris, France	101	7	13
European Insurance and Occupational Pensions Authority (EIOPA)	2010	Supports the stability of the financial system, transparency of markets and financial products as well as the protection of insurance policyholders and pension scheme members.	Frankfurt, Germany	89	6	9
European Asylum Support Office (EASO)	2010	Supports the consistent treatment of individual asylum cases in all member states.	Valetta, Malta	61	10	
European Agency for the operational management of large-scale IT systems in the area of freedom, security and justice (IT Agency)	2011	Manages large-scale information technology systems in Home Affairs.	Tallinn, Estonia	87	20	

and competencies to cope with the increased demand for regulation, member states were hesitant to oblige as they assumed that the Commission harboured integrationist ambitions. Even though governments were reluctant to endow the Commission with new regulatory tasks, they acknowledged – at the same time – the need for upgrading the EU's bureaucratic capacities, and hence agreed with the Commission on the establishment of agencies. As stated earlier, these agencies had limited powers and the composition of their management boards provided governments with significant political influence on agencies' activities (Kelemen 2002; Dehousse 2008), thereby limiting their potential to impose regulatory burdens on important domestic economic constituents and political costs on governments.

In sum, it can be argued that the establishment and the design of EU agencies are governed by functional as well as political considerations. This is also true for the timing of agencies' establishment: The political agreement on the completion of the internal market created a functional demand for more bureaucratic resources. Moreover, agencies were also established because the malfunctioning of existing governance structures frustrated governments and the Commission alike. Agencies such as the European Medicines Agency (Majone 2000; Kelemen and Majone 2012: 231–234) as well as the European Chemicals Agency replaced committee-governance structures whose institutional contribution to the realization of the regulatory goals was considered ineffective. Moreover, the establishment of some agencies followed prominent regulatory failures and environmental accidents, which pointed at the insufficiency of existing regulatory structures. The European Food Safety Authority, for example, was established after governments and the Commission failed to deal effectively with the BSE crisis. While plans for an agency on food safety had been discussed prior to the crisis, the crisis acted as a catalyst, creating sufficient political awareness and public pressure to form an agreement between governments, the Commission and the European Parliament on its establishment (Majone 2000; Kelemen and Majone 2012: 234–236). The establishment of the European Maritime Safety Agency (EMSA) followed a similar dramaturgy, with an exogenous event unsettling the institutional status quo: In the late 1990s and early 2000s the accidents of two oil tankers caused serious environmental damages along the coasts of France and Spain, which created the political momentum for the establishment of EMSA, which is tasked with the development, implementation and monitoring of legislation addressing the security of vessels and maritime safety.

The literature draws a general distinction between agencies operating in the area of social and economic regulation. Economic regulation refers to market imperfections and highlights regulatory measure to redress these, such as the protection of property rights, ensuring fair competition and market access. Social regulation is about devising rules to protect citizens, workers and consumers against the socially undesirable externalities of market integration (Wonka and Rittberger 2010; Thatcher 2011). Some EU agencies can be unambiguously assigned to one category: The EU agency dealing with trademarks (OHIM), the Agency for the Cooperation of Energy Regulators (ACER), the Body of European Regulators for Electronic Communications (BEREC) and the three financial supervisory agencies (the EBA, the ESMA and the European Insurance and Occupational Pensions Authority) are in the economic regulation camp. The European Centre for the Development of Vocational Training (Cedefop), the European Foundation for the Improvement of Living and Working Conditions (Eurofound) and the European Agency for Safety and Health at Work (EU-OSHA) address questions of social regulation.

The EMA, the Chemicals Agency (ECHA) and the European Food Safety Authority (EFSA) are normally also classified as social regulators, since their activities are meant to reduce the environmental and health-related risks of pharmaceuticals, chemicals and foodstuffs traded in the EU (Wonka and Rittberger 2010: 731–732; Thatcher 2011: 797). At the same time, however, these agencies are directly or indirectly involved in granting producers of these products the right to access the European market. Their activities thus also strongly touch upon economic issues. The agencies established during the 1990s and early 2000s mostly operate in the area of social regulation. Only more recently do we witness a wave of agency formation in the area of economic regulation. Finally, there is a third category of agencies, which does not operate in the area of economic and social regulation, but focuses on questions relating to external and internal security. These agencies are tasked with facilitating the cooperation of member states' police authorities and judiciaries and collecting specific security-related information. By Having their institutional origin in the EU's former pillar structure under the second and third pillars, the management of these agencies is dominated by governments.

EU agencies, networks, and the Commission: who regulates?

Why are EU agencies created? The brief episodes mentioned earlier suggest that the failure of existing governance structures to solve regulatory problems plays an important role in decisions to establish EU agencies. While such *functional* reasons are important in accounts on agency creation, so are *political* considerations: Member state governments as well as the Commission have very clear – and often contrary – views about the preferred design of regulatory governance arrangements, reflecting respective institutional and political preferences. We can think about functional and political explanations as complementary explanations for the creation of EU agencies: While functional explanations point towards the *demand* for EU agencies, political explanations are better suited to explain the *supply* of EU agencies.

According to the functional demand-side explanation, politicians believe that opting for an agency allows them to overcome collective action problems, which hamper the present realization of regulatory policy goals (Dehousse 2008). Two types of problems stand out in the literature to which the establishment of agencies is considered a functional remedy: First, effective regulation depends on the provision of problem-adequate expertise and information, which elected policy-makers and officials often lack. As technical issues are commonly of little salience to politicians, they have few incentives (and often few resources) to develop the necessary expertise themselves. The heterogeneity of the regulatory arena in the EU – comprising a multitude of different regulatory regimes – even exacerbates the demand for information and expert knowledge (see Wonka and Rittberger 2010: 736). From this perspective, EU agencies provide decision-makers with the necessary expertise and information to arrive at problem-adequate solutions to regulatory policy problems. Second, the creation of agencies can also be seen as a means by policy-makers to enhance the credibility of their policy commitments (see Kelemen and Majone 2012: 225–226; Wonka and Rittberger 2010: 734–735). According to this perspective, the nature of the democratic process, with elections taking place at regular intervals, renders policy decisions enacted by the current majority inherently unstable, for they can be reversed by a future governing majority (see Kelemen and Majone 2012: 225). This uncertainty about future policy decisions can be counteracted, if elected officials delegate policy-making prerogatives to independent agencies, which allow governments to lock in cherished policy objectives (see Wonka and Rittberger 2010: 737). Policy credibility not only suffers from policy uncertainty, but also from the time inconsistent preferences of elected policy-makers, which 'occurs when a government's optimal long-run policy differs from its preferred short-run policy, so that the government in the short run has an incentive to renege on its long-term commitments' (Kelemen and Majone 2012: 225). Again, governments can tie their own hands, forgoing the temptation of short-termism, and commit to regulatory policies by delegating regulatory powers to an independent agency, which operates at arm's length from elected politicians.

Yet, demand alone may not be sufficient to explain supply of EU agencies, for the creation of EU agencies may impose political costs on actors: For example the Commission may be opposed to seeing an agency endowed with regulatory tasks instead of having its powers expanded and member states may not want to see the prerogatives of domestic regulators curbed at the expense of a supranational regulatory agency. In short, we would expect that the political principals – the member states, the Commission and (as of more recently) the European Parliament – wrangle over the powers conferred to EU agencies as well as over its institutional design and the concomitant mechanisms for controlling the agency (Dehousse 2008). We thus need to look at the politics behind the creation of EU agencies and ask why the key policy-makers – the member state governments, the Commission and the European Parliament – opt for the agency solution rather than expand the regulatory powers of the Commission or leave the regulatory work to networks of national agencies. Kelemen and Tarrant (2011) suggest that member state governments, the Commission and the European Parliament hold different preferences when choosing a regulatory governance arrangement. For the Commission, the agency option is inferior to its most preferred option: seeing its own regulatory competencies enhanced. Only when this option is considered to be out of reach because of member state resistance will the Commission support the creation of EU agencies, because the Commission holds a general preference to expand the EU's regulatory reach (see Kelemen and Tarrant 2011: 927). This view is supported by empirical evidence, which indicates that EU agencies hold close working relationships with their "sister" directorates in the Commission (Egeberg and Trondal 2011).

To EU member states, EU agencies do not only bring functional benefits, such as the promotion of harmonized regulation or the reduction of political uncertainty, they also entail 'distributional consequences' (Kelemen and Tarrant 2011: 928) and pose a 'considerable risk to national autonomy in regulatory implementation' (Kelemen and Tarrant 2011: 929), which reduces member states' willingness to delegate regulatory competencies to supranational actors. To facilitate and monitor the implementation of its policies and to provide the Council and European Parliament with expertise for regulatory policy-making, EU agencies are only one of various institutional alternatives to fulfil this task. Governments and EU institutions can delegate implementing tasks to the European Commission or charge networks of national regulatory agencies with the coordination and monitoring of implementation. The Commission, agencies and regulatory networks differ with regard to their formal decision-making competencies and the resources they have at their disposal to fulfil their tasks. As discussed previously, EU agencies enjoy some institutional independence as they operate outside the Commission's bureaucracy and have their own legal personality. Moreover, they do have their own, albeit varying, administrative resources (see Table 10.1). At the same time, their competencies in EU policy-making are closely circumscribed. Based on the criteria and rules laid down in EU legislation, some agencies (e.g. Community Plant Variety Office [CPVO], Office for Harmonization in the Internal Market [OHIM], European Chemicals Agency [ECHA]) can take binding decisions (European Commission 2008: 7). The work of most agencies' is, however, restricted: They shall support the effective implementation of EU policies by collecting and disseminating information on the regulatory situation and on the implementation in member states, on one hand, and by providing (formally non-binding) advice to the Commission in EU policy-making, on the other hand. By contrast, the European Commission can adopt implementing measures, which are binding for the member states and it generally plays a powerful role in EU policy-making (see chapters by Thomson and Wonka, in this volume). European networks of national regulators, in turn, provide forums in which national regulators share their experiences in the implementation of EU policies and agree on – non-binding – common strategies to address regulatory problems. Moreover, networks provide advice to the EU's legislative institutions on matters of EU policy. Networks, however, lack delegated competencies and they do have only limited administrative resources to organize and fulfil their functions (Coen and Thatcher 2008; Kelemen and Tarrant 2011).

The functional and political accounts, which we highlighted to explain the establishment of EU agencies, also offer good guidance for explaining how political actors choose among EU agencies, networks and the Commission (see Eberlein and Grande 2005; Coen and Thatcher 2008; Thatcher and Coen 2008; Kelemen and Tarrant 2011; Blauberger and Rittberger 2014). There is relatively broad agreement in the literature that functional arguments alone are insufficient to explain why the Commission, EU agencies or regulatory networks are chosen to assist member states in regulatory implementation. Had actors been driven by functional concerns alone, the EU would see either an extension of the Commission's regulatory capacities or an increase in independent (and powerful) agencies in the regulation of public utilities, such as telecoms and energy (see Thatcher 2011). Yet, European regulatory networks are the dominant governance structures in these policy areas (Coen and Thatcher 2008). As argued earlier, the reluctance of member state governments to opt for EU agencies is explained by governments' unwillingness to accept possible redistributive effects, which result from the delegation of powers to independent agencies (Kelemen and Tarrant 2011). In economic sectors dominated by state owned firms, governments are reluctant to cease policy-making or implementing authority to supranational agencies – or the Commission – as such moves would undermine their ability to cater for important electoral constituencies. Hence, governments tend to block the establishment of EU agencies and push for the establishment of networks of national regulators, which preserve room for political manoeuvre for domestic actors. Moreover, the Commission and national agencies actively work against the creation of EU agencies, if the establishment of EU agencies threatens to undermine their own competencies (see Thatcher 2011). The Commission, however, is regularly considered to promote the establishment of agencies in policy areas where it possesses only weak competencies itself and entertains only slim prospects that this will change. In such a case, so the argument, EU agencies are seen to strengthen the EU's bureaucracy from which the Commission – through its close working ties to agencies – tends to profit indirectly (Kelemen 2002; Egeberg and Trondal 2011).

There is a tendency in the literature to treat political and functional explanations as exclusive, rather than complementary. While it is certainly true that the establishment and the design of EU agencies and networks cannot be explained by functional factors alone, reducing their existence and design to political conflicts over power and influence in these regulatory arrangements and EU regulatory policy-making is also mistaken. Governments, the Commission and the European Parliament surely care about the choice of arrangement charged with the implementation of policies, and they try to ensure that they obtain institutional design outcomes that also produce preferable policy outcomes. Yet, EU agencies are not built from scratch but often succeed networks and (comitology) committees, which – at one point – were considered incapable of effectively and efficiently handling their regulatory tasks (see Thatcher and Coen 2008). The EFSA and the EMSA have, for different reasons, been discussed as examples, whereby existing regulatory structures were deemed inefficient and – in the end – were replaced by an EU agency. At the same time, however, governments ensure that agencies' tasks are tightly circumscribed, their resources limited, and sufficient control mechanism installed, so that the functional benefits of creating an agency are not offset by a new supranational runaway bureaucracy. Moreover, the Commission, agencies and regulatory networks very often operate in parallel, thereby complementing each other's work rather than operating discretely and in isolation from each other. The Commission has, for instance, enlisted committees and networks that support its regulatory tasks (see Blauberger and Rittberger 2014; the chapter by Wonka, in this volume). Moreover, agencies regularly rely on (more or less formalized) networks and institutionalize their exchanges with national regulators and others stakeholders. Some agencies should therefore be considered as central nodes in EU regulatory networks rather than independent and self-sufficient regulators (see Levi-Faur 2011).

The effectiveness of agency governance

We have argued that policy harmonization and implementation tasks are often shared among EU agencies, national regulators, and the Commission. Recalling the functional motivation for the growth of the EU agency phenomenon, agencies are considered to play an important role in assisting domestic actors in effectively implementing EU policies. Can EU agencies live up to this expectation? Do they promote regulatory outcomes 'that are systematically more problem adequate (effective) than what can be expected from decision processes dominated by bargaining or majority voting' (Gehring 2012: 106)? In this section, we focus on the effects of agency governance for policy outcomes. We first zoom into the rule-making process and ask whether the inclusion of EU agencies in regulatory decisions transforms modes of rule making: If the functional and technocratic logic affects agency creation, it can be hypothesized that this logic also affects the modes of interaction when agencies are involved in policy-making and implementation. According to the functional logic, decision processes should be less prone to short-term oriented political bargaining and more conducive to reason-based arguing grounded in regulatory expertise. Second, we focus on the implementation of EU regulatory decisions and explore how EU agencies affect this crucial dimension of the policy process. Since the literature with regard to both themes is scant, the reported findings do not lend themselves (yet) to generalizable interpretations.

EU agencies and regulatory decision-making: Transforming bargaining into arguing?

In a recent essay, Gehring (2012) argues that in the absence of full independence, EU agencies lack the institutional capacities to act as 'trustees' of their political principals (see our discussion in section 1, as well as Wonka and Rittberger 2010). Only a trustee agent enjoying full independence is able to act in the long-term interests of governments: Trustee agents are able to overcome the so-called time inconsistency problem faced by politicians, as they are tempted by short-term political goals and preferences, which contradict and tend to undermine optimal long-term policy objective (see Majone 2001). Trustee agents evaluate 'the merits of existing options sincerely in light of externally given criteria and choose[s] the most convincing one' (Gehring 2012: 108). From this perspective, the ECB carries the traits of a trustee: it possesses a high level of independence, and its actions rest on a treaty-based commitment to keep inflation low. EU agencies, however, have only limited independence and their political principals are able to ignore or politically circumvent their recommendations. Yet, Gehring (2012) argues that despite their limited discretionary powers, EU agencies are embedded in institutional structures that promote long-term policy objective and inhibit interest-based, short-term oriented political bargaining. The adoption of binding and legally enforceable substantive decision criteria commits all decision-making parties to uphold previously defined objectives. Mandatory criteria impose legal as well as argumentative constraints on governments' abilities to pursue their parochial short-term interests (Gehring 2012: 112, 123).

Comparing the EMA and the EFSA, Gehring finds that even though the EMA lacks the independence that characterizes a trustee agent, it can still act as if it were a trustee 'because it is embedded in an institutional arrangement that commits all actors involved to general decision-making criteria' (Gehring 2012: 113). Even though the agency's formal status in the authorization of pharmaceuticals is rather weak, the Commission and the Council members can hardly ignore its scientific opinion, because the criteria on which these decisions are based are legally binding and enforceable (Gehring and Krapohl 2007; Gehring 2012: 115). A deliberative decision-making mode is thereby encouraged, because all actors are compelled to argue over the correct application of the previously defined and agreed upon authorization criteria. This decision-making setting thus empowers scientific experts, and hence the agency, and delegitimizes the pursuit of parochial and sectional interests and renders bargaining strategies ineffective.

While the EFSA enjoys a higher degree of formal independence than the EMA (see Wonka and Rittberger 2010: 731–732), decision-making on food safety often follows political considerations rather than expert advice. For instance, in the case of genetically modified (GMO) feed and foodstuffs, member states repeatedly ignored the opinions of the EFSA and the ensuing Commission proposals. Why can the member states ignore scientific expertise more easily in the case of foodstuffs compared to pharmaceuticals? Unlike the authorization of pharmaceuticals, the member states did not subscribe to binding substantive criteria for safety regulation in the case of foodstuffs. This invited interest-based bargaining in the rule-making process and provides member states as well as the Commission with ample room to pursue case-specific interests (Gehring 2012: 118).

The effect of arguing should, however, not be overestimated. An arguing mode seems most likely in the work of agencies such as EMA and EFSA, which operate in highly technical policy areas and which are indirectly involved in actual decision-making (see e.g. Skogstad [2003] on the regulation of GMO). At the same time, research on comitology shows that bargaining and arguing are not mutually exclusive and that their relative importance or prevalence in committee discussions depends on the nature of the issues addressed (Blom-Hansen and Brandsma 2009). Since comitology committees also operate in highly technical areas, we would expect similar patterns with regard to EU agencies. In our survey of the regulatory staff of nine agencies we also find that deliberation and bargaining should be considered as complementary modes of interaction without one clearly dominating the other: 48 per cent of our respondents ($N = 183$) agree that they regularly take a decision, even if consensus among the relevant members of the agency cannot be established. If arguing were the dominant mode of interaction in agency decision-making we would probably expect to find more consensus-based agreement and less reliance on voting to arrive at decisions.[3]

Do EU agencies improve the domestic implementation of EU rules?

As discussed previously, the member states and the Commission have endowed some EU agencies with the task to improve the implementation of EU rules in the member states by providing technical and scientific expertise. Thus far, the literature on how EU agencies affect the implementation of EU rules and contribute to ensure compliance is very limited. Two contributions have recently analysed the role of EU agencies in policy implementation in the transport sector (Groenleer *et al.* 2010; Versluis and Tarr 2013). Focusing on the areas of maritime and aviation safety, Groenleer *et al.* (2010) find that EU legislation in these areas tends to be transposed not only in an untimely fashion but that there is also a lack of uniform application of safety measures on the ground. The EU agencies dealing with issues of maritime and aviation safety (the EMSA and European Aviation Safety Association [EASA], respectively) have both been endowed with implementation-related tasks, which includes monitoring and inspections of member states and undertakings so as to ensure uniform safety levels as well as a level playing field (Groenleer *et al.* 2010: 1226). The study on the EMSA and the EASA shows that agencies are most effective in improving implementation, when 'they spur informal learning among national regulatory authorities' (Groenleer *et al.* 2010: 1226). The authors argue that the political interests of the member states and the Commission have led to a tight circumscription of the respective agencies' implementation tasks (e.g. inspections being non-random and results remaining confidential), hence reducing the agencies' ability to effectively improve street-level implementation by taking binding decisions (Groenleer *et al.* 2010: 1227). Given their limited formal competencies EU agencies have to rely on the voluntary cooperation and coordination of domestic regulators to improve the uniform application of EU rules. They do so by facilitating the direct communication between domestic regulators and by disseminating information on their respective practices (Groenleer *et al.* 2010: 1228). Versluis and Tarr (2013) echo this finding. In their study in the European Railway Agency (ERA), they demonstrate that the willingness of member states to draw on the information provided by the agency is conditioned by existing domestic regulatory capacity and performance:

Countries with limited regulatory capacities tend to compensate their resource limitations by relying on the expertise provided by ERA (Versluis and Tarr 2013: 16), while resourceful member states with strong regulatory traditions act more independently and are sceptical of the agency's added value in promoting domestic implementation.

The legitimacy and accountability of agency governance

Governance with and through EU agencies raises important questions about their sources of legitimacy. According to the functional argument for creating EU agencies, politically independent and impartial bureaucrats are considered to provide the kind of unbiased expertise and policy advice necessary to produce efficient regulatory outcomes. From this perspective, it is a 'category mistake' (Majone 2006: 618) to evaluate EU agencies and their role in the policy-process from the purview of *democratic* legitimacy, because the institutional design of EU agencies is built on the premise that independence and hence political non-interference in the decision-making of these organizations is a fundamental condition to obtain desired governance objectives. Instead, functionalists argue that the legitimacy enjoyed by agencies is founded on *technocratic* criteria, and hence based on the belief that decision-making follows the 'use of value-free objective criteria' (Centeno 1993: 311) and widely accepted practices to arrive at *optimal* answers to particular problems.

Both, the democratic or "input"-oriented and the technocratic or "output"-oriented view are not without problems. Applying the standards of democratic legitimacy to EU agencies overlooks that agencies are considered to perform their regulatory tasks most effectively when they are not subjected to electoral scrutiny and party-political contestation. Yet, assuming that agencies should be judged by the standard of technocratic legitimacy may be equally unruly. Shapiro (1997) has argued forcefully that technocratic legitimacy cannot be an adequate substitute for democratic legitimacy because the provision of seemingly apolitical, neutral, value-free expertise is a myth: 'If the independent agency argument is that information = technical expertise outside of politics = technocracy = non-democratic legitimacy, the response is that information is not technical but political' (Shapiro 1997: 287) for, even technocrats pursue agendas that are *political* in the very sense that they result in the allocation and distribution of values. No doubt, expertise can be used for functional or problem-solving purposes, yet it can also be cloaked as technocratic knowledge while it is actually employed for political and strategic objectives (Schrefler 2010).

Accountability as source of agency legitimacy

If evaluating EU agencies by the standards of democratic or technocratic legitimacy does not appear very promising, where are we to look for standards of legitimacy unless we are willing to accept some form of enlightened expert rule? While democratic polities obviously endow institutions, such as agencies, central banks and bureaucracies, with discretionary powers (e.g. to set regulatory standards, define interest rates or decide on policy implementation), there tends to be a great concern that the actors exercising political discretion are adequately checked and held to account. Even though EU agencies exercise limited discretionary political power, their decisions affect policy-making and hence a vast array of actors, and questions about how they are checked and to be held to account thus become pertinent. Against this backdrop, *accountability* becomes an integral component in debates about and assessments of the legitimacy of the EU in general (see Bovens *et al.* 2010: 27) and of EU agencies in particular. In a democratic polity, having a legitimate claim on the exercise of authority is premised 'on whether or not the actor is accepted as having appropriate accountability relationships with others' (Black 2008: 150).

Lupia (2003) argues that an 'agent is accountable to a principal if the principal can exercise control over the agent and delegation is not accountable if the principal is unable to exercise control. If a principal in situation A exerts more control than a principal in situation B, then accountability is greater in situation A than it is in situation B' (Lupia 2003: 35). Bovens (2007) takes issue with the equation that accountability is synonymous with control. He defines accountability as a 'relationship between an actor and a forum, in which the actor has an obligation to explain and to justify his or her conduct, the forum can pose questions and pass judgement, and the actor may face consequences' (Bovens 2007: 450). According to Bovens 'not all forms of control are accountability mechanisms' (2007: 454). First, accountability is 'an *after the fact* process' (Busuioc 2009: 607) and as such does not cover mechanisms of *ex ante* control, such as the design of founding 'contracts' defining the legal power and discretion of EU agencies. Second, the principal–agent perspective on accountability-as-control presupposes the existence of an *information* stage and a *consequence* stage, which provide the principal with information on the agent's conduct and the possibility of the former to sanction the latter in order to prevent agency drift (see Strøm 2000). Accountability contains yet another stage, a *deliberation* stage, which entails the requirement of the accountee to *explain* and *justify* her behaviour and where the accountor can ask questions (see Bovens 2007; Busuioc 2010).

Deliberation is seen as a crucial component of accountability because the principals' preferences – for instance on a complex regulatory matter or on the application of a particular method to assess a regulatory risk – are often not known to the principals themselves at the outset. A perspective that assumes given and fixed preferences will thus fall short of providing adequate benchmarks for 'real' and effective accountability. Discussions between accountor and accountee are crucial for the former 'learn to articulate his preferences or start thinking about what is really at stake, and the agent [accountee, B. R./A. W.] may learn what its principal *really* wants to see accomplished' (see Brandsma and Schillemans 2013: 957, emphasis in the original). Third, the principal–agent perspective typically highlights *hierarchical political* control, which concerns the relationship between political principals (the Council, the European Commission and, in some cases, the European Parliament) with the agent (the EU agency). Political control by the political principals constitutes only one of many possible accountability forums. Bovens (2007: 455–457) argues that public organizations, such as EU agencies, are not only held to account by their political principals they may be also legally required or feel socially compelled to explain and justify their behaviour to different *accountability forums* and hence accountors, such as professional peers and stakeholder groups. To assess the quality and the extent to which accountability is provided (or underprovided), legal accountability requirements, available instruments as well as accountability practices in different accountability stages – information, deliberation and consequences – should be analysed (Brandsma and Schillemans 2013). Since the study of EU agency accountability is still in its infancy, the ensuing section refers to a set of recent studies, which allow us to zoom into particular configurations of agency accountability.

Agency accountability in practice

Since the literature on agency accountability is still in its infancy, we focus our discussion on examples from the literature on *political* as well as *peer* accountability. In a recent study, Madalina Busuioc (2012) investigates one particular aspect of EU agency's *political* accountability, by focusing on the accountability relationship between EU agencies and their management boards (see also Busuioc 2010). The main task of management boards is to exercise oversight on how the agency and its director carry out their tasks. Agency boards comprise representatives from each member state and from the Commission (in rare cases, also from the European Parliament). In some instances, representatives of civil society organizations and stakeholder organisations are also included (see Busuioc 2012: 724). In her study, Busuioc not only assesses the legal requirements defining the accountability relationship, but also focuses on actual accountability practices as well as on the intensity of the accountability relationship. While agencies tend to comply with their formal reporting obligations vis-à-vis the management boards, thus providing sufficient information, Busuioc finds that many board members lack the managerial knowledge to assess financial and administrative matters and hence fail to carry out their supervisory role adequately. While member states, the Commission and the European Parliament tend to engage in hefty scuffles about the composition and voting rights on the boards to ensure that 'their' institution is properly represented, they appear to care less about ensuring that the representatives are adequately qualified for the task at hand (see Busuioc 2012: 726–727).

Against this backdrop, do the deliberations in management boards contribute to agency accountability? This does not seem to be the case. Effective oversight is not only hampered by a lack of managerial expertise, but also by the fact that the members of the board representing the member states are frequently full-time employees of national regulatory bodies. Busuioc argues that they care less about the overall performance of the EU agency and tend to be more concerned about how the workings of the EU agency affect their national regulatory bodies and prerogatives (see Busuioc 2012: 732). Conflicts of interests thus seem to stand in the way of effective oversight and accountability. Nationally minded management board representatives are bad news for those who hypothesize that the dynamics among board members begets learning and socialization dynamics thereby fuelling a common European outlook for problem solving. At the same time, one might also argue that it is unreasonable to expect that domestic regulators develop common regulatory perspectives, since the member states are marked by considerable political and regulatory diversity, which is reflected in regulators' perspectives. The institutional design of management boards might therefore reflect not only governments' interest in influencing agencies' actions but also their conviction that the consideration of diverging national perspectives is a precondition for EU agencies' ability to act legitimately and effectively in regulatory policy-making.

Effective accountability implies, furthermore, that – once the agency's conduct has been debated and judgment passed – consequences can be enacted. In the case of EU agencies, formal sanctions – such as dismissing the director of an agency – are rarely (if at all) used. There are two possible rationales for this observation (Busuioc 2012). First, informal controls or the mere prospect of imposing sanctions are actually quite effective. There is evidence that by withholding relevant resources (such as the refusal to adopt the agency's work program), the management board can alter the conduct of the agency. In this case, accountability is effective because of informal sanctions or because the threat of carrying formal sanction is a credible one. The second rationale highlights the potentially prohibitive costs of sanctioning for the members of the management boards. Not only is the sacking of a director likely to spark political conflict among the political principals; it could also cast a negative light on the work of the management board itself (Busuioc 2012: 731).

Political accountability has also been studied from the perspective of the European Parliament. It is only during the later waves of agency creation that the European Parliament – through the adoption of the co-decision procedure – has been able to assert its influence over the creation and design of EU agencies (Kelemen 2002; Lord 2011). Over time, the European Parliament has raised its profile and plays an increasingly important role in holding agencies to account, primarily through (partially) controlling the purse strings of agencies. The Committee on Budgets as well as the Committee on Budgetary Control are central parliamentary forums for monitoring agency conduct (Busuioc 2010; Bach and Fleischer 2012). Over time, these two committees have stepped up efforts to expand activities and practices to hold agencies to account beyond the mere requirement that agencies have to submit reports on a regular basis. This change of practice has affected Parliament's capacity as an effective accountor, as information on the agencies' conduct is more plentiful and deliberations about the agency's behaviour better informed (see Bach and Fleischer 2012). Moreover, the European Parliament not only holds EU agencies to account through ex post control mechanisms, it also uses its institutional capacity to affect the overall design of EU agency accountability (see Busuioc 2010: 156). This practice is well known to scholars of the EU's *parliamentarization*: The parliament employs its institutional power to veto policies to obtain institutional or policy gains in other areas (see the chapter by Rittberger and Winzen, in this volume).

The accountability of EU agencies cannot only be assessed by studying formal requirements and accountability practices: Wonka and Rittberger (2011) have conducted a survey among officials of seven EU agencies to tap into their perceptions on key dimensions of EU governance, including attitudes about the sources of legitimacy and accountability of EU agencies. Agency officials perceive themselves as experts in a particular field of governance who would like to see their work assessed and judged by their professional peers according to the prevailing scientific and methodological standards in their field. Our respondents thus consider *peer* accountability an important source for the legitimation of their work. This finding strongly reflects the functional argument that agencies are created to address regulatory problems in an efficient and technocratic way.

Yet, technocratic legitimacy and accountability are not the only yardsticks perceived to be important among agency officials. Political accountability is also of high relevance: The survey results indicate that agency staff members are attentive to the political preferences and sensitivities of their political principals as well as of the public at large (Wonka and Rittberger 2011: 897). Such attentiveness might exist for several reasons (Wonka and Rittberger 2011: 904–905): First, agency professionals themselves may not believe in the strict separability of (seemingly) objective facts from value judgements, which suggests that technocratic legitimacy needs to be complemented by some form of democratic legitimacy (see Brown 2009; Shapiro 1997). Second, it is also conceivable that agency staff sees a (functionally driven) need for public and political approval of their work, so that their suggestions and proposals are taken up and implemented by domestic policy makers (Scharpf 2009). This also suggests that professionally derived norms that emphasize problem-solving efficiency and the norm of democratic responsiveness are mutually reinforcing rather than exclusive or competing (Majone 2010). Finally, agencies might also consider public and political approval of their work instrumental in order to secure their organizational survival in the medium to long run.

Too much accountability?

Hardly anyone would contest the twin (normative) claim that accountability is a good thing and that more accountability is better than less accountability. The real world of accountability is more complicated. As we have seen, agencies are given some discretionary powers and hence a certain degree of formal independence to effectively fulfil their tasks. The more agencies are independent formally and factually, the more important it is – as argued in the previous section – that they are being checked and held to account. In a case study on Europol, Busuioc *et al.* (2011) have shown that accountability arrangements and factual independence do not necessarily co-evolve. As a result of the frequent interference of member states in the workings of Europol, the agency had difficulty to establish itself as an independent European law enforcement agency. Despite its limited and precarious factual independence, the perception that Europol constituted an "unaccountable European FBI" was widely shared (Busuioc *et al.* 2011: 858). Consequently, demands for more stringent accountability mechanisms have been repeatedly voiced. The Lisbon Treaty paved the way to expand mechanisms for Europol oversight to actors previously excluded from political accountability forums: the European Parliament (see Trauner 2012), as well as the ECJ. Interestingly, stepping up Europol's accountability mechanisms has not been associated with a significant expansion of its ability to act autonomously.

Busuioc *et al.* (2011) argue that the incongruence between accountability and independence could result from the specificity of the policy area: international police cooperation is an area in which the member states' willingness to grant a supranational body discretionary powers and a certain degree of independence tends to be much more tightly circumscribed than, for instance, in regulatory policy areas: Police cooperation is, after all, a matter touching on states' monopoly of the use of force and hence is particularly challenging to the sovereignty of the state. For the same reason, demands for accountability also tend to be particularly pronounced in the case of Europol. Looking beyond Europol, the authors discuss possible positive and negative dynamics between accountability and independence. Too much accountability can, for instance, stifle the agency's ability to fulfil its tasks effectively, which, in turn, tends to undermine the agency's credibility and hence the willingness of its political principals to delegate further tasks to the agency. Yet, the two can also be positively related, as effective accountability arrangements 'are likely to positively affect the credibility of an agency, which may breed trust and increase actual autonomy. In turn, such actual autonomy may be formalized as accountability forums will feel more confident that the agency is under control and, thus, more power can be delegated' (Busuioc *et al.* 2011: 862).

Conclusion

Research on EU agencies is flourishing. This chapter has demonstrated that the 'agency phenomenon' (Busuioc *et al.* 2012) can be analysed from a multitude of different perspectives. First, agency scholars have been interested in questions about institutional choice and institutional design. Agencies are not a *natural* solution to address regulatory policy problems, such as promoting the effective implementation of EU policies, but are one of several governance arrangements among which political actors can choose. European policy networks, the Commission as well as EU agencies compete and complement each other in the provision and implementation of EU regulatory policies. While institutional choice is triggered by functional demands, the supply of a particular regulatory arrangement – whether governments and the Commission opt for agencies or networks – mostly depends on power and politics: For instance, member states want to solve regulatory problems, but they also are weary of giving up too much regulatory autonomy. Hence, they place EU agencies under tight ex ante and ex post controls. Moreover, whereas the political costs of delegating authority to supranational agencies are deemed too high, policy networks, which formally do not circumscribe the authority of national regulators, are seen as apposite solutions.

Second, scholarship on EU agencies is increasingly zooming in on the implications of governance with and through agencies on the policy process and policy outcomes. For instance, many EU agencies are assigned a crucial role in implementing EU legislation, but we still know relatively little about how EU agencies affect the compliance game and how they interact with domestic authorities and regulators. Case study–based research suggests thus far that EU agencies' capacity to effect domestic implementation processes depends both on the agencies' formal mandate as well as on the resources and regulatory capacities available in the respective member states, whereby the less resourceful member states tend to demand (and accept) the expertise provided by EU agencies. Moreover, to be able to act effectively, EU agencies depend on the willingness of domestic regulators to cooperate.

Third, we have sought to highlight yet another concern of scholars studying EU agencies, how demands for agency independence to effectively solve regulatory problems can be squared with democratic control. We have shown that the agencies' principals have opted to tightly circumscribe the competencies of agencies by establishing a plethora of control mechanisms and formal opportunities to reign in the agency. How effective these controls and accountability mechanisms are to ensure that agencies are accountable and under control is subject to on-going research.

Notes

We are grateful to Sebastian Rohe for his research assistance and to Dovile Rimkute for her excellent comments.

1   These are the European Agency for the Management of Operational Cooperation at the External Borders of the Member States of the European Union (FRONTEX), the European Food Safety Authority (EFSA), the European Institute for Gender Equality (EIGE) and the European Defence Agency (EDA).

2   To compile the information on EU agencies, we consulted their homepages and annual reports (http://europa.eu/agencies/regulatory_agencies_bodies/index_en.htm), as well as

the Commission's draft general budget for 2013 (http://ec.europa.eu/budget/library/biblio/documents/2013/DB2013/DB2013-WDIII-AGENCIES.pdf) the amounts in brackets in the budget column refer to the amount of agencies' budgets earned through fees from customers and users of their services.

3   We are aware that taking a vote does not preclude *arguing* as a mode of interaction, for actors can resort to voting when they agree that they cannot come to a reasoned consensus.

References

Bach, T. and Fleischer, J. (2012) 'The Parliamentary Accountability of European Union and National Agencies', in M. Busuioc, M. Groenleer and J. Trondal (eds) *The Agency Phenomenon in the European Union: Emergence, Institutionalization and Everyday Decision-making*, Manchester: Manchester University Press.

Black, J. (2008) 'Constructing and Contesting Legitimacy and Accountability in Polycentric Regulatory Reimes', *Regulation & Governance*, **2**(2): 137–164.

Blauberger, M. and Rittberger, B. (2014) 'Conceptualizing and Theorizing EU Regulatory Networks', Regulation & Governance, DOI: 10.1111/rego12064.

Blom-Hansen, J. and Brandsma, G.J. (2009) 'The EU Comitology System: Intergovernmental Bargaining and Deliberative Supranationalism?', *Journal of Common Market Studies*, **47**(4): 719–740.

Brandsma, G.J. and Schillemans, T. (2013) 'The Accountability Cube: Measuring Accountability', *Journal of Public Administration Research and Theory*, **23**(4): 953–975. doi:10.1093/jopart/mus034.

Brown, M.B. (2009) *Science in Democracy. Expertise, Institutions, and Representation*, Cambridge, MA: MIT Press.

Bovens, M. (2007) 'Analysing and Assessing Accountability: A Conceptual Framework', *European Law Journal*, **13**(4): 447–468.

Bovens, M., Curtin, D. and Hart, P. (2010) 'The Quest for Legitimacy and Accountability in EU Governance', in M. Bovens, D. Curtin and P. Hart (eds) *The Real World of EU Accountability: What Deficit?*, Oxford: Oxford University Press.

Busuioc, M. (2009) 'Accountability, Control and Independence: The Case of European Agencies', *European Law Journal*, **15**(5): 599–615.

———. (2010) 'European Agencies: Pockets of Accountability', in M. Bovens, D. Curtin and P. Hart (eds) *The Real World of EU Accountability: What Deficit?*, Oxford: Oxford University Press.

———. (2012) 'European Agencies and their Boards: Promises and Pitfalls of Accountability beyond Design', *Journal of European Public Policy*, **19**(5): 719–736.

Busuioc, M., Curtin, D. and Groenleer, M. (2011) 'Agency Growth between Autonomy and Accountability: The European Police Office as a "Living Institution"', *Journal of European Public Policy*, **18**(6): 848–867.

Busuioc, M., Groenleer, M. and Trondal, J. (eds) (2012) *The Agency Phenomenon in the European Union: Emergence, Institutionalization and Everyday Decision-making*, Manchester: Manchester University Press.

Centeno, M.A. (1993) 'The New Leviathan: The Dynamics and Limits of Technocracy', *Theory and Society*, **22**(3): 307–335.

Chiti, E. (2013) 'European Agencies' Rulemaking: Powers, Procedures and Assessment', *European Law Journal*, **19**(1): 93–110.

Coen, D. and Thatcher, M. (2008) 'Network Governance and Multi-level Delegation: European Networks of Regulatory Agencies', *Journal of Public Policy*, **28**(1): 49–71.

Dehousse, R. (2008) 'Delegation of Powers in the European Union: The Need for a Multi-Principals Model', *Western European Politics* **31**(4): 789–805.

Eberlein, B. and Grande, E. (2005) 'Beyond Delegation: Transnational Regulatory Regimes and the EU Regulatory State', *Journal of European Public Policy*, **12**(1): 89–112.

Egeberg, M. and Trondal, J. (2011) 'EU-level Agencies: New Executive Centre Formation or Vehicles for National Control?', *Journal of European Public Policy*, **18**(6): 868–887.

European Commission (2008). European agencies – The way forward. Communication from the Commission to the European Parliament and the Council (COM(2008) 135 final).

Gehring, T. (2012) 'Deliberative Regulation through European Union Agencies and Other Network Structures', in M. Busuioc, M. Groenleer and J. Trondal (eds) *The Agency Phenomenon in the European Union: Emergence, Institutionalization and Everyday Decision-making*, Manchester: Manchester University Press.

Gehring, T. and Krapohl, S. (2007) 'Supranational Regulatory Agencies between Independence and Control: The EMEA and the Authorization of Pharmaceuticals in the European Single Market', *Journal of European Public Policy*, **14**(2): 208–226.

Gilardi, F. (2002) 'Policy Credibility and Delegation to Independent Regulatory Agencies: A Comparative Empirical Analysis', *Journal of European Public Policy*, **9**(6): 873–893.

———. (2005) 'The Institutional Foundations of Regulatory Capitalism: The Diffusion of Independent Regulatory Agencies in Western Europe', *Annals of the American Academy of Political and Social Sciences*, **598**(1): 84–101.

Groenleer, M., Kaeding, M. and Versluis, E. (2010) 'Regulatory Governance through Agencies of the European Union? The Role of the European Agencies for Maritime and Aviation Safety in the Implementation of European Transport Legislation', *Journal of European Public Policy*, **17**(8): 1212–1230.

Hofmann, H.C.H. and Morini, A. (2012) 'Constitutional Aspect of the Pluralisation of the EU Executive through "Agencification"', *European Law Review* 4: 419–443.

Jordana, J., Levi-Faur, D. and Fernández i Marin, X. (2011) 'The Global Diffusion of Regulatory Agencies: Channels of Transfer and Stages of Diffusion', *Comparative Political Studies*, **44**(10): 1343–1369.

Kelemen, D.R. (2002) 'The Politics of "Eurocratic" Structure and the New European Agencies', *West European Politics*, **25**(4): 93–118.

Kelemen, D.R. and Majone, G. (2012) 'Managing Europeanization: the European Agencies', in J. Peterson and M. Shackleton (eds) *The Institutions of the European Union*, 3rd edn, Oxford: Oxford University Press.

Kelemen, D.R. and Tarrant, A.R. (2011) 'The Political Foundations of the Eurocracy', *West European Politics*, **34**(5): 922–947.

Levi-Faur, D. (2011) 'Regulatory Networks and Regulatory Agencification: Toward a Single European Regulatory Space', *Journal of European Public Policy*, **18**(6): 810–829.

Lord, C. (2011) 'The European Parliament and the Legitimation of Agencification', *Journal of European Public Policy* **18**(6): 909–925.

Lupia, A. (2003) 'Delegation and its Perils', in K. Strøm, W. Müller and T. Bergman (eds) *Delegation and Accountability in Parliamentary Democracies*, Oxford: Oxford University Press.

Majone, G. (2000) 'The Credibility Crisis of Community Regulation', *Journal of Common Market Studies*, **38**(2): 273–302.

———. (2001) 'Two Logics of Delegation. Agency and Fiduciary Relations in EU Governance', *European Union Politics*, **2**(1): 103–122.

———. (2006) 'The common sense of European integration', *Journal of European Public Policy*, Vol. 13(5): 607–626.

———. (2010) 'Transaction-cost Efficiency and the Democratic Deficit', *Journal of European Public Policy*, **17**(2): 150–175.

Martens, M. (2010) 'Voice or Loyalty? The Evolution of the European Environment Agency (EEA)', *Journal of Common Market Studies*, **48**(4): 881–901.

Scharpf, F. W. (2009) 'Legitimacy in the Multilevel European Polity', *European Political Science Review*, **1**(2): 173–204.

Schrefler, L. (2010) 'The Usage of Scientific Knowledge by Independent Regulatory Agencies', *Governance* **23**(2): 309–330.

Shapiro, M. (1997) 'The Problems of Independent Agencies in the United States and the European Union', *Journal of European Public Policy*, **4**(2): 276–291.

Skogstad, G. (2003) 'Legitimacy and/or Policy Effectiveness?: Network Governance and GMO Regulation in the European Union', *Journal of European Public Policy*, **10**(3): 321–338.

Strøm, K. (2000) 'Delegation and Accountability in Parliamentary Democracies', *European Journal of Political Research*, **37**(3): 261–289.

Thatcher, M. (2011) 'The Creation of European Regulatory Agencies and its Limits: A Comparative Analysis of European Delegation', *Journal of European Public Policy*, **18**(6): 790–809.

Thatcher, M. and Coen, D. (2008) 'Reshaping European Regulatory Space: An Evolutionary Analysis', *West European Politics*, **31**(4): 806–836.

Trauner, F. (2012) 'The European Parliament and Agency Control in the Area of Freedom, Security and Justice', *West European Politics*, **35**(4): 784–802.

Versluis, E. and Tarr, E. (2013) 'Improving Compliance with European Union Law via Agencies: The Case of the European Railway Agency', *Journal of Common Market Studies*, **51**(2): 316–333.

Wonka, A. and Rittberger, B. (2010) 'Credibility, Complexity and Uncertainty: Determinants of Institutional Independence of 29 EU Agencies', *West European Politics*, **33**(4): 730–752.

Wonka, A. and Rittberger, B. (2011) 'Perspectives on EU Governance: An Empirical Assessment of the Political Attitudes of EU Agency Professionals', *Journal of European Public Policy*, **18**(6): 888–908.

Part III

VARIEGATED POLICY-MAKING

Chapter 11

EU enlargement

FRANK SCHIMMELFENNIG

Introduction

During the past decade, the European Union (EU) has almost doubled its membership: from 15 to 28 countries. In 2004, ten new member states acceded. Besides Malta and the Republic of Cyprus, the group consisted of eight formerly communist countries: the Baltic countries of Estonia, Latvia, and Lithuania; the Czech Republic; Hungary; Poland; Slovakia; and Slovenia. Bulgaria and Romania joined in 2007. Since then, however, the enlargement process has slowed markedly. Whereas Croatia was admitted in 2013, no other country is even close to accession. Accession negotiations with Turkey have stagnated for many years; those with Montenegro and Serbia only started in 2012 and 2014. Iceland's new government has suspended accession negotiations in 2013. For the remaining countries of the so-called Western Balkans (Albania, Bosnia-Herzegovina, Kosovo, and Macedonia), a starting date for accession negotiations has not been set yet. Other European countries such as Moldova and Ukraine do not even have an explicit membership perspective but have signed association agreements recently.[1] For a chronological overview of this process, see Table 11.1.

EU enlargement has two major facets: the EU's decision-making on enlargement and the candidates' Europeanization. On one hand, the old member states decide on the conditions of enlargement and the selection of candidates. On the other hand, the candidates are required to adopt EU rules and policies during the accession process. Both processes are closely interdependent: EU accession conditionality triggers a process of Europeanization, and the Europeanization of non-member states advances the enlargement process.

This chapter continues with an overview of the problems of enlargement for the EU and the accession countries, followed by a sketch of the main theoretical approaches used to explain enlargement and Europeanization. It then offers an analysis of the two facets of enlargement policy based on evidence from the 2004/07 eastern enlargement process, the accession negotiations with Turkey, and the current policy towards the Western Balkans. The final section draws theoretical conclusions and discusses the limits of EU enlargement.

Problems of EU enlargement

Any enlargement of an international organization offers potential benefits but is also fraught with costs for member states old and new. New member states contribute to the collective goods produced by the organization and the organization's running costs. They may enhance the organization's power, welfare, and standing. At the same time, enlargement is likely to produce 'crowding costs' because new members want a share of the collective goods. In addition, enlargement increases decision and transaction costs: administrative costs rise and communication becomes more cumbersome. The greater heterogeneity of attitudes and preferences that often comes with enlargement makes it more difficult to reach decisions, in particular under unanimity and qualified majority voting. New members are also likely to gain policy-making efficiency, welfare, power, and both international and domestic standing. In return, however, they may lose autonomy.

Table 11.1 Chronology of enlargement

Country	Signing of association treaty	Membership application	Beginning of accession negotiations	Accession
Cyprus	1972	1990	1998	2004
Poland	1991	1994	1998	2004
Hungary	1991	1994	1998	2004
Czech Republic	1991 (1993)[1]	1996	1998	2004
Estonia	1995	1995	1998	2004
Slovenia	1996	1996	1998	2004
Malta	1970	1990	2000	2004
Slovakia	1991 (1993)	1995	2000	2004
Latvia	1995	1995	2000	2004
Lithuania	1995	1995	2000	2004
Bulgaria	1993	1995	2000	2007
Romania	1993	1995	2000	2007
Croatia	2001	2003	2005	2013
Turkey	1963	1987	2005	
Iceland	1992	2009	2010 (suspended 2013)	
Montenegro	2007	2008	2012	
Serbia	2008	2009	2014	
Macedonia	2001	2004		
Albania	2006	2009		
Bosnia-Herzegovina	2008			
Kosovo				
Ukraine				
Moldova				
Georgia				
Armenia				
Azerbaijan				
Belarus				

[1] After the dissolution of Czechoslovakia on 1 January 1993, the association agreements had to be renegotiated.

In the EU, the internal market is the core collective good. In addition, the EU distributes funds across the member states, mainly for agriculture and regional infrastructure: the Common Agricultural Policy (CAP) and structural funds have comprised about 80 per cent of the EU's budget during the enlargement period. The EU's justice and home affairs policies are designed to enhance the member states' internal security and protect them from crime and undesired migration. Finally, EU membership involves particularly high autonomy costs resulting from supranational integration.

EU enlargement to the east has been characterized by fundamental structural asymmetries between members and candidates. First, the candidates have been less economically developed, poorer and, on average, more agricultural than the member states. Second, the candidates have been in a process of political and economic transition. Democracy and the rule of law have only consolidated recently, and in many cases consolidation has been unstable and incomplete. Administrative capacity has been comparatively weak. Territorial and ethnic minority conflicts have been virulent throughout the region.

From the perspective of the old member states, these asymmetries created problems for an enlarged EU and reluctance and resistance among the member states (Schimmelfennig 2003: 55–62). On one hand, the old member states generally benefit from an expanded internal market. Enlargement fully integrates a new market for their exports and investments in close proximity. In addition, the supply of cheaper resources and cheaper but qualified labour reduces costs and strengthens European competitiveness on the world market. On the other hand, those (mostly southern) member states that specialize in agriculture and the same low-tech industries as the candidates faced economic competition from the candidates' unrestrained access to the internal market. They also faced budgetary competition because the heavily agricultural and relatively poor candidates would be eligible to substantial net transfers from the CAP and the structural funds upon membership, potentially crowding out the former main beneficiaries of EU subsidies (Greece, Ireland, Portugal, and Spain). Moreover, the economic asymmetries were bound to create strong migration pressure.

Beyond economic concerns, eastern enlargement was thought to lead to a considerable increase in decision and transaction costs. This is not only because of the high number of new member states but also because of the increased heterogeneity of preferences resulting from the structural differences between old and new member states and the historical legacies of communism and ethno-nationalistic conflicts. Turkey has created two additional concerns. First, whereas most of the ex-communist candidates were small, Turkey was likely to be the largest member state by the time it would join – with uncertain consequences for the EU's internal balance of power and decision-making. Second, as a large Muslim country, it was perceived to produce additional heterogeneity.

Finally, the administrative capacity of most candidates has been weak. Because EU-level administrative capacities are weak as well, the internal market, legal integration, and policy implementation in the EU rely to a large extent on the proper functioning of nation-state administrations. So do the EU's justice and home affairs policies. Low state capacity and problems of corruption and the rule of law have thus been major EU concerns regarding the candidate countries and new members.

The candidate countries have faced huge challenges, too. On one hand, they were to profit from unimpeded access to their most important foreign market and from an increased inflow of capital. Moreover, they would receive subsidies from the EU budget that help to cushion the painful economic adaptation and catching-up processes. Last but not least, they would be entitled to participate in EU decision-making and thereby increase the influence that they lacked as small and poor states in European politics. On the other hand, however, the EU is not just a free-trade zone that requires its members to tear down trade barriers but a community of law and a market-regulating organization that obliges new members to adopt its rules. Candidates have to transpose the entire body of EU law, the *acquis communautaire*, into domestic law and to create new or reform existing domestic administrations and procedures in line with EU prescriptions.

The problems of enlargement outlined in this section bring up two sets of questions. First, why has the EU decided to embark on Eastern enlargement in spite of the substantial economic, financial, decision, and transaction costs this policy appeared to entail? And why has it admitted some countries rather than others and some countries earlier than others? Second, why has 'Europeanization' been more effective in some countries rather than others?

Theoretical approaches to enlargement

The analysis of EU enlargement and non-member Europeanization has largely followed the theoretical lead of institutional theories in International Relations, most prominently the debate between 'rationalism' and 'constructivism', two families of theories developed to explain the causes and effects of international institutions (Schimmelfennig 2003; Schimmelfennig and Sedelmeier 2005).[2] Explanations of enlargement also draw on (rational) intergovernmentalism and constructivism in the theory of European integration (Chapter 2).

Rationalist theories conceive international organizations as *clubs*, that is voluntary associations 'in the sense that members would not join (or remain in the club) unless a net gain resulted from membership (Sandler and Tschirhart 1980: 1491). In the rationalist perspective, cost-benefit calculations determine the enlargement preferences of member states and candidates. More specifically, a member state favours the admission of a non-member state – and a non-member state seeks membership – under the condition that it will reap positive net benefits from enlargement and that these benefits exceed the benefits it would secure from a different kind of relationship (such as simple cooperation or association). Enlargement then takes place if, for both the member states and the candidate countries, marginal benefits exceed marginal costs. If individual states incur net costs, enlargement can still result from side payments or unequal bargaining power. For instance, member states that expect net losses will still agree to enlargement if they obtain full compensation by the winners. In addition, the losers will consent to enlargement if the winners are able to threaten them credibly with exclusion (and if the losses of exclusion exceed the losses of enlargement).

According to *constructivist institutionalism*, enlargement politics will generally be shaped by ideational, cultural factors. The most relevant of these factors is 'community' or 'cultural match', that is, the degree to which the actors inside and outside the organization share a collective identity and fundamental beliefs. Studying enlargement in a constructivist perspective, then, primarily consists in the analysis of social identities, values, and norms, not the material, distributional consequences of enlargement for individual actors (Schimmelfennig 2001; Sedelmeier 2005). Whether applicant and member states regard enlargement as desirable depends on the degree of community they perceive to have with each other. The more an external state identifies with the international community that the organization represents and the more it shares the values and norms that define the purpose and the policies of the organization, the more it aspires to membership and the more the member states are willing to admit this country. If enlargement decisions are contested, constructivists expect to see an arguing process to determine which decision is most in line with the collective identity, the constitutive beliefs and practices of the community, and the norms and rules of the organization.

A similar theoretical distinction can be made for the 'other side of enlargement', that is the Europeanization of candidate countries. In the rationalist perspective, Europeanization is again driven by cost–benefit calculations. According to the *external incentives model* (Schimmelfennig and Sedelmeier 2004, 2005), the EU pursues a strategy of conditionality in which the EU sets its rules as conditions that non-member countries have to fulfil in order to receive EU rewards. These rewards consist of assistance and institutional ties ranging from trade and cooperation agreements via association agreements to full membership. The non-member state fulfils EU conditions if the benefits of EU rewards exceed the domestic adoption costs. The adoption of EU rules and policies then depends on the size and speed of EU and the size of domestic adoption costs. In addition, however, conditionality needs to be credible; that is candidate countries need to be certain they will not receive the reward unless they meet the conditions and that the EU will not withhold the reward in case of compliance.

By contrast, the *social learning model* builds on constructivist assumptions. Its most general proposition claims that a state adopts EU rules if it is persuaded of their appropriateness. In turn, the persuasive power of the EU depends on legitimacy, identity, and resonance. Legitimacy refers to the quality of the EU rules, the rule-making process, and the process of rule transfer. In this perspective, the legitimacy of EU rules and, as a result, the likelihood of rule adoption, increase if rules are formal, member states are subject to them as well, the process of rule transfer fulfils basic standards of deliberation, and EU rules are shared by other international organizations. As for identity, the likelihood of rule adoption is expected to increase with the identification of the target state and society with the EU community. Finally, rule adoption will be facilitated if conflicting domestic rules are absent or delegitimated and if EU rules tie in with existing or traditional domestic rules (resonance).

From partnership to association

Almost immediately after the beginnings of democratic transition in Eastern Europe, the European Community started to expand its relations with the Central and Eastern European countries (CEECs) and to assist their political and economic transformation. Already in 1988, it established diplomatic relations with its Eastern counterpart, the Council for Mutual Economic Assistance (CMEA), and concluded a first Trade and Cooperation Agreement with Hungary. Similar agreements followed with the other CEECs including the Soviet Union (in December 1989). In 1989, the Commission also began to coordinate the economic assistance of the entire G24 group of western states and issued its Phare programme of economic and technical aid for Poland and Hungary. Later it was extended to further CEECs and was complemented by a similar program for the successor countries of the Soviet Union (Tacis). Finally, in April 1991, the European Bank for Reconstruction and Development was founded to support the development of a private sector and a functioning market economy in the transformation countries.

The early negotiations and agreements between the European Community (EC) and the CEECs already show a central feature of the entire enlargement process: political conditionality. In January 1989, the European Parliament demanded that 'reference to human rights should figure' in the trade and cooperation agreements the EC was beginning to negotiate with the CEECs,[3] and in November, the European Council established that 'initiatives aimed at the countries of Eastern Europe as a whole are applicable only to those which re-establish freedom and democracy'.[4] After the dissolution of the Soviet Union, the Commission confirmed that 'negotiating . . . new types of agreements has to be subject to political conditions (respect of human rights and democratic freedoms, guarantees for minorities, etc.).[5] In May 1992, the Council agreed on a general 'human rights clause' to be added to all agreements with third states, which stipulated suspension in case of non-compliance. In November 1992 and July 1993, the EC extended this political conditionality to Phare and Tacis assistance.

Already in December 1990, the EC began to negotiate association agreements with the first group of CEECs. They provided for a political dialogue on foreign policy issues, the intensification of economic, financial, and cultural cooperation, and the adaptation of (market-related) legislation in the CEECs to EC law. The substantive core of the association agreements, however, was a progressive liberalization of the trade in goods. By contrast, they did not contain an explicit membership perspective except for a reference to future membership as 'their', that is the CEECs', but not the Community's 'final objective'.[6] The first 'Europe Agreements' were concluded with the Czech Republic, Slovakia, Poland, and Hungary. The Baltic countries, Bulgaria, Romania, and Slovenia followed until the mid-1990s.

Turkey has had an association agreement with the EC since 1964 (Ankara Agreement). The customs union it envisaged has been in place since the end of 1995. Just as the Europe Agreements, the Ankara Agreement only contains vague references to membership: 'the Contracting Parties shall examine the possibility of the accession of Turkey to the Community', as soon as the economic association and the customs union had 'advanced far enough'.

A new round of association began in 1999 when, under the impression of the Kosovo conflict, the EU offered the countries of the Western Balkans Stabilization and Association Agreements (SAAs). The first SAAs were signed with Croatia and Macedonia in 2001; in the meantime, SAAs have been concluded with all countries of the Western Balkans except Kosovo, but the agreement with Bosnia-Herzegovina is yet to enter into force (see Table 11.1). From the beginning, the SAA process came with a membership perspective. At the Thessaloniki European Council in 2003, the EU heads of state and government confirmed that all countries of the Western Balkans were potential candidates for membership.

Finally, in the context of its Eastern Partnership with Belarus, Moldova, Ukraine, and the countries of the southern Caucasus (inaugurated in 2009), the EU is negotiating another round of association agreements including 'deep and comprehensive free trade agreements'. These agreements build on the Partnership and Cooperation Agreements, which the EC had concluded with almost all former republics of the Soviet Union during the 1990s, and are similar to the Europe Agreements with the CEECs – including leaving 'open future developments' in relations with the EU.[7] Association is again subject to political conditionality: the EU has excluded autocratic Belarus from negotiations; and it refused to sign the association agreement with Ukraine, initialled in 2012, for some time because of democracy and rule of law concerns. The refusal of Ukrainian president Yanukovich to sign the agreement with the EU triggered the Maidan mass demonstrations in late 2013. In June 2014, the EU signed association agreements with Georgia, Moldova, and Ukraine whereas Armenia opted for the customs union with Russia.

If we add the Euro-Mediterranean Association Agreements with most MENA (Middle Eastern and Northern African) countries in the context of the Barcelona Process (since 1995), the EU has concluded, or is in the process of concluding, association agreements with all countries in its neighbourhood. But why and how do countries move from association to full membership?

From association to membership

Conflicting member state preferences

The CEECs were not satisfied with support and association but quickly demanded full membership at the beginning of the 1990s. This demand met with divergent member state preferences that mainly reflected an unequal distribution of enlargement costs and benefits. First, eastern enlargement was contested as such. Whereas the 'drivers' advocated an early and firm commitment to Eastern enlargement, the 'brakemen' were reticent and tried to put off the decision. Second, member states debated the scope of eastern enlargement. Here, one group of countries pushed for a limited (first) round focusing on the central European states; others favoured an inclusive approach. Table 11.2 shows the distribution of preferences on these two issues (see Schimmelfennig 2001: 48–53).

The distribution of preferences largely corresponded with the geographical distance between the member states and the CEECs. Except for Greece and Italy, the drivers neighboured the CEECs, and with the exception of the UK, the more distant member states belonged to the brakemen. The countries of the 'central region' of the EU preferred a limited (first round of) enlargement, whereas the northern countries (except Finland) and the southern countries favoured a more inclusive approach.

In general, international interdependence increases with geographical proximity. Member states on the eastern border of the Community were more sensitive to negative developments in the CEECs – such as economic crises, wars, migration, and environmental degradation – than the more remote members. For them, enlargement was an instrument to stabilize the CEECs and control the negative externalities of transformation. In addition, geographical proximity creates opportunities for economic gains from trade and investment, for instance, by reducing the costs of transport and communication. Member states close to the CEECs therefore stood to gain most from market integration. For these reasons, member states are generally interested in the accession of those states on which they border or which are in close proximity. This explains member state preferences on the scope of enlargement.

Table 11.2 Member state enlargement preferences

	Limited enlargement	Inclusive enlargement
Drivers	Austria, Finland, Germany	Denmark, Sweden, UK
Brakemen	Belgium, Luxembourg, Netherlands	France, Greece, Ireland, Italy, Portugal, Spain

However, the unequal gains from controlling negative and exploiting positive interdependence do not fully account for the divergence. To explain why Greece and Italy, two neighbours of the CEECs, joined Ireland, Spain, and Portugal as brakemen, we need to include the trade and budgetary competition that was to affect the low-tech producers and net recipients among the member states most strongly. Finally, geopolitical interests had an influence. France, in particular, was concerned that the community balance of power would shift east and in favour of Germany, the most important economic partner of the CEECs. In addition, the Italian government feared that eastern enlargement would divert the EU's attention and funding from the Mediterranean region. In contrast, the strong and early British commitment to enlargement is generally attributed to expanding the zone of liberal democracies and free markets – and the 'europhobia' of the Conservatives who regard a territorial expansion of the Community as an obstacle to its further deepening.

Similar preference patterns can be observed in later enlargement rounds. The new eastern border countries of the EU such as Poland have become the strongest supporters of a membership perspective for Ukraine, and Austria, Greece, Italy, and Slovenia have been the strongest supporters of enlargement to the neighbouring Western Balkans (Smeets 2012: 88). Germany has become less enthusiastic about further enlargement after its own eastern neighbours became members, whereas Britain has consistently remained a pro-enlargement member state, and France has continued to be reluctant towards enlargement to the east.

Member state preferences on Turkey have partly differed from this pattern. First, they have had a strong party component. Christian Democrat and conservative parties have generally been opposed to or reluctant towards Turkish membership on cultural grounds. In March 1997, for instance, the group of the European People's Party in the European Parliament framed the EU as a Christian community and categorically excluded the membership of a Muslim country. The conservative heads of government of Belgium, Germany, Ireland, and Spain supported this declaration (Reuter 2000: 51). Second, because of territorial conflicts with Turkey, the neighbouring countries Greece and Cyprus have not been supporters but opponents of Turkish membership for most of the time (Schimmelfennig 2009: 416–19).

Because member state preferences vary across time and candidates, and Turkey has proved to be a special case, it is difficult to find generalizable explanations. It is clear, however, that member states have always held conflicting preferences on enlargement in the past two decades. Regarding the admission of the CEECs, they reflect different patterns of interdependence and enlargement costs; in the case of Turkey, they stem from different cultural conceptions of the EU's collective identity in addition. Because of the conflicting member state preferences, association constituted the most efficient design for EU relations with its Eastern neighbours. On one hand, it enabled the old member states to intensify their economic involvement in neighbouring markets. On the other hand, it protected the potential losers of enlargement against the costs of trade and budget competition by equipping them with 'antidumping' and 'safeguard' measures and by blocking the candidates' access to the Community budget. Moreover, despite constant complaints about the EC's failure to commit itself to enlargement, the eastern neighbours have regularly accepted association because it was still preferable to a weaker or no institutionalized relationship with the EC.

This account generally corroborates the rationalist, intergovernmentalist analysis of enlargement as driven by cost–benefit calculations and bargaining power. But why did the Community finally commit itself to eastern enlargement and the opening of accession negotiations with Turkey even though the constellation of preferences and bargaining power did not improve in favour of the candidates?

Reaching agreement to enlarge

The drivers represented not only a minority of member states but also wielded less bargaining power than do the brakemen. Even for Germany, the greatest potential beneficiary of eastern enlargement, the CEECs were of far smaller economic and political importance than the brakemen states. Under these circumstances, the drivers had no attractive outside options and could not credibly threaten the brakemen with exit or alternative agreements. In the absence of bargaining power, the drivers therefore turned to normative pressure based on the collective identity and the core political principles of the Community to obtain enlargement.

The institutionalized collective identity of the EU is that of a community of European, liberal-democratic states. In its current version, the Treaty on European Union states in Article 2 that the 'Union is founded on the values of respect for human dignity, freedom, democracy, equality, the rule of law and respect for human rights, including the rights of persons belonging to minorities'.[8] Any European state which respects these principles can apply for membership (Art. 49 TEU).

The main strategy of the proponents of enlargement consisted in constructing enlargement as an issue of identity, values and norms, and opposition to enlargement as a betrayal of the Community's principles, purpose and past promises (see Schimmelfennig 2001: 62–76). In a first step, the CEECs invoked the pan-European, liberal identity of the community and claimed to share this identity. According to this line of argument, the CEECs have traditionally shared the values and norms of European culture and civilization, demonstrated this orientation in the revolution of 1989, and 'returned to Europe' after the Cold War period of artificial separation. Advocates then framed enlargement as an issue of the EU's identity, arguing that it ought not to be seen and decided from the vantage point of national interests and material cost–benefit calculations. They referred to the constitutive values and norms of the EU and the intentions of the founding fathers of the Community and demanded that the member states base their decisions on historical and political criteria and on the long-term collective goals of pan-European peace, stability, and welfare. Finally, they accused the reticent EU member states of acting inconsistently and betraying the fundamental values and norms of their own community if they continued to privilege their individual economic or geopolitical interest and to procrastinate. They appealed to the 'bad historic conscience' of the member states by denouncing their reticence as a new 'Yalta' or 'Iron Curtain' and demanded to be treated according to the standards of earlier enlargement rounds – above all the overriding goal of democracy promotion in the southern enlargement of the 1980s.

The most systematic and formal attempt to rhetorically commit the Community to Eastern enlargement can be found in the Commission's report to the Lisbon summit in June 1992, titled 'Europe and the Challenge of Enlargement'. The Commission referred to the Community's vision of a pan-European liberal order as creating specific obligations in the current situation: 'The Community has never been a closed club, and cannot now refuse the historic challenge to assume its continental responsibilities and contribute to the development of a political and economic order for the whole of Europe'.[9] It was difficult for the brakemen to rebut these arguments without, at the same time, casting doubts on their own commitment to the institutionalized identity and fundamental norms of the EU. Consequently, they did not publicly reject eastern enlargement for instrumental reasons. The fact that the Commission's report, which presented enlargement as inevitable, was attached without discussion to the Conclusions of the Presidency at Lisbon and 'hardly discussed by the member states and certainly not disputed in the many hours of discussion and negotiation leading up to the' Copenhagen summit in June 1993 indicates the effectiveness of normative pressure for the 'silencing' of the brakemen (Mayhew 1998: 25–7).

At the Copenhagen summit, the EU offered the CEECs a general membership perspective – under the condition that they develop stable democratic institutions, a functioning market economy, and the capacity to cope with competitive pressure in the internal market and adopt and implement the *acquis communautaire*. These 'Copenhagen Criteria' put the treaty-based enlargement criteria in more concrete terms, clarified the priority of political conditions related to the EU's liberal-democratic identity, and have since become the basis of the EU's evaluation of candidates for membership and enlargement decisions.

The selection of candidates

After the member states had made the principled decision to expand to the East, the selection of candidates was the next step in the enlargement process. According to the fundamental community norms and the political conditionality of the EU, the selection mainly followed political criteria of liberal-democratic consolidation. Table 11.3 ranks the CEECs (and Turkey in comparison) according to the status of their relationship with the EU in 1997, 1999, 2004, and 2013 together with their Freedom House ratings, a widely used indicator of democratic consolidation.

It shows, first, that countries generally need to be consolidated democracies ('free') to be admitted to accession negotiations. According to the Freedom House data, Turkey is the only exception. As of 2013, this also holds the other way around: all free countries have been admitted to accession negotiations. The data suggest that liberal democracy is in general both a necessary and sufficient condition of accession to the EU. Second, association is possible for hybrid ('partly free') but not autocratic ('not free') regimes. Third, whereas the EU has generally respected the differences between the levels of democracies among the candidates in making enlargement decisions, the absolute levels necessary to become associated or start accession negotiations have slightly decreased over time.

Table 11.3 Selection of CEECs for EU association and accession

Status	Country	1997 P/C¹	1997 Freedom Index	1999 P/C	1999 Freedom Index	2004 P/C	2004 Freedom Index	2013 P/C	2013 Freedom Index
EU member	Czech Rep.	1/2	Free	1/2	Free	1/2	Free	1/1	Free
	Estonia	1/2	Free	1/2	Free	1/2	Free	1/1	Free
	Hungary	1/2	Free	1/2	Free	1/2	Free	1/2	Free
	Poland	1/2	Free	1/2	Free	1/2	Free	1/1	Free
	Slovenia	1/2	Free	1/2	Free	1/1	Free	1/1	Free
	Latvia	2/2	Free	1/2	Free	1/2	Free	2/2	Free
	Lithuania	1/2	Free	1/2	Free	1/2	Free	1/1	Free
	Slovakia	2/4	Partly free	2/2	Free	1/2	Free	1/1	Free
	Bulgaria	2/3	Free	2/3	Free	1/2	Free	2/2	Free
	Romania	2/3	Free	2/2	Free	2/2	Free	2/2	Free
EU accession talks	Croatia	4/4	Partly free	4/4	Partly free	2/2	Free	1/2	Free
	Montenegro	–	–	–	–	–	–	3/2	Free
	Yugoslavia (Serbia)	6/6	Not free	6/6	Not free	3/2	Partly free	2/2	Free
EU association	Macedonia	4/3	Partly free	3/3	Partly free	3/3	Partly free	3/3	Partly free
	Albania	4/4	Partly free	4/5	Partly free	3/3	Partly free	3/3	Partly free
	Bosnia-H.	5/5	Partly free	5/5	Partly free	4/4	Partly free	4/3	Partly free
no association	Ukraine	3/4	Partly free	3/4	Partly free	4/4	Partly free	4/3	Partly free
	Moldova	3/4	Partly free	2/4	Partly free	3/4	Partly free	3/3	Partly free
	Belarus	6/6	Not free	6/6	Not free	6/6	Not free	7/6	Not free
	Russia	3/4	Partly free	4/4	Partly free	5/5	Partly free	6/5	Not free
	Turkey	4/5	Partly free	4/5	Partly free	3/3	Partly free	3/3	Partly free

¹P stands for political rights; C, for civil liberties.

Opening accession negotiations with Turkey

In 1997, the EU refused to grant Turkey the largely symbolic status of an official candidate for membership. Two years later, the opening of accession negotiations with the remaining Central and East European (CEE)–associated countries, including Bulgaria and Romania, and the promise of eventual membership to the countries of the Western Balkans made this decision more and more awkward. In this situation, the advocates of Turkish membership invoked the credibility of the EU and referred to its obligation to heed past promises and to treat Turkey on an equal footing with the CEECs. The main reasons for accepting Turkey as a candidate for membership were, however, strategic and domestic.[10]

For one, the member states were surprised by the harsh reaction of the Turkish government to their 1997 decision. Turkey blocked meetings of the EU–Turkey Association Council, suspended talks on the solution of the Cyprus conflict, and threatened to veto the use of North Atlantic Treaty Organization (NATO) facilities for EU military missions. There was a widespread perception that the EU had to make an accommodative gesture to safeguard the strategic partnership and to ensure Turkey's cooperation on security issues (Önis 2000: 470). In contrast to the CEECs, Turkey wielded real bargaining power because of its strategic importance and institutional power in NATO.

Crucially, a change in German and Greek preferences made this concession possible (Müftüler-Bac and McLaren 2003). Whereas the new German government under Chancellor Schröder had already declared itself in favour of 'candidacy status' at the Cologne Council of June 1999, Greece still blocked any new conclusions on Turkey. It required the change at the top of the Greek foreign ministry and the improved climate after the earthquakes in the summer of 1999 to overcome Greek resistance. As a result, 'for the first time in EU history, no country was determined to prevent Turkey from becoming an eventual member' (Rumford 2002: 55).

The common policy decided at the Helsinki Council reflected member state agreement on enhancing Turkey's status but not a consensus on the desirability of Turkish membership. In addition, it was certainly facilitated by the perception that actual accession negotiations would be a matter of the distant future. At the same time, the new status changed the institutional context of future decisions on Turkey's membership: it considerably strengthened the rather vague membership commitment of the association agreement; it strengthened the role of the Commission in the process; and it constrained the EU to use the same criteria for Turkey that it had used for the CEECs. Consequently, Turkey's application would be judged primarily on liberal-democratic merits. Cultural, religious arguments were excluded from the assessment, and criteria of economic performance were of secondary importance only. As a result, the credibility of Turkey's membership perspective was significantly enhanced: it became worthwhile for the Turkish government to take on domestic reform.

From 2001 to 2005, Turkish governments engaged in an unprecedented series of reforms in the areas of civilian control of the military, human rights, and minority rights that brought Turkey to the threshold of democratic consolidation (see Table 11.3). These reforms prompted the Commission to recommend opening accession negotiations in 2004, and the member states followed this recommendation under the condition that Turkey adopt six additional pieces of legislation and sign an Additional Protocol to the association agreement that would extend the Customs Union to all new member states including Cyprus. When Turkey complied with these conditions, accession negotiations were opened in 2005, even though the preferences of major member governments (France and Germany, in particular) had turned against Turkish membership and several member states had tried to block negotiations at the last minute.

As in the case of the CEECs, the process leading to accession negotiations with Turkey shows the effects of entrapment: after Turkey had fulfilled its part of the political conditionality deal, even the opponents of Turkish membership were compelled to keep their part of the promise as well and could not legitimately deny negotiations. However, the opponents of Turkish membership could only be made to acquiesce in accession negotiations as long as Turkey continued to comply with EU norms and keep its own promises. When Turkey failed to implement the Additional Protocol in 2006, the EU blocked the opening of eight negotiation chapters. Because of vetoes by France and Cyprus, 11 further chapters have been blocked. Only one chapter is closed. Negotiations are close to standstill.

In general, EU decision-making on enlargement corroborates the central constructivist hypothesis about the expansion of international communities: membership increases as outside states adopt the community's collective identity, values, and norms. The identity of the EU as a pan-European liberal international community has shaped both the general decision to expand and the selection of candidates. The process, however, was one of social influence and normative pressure to overcome the self-interested opposition of the brakemen. That the decision to enlarge was made and maintained in spite of adverse constellations of preferences and bargaining power can be attributed to a kind of ideational path dependency: the member states were 'rhetorically entrapped' by their past commitments and constrained by the incremental dynamic and the institutional momentum of the enlargement process.

Accession negotiations

The EU as a collective conducts its accession negotiations bilaterally with each individual applicant country. The concept of 'negotiations', however, suggests an openness that does not exist in the accession process. The substantive outcome of the negotiations is largely predetermined by the special characteristic of the EU as a community of law: the applicants' adoption of the entire body of EU legislation and policies codified in the *acquis communautaire*. Accession negotiations then mainly consist in a process of rule transfer, 'screening' and 'reporting', in which the Commission explains the *acquis* to the applicants, assesses their deficits, and monitors their progress in adopting the *acquis*. The only true negotiations concern the possibility and length of 'transition periods' during which the application of EU rules in the new member states is suspended after accession. Thus, accession negotiations are apparently structured highly asymmetrically in favour of the member states. Yet the *acquis* binds the EU as well as the applicants. In principle, the incumbent members can require the applicants to adopt only those rules that they follow themselves, and they can restrict or suspend costly rights and expenditures only for a limited period.

For the accession negotiations, the *acquis* is subdivided into 'chapters', currently 35 in the case of Montenegro and Turkey. After an initial 'screening' is completed, negotiations begin. Traditionally, they have started with the 'easy' chapters, which create no controversy and no demands for transition periods. One lesson learned from the negotiations (and in particular those with Bulgaria and Romania) was, however, that this approach has left too little time to deal properly with difficult issues such as judicial reform and the fight against corruption. For this reason, the Commission has changed the order of issues in the accession negotiations with Croatia.

All in all, the EU and the CEECs have agreed on 322 transition periods in the accession treaties of the 2004 enlargement, most of them in agriculture, taxation, and environmental policy. Similar temporary exemptions apply to the treaties with Bulgaria, Romania, and Croatia. For instance, the environmental *acquis* could have meant a substantial financial burden for the candidate countries if they had had to meet the standards of the old members. It was considerably reduced, however, by excluding those standards that do not immediately affect the internal market (such as the quality of drinking water). The chapter on the free movement of persons was complicated by fears of uncontrolled and massive migration, in particular in the former border countries of Austria and Germany. Here the EU imposed a transition period of up to seven years on the candidate countries, during which the old members were allowed to restrict the free movement. In return, however, the Union felt obliged to accommodate domestic concerns of some of the CEECs and permit them to restrict the acquisition of land by foreigners for the same time. Finally, in the course of the negotiations on the agricultural chapter, the EU gave up its plan to exclude the new members from the 'direct payments' regime. Since the direct payments are part of the agricultural *acquis*, this plan stood on shaky legal grounds anyhow. Instead, direct payments to the farmers of the new members have increased steadily during a transition period of 10 years.

The accession negotiations thus help member states to retrieve some of the losses they incur through enlargement by excluding the new member states temporarily from those rights and benefits of membership that produce particularly strong concerns among voters and interest groups (Plümper and Schneider 2007; Schneider 2009). However, the results were less unfavourable to the newcomers than expected given the highly asymmetrical bargaining power between old and new members. The *acquis* proved to be a stable bulwark against a permanent discrimination of the new members; transition periods in favour of the old members were balanced by those favouring the new members; and, finally, the old members accepted that no new member should become a net contributor to the EU budget.

Conditionality and Europeanization

Political conditionality and democratic consolidation

Political conditionality has had a decisive influence on the selection of candidate countries: the fundamental liberal principles of legitimate statehood constitute the most important filter for entry into the EU. But did it also have an impact on the outside countries themselves? Did it contribute to their democratic consolidation? Comparative analysis shows that the EU had the most significant impact in one specific group of transformation states – unconsolidated democracies with mixed party constellations – and that this impact depended on both a credible membership perspective and low domestic power costs. In contrast, EU political conditionality has been largely redundant in the forerunners of democratization and ineffective below the threshold of membership incentives and vis-à-vis consolidated autocracies (Kelley 2004; Kubicek 2003; Schimmelfennig 2005; Schimmelfennig *et al.* 2006; Schimmelfennig and Scholtz 2008; Vachudova 2005).

In the forerunner democracies, EU political conditionality has been largely redundant. Poland, the Czech Republic, Slovenia, and Hungary had been well on the way towards democratic consolidation before the EU had made its decision to enlarge and set the political conditions for opening accession negotiations. In addition, the endogenous forces for liberal democracy in these countries were so dominant that they would most likely have continued on the path to democratic consolidation without political conditionality. In the forerunner countries, all major parties based their legitimacy claims and programs on liberal reform and integration into the Western organizations. Thus, the perceived costs of political adaptation were low and did not change after changes in government.

At the other extreme, EU conditionality was not strong enough to produce democratic change in the autocratic or authoritarian countries of the region (such as Belarus, Russia, and Serbia under Milošević). For the ruling elites of these countries, the costs of political adaptation to EU conditions were always high because compliance would have affected their core practices of power preservation (for instance control of the media, manipulation of elections, concentration of competences in the executive). Consequently, domestic power concerns clearly dominated the external incentives of European integration.

The impact of EU political accession conditionality has been most significant in those CEECs that were situated between these extremes. In the forerunner democracies, the EU furthered compliance with those rules that are not generally shared by liberal parties. In CEE, this has mainly been the case with minority protection. Most visibly in the Baltic countries, accession conditionality strengthened moderate forces in the government and built up sufficient pressure for parliaments to pass contested minority legislation.

Most important, however, EU political conditionality has had a major impact in 'mixed countries' with both major liberal and anti-liberal parties, in which there was no elite consensus on liberal-democratic reform and Western integration. Liberal parties or coalitions have been able to come to power in these systems but did not exclusively shape their post-communist development. Either superficially reconstructed communist parties initiated (but also slowed down and distorted) democratic transition from above (such as in Romania). Or reform-adverse nationalists and populists benefited from the failure of reform-oriented parties to provide for economic recovery or efficient governance. In most of these countries, governmental authority has shifted more than once between the two camps.

First, EU accession conditionality helped to consolidate the liberal forces in the mixed countries. Even though the EU does not have a decisive influence on elections and the defeat of anti-liberal parties in Slovakia, Romania, Bulgaria, Croatia, and Serbia between 1996 and 2000 is best explained by domestic factors, political conditionality motivated the often fragmented democratic opposition to join forces for the elections and, after their victory, to preserve coalition discipline. This is best observed in Slovakia, where an extremely heterogeneous multiparty coalition under Prime Minister Dzurinda survived until 2003, when accession was secured.

Second, when liberal parties were in government, the liberal domestic changes they institutionalized led to progress in EU integration, and the benefits of EU integration subsequently raised the stakes in democratic consolidation and increased the costs of any future reversal. Populist parties therefore adapted their political goals in order to preserve the achieved benefits of integration. After the major nationalist-authoritarian parties of Croatia (HDZ), Romania (PDSR) and Slovakia (HZDS) had been voted out of government, Romania and Slovakia started accession negotiations with the EU, and Croatia became an EU associate and applied for membership. During the same time, these parties modified their programs and presented themselves as unequivocally pro-integration. When the PDSR and the HDZ were back in power in 2000 and 2003, they stayed the course of reform and integration. Thus, the lock-in effects of European integration create path-dependency across changes in government and, eventually, can change the party constellation from mixed to liberal.

Acquis conditionality and rule transfer

Acquis conditionality takes centre stage during the accession negotiations between the EU and the applicant states. Whereas the success of political conditionality depended on both the credibility of the membership perspective and low domestic costs, and its impact was mainly felt in CEECs with mixed party constellations, the impact of *acquis* conditionality has been highly pervasive in all countries that passed the threshold of accession negotiations and covered not only basic political institutions but the whole range of EU policies (Schimmelfennig and Sedelmeier 2004, 2005).

Studies in this area show that the key condition for the success of EU rule transfer is the high credibility of *acquis* conditionality. There was some adoption of *acquis* rules even before the EU's conditionality was spelled out, but it was patchy and selective. In addition, CEE governments often adapted EU rules or mixed EU rules with other models. However, once a policy issue became subject of the accession negotiations and *acquis* conditionality, rule adoption increased dramatically and became a consistent feature across countries and issue areas. The massive benefits of EU membership being within close reach, the fulfilment of EU *acquis* conditions became the highest priority in CEEC policy-making and crowded out alternative models (such as rules of other international organization or third countries like the US) as well as domestic opposition and obstacles.

The importance of domestic power costs thus contrasts sharply from political conditionality. As *acquis* conditionality does not concern the political system and bases of political power as such, governments generally do not have to fear that the costs of rule adoption in individual policy areas will lead to a loss of office. Costs are thus unlikely to be prohibitive. Moreover, once a credible membership perspective has been established, adoption costs in individual policy areas are discounted against the (aggregate) benefits of membership rather than just the benefits in this particular policy area. As a consequence, variation in adoption costs merely explains variation in the *speed* (not the fact) of rule adoption across issue areas and countries. Where those costs were high, governments tended to comply only in the final stage of the accession negotiations. But comply they did.

The credibility of *acquis* conditionality tends to diminish towards the end of the accession negotiations, however, especially after accession treaties have been signed (Steunenberg and Dimitrova 2007). At this point, it becomes close to impossible politically for the EU to stop the accession process. As a result, the candidates' readiness to make costly adaptations wanes. Starting with the accession treaties for Bulgaria and Romania, the EU has therefore introduced safeguard clauses into the accession treaties that allow the EU to monitor and sanction the new members' behaviour for several years after accession. In addition, participation in the Schengen regime and the euro-zone is not automatic for new members but depends on additional conditions and the consent of the member states.

The pervasiveness of *acquis* conditionality, the sheer quantity of rules that had to be transposed and the enormous time pressure of the accession process made *acquis* transfer a highly technocratic process. On the part of the EU, it is the Commission bureaucracy that specifies, explicates, and monitors the demands on the applicant states. On the side of the accession countries, it negotiates with the chief negotiators and their teams, delegations of line ministries or even with inter-ministerial coordination units specifically created for the accession negotiations. Thus, the accession processes further contributed to the centralization and strengthening of the executive; societal interest groups and parliaments were marginalized (Grabbe 2001: 1016–18; Bruszt and Stark 2003: 78). During the accession negotiations, the parliamentary agenda was primarily set from the outside. The applicant states introduced accelerated procedures for adopting EU rules and were under pressure to pass – and often rubberstamp – the *acquis*-related legislation at high speed to provide for accession in time.

The technocratic tendencies of *acquis* transfer were strengthened by the implantation of the 'regulatory state' in the CEECs. The expansion of the regulatory state is a typical feature of the development of western democracies but even more characteristic for the political system of the EU (Majone 1996). It is the main purpose of the regulatory state to correct 'market failure' through regulation – in contrast with the politics of redistribution of the 'welfare state' and the politics of macroeconomic stabilization of the 'intervention state'. Correspondingly, the *acquis* transfer to the CEECs consisted predominantly in the transfer of organizations and rules for market regulation that had no roots there. Numerous regulatory policy areas such as environmental and consumer protection, product safety, regional policy and competition policy were either added to the portfolio of traditional policies or at least strongly expanded. At the same time, *acquis* conditionality led to a mushrooming of the technocratic agencies of the regulatory state: independent central banks, competition authorities, offices for environmental protection, transport and food safety agencies, and many more (Grzymala-Busse and Innes 2003: 70–1; Maniokas 2002).[11]

Conclusion

In the past 10 years, the EU has almost doubled its membership. Enlargement has been the EU's major response to the end of the Cold War and its unique contribution to the 'third wave of democratization' and the reunification of Europe. There is no doubt that Eastern enlargement counts among the historic achievements of the EU; enlargement is rightly depicted as the EU's most successful foreign policy tool.

It is remarkable that this massive enlargement has taken place in spite of strongly perceived efficiency, distribution, and decision-making problems, stringent demands for rule adoption in the accession countries, and widespread scepticism among the member states. Enlargement has not been a consensual strategy ready to be applied when the conditions were right but a contested and incremental process, in which norms and interests have interacted in a complex way.

The main theories of European integration cover different aspects of this process (see Chapter 2). In general, intergovernmentalism is best at explaining the preferences and negotiating behaviour of the actors. First, the enlargement preferences of the member states and the candidates' responses to EU conditionality have varied with the distribution of enlargement benefits and costs. Second, negotiations on association and accession as well as EU political and *acquis* conditionality have been characterized by tough bargaining including threats to block or delay enlargement. The rational intergovernmentalist external incentives model also explains the outcomes of non-member Europeanization in general. Yet contrary to intergovernmentalist expectations, the actors with superior material bargaining power did not generally prevail in the internal EU or the EU–CEE negotiations.

Rather, the actors and their negotiations were constrained by fundamental community norms derived from the collective identity of the EU – emphasized by constructivism – and by path dependencies emphasized in supranationalist accounts of European integration. Community norms defined the content of the conditions in EU political and *acquis* conditionality, provided legitimacy to the pro-enlargement coalition, and softened the EU-candidate asymmetry in the accession negotiations. Past identity commitments, promises, and enlargement practices bound the opponents of the present enlargement and could be used by the drivers to rhetorically entrap them and to keep the enlargement process on track. In the candidate countries, progress in integration effectively locked in domestic reform and generated programmatic change in authoritarian parties. The two faces of enlargement, the accession process and the Europeanization process, have proved interdependent and mutually reinforcing: while the democratic transformation and Europeanization of the candidates put pressure on the EU to expand, EU accession conditionality put pressure on the CEECs to reform and adopt EU rules.

Why has the enlargement slowed down then after 2005? I suggest that this has less to do with the results of the enlargement process than with the remaining potential candidates for membership. In general, few of the expected problems of enlargement have materialized. First, in spite of illiberal tendencies in Hungary and Romania (Sedelmeier 2014), there has not been a general backlash in democratic consolidation after the end of EU political accession conditionality, even though the pace of reform has slowed down (Levitz and Pop-Eleches 2010). Second, the new member states belong to the best formal compliers with EU law (Sedelmeier 2008), although this picture may mask severe problems of implementation on the ground (Falkner and Treib 2008). Third, EU membership has benefitted the economies of the new member states on the whole (Epstein 2014; Jacoby 2014). Finally, enlargement has not had disruptive effects on EU decision-making capacity.

In spite of the 'enlargement fatigue' setting in after the failed referendums on the Constitutional Treaty and the conclusion of accession negotiations with Bulgaria and Romania, the EU has generally continued to apply its political accession conditionality consistently and even relaxed its requirements to accommodate the remaining candidates or potential candidates for membership (Schimmelfennig 2008). First, however, the limitation of enlargement to European countries creates a natural ceiling. Although the borders of 'Europe' are constructed and malleable, the pool of future candidates is shrinking: the further to the east a country is located, the more debate there is about its 'Europeanness'.

Second, even those non-member states, which are generally viewed as 'European', often lack the prerequisites for successful democratization and governance capacity, which are necessary to advance towards full membership. In other words, the EU has successfully integrated the 'easier cases' among the transition countries and is now faced with those countries that have the poorest socio-economic conditions and the most difficult historical legacies for democratic consolidation and stability. That the EU has not offered Moldova or Ukraine a credible membership perspective has certainly not helped democratic consolidation in these countries. But even in countries with such a perspective (e.g. Albania or Bosnia-Herzegovina), the democratization process has stagnated for many years. As the EU's enlargement process is mainly driven by successful democratic consolidation as a necessary condition to overcome scepticism among the old member states and to fulfil the EU's political accession conditions, poor prerequisites for democracy and the rule of law translate immediately into poor prospects for enlargement.

Notes

1   This chapter does not deal with EU enlargement in Western Europe.
2   This section draws strongly on Schimmelfennig and Sedelmeier (2002: 508–15; 2004: 663–68).
3   Agence Europe, 20 January 1989.
4   Agence Europe, 22 November 1989.
5   Agence Europe, 27 February 1992.
6   Sedelmeier and Wallace (2000: 438). On the association negotiations in general, see Torreblanca (2001).
7   See draft agreement between the EU and Ukraine.
8   At the time, it was Article 6(1) TEU.
9   European Commission, *Europe and the Challenge of Enlargement* (Agence Europe, Europe Documents 1790, 1992). On the relevance of the 'responsibility' theme, see Sedelmeier (2000).
10 This section is based on Schimmelfennig (2009).

References

Bruszt, L. and Stark, D. (2003) 'Who Counts? Supranational Norms and Societal Needs', *East European Politics and Societies*, 17: 74–82.

Epstein, R. (2014) 'Overcoming 'Economic Backwardness' in the European Union', *Journal of Common Market Studies*, 52: 17–34.

Falkner, G. and Treib, O. (2008) 'Three Worlds of Compliance or Four? The EU-15 Compared to New Member States', *Journal of Common Market Studies*, 46: 293–313.

Grabbe, H. (2001) 'How Does Europeanization Affect CEE Governance? Conditionality, Diffusion and Diversity', *Journal of European Public Policy*, 8: 1013–31.

Grzymala-Busse, A. and Innes, A. (2003) 'Great Expectations: The EU and Domestic Political Competition in East Central Europe', *East European Politics and Societies*, 17: 64–73.

Jacoby, W. (2014) 'The EU Factor in Fat Times and in Lean: Did the EU Amplify the Boom and Soften the Bust?', *Journal of Common Market Studies*, 52: 52–70.

Kelley, J.G. (2004) *Ethnic Politics in Europe. The Power of Norms and Incentives*, Princeton: Princeton University Press.

Kubicek, P.J. (2003) (ed.) *The European Union and Democratization*, London: Routledge.

Levitz, P. and Pop-Eleches, G. (2010) 'Why No Backsliding? The European Union's Impact on Democracy and Governance before and after Accession', *Comparative Political Studies*, 43: 457–85.

Majone, G. (1996) *Regulating Europe*, London: Routledge.

Maniokas, K. (2002) *EU Enlargement and Europeanization: When a Patchwork Becomes a Blueprint. Summary*, Mimeo.

Mayhew, A. (1998) *Recreating Europe. The European Union's Policy towards Central and Eastern Europe*, Cambridge: Cambridge University Press.

Müftüler-Bac, M. and McLaren, L.M. (2003) 'Enlargement Preferences and Policy-making in the European Union: Impacts on Turkey', *Journal of European Integration*, 25: 17–31.

Önis, Z. (2000) 'Luxembourg, Helsinki and Beyond: Towards an Interpretation of Recent Turkey-EU Relations', *Government and Opposition*, 35: 463–83.

Plümper, T. and Schneider, C. (2007) 'Discriminatory European Union Membership and the Redistribution of Enlargement Gains', *Journal of Conflict Resolution*, 51: 568–87.

Reuter, J. (2000) 'Athens Türkeipolitik im Wandel. Griechisch-türkische Beziehungen vor und nach dem EU-Gipfel von Helsinki', *Südosteuropa-Mitteilungen*, 40: 47–64.

Rumford, C. (2002) 'Failing the EU Test? Turkey's National Program, EU Candidature and the Complexities of Democratic Reform', *Mediterranean Politics*, 7: 51–68.

Sandler, T. and Tschirhart, J.T. (1980) 'The Economic Theory of Clubs: An Evaluative Survey', *Journal of Economic Literature*, 18: 1481–1521.

Schimmelfennig, F. (2001) 'The Community Trap: Liberal Norms, Rhetorical Action, and the Eastern Enlargement of the European Union', *International Organization*, 55: 47–80.

Schimmelfennig, F. (2003) *The EU, NATO and the Integration of Europe. Rules and Rhetoric*, Cambridge: Cambridge University Press.

Schimmelfennig, F. (2005) 'Strategic Calculation and International Socialization: Membership Incentives, Party Constellations, and Sustained Compliance in Central and Eastern Europe', *International Organization*, 59: 827–60.

Schimmelfennig, F. (2008) 'EU Political Conditionality after the 2004 Enlargement: Consistency and Effectiveness', *Journal of European Public Policy*, 15: 918–37.

Schimmelfennig, F. (2009) 'Entrapped Again: The Way to EU Membership Negotiations with Turkey', *International Politics*, 46: 413–31.

Schimmelfennig, F. and Sedelmeier, U. (2002) 'Theorizing EU Enlargement: Research Focus, Hypotheses, and the State of Research', *Journal of European Public Policy*, 9: 500–28.

Schimmelfennig, F. and Sedelmeier, U. (2004) 'Governance by Conditionality: EU Rule Transfer to the Candidate Countries of Central and Eastern Europe', *Journal of European Public Policy*, 11: 661–79.

Schimmelfennig, F. and Sedelmeier, U. (2005) (eds) *The Europeanization of Central and Eastern Europe*, Ithaca: Cornell University Press.

Schimmelfennig, F. and Scholtz, H. (2008) 'EU Democracy Promotion in the European Neighborhood. Political Conditionality, Economic Development and Transnational Exchange', *European Union Politics*, 9: 187–215.

Schimmelfennig, F., Engert, S., and Knobel, H. (2006) *International Socialization in Europe: European Organizations, Political Conditionality, and Democratic Change*, Basingstoke: Palgrave Macmillan.

Schneider, Christina J. (2009) *Conflict, Negotiations, and EU Enlargement*, Cambridge: Cambridge University Press.

Sedelmeier, U. (2000) 'Eastern Enlargement: Risk, Rationality, and Role-Compliance', in M. Green Cowles and M. Smith (eds) *Risks, Reforms, Resistance and Revival*, Oxford: Oxford University Press.

Sedelmeier, U. (2005) *Constructing the Path to Eastern Enlargement. The Uneven Policy Impact of EU Identity*, Manchester: Manchester University Press.

Sedelmeier, U. (2008) 'After Conditionality: Post-Accession Compliance with EU Law in East Central Europe', *Journal of European Public Policy*, 15: 806–25.

Sedelmeier, U. (2014) 'Anchoring Democracy from Above? The European Union and Democratic Backsliding in Hungary and Romania after Accession', *Journal of Common Market Studies*, 52: 105–21.

Sedelmeier, U. and Wallace, H. (2000) 'Eastern Enlargement. Strategy or Second Thoughts?', in H. Wallace and W. Wallace (eds) *Policy-Making in the European Union*, 4th edn, Oxord: Oxford University Press.

Smeets, S. (2012) 'And *All* Must Have Prizes?' Council Negotiations and the European Perspective of the Western Balkans (2000–2010), PhD dissertation, Radboud University of Nijmegen.

Steunenberg, Bernard, and Dimitrova, A. (2007) 'Compliance in the EU Enlargement Process: The Limits of Conditionality', *European Integration online Papers*, 11: 1–18.

Torreblanca, J.I. (2001) *The Reuniting of Europe. Promises, Negotiations and Compromises*, Aldershot: Ashgate.

Vachudova, Milada A. (2005) *Europe Undivided: Democracy, Leverage, and Integration after Communism*, Oxford: Oxford University Press.

Chapter 12

The EU as an international actor

MICHAEL SMITH

Introduction

From the beginning, the European Community and now the EU have had to exist in a changing international context; indeed, many treatments of the history of European integration place great weight on the international dimension of both the foundation and the development of the phenomenon (W. Wallace 1990; Pinder 1991a; Story 1993; Dinan 2004). The EU, as will be shown in more detail later in this chapter, is also a major presence in the contemporary global arena. It is thus not surprising that there should have been consistent and growing attention to the international 'credentials' of the EC and then the EU.

To state this position, though, is to beg a central question. Although the EU is a major component of the contemporary world arena, just what is its status, role and impact? At one end of the spectrum, there are those who can discern a progression in the EU towards full-fledged international 'actorness', comparable to that of the national states that comprise the major concentrations of power in world politics. But such views have to wrestle with the inconvenient fact that the EU is not a 'state' in the accepted international meaning of the term, although it undoubtedly demonstrates some 'state-like' features. Notwithstanding its ability to act in the economic and diplomatic fields, the EU has been slow to develop a coherent security policy or even the beginnings of a European-level defence policy (Hill, 1990, 1993, 1995; Smith 1994b, 2005; Cameron 1999, 2012; Gnesotto 2004; Howorth 2007, 2011).

Thwarted in the search for an EU version of statehood, others have attempted to define the EU as a growing and increasingly structured 'presence' in the international arena, with its own forms of international behaviour and influence, and most significantly an important place in the foreign policies of other international actors, whether they be states or non-state groupings (Allen and Smith, 1990, 1998). Thus, the EU cannot be avoided by national foreign policy makers, nor can it be bypassed by international organisations such as the United Nations. This approach has its undoubted advantages, not least that of finessing the issue of statehood, but it also begs major questions. Perhaps most important, it raises the issue of relations between the EU's 'presence' and the persistence of the essentially national powers of the EU's member states themselves (Hill 1995; Manners and Whitman 2000).

Whatever the position taken on the EU's claims to 'actorness' or 'presence' in the international arena, the analyst must take into account two crucial aspects of the EU's international existence. First, the EU is not simply an 'actor' or a 'presence' but also a *process*; a set of complex institutions, roles and rules which structure the activities of the EU itself and those of other internationally significant groupings with which it comes into contact. Second, the EU as 'actor', 'presence' and process exists today in a world which has *changed* greatly, not to say fundamentally, since the foundation of the European Coal and Steel Community (ECSC), the Treaty of Rome or even the Single European Act in the mid-1980s.

Since the late 1990s, it might be argued, a number of these pressures have converged to provide a new impetus for the development of the EU's international 'actorness'. Whilst the Treaty of Amsterdam (1997) was widely perceived to have fallen short of its aims in a number of areas, it did make some significant revisions to the Common Foreign and Security Policy (CFSP). It gave the European Council responsibility for the framing of 'common strategies' to guide foreign ministers, it regularised the budgetary situation of CFSP, it established a Policy Planning Unit to provide the beginnings of an intelligence and planning capability and it provided for the appointment of a 'high representative' to act as the figurehead for CFSP. These detailed changes were given new focus by the emergence during 1998 and 1999 of important new initiatives designed to formalise a 'defence policy' element in the CFSP, and by the drive by the British and French governments in particular to add strength to the EU's security and defence activities. By the time of the Treaty of Nice in 2000, the 'muscles' of an emerging EU defence policy were more clearly defined, and by 2003–2004 these were employed in the EU 's first coordinated military operations. At the same time, the production of the Constitutional Treaty from 2002 onwards, and then the Lisbon Treaty ratified in 2009, led to further formalisation of both the foreign and the defence policy structures of the Union. The question remained, however, how far these initiatives would go and how much they would change the EU's operations in specific international arenas, in particular when the interests of the United States were engaged or when the coercive as opposed to persuasive use of military assets was at issue (Cameron 1999: chap. 8–9; Everts *et al.* 2004; Howorth 2000, 2007, 2011).

Two central questions thus act as the focus for this chapter. First, what is the evidence that the EU is moving towards full-fledged 'actorness' in the international arena, adding new focus and impact to its established presence and processes? Second, what role does the EU play in the new Europe and the new world of the twenty-first century, and how does that role reflect the unique status of the EU? Based on the discussion of these two areas, the chapter also attempts to project the possible future development of the EU's international role.

The structure of the chapter reflects the agenda set out earlier. First, it deals with the foundations, both institutional and political, of the EU's international role and impact. Second, it assesses the pattern of issues, interactions and relationships that constitute the substance of the EU's international life, and finally, it evaluates the models available to describe and explain the EU's international policy making. The institutional focus is on developments up to and including the Lisbon Treaty, and on the consequent changes involving the introduction (for example) of the European External Action Service (EEAS); in its conclusions the chapter evaluates the prospects for the 'actorness' of the EU that have emerged between 2009 and 2013, and attempts to project these over the next five years or so.

The foundations

As already noted, the EU derives much of its international role and impact from the foundations on which it is built. Perhaps the most obvious, yet also problematical of these foundations, is the EU's international 'weight'. In particular, the fact that the EU accounts for a large proportion of the world's economic activity and is the world's champion trader, creates an inevitable focus on the extent to which and the ways in which the weight is translated into international outcomes. The difficulty, as Chris Hill has ably pointed out, is that there is a 'capability-expectations gap': to put it bluntly, the EU does not deliver consistently on the raw material given to it by the economic prosperity and muscle of the system it has developed. By implication, the conversion of muscle into meaningful action is deficient (Hill 1993, 1998). This theme will be developed further later in the chapter, but at this stage it leads directly into a discussion of the institutions and the politics of EU external policy making.

The EU's international role rests explicitly on the constitutional base established in the treaties, but that base is neither comprehensive nor unambiguous. It is least unambiguous in the area of the Common Commercial Policy (CCP) and the EU's international trade policies. Article 113 of the Treaty of Rome (later article 133 in the Consolidated Treaties and Article 207 in the Lisbon Treaty) gave the EC responsibility for conducting the trade relations of the Community with the rest of the world, and from it grew a complex web of both institutions and relationships. In important ways, the CCP was inevitable given the establishment of the customs union and the Common External Tariff; the need to manage the external trade relations of the Community, and to conduct relations with international partners, was a logical outcome of the establishment of the customs union, and the acquisition of international competence was one of the first items on the Commission's agenda (Smith 2005).

During the 1950s, 1960s and 1970s, therefore, the EEC developed a complicated network of international agreements, and came to play an important role in the development of the world trading system. The Commission was recognised as the voice of the EEC in the conduct of international trade negotiations, and the enlargement of the Community during the 1970s further increased the range and scope of its international economic involvement. Another impact of the enlargement was the need to develop and implement a more comprehensive Community policy on international development assistance, and this led to the so-called Lomé system based on the Convention signed in 1975 and then later revisions. But this was a partial international role at best: the Community and the Commission had competence in trade negotiations, but even in this area there was a division of powers between the Commission and the Council of Ministers; when the Commission negotiated on international trade, it was on the basis of a mandate from the Council and with the close attention of what became known as the '113 Committee' (later the '133 Committee' and now the Trade Policy Committee) of national trade officials. In the area of development policy there was even more of a 'mixed' system in which the views and resources of member states remained central. Although other aspects of international economic relations such as monetary policy and investment were in many respects crucial to the development of the Community, they were not the subject of Community-level policy making. Even the establishment of the European Monetary System in the late 1970s did not extend Community competence fully into this area, since the system was effectively operated by the central banks of the member states (Tsoukalis 1997).

If the initial competence of the Community was limited in the field of international economic policy, it was almost non-existent in the field of what some would call 'real' foreign policy: the 'high politics' of diplomacy, defence and security. What emerged in this area during the 1970s was not a Community policy, but a series of mechanisms through which the national foreign policies of the EC's members could be more closely coordinated. By the end of the 1970s, this had evolved into the framework known as European Political Cooperation (EPC), which effectively acted as a procedural device for the management of common interests. But the member states had not yielded any of their formal freedom of action to the Community, and they retained the right to pursue purely national policies at the same time as participating in the EPC mechanism (Allen *et al.* 1982; Hill 1983).

This meant that by the early 1980s, there was only a patchy and partial basis for the development of the EC's international role. There were areas of intense and continuous activity, for example in the conduct of trade policy and the implementation of the Lomé Conventions; there were areas of intense but temporary activity, such as those centred around the energy crises of the 1970s or the issue of economic sanctions as Soviet–American tensions waxed and waned, but in many areas including the politics of national security, the national policy mechanisms of EC members remained almost untouched.

During the 1980s, however, there were important changes both in the international conditions and in the institutional base for EC international policy making. At the international level, it became apparent more and more that the separation of 'economic' and 'political' or 'security' issues was artificial. Indeed, many of the most pressing international problems were intractable precisely because of the ways in which the economic, the political and the security elements were intertwined and interdependent. Not only this, but in the world political economy itself there was an increasing awareness of the issues arising from technological change and shifts in competitive advantage (Smith and Woolcock 1993; Stubbs and Underhill 2005).

At the Community level, one response to the latter development was the Single Market Programme. It is possible to see the Commission White Paper of 1985 and the subsequent legislative programme simply as a process dealing with the internal economic activity of the EC, but it was apparent to many from the outset that this was also a programme designed to enhance the international presence and impact of the EC and its economic groupings. This implied a major increase in the international activity of the Community, not only to ensure that the single market was effectively integrated with the international economic framework but also to defuse the often suspicious reactions of economic partners and rivals such as the United States or Japan (Ishikawa 1989; Hufbauer 1990; Redmond 1992; Smith and Woolcock 1993; Hocking and Smith 1997).

Alongside this, though, went crucial developments in the area of 'high politics', which gave the Community and its members both the incentive and some of the instruments to develop policy in new domains. One such development, already noted, was the linkage between economic and security aims in the world arena, at its most obvious in the use of economic sanctions against (for example) the Iranians, the USSR and South Africa. In these cases, however much the member states might have wished to act on a national basis, they could not do so effectively because of the concentration of commercial policy powers at the Community level (Allen and Pijpers 1984; Pijpers *et al*. 1988; Nuttall 1992).

Another set of significant international policy developments arose from the further evolution of EPC. During the 1980s, a process which remained resolutely intergovernmental was given further definition and a more formal institutional framework. The Single European Act for the first time created a treaty base – albeit an explicitly intergovernmental one – for the EPC mechanisms. It also formalised the 'troika' through which successive Council presidencies ensured continuity, and it established a permanent though small EPC secretariat. It even went so far as to introduce the word 'security' into the EPC framework, although there was a firm restriction to the 'political and economic aspects' of security issues (Pijpers *et al*. 1988; Nuttall 1992).

By the late 1980s, then, the framework for EC international policy consisted effectively of two strands: the Community strand as applied through the CCP and its instruments (with the additional but related dimension of development policy), which was given added force by the external impact of the single market; and the intergovernmental strand as exemplified in Title III of the Single European Act and EPC mechanisms. At the same time, there was an increasing consciousness of the artificiality of distinctions between 'high' and 'low' politics or between economics and security. The lesson was borne in with unprecedented force by the events of 1989 in Europe, with the fall of the

Berlin Wall and the subsequent more or less peaceful revolutions in central and Eastern European countries (W. Wallace 1990; Pinder 1991b; Allen and Smith, 1991–92).

It was in this context that the Maastricht Treaty in EU attacked the issues of the 'second pillar' or foreign and security policy. Indeed, it was because of this context that the EC's members felt the need to go beyond the limits of intergovernmental cooperation so far established and to develop new mechanisms for foreign policy coordination. Whilst the external commercial policy powers of the Community were hardly altered by the TEU, the provisions on a common foreign and security policy in the treaty broke new ground both in terms of substance and in terms of the organisational framework. The treaty declared the members' determination to establish a common foreign and security policy, which would lead in time to a common defence policy and even to a common defence (by implication, a military community to stand alongside the economic one in the framework of the Union). The existing Western European Union was defined as the defence arm of the Union, with provision for a growing together of the two organisations and a definitive review of their relations in the 1996 Inter-Governmental Conference (IGC) (Rummel 1992; Norgaard *et al.* 1993; Forster and Wallace 1996; Regelsberger *et al.* 1997; Keukeleire and MacNaughtan 2008: chap. 2; Cameron 2012: chap. 2).

To support this set of aims and intentions, the Treaty on European Union (TEU) established new procedures. The Commission was given a (non-exclusive) right of initiative in the CFSP field, whilst the intergovernmental character of the framework was preserved by the guiding role of the European Council and the continued location of the primary operational responsibilities with the Council of Ministers. For the first time, voting procedures including majority voting were introduced to the domain of foreign policy, although there were strong safeguards for national positions. The common diplomatic positions generated by the EPC mechanism were supplemented by potential 'joint actions' within agreed limits, raising a number of issues about resourcing and the role of the Commission in implementing foreign policy decisions (Laursen and Vanhoonacker 1992; Rummel 1992; Norgaard *et al.* 1993; Regelsberger *et al.* 1997; Cameron 1999: chap. 2–4).

As noted earlier in the chapter, the Treaty of Amsterdam in many ways continued the processes set in motion by the TEU. Indeed, since the TEU only entered into force in late 1993, the CFSP provisions had had little time to develop before they were once again subject to review. In addition to the procedural innovations summarised earlier – 'common strategies', the budgetary provisions, the Planning Unit and the 'high representative' – Amsterdam also introduced general provisions for 'flexibility', and for an extension of Qualified Majority Voting (QMV), whereby those member states wishing to move more rapidly, or to take more muscular action, might hope not to be impeded by the others. The Treaty also introduced into the CFSP the so-called Petersberg tasks relating to humanitarian intervention and peacekeeping activities, and foreshadowed the eventual absorption of the Western European Union (WEU) into the Union. These measures were not insignificant; indeed, they could form a basis for creative exploitation of the potential in the CFSP, as long as the political will was to be found. But it is open to question whether in themselves they resolved the 'unstable compromise' hammered together at Maastricht in 1991 (Forster and Wallace 1996; Cameron 1999: chap. 5).

The Treaty of Nice in 2000 did little to alter the detailed provisions for CFSP, but as noted earlier it reflected in the provisions on the Common Security and Defence Policy (CSDP) the major steps undertaken since the Franco-British St Malo summit of 1998. Thus, by the time the Constitutional Convention started its work in 2004, the provisions for a 'European foreign policy' showed significant changes with the introduction of what some described as a 'fourth pillar' dealing with the military aspects of the Union's external policies. The Western European Union, a previously independent European security organisation, had been effectively absorbed into the Union, and military uniforms were an increasingly salient feature of everyday life in the Brussels administration.

Later parts of the chapter will deal with the practical impact of these CFSP and CSDP provisions, but at this stage a review of the position reached in the TEU (and as modified at Amsterdam and Nice) is in order. Three interim conclusions are apparent. In the first place, the longstanding foundations of the EC's external policy powers in the field of trade and related areas continued to flourish, reinforced by the impact of the single market programme and the intensification of international economic interdependence. Second, the 'civilian power' of the Community had been supplemented through inter-governmental channels by the increasingly 'high politics' of EPC, then the CFSP and finally the CSDP. Not only this, but in a number of cases it had been demonstrated that the Community and its powers were essential to the successful pursuit of diplomatic objectives in the area of 'high politics'.

Finally, although this may appear to have been an inexorable advance towards the construction of an integrated Union foreign policy, and thus the achievement of full international 'actorness' on the part of the Union, there were a number of reasons to be cautious in making such judgements. The CFSP and the CSDP remained intergovernmental, albeit much more effectively institutionalised than the original EPC framework. Member states might recognise the logic of fuller EU responsibilities for foreign policy, but certainly in the case of the major members they would be reluctant to give up the core elements of sovereignty and national security. And perhaps above all, the fluid and potentially dangerous situation in the 'new Europe' and the broader 'new-world disorder' was always capable of placing severe strains on the coordination mechanisms available even under the TEU, Amsterdam and Nice. With this, it is appropriate to turn to the Constitutional Treaty and the Treaty of Lisbon, which appeared to herald a new and transformative phase in the development of the EU's external policy-making.

Amongst other consequences of the Nice Treaty, one of the most significant was the recognition by member states that in the light of major enlargement, the institutional framework for 'European foreign policy' and broader external action would require further modification. As in previous bouts of institutional renegotiation, there were several different positions among the member states on this issue, ranging between those who wanted simply an incremental development of the existing mechanisms and those who wanted a transformation, with the establishment of a 'foreign minister' and a full-blown diplomatic service for the Union. At a relatively early stage in the deliberations of the Convention, it became clear that there was broad support for an extension and consolidation of cooperation and for linkages between the Community-based focus on commercial and foreign economic policies and the more 'political' aspects of diplomacy and security. It must be remembered that these discussions were taking place in the shadow of major intra-EU disputes accompanying the Iraq War of 2003, and the subsequent elaboration of the EU's Security Strategy (see the later discussion). It is noteworthy, then, that there was broad agreement on the need to bring together the 'external action' of the Union in one part of the projected treaty, and to provide it with mechanisms for institutional coordination and linkage between the various 'pillars' of European external policy-making (Keukeleire and MacNaughtan 2008: chap. 2; Cameron 2012: chap. 3–4).

In principle, the Constitutional Treaty and then the Lisbon Treaty provided for the disappearance of the 'three pillars' of Union policy-making, and their integration into one part of the institutional framework, that dealing with 'external action'. But it was noticeable that although this merger was formally proclaimed as one of the key achievements of the Lisbon Treaty, in reality the distinction between modes of policy-making still persisted. It was still possible in trade policy, for example, to discern the working of the old 'Community method', and in the CFSP to recognise the familiar 'second pillar' processes with their dominant intergovernmental characteristics. But there was also an increasing number of areas in which this distinction was very difficult to uphold – for example the development of 'neighbourhood policy' after the 2004 enlargement and the increasing prominence of environmental policy or development policy – meant that there was a growing need for new mechanisms of coordination quite apart from the institutional formalities.

The major institutional innovations of the Lisbon Treaty in external policy terms were thus at one level those of principle. But clearly also, there were several new formal institutions to be considered. The most prominent of these was the EEAS: a new form of multinational diplomatic service that was not quite a foreign ministry but which also covered ground that conventional foreign ministries often did not – for example the CSDP, which in national foreign ministries is often 'off-limits' because of the existence of powerful defence ministries, or major areas of development policy that are often separately conducted at national level. At the top of the EEAS, the High Representative for Foreign Affairs and Security Policy was formalised as the key official, and given a dual role as not only the head of the EEAS but also a vice-president of the Commission (hence the commonly used acronym 'HRVP').

In many ways, this set of innovations seemed to provide for a transformation of EU external action. But the message of the earlier parts of this chapter should be remembered: in the development of EU external action and 'European foreign policy', the impact of external events and of the real-world linkages between issues can be as powerful if not more powerful than the frameworks established in treaties. One of the key tests of the post-Lisbon policy framework was thus likely to centre on the extent to which it gave the Union a firm basis for coordination in complex and turbulent contexts of the kind that have been all too typical of the twenty-first century. This is the cue to turn to matters of policy substance, the second part of the analytical framework proposed here.

The substance of policy

In order to arrive at a more precise description of the EU's international connections, and to explore the ways in which they affect policy making, this part of the chapter examines four aspects of the problem. First, it evaluates the *agendas* on which the EU's international activities are focused. Second, it identifies the *arenas* within which the EU is involved. Third, it looks at the *relationships* that are central to the EU's international existence. Finally, it reviews the *levels* at which EU actions are shaped and take place, and provides some brief examples of the implications of multilevel policy making. Whilst these four aspects are separated here for analytical purposes, in reality they are often closely – indeed, inextricably – linked. The final section of the chapter attempts to bring them together in an examination of modes of EU policy making.

Agendas

The longest established agenda for action at the European level is that of trade and commercial relations, including development policies. As the EU has evolved, it has spawned an extensive set of international trade and aid agreements, which some have described as a 'pyramid of privilege'. The extent and complexity of this network reflect the centrality of the trade and aid agenda to the EU; after all, this was the original *raison d'etre* of the EEC, and the focus of the earliest common policy efforts of the Community in the international field. Thus, today, the Union finds itself deeply and continuously engaged in international trade negotiations, either on a bilateral basis, or on an inter-regional basis, or in the context of the World Trade Organization. At the same time, it deals with less developed countries, particularly those of the African, Caribbean and Pacific (ACP) grouping in the framework of the Cotonou Agreement, which replaced the series of Lomé Conventions in 2000, and in the context of the Economic Partnership Agreements (EPAs) which are the key means of pursuing the Convention (Carbone 2007; Holland and Doidge 2012). During the 1990s and early 2000s, a novel trade and aid agenda emerged, centred on the development and stabilisation needs of what came to be called the enlarged EU's 'neighbourhood', including the former Soviet bloc and the Mediterranean (Hine 1985; Edwards and Regelsberger 1990; Pinder 1991b; Dent 1997; Piening 1997; Dannreuther 2004; K. Smith 2011; Cameron 2012: chap. 8).

Trade, aid and commercial agreements are thus at the core of the EU's international agenda. As the growth of international interdependence and interpenetration has proceeded since the 1980s, this traditional focus has been joined by another: the links between markets and regulatory structures within and outside the EU. The Single Market Programme was launched in a different world from that of the Treaty of Rome or the CAP – a world in which the seemingly 'domestic' concerns of market regulation, standards setting and competition policies were becoming the stuff of international politics through processes loosely termed 'globalisation'. As a result, the EC and then the EU have had to develop new structures and procedures to deal with such matters as public procurement, mergers and acquisitions, market access and environmental regulation at the international level (Woolcock 1992, 2012; Harrison 1994; Woolcock and Hodges 1996; Hocking and Smith 1997; M. Smith 1999; Young 2002).

The agenda for diplomacy, security and defence was for a long time separated from the more central economic and commercial EU agendas, but as time has gone on it has become increasingly difficult to maintain the distance between matters of economic welfare and matters of national or European security. The intertwining of these areas became especially apparent in the aftermath of the collapse of the USSR; not only had the geopolitical division of Europe disappeared, but the functional division in the EU between civilian and security agendas had also (Laffan *et al.* 2000: chap. 3). No clearer example of this new logic could be found than in the events and processes surrounding the development of the 'European defence identity' after 1998. Whilst the formal institutionalisation process revolved around successive political 'summits', first between the British and the French at St Malo in the autumn of 1998, then in the European Councils of Cologne and Helsinki during 1999 and in the intergovernmental conference leading up to the Treaty of Nice, there was also a move during the same period to set up a European Aerospace and Defence corporation, to express the growing feeling that the EU's defence industries should consolidate and integrate. During the mid-2000s, there were active moves towards the establishment of a European arms procurement agency – the potential 'customer' for the products of a consolidated Union defence industrial complex (Howorth 2007, 2011).

Arenas

For many years, from the 1960s to the late 1980s, the EC's dominant arena of action, its main reference point for any sort of international identity, was the western system and in particular the economic structure built around the North Atlantic area (Allen and Smith 1991–92; Smith and Woolcock 1993; Story 1993). Just as the policy agenda for the EU has been transformed since the 1980s, so has the arena for its international actions. Whilst the long established institutional arrangements have not disappeared, they are implanted in a radically changed context, and have been joined by a number of novel arrangements reflecting the needs of the post–Cold War world. Many of these new arrangements reflect the linkages between agendas already noted: for example, the influence of the Organization on Security and Co-operation in Europe with its focus on non-military as well as military aspects of security, or the role of the European Bank for Reconstruction and Development in the political and economic stabilisation of the 'new Europe'. The EU finds itself not only in a transformed world arena but also in a newly institutionalised and rapidly developing European order, and this is a challenge to international action (Allen and Smith 1991–92; Smith and Woolcock 1993; Carlsnaes and Smith 1994; Laffan *et al.* 2000; K. Smith 2003, 2011).

The challenge is complicated further by two sets of contradictions, which surround and penetrate the arenas for EU action. First, there is the coexistence of new and developing institutions with persistent disorder and conflict. This contradiction was first clearly seen in the conflicts that erupted in the former Yugoslavia during the 1990s. Although there was no shortage of institutions with roles and responsibilities, one of which was the EU itself, they were challenged and often defeated by the mercurial and combustible array of contending forces with an interest in chaos and destruction.

An arguably even more dramatic illustration of this problem came in the wake of the attack on the World Trade Centre and the Pentagon in the US on 11 September 2001. In many ways, this highlighted the fact that the EU had been insulated for a generation from the impact of global disorder; after '9.11', the intimate linkages between the EU's roles in the European order and the broader global disorder posed severe problems of management at the European level, spanning areas such as justice and home affairs, the developing European security and defence institutions and the engagement of North Atlantic Treaty Organization (NATO) and other bodies in the 'war on terror'. The contradictions and tensions were underlined further by the US-led attack on Iraq in 2003, in which both the European and many global institutions proved incapable of meeting the challenges (Peterson and Pollack 2003). In 2011, the eruption of the 'Arab Spring' along the southern shores of the Mediterranean, in Egypt and eventually in Syria provided another acute test of the EU's position: here was a key part of the 'neighbourhood' in which there was a long-standing EU presence, but in which the problems of institutional coordination were acute; even in the presence of the post-Lisbon institutions for 'external action', it was very difficult for the EU to come to terms with the intricate linkages between politics, economics and security.

A second set of contradictions surrounds the EU's role in the world political economy, where the coexisting forces of globalisation and regionalisation have given rise to major policy dilemmas and problems of management. The result of these contradictions is a complex, multilayered and often apparently uncontrollable set of policy arenas, in which the EU is not the only body subject to challenge (Laffan *et al.* 2000: chap. 3–4). On issues such as the management of the global environment, the EU has solid credentials arising from its internal regulatory processes, but finds itself engaged in a global arena where there is a constant and ever-more politicised tension between management through national authorities, regional bodies and multilateral or global institutions (Vogler 2011). Also, often these fluctuating tensions bring to the fore EU relationships with major trading and political partners.

Relationships

Certain relationships are central to the international policies of the EU, demanding continuous management and producing a series of interrelated challenges and opportunities. The most intense, highly developed and longest established is that with the US. Together, the EU and the US account for nearly half of the world economy, and their relationship is both extensive and rich. It is one from which both parties benefit considerably and in which the balance of economic advantage is relatively even. Not only this, but the EU–US relationship is implanted in the broader security relationship expressed through NATO and other institutions (Smith and Woolcock 1993; Frellesen and Ginsberg 1994; Featherstone and Ginsberg 1996; Peterson 1996; Guay 1999; Pollack and Shaffer 2001; McGuire and Smith 2008; Smith and Steffenson 2011).

Given the intensity of the interdependence between the two partners, it is not at all surprising that there will be a continuous flow of disputes between them, particularly in areas of important trade or financial competition. Thus, the relationship in the 1990s and early 2000s was beset by disputes over agricultural trade, over the openness of the Single Market to US financial and other institutions, and over politically symbolic high-technology projects such as the European Airbus. Not only this, but also an emerging new agenda of disputes over such areas as genetically modified foods, competition policy and taxation regimes has created a new set of challenges in the new millennium. The point is that whilst challenging, such issues are dealt with on the whole in the cooperative mode, with the intention of resolving differences and building new procedures. This aim was first expressed in the Transatlantic Declaration of November 1990, which spawned a set of specialist working groups and other forms of cooperation on significant issues (Frellesen and Ginsberg 1994). It was followed in the mid- and late 1990s by the New Transatlantic Agenda of 1995 and the Transatlantic Economic Partnership (TEP) of 1998 (Smith 1998a; Pollack and Shaffer 2001; Steffenson 2005; Smith and Steffenson 2011). In 2007, the TEP was reinvigorated with the establishment of the Transatlantic Economic Council to provide a focus for the management of potential disputes and the development of new forms of cooperation, and by 2013, there was a major push for a Transatlantic Free Trade Agreement to express the high levels of integration between the two partners.

The end of the Cold War put a new complexion on important aspects of EU–US relations. On one hand, it found the EU anxious to develop new international roles in the development of the 'new Europe', often in areas where the US found it difficult to respond. On the other, it became apparent that the role of the EU in high politics and security had severe limitations; there were still areas in which and ways in which only the US had the capacity to act, particularly where this implied the rapid mobilisation of major military assets (as in the former Yugoslavia and more recently in Afghanistan and Iraq). Although the Maastricht agreements established the CFSP, and recognised the growing linkage between the EU and the Western European Union in the evolution of security policy, this did not and could not make it the equal of the US in theatres of active military conflict (Smith and Woolcock 1994; Allen and Smith 1998; Everts *et al.* 2004). As noted earlier in the chapter, from 1998 onwards there were apparently fundamental shifts in the EU's ability to muster a 'hard security' capability, with plans to set up a 60,000-strong EU Rapid Deployment Force and to enter actively into peacekeeping and peace-building operations. Significantly, the US government expressed reservations both about the feasibility and the appropriateness of this enterprise – reservations which for many were borne out by experience first in Kosovo during 1999 and later in the 'war on terror' and the attack on Iraq. In the first of these, NATO proved the only viable means of collective action, whilst in the second and third cases, the EU was to all intents and purposes by-passed both by the US and by key EU member states such as the UK. Notwithstanding the later evidence of the EU's capacity to manage or to contribute to the post-conflict stabilisation processes in Kosovo and Afghanistan, the record in such EU–US collisions was not a happy one (Peterson and Pollack 2003). As noted earlier, when the Arab Spring erupted in 2011, the EU was still not capable of mounting a military response, and almost by default military action in Libya was taken by the UK and France, with the US 'leading from behind' and NATO also implicated.

The relationship between the EU and the US has thus been and will continue to be a central policy concern. Less comprehensive, but no less sensitive at times, has been the relationship with Japan and alongside it those with China and the Asia-Pacific region. In the case of Japan, the texture of the relationship is primarily that of economic interdependence and economic competition, with the Japanese enjoying a considerable credit balance in the areas of trade and financial services. Thus, the EU has found itself dealing with the Japanese on a succession of more or less serious trade disputes, most notably in the areas of automobiles and consumer electronics. Although the early 1990s produced an EU–Japan Declaration modelled after the Transatlantic Declaration, the effective scope of collaboration between the two partners remained significantly less ambitious and intensive. Partly this is a reflection of history; partly it reflects the relative distance and lack of complementarity between the two entities; nonetheless, there is a growing need to organise the relations between the two (Gilson 2000).

With China, the EU during the 1990s and early 2000s experienced a rapidly growing relationship, but one bedevilled by trade disputes as the Chinese expanded their overseas trade, and by lingering tensions over human rights. The trajectory of the EU–China relationship, though, means that it has effectively supplanted that with Japan as the second-most salient relationship in the EU's external relations, creating new institutional contacts such as those in the World Trade Organization but also creating a series of new bilateral economic challenges. Not only this, but the development of competition between China and the US has also created a new challenge for the EU as the US under President Barack Obama conducted a strategic 'pivot' towards the Asia-Pacific. At the same time, the EU has made significant efforts to establish inter-regional contacts with the countries of Southeast Asia, through agreements with the members of the Association of Southeast Asian Nations, and to bring together all of its Asia-Pacific partners in the Asia-Europe Meetings, the first of which was held in 1996 (Smith 1998b; Maull *et al.* 1998; Dent 1999; Wiessala 2002). Parallel efforts have been made to increase and to institutionalise contacts with Latin America and Africa through a series of inter-regional conferences and networks aimed at promoting both economic transactions and political dialogue. As with EU–China relations, in each of these areas the 'US factor' is also a key component of the EU's capacity to get involved and to act.

In respect of the 'new Europe', there have been two components to the EU's international activity since the early 1990s. On one hand, there was the need during the early 1990s to incorporate three new members – Finland, Sweden and Austria (see Chapter 13, in this volume). On the other hand, there was the establishment and intensification of relations with the countries of the former Soviet bloc, either on the basis of 'arm's-length' relationships based on trade and assistance or (as in the case of the 'Visegrad countries') on the basis of increasingly close linkages and eventual membership of the Union itself (Pinder 1991b; H. Wallace 1991; Carlsnaes and Smith 1994; Henderson 1999; K. Smith 1999). The eastern enlargement that took place during 2004, with the prospect of further new entrants as early as 2007, led to a further reorientation of both the economic and the political-security aspects of EU external policies, particularly as a result of the new 'geopolitics' and 'geoeconomics' implied by a shift to the east and to a common border with the former Soviet Union. Coupled with the continuing attention to the Mediterranean and the 'south', this was the key stimulus to the development of a new 'neighbourhood' policy from 2002 to 2004 aimed at stabilising and managing the new neighbours who had no prospect of early membership in the Union – or in some cases, no realistic prospect at all (Dannreuther 2004; K. Smith 2011).

For the EU's international activities and policies, the overall impact of these changes in agendas, arenas and relationships has been profound. Whilst the Cold War years were far from simple, they at least made it possible for EC leaders to focus on 'civilian' activities and to operate within a well-defined set of institutional and political arrangements. A combination of factors ranging from the Single Market Programme through the collapse of the USSR to the transformation of the global economy and the 'war on terror', followed in 2008 and after by the global financial crisis, has made redundant a number of the longstanding assumptions on which the EC's international role was founded. This has meant a series of unavoidable challenges both for EU policy makers and for the EU's institutions (W. Wallace 1990; Keohane *et al.* 1993; Story 1993; Laffan *et al.* 2000; Hill and Smith 2011).

Levels

Not the least of these challenges has been that of dealing with the implications of multilevel politics and diplomacy. The EU has found in a number of contexts that it has to reconcile its own – often limited – capacity to act with the needs and demands of international institutions, major political and trading partners, and not least its own member states and their governments. Two examples suffice for demonstrating this set of interlocking dilemmas.

First, in the area of traditional EC/EU action, there is the experience of the negotiations in the World Trade Organisation, centred on the attempt to conclude the so-called Doha Development Round, which began in 2002 and continued at the time of this writing. Over an extended period, the EU had to project its trade policy competence into new areas, meeting competition and conflicting demands from the USA, developing countries and a range of agricultural interests. At the same time, the continued deepening of the Single Market strengthened key areas of EU international activity such as competition policy, radically changing and extending the perception of the EC as an international economic force. Not only this, but the divergent interests of EC members were underlined by the demands of the international negotiation process, and fed back into it often with widespread and potentially damaging implications (Smith 2011; de Burca and Scott 2001; Young 2002; Meunier and Nicolaïdis 2011; Woolcock 2012). The extended duration and inconclusive nature of the negotiations also meant that they were prey to developments in the broader global political economy, most notably the financial crises of 2008 and after, which created further dilemmas for the EU. Whilst this can be seen as a challenge mainly for policy makers at the EU level, it is also a key example in the growth and problems of 'global governance' in the economic sphere.

A second and very different example is provided by the EU's involvement in the conflicts in former Yugoslavia – from the independence of Croatia and Slovenia in 1991, through the Bosnian conflict of 1992–95 to the Kosovo crisis of 1999. In this most dangerous series of post–Cold War European conflicts, the assumption at the outset was that the EU would have a special role and responsibility, not least because the US proved unwilling to become directly engaged. A number of – often tragic – dilemmas ensued for the EU and its members. First, there was the problem of the recognition of Slovenia, Croatia and, finally, Bosnia-Herzegovina, in which the tensions among EU members were apparent throughout. Then, there was the problem of dealing with the escalation of the conflict, particularly in Bosnia – a conflict that exposed to the full the lack of military muscle behind the EU's position, and the overlapping concerns and competences of the UN, the EU and other organisations such as the Conference on Security and Cooperation in Europe (CSCE). Third, there was the issue of stabilisation and the creation of safe areas for the ravaged population of Bosnia – a task to which the EU was in many respects peripheral, and in which the interaction of the UN and NATO came to play a central part. Whilst playing a dogged and persistent diplomatic role, backed up by economic sanctions, the EU inevitably found it difficult if not impossible to go beyond exhortation and indirect pressure (Nuttall 1994; Zucconi 1996). By the time the Kosovo crisis became acute in 1999, expectations of EU action were understandably modest, and indeed, the EU itself played no significant role in the military campaign. On the other hand, the Union was able to take a positive lead in post-war reconstruction, and mounted an important long-term initiative in the shape of the Stability Pact for the Balkans, which coupled short-term stabilisation measures with the long-term prospect of EU membership for some if not all of the region's regimes. As noted earlier, some of the same challenges arose for the EU in coping with the Arab Spring from 2011 onwards, and in some respects, despite the enhancement of the EU's foreign and security policy apparatus in the Treaty of Lisbon, the same issues arose.

A third and in some respects even more challenging set of issues for the EU arose out of the 'war on terror' after the events of 11 September 2001, and the subsequent attack on Iraq. As noted earlier, this was a major challenge for the EU in terms of its policy competence, but it was also a challenge at a host of interrelated levels of policy and action. Within the EU there was the need to manage the impact of the war on terror on policy areas as diverse as transportation and justice and home affairs; this intersected with the need to manage relationships between member states, which were often at odds, to manage transatlantic relations, to operate within the UN and other global institutions, and to link these activities with others in policy areas ranging from trade to military security and defence (Peterson and Pollack 2003).

The conclusion here is not that the EU succeeded or failed in either the GATT/WTO context or former Yugoslavia, or in the war on terror and Iraq. The point is to show the ways in which since the early 1990s, the EU has been faced with profoundly challenging tasks in the international field. The evolution both of the world economy and of the post–Cold War international order created opportunities for a more expansive and ambitious EU role, but it also raised questions about the extent to which the EU policy process was capable of defining and pursuing appropriate and effective international action, and about the risks that were run in so doing (Allen and Smith 1991–92, 1998). Those questions are the starting point for the next section.

Modes of international policy making in the EU

From the preceding discussion, it should be clear that the EU has important roles to play in the contemporary international arena. Chris Hill (1993, 1998) has identified both a number of functions the EC and the EU have played in the international system up to the late 1990s and a number of potential future roles or functions. In the past, the EC performed the roles of regional stabiliser in Western Europe, co-manager of world trade, a principal voice for the developed world in relations with the less-developed countries, and provider of a second Western voice in international diplomacy. For the future, Hill discerned in 1998 a number of conceivable roles: a replacement for the USSR in the global balance of power; a regional pacifier; a global intervenor; a mediator of conflicts; a bridge between the rich and the poor; and a joint supervisor of the world economy. But to list these past and possible future roles is to identify a central problem, which Hill has encapsulated in the notion of the 'capability-expectations gap' (see the earlier discussion): to put it simply, the EU can seem a desirable or logical actor in many international contexts, but this tells us nothing about its prospects of influence or effectiveness. Further studies of the EU's roles in international politics provide additional evidence of this conundrum, by identifying the tensions between role conceptions, role performance and role evaluation in EU external policy making (Elgström and Smith 2006).

In this part of the chapter, it is suggested that one crucial element in the resolution of this problem is the study of *modes of EU international policy making*. From the evidence produced so far, three such modes of policy can be identified and will be examined here (see White [2001] for a related classification):

First, there is what for a long time could be termed *Community policy making*: the development of the instruments and processes typical of the European Community and of its role in the world political economy.
Second, there is what can be described as *Union policy making*: the policy processes generated by the interaction of member governments and European institutions

in the context of the Treaties and their practical application, which became institutionalised in the 'three pillars' of the Maastricht Treaty.

Finally, there is the style of policy which can best be described as *negotiated order*: the response of both Community and Union to the multilayered political and economic environment in which they are implanted, and the outcome of the complex exchange relationships in which the member states and other actors are involved.

All three of these policy modes are affected and focused by a number of key dilemmas and assumptions, which have been ably evaluated by Hill and other analysts. They have to cope with the problem of *competence and consistency* within the EU, and the matching of institutional means to appropriate and agreed purposes. They must deal with the *intersection of economic, political and security issues* in the contemporary international arena. They confront the test of *multilayered policy making and a multiplicity of policy actors* which is characteristic of the contemporary European and international milieu. And finally, they face the need to account for *the proliferation of institutions and instruments* which is equally central to the management of international policies in the new millennium.

Community policy making

The longest established and most highly developed form of EU policy process in the international sphere has been that of *Community policy making*. This is the external policy mode first encapsulated in the Common Commercial Policy and other parts of the Treaty of Rome dealing with the negotiation and conclusion of international agreements. The key elements of this policy mode were thus the concept of Community competence expressed through the Commission, and the development of policy instruments at the European level. They reached their highest point of development in the Community's role with respect to the General Agreement on Tariffs and Trade (GATT) and the World Trade Organization (WTO), and in the use of policy instruments such as antidumping regulations. More recently, they were extended into areas such as the international regulation of competition and the international coordination of policies in such areas as standards setting or public procurement; less certainly, they have also been extended into more contested areas such as international regulation of air transport and the environment. In many ways, as can be seen from these examples, the policy style is an external expression of internal Community powers and concerns. As such, it has long formed the core of the Community's claims to international 'actorness'.

It might be thought that in this policy mode, the development of internal Community competence would inexorably be reflected in the extension of its exclusive international competence. In fact, and significantly for those who see the EU as an international actor in the making, there were distinct variations both in the coverage of the process and in the extent to which it can be halted or reversed. Two examples illustrate the point. First, the negotiation and conclusion of international agreements by the Community through the Commission was (and remains even after Lisbon) crucially dependent on agreement between the member states in the Council of Ministers. For GATT/WTO negotiations, they give the mandate to the Commission, and it is they who finally conclude the agreements after the involvement of the European Parliament and the Commission. In the early 1990s, the Court of Justice concluded that even the trade policy powers of the Community exercised through the Commission were limited. To be specific, areas of trade negotiation going beyond traditional trade in goods were the joint responsibility of the Community and the member states (so-called mixed agreements). The Court's opinion, delivered in November 1994, clearly implied a set of boundaries to the Common Commercial Policy which had not been suspected previously, and which led to a series of tensions in the policy-making process during the later 1990s (Meunier and Nicolaidis 1999; Smith and Woolcock 1999). These tensions were effectively resolved by the time the Treaty of Nice was agreed in 2000, but it can be seen that as the internationalisation of successive areas of economic and related activities take place, there can still be 'boundary problems', raising the question of EU competence.

The Lisbon Treaty, of course, seemed to be based on the assumption that this mode of international policy making would be absorbed into the broader realm of EU 'external action'. Whereas previously the notion of international legal 'personality' had been limited strictly to issues of Community competence, the Treaty extended this to all acts of the Union. It also gave an expanded role in the conclusion of international agreements to the European Parliament, which now has to 'assent' to any significant trade and other agreements entered into by the Union. The treaty also extended the Union's competence into the area of investment as well as that of commercial policy, thereby bringing under the umbrella a key element in the globalisation process. But one question that inevitably arises is, to what extent have the distinctions between different modes of EU policy making been eliminated by the Lisbon institutional innovations?

Union policy making

Community policy making has been a crucial but incomplete model for the conduct of the EU's international business. Alongside it there developed during the 1990s what is termed here *Union policy making*. The keynote of this mode of policy making was the intensive and continuous coordination of national policies, rather than the application of agreed common policies. Central to its development was the evolution of EPC and then the establishment of the CFSP and eventually the CSDP, but these are not the only examples. In this policy mode, the Commission is not the exclusive bearer of the Community (or now, the Union) mandate: rather, it is fully associated with the process and a vital source of information, advice and initiatives alongside increasingly 'Europeanised' national governments.

It is clear that this mode of international policy making falls close to the intergovernmental mode of general EU policy making. But there are important, not to say crucial, differences. In particular, the role of the Commission as an active and continuous participant, and a vital facilitator of action, has been distinctive; indeed, in some areas such as the imposition of sanctions or the provision of humanitarian or technical assistance, the Commission and the Community could be the only possible implementers of policy.

One dramatic example of this came in the Bosnian conflict, where during 1994 the EU installed an administrator to run the city of Mostar. This 'pro-consul' had wide-ranging powers, including that of derogating from the Bosnian constitution. Whilst the administrator was put in place through the CFSP, the infrastructure for the office and the financial resources were to an important extent provided through the Commission and the Community budget. A complex form of words expressed the equally complex reality: the policy was to be implemented by 'the member states of the EU working within the framework of the Union and in close association with the European Commission'. This appears to demonstrate that Union policy making, far from marking a retreat to intergovernmentalism, marked a new departure and a creative way of bringing the various EU institutions and the member governments together. As noted earlier, the ways in which the EU operated during the Kosovo crisis of 1999 also raised the prospect of linkages between Union membership and regional stabilisation in a novel way. Other early joint actions in South Africa and in Russia (in each case primarily the monitoring of elections) were less dramatic but raised the same issues and possibilities; much later, the involvement of the Union in security and policing activities both in former Yugoslavia and elsewhere again demonstrated the complex management processes at work.

In the Lisbon Treaty, as noted earlier, it might have been assumed that there has been a major extension of 'Union policy-making'. After all, the Union is now defined as the key actor and the extension of legal personality to the Union gives it new credentials. To that extent, all 'European' policy-making is now Union policy-making, and the addition of the External Action Service and the high representative/vice-president to the institutional mix confirms this position. But it is clear that rather than reflecting a smooth and seamless transition to a fully 'Unionised' policy process, there is still a considerable difference between policies at different points on what has become a spectrum of policy processes and instruments. Trade policy is still made essentially within the Commission, and within Directorate-General for Trade (DG Trade), whereas the CFSP and CSDP retain their distinctively intergovernmental features – and in between, there are many areas in which policy-making is essentially mixed, such as development policy (Carbone 2007; Holland and Doidge 2012). But the fact that international policy-making is now a spectrum rather than a set of distinct 'pillars' does create the possibility of further cross-overs, processes of cooperation and the learning of new habits that over time could result in the elimination of at least some of the distinctions.

International policy as negotiated order

Such developments give support to a third mode of international policy making in the EU; indeed, the three modes being examined here represent coexisting tendencies rather than competing and mutually exclusive models. Given the complex institutional relationships and processes of exchange between 'European' bodies, member governments and other actors in the Union's international policy process, it could be argued that the EU in its international activities constitutes an evolving *negotiated order*. Within the administrative, institutional and political structures established over the life of the Community and the EU, there is a constant, rule-governed process of negotiation among actors which produces policy positions and international policy outcomes. Process is as important as outcome, and it is thus inappropriate to apply to the EU the concepts of statehood or foreign policy which are typical of conventional international relations models and approaches (Allen and Smith 1990; Smith 1994a; Elgström and Smith 2000).

It is important to note that this perspective on the international policy process in the EU coincides with new patterns of analysis for the global arena more generally, which stress precisely the multilevel, institutionalised and rule-governed behaviour to which attention has been drawn in this chapter (Hocking and Smith 1997: chap. 1–2; Prakash and Hart 1999; Pollack and Shaffer 2001; Stubbs and Underhill 2005). In the more strictly EU context, such an approach leads in a number of directions. First, it draws attention to the ways in which 'Community policy making' as outlined previously is itself a focus for negotiation and exchange between a number of actors. To give but one example, the new Commission installed in 1999 – and its successors installed in 2004 and 2009 – had within them at least six Commissioners with substantial international policy responsibilities, and the process of allocating these responsibilities had, in each case, been a source of considerable negotiation. The appointment of Chris Patten as a kind of 'lead Commissioner' for external policies, and the development of consolidated coordination mechanisms not only between the Commissioners concerned but also between Patten and the 'high representative' for CFSP, Javier Solana, symbolised a major effort to ensure consistency among the various channels of EU external policy in conditions of complex policy making. This was given a much more formal and elaborate expression under the Treaty of Lisbon with the establishment of the EEAS and the HRVP, but the transition to the new set of arrangements created a new set of 'negotiations' about the role and purpose of these new participants in the policy process (Hocking and Smith 2011; Vanhoonacker *et al.* 2012).

A second feature of EU international policy making which is captured by a 'negotiated order' focus is that in many cases the EU's international activities are undertaken in a multilevel negotiation context. The example of the Doha Development Round cited earlier in this chapter is perhaps the most significant recent instance of the ways in which negotiations within the WTO, within the Commission, within and between the EU institutions and the member states all came together to provide a potent mix of overlapping and often irreconcilable claims. There are, however, many other instances of such relationships: the EU–US partnership, the attempts through negotiation to consolidate the post–Cold War European order, the negotiations attending the accession of new members, the development of global environmental governance.

In this view, then, the EU's international positions and actions are both the product of an institutionalised negotiation process and frequently part of such a process in the international arena. As such, they not only epitomise many features of the changing world political economy in the twenty-first century, but they also focus them in a very distinctive way. A key area of policy analysis for the foreseeable future will be the ways in which this situation plays out for the enlarged EU, in particular in the context of the 'new Europe' and the 'neighbourhood'.

Conclusion: towards an EU foreign policy?

This chapter started by examining briefly the debates which have centred around the EU's credentials as an international actor, and by suggesting the significance of the developments that have taken place in the EU's international involvement. Often, the debates and the significance are placed into the context of a broader debate about statehood, foreign policy and the EU's approximation to the conventional model of both. The argument in this chapter has tested both the substantive basis for claims about the EU's international significance and the broader conceptual claims made by those who foresee the emergence of a 'foreign policy' conducted by the Union or its representatives.

The general conclusions from the argument are threefold:

- First, that the EC and now the EU have long-established and material foundations for their presence and impact in the international arena. These foundations are the reflection of the economic and political weight of the EU, of its institutional capacity and of the ways in which it has enlarged its tasks and roles in the changing world arena. But they are not monolithic, nor do they suppress the claims or the prerogatives of the member states. Indeed, as the EU has entered new areas of activity, it has occasionally seemed to reach the limits of its capacity to lay claim to the new territory on which it finds itself.

- Second, that the substance of EU international policy betrays not only the value placed on the EU both by its members and by others as an international role player but also the limitations imposed by the ways in which the EU is constrained in its mobilisation of resources. Whilst this is particularly apparent in the area of international security and defence policy, there is no shortage of other examples to illustrate the 'capability-expectations gap' (or rather the multiple 'capability-expectations gaps') in the EU's international existence.

- Third, that one way of taking further an appreciation of the distinctive nature of EU international policy is to focus on modes of policy making. There is no single mode of such policy making, and therein lies part of the unique character of the European construction. There are elements of 'Community policy making', of 'Union policy making' and of 'negotiated order' in all aspects of the EU's international policy, and whilst the Lisbon Treaty has formally declared the abolition of the 'three pillars' in EU policy making, this has been replaced by a complex spectrum of policy-making processes reflecting these three modes. The challenge for analysis lies in interpreting the conditions in which they interact to produce distinctive mixes of policy making and EU external action, and thus shape the EU's evolving roles in the world arena.

References

Allen, D. and Pijpers, A. (1984) *European Foreign Policy Making and the Arab-Israeli Dispute*. The Hague: Nijhoff.

Allen, D. and Smith, M. (1990) 'Western Europe's Presence in the Contemporary International Arena.' *Review of International Studies* 16(1), January: 19–39.

Allen, D. and Smith, M. (1991–92), 'The European Community in the New Europe: Bearing the Burden of Change.' *International Journal* XLVII (1), Winter: 1–28.

Allen, D. and Smith, M. (1998) 'The European Union's Security Presence: Barrier, Facilitator or Manager?' in Rhodes, C. (ed.) *The European Union in the World Community*. Boulder, CO: Lynne Rienner.

Allen, D., Rummel, R. and Wessels, W. (1982) *European Political Cooperation: Towards a foreign policy for Western Europe?* London: Butterworth.

Cameron, F. (1999) *The Foreign and Security Policy of the European Union: Past, Present and Future*. Sheffield: Sheffield Academic Press.

Cameron, F. (2012) *An Introduction to European Foreign Policy*. 2nd edition. London: Routledge.

Carbone, M. (2007) *The European Union and International Development: The Politics of Foreign Aid*. London: Routledge.

Carlsnaes, W. and Smith, S. (eds.) (1994) *European Foreign Policy: The EC and Changing Perspectives in Europe*. London: Sage.

Dannreuther, R. (ed.) (2004) *European Union Foreign and Security Policy: Towards a Neighborhood Policy*. London: Routledge.

de Burca, G. and Scott. J. (2001) *The European Union and the World Trade Organisation: Legal and Constitutional Issues*. Oxford: Hart Publishing.

Dent, C. (1997) *The European Economy: The Global Context*. London: Routledge.

Dent, C. (1999) *The European Union and East Asia: An Economic Relationship*. London: Routledge.

Dinan, D. (2004) *Europe Recast: A History of European Integration*. Basingstoke: Palgrave Macmillan.

Edwards, G. and Regelsberger, E. (eds.) (1990) *Europe's Global Links: The European Community and inter-regional cooperation*. London: Pinter.

Elgström, O. and Smith, M. (eds.) (2000) 'Negotiation and Policy-Making in the European Union: Processes, System and Order.' Special Issue of the *Journal of European Public Policy*, December.

Elgström, O. and Smith, M. (eds.) (2006) *The European Union's Roles in International Politics: Concepts and Analysis*. London: Routledge.

Everts, S., Freedman, L., Grant, C., Heisbourg, F., Keohane, D. and O'Hanlon, M. (2004) *A European Way of War*. London: Centre for European Reform.

Featherstone, K. and Ginsberg, R. (1996) *The United States and the European Community in the 1990s: Partners in Transition*. 2nd edition. London: Macmillan; New York: St Martin's Press.

Forster, A. and Wallace, W. (1996) 'Common Foreign and Security Policy: A New Policy or Just a New Name?' in Wallace, H. and Wallace, W. (eds.) *Policy-Making in the European Union*. Oxford: Oxford University Press.

Frellesen, T. and Ginsberg, R. (1994) *EU-US Foreign Policy Cooperation in the 1990s: Elements of Partnership*. Brussels: Centre for European Policy Studies.

Gilson, J. (2000) *Japan and the European Union: A Partnership for the Twenty-First Century?* Basingstoke: Macmillan.

Gnesotto, N. (ed.) (2004) *European Security and Defence Policy: The First Five Years (1999–2004)*. Paris: European Union Institute for Security Studies.

Guay, T. (1999) *The European Union and the United States: The Political Economy of a Relationship*. Sheffield: Sheffield Academic Press.

Harrison, G. (ed.) (1994) *Europe and the United States: Competition and Cooperation in the 1990s*. Armonk, NY: Sharpe.

Henderson, K. (ed.) (1999) *Back to Europe: Central and Eastern Europe and the European Union*. London: UCL Press.

Hill, C. (ed.) (1983) *National Foreign Policies and European Political Cooperation*. London: George Allen and Unwin.

Hill, C. (1990) 'European Foreign Policy: Power Bloc, Civilian Model – or Flop?' in Rummel, R. (ed.) *The Evolution of an International Actor: Western Europe's New Assertiveness*. Boulder, CO: Westview Press.

Hill, C. (1993) 'The Capability-Expectations Gap, or Conceptualising Europe's International Role.' *Journal of Common Market Studies* 31(3), September: 305–28.

Hill, C. (ed.) (1995) *The Actors in European Political Cooperation*. London: Routledge

Hill, C. (1998) 'Closing the Capabilities-Expectations Gap?' in Peterson, J, and Sjursen, H. (eds.) *A Common Foreign Policy for Europe? Competing Visions of the CFSP*. London: Routledge: 18–38.

Hill, C. and Smith, M. (eds) (2011) *International Relations and the European Union*. 2nd edition, Oxford: Oxford University Press.

Hine, R. (1985) *The Political Economy of European Trade*. Brighton: Harvester-Wheatsheaf.

Hocking, B. and Smith, M. (1997) *Beyond Foreign Economic Policy: The United States, the Single European Market and a Changing World Economy*. London: Cassell/Pinter.

Hocking, B. and Smith, M. (2011) 'An Emerging Diplomatic System for the EU? Frameworks and Issues.' *Cuadernos Europeos de Deusto* 44: 19–42.

Holland, M. and Doidge, M. (2012) *Development Policy of the European Union*. Basingstoke: Palgrave Macmillan.

Howorth, J. (2000) *European Integration and Defence: The Ultimate Challenge?* Chaillot Paper 43, Paris: Institute for Security Studies of the WEU.

Howorth, J. (2007) *Security and Defence Policy in the European Union*. Basingstoke: Palgrave Macmillan.

Howorth, J. (2011) 'The EU's Security to Defence Policy: Towards a Strategic Approach' in C. Hill and M. Smith (eds.) *The International Relations of the European Union*. 2nd edition. Oxford: Oxford University Press.

Hufbauer, G. (ed.) (1990) *Europe 1992: An American Perspective*. Washington, DC: Brookings Institution.

Keohane, R., Nye, J. and Hoffmann, S. (eds.) (1993) *After the Cold War: International Institutions and State Strategies in Europe, 1989–1991*. Cambridge, MA: Harvard University Press.

Keukeleire, S. and MacNaughtan, J. (2008) *The Foreign Policy of the European Union*. Basingstoke: Palgrave Macmillan.

Laffan, B., O'Donnell, R. and Smith, M. (2000) *Europe's Experimental Union: Rethinking Integration*. London: Routledge.

Laursen, F. and Vanhoonacker, S. (eds.) 1992. *The Intergovernmental Conference on Political Union: Institutional Reforms, New Policies and International Identity of the European Community*. Maastricht: European Institute of Public Administration.

Manners, I. and Whitman, R. (eds.) (2000) *The Foreign Policies of European Union Member States*. Manchester: Manchester University Press.

Maull, H., Segal, G. and Wanandi, J. (eds.) (1998) *Europe and the Asia-Pacific*. London: Routledge.

McGuire, S. and Smith, M. (2008) *The European Union and the United States: Competition and Convergence in the Global Arena*. Basingstoke: Palgrave Macmillan.

Meunier, S. and Nicolaidis, K. (1999) 'Who Speaks for Europe? The Delegation of Trade Authority in the EU.' *Journal of Common Market Studies* 37(3), September: 477–502.

Meunier, S. and Nicolaïdis, K. (2011) 'The European Union as a Trade Power' in C. Hill and M. Smith (eds.) *International Relations and the European Union*. 2nd edition. Oxford: Oxford University Press.

Norgaard, O., Pedersen, T. and Petersen, N. (eds.) (1993) *The European Community in World Politics*. London: Pinter.

Nuttall, S. (1992) *European Political Cooperation*. Oxford: Clarendon Press.

Nuttall, S. (1994) 'The EC and Yugoslavia – deus ex machina or machina sine deo?' in Nugent, N. (ed.) *The European Union 1993: Annual Review of Activities*. Oxford: Blackwell: 11–26.

Peterson, J. (1996) *Europe and America in the 1990s: Prospects for Partnership*. 2nd edition. London: Routledge.

Peterson, J. and Pollack, M. (2003) *Europe, America, Bush: Transatlantic Relations in the Twenty-First Century*. London: Routledge.

Piening, C. (1997) *Global Europe: The European Union in World Affairs*. Boulder, CO: Lynne Rienner.

Pijpers, A., Regelsberger, E. and Wessels, W. (eds.) (1988) *European Political Cooperation in the 1980s: A Common Foreign Policy for Western* Dordrecht: Nijhoff.

Pinder, J. (1991a) *European Community: The Building of a Union*. Oxford: Oxford University Press.

Pinder, J. (1991b) *The European Community and Eastern Europe*. London: Royal Institute of International Affairs/Pinter Publishers.

Pollack, M. and Shaffer, G. (eds.) (2001) *Transatlantic Governance in the Global Economy*. Lanham, MD: Rowman & Littlefield.

Prakash, A. and Hart, J. (eds.) (1999) *Globalisation and Governance*. London: Routledge.

Redmond, J. (ed.) (1992) *The External Relations of the European Community: The International Response to 1992*. London: Macmillan.

Regelsberger, E., de Schoutheete de Tervarent, P. and Wessels, W. (eds.) (1997) *Foreign Policy of the European Union: From EPC to CFSP and Beyond*. Boulder, CO: Lynne Rienner.

Rummel, R. (ed.) (1992) *Toward Political Union: Planning a Common Foreign and Security Policy in the European Community*. Boulder, CO: Westview Press.

Smith, K. (1999) *The Making of EU Foreign Policy: The Case of Eastern Europe*. London: Macmillan.

Smith, K. (2003) *European Union Foreign Policy in a Changing World*. Cambridge: Polity Press.

Smith, K. (2011) 'Enlargement, the Neighbourhood and European Order' in C. Hill and M. Smith (eds.) *International Relations of the European Union*. 2nd edition. Oxford: Oxford University Press.

Smith, M. (1994a) 'Beyond the stable state? Foreign policy challenges and opportunities in the new Europe' in W. Carlsnaes and S. Smith (eds.) *European Foreign Policy: The EC and New Perspectives in Europe*. London: Sage.

Smith, M. (1994b) 'The European Union, foreign economic policy and a changing world arena.' *Journal of European Public Policy* 1(2), Autumn: 283–302.

Smith, M. (1998a) 'Competitive Cooperation and EU-US Relations: Can the EU be a Strategic Partner for the US in the World Political Economy?' *Journal of European Public Policy* 5(4), December: 561–77.

Smith, M. (1998b) 'The European Union and the Asia-Pacific' in McGrew, A. and Brook, C. (eds.) *Asia-Pacific in the New World Order*. London: Routledge.

Smith, M. (1999) 'The European Union' in Hocking, B. and McGuire, S. (eds.) *Trade Politics: International, Domestic and Regional Perspectives*. London: Routledge.

Smith, M. (2005) 'The Commission and external relations' in Spence, D. (ed.) *The European Commission*. 3rd edition, London: John Harper Publishing.

Smith, M. and Woolcock, S. (1993) *The United States and the European Community in a Transformed World*. London: Royal Institute of International Affairs/Pinter Publishers.

Smith, M. and Woolcock, S. (1994) 'Learning to cooperate: the Clinton administration and the European Union', *International Affairs* 70(3), July: 459–76.

Smith, M. and Woolcock, S. (1999) 'European Commercial Policy: A Leadership Role in the New Millennium?' *European Foreign Affairs Review* 4(4), Winter: 439–62.

Smith, M. and Steffenson, R. (2011) 'The EU and the united States' in C. Hill and M. Smith (eds) *International Relations and the European Union*. 2nd edition. Oxford: Oxford University Press.

Steffenson, R. (2005) *Managing EU-US Relations: Actors, Institutions and the New Transatlantic Agenda*. Manchester: Manchester University Press.

Story, J. (ed.) (1993) *The New Europe: Politics, Government and Society since 1945*. Oxford: Blackwell.

Stubbs, R. and Underhill, G. (eds.) (2005) *Political Economy and the Changing Global Order*. 3rd edition. Toronto: Oxford University Press.

Tsoukalis, L. (1997) *The New European Economy Revisited*. Oxford: Oxford University Press.

Vanhoonacker, S., Pomorska, K. and Petrov, P. (eds.) (2012) 'The Emerging EU Diplomatic System.' *Special Issue of The Hague Journal of Diplomacy*, 7(1).

Vogler, J. (2011) 'The Challenge of the Environment, Energy and Climate Change' in C. Hill and M. Smith (eds.) *International Relations and the European Union*. 2nd edition. Oxford: Oxford University Press.

Wallace, H. (ed.) (1991) *The Wider Western Europe: Reshaping the EC/EFTA Relationship*. London: Royal Institute of International Affairs/Pinter Publishers.

Wallace, W. (1990) *The Transformation of Western Europe*. London: Royal Institute of International Affairs/Pinter Publishers.

White, B. (2001) *Understanding European Foreign Policy*. Basingstoke: Palgrave/Macmillan.

Wiessala, G. (2002) *The European Union and Asian Countries*. Sheffield: Sheffield Academic Press.

Woolcock, S. (1992) *Market Access Issues in EC/US Trade Relations: Trading Partners or Trading Blows?* London: Royal Institute of International Affairs/Pinter Publishers.

Woolcock, S. (2012) *European Union Economic Diplomacy: The Role of the EU in External Economic Relations*. Aldershot: Ashgate.

Woolcock, S. and Hodges, M. (1996) 'EU Policy in the Uruguay Round' in Wallace, H. and Wallace, W. (eds.) *Policy-Making in the European Union*. Oxford: Oxford University Press.

Young, A. (2002) *Extending European Cooperation: The European Union and the 'New' International Trade Agenda*. Manchester: Manchester University Press.

Zucconi, M. (1996) 'The European Union in the Former Yugoslavia' in Chayes, A. and Chayes, A. (eds.) *Preventing Conflict in the Post-Communist World: Mobilizing International and Regional Organizations*. Washington, DC: Brookings Institution.

European regulation

MARK THATCHER

The EC's central policy activity is regulation rather than distribution or redistribution: its expenditure, revenues and staffing have remained small compared to those of national governments. In contrast, its regulatory role has grown rapidly between the 1980s and today, as part of a general trend towards the 'regulatory state' in Europe (see Majone 1996; Héritier and Thatcher 2002; Moran 2002, 2010). The EC has extended its activities into new policy areas and deepened its role in its existing policy domains. The financial and economic crisis after 2007 has been followed by further expansion and greater visibility, especially in governing markets. Aided by the doctrine of legal supremacy of Community law, it has become the most significant source of regulation in Europe. Indeed, it is frequently seen as a central to the spread of 'neo-liberalism' in Europe (Crouch 2011; Schmidt and Thatcher 2013).

The chapter examines the development of EC regulation.[1] It begins by mapping the expansion which has taken diverse forms and varied across policy domains. Many factors and actors are responsible for that expansion, and analysis is linked to wider debates about European integration. Hence, the chapter puts forward three analytical lenses to examine the growth of EC regulation. Thereafter, it considers the impacts of EC regulation, 'Europeanisation' and issues of implementation/compliance and the limits of EC regulation.

EC regulation: forms and growth

Several different definitions of 'regulation' exist. Economists usually emphasise rules to correct market failures (see Gaitsos and Seabright 1989), whereas political scientists and sociologists have broader conceptions that include rules governing state activity and can extend to all forms of social control and influence (Baldwin *et al.* 2011; Majone 1996). Its 'central meaning' (Selznick 1985) is 'sustained and focused control by a public agency over activities that are valued by the community'. Control through regulation involves rules, although these can vary from formal legislation to informal norms.

EC regulation covers this spectrum. It includes treaty articles that define the competencies and policy domains of the EC and secondary legislation regulations, directives and decisions. Regulations, and some treaty articles and directives are directly effective and hence can be used by litigants in national courts; in addition, the doctrine of 'indirect effect' allows EC law to influence national law. The EC also uses non-binding forms of regulation, often called 'soft law', which include recommendations, resolutions and declarations. Finally, the EC exercises regulatory influence by activities such as benchmarking, attempts to spread 'best practice', studies, conferences and encouragement of reform. These can aid the development of European norms and standards of behaviour.

EC regulatory activities have expanded far beyond those existing in 1958 in terms of legal competencies, legislation and policy fields. The EC's initial focus was on creating a free trade area through removing barriers to trade ('negative integration'), in particular tariff barriers. Thereafter, EC action extended to non-tariff barriers to trade, from product standards to bans on monopolies and restrictive rules on the supply of activities ranging from telecommunications to financial services. However, whilst liberalisation measures are its most visible forms of regulation, the EC has not 'deregulated'. On the contrary, it has engaged in considerable 're-regulation', corresponding to 'positive integration', setting rules governing competition and 'harmonisation' or minimal standards.

EC regulation covers focused, 'vertical' fields such as sectoral regulation for pub-lic utilities, agriculture, pharmaceuticals, financial services and professional services. However, it also takes 'horizontal' cross-sectoral forms – not just general competition policy but also increasingly social, consumer and environmental regulation. Not only does it structure markets, but with economic and monetary union, it is also increasingly extending to fiscal policies (see Schelkle 2009). Numbers also indicate the expansion of EC regulation. In 1970, 20 directives and 46 regulations were passed; in 1980, the figures were 57 directives and 113 regulations; in 1999, there were 169 directives and 1,316 regulations; in 2012, the Commission made proposals for 168 legislative acts, of which 137 were draft regulations and 31 draft directives, by 2014 the EU listed 22317 legislative acts in force (Commission of the European Communities 2003, 2012, 2014).

Whilst the overall picture is of EC regulatory growth, the speed, timing and extent of EC regulation have varied across policy domains. The most detailed EC regulation has been in economic regulation, especially covering competition. Even here, however, there have been cross-sectoral differences – for example telecommunications have seen more detailed and earlier regulation than postal services. In other fields, EC action has been more recent and remains less developed – for instance food safety and labeling or privacy. Nevertheless, fewer and fewer areas of policy lack an EC regulatory presence.

The process of EC regulatory expansion has taken place through several related channels. Regulatory powers and competencies have been explicitly given to the EC by member states via treaties as the EC's policy domains have been progressively extended. Under the 1958 Treaty of Rome, the EC's core powers mostly concerned building free-trade area–removing restrictions on the free movement of goods, persons, services and capital. The 1980s and 1990s saw member states provide further regulatory areas and powers to EC institutions via new Treaties. The Single European Act added explicit horizontal competencies, including the health and safety of workers, environmental pro-tection, research and development and economic and social cohesion. Crucially, it intro-duced qualified majority voting for certain fields; the most notable example concerned the Internal Market Programme (the '1992 Programme'). The Maastricht Treaty provided further explicit policy fields for EC regulation, notably consumer protection, public health and education. It also included social regulations, albeit in a separate social protocol that applied to all member states except Britain. Moreover, it widened the scope of qualified majority voting to areas such as consumer protection, the environment and some parts of social policy. The 1997 Treaty of Amsterdam, the 2001 Treaty of Nice and the 2007 Treaty of Lisbon continued the expansion of EC competencies in social policy, the environment, employment and international negotiations and the extension of qualified majority voting.

The greatest direct source of increased EC regulation has been through programmes and secondary legislation (directives and regulations) agreed by the Council of Minis-ters and, in the 1990s, also the European Parliament. The most trumpeted extension after the initial foundation of the EC, was the 1992 Programme (Commission of the European Communities 1985; Armstrong and Bulmer 1998; Egan 2001). This involved 300 legislative proposals to remove trade barriers within the EC through opening mar-kets, removing non-tariff barriers and setting EC standards. However, in many other fields, the expansion of EC regulation has taken place through gradual accretion over time – seen for example in social policy, environmental protection or employment. Pass-ing secondary legislation has been made easier by the extension of qualified majority voting and its volume rose sharply after the Single European Act.

Another, vital source of EC regulatory expansion has been European Court of Justice decisions (see Stone Sweet and Caporaso 1998; Stone Sweet and Brunnell 2012). An important example is Article 34 TFEU (Treaty on the Functioning of the European Union) which prohibits member states from introducing quantitative restrictions on imports from other member states or measures having 'equivalent effect'. The European Court of Justice (ECJ) stated (in the Dassonville case of 1974, ECJ 1974) that "all trading rules enacted by member states which are capable of hindering, actually or potentially, intra-Community trade" were covered by Article 34. It therefore greatly extended the ECJ's powers to strike down a host of national rules that, regardless of intention or even current effects, could reduce trade among member states.

Since 2000, there have been attempts to increase the use of 'soft law' and new forms of governance. Initially, this was titled 'the open method of coordination' and was promoted by the Commission, but today the more general phenomenon is often analysed in terms of 'experimentalist governance' (Commission of the European Communities 2001; cf Sabel and Zeitlin 2010; Héritier and Rhodes 2011). The importance and especially the novelty of such new forms have been questioned, notably whether they operate under the 'shadow of hierarchy' and hence depend on the legal framework and power relations (Börzel 2010), but they offer a further source of regulatory expansion.

Equally, new institutional arrangements linking the national and EU levels have provided a further source of regulation. In the late 1990s, 'networks' of national regulatory agencies (NRAs) were increasingly used by the EU (Coen and Thatcher 2008). In many domains they have been superseded by new European regulatory agencies (Wonka and Rittberger 2010; Rittberger and Wonka 2011). Important examples include competition telecommunications, electricity and gas authorities (Thatcher 2011). These are potentially significant in producing soft-law forms of regulation such as codes and norms. Equally, they may strengthen European epistemic regulatory communities and encourage cross-national policy learning and transfer. Thus, they may represent a significant stimulus to new forms of governance whereby the EC regulates through coordination. However, behind the networks lies traditional 'hard law': the Commission has formal legal powers to oblige NRAs to notify it and other NRAs over measures that may affect trade among member states and to order the NRA to withdraw measures; examples include network industries and general competition authorities (Coen and Thatcher 2008; Wilks 2005).

Explaining EC regulatory expansion

Many related factors have driven the expansion of EC regulatory activity: the interests and role of the Commission; the ECJ and the EC's legal framework; decisions by national governments; national regulatory inadequacies; interest groups and increased transnational trade; the dynamics of EC policy making. Assessing the balance of importance among these factors, and especially the weight of supranational actors (the Commission and ECJ), transnational trade and decisions by national governments, relates closely to general debates on European integration – particularly those among inter-governmentalism, neo-functionalism and more recent multilevel governance, policy transfer and delegation approaches (see Moravcsik 1993; Sandholtz and Stone Sweet 1998, 2012; Hooghe and Marks 2001; Radaelli 2000; Pollack 2003, 2012; Bulmer *et al.* 2007).

The relative importance of the different factors has also varied from one policy domain to another, because of variations in Commission powers and resources, ECJ case law, treaty articles, the position of national governments, exposure to transnational trade and interests and the extent of domestic regulatory inadequacies. No single approach or factor can explain EC regulatory growth. Instead, what is put forward below are three analytical 'models' or lenses, with empirical examples, which themselves relate to broader theoretical frameworks for analysing EC integration.

A neo-functionalist or 'top-down' model of EC regulatory growth

This model emphasises the roles of the EC Commission, the ECJ and powerful interest groups, especially firms who engage in cross-border trade. It sees EC regulation as largely driven by these actors, often against the will of national governments.

A key starting point is Commission activism. The Commission has been a central actor in EC regulatory expansion, putting forward new ideas, pressing for action and proposing specific action. At times, it has launched headline-catching ambitious initiatives; the 1992 Programme for the internal market was the most prominent example. More generally, however, it has taken a less public but perhaps more effective strategy involving incremental steps and persistence even in the face of inertia and opposition by member states. The Commission has tended to follow a long process of garnering support before acting, for example holding conferences and workshops with experts and interested groups, issuing Green Papers, commissioning studies and seeking to accommodate different points of view. It has then made specific legislative proposals and been able to offer a direction for regulation, with opponents left facing considerable momentum and a well-developed agenda. Merger control illustrates Commission patience and persistence: discussion of empowering the Commission to vet large cross-border mergers began in 1973 and eventually led to the 1989 Merger Regulation, which covered notification and approval of mergers (Cini and McGowan 2009). Similar stories of the Commission continuing its efforts until circumstances were propitious can be told in many other fields, such as the environment, occupational safety, social policy or gender discrimination (see Richardson 1994; Cichowski 2007; Jordan and Adelle 2012; Mazey 2012; Stone Sweet and Brunnell 2012).

The Commission has been able to utilise its legal monopoly over secondary legislative proposals, together with great influence as an 'agenda setter' at the centre of many European networks (Princen 2011). Within the Commission, different DGs compete with each other for prestige and territory, creating further pressures for action; for example, in the late 1980s, DGIV (the competition directorate) was spurred into activity as its rival, DGIII (at that time, both industry and internal market) used the 1992 Programme to expand its role. Perhaps most important of all, the Commission has been able to wait, taking time to place new ideas of increased EC regulation in the European policy space, testing out the balance of forces, gradually creating a climate of opinion and coalition supportive of its ideas, refining those ideas to match the balance of forces and finally, making proposals at suitable times or simply repeating them until accepted.

Yet the Commission has not been able to expand EC regulation on its own. A key ally has often been the ECJ, which has frequently supported the expansion of EC competencies and regulation, taking a broad view of the scope of EC powers and legislation. The

ECJ's decisions that directives could be directly effective made passing such secondary legislation an attractive and relatively easy method of EC action, especially in combination with the doctrine of the supremacy of EC law. Moreover, the ECJ has offered wide interpretations of Treaty provisions and secondary legislation. Thus for example, in a series of cases under Article 157 TFEU (equal pay for equal work), and other directives on equal pay for work of equal value (Directive 75/119), equal treatment in employment (Directive 76/207) and equal treatment in social security matters (Directive 97/7) it took a broad view of payment and discrimination so that it interpreted Article 157 to mean equal pay for work of equal value, found that discrimination could be indirect and included pensions and retirement ages, even though these had been excluded from the Directives (Stone Sweet and Caporaso, 1998, pp. 121–127). The ECJ has played a key role in the expansion of many other areas of EC regulation, from competition policy to the environment (see Weiler 1991; Gerber 1994; Bulmer 1998; Stone Sweet and Caparoso 1998; Stone Sweet et al. 2001; Cichowski 2007).

ECJ rulings have not only strengthened EC regulatory capacities, but also created incentives for secondary legislation. The best-known example is the Cassis de Dijon case (ECJ 1979): the ECJ ruled that goods legally produced in one member state, according to its rules and regulations, could be sold in other member states. "In the absence of common rules", it was for individual member states to set their own rules, but other member states could not impose national restrictions that hindered trade (being caught by Article 34 TFEU) except under limited circumstances (set out in Article 36 TFEU, including for instance, public morality, public policy or health and safety). Such rulings put pressure on member states to pass EC secondary legislation, in order to avoid uncertainty and to play a part in the detail of regulation rather than merely following judicial decisions (see Bulmer 1998). The jurisprudence of the Dassonville and Cassis cases produced great impetus for legislation to set standards, since otherwise member states would have to accept the standards of other member states, over which they had no control, and/or justify restrictions in a possible flood of court cases, causing uncertainty and damage to trade. These cases were followed by the Internal Market Programme (1992) and the 'new approach' to harmonisation and standardization in the 1980s whereby the EC set minimum standards rather than pursuing full harmonisation which had largely failed (Pelkmans 1987).

However, the ECJ is reliant on cases being brought before it, whilst the Commission is a small bureaucracy, dependent on other actors to provide it with information, expertise, political support and legitimacy. A neo-functionalist model underlines how interest groups such as firms, trade unions and pressure groups in areas such as the environment or gender equality have sought increased EC regulation. They have done so at the EC level, especially as the Brussels bureaucracy is remarkably permeable and open to lobbying (Coen and Richardson 2009), and at the national level. They have offered information to the Commission as part of their strategies of influencing EC regulation (Broscheid and Coen 2003). Frequently such activity has been linked to the growth of transnational trade, which has provided important incentives for EC integration (see Sandholtz and Stone Sweet 1998, 2012).

Internationalising firms (sometimes in conjunction with national associations and governments) have urged EC action to open up closed domestic markets and to establish a single set of predictable rules across the EC (Coen 1998). Thus, for example companies such as BT and large City institutions, supported by the supposedly

'Euro-sceptical' British governments of the 1980s and 1990s, urged EC measures to liberalise areas such as financial services, airlines or telecommunications (see Hayward 1995). Conversely, firms facing 'dumping' or 'unfairly' subsidised foreign competitors (industries such as consumer electronics, steel or coal) have sought EC protection. Equally, in international 'standards battles', European firms and policy makers have turned to the EC to create Europe-wide standards in areas ranging from mobile communications to environmental requirements. Thus, a neo-functionalist model analyses EC regulation as the product of a coalition or at least cooperation between the Commission, the ECJ and interest groups that is sufficiently powerful to overcome resistance by national governments.

An inter-governmental or delegation model of EC regulation

An alternative model, however, sees EC regulation as desired and indeed intended by national governments. Far from the regulations being imposed on them, governments choose to delegate to the Commission and ECJ to resolve problems such as lack of credible commitment, dealing with information asymmetries or aiding monitoring and compliance across nations (Pollack 2003). This model underlines that national governments have chosen to provide increasingly wide regulatory powers to the EC under successive Treaties. When faced with insistent opposition from a small minority (often Britain), they have found ways to circumvent it–for example, through the Social Protocol to the Maastricht Treaty signed by all member states except Britain. Moreover, governments have made passing secondary regulatory legislation easier by extending qualified majority voting and restricting the requirement of unanimity in the Council of Ministers in the Single European Act and later treaties; individual member states have found themselves obliged to compromise and trade.

National governments have accepted initiatives to expand EC regulation. As early as 1962, they passed Regulation 17 (Council of the European Communities 1962), whereby the Commission implemented competition law, including acting against anti-competitive agreements and abuse of a dominant position and granting exemptions under Articles 101, 102 and 106 TFEU. Later, they welcomed the 1992 Programme and accepted EC directives for environmental protection in the 1970s and 1980s. Even in an area such as social policy, apparently far removed from ending barriers to trade, they accepted EC regulatory action. At times, member states have used broad Articles to extend the EC's regulatory activities. In particular, Article 352 TFEU operated as a 'catch-all' provision, as it allowed the EC action that is necessary to attain EC objectives but for which powers were not provided for explicitly in the treaty; it was used to initiate EC regulation in several fields, including social security for migrants, the environment and equal treatment in employment. Later on, explicit treaty articles followed, in effect ratifying the EC's entry into new areas.

Telecommunications provides a good example of the 'partnership' between the Commission and national governments (Thatcher 2001). The latter had formal and informal institutional controls over the Commission that made it very sensitive to their preferences over the substance of telecommunications regulation. These controls were seen in the participation of national governments at all stages of decision making, incrementalism decision making, compromises and linkages in policy choices and room for significant national discretion in implementation of EC regulation. The Commission engaged in extensive consultation with governments and then made detailed proposals for EC directives that were largely accepted by national governments. Far from the Commission imposing EC regulation, it engaged in a partnership with national governments in which they agreed on expanded EC legislation.

Why should national governments accept or welcome increased EC regulation? Principal–agent models point to several reasons (Pollack 2003, 2010). First, national policy makers may be faced with potential gains from coordination. These may arise from interdependence and 'regulatory externalities' in which the decisions of national regulators have effects on other EC member states; the clearest example is pollution, where discharges in one country affect other countries (e.g. waste in the North Sea or air pollution in border areas). But whilst nation-states may gain from cooperation, they face international prisoners' dilemmas (Gaitsos and Seabright 1989). Thus, for instance the benefits of regulatory decisions in one member state (for instance higher pollution standards) may be negated by decisions in another, leaving the first with higher costs. Moreover, national regulators may also engage in strategic behaviour, whereby some or all of the costs of their decisions are borne by other nations; one example is member states competition in increasing state subsidies to non-viable firms, negating their effects and using resources that could be better used for other purposes. Cross-national cooperation faces information and transaction costs, arising, for example, from cheating, enforcement, discretion, differing cultures and organisational barriers to trading national gains and losses across policy fields (see Majone 1996, chap. 4). EC regulation allows cooperation and coordination to capture externalities, for example by setting common rules for state aids, pollution or standards. It offers a mechanism to establish rules that member states can accept more easily in the knowledge that other member states are placed under the same rules, making cheating and gaining regulatory advantages more difficult. In other words, the EC acts as a credible supranational monitor, arbitrator and enforcer (Pollack 2003).

EC regulation may also enhance credible commitment by governments. Such commitment is important if governments, firms and investors rely on long-term policies being followed. For example, they may need to be reassured that competition policies will be enforced in practice or that standards will be followed before investing or implementing difficult policies such as reducing state aid or complying with expensive standards. Governments may wish to provide such reassurance, since it will lead to beneficial outcomes such as higher investment, but lack credibility to make promises because of short-term incentives, especially electoral ones. In contrast, the EC as a non-majoritarian supranational organisation offers greater credibility for long-term promises, lowering the costs of regulation (e.g. enforcement costs) and increasing benefits (Majone 2000).

A third reason for governments to delegate regulation to the EC is blame shifting. EC regulation can provide a good external reason for decisions that face powerful domestic opposition, such as ending monopolies, reducing state aid, altering standards or privatisation to name but a few. These reforms may be desired for both EC and non-EC reasons but be unpopular domestically. A general analysis is that national governments are able to engage in a 'two-level game' (Putnam 1988; Evans *et al.* 1993), whereby they pursue their domestic interests at the EC level, avoiding or reducing domestic obstacles to their policies.

A dynamic 'governance' model

The third 'model' looks at how processes arising from interactions between the EC, national and international levels create pressures and incentives for an expansion of EU regulation. These processes can include regulatory competition, the growth of epistemic communities and cross-national policy transfer. The model is thus rather eclectic and encompasses several theoretical literatures, both rational choice and 'constructivist', but the central common feature is that events at the EU level influence and are themselves influenced by events at the national and international levels, resulting in greater EC regulation.

At the EU level, institutions are not inert but can actively engage in processes to work around the supposed 'joint decision trap' of multiple veto points and players (Falkner 2011). Thus they may alter arenas, so that regulation is considered in arenas favourable to it or they can alter opportunity structures, for instance by increasing pressures on governments. The coalition of the Commission and EC is particularly powerful here. The Commission in particular is seen as pursuing a political strategy of pursuing European integration, using conceptions of the single market to build alliances and legitimate the expansion of EC regulation (Jabko 2006).

Member states are frequently in competition with each: they seek to 'export' their regulatory model to the EC level, because this provides domestic companies with competitive advantages and requires little national adaptation. In the EC, there are often important first-mover advantages, notably in defining problems and setting agendas (Peters 1994). At the same time, member states may seek to respond to the danger of regulatory competition by cooperation through the EU. In competition and cooperation, the Commission plays a key role as a gatekeeper, because of its position at the centre of many European networks and its monopoly over legislative proposals. Member states therefore have an incentive to act quickly and offer nationally advantageous ideas for EC regulation to the Commission, before other countries enter the field and offer their own agendas and suggestions. The Commission is unlikely to accept proposals that reduce its powers and competencies. The result is a dynamic towards increased EC regulation, based on member states suggesting EC action. Examples can be found in many policy areas, from pollution control to electricity regulation, as national policy makers vie for the ear of the Commission and influence over EC regulatory development.

The interaction between negative and positive integration offers another dynamic that sustains EC regulatory growth. Attempts to end non-tariff barriers creates strong forces for EC re-regulation, since national standards and norms can and often do operate as non-tariffs barriers. Moreover, they raise the problem of standards: if no EC standards are set and if member states are obliged to allow entry of products regardless of domestic standards, there are dangers of 'races to the bottom', as firms in EC countries with lower and less costly standards enjoy competitive advantages leading to the progressive reduction of standards (Dehousse 1992). Moreover, as markets are opened up, firms seek certainty about standards in order to plan ahead and compete effectively. Hence, the internal market and liberalisation of markets such as telecommunications have seen both the removal of non-tariff barriers to trade and the development of EC regulatory standards. These range from minimum standards to voluntary Europe-wide norms to compulsory harmonised standards in fields ranging from electronic equipment to environmental standards (see Holzinger and Knill 2004; Cichowski 2007).

A third process involves the EU encouraging policy learning, policy coordination and the development of European epistemic or policy communities. This may happen formally, notably through committees or the open method of coordination. However, it can also take place informally, as the EU encourages the development of cross-national networks. Such processes can alter policy preferences of member states, as well as their strategic calculations and their ability to link different policy areas and hence trade-off gains and losses. The results can be seen in 'hard' regulation, that is the production of EC legislation; thus, it is argued that the process of liberalising the electricity market saw modifications in national governments' preferences over competition (Eising 2002). However, such processes are most likely to have greatest initial effects through the production of EC norms. Thus, for instance work on experimentalist governance argues that recursive processes have driven the growth of new forms of regulatory governance, from the use of forums to soft law (Sabel and Zeitlin 2010).

Finally, more ideational and 'constructivist' approaches emphasise how socialisation, learning and the development of common identities can alter actor preferences and hence definitions of self interest (Saurugger 2013). Such constructivism may be limited, in that ideas are seen as 'strategic instruments' used by actors such as the Commission to justify expanding its regulatory powers (Jabko 2006), or they can be seen as the 'glue' that holds different coalitions together in fields ranging from gambling regulation to financial regulation (Della Sala 2010; Quaglia 2010). At the more 'contructivist' end, work on 'discursive institutionalism' argues that discourse affects which solutions are regarded as legitimate and hence acceptable (V. Schmidt 2002, 2010). In the field of food safety, for instance a new discourse since the 1990s has aided the growth of EC regulation by legitimating the need to protect consumers' health, in contrast to traditional producer-focused policy (Paul 2012). All these approaches, however, share the view that EC regulation emerges from shared processes that involve interactions of actors and in which ideas are crucial.

Europeanisation and EC regulation

Much attention has been paid to the effects of EC regulation at the national level – i.e., 'Europeanisation' (Green Cowles *et al.* 2001; Featherstone and Radaelli 2003; Radaelli and Schmidt 2004). Assessing the impacts of EC regulation within member states is far from easy since they have varied, both from one sector to another and across member states. At one extreme, in certain sectors there has been little EC regulation, and/or EC measures had already been introduced by some member states so that the EC was following rather than leading; in addition, EC rules may not have been implemented in practice, their impact being more apparent than real. Moreover, the EC has only been one force for regulatory change, as other factors such as globalisation have been at work (see Smith 2010). At the other extreme, EC regulation has caused major repercussions in markets, institutions and strategies in member states, with claims of a move towards a European 'regulatory state' (McGowan and Wallace 1996). Despite these problems in assessing the impacts of EC regulation, certain traits can be sketched.

A key impact has been on domestic institutional change. National markets have been opened to competition at least in terms of formal rules. The EC has contributed to ending legal monopolies lying at the heart of states, such as telecommunications, energy and railways (Thatcher 2007). It has also aided the spread of independent regulatory authorities, has provided re-regulatory rules and sometimes has provided impetus for privatization (Schneider *et al*. 2005; Clifton *et al*. 2006; Schmitt 2013).

EC regulation has encouraged the internationalisation of European firms through cross-border mergers and takeovers that have often been aimed at becoming European-wide suppliers, from banking and insurance mergers to cars and pharmaceuticals (Clifton *et al*. 2011). It has also aided the entry of foreign suppliers (European and subsidiaries of non-European firms) into previously closed national markets in sectors ranging from the utilities or financial services to manufactured goods. It has increased pressures on publicly owned enterprises which have lost many of their legal monopolies and found their privileged relationships with governments under scrutiny by the Commission, especially under state aid provisions.

Some Europeanisation has occurred by imposition of EC regulation on member states. However, other processes seem to be more important. The EC has aided policy transfer and policy learning (cf Radaelli and Dunlop 2013). Thus for instance, the EC encouraged the spread of the 'British model' of regulating the electricity sector (complete liberalisation, regulated access to the transmission infrastructure, simple authorisation of new capacity, legal separation of transmission and supply and independent sectoral regulators) although these features were not required by EC law (Bulmer *et al*. 2007). Even in telecommunications, where a detailed EC regulatory regime has developed, the main impacts have been to provide legitimation and explanation for national governments to pursue policies desired for non-EC reasons (Thatcher 2007; see Radaelli and Schmidt 2004). Thus, for instance governments in France and Italy used EC regulation to justify privatisation of Telecom Italia or France Télécom, which they sought for other reasons, notably raising money for budgets (Thatcher 2007). Indeed, national governments can use EC regulation as part of their domestic political strategies, including bypassing or overcoming domestic obstacles to reform (Fontana 2011).

Limits on EC regulation

In analysing EC regulation, it is too easy to lose sight of the real limits on its growth and significance: increased activity is only one indicator of importance and the expansion of EC regulation must be analysed in the context of its impact on member states. Even when the EC has considerable formal powers, it faces limits which can prevent it from taking a distinctive path, resulting in it having 'power without purpose' (see Posner and Véron 2010). Closer examination reveals several factors that constrain the EC.

Veto points and the power of member states

There are many 'veto points' in the EC's decision-making processes that allow key actors, particularly member states, to block, hinder or delay EC regulation. Treaty amendments to provide the EC with new powers are slow and require approval by all member states. Passing secondary legislation, the key means of EC regulation, is now mostly covered by the co-decision procedure that gives powers to three actors (the Commission, the Council and the European Parliament) each with its own interests.

The comitology process, a central method of moving from general principles and aims to specific EC requirements, involves national officials (see Vos 1997). The Commission itself is a collegial body, headed by the appointees of national governments (although the Amsterdam Treaty slightly strengthens the president). Regulatory decisions, including 'technical' ones in a highly juridicised environment such as the application of competition policy, must be approved by the College of Commissioners, leading to intense and often highly politicised battles (Cini and McGowan 2009). Individual Commissioners must therefore build alliances within the College and watch carefully the reactions of national governments.

The resources of the Commission

Although the scope of EC regulation and the amount of legislation have expanded, the Commission remains a small organisation with severely constrained material resources. It has very few staff and low expenditure, especially relative to national bureaucracies and large firms. Even DG Competition, responsible for policing and sometimes enforcing competition policy has a tiny staff (approximately 400) relative to the breadth and importance of its tasks. Yet producing regulation is frequently difficult, and highly technical. The Commission therefore has to be very selective in where to attempt to regulate. Moreover, it relies heavily on other actors for information and expertise, including national governments and regulators, firms and interest groups. National officials play a key role in the preparation of legislative proposals (including through COREPER) and then, after directives have been passed, in fleshing out 'technical' matters through the comitology system. Through these committees, national officials are intimately involved in passing most EC regulatory legislation, in advising, managing and making detailed rules. In addition, Commission staffing is constantly a problem, and many officials in Brussels are in fact seconded national officials and experts.

Implementation and compliance

Closely linked to lack of Commission resources is the fact that most EC legislation is broad, and offers only a framework for decision making within member states. Directives are only binding as to their objectives and not their means. Almost all implementation is undertaken by national regulators. Although new EC regulatory agencies have been created, the process has been slow, and important, these bodies have limited powers, relying heavily on national bodies both for membership and implementation, while the Commission maintains important final powers over their decisions (Levi-Faur 2011; Thatcher 2011).

These features make effective enforcement by the EC difficult. There can be considerable gaps between EC rules and their operation in practice. If member states oppose EC regulation and lose, they can be tempted to seek a 'second round' by resisting effective implementation. However, even when member states agree to EU legislation, they may fail to implement it, due not only to 'opposition through the backdoor' but also administrative weaknesses, difficulties in interpreting it and linkage with other issues (Falkner *et al.* 2008). The Commission lacks resources to pursue all member states over implementation, even if it so wished. Moreover, infringement proceedings are slow and difficult. Private litigants within member states can play a part, but legal action is frequently financially costly, damaging to relationships with national actors and unlikely to offer swift results that may be required in fast-moving markets.

Existing national regulation and regulators

The decentralised nature of most EC regulation makes the national level very important for regulation in practice. Key decisions are still made within nation-states, on matters such as ownership or the institutional structure of domestic regulators. National institutions such as public ownership or the existence and powers of independent agencies, influence decision making. Legally, the EC cannot require changes in ownership (under Article 345 TFEU). Yet ownership can affect the impact of EC regulation; for example public ownership of commercial enterprises poses significant difficulties over matters such as distinguishing state aid and new capital injections and can create incentives for governments to favour state-owned companies. The EC has been unable to break up large oligopolistic or monopolistic suppliers – even in markets subject to considerable EC regulation, powerful national champions such as France Télécom, Deutsche Telekom, EdF, Deutsche Post, Royal Mail and La Poste continue to enjoy strong positions in domestic telecommunications, electricity and postal markets. EC structural intervention has been largely confined to occasions of takeovers and mergers, and even on these, its requirements have been limited to the disposal of limited parts of businesses. Member states retain great freedom over the organisational features of national regulatory authorities, as EC requirements are often limited; hence, for instance in utilities regulation, EC directives typically demand that national regulatory authorities be organisationally separate from suppliers and that they must act fairly and transparently, but add little detail about decision-making procedures and processes.

EC regulation also leaves much room for national choices in features other than organizational structures, especially in re-regulation, for instance over social obligations, tariffs or professional registration requirements (Héritier 2002). One reason is that re-regulation often depends on mutual recognition (of standards among member states), which is subject to minimum standards and exceptions, leaving much room for national discretion. Moreover, even when domestic markets such as road haulage or insurance have been liberalised following EC regulation, they have continued to be dominated by domestic firms (S. Schmidt 2002). The result is that even within policy fields with a fairly high degree of EC regulation such as the utilities, considerable national variations continue (Coen and Héritier 2006).

Interest groups

The EC is highly dependent on interest groups to persuade national policy makers to accept its regulation, for information, for expertise and for monitoring implementation and challenging non-compliance (if necessary through litigation). Its scope to regulate in the face of well-organised hostile interests is therefore limited. Indeed, it is subject to powerful lobbying, especially by large firms and their associations (Coen 1998;

Broscheid and Coen 2003; Coen and Richardson 2009). This holds true even in competition policy, where the Commission offers informal guidance and negotiates with firms to obtain agreements, and seeking to avoid lengthy legal proceedings that will take up time and resources; thus, for example between 1990 and 2009, only mergers notified to the Commission were prohibited.

International regulation

Since the 1990s, international regulation has expanded, notably the General Tariff and Trade Agreement and World Trade Organization (WTO). International trade negotiations may have strengthened EC regulation, as the Commission frequently represented the EC, member states were obliged to cooperate with it due to shared competencies and as the Community sought to maximise its influence by establishing common positions. However, EC regulation is now subject to the WTO and legislation and decisions that affect international trade are liable to challenge under WTO rules. As a result, much of EC regulation, from food health and safety rules to product standards or EC content requirements is open to attack; this process has already begun, often led by US multinationals and public officials, seen recently in disputes over genetically modified food.

The legitimacy of EC regulation

EC regulation suffers from significant problems of legitimacy (see Schmidt 2006). Under the first pillar of the EU, the EC has supranational competencies and, hence, can impose regulation on unwilling member states. Yet passing legislation is shared between the Commission, the Council of Ministers and the European Parliament, with the ECJ playing a crucial role. The constitutional basis of the EC is therefore hybrid between elected (directly or indirectly) and non-majoritarian bodies. EC decision-making procedures appear opaque, for example debates within the Council and the Commission are not published, there is no overall code of conduct on how regulatory decisions should made, and the comitology system is closed and largely private. Lines of accountability are multiple and unclear, especially after the strengthening of the European Parliament's powers under the Maastricht and Amsterdam Treaties; the Commission answers to both it and the Council. Because of its limited resources and the power of national interests at all stages of regulation, the Commission's expertise, effectiveness and independence are open to severe questioning. Such problems rise rapidly to the surface whenever controversial decisions are taken that involve powerful national interests, as evidenced in the bovine spongiform encephalopathy (BSE – 'mad cow disease') crisis or regulation of state aid.

Conclusion

EC regulation has grown, expanding from removal of tariffs to dealing with non-tariff barriers and introducing Community re-regulatory standards and rules. It has spread across many sectors, from utilities to food. Its development has been the product of many factors: Commission activism, ECJ rulings, delegating by national governments and pressure by interest groups have all played a part. To create analytical simplicity and to link to broader claims about European integration, the chapter has offered three analytical lenses: a top-down view in which the expansion of EC regulation has been led by the Commission and ECJ, a delegation model in which national governments have chosen to delegate to the EC and a dynamic framework in which EC regulation is the result of processes arising from interactions between different levels of decision making.

As EC regulation has increased, greater attention is being paid to its content and especially its role in the spread of 'neo-liberalism' in Europe (Crouch 2011; Thatcher 2013). This underlines the importance of EU regulation in Europe's political economy and its interactions with national policy making.

Note

1   References are to the European Community since almost all regulation discussed here falls under the EC pillar of the EU.

References

Armstrong, K. and Bulmer, S. (1998) *Governance of the Single European Market*. Manchester: Manchester University Press.

Baldwin, R., Cave, M. and Lodge, M. (2011) *Understanding Regulation*, 2nd ed. Oxford: Oxford University Press.

Börzel, T. (2010) 'European Governance- Negotiation and Competition in the Shadow of Hierarchy', *Journal of Common Market Studies* 48(2): 191–219.

Broscheid, A. and Coen, D. (2003) 'Insider and Outsider Lobbying of the European Commission', *European Union Politics* 4(2): 165–189.

Bulmer, S. J. (1998) 'New Institutionalism and the Governance of the Sungle European Market', *Journal of European Public Policy* 5(3): 365–186.

Bulmer, S., Dolowitz, D., Humphreys, P. and Padgett, S. (2007) *Policy Transfer in the European Union. Regulating the Utilities*. London: Routledge

Case 8/74, Procureur du Roi v. Dassonville [1974] ECR 837.

Case 120/78, Rewe [1979] ECR 649. [Cassis de Dijon].

Case 156/84 [1987] ECR 4487.

Case 202/88 French Republic v. Commission [1991] ECR I-1223.

Cichowski, Rachel (2007) *The European Court and Civil Society: Litigation, Mobilization and Governance*. Cambridge: Cambridge University Press.

Cini, M. and McGowan, L. (2009) *Competition Policy in the European Union*, 2nd ed. Basingstoke: Macmillan.

Clifton, J., Comín, F., and Fuentes, D. (2006) 'Privatizing Public Enterprises in the European Union 1960–2002: Ideological, Pragmatic, Inevitable?', *Journal of European Public Policy* 13(5): 736–756.

Clifton, J., Comín, F., and Fuentes, D. (2011) 'From National Monopoly to Multinational Corporation: How Regulation Shaped the Road towards Telecommunications Internationalisation', *Business History* 53(5): 761–781.

Coen, D. (1998) 'The European Business Interest and the Nation State: Large-firm Lobbying in the European Union and Member States', *Journal of Public Policy* 18(1): 75–100.

Coen, D. and Héritier, A. (2006) *Refining Regulatory Regimes: Utilities in Europe*. Northampton: Edward Elgar.

Coen, D. and Richardson, J. (eds.) (2009) *Lobbying the European Union: Institutions, Actors, and Issues*. Oxford: Oxford University Press.

Coen, D. and Thatcher, M. (2008), Network governance and delegation: European Networks of Regulatory Agencies, *Journal of Public Policy* 28(1): 49–71.

Commission of the European Communities (1985) *Completing the Internal Market: White Paper from the Commission to the European Council*. Luxembourg: Office for Official Publications of the European Communities.

—— (2001) *European Governance: A White Paper*, COM(2001) 428. Brussels: Commission of the European Communities.

—— (2003) Directory of Community Legislation in Force and Other Acts of the Community Institutions., 41 rev. ed., vols 1 and 2. *Official Journal of the European Communities*. Brussels: Stationery Office Books.

—— (2012) *General Report on the Activities of the European Union*. Brussels: Commission of the European Communities.

Council of the European Communities (1962) *Council Regulation 17/62*, 1962 O.J. 204.

Commission of the European Communities (2014), *Directory of European Union Legislation*, http://eur-lex.europa.eu/browse/directories/legislation.html, accessed 1 December 2014.

Crouch, C. (2011) *The Strange Non-death of Neo-liberalism*. Cambridge: Polity Press.

Dehousse, R. (1992) 'Integration v. Regulation? On the Dynamics of Regulation in the European Community', *Journal of Common Market Studies* 30(4): 383–402.

—— (1997) 'Regulation by Networks in the European Community: The Role of European Agencies', *Journal of European Public Policy* 4(2): 246–261.

Della Sala, V. (2010) 'Stakes and states: gambling in the single market', *Journal of European Public Policy* 17(7): 1024–1038.

Egan, M. (2001) *Constructing a European Market*. Oxford: Oxford University Press.

Eising, R. (2002) 'Policy Learning in Embedded Negotiations: Explaining EU Electricity Liberalization', *International Organization* 56(1): 85–120.

Evans, P., Jacobson, H. and Putnam, R. (eds.) (1993) *Double-Edged Diplomacy: International Bargaining and Domestic Politics*. Berkeley: University of California Press.

Falkner, G. (ed.) (2011) *The EU's Decision Traps: Comparing Policies*. Oxford: Oxford University Press.

Falkner, G., Treib, O., Holzleithner, E. and Causse, E. (2008) *Compliance in the Enlarged European Union: Living Rights or Dead Letters?* Aldershot: Ashgate.

Featherstone, K. and Radaelli, C.M., (eds.) (2003) *The Politics of Europeanization*. Oxford: Oxford University Press.

Fontana, M.-C. (2011) 'Europeanization and Domestic Policy Concertation: How Actors Use Europe to Modify Domestic Patterns of Policy-making', *Journal of European Public Policy* 18(5): 654–671.

Gaitsos, K. and Seabright, P. (1989) 'Regulation in the European Community', *Oxford Review of Economic Policy* 5(2): 37–60.

Gerber, D. J. (1994) 'The Transformation of European Community Competition Law?', *Harvard International Law Review* 35(1): 97–147.

Green Cowles, M., Caporaso, J. and Risse, T. (eds.) (2001) *Transforming Europe*. Ithaca: Cornell University Press.

Hayward, J. E. S. (Ed.) (1995). *Industrial Enterprise and European Integration*. Oxford: Oxford.

—— (2002) 'Public-interest Services Revisited', *Journal of European Public Policy* 9(6): 995–1019.

Héritier, A. and Thatcher, M. (eds.) (2002) 'Regulatory Reform in Europe', special issue, *Journal of European Public Policy* 9(6).

Héritier, A. and Rhodes, M. (eds.) (2011) *New Modes of Governance in Europe: Governing in the Shadow of Hierarchy*. Basingstoke: Palgrave Macmillan.

Holzinger, K. and Knill, C. (2004) 'Competition and Cooperation in Environmental Policy', *Journal of Public Policy* 24(1): 25–47.

Hooghe, L. and Marks, G. (2001) *Multi-level Governance and European Integration*. Lanham, MD: Rowman & Littlefield.

Jabko, N. (2006) *Playing the Market: A Political Strategy for Uniting Europe, 1985–2005*. Ithaca: Cornell University Press.

Joined Cases C-271/90, C-281/90 and C-289/90 Spain, France, Belgium and Italy v. Commission [1992] ECR I-5833.

Jordan, A. J. and Adelle, C. (ed.) (2012) *Environmental Policy in the European Union: Contexts, Actors and Policy Dynamics* (3 ed.). London and Sterling: Earthscan.

Levi-Faur, D. (2011) 'Regulatory Networks & Regulatory Agencification', *Journal of European Public Policy* 18(6): 810–846.

Majone, G. (ed.) (1996) *Regulating Europe*. London: Routledge.

—— (2000) 'The Credibility Crisis of Community Regulation', *Journal of Common Market Studies* 38(2): 273–302.

Mazey, S. (2012) 'Policy Entrepreneurship, Group Mobilisation and the Creation of a New Policy Domain: Women's Rights and the European Union' in Richardson, J. (ed.), *Constructing a Policy-making State? Policy Dynamics in the European Union*. Oxford: Oxford University Press.

McGowan, F. and Wallace, H. (1996) 'Towards a European Regulatory State', *Journal of European Public Policy* 3(4): 560–576.

Moran, M. (2002) 'Understanding the Regulatory State', *British Journal of Political Science* 32, 391–413.

—— (2010) 'The Rise of the Regulatory State' in *The Oxford Handbook of Business Government Relations*. Oxford: Oxford University Press.

Moravcsik, A. (1993) 'Preferences and Power in the European Community: A Liberal Intergovernmentalist Approach', *Journal of Common Market Studies* 31(4): 473–524.

Paul, K. (2012) 'The Europeanization of Food Safety: A Discourse-analytical Approach', *Journal of European Public Policy* 19(4): 549–566.

Pelkmans, J. (1987) 'The New Approach to Technical Harmonisation and Standardisation', *Journal of Common Market Studies* XXV(3): 249–269.

Peters, B. G. (1994) 'Agenda-Setting in the European Community', *Journal of European Public Policy* 1(1): 9–26.

Pollack, M. (2003) *The Engines of European Integration*. Oxford: Oxford University Press.

—— (2010) 'Theorizing EU Policy-Making' in Wallace, A., Pollack, M. and Young, A. (eds.), *Policy-Making in the European Union*, 6th edition, New York: Oxford University Press, 2010, pp. 14–43.

—— (2012) 'Realist, Intergovernmentalist, and Institutionalist Approaches' in Jones, E., Menon, A., and Weatherill, S. (eds.), *The Oxford Handbook of European Governance*. Oxford: Oxford University Press.

Posner, E. and Véron, N. (2010) 'The EU and Financial Regulation: Power without Purpose?', *Journal of European Public Policy* 17(3): 400–415.

Princen, S. (2011) 'Agenda-setting Strategies in EU Policy Processes', *Journal of European Public Policy* 18(7): 927–943.

Putnam, R. D. (1988) 'Diplomacy and Domestic Politics: The Logic of Two-Level Games', *International Organization* 42(3): 427–460.

Quaglia, L. (2010) 'Completing the Single Market in Financial Services: The Politics of Competing Advocacy Coalitions', *Journal of European Public Policy* 17(7): 1007–1023.

Radaelli, C. (2000) 'Policy Transfer in the European Union', *Governance* 13(1): 25–43.

Radaelli, C. and Dunlop, C. (2013) 'Learning in the European Union: Theoretical Lenses and Meta-theory', *Journal of European Public Policy* 20(6): 923–940.

Radaelli, C. and Schmidt, V. (eds.) (2004) 'Europeanisation, Discourse and Policy Change', special issue, *West European Politics* 27(2).

Richardson, J. (1994) 'EU Water Policy: Uncertain Agendas, Shifting Networks and Complex Coalitions', *Environmental Politics* 3(4): 139–167.

Rittberger, B. and Wonka, A. (2011) 'Agency Governance in the European Union', special issue, *Journal of European Public Policy* 18(6): 779–925.

Sabel, C. and Zeitlin, J. (eds.) (2010) *Experimentalist Governance in the European Union: Towards a New Architecture*. Oxford: Oxford University Press.

Sandholtz, W. and Stone Sweet, A. (eds.) (1998) *European Integration and Supranational Governance*. Oxford: Oxford University Press.

Sandholtz, W. and Stone Sweet, A. (2012) 'Neo-functionalism and Supranational Governance' in Jones, E., Menon, A., and Weatherill, S. (eds.), *The Oxford Handbook of European Governance*. Oxford: Oxford University Press.

Saurugger, S. (2013) 'Constructivism and Public Policy Approaches in the EU: From Ideas to Power Games', *Journal of European Public Policy* 20(6): 888–906.

Schelkle, W. (2009) 'The Contentious Creation of the Regulatory State in Fiscal Surveillance', *West European Politics* 32(4): 829–846.

Schmidt, S. (2002) 'The Impact of Mutual Recognition – Inbuilt Limits and Domestic Responses to the Single Market', *Journal of European Public Policy* 9(6): 935–953.

Schmidt, V. (2002) *The Futures of European Capitalism*. Oxford: Oxford University Press.

—— (2002) *The Futures of European Capitalism*. Oxford: Oxford University Press.

—— (2006) *Democracy in Europe*. Oxford: Oxford University Press.

—— (2010) 'Taking Ideas and Discourse Seriously: Explaining Change through Discursive Institutionalism as the Fourth New Institutionalism', *European Political Science Review* 2(1): 1–25.

Schmidt, V. and Thatcher, M. (eds.) (2013) *Resilient Liberalism in Europe's Political Economy*. Cambridge: Cambridge University Press.

Schmitt, C. (2013) 'The Janus Face of Europeanisation: Explaining Cross-sectoral Differences in Public Utilities', *West European Politics* 36(3), 547–563.

Schneider, V., Fink, S. and Tenbucken, M. (2005) 'Buying Out the State', *Comparative Political Studies* 38(6): 704–727.

Selznick, P. (1985) 'Focusing Organizational Research on Regulation' in R. Noll (ed.), *Regulatory Policy and the Social Sciences*. Berkeley: University of California Press.

Smith, M. (2010) 'Single Market, Global Competition: Regulating the European Market in a Global Economy', *Journal of European Public Policy* 17(7): 936–953.

Stone Sweet A. and Caporaso J. A. (1998) 'From Free Trade to Supranational Polity: The European Court and Integration' in W. Sandholtz and A. Stone Sweet (eds.), *European Integration and Supranational Governance*. Oxford: Oxford University Press.

Stone Sweet, A. and Brunell, T. (2012) 'The European Court of Just, State Noncompliance, and the Politics of Override', *American Political Science Review* 106(1): 204.

Stone Sweet, A., Sandholtz, W. and Fligstein, N. (eds.) (2001) *The Institutionalization of Europe*. Oxford: Oxford University Press.

Thatcher, M. (2001) 'The Commission and National Governments as Partners: EC Regulatory Expansion in Telecommunications 1979–2000', *Journal of European Public Policy* 8(4): 558–584.

—— (2007) *Internationalisation and Economic Institutions: Comparing European Experiences*. Oxford: Oxford University Press.

—— (2011) 'The Creation of European Regulatory Agencies and its Limits: A Comparative Analysis of European delegation', *Journal of European Public Policy* 18(6): 790–809.

——— (2013) 'Supranational Neo-liberalization: The EU's Regulatory Model of Economic Markets' in Schmidt, VA and Thatcher, M (eds.), *Resilient Liberalism in Europe's Political Economy*. Cambridge: Cambridge University Press.

Vos, E. (1997) The Rise of Committees, *European Law Journal* 3,3: 210–29.

Weiler, J. (1991) 'The Transformation of Europe', *Yale Law Journal* 100: 2403–2483.

Wilks, S. (2005) 'Agency Escape: Decentralisation or Dominance of the European Commission in the Modernisation of Competition Policy?', *Governance*, Summer 2005.

Wonka, A. and Rittberger, R. (2010), 'Credibility, Complexity and Uncertainty: Explaining the Institutional Independence of 29 EU Agencies', *West European Politics* 33(4): 730–752.

Chapter 14

European macroeconomic governance

ERIK JONES AND GREGORY W. FULLER

Macroeconomic governance was the last economic policy area to develop within the process of European integration; it remains a work in progress. Moreover, the division of labor between European Union (EU) institutions and across the different levels of European governance is often difficult to pin down. Sometimes it is straightforward; other times, it is not.

The purpose of this chapter is to provide an overview of what European macroeconomic governance looks like at present. The picture it offers is like a snapshot of a moving object. It remains blurred at the edges of what is European, what is macroeconomic, and what is governance. It also blends across the many actors, instruments, targets, and procedures involved.

The direction of motion is clear even if the contours are not sharply delineated. The EU is heading for stronger forms of cross-country coordination, with stricter controls on the room for maneuver within the member states. The monetary union is expanding. The mechanisms for fiscal policy coordination are tightening. The scope of multilateral surveillance is broadening. And the respective roles of the European Central Bank and the European Commission are becoming more prominent.

This movement toward greater coordination and tighter constraints is not necessarily positive. Coordination can be misdirected, constraints can be too rigid, and shared institutions can be overexposed. The signs of stress are apparent in the volatility of financial markets, the divergence in growth rates, the rise of unemployment, and the loss of public confidence in European institutions.

The challenge is to diagnose the problem and not just to recognize the symptoms. Such diagnosis is a source of disagreement both within and across EU member states. You can see this disagreement in popular debates about austerity and competitiveness. You can also find it in more technical arguments about financial imbalances, prudential oversight, collateral rules, and monetary financing.

Such disagreement explains why European macroeconomic governance has become so important. Member state governments face a choice between working together and acting alone. That choice hinges on what policymakers think went wrong within the original European macroeconomic policy framework, how they believe they should respond using the instruments at their disposal, and how well they think different national policies will fit together at the European level.

This chapter has four sections. The first introduces the broad framework for macroeconomic governance within the EU as described in the 'Treaty on the European Union' and 'Treaty on the Functioning of the European Union'. The second explains how that framework emerged out of challenges experienced in the 1990s and early 2000s. The third surveys European efforts to reforge the macroeconomic governance framework in order to provide an adequate response to the economic and financial crisis. The fourth section presents a preliminary assessment of the progress that has been made.

The European macroeconomic policy framework

Macroeconomics deals with aggregates or collectives and not individuals. When macroeconomists talk about inflation, exchange rates, output growth, or unemployment, they are assuming the existence of a group. Inflation measures the rate of change in an array of prices across a range of different actors. Exchange rates imply the existence of different currency areas. Output is aggregate production over a given time; growth is how much that output changes from one period to the next. Unemployment measures the cohort without work, usually as a ratio of the population that is eligible, holding, or looking for employment.

This notion of aggregation or collective is central to macroeconomics. It is also important to European integration and to Europe, particularly when 'Europe' is supposed to do something in policy terms. Depending upon the context, the European Union is either a group of member states or a unitary actor in its own right. It can also be both things at once – a set of member states that remain distinctive and yet still work in coordination.

This variation in how 'Europe' behaves as a policy actor is obviously political. It is also policy relevant insofar as it affects the design and targeting of instruments. Some instruments, like the common monetary policy within the single currency, operate across many countries at once. Other instruments, like fiscal policy, work interdependently from one country to the next. Still other instruments, like market structural reforms, have more localized implications.

The challenge is to use these instruments harmoniously toward the achievement of a coherent and consistent set of goals. The danger is that they will work at cross-purposes such that success in one policy area, member state, or locality, comes at the expense of another. Article 3 of the Treaty on European Union sets out the macroeconomic objectives of the European Union. The most important of these are 'balanced economic growth', 'price stability', and 'full employment'. The same article also stresses the goal of a 'competitive social market economy', 'social progress', and 'protection and improvement of the quality of the environment'. These are not strictly macroeconomic objectives, but they are influenced by macroeconomic performance. Efforts to pursue these broader objectives have an impact on macroeconomic outcomes as well.

The Treaty on the Functioning of the European Union sets out the mechanisms for achieving these goals – both macroeconomic and related. It starts with the allocation of competences. Article 2 establishes the basic principles for assigning competences to different levels of government. It also highlights economic policy as a special case: 'The Member States shall coordinate their economic and employment policies within arrangements to be determined by this Treaty, which the Union shall have competence to provide'. Article 3 makes it clear that monetary policy is a European competence for those member states that have adopted the euro as a common currency. Article 4 lists market-structural matters such as those related to the internal market, social policy, regional policy, and environmental policy as shared competences. Article 5 returns to the role of Europe in coordinating the separate economic policies of the member states by setting the broad guidelines for policy action across different areas and in different countries.

The specific provisions for implementing the various aspects of the macroeconomic policy framework come much later in the document. Economic and monetary policy fall under Title VIII of the Treaty (meaning Articles 119–144); Employment falls under Title IX (Articles 145–150). As anticipated, the emphasis is on European coordination of national action; monetary policy for those countries within the euro is the exception.

Multilateral surveillance

The basic framework for policy coordination rests on the commitment that the 'Member States shall conduct their economic policies with a view to contributing to the achievements of the objectives of the Union' (Article 120) and 'as a matter of common concern' (Article 121, para. 1). This commitment applies to all member states without exception. In practice, however, the implications differ from one country to the next depending upon a wide range of variables relating to, inter alia, their relative size, geographic location, industrial structure, welfare state design, and position in the marketplace. The implications also differ across policy areas – meaning not just fiscal policy or, for those outside the single currency, monetary and exchange rate policy, but also related issues such as employment promotion, social protection, business regulation, and the environment.

This is where the broad guidelines become important. The European Commission makes specific recommendations to the Council of the European Union about what each member state should do across many policy areas in order to improve macroeconomic performance. The Council then shepherds these recommendations through the European Council and the European Parliament until there is agreement about what is supposed to happen in the near future both across countries and at the European level. Following that, the member states provide regular reports on what they have done and with what effect, and the European Commission checks what the member states report against the legislative record and the economic data. If there is a discrepancy, the European Commission can issue a warning to the member state in question and a report back to the Council. In turn, the Council can recommend remedial action to the member state, which triggers another round of reporting and auditing.

The treaty offers very little in the form of sanctions to ensure compliance within this context. If a member state government fails to do something set out in the broad guidelines, the worst punishment that the Council can threaten is 'to make its recommendations public' (Article 121, para. 4). Nevertheless, by placing too much emphasis on the sanctions, it is easy to miss the broader point. Most member state governments do not want to implement policies that work at cross purposes with what they are doing in other areas or with what is being done in other countries. That not only wastes time but also prevents them from achieving their policy objectives. Governments do not want to antagonize their neighbors either, by inadvertently pushing problems from one country to the next. And they do not want to absorb the problems – such as unemployment – that other member states are hoping to escape. Hence, member state governments are eager to know that the policy they implement has the best possible prospects of achieving its objectives without imposing costs that other countries will find unacceptable. The multilateral surveillance procedures help Member State governments manage their interdependence.

Fiscal policy

The coordination of fiscal policy is more challenging both because most trade-offs are unavoidable and because the unintended consequences of excess – such as inflation or insolvency – are hard to contain within national boundaries. By implication, every member state government wants as much freedom as possible in determining its own finances and as much control as possible over everyone else. These two positions are hard to reconcile equitably across the European Union as a whole and so the Treaty on the Functioning of the European Union has to strike a balance between the amounts of freedom national governments are willing to surrender in order to attain some measure of control over other member states.

The usual pattern of multilateral surveillance is only one part of a three-part process for fiscal policy coordination. The other two parts are the restrictions on public financing and the prohibition against excessive deficits. The Treaty on the Functioning of the European Union prefaces these other aspects with an escape clause (Article 122) saying that the usual rules need not apply when a country faces 'severe difficulties' in a specific sector of the economy, like energy, or when suffering from 'natural disasters or exceptional circumstances beyond its control'. The goal is to ensure that Member States formally retain discretion that they are likely to exercise in extremis and which the EU would be foolish to deny.

The no bailout provisions make it clear that the member states must rely on their own resources to finance government outlays. Member state governments, including their regional and local subsidiaries, may not borrow from one another or from their national central banks (Article 123) and they may not have preferential access to financial institutions (Article 124). Similarly, the institutions of the European Union may not purchase debt directly from national, regional or local governments (Article 125). There are a few exceptions to these provisions. Member state governments can underwrite project financing jointly with each other and with European institutions. Governments can have privileged relationships with primary dealer banks that specialize in the placement of newly issued sovereign debt. And national central banks and the European Central Bank can purchase sovereign debt in secondary markets as necessary for the conduct of monetary policy. The point is simply that these types of relationships cannot be used as an illicit source of government finance.

The reason is that member state governments 'shall avoid excessive deficits' (Article 126, para. 1). The notion of excess here goes beyond the positive commitment to set economic policy in the common interest insofar as it underscores the capacity of member state governments to use fiscal policy to do harm – to themselves and to the European Union as a whole – even if unintentionally. The Treaty includes a pair of reference values established during the Maastricht Treaty negotiations in the early 1990s (set out in a separate protocol). It also provides an elaborate procedure for monitoring member state performance, alerting and reporting when there is a problem, recommending corrective action to member state governments, and checking whether the member states respond accordingly. In contrast to the more general process of multilateral surveillance, the Council may also decide (by qualified majority vote) that the failure of a government to comply with its recommendations is sufficiently problematic to warrant a corrective sanction: it can make the recommendations public; it can cut off access to lending from the European Investment Bank; it can instruct the member state to make a non-interest-bearing deposit until the excessive deficit is correct; and it can 'impose fines of an appropriate size' (Article 126, para. 11).

The point to note about this more restrictive aspect of fiscal policy coordination is that it has very little to do with the size of the public sector in the economy. The treaty does not restrict member state governments from having large social welfare benefits, and it does not enjoin them to do so either. Instead, it focuses more narrowly on the balance between revenues and expenditures. So long as member state governments live within their means, they are free to work with very few resources or to play a more prominent role in the economy. There may be some argument about the appropriate size of the public sector in promoting the more general goals of Europe within the context of multilateral surveillance. However, that is not the focus for fiscal policy coordination, which is more narrowly defined.

Monetary policy

The scope of monetary policy coordination is more restrictive than it is for fiscal policy. For Member States that have adopted the euro as a common currency, the European System of Central Banks (ESCB) is the sole responsible actor. Its 'primary objective' is 'to maintain price stability' (Article 127, para. 1). Without prejudice to that objective, 'the ESCB shall support the general economic policies of the Union'. In this way, monetary policy supplements the broad guidelines at the heart of multilateral surveillance. This is not to imply, however, that other actors have an influence on how the common monetary policy is conducted. On the contrary, the ESCB is prohibited from seeking instruction even as both other European institutions and the Member State governments are prohibited from exercising influence (Article 130). Moreover, this political independence covers not only the ESCB as a collective actor but also the separate national central banks (Article 131).

The central institution of the ESCB is the European Central Bank (ECB), which comprises a Governing Council for decision-making and an Executive Board for implementation in cooperation with the national central banks. The balance of power is decentralized and leans toward the member states. National central bank representatives make up the overwhelming majority of ECB Governing Council members; national central banks provide the main engine for the open market operations necessary to change policy rates; and national central banks maintain working balances of foreign exchange reserves and other trading assets many times larger than the asset portfolio of the ECB. Finally, the ESCB also involves those countries that have not adopted the euro as a common currency – both those waiting to join, and those that have negotiated an opt-out such as the United Kingdom or Denmark.

This organizational decentralization is at odds with the centralized nature of the ESCB's mandate and targets. According to both the Treaty on the Functioning of the European Union and the statutes that govern the ESCB and the ECB, only European monetary authorities have the right to interpret and operationalize their mandate (Article 127, para. 2). They decide what constitutes price stability, how it is measured and anticipated, and what to do if it appears to be in jeopardy. Initially, the ECB worked from two different frames of reference. It looked at medium-term expectations for inflation performance and it compared that to the actual growth in broad money aggregates (also known as M3). The reference values it used were for the monetary union as a whole and not for individual participating member states. The goal was to keep expected price inflation below 2 per cent on an annualized basis; in monetary terms, this meant that M3 should grow at around 4.5 per cent per annum. Over time, however, the emphasis in policy targeting shifted more toward expected inflation, which the Governing Council aimed to keep below but close to 2 per cent, and away from monetary targeting. The Governing Council retained the reference value for M3 growth, but it also tolerated wide deviations.

The situation outside the euro area is slightly different. With the exception of the United Kingdom and Denmark, all EU Member States have an obligation to prepare for eventual entry into the single currency. Hence, these countries also have an obligation to work toward monetary convergence, which is still measured using the monetary reference values embedded in the 1992 Maastricht Treaty: an inflation rate within 1.5 percentage points of the three best performers and a long-term nominal interest rate within 2 percentage points of the three best performers in terms of price inflation. The EU has no sanction for failure to achieve monetary convergence or even for failure to try. For example, Sweden is obliged to prepare for membership and yet has chosen not to make the effort. Nevertheless, the requirement to achieve monetary convergence plays a role in the pattern of multilateral surveillance and (obviously) also in terms of eventual qualification for adoption of the euro (Article 140).

The most curious element in the pattern of monetary convergence for those countries that have not adopted the euro as a single currency is that the point of reference is not the euro area as an aggregate. It is not even the three best countries in terms of inflation performance that have adopted the euro. Instead, it is the three best inflation performers across the European Union, with the implication that countries seeking to join the single currency could do better than most countries that have already adopted the euro and yet still not qualify.

Exchange rate policy

The third main macroeconomic instrument is exchange rate policy. Here the rules are ambiguous. Those countries that have not adopted the euro as a common currency are required to treat 'exchange rate policy as a matter of common interest' (Article 142). In practice, this means they should participate in a fixed but adjustable exchange rate mechanism modeled on the old European Monetary System but with the euro at its center. Such systems are asymmetric in practice and place the burden of adjustment onto the country with the weaker currency. Therefore, the Treaty on the Functioning of the European Union includes provisions to extend financial support to countries that experience a balance of payments crisis (Article 143). In the event that the European Union is unable to provide assistance, the treaty also offers member state governments the possibility to introduce temporary protectionist measures in order to stabilize the balance of payments and so also the value of their currency relative to the euro.

The exchange rate policy of the single currency is more amorphous. Like monetary policy, the exchange policy of the euro area should have a primary objective to maintain price stability. Without prejudice to that objective, the exchange rate policy can also 'support the general economic policies in the Union' (Article 119, para. 2). This much is straightforward. The complications arise in terms of institutions and structures. An exchange rate policy can take one of three forms: it can lack formal targets, it can establish formal targets by internal commitment, and it can set formal targets by agreement with third parties, bilaterally with other countries, or multilaterally through international organizations.

The default exchange rate policy operates without formal targets. In this case, the external value of the euro is the result of market forces as influenced by the monetary policy of the ESCB. Exchange rates matter only insofar as they have an impact on domestic price stability that needs to be offset through other measures. The Governing Council of the ECB could choose to pursue a more active strategy, but that choice does not constrain its independence. Under this default option, the Governing Council determines whether it makes sense to pay attention to exchange rates, it assesses how much the influence of exchange rates on domestic prices needs to be accommodated when setting monetary policy instruments, and it decides whether it is worth trying to influence the external value of the euro.

A more active exchange rate policy pays more explicit attention to the external value of the euro. This would happen if the Council of the European Union decided to set 'general orientations for exchange rate policy in relation to [other] currencies' (Article 219, para. 2). In this case, the Governing Council has to focus on more or less formal targets for the value of the euro in terms of specific reference currencies, setting monetary instruments and engaging in foreign exchange interventions in order to harness the exchange rate to the promotion of price stability. Such guidelines would necessarily constrain the independence of the ESCB and so can only be adopted on the recommendation of the ECB or on the recommendation of the European Commission in consultation with the ECB.

The other possibility for exchange rate policy binds the European Central Bank to regulate the external value of the euro through 'formal agreements on an exchange rate system for the euro in relation to the currencies of third States' (Article 219, para. 1). Here, too, the Treaty makes this possible only if the ECB recommends such action or if the European Commission recommends it after consultation with the ECB. The Treaty also requires that the Council of the European Union act unanimously, that it consult the European Parliament, and that it associate the European Commission fully in any resulting negotiations. The reason for establishing such a high decision-making threshold is to ensure again that the exchange rate policy does not come into conflict with the primary objective to maintain price stability.

This danger of conflict explains why the default option of having no targets for the external value of the euro is easier to implement than any general guidelines or formal commitments. The instruments used for monetary policy are the same as those used for exchange rate policy. However, domestic price inflation does not always move together with the external value of the currency in a way that would require the same policy response. Sometimes a higher rate of domestic inflation coincides with a fall in the value of euro; sometimes it happens to coincides with a rise. According to the primary objective set out in the European treaties, monetary policy instruments should move in the same direction in both cases in order to respond to the threat of inflation. The impact of those policies changes in terms of exchange rates would be very different. Neither broad guidelines nor formal commitments to third countries can make that tension go away.

Market-structural reform

The role of macroeconomic policy instruments is to balance growth, lower unemployment, and maintain price stability. However, the control that governments have over these variables is imperfect and the interaction between government policies across countries or from one policy domain to the next creates inefficiencies and other unintended consequences. The pattern of multilateral surveillance to ensure compliance with broad policy guidelines can alleviate some of this problem by improving the flow of information about what policies are necessary for individual governments and about how those policies are likely to interact. Fiscal policy coordination can ensure that governments do not actively undermine market conditions for one another or inadvertently shift responsibilities from one country to the next. Monetary policy can help to maintain stable prices. And exchange rate policy can add very little beyond that objective. Therefore, the role of market-structural reform is to fill the gaps in macroeconomic performance.

This role is easiest to see with respect to employment. Governments have three ways of dealing with unemployment. One is that they can race to cut costs and benefits in order to make it easier for domestic firms to steal away markets from their competitors. This strategy increases employment in domestic industry, but at the cost of a reduction in social welfare and by effectively pushing unemployment elsewhere. For the European Union as a whole, this is a negative sum game insofar as everyone is worse off as an aggregate (even if some countries are relatively better). Therefore the Employment Title of the Treaty on the Functioning of the European Union emphasizes the importance of 'developing a coordinated strategy' and 'promoting employment as a matter of common concern' (Articles 145 and 146).

A second way of addressing unemployment is to apply some kind of macroeconomic stimulus by increasing net fiscal spending, lowering interest rates, or depreciating or devaluing the currency. Such stimuli work by driving up domestic demand or by encouraging foreign demand for domestic exports. However, they do so only by increasing the burden of public indebtedness, encouraging the growth of liquidity, and raising the relative price of imports. In turn, such actions threaten to undermine domestic price stability while at the same time creating longer-term problems associated with government insolvency and market expectations. The European Treaties discourage such actions through the prohibition on excessive deficits, the priority given to price stability, and the implicit subordination of exchange rate policy to monetary policy. Macroeconomic stimulus remains available as a policy remedy provided that it is not excessive and it does not jeopardize price stability. Nevertheless, the Treaties make it clear that such stimulus operates within strict limits.

The third way for governments to tackle unemployment is to make sure that workers who lose jobs in declining sectors of the economy have an easy time finding a new source of employment even without some form of macroeconomic stimulus. This is where the Employment Title places emphasis – on 'promoting a skilled, trained and adaptable workforce and labor markets responsive to economic change' (Article 145). The mechanisms it uses are very similar to the general multilateral surveillance. The difference is that they focus on employment. They also stress the importance of 'developing exchanges of information and best practices' (Article 149). The goal is not to compel member states to follow the same formulas; rather, it is to empower them to seek solutions that are appropriate to their concerns.

The success of European efforts to manage unemployment through market structural reforms depends upon the willingness of member state governments to re-examine a host of other related institutions. The treaties do not specify how the member states will address this broader range of issues; instead, that process developed out of the pattern of multilateral surveillance and alongside the European employment strategy. Originally, this more comprehensive approach to market structural reform included active labor market policies, product market reforms, and macroeconomic dialog with stakeholders in labor and industry. This broader framework generalized the sharing of information and best practice as part of an open method of coordination. Such coordination relied more on peer review than enforcement. The incentives for Member State compliance derived from the 'naming, shaming, and faming' of individual performance relative to specific targets and general benchmarks.

Experience before the crisis

The macroeconomic framework set out in the European treaties resulted from a long and at times unhappy evolution (Jones 2006). Nevertheless, many of the original institutions proposed in the 1992 Maastricht Treaty are still intact. So are the main additions included in the 1997 Amsterdam Treaty. Indeed, what is surprising about the most recent Treaties is how little has changed over the years. The explanation is not that the European macroeconomic policy framework proved to be so effective. Rather, it is that the member states could not agree on any alternative. For example, efforts to open the macroeconomic framework for renegotiation during the 2002–2003 European Convention failed.

The only changes that were made during the first decade of the single currency were at the margins of the process of macroeconomic policy coordination and usually outside the language of the treaties. The changes introduced by the ECB in its interpretation of price stability and to the overarching framework for the conduct of monetary policy are one example. The 2005 revisions to the legislative procedures underpinning the process of fiscal policy coordination is another. The tighter focus on jobs and growth that the European Commission tried to introduce into the open method of coordination is a third.

The details of these changes are both too subtle and too numerous to warrant extended exposition. Suffice it to say that the revisions offered only modest improvements on the original designs. The reasons why they came about are more significant because they reveal the underlying tensions in the macroeconomic policy framework. A thumbnail of three of these reasons shows the extent to which the European macroeconomic framework has been contested.

The limits of money

The first major conflict started even before the single currency came into being. The October 1998 German parliamentary elections resulted in a victory for the center-left and an unprecedented national coalition of social democrats and greens. The new Social-Democratic German finance minister, Oskar Lafontaine, wasted little time raising concerns about the high rate of unemployment and the ineffectiveness of European macroeconomic policy coordination to forge a response. He called explicitly on the newly empowered European Central Bank to target its monetary policy instruments to stimulate growth. The inaugural president of the ECB, Wim Duisenberg, responded that he could not bow to political pressure. The primary objective of the ECB, Duisenberg insisted, is to maintain price stability. Worse, Duisenberg intimated that Lafontaine's actions were having the unintended effect of preventing the ECB from lowering its policy rates because even the appearance of doing so under pressure might damage the ECB's credibility in the markets. Lafontaine resigned in March 1999 and the ECB's Governing Council voted to lower its interest rates a month later.

Unemployment improved both in Germany and elsewhere from 1999 to 2001, driven mainly by the knock-on effects of the dot-com bubble in the United States. Meanwhile, European policymakers accepted that they could not browbeat the ECB into targeting its monetary policy instruments to promote growth and ECB officials honed the argument that their unique contribution to the macroeconomic framework is to maintain price stability and anchor expectations about future inflation. This did not end the conflict between policy instruments, however, because the exchange rate between the euro and the dollar depreciated both unexpectedly and dramatically. The euro launched at a value of US$1.17 in January 1999 and fell soon thereafter. The euro reached parity with the dollar by early 2000, having lost 16 per cent of its initial value, and then dropped another 13 per cent by the following September. ECB President Duisenberg struggled to find an appropriate response. He tried intervening in the market with only limited success. Pressure mounted that he should take more decisive action. Ultimately, however, Duisenberg had to admit that such action was beyond his power.

The lesson that emerged from this combined experience was that the ECB would not take action to stimulate economic performance and it could not take action to influence the external value of the euro. More important, European policymakers recognized that the ECB could not maintain its political independence if it faced a trade-off in its policy objectives – such as inflation versus unemployment – and that ECB presidents would be wise to avoid talking about the external value of the euro altogether. Monetary policy-making is a limited endeavor. It can contribute to the broader European macroeconomic policy framework, but it should not be overburdened.

Fiscal intransigence

The experience with fiscal policy was similarly disappointing. Although unemployment fell during the first two years of the single currency, it leapt up again during the recession that started when the dot-com bubble burst in the United States in 2001. At the same time, tax revenues declined with the slowing down of economic activity and expenditures rose with the increase in welfare payouts for jobless workers and other related benefits. The effect on fiscal deficits was to increase them automatically – which is what is supposed to happen in times of recession. The problem was that these increases were excessive according to the standards set out in the European treaties and so the question was what the member states would do to correct the situation.

The answer reveals a lot about the relative restrictiveness of the multilateral surveillance and excessive deficits procedures. The multilateral surveillance procedure supports the implementation of the European Union's broad economic policy guidelines and culminates in the case of non-compliance with the publication of the policy recommendations made by the European institutions that the member state government chose not to follow. For example, in April 2000 the Irish government agreed to increase the size of its government surplus – meaning the excess in tax receipts over government expenditures – in order to slow the country's overheating economy. The Council of Economics and Finance Ministers (Ecofin Council) argued that this action would be in the broader public interest. By December 2000, however, the Irish government no longer agreed. Instead of increasing its surplus, it decided to lower it slightly during the run-up to elections the following spring. The Ecofin Council responded the following February (2001) by issuing a reprimand that the Irish government very publicly ignored. As it turned out, the bursting of the dot-com bubble was enough to slow the Irish economy without further tax rises and so the Ecofin Council quietly let the matter drop.

By February 2002, however, the focus was on Germany not Ireland and the context was the excessive deficits procedure and not multilateral surveillance. German government finances had veered sharply into the red, moving from a surplus in 2000 to a deficit just above the European threshold value in 2001. Nevertheless, the Ecofin Council decided not to take action. It accepted reassurances from the German government that it would correct the problem instead. During the course of 2002, however, the German fiscal situation got worse rather than better. The Ecofin Council found itself with no choice but to initiate the procedures for monitoring German public finances more closely and to make appropriate recommendations for policy revision. When the German government failed to comply with these instructions, the Ecofin Council met in November 2003 to consider the possibility of sanctions. Other large countries like France and Italy had similar difficulties, both actual and impending. What these large countries decided together with Germany was to hold the entire excessive deficits procedure in abeyance – accepting the need to take policy action but refusing to make legally binding commitments to European institutions.

This move to step outside the treaty-based procedures was unlawful, at least according to the decision rendered by the European Court of Justice the following summer. Nevertheless, it accurately reflected the unwillingness of member state governments to accept what they regard as unreasonable constraints on their macroeconomic room for maneuver. It also reflected the inability of the Ecofin Council to generate a qualified majority willing to impose sanctions on a large Member State. A small country like Ireland could be reprimanded; a large country like Germany received different treatment.

Market-structural inertia

The open method of coordination was no more successful at generating decisive action than the excessive deficits procedure. The reason for the failure, however, was different. Where member state governments only reluctantly accepted constraints on fiscal policy, they enthusiastically embraced the opportunity to share information and best practice. They also lauded the strategic objective of reshaping the EU into the world's most competitive and dynamic knowledge-based economy by the end of the decade. What they lacked was a clear sense of priority. They also lacked the willingness to take on entrenched vested interests.

This criticism of market structural reform efforts emerged out of the mid-term review of the Lisbon strategy that brought together diverse market processes within the open method of coordination. That review took place in two stages. First, former Dutch prime minister Wim Kok (2004) issued a reflection group report based on deliberations among senior European politicians. Then the European Commission drafted a formal review based on the Kok Report findings. The message coming out of this two-stage review process was that the combination of market structural reform efforts was insufficient to fill the gaps in the macroeconomic policy framework. Far from transforming Europe into the world's most competitive economy, the Lisbon strategy inadvertently squandered the attention of European policymakers and so placed both European competitiveness and the European social model in jeopardy. To be successful, market-structural reform efforts would need to focus more narrowly on their contribution to macroeconomic performance; specifically, they would need to promote growth and employment.

The difficulty with focusing the open method of coordination more narrowly, however, is that it requires the member states to take benefits away from entrenched vested interests. To give an example, the center-left Italy government led by former European Commission president Romano Prodi that came into office in April 2006 tried to take on licensed and professional services (like taxi drivers, lawyers, and notary publics). The goal was to increase competition and lower costs in order to stimulate the moribund Italian economy. The results were unimpressive. The Prodi government managed to remove some of the privileges of the professional classes (such as lawyers), but it could not loosen the grip of licensed professional services (such as taxi drivers). Worse, the Prodi government fell prematurely and the subsequent center-right government under Silvio Berlusconi reversed many of the gains it had made.

Of course, Italy is an outlier, and much of the writing on the Italian case is exaggerated. European governments are capable of significant reform efforts. Nevertheless, they usually involve a slow and painstaking process with long lag times between the institutional changes and the macroeconomic benefits. Here it is useful to think of the German case. The center-left government that came to power in 1998 moved strongly to the center after Lafontaine resigned as finance minister. It also embarked on a significant multistage reform of German labor markets. This reform was both painful and unpopular. Moreover, it took three to five years to yield significant benefits in terms of lower unemployment and higher growth. That time lag is as long as a parliamentary mandate. The German social democratic party lost two million voters between 2002 and 2005; it lost another six million between 2005 and 2009. Now that the benefits of the labor market reforms it introduced are widely recognized, moreover, the social democratic party receives little credit for its efforts. It is hardly surprising, therefore, that politicians are so reluctant to engage in aggressive market structural reform. As long-term Luxembourg prime minister Jean-Claude Juncker once commented: 'we all know what to do; we just don't know how to get re-elected after we've done it'.

Absent alternatives

The European macroeconomic framework embedded in the 2009 Lisbon Treaty was far from ideal. Critics complained that it targeted monetary policy too narrowly, it ignored exchange rates entirely, it constrained fiscal policy excessively, and it placed too much emphasis on market structural reforms that were too slow to materialize. European macroeconomic performance was overly sluggish as a consequence, particularly when compared to the more dynamic economy in the United States and even more obviously when compared with the dramatic rise of China. Prominent economists wrote popular books excoriating the European model for economic governance (Alesina and Giavazzi 2008). Prominent political scientists wrote similar books questioning whether Europe's economic malaise was undermining popular support for the European project (Hix 2008).

European politicians acknowledged this criticism and yet could offer no comprehensive alternative. They could not see how to make monetary policy more flexible without jeopardizing the political independence of the ECB. They could not target the external value of the euro more effectively without sacrificing the goal of domestic price stability. They could not loosen the constraints on fiscal policy without inviting moral hazard and they could not tighten the constraints without inviting further defection. Worse, they could not admit that the same fiscal rules might have different implications for larger and smaller member states. Finally, they could not come up with a formula to encourage member state governments to reform their market structural institutions at a faster pace.

Crisis and innovation

The onset of the European economic and financial crisis made it impossible for Europe's policymakers to remain complacent. The impact was not immediate. The first signs of trouble emerged in August 2007 when a major French bank had to close one of its investment funds due to the losses it incurred in the United States. The tension soon spread to the United Kingdom, where some of the larger regional mortgage banks relied excessively on access to interbank lending in order to finance their assets. The Northern Rock was the first of these banks to go under; Bradford & Bingley was not far behind. Then the losses began to accumulate in some of the larger Belgian and Dutch banks. Specialized mortgage lenders and large regional banks in Germany were also hurt. Nevertheless, the general European attitude was undaunted. The crisis was American; Europe's economies may be sluggish, but they were not as reckless as those across the Atlantic.

This position began to falter soon after the failure of the U.S. investment giant Lehman Brothers in September 2008. Some of the smaller, peripheral countries of Europe were the first to suffer – including Iceland, Ireland, Latvia, Hungary, and Greece. The smallest of these were obvious victims of financial mismanagement. Ireland and Greece were different. These countries had financial problems, but the implications were macroeconomic, and the potential for contagion to other parts of Europe could not so easily be contained. The question was whether Europe's macroeconomic framework was sufficiently resilient to meet the challenge. The answer was quick in coming.

In October 2008, the Irish government made the unprecedented decision to underwrite the liabilities of the country's entire banking system. In doing so, it instantly reversed more than a decade of fiscal consolidation. The ratio of Ireland's debt to gross domestic product was just 25 per cent in 2007; it was 44 per cent by the end of 2008 and 65 per cent in 2009. The European Commission estimates that it rose to just more than 122 per cent in 2013 and expects it to begin to decline gradually thereafter. Also in October 2008, the Greek center-right government restated its fiscal accounts, increasing the size of its reported deficit marginally. The market response was violent. The spread of

Greek long-term interest rates over those in Germany doubled in just a few days and continued to widen gradually through the end of the year. When the Standard & Poor's ratings agency downgraded Greece in January 2009, this market pressure increased. It only abated in February, once the Social Democratic German finance minister Peer Steinbrueck made it clear that no government in the euro area would be allowed to become insolvent. Steinbrueck's assistant clarified later that this commitment held no matter what the no bailout clauses of the European Treaties might say (Benoit and Barber 2009).

Steinbrueck's commitment was a stop-gap measure, later reversed when his party lost power in the 2009 parliamentary elections. It was not, however, the only attempt to modify the European macroeconomic policy framework to make it more resilient. On the contrary, European policymakers developed a host of new strategies – and resurrected some old ones – for governing the euro area. The general shift in approach was comprised of three elements: first, changes to the formal governance framework such as the so-called fiscal compact and the 'six-pack' and 'two-pack' reforms; second, institutional innovations such as the European Stability Mechanism (ESM); and, third, the increasing reliance on the ECB as the problem-solver when formal rules and institutions failed. A fourth potential response to the crisis – the creation of common debt instrument (or 'eurobond') to circulate across the euro area – remains controversial.

Formal rule changes

Three alterations to the European macroeconomic governance framework are of particular importance. The first is the so-called six-pack of new rules which aim to reestablish the authority of the procedures for governing excessive deficits, widen macroeconomic governance beyond the realm of national fiscal policy, and bring member state budgets under closer surveillance by the European Council and Commission. The second is the Treaty on Stability, Coordination and Governance (TSCG), more colloquially known as the 'fiscal compact'. The third is the two-pack of regulations adopted in May 2013 and intended to strengthen EU control over the budgetary decisions made by the member states.

Many of the six-pack provisions – embodied in five pieces of legislation and one EU directive which entered into force on 13 December 2010 – are intended to repair the damage done by the French and German defections from the procedures for fiscal policy coordination in November 2003. The new rules add detail to the chronology of the excessive deficit procedure and make moving from one step of the process to the next more automatic: states in violation of the rules are first privately warned by the European Commission and given six months to present a plan for annual 0.5 per cent reductions to their deficits. If they do not present an acceptable plan, their breach is made public and they are given an additional two months to respond. If an acceptable plan is still not forthcoming, the European Council must decide within 16 months whether it wishes to pursue sanctions (European Council 2011b).

If the European Council does seek sanctions, the European Commission is then tasked with proposing an appropriate punishment. These can include compulsory deposits of up to 0.2 percent of GDP, to be withheld in either interest-bearing or non-interest-bearing accounts until the situation is resolved. Outright fines of the same amount are also permitted in particularly egregious cases, or when member states have been found to have manipulated their economic statistics (European Council 2011a). The European Council, on receiving the Commission's recommended punishment, has 10 days in which it can overrule the punishment by qualified majority vote before the sanction goes into effect (European Council and European Parliament 2011d).

This revised set of procedures for fiscal policy coordination differs somewhat from the original procedures used to restrain excessive deficits. Specifically, the new rules make it more difficult for the European Council to stop the process once it has recommended pursuing sanctions. Once begun, the excessive deficit procedure moves ahead unless there is a vote to block it – though the Council still has the discretionary power to decide whether to start the process at all. In another departure from the original procedures, sovereign debt amounting to more than 60 per cent of GDP triggers the same process unless the member state in question can demonstrate that they will bring their debt–to–gross domestic product (GDP) ratio below 60 per cent within 20 years.

Two additional provisions included in the six pack – regulations 1174/2011 and 1176/2011 – extend the EU's macroeconomic oversight beyond government spending. Under the new regulations, a 'scoreboard' tracks various economic indicators for each member state, including asset and credit markets, unemployment rates, balance of payments, exchange rates, productivity measures, and export performance. Should any state breach targeted 'alert level' thresholds for any of these variables, the European Commission has the option of triggering a process similar to the revised excessive deficit procedure, though with a smaller maximum penalty of 0.1 per cent of GDP (European Council and European Parliament 2011a, 2011b).

The final element of the six pack calls for tighter macroeconomic coordination between EU member states. It establishes an annual timetable for budgetary planning in which every state submits their medium-term budgetary objectives to the European Commission and Council. If these objectives are seen as unrealistic, the Council can issue private or public rebukes as well as use the sanctions permitted under the macroeconomic imbalances procedure to bring non-compliant states into line (European Council and European Parliament 2011c).

The six pack, which applies to the whole of the EU, is buttressed within the euro area by the fiscal compact. Signed by all EU members except the United Kingdom and Czech Republic in early 2012, the fiscal compact entered force at the start of 2013, following ratification by 12 euro-area members. While non-euro-area members are signatories to the treaty, only contracting parties using the common currency are bound by its provisions – though countries outside the euro area can volunteer to participate. Content-wise, the fiscal compact largely duplicates the provisions of the six-pack. Unlike the six-pack, however, the fiscal compact is an intergovernmental agreement calling for new rules written into domestic – preferably constitutional – law (TSCG, 2012).

Nevertheless, the fiscal compact does slightly alter the six-pack's framework for macroeconomic governance in the euro area, particularly through its balanced budget rule. The treaty calls for a maximum budget deficit of 0.5 per cent of GDP (or 1 per cent of GDP for low-debt countries), effectively requiring fiscal compact members to run near-balanced budgets in times of normal economic growth. While this may seem a significant tightening when compared to the original reference values for an excessive deficit, it is not: the target written into the fiscal compact refers to structural budget deficits – that is the budget deficit that would exist assuming the country was producing at full output. In contrast, the references values used in the excessive deficits procedure refer to the general budget deficit, which does not adjust for cyclical downturns. A country in a recession could therefore run a budget deficit greater than 0.5 per cent of GDP and not breach the provisions of the fiscal compact so long as it could argue that the deficit would be less than 0.5 percent of GDP if economic conditions were normal.

The enforcement mechanism in the fiscal compact also differs from that of the six-pack. While the European Commission continues to take the lead in recommending corrective measures for countries in breach of the budget rule, the European Court of Justice (ECJ) punishes rule breakers. Alternatively, the treaty allows contracting parties the right to circumvent the Commission altogether and bring a case directly to the ECJ if they feel that another country is in violation of the limits. The ECJ has the power to fine misbehaving governments up to 0.1 per cent of GDP, which euro-area members would pay into the European Stability Mechanism.

The EU adopted two further regulations (the two pack) to enhance the European Commission's powers to supervise member states' budgets. Originally, the Commission had hoped that the two-pack would be adopted by the end of 2012; that target was missed as the European Council and Parliament continued to negotiate the final text of the regulations. Discussions dragged into January 2013, leading Economic and Monetary Affairs commissioner Olli Rehn to appeal to both the Council and Parliament to speed the process (Rehn 2013). The two regulations were finally adopted the following May.

One of the regulations (473/2013) obliges all euro area governments to submit their annual budgets – on top of the medium-term budgetary objectives required under the six-pack – to the Commission for an assessment of their compatibility with EU rules. The other (472/2013) compels member states in 'serious difficulties with regard to their financial stability' to seek the assistance of the European Commission and the ECB in crafting crisis-response policies. Moreover, it forces them to accept outside technical assistance if they are deemed unable to carry out reforms on their own. Such 'enhanced surveillance' would only apply to states receiving EU emergency funds – currently Greece, Ireland, and Portugal. However, the Commission would also gain the power to make a statement of no confidence in states' capacities to resolve their own difficulties, giving the EU far greater leverage over policymaking in states teetering on the brink of macroeconomic collapse.

Institutional innovation

The new rules developed after 2009 were chiefly intended to avert the next crisis – new governance structures could do little to address economies already suffering. Something else was required to deal with the more acute challenges posed by macroeconomic instability in the European periphery: by the end of April 2010, it had become apparent that Greece was not going to be able to deal with its rising cost of borrowing. Nor was it likely that other troubled countries, particularly Ireland, would be able to pay the cost of borrowing from private capital markets. Euro area countries consequently agreed in May 2010 to set aside €500 billion to support troubled euro area governments cut off from financial markets. These initial funds were split between two hastily assembled financial entities: the €440 billion European Financial Stability Facility (EFSF) and the €60 billion European Financial Stability Mechanism (EFSM).

The EFSF raised funds by issuing bonds or other securities guaranteed by proportional contributions from all members of the euro area. The EFSM operated in a similar fashion, but secured its borrowing on the EU budget itself. Funds raised by both entities could then be lent to countries in financial distress. Over more than two years in operation, the EFSF and EFSM developed programs for Portugal, Ireland, and Greece (although the initial 2010 Greek bailout has remained governed by a separate one-off agreement). These loans were offered with strict conditionality – allowing the EU as creditor to exercise a great deal of leverage over domestic policymaking. This is, in effect, a harsh form of macroeconomic governance: if states cannot follow the rules and stabilize themselves, the EU effectively stages an intervention and compels change from the outside. This power, largely exercised on an ad hoc basis thus far, will be codified by the approval of the two-pack.

Despite successfully averting uncontrolled default by Greece, Ireland, and Portugal, the EFSF and EFSM were intended as temporary measures and had no basis in European treaties. Indeed, the legality of the entities was open to question. The no-bailout clause in the Treaty on the Functioning of the European Union officially barred the EU from assuming liability for member states. The thin rationale for the EFSF and EFSM rested on the premise that the EU was not assuming member states debts, but was simply providing a facility which could ensure that their debts were repaid (House of Lords Select Committee 2011). In other words, bailing out a government through an EFSF or EFSM loan did not directly generate new liabilities for euro-area members (the creation of the EFSF and EFSM had done that already).

At the December 2010 meeting of the European Council, it was agreed that the EU needed a permanent mechanism which could act when EU's normal macroeconomic governance framework failed to produce sound national economic policies. This resulted in the founding of the permanent European Stability Mechanism (ESM). It was further agreed – at German insistence – that such a facility needed to be explicitly authorized by treaty. The European Council responded by making a two-sentence amendment to Article 136 of the Treaty on the Functioning of the European Union which allowed the euro area's governments to create a stability mechanism to secure the stability of the single currency. The finance ministers of the 17 euro-area members subsequently signed the Treaty Establishing the ESM, which entered force in late September 2012.

The ESM, which began operations in late 2012, completely assumed the roles formerly played by the EFSF and EFSM as of July 2013, when the two original entities were phased out. The new organization – with a raised lending capacity of €700 billion – raises funds through the issuance of medium- and long-term debt backed by €80 billion of paid-in capital and an additional €620 billion of callable capital provided by ESM members (Treaty Establishing the ESM 2012). The permanent body is intended to prevent the sort of uncertainty which prevailed in the early days of the sovereign debt crisis, ensuring that financing will remain available even if the formal rules regime fails to prevent new bouts of macroeconomic instability.

A more powerful ECB

While the ESM is seen as the future guarantor of financial stability – and has the final word on how financially troubled governments are to adjust – it has limitations. As initially envisioned, the ESM could only lend to national governments, rendering it unable to prevent a banking crisis from metastasizing into a sovereign debt crisis. Moreover, its €700 billion size is insufficient to bail out larger euro-area economies such as Italy. As the EU's sovereign debt crisis has worn on, these limitations have repeatedly pressed the ECB into extraordinary action: The ECB has stepped up its purchases of sovereign debt and stepped between banks and national governments, hoping to keep down sovereign borrowing costs and reduce the dangerous mutual exposure between governments and their domestic financial institutions. The new activist ECB has consequently become a much larger player in European economic governance, adopting the role of lender of last resort for both banks and governments.

While the ECB is prohibited by treaty from directly buying government bonds in primary markets, it is permitted to buy them in secondary markets – although only if such transactions are necessary for ensuring financial stability or conducting interest rate policy. By acting as a buyer on the market for sovereign debt, the ECB can drive up demand for distressed sovereigns and thus push their respective yields toward the ECB's targeted interest rate. This achieves two further goals which, while desirable, are not part of the ECB's mandate: first, it reduces the exposure of national banking systems to default by their government by taking sovereign bonds out of the domestic economy and placing them on the ECB's own balance sheet. Second, the ECB's involvement as buyer of last resort depresses the panic selling of government bonds in other troubled economies, keeping their cost of borrowing down: investors are less tempted to dump their holdings of sovereign debt if they know the ECB will buy their assets in the event of a crisis.

The ECB began buying sovereign bonds in May 2010, a move ostensibly justified by the fact that ECB's low official interest rate was not being transmitted to the euro area periphery, where fears over a euro-area exit had pushed interest rates higher. The policy, known as the Securities Markets Program (SMP), aimed to bring the cost of borrowing in countries down toward the ECB's official rate. Initially limited to Greek bonds, the program was eventually extended to Ireland, Portugal, Italy, and Spain. Intermittent purchases, particularly in late-Spring 2010 and at the end of 2011, brought more than €200 billion in the government debt of the peripheral euro-area countries onto the ECB's balance sheet by the time the program shut down in September 2012.

Despite some success at bringing interest rates down, the SMP was subject to restraints – particularly on the quantity of bonds which the ECB was willing to purchase – which limited its effectiveness. The SMP was shut down in late 2012 as the ECB adopted a new program to purchase the short-term sovereign debt of distressed countries that still have access to private capital markets. The ECB dubbed these purchases Outright Monetary Transactions (OMT), because the goal is to set a floor under sovereign debt prices and so protect governments from unwarranted speculation in the markets. OMT differs from SMP in that there is no ex ante limit on the amount of debt that the ECB will buy.

The ECB justified this new program by arguing that it is essential to eliminate 'convertibility risk', or what it argued is the mistaken perception in the markets that the euro might break up into separate national currencies. ECB president Mario Draghi insisted that he would do everything within his power to prevent that from happening. In this way, he promised to prevent the disintegration of European financial markets. That objective is squarely within the mandate of the ECB. Nevertheless, by promising unlimited purchases of short-term government debt, OMT effectively turns the ECB into a lender of last resort for euro-area governments. In order to avoid the abuse of this facility by profligate governments, OMT debt purchases are only available to states which have signed up to an ESM program, making OMT assistance conditional on the same sort of strict conditions that come with ESM loans.

The announcement that the ECB would purchase unlimited amounts of short-term sovereign debt for governments in need of assistance and willing to accept conditionality immediately reduced the cost of borrowing in the peripheral countries of the euro area. In that sense it was a success. It remained controversial nonetheless. The German Bundesbank and its president Jens Wiedmann objected strenuously and argued that the ECB was moving dangerously close to directly financing irresponsible governments. ECB president Draghi, backed by the EU's political leaders, countered that such an ambitious program was necessary in order to fend off speculative attacks on the bonds of large countries such as Spain or Italy – countries whose outstanding sovereign debts could not be credibly backstopped by the €700 billion ESM (Ewing and Erlanger 2012).

The ECB's remit has also grown in the realm of banking supervision. In an attempt to streamline the patchwork assembly of national financial regulators, the EU has taken a number of steps toward the creation of a Single Supervisory Mechanism (SSM) for overseeing all 6,000 banks within the euro area. The ECB has been tasked with acting as direct supervisor for the largest of these banks – those with more than €30 billion in assets or more than 20 per cent of national GDP on their balance sheets – and with indirectly managing smaller banks through national authorities. Once established, euro-area heads of government have envisioned the SSM allowing the ECB to recapitalize distressed banks directly through the ESM. This would mean that the costs of bank bailouts would be met by the ESM rather than by the government of the banks' home country (European Council 2012). This would, for instance, allow a recapitalization of the Spanish banking system without substantially raising the debt load of the Spanish government.

Taken together, these decisions reflect a conscious choice by the ECB to act as the ultimate guardian of the euro area's macroeconomic stability: where existing rules and institutions leave gaps, the ECB has been willing to fill them. Along the way, the ECB has moved well beyond its price stability mandate. Instead, the ECB has become Europe's last bulwark against macroeconomic catastrophe: as regulator, it has gained the power to ensure that financial market instability does not cause wider economic instability; as the buyer of last resort for government securities, it can now provide time for even the largest countries to adjust to economic difficulties. The ECB's decisions have also nudged the EU toward communal responsibility for national debt commitments. ESM-financed national bank bailouts and ECB purchases of sovereign bonds both create new sources of indirect liability for the commitments of other governments – arguably in violation of the spirit of the no-bailout clause.

The eurobond debate: a next step?

For some commentators, the next step in constructing a coherent macroeconomic governance framework for the euro area requires the mutualization of at least a part of the sovereign debt of euro area countries through the creation of jointly underwritten 'eurobond'. The advantage of having such common instruments is that they can be used to create market incentives for debt reduction, they can help break the link between national governments and their banking systems, and they can reduce capital flight by creating a relatively risk-free asset which circulates throughout the euro area. Sceptics argue, however, that eurobonds constitute the ultimate breach of the no-bailout clause and would invite profligate countries to spend freely while more responsible states pick up the bill. They also argue that any future communal debt instrument – if one is to exist at all – will be predicated on the strict and universal adherence to the macroeconomic governance framework established in the six-pack, fiscal compact, and two-pack.

The case for eurobonds rests on three arguments (Delpa and Von Weiszäcker 2010; Jones, 2010). First, that by allowing only a portion of national debt to be communally guaranteed, the price differential between joint debt and national debt will create a market-based incentive for states to reduce borrowing toward the maximum amount of joint debt permitted. Second, that the creation of a pan-European debt instrument would reduce the exposure of banks to default by their home country government by offering them an alternative asset. Likewise, national governments would face a far larger – and thus cheaper – market for loanable funds. Third, the presence of a high-quality asset which circulates across borders would make it unnecessary for frightened investors to pull funds out of a troubled national economy and thus greatly reduce the threat of sudden stops and capital flow reversals. Instead of starving troubled economies of needed capital, skittish investors could simply move their money into eurobonds. In effect, the eurobond would address many of the same deficiencies in the current European macroeconomic governance framework that the ECB has been forced to deal with thus far.

The European Commission (2011) produced a green paper on the feasibility of a jointly underwritten debt instrument and the idea has powerful backers such as long-time Eurogroup president Jean-Claude Juncker and former Italian prime minister Mario Monti. Yet the opposition is stronger. German public opinion is firmly against any notion of debt mutualization. So too are the governments of Finland, the Netherlands, and Slovakia. And while detractors of the idea – most important, the German government of Chancellor Angela Merkel – concede that common debt instruments may be desirable in the long run, they maintain that a functioning fiscal union is a necessary pre-condition. Faced with such strong opposition, the eurobond idea is likely to remain at the periphery of the European macroeconomic governance debate.

Assessing the future of European macroeconomic governance

The success of recent efforts to reform European macroeconomic governance continues to be uncertain. In that sense, not all work is progress. The new formal commitments to fiscal consolidation and mutual surveillance are significant – collectively representing the most important steps to enhance European macroeconomic governance since the original adoption of the Maastricht Treaty. However, they bear the same weaknesses which undermined the original procedures for managing excessive government deficits.

The new rules effectively constitute a set of politically onerous commitments to be enforced through problematic sanctioning procedures. Large potential for uneven application of the rules remains, with the six-pack giving the European Council broad discretionary powers over when the rules will or will not be enforced. The dilemma at the core of the 2003 breach of the procedures for handling excessive deficits is still a problem: what happens if one of the large and politically influential states decides to break the rules again? The difficulty with enforcing the fiscal compact is lessened – though not rendered completely moot – by placing Commission or ECJ in charge of the process. Even then, however, there is a basic problem with the sanctions envisioned for rule-breaking states. States in violation of the rules – almost by definition, governments in fiscal disarray – face financial penalties, fines which would further reduce their already limited financial resources. These problems make it difficult to envision the new rules being enforced for either powerful or the most deeply troubled member states.

While the somewhat unrealistic effort to create a new ideal form of macroeconomic governance ideal seems doomed to repeat past failures, the EU's narrower crisis-response measures are more encouraging. The establishment of a crisis resolution mechanism in the ESM is a long-overdue piece of the euro area's institutional puzzle. Should the European Union manage to construct a viable arrangement for banking supervision and deposit insurance, it will have done much to limit the lasting damage that financial volatility can do to macroeconomic performance.

Finally, while the speed, agility, and pluck of the ECB over the last several years is worthy of praise, it cannot continue indefinitely as the euro area's macroeconomic firefighter. As the EU has muddled through this crisis, it has largely done so at the mercy of the ECB's ability to make major decisions and make them well. The formal rule making which has taken place has largely been oriented toward an idealized future which takes stability as a starting point. The ESM has helped, but ultimately cannot cope with a systemic crisis in the euro area's largest economies. Nothing has convincingly drawn a line under the crisis.

Ultimately, this failure has stemmed from the fact that all available solutions are politically controversial: the political will for supporting ESM or EU-enforced austerity in debtor countries has been stressed to the breaking point, with the clearest evidence coming from Italy. The technocratic Mario Monti was the clear loser in the February 2013 parliamentary elections; his successor, Enrico Letta, was unable to make any great strides with an economic reform agenda; and Letta's successor Matteo Renzi has openly announced his intention to ignore European fiscal requirements. Likewise, the acrimonious debate over eurobonds indicates unwillingness to move toward communal responsibility for sovereign debt. Debt forgiveness is similarly politically fraught. In sum, very few options remain on the table and, as the recent dissent over OMT shows, there are limits to what the ECB can do. Muddling through has thus far led Europe out of the worst phases of the crisis, but it has not ensured that Europeans are safe from a return to the volatility of the recent past.

References

Alessina, Alberto, and Francesco Giavazzi (2008). *The Future of Europe: Reform or Decline*. Cambridge: MIT Press.

Benoit, Bertrand, and Tony Barber (2009). 'Germany Ready to Help Eurozone Members.' *Financial Times* (18 February).

Delpa, Jacques, and Jakob von Weiszäcker (2010). 'The Blue Bond Proposal.' Bruegel Policy Brief 2010/03. Brussels: Bruegel.

European Commission (2011). 'Green Paper on the Feasibility of Introducing Stability Bonds.' COM(2011) 818 Final.

European Council (2011a). 'Council Directive 2011/85/EU of 8 November 2011 on Requirements for Budgetary Frameworks of the Member States.' *Official Journal of the European Union* L 306/41 (November 8).

European Council (2011b). 'Council Regulation (EU) No 1177/2011 of 8 November 2011 Amending Regulation (EC) No 1467/97 on Speeding up and Clarifying the Implementation of the Excessive Deficit Procedure.' *Official Journal of the European Union* L 306 (November 23).

European Council (2012). 'Council Agrees Position on Bank Supervision.' Press Release 528. Brussels: Council of the European Union.

European Council (2012) 'Treaty Establishing the European Stability Mechanism'. Brussels: European Council (T/ESM 2012/en 1) http://www.european-council.europa.eu/media/582311/05-tesm2.en12.pdf.

European Council and European Parliament (2011a). 'Regulation (EU) No 1174/2011 of the European Parliament and of the Council of 16 November 2011 on Enforcement Measures to Correct Excessive Macroeconomic Imbalances in the Euro Area.' *Official Journal of the European Union* L 306 (November 16).

European Council and European Parliament (2011b). 'Regulation (EU) No 1176/2011 of the European Parliament and of the Council of 16 November 2011 on the Prevention and Correction of Macroeconomic Imbalances.' *Official Journal of the European Union* L 306 (November 16).

European Council and European Parliament (2011c). 'Regulation (EU) No 1175/2011 of the European Parliament and of the Council of 16 November 2011 Amending Council Regulation (EC) No 1466/97 on the Strengthening of the Surveillance of Budgetary Positions and the Surveillance and Coordination of Economic Policies.' *Official Journal of the European Union* L 306 (November 16).

European Council and European Parliament (2011d). 'Regulation (EU) No 1173/2011 of the European Parliament and of the Council of 16 November 2011 on the Effective Enforcement of Budgetary Surveillance in the Euro Area.' *Official Journal of the European Union* L 306 (November 23).

Ewing, Jack, and Steven Erlanger (2012). 'Huge Step Taken by Europe's Bank to Abate a Crisis.' *The New York Times* (September 6).

Hix, Simon (2008). *What's Wrong with the European Union & How to Fix It*. Cambridge: Polity.

House of Lords Select Committee (2011). 'Amending Article 136 of the Treaty on the Functioning of the European Union.' London: Parliament of the United Kingdom.

Jones, Erik (2006). 'European Macroeconomic Governance.' In Jeremy Richardson, ed. *European Union: Power and Policymaking*. London: Routledge, pp. 329–349.

Jones, Erik (2010). 'A Eurobond Proposal to Promote Stability and Liquidity while Preventing Moral Hazard.' ISPI Policy Brief N. 180 (March). Milan: ISPI.

Kok, Wim (2004). 'Facing the Challenge: The Lisbon Strategy for Growth and Employment.' Brussels: European Commission (November).

Rehn, Olli (2013). 'Vice-President Rehn's Remarks at the ECOFIN'. Presented at the ECOFIN Council Meeting of 22 January 2013, Brussels.

Treaty on Stability, Coordination and Governance (TSCG) (2012). Brussels: Council of the European Union.

Chapter 15

Covert integration in the European Union

ADRIENNE HÉRITIER

Introduction

In the European Union, over time, integration has deepened in many policy areas (Wallace *et al.* 2005; Richardson 2012). This deepening has not only occurred via the main political arenas, but to a considerable extent through covert channels of integration. Covert integration or integration 'by subterfuge' occurs outside the formal political decision-making arenas without being explicitly mandated by formal political actors. As such it is politically less cumbersome and faster. However, because of its covert nature may subsequently lead to political backlash.

The most important *patterns of covert deepening integration* are the following: (a) members' formal political commitment to framework policy goals which may be redefined more stringently during implementation by executive or judicial actors; (b) international agreements framed in general terms – through executive judicial action – may lead to a competence shift and more stringent supranational regulation; (c) the use of soft, voluntary modes of policy making may give rise to a deepening formal integration; (d) delegating policy-making to independent regulatory bodies and the linked building of administrative capacity may result in a strengthening of supranational policy making; and (e) the introduction of parallel options of regulation, European and national, may lead to a crowding out of national regulation. Whilst covert integration may provide effective solutions to important problems of collective action, it also creates problems of democratic legitimation from the viewpoint of legislators and citizens because it shifts power from national to supranational actors and from legislative to executive and judicial actors. In a time of international market pressure and fiscal crisis with concerns about the lack of coordination of national measures in fields as diverse as market integration, fiscal, environmental and social policy, it could be argued that any type of deepening integration is desirable. However, a lesson from this analysis could be that if integration happens 'backstage' and not openly in the main political arena with the support of the majority of member states and their electorates, it may lead to a backlash at a later point in time if things should turn out not as successful as anticipated.

This chapter theorizes and analyses the conditions and processes of covert integration and its 'stopping points' and illustrates them with concrete policy examples. It concludes by discussing some implications for democratic decision-making.

Definitions of concepts and theoretical arguments

Covert integration is defined as a *process* which takes place *outside* the formal regional political decision-making arena. *Deepening integration* refers to an *outcome* and is defined at two dimensions: (1) a transfer of policy-making competences to the higher level/ supranational level and/or (2) the 'demandingness' and 'detailedness' of policy prescriptions issued by the supranational level.

The article builds on but goes beyond two big strands of theory: (1) European integration theory, in particular on the literature on 'escaping the deadlock' in intergovernmental decision-making, on one hand, and (2) theory of institutional change, on the other.

Theories of regional integration and European integration constitute important starting points for the analysis. *Neofunctionalist explanations* of regional integration focus on the societal demand which presses for more integrated forms of formal political decision-making (Haas and Schmitter 1964; Nye 1965; Mattli 1999). It analyses political, social, economic and cultural factors and their spillover effects which, in turn, create a demand for further steps of political integration (Haas 1967; Nye 1968) eventually leading to a "shifting of loyalties" to the supranational level. The study of the EU as a political system by Lindberg and Scheingold emphasized three integration mechanisms of logrolling and side payments, actor socialization, and feedback. Inputs as political demands, support and leadership are transformed into outputs in the form of policies and decisions (Lindberg and Scheingold 1970). In this decision-making system the independent Commission plays an important role because it actively tries to build coalitions to overcome national resistance to new policies and decisions and exercise supranational leadership (Laursen 2003: 9). Later neofunctionalist studies of European integration also focus on supranational institutions (Pollack 1996; Sandholtz and Stone Sweet 1998) and the promotion of ideas in view of a functional demand (Wiener and Diez 2003; Hooghe and Marks 2009). Pierson (1996), adopting a historical institutionalist approach to European integration, builds on neofunctionalist arguments pointing to the gaps which emerge in member states' control over supranational actors, as well as unintended consequences. These gaps are difficult to close because supranational actors enjoy some autonomy, political decision-makers have restricted time horizons and shifting preferences, and there may be institutional barriers to reform and various costs of change (Pierson 1996).

The chapter starts from a *neofunctionalist* perspective emphasizing a possible gap between original integration decisions and unintended deepening integration consequences. It points to supranational initiatives in seeking to bring about integration. The non-majoritarian 'engines of integration' (the Commission and the European Court of Justice [ECJ]) are widely believed to be very effective at supplying more integration by stealth (Pollack 2003). In the present argument initiatives by supranational actors (the Commission and the ECJ) constitute important preconditions for opening processes of covert integration (Héritier 1997, 2003, 2007, 2012).

Intergovernmentalism as a theory of regional integration analyses the bargaining processes between governments intent on joint action, however, also seeking to preserve as much as possible of their national sovereignty, therefore, tending to agree on the smallest common denominator. Keohane and Hoffman (1991) emphasize the important role of institutions in cooperation and conflict in international politics. Steps of integration are negotiated and decided in the central formal political arena. Liberal intergovernmentalism in a first step focuses on the preference formation in domestic political processes in order to explain in a second step the negotiation outcomes at center stage (Moravcsik 1993, 1998). The outcome of these decision processes in the central political arena constitutes the *starting point* of the analysis here.

The work on *escaping the deadlock in intergovernmental decision-making* links perspectives of intergovernmentalism and neofunctionalism on how to avoid stalled intergovernmental decision-making processes. It emphasizes possible escape routes from gridlock (Héritier 1997). However, a systematic conceptualization and theorization of different channels of covert deepening integration, its conditions, mechanisms and outcomes for the European Union is still underdeveloped (see Héritier 1997; Scharpf 1999; Tallberg 2000; Majone 2005; Falkner 2012; Genschel and Jachtenfuchs 2014). Assuming decision-making deadlock because of divergent preferences, Héritier (1997) maps and explains a number of escape routes or "subterfuge" out of deadlock, such as switching negotiation arenas and multilevel games, and the early self-commitment of actors. Scharpf (1999) pointed out the political slowness and costliness of positive integration through intergovernmental decision-making and the resulting asymmetry between Court and Commission driven negative integration leading to deepening integration. Falkner (2012) conceptualizes and theorizes different avenues of escaping the 'joint-decision-making trap', that is a decision-making situation in which the status quo cannot be changed without the support of all actors depending in turn on the confirmation of their respective constituencies, developed by Scharpf (1988). She distinguishes various patterns of deepening integration, and differentiates between supranational hierarchical steering (ECJ and Commission decisions), playing the treaty-base game and arena shifting, on one hand, and socialization processes, on the other. These processes lead to a convergence of preferences of actors induced by following the same values of integration (Falkner 2012). Genschel and Jachtenfuchs (2014) analyse how more integration with respect to member states' core powers may be accounted for. Based on a demand and supply model they emphasize that in a process of 'disintegration' there are no non-majoritarian actors, such as the Commission and the ECJ, with an institutional self-interest which would contain inroads into national sovereignty cores. While member states willing to adopt disintegrative decisions need to achieve unanimity in most areas of core state powers (Genschel and Jachtenfuchs, 2014: 19). It is the objective of this chapter to build on this literature and contribute to a further conceptualization and theorization of different channels of covert deepening integration, its conditions, mechanisms and outcomes for the European Union and to illustrate them by individual examples of European policy making.

Covert integration: why, how, and to what effect?

Why and how do different patterns of covert integration emerge, patterns that may lead to a deepening of integration, that is more demanding and detailed common policy requirements and a power shift to the supranational level and from the legislator to the executive and judiciary? Different strands of theory offer different answers. I use *rational choice institutionalism* to explain covert processes of institutional and policy change.

Rational institutionalist explanations

This explanation builds on the *theory of continuous institutional change* (Héritier 1997, 2007, 2012; Farrell and Héritier 2003, 2004; Stacey and Rittberger 2003) which may also be applied to the change of policy measures. It emphasizes the renegotiation or re-interpretation of incomplete institutional rules and policies. Channels of covert integration may be considered as an institutional and a policy change that emerges once a formal political decision of integration has been taken that offers the possibility to be renegotiated and specified in the course of its application. The explanation is based on the assumptions of goal-oriented, boundedly rational actors, seeking to maximize their institutional power and thereby their power over policy outcomes. Answers to why patterns of deepening integration appear may be derived from the existence of external problem pressure, specific institutional conditions and the relative bargaining power of the involved actors when redefining incomplete institutional or policy rules.

Pattern 1: "Deepening integration through general commitment". I argue that – given problem pressure and a demand for a coordination of national policies – it is crucial whether decisions to coordinate at the higher level represent complete or incomplete contracts. If member states have similar preferences and agree in a detailed decision to upload competences to the higher level which also clearly circumscribes the power given to supranational actors, a limited transfer of national powers has occurred in a complete contract and in an overt way in the main political arena. If, by contrast, member states have diverse preferences regarding the desired policy solutions and appropriate limits of supranational power, the outcome of the decision process in the main arena is likely to be vaguely formulated as an incomplete contract and/or at the lowest common denominator. An incomplete contract – for strategic reasons and reasons of substantive uncertainty (Cooley and Spruyt 2007) – leaves many details yet to be specified, and thereby opens the door for subsequent institutional and policy changes (Héritier 2007). These changes often happen outside the formal political arena. The renegotiation may give rise to informal rules regarding the handling of national powers emerging alongside the formal political arena. The outcome of the re-bargaining of the incomplete contract will be determined by the most powerful actors (as defined by their fallback position), the existing decision-making rule and exogenous events. When specifying the incomplete contract supranational executive actors may form an alliance with judicial actors in interpreting the details of the contract and – through court rulings – make an inroad into national competences previously not formally mandated.

In short, a deepening integration may result from the fact that – given external problem pressure – the formal political decision-makers (because of diverging preferences and consensus or unanimity rules) commit themselves to only vaguely formulated institutional rules or policy goals. Given the ambiguity of the rule or policy mandate, implementing actors, that is executive actors, and judicial actors, are able to redefine the generally stated goal. Depending on the preferences and the relative power of the actors involved in the renegotiation of the incomplete contract and given institutional restrictions deepening integration may ensue (Héritier 2007).[1] This leads to *conjecture 1* that *"an incomplete institutional rule or policy may lead to a deepening of integration in the course of its application if pro-integration executive and judicial actors with pro-integration preferences specify the incomplete rule".*

Pattern 2: "Deepening integration through external contracts". Regional polities are complex policy systems by and in themselves. They are faced with internal complexity and diversity but – additionally – with close links with the international environment. In other words, internal decision-making processes and the resulting policy solutions, as well as internal decision-making structures and institutional rules, are affected by existing international agreements, bilateral treaties and transnational governance in all areas of policy making (Katsikas 2011). How does the power of external challenges meet with established decision-making processes in the EU? Under which conditions do they give rise to covert patterns of deepening integration? Since it is assumed that there are ambiguous provisions in the treaty with external actors, it is expected that in the course of its application it may be renegotiated or re-interpreted by executive and judicial actors and thereby – because of contractual obligations with external actors – lead to more deepening of integration in a regional polity.[2] In short, assuming ambiguity in elements of a policy agreement concluded with an external actor (e.g. another regional polity or other non-state actors), executive and judicial implementing actors with pro-integration preferences may redefine the generally stated goal of the contract. Under *conjecture 2* it is therefore submitted that *"if agreements with external actors include vague provisions which are specified by implementing executive actors or courts with pro-integration preferences, deepening integration will follow"*.

Pattern 3: "Deepening integration through delegation to independent regulators". A related rational institutionalist explanation based on the principal–agent approach suggests the emergence of deepening integration if the specification of the general policy goal is deliberately taken out of the political arena and the power of detailing a policy and regulatory capacity is transferred to an independent regulatory authority or a technical body at the supranational level (Radaelli 1998; Gilardi 2001; Mattli 2003; Coen and Héritier 2005). The causes and political motives behind the act of delegation (McCubbins, 1985: 721; Majone 1994) have been extensively discussed in the literature, the most frequently mentioned motivations being substantive uncertainty and the need for expertise, political uncertainty, policy credibility, and blame shifting. The principal agent approach starts out from the assumption that the agent through his policy expertise has an informational advantage over the principal (Fiorina, 1982, 1986; McCubbins, 1985; McCubbins *et al.*, 1987; Horn and Shepsle, 1989; Epstein and O'Halloran 1999; Franchino, 2002, 2004, 2007; Pollack, 2003; Miller, 2005). Political uncertainty refers to the wish to ensure policy stability over time, that is the wish of governments to protect their policy choices from being dismantled by their successor governments (Moe 1990; credible commitment Majone 1994). A different form of political uncertainty argument was presented by Fiorina (1982) who argued that interest groups with diverse preferences might mutually block each other in the legislative process and might therefore be unable to come to an agreement supporting detailed legislation. In order to avoid stalled decision-making, legislators linked with different interest groups will agree that authority be delegated to bureaucracy or agencies with the task to take detailed decisions, while legislation takes only the form of framework legislation. The shifting of responsibility or 'blame shifting' (Fiorina 1982) is another important reason for delegation that is discussed in the literature. If the electoral costs of regulation are expected to be greater than the benefits a rational legislator would delegate rather than legislate.

When delegating, principals still seek to control – to some extent – the agent's activities. In *ex ante* controls they insert incentives into the contract that seek to align the agent's preferences with those of the principals. In ex post controls they use rules to control the agent and to avoid agency drift,[3] such as the assigning of the burden of proof to one specific party, the prescription of consultation, transparency and public disclosure rules; they also may limit the time of delegation (McCubbins *et al.*, 1987; Epstein and O'Halloran, 1999; Franchino, 2004). McCubbins and Schwartz (1984), highlight mechanisms of *ex post* contractual control that allow a principal to discover problems of agency drift. Legislators can either seek to control bureaucrats by gathering their own information or force the agent to disclose information at oversight hearing ('police patrol' oversight), or they can turn to those interest groups affected by the agent's decisions ('fire alarm' oversight).

Hence, assuming that the agent is more integration friendly than the principals, it is argued that delegation will result in agency drift unless the agent is kept under tight control. This leads to *conjecture 3a*, *"in policy areas under delegation there will be more indirect deepening of integration than in policy areas without delegation"*, and *conjecture 3b*, *"if principals do not engage in control over the agent, delegation will lead to deepening integration."*

Pattern 4: "Deepening integration through soft modes of governance" refers to the possibility that deepening integration may result from a general commitment to a policy goal that is non-binding. In recent years new modes of governance, not based on legislation have increased in salience in European policy-making. They have been advocated as a panacea for speeding up European decision making which has often ended up in gridlock (Héritier 1999; 2003). One reason is that European integration has reached a stage where the core activities of the member states are addressed. In these areas member states' political support for harmonization through legislation is very difficult to gain because governments see their sovereignty endangered. Hence, a method of cooperation has been developed to avoid the classical form of legislation through directives and regulations. Instead, it relies on an open method of coordination (Scott and Trubek 2002; Sabel and Zeitlin 2007) or on voluntary agreements between private actors. From a rational institutionalist perspective it is argued that – given external problem pressure – members agree that action is needed but hesitate to transfer formal competences to the supranational level. In order to initiate measures of collective action they therefore engage in 'soft' measures, such as the exchange of information regarding their policy goals, information about which instruments they apply to reach these policy goals, and the publication of the results of their endeavours in terms of policy outputs (legislation), but also outcomes (resources invested) and their impact (contribution to the solution of the policy problem). These results may be published in an overall benchmarking exercise, showing how countries perform in order to incite the laggards to catch up with the leaders. But all this happens on a strictly voluntary basis. No formal controls are applied by the supranational level, nor are there sanctions in case a member state disregards the defined policy goals. Instead, the member states only commit themselves to voluntary coordination linked with informal sanctions such as a loss of reputation in case of non-compliance (DeLaPorte and Pochet 2002; Sabel and Zeitlin 2007; de Ruiter 2008; Héritier and Lehmkuhl 2008). Elsewhere I have argued that it makes a difference whether soft modes of governance are employed in policy issues in which all gain from cooperation or they are employed in policy areas in which there are clear losers and winners. In the latter case, it is unlikely that the losers would voluntarily observe the defined policy goals (Héritier 2003). Hence, we may expect that if all members gain from the coordination of policies, or agree with the deepening of integration on a voluntary basis it will happen. This leads to *conjecture 4: "in the absence of similar pro-integration preferences of members, soft modes of governance will not lead to deepening integration"*.

Pattern 5: "Deepening integration through regulatory venue shopping" assumes the existence of several national and supranational options of regulation from which members may choose. Jupille, Mattli and Snidal focus on the "potentially rich range of institutional alternatives available to states . . . on international institutional choice as an unfolding process regarding *which* institution to choose from among a range of alternatives" (2011: 1). They argue that institutional selection is most likely when several existing institutions "occupy the same issue space" and could handle the problem, but none is 'focal' (ibid.: 11). Different jurisdictions might partially overlap with respect to specific issues and actors. As a result an existing institution for an existing issue "can be undermined by competition of other institutions seeking to take on this issue" (ibid.: 11). Alternative institutional venues may be actively created by actors for exactly this purpose (Alter and Meunier 2009). At the same time the possibility of choosing between regulatory options may also facilitate exit from one regulatory arena and thereby non-compliance with strict regulations (Alter and Meunier 2009).

In an issue space with multiple regulatory options or institutions, in our case the supranational regulatory option which also covers transborder aspects, may be more attractive. It is therefore expected that national actors would prefer the supranational regulation to their national regulation *if* the supranational regulation is not stricter than its own national regulation. This may result in supranational regulation crowding out national regulation. Under *conjecture 5*, I therefore submit that "*given a choice between regulatory arenas, actors will choose the supranational offer, thereby rendering national regulatory arenas obsolete; therefore deepening integration will ensue*".

In the following the patterns of covert integration presented earlier are illustrated by recent examples of policy making in the EU.

Empirical illustrations

Pattern 1: "deepening integration through general commitment"

Under this pattern it is expected that "an incomplete institutional rule or policy may lead to a deepening of integration in the course of its application if executive and judicial actors with pro-integration preferences specify the incomplete rule/policy".

Example: Regulation on the Prevention and Correction of Macroeconomic Imbalances (EU 1176, 2011)

The first example refers to a new institutional rule in the application of delegated and implementing acts under the six-pack regulations revising the Stability and Growth Pact. In the Regulation on the Prevention and Correction of Macroeconomic Imbalances some vague provisions were introduced that need specification through delegated legislation. The Treaty on the Functioning of the European Union (TFEU; 2009) distinguishes, for the first time, between legislative delegation and executive delegation and provides for two separate procedures for "delegated acts" and "implementing acts' (Ponzano 2010). Under "delegated acts" (Art. 290 TFEU), the Commission – by legislation – may be delegated the power to adopt acts of general scope supplementing or amend-ing certain non-essential elements of the legislation in question. The legislators must explicitly define the objective, content, scope and duration of this delegation. They also can choose the mechanism or mechanisms in order to control the Commission when it applies these delegated powers, revocation and objection. In the case of revocation, either the Council or the Parliament may revoke a delegation. Similarly, an objection on the part of either the Council or the Parliament would prevent an individual "delegated act" from entering into force (see also Blom-Hansen 2011).

The new provisions of the Lisbon Treaty leave open many questions as to how dele-gated acts (Art. 290) and implementing acts (Art. 291) should be applied. In other words the provisions constitute an incomplete contract. As a rule, when the Commission pro-poses a 'delegated act' a conflict ensues between the Parliament, the Council and the Commission. The Council seeks to oppose it entirely or to reduce its scope, or to trans-late it into an implementing act. Frequently, in order to come to an agreement packages are struck across various issues as to whether to use "delegating" or implementing acts (Interview Commission, January 2012).

An instance of such a conflict over the choice of either Art. 290 or Art. 291 in recent legislation[4] is precisely the adoption of the Regulation on the prevention and correction of macro-economic imbalances. When deciding how to flesh out the scoreboard regime, that is the indicators used to measure and monitor macroeconomic and macrofinancial imbalances, the Commission and the Parliament favoured 'delegated acts' (Art. 290) whilst the Council wished to use an implementing act (Art. 291) for the reasons described previously. A deadlock ensued which after a round of negotiations led to the use of an informal new type of procedure which is *neither* Art. 290 nor Art. 291, the 'compromise'. The respective recital 12 of the regulation says,

> The Commission should closely cooperate with the European Parliament and the Council when drawing up the scoreboard and the set of macroeconomic and macrofinancial indicators for Member States. The Commission should present suggestions for comments to the competent committees of the European Parliament and of the Council on plans to establish and adjust the indicators and threshold. The Commission should inform the European Parliament and the Council of any changes to the indicators and threshold and explain its reasons for suggesting such changes.

Note the difference to the 'real' use of a delegation act used in another six-pack regulation on the effective enforcement of budgetary surveillance in the euro area.[5] It states, as prescribed in the Comitology Regulation of 2010, that the Commission shall be empowered to adopt "delegated acts" regarding the criteria establishing fines, procedures for investigations (Art. 8.4); that the Commission shall draw up a report in respect of the delegation of power; and that the delegation may be revoked at any time by the Parliament or by the Council (Art. 11.2, and 3).

What is striking from our theoretical perspective of covert institutional change under pattern one is that the existing formal rules constitute ambiguous terms of contract, which in the situation of a decision stalemate – were re-bargained and transformed in such a way as to overcome the impasse. By so doing the power of the Commission was clearly strengthened.

Pattern 2: "deepening integration through external contracts"

Pattern 2 posits that "if agreements with external actors include vague provisions which subsequently are specified by implementing executive actors or courts with pro-integration preferences, deepening integration will follow".

Example: The Open Skies Agreement between the EU and the US of 2007/2011

In 2003 the Council of Ministers gave the Commission a mandate to negotiate with the US a liberalization of the EU–US aviation market with full possibility of free foreign investment and control and the delivery of airport services without restrictions, including cabotage, that is the right of a foreign carrier to operate purely domestic flights. The Open Skies Agreement (OSA) concluded in 2007 introduced the liberalization of aviation services between any city in the US to any city in the EU, a right of cabotage for the US, but no liberalization of ownership and control. The agreement of 2007 also makes liberalization subject to jointly agreed regulatory provisions – 'convergence'. It takes the highly unusual step of establishing a common decision-making institution, the joint committee, in view of achieving full-range regulatory convergence. This applies to such diverse policy areas as (a) health and safety and (b) competition and state subsidies, as well as (c) ownership and control, (d) environmental standards, (e) labour relations, and (f) consumer protection (Delreux 2011; Héritier and Karagiannis 2011).

As mentioned, the agreement of 2007 was biased in favour of the US as regards two crucial dimensions, namely cabotage and ownership rights. In consequence, renegotiation was the condition under which the EU accepted the 'biased' negotiation outcome of OSA 2007. In the second round the American negotiator basically sought to maintain the status quo of what had been negotiated under stage one to fend off the European request of liberalization of ownership and control. For this purpose, the US – in a clever move – introduced a counter-request which for the Europeans was very difficult to fulfil, that is the request of lifting night flight prohibitions, and successfully used it as a bargaining chip. The outcome was the institution of a conditional procedure called 'asymmetric basket'.

Art 21.3 of the Protocol to amend the Air Transport Agreement between the US and the EU states that

> if the laws and regulations of each Party permit majority ownership and effective control of its airlines by the other Party or its nationals . . . airlines of the U.S. shall have the right to provide scheduled passenger combination services between points in the EU and its Member States and five countries, without serving a point in the territory of the US.

And Art.21.4 if

> the laws and regulations of the EU and its Member States with regard to the imposition of noise-based operating restrictions at airports having more than 50.000 annual movements of civil subsonic jet aeroplanes provide that that **the European Commission has the authority to review the process prior to the imposition of such measures, and where it is not satisfied that the appropriate procedures have been followed . . . to take that case, prior to their imposition, appropriate legal action regarding the measures in question** [emphasis added A.H.], airlines of the EU shall have the right to provide scheduled passenger combination services between points in the US and five additional countries, without serving a point in the territory of the EU and its Member States. [Emphasis added.]

In other words, the provisions under Art. 21 introduced discretion for the Commission to decide to refer the issue of night flight prohibitions in European cities to the ECJ *before* they are put into practice. During the negotiations the US negotiator frequently invited the EU negotiator to impose a lift of night-flight prohibitions, ignoring the fact that formally the Commission has no powers to impose such bans on European cities. Nevertheless, the outcome of this negotiation was a conditional empowerment of the Commission to take member states to court *before* the imposition of a night-flight ban.

Hence, in the light of our theoretical argument, a vague term in the agreement gives discretion to the Commission to take such action, clearly empowering the Commission in noise-emission control. Bearing in mind the 'conditional asymmetric basket mechanism' it is likely that European carriers will pressure their countries to lift night bans and subject them – as requested by the US – to the corresponding International Civil Aviation Organization's notoriously lenient rules. The Parliament in its resolution on OSA 2011 emphasized that various aspects of aviation regulation, including noise restrictions and night flight limitations, should be determined at the local level in compliance with the subsidiarity principle.

Pattern 3: "delegation to an independent regulator"

Under this pattern it is expected that "in policy areas under delegation there will be more indirect deepening of integration than in policy areas without delegation".

Example: delegation to the European Central Bank

The European Central Bank (ECB) was delegated the task to conduct European monetary policy. The Statute of the ESCB (European System of Central Banks), as laid down in the protocol to the Maastricht Treaty, empowers the ECB with the primary monetary policy objective of achieving price stability. The bank is independent within a clear and precise mandate, and is accountable to the citizens and elected representatives for the execution of this mandate (Scheller 2006). To obtain its main objective of price stability, the ECB sets key interest rates for the eurozone seeking to keep inflation rates below but close to 2 per cent over the medium term. The ECB is also the sole issuer of bank notes and bank reserves for the euro area. It manages, moreover, the eurozone's foreign currency reserves to keep exchange rates in check and supports national authorities in supervising financial markets and institutions.

Recently, there have been heated debates about whether the ECB has gone beyond the mandate delegated to it by member states. This is because in the course of the present European sovereign debt crisis the ECB has taken new innovative measures. It repeatedly engaged in rounds of indirect government bond purchases. Basically, it can purchase bonds of the struggling GIPSI (Greece, Ireland, Portugal, Spain or Italy) governments in two ways: directly or indirectly by making additional loans to commercial banks that in turn acquire GIPSI bonds (White www.freebanking.org/2012/09/07/). The ECB declared that it would not refinance the European Stability Mechanism (ESM) by giving it a mechanism with a banking license. However, it decided that it will support any ESM bond/purchase operations with potentially unlimited amounts of interventions in the secondary market,[6] albeit limited to shorter maturity. The president of the ECB, Mario Draghi, described the new bond-buying program of July 2012, the Outright Monetary Transactions (OMT), intending to ease financial conditions for member states in financial and fiscal crisis, as clearly within the mandate of monetary policy. Yet, formally, the ECB is prohibited from directly financing governments which renders its purchases of governments bonds – even in the secondary market – highly controversial.

These crisis driven activities raised questions of whether the ECB has stepped outside its traditional role and gone beyond its mandate. It was argued that due to the slowness of European political decision makers, that is governments, a vacuum was created that resulted in the ECB being "the only institution in the euro area capable of intervening promptly and decisively, into territory far outside its custom and practice" (*The Economist* 2011; Schelkle 2012). "The ECB has shown it is willing to step in when fiscal authorities have not, . . . but also knows it is stretching its mandate" (Begg 2012, quoted in Alessi 2012:4). Critique from Germany was particularly acute. The chief of the German Bundesbank, Jens Weidmann, challenges the ECB's bond-buying and argues that the ECB is engaging in "monetary financing" or providing direct financial support to governments which is illegal under the EU Treaty. The broader debate, however, is whether the ECB should engage in bond-buying in eurozone countries threatened by sovereign debt crisis, and – if so – which kind of budgetary and structural conditions should be attached to it (Wolff 2012, cited in Alessi 2012:7).

From the perspective of our theoretical argument, the recent activities of the ECB offer an example of an agent which – forced by external shocks – engages in a redefinition of its mandate leading to a deepening of integration and, as a result, meets with attempts of some principals to contain the redefinition.

Pattern 4: "deepening integration through soft modes of regulation"

Under pattern 4 it is argued that "in the absence of similar pro-integration preferences of members, soft modes of governance will not lead to deepening integration".

Example: temporary workers agreement

The attempt to reach an agreement that improves the legal rights and the compensation of temporary workers hired by agencies is an example of a clear redistributive issue between employers and employees in which the concerned actors do *not* hold similar preferences (Héritier 2003). In the case of temporary workers the normal avenue of legislation was not chosen. Rather was an attempt made to solve the problem by soft regulation under the social dialogue allowing social partners to come to a voluntary accord. This agreement was subsequently to be enacted by the Council of Ministers. However, the negotiations quickly showed that an agreement could not be reached between Union of Industrial and Employers' Associations of Europe (UNICE) and European Trade Union Association (ETUC). While both parties agreed on the principle of equal treatment for equal work, they disagreed about what constitutes a comparable worker. ETUC argued that the basis for any deal must be the principle that agency workers are given the same rights as workers in the company where they are temporarily employed. The employers' associations accepted the introduction of a non-discrimination clause, but insisted that it is enough to ensure that such workers are granted minimum employment standards by their agencies. They also argued that since member states have very different traditions in regulating labour relations that are institutionally deeply entrenched, the principle of subsidiarity should be respected allowing member states to use both comparisons, that is the comparison to the workplace where workers are temporarily employed and the comparison to the agency for which they do the temporary work (Harvey 2002).

Moreover, what emerged in the course of the negotiations was that not only a redistributive issue of costs imposed upon employers and benefits to employees were at stake but a institutional redistributive issue was as well. This issue concerned the division of institutional power between national roof associations and sectoral associations and between European associations and national associations. The conflict was particularly acute among the trade unions. While the delegation of UNICE was able to come up with a compromise position, albeit only on the smallest common denominator, ETUC was not able to reach such a compromise among its members. As a consequence, the talks ended in deadlock. After almost two years the social dialogue negotiations failed, and the Commission drew up a draft directive which was subsequently adopted.

The experience of the temporary workers shows that voluntary accords as a soft mode of governance does not necessarily lead to deepening integration in the case of diverging preferences if a redistributive issue is at stake.

Pattern 5: "deepening integration through regulatory venue shopping"

Under this pattern it is expected that "given a choice between regulatory arenas, actors will – ceteris paribus – choose the supranational offer rendering national regulatory arenas obsolete; therefore deepening integration will ensue".

Example: the proposed Regulation on a Common European Sales Law

The Commission in its explanatory memorandum on a Regulation on a Common European Sales Law (CESL) states that the proposed regulation would establish a second contract law regime within the national law of each member state (Commission explanatory memorandum of 15429/11, COM (11) 635, p.5), or a new 28th regime of contract law alongside the existing frameworks that apply in the 27 member states.

The CESL would be used by parties to govern cross-border transactions where at least one of the parties is based in the EU and where both parties have expressly agreed to its application. CESL would be used where contracts exist for the sale of goods between businesses and consumers and for transactions between businesses where at least one of the parties is a small or medium enterprise.

A number of member states objected to the proposal. Thus, the UK government and the House of Commons in its Reasoned Opinion argue that the CESL does not comply with the principles of subsidiarity and solidarity. Furthermore, confusion and legal complexity would ensue if each member state could apply its own different interpretation of the CESL. It sees the risk that the CESL could replace national consumer laws, stating that, if there is a choice of applicable law, there is the possibility that the CESL might offer less protection than the domestic laws of a particular member state (House of Commons Reasoned Opinion 2011). The UK was joined in these objections by the Austrian Federal Council, the Belgian Senate, and the German Bundestag. Representatives of the Austrian Federal Chamber of Law argued that an optional instrument would mean that, when traders decide which law to apply, European or national law, business would always choose the law which would benefit them and not the consumers (Austrian Federal Chamber of Labour, http://www.akeuropa.eu/en/criticism-of-eu-proposal-on CESL). The German Bundestag also unanimously concluded that the proposal does not comply with the principle of subsidiarity (PE478.528v01-00; CM/887301EN.doc).

Similarly, legal scholars pointed out that a narrow concept of consumer may create an incentive of traders to circumvent mandatory provisions in borderline cases. And that a "simple choice of the CESL which for the consumer is usually done on a 'take-it-or-leave it' basis should be seen as problematic. It involves a complete shift in jurisdiction on contract and consumer law matters and results in the end in a de facto 'full harmonisation' which had just been rejected in the debate on the CRD" (Micklitz and Reich 2012: 2).

For national parliaments to stop a Commission initiative under the Lisbon Treaty's "yellow card" mechanism, 18 votes of 54 votes (2 per national parliament) would have been necessary. The four reasoned opinions mentioned earlier fell short of the necessary one-third threshold. However, in May 2012, also Hungary, the Netherlands, Slovenia and Finland expressed that they remain unconvinced by the proposal, while support was coming from Poland, Lithuania, Latvia, Greece, Estonia, Malta and Bulgaria (http://www.ecommerce-europe.eu/news/2012/12). The EP by 416 votes to 159, with about 65 abstentions, adopted in February 2014 a legislative resolution on an optional Common European Sales Law (CESL). The decision making process has not been concluded at the time of writing.

The conflict around the proposed CESL shows that introducing a choice between competing national and European legislation may lead to a shift in institutional competences if the European option is chosen over the national one, that is a de facto deepening of institutional competences at the European level. Interestingly, however, it also shows that it may be linked to a substantive dilution of the stringency of national (consumer) regulation if member states primarily opt for the less-stringent European regulation.

Conclusion

This chapter argues that deepening integration in the European union takes place not only front stage but also backstage. Important steps of deepening integration occur not only in the formal central political arena but also through five mechanism of covert integration without being visible to the European public. These mechanisms are members' formal political commitment to framework policy goals which may be redefined more stringently during implementation by executive or judicial actors; international agreements framed in general terms – through executive judicial action – may lead to a competence shift and more stringent supranational regulation; the use of soft, voluntary modes of policy making may give rise to a deepening formal integration; delegating policy-making to independent regulatory bodies and the linked building up of administrative capacity may result in a strengthening of supranational policy making; and the introduction of parallel options of regulation, European and national, may lead to a crowding out of national regulation. By implication covert integration should be less likely to happen if contract terms are specific, if there are similar preferences under soft modes, if there is no delegation to independent authorities and no parallel policy options. The analysis of the democratic institutional implications of covert integration and the concomitant power shifts between legislative, executive and judicial actors at the European level and between legislative, executive and judicial actors across the different levels of government is only in its beginnings (see for instance Menon and Weatherill 2002; Scharpf 2010). *As it was shown earlier, the shift of power to the supranational level and at the supranational level from legislative to executive actors, that is the Commission or the ECB or independent regulators, may trigger popular protest by voice. This is most likely to happen in times of crisis. Avenues for chanelling such voice are the elections to the EP, or the rejection of treaty changes in national referenda. So far, in times of financial and economic crisis, when the policy implications of covert integration become widely felt in countries under stress, popular discontent has been mainly addressed at national governments. Their capacity of "democratic legitimacy intermediation" (Scharpf 2013), however, may be put under serious strain.*

Notes

1   S. Schmidt (2012: 3) points out that case law often is "fuzzy" and in turn may create new legal uncertainty in drawing "the line between the remaining national competences and European obligations". Thereby it gives private actors and the legislature "an incentive to settle on the most far-reaching interpretation of the ambiguous case law, as otherwise an interpretation of secondary law in the light of case law may again fail to secure legal certainty" (ibid.: 23). Schmidt thereby underlines a highly interesting corollary of the pattern of judicial specification of incomplete contracts addressed here.
2   The research on the rational design of international institutions by Koremenos *et al.* (2001) asks why international agreements are designed in different ways as regards geographical scope and membership, decision-making rules, (de)centralization and in-built flexibility clauses to adjust to external shocks. This last aspect focuses on the conditions under which international institutions are being renegotiated or automatically adjusted. However, this change over time is intentionally included in the contract from the very beginning.
3   McCubbins, Noll and Weingast (1989) define bureaucratic discretion and latitude as those actions that no political coalition can overturn. Epstein and O'Halloran describe bureaucratic drift as "the ability of an agency to enact outcomes different from the policies preferred by those who originally delegated power" (1999: 25).
4   Other recent instances of a conflict between the Council, the Parliament and the Commission about the selection of a delegated or implementing act are the Cross-Border Health Care Directive and the Novel Food Directive.
5   Regulation (EU) No 1173/2011 of the European Parliament and of the Council of 16 November 2011 on the effective enforcement of budgetary surveillance in the euro area.
6   An ESM fund endowed with limited funds cannot work as a backstop mechanism in case of liquidity crisis, especially if a large member state is in financial difficulties.

References

Alessi, C., 2012, *The Role of the European Central Bank*, Council of Foreign Relations, September.
Alter, K. J., and S. Meunier, 2009, The Politics of International Regime Complexity, *Perspectives on Politics*, 7(1), 13–24.
Austrian Federal Chamber of Labour, http://www.akeuropa.eu/en/criticism-of-eu-proposal-on CESL).
Blom-Hansen, J. 2011, The EU Comitology Szstem: Taking Stock Before the New Lisbon Regime, *Journal of European Public Policy*, 18, 4, 607–17.
Coen, D., and A. Héritier, 2005, *Refining Regulatory Regimes, Utilities in Europe*, Edward Elgar.
Cooley, A., and H. Spruyt, 2007, *Contracting States. Sovereignty Transfers in International Relations*, Princeton University Press.
DeLaPorte C. and P. Pochet, 2002, eds., *Building the Social Europe through the Open Method of Co-ordination*, Peter Lang.

Delreux, T., 2011, The Relation between the European Commission and the EU Member States in the Transatlantic Open Skies Negotiations: An Analysis of Their Opportunities and Constraints. *Journal of Transatlantic Studies*, 9(2), 113–135.

de Ruiter, R., 2008, Developing Multilateral Surveillance Tools in the EU, *West European Politics*, 31(5), 869–914.

The Economist, (2012), October

Epstein, D. and S. O'Halloran, 1999, *Delegating Powers: A Transaction Cost Politics Approach to Policy Making Under Separate Powers*, Cambridge University Press.

Falkner, G., Ed., 2012, *In and Out of EU Decision Traps: Comparative Perspectives*, Oxford University Press.

Farrell, H. and A. Héritier, 2003, Formal and Informal Institutions under Codecision: Continuous Constitution Building in Europe, *Governance*, 16(4), 577–600.

Farrell, H. and A. Héritier, 2004, Interorganizational Cooperation and Intraorganizational Power: Early Agreements under Codecision and Their Impact on the Parliament and the Council, *Comparative Political Studies*, 37(10): 1184–1212.

Fiorina, M. P., 1982, Legislative Choice of Regulatory Forms: Legal Process or Administrative Process?, *Public Choice*, 39(1), 33–66.

Fiorina, M. P., 1986, Legislator Uncertainty, Legislative Control, and the Delegation of Legislative Power, *Journal of Law, Economics, & Organization*, 2(1), 33–51.

Franchino, F., 2002, Efficiency or credibility? Testing the Two Logics of Delegation to the European Commission, *Journal of European Public Policy*, 9(5), 677–694.

Franchino, F., 2004, Delegating Powers in the European Community, *British Journal of Political Science*, 34(2), 269–293.

Franchino, F., 2007, *The Powers of the Union: Delegation in the EU*, Cambridge University Press.

Genschel, P., and M. Jachtenfuchs, 2014, eds., *Beyond the Regulatory Polity. European Integration of Core State Powers*, Oxford University Press.

Gilardi, F., 2001, Policy Credibility and the Delegation to Independent Regulatory Agencies: A Comparative Empirical Analysis, *Journal of European Public Policy*, 9(4), 873–893.

Haas, E. B., 1958, *The Uniting of Europe; Political, Social, and Economic Forces, 1950–1957*, Stanford University Press.

Haas, E. B., 1967, The Uniting of Europe and the Uniting of Latin America, *Journal of Common Market Studies* 5, 315–343.

Haas, E. B., 1975, On Systems and International Regimes, *World Politics: A Quarterly Journal of International Relations*, V, 147–174.

Haas, E. B., and P. C. Schmitter, 1964, Economics and Differential Patterns of Political Integration: Projections about Unity in Latin America, *International Organization*, 18(4), 705–737.

Harvey, M., 2002, *The Social Dialogue as a Form of Network Governance: lessons from the failure of the framework agreement on temporary agency work*, Paper, Annual Pan-European Conference on European Union Politics, Bordeaux.

Héritier, A., 1997, Policy-making by Subterfuge: Interest Accommodation, Innovation and Substitute Democratic Legitimation in Europe – Perspectives from Distinctive Policy Areas, *Journal of European Public Policy*, 4(2), 171–189.

Héritier, A., 1999, *Policy Making and Diversity in Europe – Escaping Deadlock*, Cambridge University Press.

Héritier, A., 2003, New Modes of Governance in Europe: Increasing Political Capacity and Policy Effectiveness? in T. A. Börzel and R. A. Cichowski (eds.), *Law, Politics, and Society*, Oxford: Oxford University Press, pp. 105–126.

Héritier, A., 2007, *Explaining Institutional Change in Europe*, Oxford: Oxford University Press.

Héritier, A., 2012, Institutional Change in Europe: Co-decision and Comitology Transformed, *Journal of Common Market Studies*, Special Issue, W. Mattli and A. Stone Sweet, eds., 50(1), 38–54.

Héritier, A. and D. Lehmkuhl, 2008, The Shadow of Hierarchy and New Modes of Governance, in Héritier, A., D. Lehmkuhl, D. Coen and M. Thatcher, The Shadow of Hierarchy and New Modes of Governance: Sectoral Governance and Democratic Government, *Journal of Public Policy*, Special Issue, 1–17.

Héritier, A. and Y. Karagiannis, 2011, The New Institutions of Transatlantic Aviation, *Global Policy*, 2, 152–162.

Hooghe, L. and G. Marks, 2009, A Postfunctionalist Theory of European Integration: From Permissive Consensus to Constraining Dissensus, *British Journal of Political Science*, 39(1), 1–23.

Horn, M. J. and K. A. Shepsle, 1989, Commentary on "Administrative Arrangements and the Political Control of Agencies": Administrative Process and Organizational Form as Legislative Responses to Agency Costs, *Virginia Law Review*, 75(2), 499–508.

House of Commons Reasoned Opinion, 2011, 12 August.

Jupille, J., W. Mattli, and D. Snidal, 2011, *International Institutional Choice: Cooperation, Alternatives and Strategies*, Cambridge University Press.

Katsikas, D., 2011, Global Regulation and Institutional Change, *West European Politics*, 34(4), 819–837.

Keohane, R. and Hoffman, S., 1991, *The New European Community: Decision Making and Institutional Change*, Westview Press.

Koremenos, B., C. Lipson, D. Snidal, 2001, The Rational Design of International Institutions, *International Organization*, 55(4), 761–99.

Laursen, F., 2003, *Comparative Regional Integration: Theoretical Perspectives*, Ashgate.

Lindberg, L. N., and S. A. Scheingold, 1970, *Europe's Would-be Polity: Patterns of Change in the European Community*, Prentice Hall.

Majone, G., 1994, The Rise of the Regulatory State in Europe, *West European Politics*, 17(3), 77–101.

Majone, G., 2005, *Dilemmas of European Integration. Ambiguities and Pitfalls of Integration by Stealth*, Oxford University Press.

Mattli, W., 1999, *The Logic of Regional Integration: Europe and Beyond*, Cambridge University Press.

Mattli, W., 2003, Setting International Standards: Technological Rationality or Primacy of Power?, *World Politics*, 56(1), 1–42.

McCubbins, M. D., 1985, The Legislative Design of Regulatory Structure, *American Journal of Political Science*, 29(4), 721–748.

McCubbins, M. D., R. G. Noll, and B. R. Weingast, 1987, Administrative Procedures as Instruments of Political Control, *Journal of Law, Economics, & Organization*, 3(2), 243–277.

McCubbins, M.D. and T. Schwartz, 1984, Congressional Oversight Overlooked: Police Patrols versus Fire Alarms, *American Journal of Political Science*, 28, 1, 165–79.

Menon, A., and S. Weatherill, 2002, Legitimacy, Accountability and Delegation in the European Union, in A. Arnull and D. Wincott, eds., *Accountability and Legitimacy in the European Union*, Oxford University Press, pp. 113–132.

Micklitz and Reich 2012

Miller, G. J., 2005, The Political Evolution of Principal-Agent Models, *Annual Review of Political Science*, 8(1), 203–225.

Moe, T. M., 1990, Political Institutions: The Neglected Side of the Story, *Journal of Law, Economics, & Organization*, 6, 213–253.

Moravcsik, A., 1993, Preferences and Power in the European Community: A Liberal Intergovernmentalist Approach, *Journal of Common Market Studies*, 31(4), 473–524.

Moravcsik, A., 1998, *The Choice for Europe: Social Purpose and State Power from Messina to Maastricht*, Cornell University Press.

Nye, J. S., 1965, Patterns and Catalysts in Regional Integration, *International Organization*, 19(4), 870–884.

Nye, J. S., 1968, Comparative Regional Integration: Concept and Measurement, *International Organization*, 22(4), 855–880.

Pierson, P., 1996, The Path to European Integration, *Comparative Political Studies*, 29(2), 123–163.

Pollack, M. A., 1996, The New Institutionalism and EC Governance: The Promise and Limits of Institutional Analysis, *Governance*, 9(4), 429–458.

Pollack, M. A., 2003, *The Engines of European Integration: Delegation, Agency, and Agenda Setting in the EU*, Oxford: Oxford University Press.

Ponzano, P. 2010, *La nouvelle comitologie et les actes délégués*, Manuscript, European University Institute, Florence.

Radaelli, C., 1998, *Governing European Regulation: the Challenges Ahead*, Robert Schuman Center, European University Institute Policy Paper.

Richardson, R., ed., 2012, *Constructing a Policy-making State? Policy Dynamics in the European Union*, Oxford University Press.

Sabel, C. F., and J. Zeitlin, 2007, *Learning from Difference: The New Architecture of Experimentalist Governance in the European Union*, European Governance Papers (EUROGOV).

Sandholtz, W., and A. Stone Sweet, 1998, *European Integration and Supranational Governance*, Oxford University Press.

Scharpf, F. W., 1988, The Joint-Decision Trap: Lessons from German Federalism and European Integration, *Public Administration*, 66(3), 239–278.

Scharpf, F. W., 1999, *Governing in Europe: Effective and Democratic?*, Oxford University Press.

Scharpf, F. W., 2010, *Community and Autonomy: Institutions, Policies and Legitimacy in Multilevel Europe*, Campus Verlag – Publication Series of the Max Planck Institute for the Study of Society.

Schelkle, W., 2012, European Fiscal Union: From Monetary Back Door to Parliamentary Main Entrance, *CESifo Forum*, 13(1), 28–34.

Scheller, H. K., 2006, *The European Central Bank: History, Role and Functions*, 2nd ed., European Central Bank.

Schmidt, V. A., 2008, Discursive Institutionalism: The Explanatory Power of Ideas and Discourse, *Annual Review of Political Science*, 11(1), 303–326.

Scott, J., and D. M. Trubek, 2002, Mind the Gap: Law and New Approaches to Governance in the European Union, *European Law Journal*, 8(1), 1–18.

Stacey, J., and B. Rittberger, 2003, Dynamics of Formal and Informal Institutional Change in the EU, *Journal of European Public Policy*, 10(6), 858–883.

Tallberg, J., 2000, The Anatomy of Autonomy: An Institutional Account of Variation in Supranational Influence, *Journal of Common Market Studies*, 38(5), 843–864.

Wallace, W., H. Wallace, and M. Pollack, eds., 2005, *Policy-Making in the European Union*, Oxford University Press.

Weatherill, S. R., 2009, Competence and Legitimacy, in C. Barnard and O. Odudu, eds., *The Outer Limits of European Union Law*, Hart Publishing, pp. 17–34.

Weiler, J.H.H., 1993, Journey to an Unknown Destination: A Retrospective and Prospective of the European Court of Justice in the Arena of Political Integration, *Journal of Common Market Studies*, 31(4), 417–446.

Weiler, J.H.H., 1999, *The Constitution of Europe: "Do the New Clothes Have an Emperor?" and Other Essays on European Integration*, Cambridge University Press.

Wiener, A. and T. Diez, 2003, *European Integration Theory*, Oxford University Press.

Implementation

Christoph Knill

What happens to a European law or program after its official passing at the European level? How do the formal transposition and the practical application of legal acts take shape at the national level? Which problems and deviations from the European objectives can be observed? At the first glance, it could be assumed that questions like these are relatively trivial. Why should there subsequently emerge problems in the execution of an apparently well-devised measure that was accepted by the Council of Ministers? The fact that political reality presents itself more complex, not exclusively becomes apparent in the far-reaching implementation deficits generally observed for the European policies. Implementation research also demonstrated already in the 1970s and 1980s that even with national programs, great deviations and shifts in objectives can occur during the execution phase. During implementation, administrative agencies by no means always follow unrestrictedly the political guidelines and even if they do so, in some cases the results remarkably deviate from the political expectations. In their classical study, Pressman and Wildavsky (1973) even argued that the effective transposition of political programs is rather an exception than the rule because the cooperation of a vast number of actors involved inside the implementation chain is necessary (including political decision-makers, responsible administrative agencies at different institutional levels and various societal interest groups as well as policy addressees), all trying to influence the execution according to their interests.

The general finding that shifts in policy objectives and deviations from the original political intentions are frequently observed during the implementation stage can be expected to be of particular relevance when it comes to the implementation of EU policies. This arises primarily from the fact that in executing EU measures a vast number of actors at different institutional levels are involved. Additionally, the Commission, monitoring the transposition of the Community law in the member states as the 'guardian of the treaties', possesses comparatively few resources to hierarchically ensure the cooperation of the public and private actors participating in the implementation process.

In view of this general assessment, it is the objective of this chapter to investigate the implementation of EU policies from an empirical and theoretical perspective. It proceeds as follows. In the first part, the institutional, political and empirical background with regard to the implementation of EU policies is presented. What are the institutional framework conditions that are relevant for the execution of European policies? How large is the European implementation deficit, and which measures were adopted in order to reduce it? This stock taking forms the basis for subsequent conceptual and theoretical considerations.

In the second part of this chapter, the focus is on different analytical perspectives on the implementation process and their implications for measuring implementation effectiveness. So the identification of deviations from the original political intentions during the implementation stage is closely associated with a distinctive analytical perspective on the implementation process: the so-called top-down approach that makes a clear distinction between the stages of policy formulation and policy implementation (Hill 2009: 196). It is only on this basis that an actual comparison between policy requirements and their degree of implementation is possible (Knill and Tosun 2012: 155–156). This view, however, is not uncontested in the literature. Hence, advocates of the bottom-up perspective emphasize that a clear-cut distinction between different stages should be given up in favour of an approach that explicitly acknowledges that policy formulation can continue and is even appropriate during the implementation stage in order to allow for policy designs and solutions that take into account the particular conditions at the 'street level'. In view of this debate – which in recent years has been enriched by authors emphasizing the need for a synthesis of both perspectives (see O'Toole 2003; Winter 2003) – the second part of this chapter is dedicated to a discussion of different analytical lenses on the implementation process.

Apart from this conceptual debate, the central focus of the relevant literature is on the theoretical factors that account for varying degrees of implementation effectiveness across different policies and countries. In this regard, a broad number of causes has been suggested and tested in various settings. In recent years, especially research on the implementation of EU policies in the member states strongly stimulated the theoretical debate. The third part of this chapter hence concentrates on the central theoretical factors affecting implementation effectiveness and their empirical illustration.

The implementation of EU policies: institutional framework, political background and empirical assessment

Considering the political and scientific discussion about the implementation of European policies, two aspects in particular appear rather striking. First, an explanation is needed for the fact that it is only since the mid-1980s that the implementation of EU policies has been perceived as a political problem. Second, existing studies point to fundamental problems with regard to the measurement of implementation deficits. In particular, empirical assessments can noticeably vary depending on the chosen scale. However, before turning to these issues, the institutional framework is sketched out, in which the implementation of EU policies takes place.

Institutional framework

In the EU, there is a clear-cut distribution of competence concerning the implementation of common policies in the member states. Responsibility for the execution of the Community law generally lies with the member states (article 4(3) TEU). The Commission as the 'guardian of the treaties' is responsible for controlling the transposition and application of Community law in the member states (article 17(1) TEU). For ensuring the correct implementation of European measures, the Commission, in accordance with article 258 TFEU, can instruct an infringement procedure against member states that did not fulfil the commitments resulting from Community law. But before such a procedure is instructed, the Commission takes various formal and informal steps to warrant the proper transposition of the legal acts. In this respect, the following steps can be distinguished.

If the Commission believes that there is an infringement against Community law in a member state, it first takes up informal contacts with the competent national authorities in order to discuss the details and possible problems concerning the execution of the affected measure. Depending on the results of these informal discussions, the Commission can instruct the second step of the procedure, which consists of a reminder letter from the Commission to the member state. In this way, the member state shall be given the opportunity to clarify potential obscurities and problems within the implementation process and eliminate them if necessary. If a consensual solution is not found even at this level, in a third step, the Commission gives a reasoned opinion explaining to what extent the affected member state has infringed the Community law. Beyond that, the state will be given a time limit within which the detected implementation deficits have to be redressed.

If the Member State does not comply with the obligations resulting from the reasoned opinion within the given time limit, the Commission can appeal to the European Court of Justice (ECJ). The Court finally decides whether a member state has infringed an obligation of the treaty. The member state is then obliged to take the requisite steps resulting from the sentence of the ECJ. But the EU only has humble sanctioning measures at its disposal for pushing through such obligations. The sanctioning potential has been somewhat widened, however, with the Maastricht Treaty which allows for the imposition of a fine on member states not fulfilling their obligations emerging from European law (article 260(2) TFEU).

Before appealing to the ECJ, however, in many instances bilateral negotiations between the Commission and the Member State in question are taking place with the objective of finding a consensual solution 'at the last minute'. Correspondingly, as shown in Figure 16.1, the number of commencements of proceedings before the ECJ is very low in relation to reminder letters and reasoned opinions.

For instructing infringement proceedings, three constituent facts are to be distinguished: (1) the late or non-notification of transposition measures in the member states, (2) the incorrect or incomplete transposition and (3) the incorrect application of

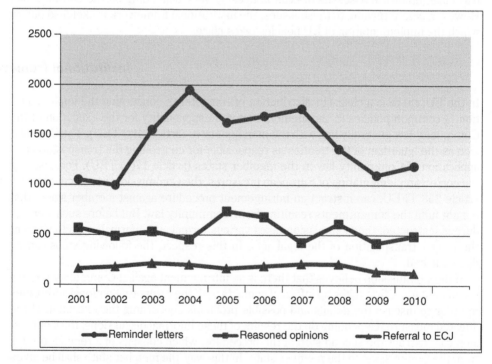

Figure 16.1 Number of infringements (according to proceeding)
Source: European Commission (2006, 2011).

Table 16.1 Investigative criteria for the introduction of infringement proceedings

	Focus	*Criteria*
Formal Transposition	• Legal and administrative provisions for the transposition of European law into the national legal and administrative system	• Time frame (Commission notification) • Completeness • Correct integration into the regulative context
Practical Transposition	• National regulation practice (regulatory style, organisational and administrative structures)	• Correct application and adherence to legal guidelines

Community law. While the first two aspects refer to the formal transposition, the third factor relates to the practical application of the Community law (see Table 16.1).

With regard to the formal transposition, the focus is on the respective legal and administrative provisions, which were fared to incorporate the legal and institutional requirements resulting from European policies into the national legal order. In this context, effective implementation not only implies the timely and complete adaptation to European requirements but also requires the corresponding integration of these rules into the existing regulatory context. When it comes to the practical transposition of European policies, the activities of implementers and policy addressees are at the centre of attention. To what extent did the legal modifications indeed result in corresponding adjustments in national regulation practice? Are the European requirements (e.g. threshold values, the foundation of new administrative agencies or the modification of existing administrative procedures) actually complied with (Knill and Lenschow 1999: 595; Weale *et al*. 2000: 297)?

Politicisation of implementation problems

Until the mid-1980s, problems of implementation of Community law played a minor role on the political agenda. The rather late politicisation of implementation deficits does not mean, however, that such deficits have been absent in the previous decades. It has rather been in the interest of the Commission and the member states to neglect implementation problems with regard to Community law.

The Commission as well as the member states for a long time primarily concentrated their activities on policy-making. The focal point of the European integration was rather on the formulation of Common policies and less on their implementation. On the side of the Commission, this orientation was favoured by its own institutional interests in expanding its political authority. In this situation, fortified interventions by the Commission in order to control and monitor the implementation effectiveness of EU policies would have endangered the political support of the member states for the expansion of political competence at the European level. The Commission's position was broadly congruent with the objectives of the member states that were, for obvious reasons, hardly interested in exposing their respective problems and failures in the transposition of European policies (Knill and Liefferink 2007: 150–151).

This initial constellation of interests, which largely favoured the depoliticisation of implementation problems, changed during the 1990s. The implementation effectiveness of European policies increasingly moved to the centre of political and scientific attention. First, the objective of completing the integration of the Common Market until 1992, as defined by the Single European Act (SEA), implied that questions about the effective transposition of Community law gained political significance (Weiler 1988). Beyond this, the increasing politicisation of implementation problems was facilitated by various judgements of the ECJ. In this context, the principles of supremacy and direct effect of Community law (which were not mentioned in the constituting treaties) have to be stressed in particular. The ECJ not only clarified that Community law is to be regarded as superior in case of a collision between European and national rules. At the same time, the Court stated that European legal acts – independent of their national implementation – are directly effective at the national level (Knill and Lenschow 2000; Knill and Liefferink 2007: 147–148).

As a result of these developments, the implementation effectiveness of European policies became a central issue on the political agenda. However, the mere observation that the implementation of EU policies became an increasingly politicised issue does not allow us to draw conclusions on the actual size of the European implementation deficit. This question as well as the related problems in measuring and judging are analysed in the following section.

Problems of measurement and data

Existing empirical data hardly allow for a comprehensive assessment of the implementation effectiveness of EU policies. In view of lacking alternative resources, comprehensive information on implementation across policies and member states can only be obtained from the data provided by the Commission. Of particular relevance in this respect are the annual reports on the application of Community law in the member states, which the Commission has been publishing since 1984. Although the data provided in these reports are currently the only comprehensive source for judging the implementation effectiveness of European policies, they allow only to a very limited extent for reliable statements about general tendencies. This can be traced to several problems that are resulting from the interpretation of the data.

First, it is averted that from the observed increase in the number of introduced infringement proceedings, opinions and reminder letters, a rise in implementation deficits cannot be concluded. Hence, Jordan (1999: 81), for instance, stresses that 'the recent rise in complaints and infringement proceedings may simply reflect the Commission's determination to tighten up on enforcement rather than increasing lawlessness among member states'. From this perspective, the augmenting implementation deficits rather reflect modified political priorities of the Commission than an aggravation of actual implementation problems.

A second problem refers to the fact that the data published by the Commission is partially inconsistent. For example, over the years the Commission has changed the basis for the collection and assignment of implementation failures (such as the amount of infringement proceedings). The same applies to the criteria of the allocation of individual measures to policy sectors, implying, for instance, that implementation deficits for directives restricting the use of chemicals in the agricultural industry have sometimes been allocated to agriculture and sometimes to the environmental sector. The frequent modifications of the basis for the data collection severely restrict the opportunities to make valid statements with regard to the development of the European implementation deficit over time and across countries and policies (Börzel 2001: 810–811; Knill and Liefferink 2007: 157–160).

Third, the data from the Commission are incomplete in various regards. On one hand, it only includes those violations against Community law, which the Commission has discovered itself or to which it turned its attention after complaints by domestic interest groups or citizens. On the other hand, the 'clearing quota' of the Commission concerning the formal and the practical implementation is unevenly distributed. So, the deficits of the member states in the formal transposition of European requirements into national law can still be ascertained quite easily. The detection of implementation deficits is much more difficult, however, when it comes to the practical application of the Community law. In view of its limited financial and personal resources, the Commission is hardly able to monitor and control the practical implementation of EU policies in the member states, but has to rely on the information provided by national authorities or complaints. As shown in Table 16.2, the number of infringement proceedings originating from complaints is much higher than the cases detected by the Commission. The implementation statistics of the Commission therefore primarily refer to the problems of formal transposition; the probably more severe problems of practical application are not sufficiently captured (Weale *et al.* 2000: 299).

A fourth difficulty results from the comparative interpretation of the Commission data. These data often tell more about the political and administrative differences between the member states than about possible domestic differences in the quality of the implementation of Community law (Knill and Liefferink 2007: 158; Krämer 2000: 143). Member states with a federal structure, for instance, typically have greater problems with the formal implementation than unitary states. This finding results from the

Table 16.2 Origin of conjectural treaty infringements

Year	Complaints	Cases detected by the Commission	Failure to notify	Total
2002	1,431	318	607	2,356
2003	1,290	253	1,166	2,709
2004	1,146	328	1,519	2,993
2005	1,154	433	1,066	2,653
2006	1,049	565	905	2,518
2007	958	512	1,196	2,666
2008	1,038	369	816	2,223
2009	772	356	531	1,659

Source: European Commission (2011).

fact that legal transposition generally entails comprehensive coordination requirements with individual sub-states or regions that are responsible for the practical implementation (see for instance König and Luetgert 2008).

Moreover, the amount of implementation failures per member state can be strongly affected by existing administrative capacities for controlling and monitoring the enforcement of EU policies (Hille and Knill 2006). Problems of practical implementation can be identified only if domestic administrations have sufficient resources to measure and control the compliance with European requirements. As a consequence, the implementation performance of member states with a low administrative capacity might be less successful than suggested by the Commission data. So, the implementation of the 1980 Drinking Water Directive at first glance seemed to be very successful in Spain, simply because of the fact that the national water authorities did not dispose of the necessary technical equipment in order to detect the small limit values for nitrates and pesticides, as they were defined by the directive. In Germany, by contrast, where the necessary measurement technology was available, non-compliance with the strict European standards resulted in infringement proceedings initiated by the Commission (Knill 2001: 153–154).

In addition to these problems inherent to the Commission statistics, existing studies on the implementation of EU policies suffer from certain methodological weaknesses which make general statements about factors affecting the implementation effectiveness of EU policies rather difficult. While case studies suffer from basic problems of generalisation, quantitative studies typically suffer from the problem that they rely on variables that are easy to measure but are maybe not the theoretically most interesting ones (Mastenbroek 2005: 1113). These variables include, for instance, failures of notification or formal transposition or the initiation of infringement proceedings. This way, the issues of practical application and potential problems emerging during this stage are systematically excluded (Knill and Liefferink 2007: 159–160).

Empirical findings

Although there is no solid data basis yet that allows for a comprehensive assessment of the implementation effectiveness of EU policies, it is nevertheless possible to identify certain general patterns. They can be derived not only from a careful interpretation of the Commission's data but also from the results of various research projects on the implementation of EU policies in different policy fields (Börzel 2000; Falkner et al. 2005; Hille and Knill 2006; Knill and Lenschow 1999, 2000; Mastenbroek 2005; Steunenberg and Toshkov 2009). To be sure, these findings hardly provide a solid basis for answering the question whether the intensified politicization of implementation deficits, as it has been observed since the mid-1980s, indeed correlates with a real increase in implementation problems or whether it is just the result of a shift in political priorities and the perception of problems. However, regardless of these problems, we are at least able to single out stable empirical trends.

A first pattern that is rather striking in this respect refers to the fact that the implementation effectiveness of EU policies strongly varies across policy sectors. Comparative data reveal that implementation problems are much more pronounced for policies directed at environmental protection, the integration of the internal market, justice affairs and taxation than is the case for other policy fields of the Community.

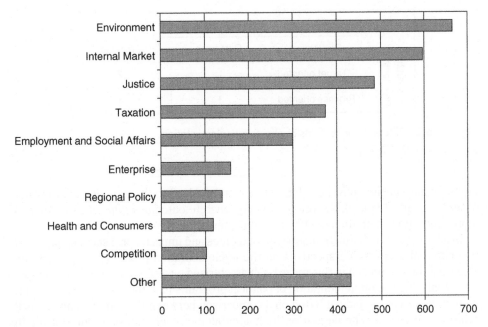

Figure 16.2 Complaints under investigation (end of 2010, by sector)
Source: European Commission (2010).

Second, and in contrast with the pattern observed across policy areas, differences in the implementation performance of the member states are by far less pronounced than one might have expected. In particular, the often stated hypothesis of the so-called Mediterranean syndrome, which expects that southern member states implement EU policies less effectively as a result of lacking administrative resources, is not confirmed (Börzel 2000). Implementation deficits rather vary in a relatively unsystematic manner across countries, regardless of their geographic location (Knill and Liefferink 2007: 155–157). This holds true, in particular, if implementation effectiveness is not only measured by focusing on the formal transpositions of EU policies, but also by considering the dimension of practical application.

Concepts for analysing and measuring implementation

Any judgement, whether a measure was implemented successfully or not, strongly depends in the way effective implementation is operationalised (Hill 2009). Generally, the conceptions that are conceivable in this context can be divided along two dimensions that refer to the analytical focus and the underlying perspective of research (see Figure 16.3).

The first dimension refers to the distinction between policy outcomes and policy impacts. With a focus on policy outcomes, effective implementation is already assumed, if the legal transposition and the practical application correspond to the objectives defined by the policy under investigation. Yet, it remains excluded, if and to what extent the objectives of a policy are actually achieved (policy impacts). Did the introduction of

		Analytical Focus	
		Outcomes	Impacts
Research Perspective	Target oriented	1	2
	Process oriented	3	4

Figure 16.3 Different conceptions of effective implementation
Source: Weale (1992: 45).

limits for automobile emissions, for instance, indeed lead to the intended improvement of the air quality? Hence, the orientation on concrete outcomes implies a substantially more pretentious definition of effective implementation.

In addition to the distinction between outcomes and impacts, on a second dimension, two different research perspectives on the implementation process can be identified. The traditional approach in this regard is characterized by a so-called top-down perspective. Analysing the implementation of political programs in a 'top down' manner, implementation success is judged based on a comparison between the intended and actually achieved outcomes. The degree of the goal attainment serves as an indicator for the implementation success; effective implementation implies a match between objectives and outcomes. If the objective of European legislation is, for instance, to set a certain standard for industrial emissions into the air, effective implementation is achieved as soon as the prescribed level is complied with throughout the Community (Hill 2009: 196; Knill and Tosun 2012: 153).

This perspective is frequently grounded on a highly simplified model of political steering. Governments and legislators are assumed to have homogenous preferences, implying clear and unambiguous standards and guidelines for administrative authorities responsible for implementation and enforcement. From analysing potential implementation deficits, conclusions on an improved design of future policies shall be drawn (concerning, for instance, policy objectives, the allocation of resources or the structures of the coordination and control of subordinate administrative agencies). At the same time, however, this perspective has been criticized for insufficiently taking into account the capacities of actors opposing against a certain policy to intervene into the implementation process (Winter 2003: 212). Moreover, the perspective excludes the important role and relevance of administrative actors that actually are involved in the execution of a certain policy program.

By contrast, the conception of an effective implementation, as it is generally underlying the 'bottom-up' perspective, is primarily process oriented. Policy objectives and instruments are no longer defined as benchmarks to be reached; instead, it is expected that they may undergo modifications during the process of policy implementation. Implementers should have flexibility and autonomy to adjust the policy in the light of particular local requirements, changes in the perception or constellation of policy problems and new scientific evidence on causal relationships between means and ends. Hence, effective implementation is not measured by the attainment of a certain centrally defined objective, but judged by the extent to which the perceived outcomes correspond with the preferences of the actors involved in the implementation process. The crucial question for evaluating implementation success is to what extent a certain policy did allow for processes of learning, capacity building and support building in order to address policy problems in a decentralised way consistent with the interests of the actors involved (Ingram and Schneider 1990, 1997).

This conception challenges the simplifying assumptions of the top-down perspective and tries to take into account the complexity of implementation processes. Thus, it is emphasised that the formulation of clear-cut objectives often contrasts with the interests of politicians who have a preference for vague and ambiguous rather than for clear-cut objectives in order to make an easy evaluation and detection of potential failures more difficult. In addition, the bottom-up perspective takes account of the fact that implementation processes are hardly characterised by a clear delineation of competencies between the involved political and administrative actors at different institutional levels. Implementation rather often implies complex interactions between public and private actors and organisations at the European, national, regional or local levels with potentially diverging interests, beliefs and perceptions with regard to the underlying policy problem. From this perspective, implementation is to a lesser extent based on hierarchically defined and controlled requirements but is understood as a bargaining process between a great number of organisations and administrative agencies participating in the implementation process. Bargaining at the same time implies that during the implementation phase, initial policy objectives might undergo significant modifications (Winter 2003).

Not least because of the fact that both analytical perspectives on the implementataion process are characterized by mutual strengths and weaknesses the current theoretical discussion attempts to combine both approaches. One possibility is to integrate both approaches into one model (Goggin *et al.* 1990; Winter 2003). Other authors (Matland 1995; Sabatier 1986) identify additional scope conditions that in a given constellation render a distinctive approach more or less analytically promising or suitable. These conditions include, for instance, the ambiguity of political objectives or the level of political conflict surrounding a policy decision (Knill and Lenschow 2000).

With regard to the analysis of the implementation of European policies, however, typically a target-oriented perspective is applied, evaluating implementation performance by comparing policy objectives and outcomes (box 1 in Figure 16.3). It is asked to what extent the necessary legal and administrative conditions were created in order to meet the objectives of European measures. It is therefore the manner of the legal and practical implementation of European policies rather than the evaluation of policy outcomes, which mostly serve as an indicator for assessing implementation effectiveness. Although this perspective implies a somewhat restricted focus, it bears several analytical advantages.

First, in this way, conceptual problems (which are confronted with alternative definitions) are avoided. A focus on policy impacts is analytically problematic as it obscures the actual link between policy instruments and their effects. Whether policy objectives are achieved not only depends on the deliberate choice of policy instruments, but also on contingencies of the political, economic, and social policy contexts. Hence, this perspective passes over important questions such as 'How do we know whether air water quality has improved as a result of European legislation rather than as the consequence of other factors completely independent from European developments, such as modified weather conditions, privatisation, or economic decline?' It ignores that the success of policy implementation in terms of policy impacts is not predictable given the scientific uncertainties and socio-economic complexities underlying a given problem constellation (Baier, March and Sætren 1990). The application of a process-oriented bottom-up perspective, by contrast, is yet characterised by the absence of a baseline for evaluating implementation results. It fails to offer a measuring rod for learning, capacity or support. When do these processes actually occur and work successfully? Moreover, and maybe even more significantly from the perspective of evaluating the impact of different policy instruments, this definition ignores the nature of the link between the (EU) policy and the local process of learning and problem solving. After all, local processes could have entirely different origins. In order to assess whether the EU policy has had any impact on these local processes, we need to observe whether its 'instructions' – however open they might be – have been complied with (Knill and Lenschow 2000).

Second, a focus on policy outcomes (i.e., the formal and practical implementation of EU policies) provides the opportunity to compare implementation results even of widely different measures. By contrast, it would be problematic to measure and hence compare the contributions of different policies (e.g. the Directive for Free Access to Environmental Information and the Large Combustion Plant Directive) with respect to their achievement of certain policy outcomes (such as air quality; Knill and Lenschow 1999: 596). Against this background, a focus on the impacts of EU policies in the member states generally appears to be an appropriate measurement rod for judging their implementation effectiveness.

How to explain variation in implementation effectiveness?

Despite significant efforts during the 1970s and 1980s, where implementation research was a 'flourishing industry', theory building remained comparatively underdeveloped. With the increasing number of case studies it became more and more apparent that, given the high variety, singularity and contingency of implementation results, the ambitious plans for developing comprehensive and general theoretical models had to be abandoned (see Hill 2009; Knill and Tosun 2012: 161–171; Mayntz 1983). These theoretical deficits are further aggravated by the fact that the concept of implementation effectiveness is operationalised differently in the literature.

This general picture, however, does not mean that no specific theoretical approaches for the analysis of European implementation processes were developed. This is facilitated by the fact that analysing the implementation of EU policies – compared to the analysis of domestic policies – offers an important methodological advantage. We are able to investigate the implementation of policies whose requirements are identical for all member states in a cross-country comparison. Moreover, it can be analysed how different countries cope with different types of policies enacted at the EU level. On this basis, a range of factors has been identified that are generally expected to play an important role in the implementation process and hence should be considered as potential explanations for varying degrees of implementation effectiveness. In the following, these factors are discussed in closer detail.

Deficient policy design

Many implementation problems have their roots in deficient policy formulation (Winter 2003). Such problems of policy design can first of all be the result of vague and ambiguous policy objectives and requirements. Often, it is only based on such vague formulation that the adoption of a policy is possible at all in order to allow for a compromise between opposing actor coalitions. In addition, the high degree of distributional conflict and politicization favours a negotiation context that is dominated by bargaining rather than problem-solving; that is the involved actors are primarily concerned with potential losses and gains rather than analysing more thoroughly the extent to which there actually exists a sound causal relationship between policy objectives and the suggested policy instruments. As a result, distributional conflicts might lead to the formulation of ill-designed policies that are characterised by wrong assumptions about the causal relationship between policy problems and politically adopted remedies. Finally, conflicts not sufficiently resolved during the formulation stage bear a high risk of popping up again during the implementation process, hence leading to far-reaching implementation deficits.

The likelihood of deficient policy designs is not only affected by the degree of distributional conflicts characterizing a certain policy discussion. It also varies with the number of actors that are involved in the decision-making process. The higher the number of actors with veto potential and the more complex the overall decision-making structures, the higher is the probability for compromises based on vague and open formulations and hence inconsistencies in policy design (Knill and Tosun 2012: 162).

Complex decision-making procedures at the EU level render EU policies particularly vulnerable to design deficits. This can be traced to the fact that policy adoption requires the accommodation of a broad range of heterogeneous interests of national governments and European institutions (the Council, the Commission, and the European Parliament). In many cases, conflicts of interests can only be resolved by vague and open wording in legal documents that allow the member states much leeway for 'minimalist' implementation, that is implementation at a lower level than originally envisioned.

For instance, many environmental policy measures in the EU grant the member states a great degree of freedom when it comes to implementation. In principle, this is with good reason, as it allows the member states to accommodate their specific economic and ecological interests. At the same time, however, this freedom leads to cross-country differences in the application of EU rules which were originally intended to be uniform. This, in turn, may be interpreted as a form of renationalisation of European environmental policies (Knill and Liefferink 2007: 201).

An important example of such regulations is formed by the series of directives on water quality, for instance for bathing water or shellfish water, where the countries themselves are free to define the bodies of water to which the directives apply. This form of self-definition, combined with the unclear wording of the classification criteria, basically leaves it open to the member states if they want to apply the directive or not, depending on their specific environmental policy goals. In the Directive on the Quality of Bathing Water, for example, bathing water is defined as a body of water 'in which bathing is explicitly authorized by the competent authorities of each member state, or bathing is not prohibited and is traditionally practised by a large number of bathers' (Directive 76/160/EEC. Article 1(2)). This definition clearly leaves a lot of room for

383

interpretation. The countries do indeed have to implement the directive, but the decision whether it is applied effectively is in practice up to the member state authorities. In extreme cases, the countries can let the directive 'run idle', by completely refraining from identifying bodies of water of the concerned type or by only designating those bodies of water that are guaranteed to comply with the quality standards anyway. An instructive example of this is how the UK dealt with the Directive on Shellfish Water. The responsible authorities were explicitly instructed by the Department of the Environment to initially designate only a small number of bodies of water which fulfilled the European standards anyway, in order to save any potential costs for the installation of control and filter technology (Knill and Liefferink 2007: 202–203).

Besides these regulations with their explicit renationalisation effects, vaguely defined legal terms in the directives generally leave much room for interpretation during national implementation. Vague legal concepts can be of a very different calibre, such as 'a large number' of bathers in the example mentioned earlier, or the weighing of 'state of technology' and 'economic feasibility' considerations with regard to the definition of approval requirements for industrial installations. Very different judgements can be made when deciding if a measure is 'economically reasonable' or if the requirements linked to the current 'state of technology' are fulfilled. The same holds for the question what should be regarded as 'a large number' of bathers.

If we look at the overall possibilities that vague legal terms and regulations with renationalisation effects in the European measures entail, the member states have considerable room to manoeuvre despite the seemingly 'uniform' design of many EU policies. This, in turn, results in a differentiation of policy effects at the national level. In most cases, such differentiation leads to a 'watering down' of the original policy objectives. Hence, regulations allowing for deviations from the initial policy can be characterised as programme deficits. They are part of the story behind the implementation deficits of EU policy.

Control deficits

Principal–agent theories constitute an important starting point for the explanation of implementation deficits. In these theories it is assumed that implementation problems result from the differences between policy objectives and their actual implementation through the responsible administrative agencies. This difference is seen as an unavoidable consequence emerging from the configuration of modern political-administrative systems that are characterized by the delegation of competencies to subordinate administrative authorities. This delegation is of particular relevance with regard to the distinction between the tasks of policy formulation (usually taking place at the EU level) and the implementation of these policies (which is usually the responsibility of the member states).

Delegation entails the problem of 'agency drift'. The agents, that is the subordinate administrations, cannot be completely controlled by their political principals. Control deficits emerge from information asymmetries, implying that administrative agents enjoy considerable discretion in fulfilling their tasks and can pursue objectives that partially deviate from the goals of their principals. From this perspective, implementation problems are particularly likely in constellation in which administrative agents interpret policy requirements differently than their principals in view of their own perceptions, interests, resources and information.

These problems, that are inherent to the configuration of political-administrative systems, are further aggravated by two factors. On one hand, high organisational complexity might increase the number of agents and government levels that are involved in the implementation process and hence increase the potential of 'agency drift'. On the other hand, high scientific or technological complexity of the underlying policy problems increases the chances for different interpretations of policy objectives by principals and agents.

The political system of the EU displays various characteristics that favor the emergence of control deficits during the implementation stage of EU policies. On one hand, in the implementation phase of European policies a shift in focus takes place from the supranational to the national level. Except for a few exceptions such as competition policy, the EU is as a rule dependent on the cooperation of the member states in the implementation of its programs. The central role of the member states implies that the implementation of EU policies is generally characterized by a high number of 'clearing points' (Pressman and Wildavsky 1973) at different institutional levels. Depending on the configuration of the national political systems, this might include not only authorities at the national, but also at the subnational and local level. As argued by Pressman and Wildavsky (1973), deviations in policy goals are likely if action depends on a number of actors that must cooperate in order to achieve the intended policy goals. Hence, the longer the implementation chain and therewith the greater the number of actors involved in the process, the more difficult becomes implementation.

On the other hand, as we have seen earlier, the possibilities of the Commission to control and sanction the implementation of EU policies in the member states are fairly limited. This is first illustrated by the fact that the Commission rarely makes use of its formal possibility to start infringement proceedings when detecting implementation problems. Implementation problems are more a matter of bilateral bargaining between the Commission and individual member states rather than being determined legally. Second, we have also seen that effective control of implementation processes by the Commission is restricted as a result of information asymmetries. This holds true in particular when it comes to questions of practical application of EU law. Here, the Commission is strongly dependent on official complaints from domestic actors, given its limited resources and competencies to directly observe implementation processes in the member states.

Choice of policy instruments

An important theoretical debate in implementation research centers on the question whether the choice of policy instruments makes a difference for implementation effectiveness (May 2003). However, this debate still suffers from the problem that so far no generally accepted classification of instruments has emerged. There exists a broad number of suggestions (for an overview see Salomon 2002), reaching from primarily descriptive assessments to more analytically ground typologies that different between three basic instrument types: instruments prescribing behavioral changes, instruments providing negative or positive incentives for behavioral changes and instruments directed at increasing implementation capacities (e.g. setting up structures, information or participation rights; Ingram and Schneider 1997).

In addition to the classification problem, research so far has not come up with sound theoretical statements on causal relationships between instrument choice and implementation effectiveness. We are rather confronted with contradictory statements in the literature. For instance, Ingram and Schneider (1997) argue that in constellations of low support for a policy, instruments emphasising learning and support building will lead to better implementation performance than detailed intervention. This view contrasts with an argument advanced by Cerych and Sabatier (1986), stating that clear and specific objectives might enhance learning by lower-level agents because it produces obvious performance indicators. Another example is the recommendation to apply instruments emphasizing participation and support building in constellations characterised by high uncertainty and complexity in order to allow for sufficient flexibility to react to new developments in the light of specific context conditions and the generation of ideas useful for the further evolution of a policy (Ingram and Schneider 1997). Again, there are also good arguments to justify detailed intervention in such constellations. First, too much discretion for subordinate agents might imply that nothing happens at all. Second, even an interventionist policy that takes little account of the given complexity might succeed in stimulating learning processes by trial and error (Knill and Lenschow 2000).

The previously mentioned theoretical problems are joined by another research deficit resulting from the fact that so far few efforts have been made to analyse potential implementation impacts emerging from possible combinations of different types of instruments (May 2003: 225). Relevant studies have dealt primarily with intrinsic characteristics of instruments and their impact on implementation effectiveness (Salomon 2002). Potential interactions between different instruments and possible effects of different combinations of instruments were previously only rarely investigated (Gunningham and Grabosky 1998).

Regardless of the described theoretical and analytical problems, the question of instrument choice and its implication on implementation effectiveness constitutes a topic of high political relevance. This can be observed in particular with regard to the EU. Here, it is notably the European Commission, which since the mid-1990s promoted a change in the choice of instruments. This is characterised by the fact that in addition to traditional hierarchical control approaches, increased incentive-based 'economic' instruments and information-based instruments (which emphasize the improvement of information and opportunities for participation of social actors) should be used. Moreover, a general tendency for governance approaches relying on general frameworks rather than detailed regulations and the emphasis on procedures rather than specific substantial requirements (Knill 2008; Knill and Lenschow 2000; Knill and Liefferink 2007).

So far, however, existing studies point out that in practice the resulting changes in instrument choice are much less pronounced as one might expect from the declarations of the Commission. Still provide traditional forms of hierarchical intervention far the most important group of policy instruments applied at the EU level (Holzinger *et al.* 2006). A potential explanation for this finding refers to the fact that the possibility of substitution of hierarchical instruments is often limited. This applies, for instance, to the whole area of harmonization of national laws and regulations to establish the Common market.

In addition, comparative studies of the implementation effectiveness of different European policy instruments show that there exists no systematic causal relationship between the choice of instruments and implementation effectiveness; hence underlining the general theoretical ambiguity of implementation research with regard to this aspect (Knill 2008; Knill and Lenschow 2000). Between instrument choice and implementation effectiveness there is obviously no simple causal relationship.

This aspect has been identified especially in the field of environmental policy. EU environmental policy had traditionally relied on instruments associated with hierarchical intervention and command-and-control regulation. Typical for this approach were highly detailed legal rules and standards which left the member states comparatively little discretion during the implementation. In many cases, EU policies not only defined detailed procedural rules, but also specified contained substantive objectives in terms of content (such as emission or quality standards) that had to be complied with by the member states, regardless of potentially differing environmental conditions and problems at the domestic level. Notwithstanding the definition of ambitious and detailed policy requirements from the European level, however, the implementation deficit in environmental field continuously increased.

In response to these problems, the Commission strongly promoted the development of so-called new instruments from the early 1990s onwards. New instruments were expected to improve the implementation effectiveness of environmental policy in basically two ways. First, they purportedly left member states more leeway to comply with EU requirements by taking account of domestic context conditions. In contrast to the detailed and substantive, standard-oriented 'old' instruments that are to be uniformly implemented regardless of the physical, economic or political context, new instruments focus on establishing basic procedures for improving environmental awareness and behaviour and no concrete environmental targets are set. Second, new instruments also target the policy context directly and aim to change context factors in order to facilitate the formal and practical implementation of environmental policy in general. Here we can distinguish two strategies: the mobilisation of society through more transparent processes and participatory opportunities as well as the provision of economic incentives for industrial self-regulation.

Comparative research, however, shows that there is obviously no direct causal relationship between the choice of European policy instruments and implementation effectiveness. Instead, successes and failures vary across policies and countries, without indicating a direct causal linkage between instrument type and implementation performance. The formal and practical transposition of new instruments poses by no means fewer problems than it is the case for old instruments (Börzel 2000; Knill 1998; Knill and Lenschow 2000).

Institutional design

Except for very rare cases where policies to some extent 'are self-implementing' (e.g. the change of key interest rates by the European Central Bank that for their proper observance need not be backed by a comprehensive inspection apparatus), the implementation of policies generally requires the establishment of institutional structures and arrangements: 'Policy implementation requires institutions to carry the burden of transforming general policy intent into an array of rules, routines and social processes that can convert policy intention into action' (O'Toole 2003: 234). In other words, policies generally have institutional implications, that is requirements for the establishment of appropriate structures and procedures for their proper implementation.

Generally a distinction can be made between policies that can be implemented by single organizations or authorities (Torenvlied 1996), and measures for those proper implementation entails horizontal and vertical coordination across several administrative units and levels (Hjern and Porter 1981). It is obvious that in the latter case much greater challenges for effective implementation exist than in the case of an integrated implementation structure: 'Between or among organizations, the differing routines and specialized languages, not to mention distinct ways of seeing the world mean, that poses particularly daunting challenges interorganisational implementation (O'Toole 2003: 235).

These challenges are based on the fact that the implementation of a policy in this way requires major changes in existing institutional structures. This aspect is of key importance in multilevel systems like the EU. The fact that EU member states are legally obliged to implement European model specifications that do not originate in their own national contexts, already as such bears potentially high costs of institutional adjustment. These potential pressures of institutional adjustment vary in the extent to which the European requirements differ from given institutional arrangements in the member states (Knill 2001).

In light of these considerations, the institutional compatibility of new requirements and existing arrangements is emphasised as important explanatory factor for implementation effectiveness in the literature, in particular with regard to the domestic implementation of EU policies. The central argument here is that it is to a lesser extent the choice of the instrument per se that affects the implementation success of European politics but the extent of institutional adjustment pressures, which emanate from these policies on national regulatory patterns and administrative structures (Blauberger 2009; Kaeding 2008; Knill 2001; Knill and Lenschow 1999; Skjærseth and Wettestad 2008; Thomson 2009; Toshkov 2008).

The institutional perspective rests on two central assumptions that are introduced before we look at the consequences with regard to implementation effectiveness: (1) Effective implementation is generally a question of effective institutional adaptation, and (2) the extent of institutional change is limited by the given institutional arrangements.

Although policies and respective political debates are primarily directed at the specification of policy contents and instruments rather than institutional arrangements, it should not be overlooked that there is often a tight linkage between policy content and corresponding institutional implementation requirements. Therefore, decisions on instruments to a certain extent always entail decisions on corresponding institutional arrangements for their proper application. While being aware of the fact that the degree to which policy contents and institutional implications are coupled may vary from policy to policy and from sector to sector, it cannot be ignored that the growing importance of EU policies leaves its mark on domestic institutions. Consequently, implementation problems can be conceived as problems of institutional change (Knill and Lenschow 1999: 608–609).

The connection between instruments and institutions has long been acknowledged in the implementation literature. However, institutions were basically analysed from the perspective of adequate design. Analysts coming from the top-down perspective developed optimal structural and organisational arrangements that would permit effective implementation of a certain policy (see Pressmann and Wildavsky 1973). This thinking relies on the implicit assumption that national institutions would easily adapt to the suggested 'model' structure. Problems of institutional change were ignored. The bottom-up perspective assumes a similar malleability of existing institutional factors. Here, analysts are interested in the impact of varying institutional designs on the skills, resources and capacities of relevant actors. They are interested in the perfect design that serves to equip the implementing authorities with sufficient financial, legal and personal resources.

Without denying the importance of adequate institutional design, such a perspective remains incomplete as long as it ignores the problems associated with the process of adjusting the existing institutional arrangements to the defined 'ideal' arrangements. It is in particular this latter aspect and to lesser extent the knowledge of the correct institutional design that makes the implementation of public policies problematic.

This leads us to the second basic assumption of the institutionalist perspective: Effective institutional adaptation to external requirements can only be expected within certain limits. It is one of the few generally accepted findings in the otherwise diverse institutionalist literature (Hall and Taylor 1996) that institutional change, regardless if required explicitly or implicitly, rarely takes place in a smooth and unproblematic way. Existing institutions 'matter' and they do so mainly by constraining the options for future changes and adaptations.

The emphasis on institutional stability and continuity is yet not synonymous for a static understanding of institutional development. Rather institutions virtually find themselves in a permanent process of adaptation to their environment. However, the scope of these adaptations is restricted by the structuring effects of existing institutional arrangements. Institutional change is hence often limited to aspects that do not question the very identity of an institution (March and Olsen 1989; Thelen and Steinmo 1992).

This abstract argument is of limited explanatory value, however, as long as we do not have criteria in order to judge in which constellations institutional requirements exceed the adaptation capacity of national institutions and when not. To cope with this problem, Knill and Lenschow (1998) suggest a distinction between three levels of adaptation pressure, each of them being linked to different expectations with regard to implementation effectiveness (see Figure 16.4). This distinction is based on the understanding that institutionally grown structures and routines prevent easy adaptation to exogenous pressure (DiMaggio and Powell 1991; March and Olsen 1989). Hence, domestic adaptation appears to be more likely in cases where European policies imply incremental rather than fundamental departures from existing arrangements at the domestic level.

The first scenario refers to constellations of low adaptation pressure. In this case, the institutional implications of new policies are completely in line with existing arrangements; that is none or only marginal changes are demanded. Implementation therefore is expected to be rather effective, as institutional adjustment requirements are very limited or completely absent.

In the second scenario of high adaptation pressure, by contrast, new requirements exceed the adjustment capacities of existing institutions. Ineffective implementation is the probable consequence. Such constellations can be expected, for instance, when EU requirements are in contradiction with institutionally strongly entrenched elements of national regulatory arrangements (see Krasner 1988).[1] Such contradictions occur, for instance, if EU policies require changes in domestic regulatory styles and structures that represent general patterns of national state, legal and administrative traditions and that are strongly rooted in a country's political, administrative and legal system.

The third scenario of moderate adaptation pressure refers to constellations in which new policies require substantive adjustments of existing institutions, however, without challenging well-entrenched core patterns of the political, legal and administrative system. While in such cases there is a higher probability for an effective implementation of these policies, effective implementation, nevertheless, cannot be taken for granted. In contrast with the two other scenarios, in these cases a mere institutional perspective is not sufficient to develop hypotheses on the expected implementation performance (in terms of domestic institutional adjustments to new requirements). To answer this question we have to complement our analysis with a second explanatory step which considers the particular interest constellation and institutional opportunity structures at the domestic level. To what extent is there sufficient public support for adjusting to new requirements? To what extent have actors who support regulatory change sufficient powers and resources to realise their interests? Institutional adaptation and hence effective implementation can only be expected if they are facilitated by favourable context conditions in that respect (Knill and Lehmkuhl 2002; Knill and Lenschow 1998).

Preferences and strategies of the involved actors

Not least against the background of the described limitations of the explanatory value of institutionalist approaches various studies emphasize the importance of the preferences and strategies of actors involved in the implementation process (Knill and Lehmkuhl 2002; Steunenberg 2007).

The basic assumption underlying this reasoning is that actors such as political parties, bureaucracies and interest groups occupy a central role in the implementation process. With regard to the implementation of EU policies, for instance this implies that high explanatory importance is associated with domestic factors. The latter relate in particular to the interests of the involved actors and the national institutional opportunity structures that influence the strategic options of these actors in pursuing their

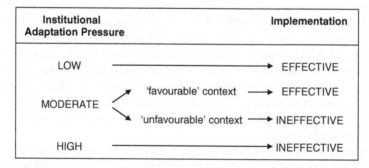

Figure 16.4 Institutional adaptation pressure and implementation effectiveness
Source: Knill and Lehmkuhl (2002).

interests (Steunenberg 2007). This way, the implementation effectiveness of European policies is explained on the basis of national interest constellation and existing institutional opportunity structures (Hartlapp 2009; Knill and Lehmkuhl 2002).

One example is the investigation of Treib (2003), focusing on the implementation of six EU labor policies in four member states. He comes to the conclusion that political parties and their programs have an effect on the implementation of European directives. He stresses that rather than the level of institutional adjustment pressure per se, the way domestic actors cope with these pressures is of crucial importance for understanding implementation effectiveness. In this context, the way political actors perceive such adjustment pressure is strongly affected by their party political affiliation. From the 'parties-do-matter' hypothesis, expectations on two implementation patterns can be derived that refer explicitly to coalition governments. First, if EU requirements are in line with the party-politically defined interests of the coalition partners, effective implementation regardless of the level of adaptation pressure is expected. Second, ineffective implementation is the likely scenario if one or more coalition partners oppose the given policy as it runs counter to their political objectives.

However, in addition to political actors also other national stakeholders might play an important role in the implementation process. Steunenberg (2007), for example shows that in addition to the preferences of party politicians, the preferences of administrative actors are important. This is true not only for potential self-interests of the government bureaucracy, which plays an important role in shaping the formal implementation, but also for subordinate administrative units that are involved in the practical implementation stage (Knill 2001).

Administrative capacities

While the factors discussed so far in particular focused on the willingness of the involved actors to achieve effective implementation, the focus on administrative capacities entails a different perspective that is concerned with the ability rather than the willingness to effectively comply with given policy requirements. In other words, varying implementation effectiveness is explained by different capacities, which affect the opportunities available for effective formal and practical implementation. In this context, particular emphasis is placed on human capacity (administrative and technical expertise) as well as financial, technical and organizational resources. The less developed these capacities, the more important becomes the allocation of existing resources in the light of political priorities. Depending on the importance of effective implementation of a certain policy on the political agenda, therefore, more or less severe effects emerging from a lack of administrative capacity on the implementation effectiveness may be expected.

On this basis, for example differences in implementation effectiveness between economically stronger and weaker developed EU member states have been postulated (Hille and Knill 2006). Accordingly, Pridham (1994), for instance, expected a generally ineffective implementation of European policies in the southern member states of the EU (Mediterranean syndrome), assuming that in comparison to their northern neighbors, much less pronounced administrative resources for proper transposition and enforcement are available in these countries. Although this argument is controversially discussed in the literature (Börzel 2000), it might play an important explanatory role in particular in constellations in which it comes to the implementation of rather encompassing or complex policies (Featherstone and Papadimitriou 2008).

Conclusion: how to improve the implementation of EU policies?

The empirical and theoretical analysis of the implementation of European policies suggests several conclusions which have to be taken into account when trying to improve the EU's implementation performance. First, the formal and practical implementation of EU policies is in general a highly complex process, which can not only be analyzed from different analytical perspectives (top down versus bottom up) but is also influenced by a variety of factors.

Second, empirical evidence shows that the implementation effectiveness of EU policies can hardly be fully explained by looking at country-specific factors. The formal transformation and practical application of Community law reveals no clear pattern of member states typically implementing EU policies either effectively or ineffectively. Rather, the performance of each member state varies to a great extent from policy to policy and from sector to sector.

Third, potential factors affecting the implementation effectiveness of EU policies can be summed up in six groups, including program deficits, control deficits, instrument choice, institutional compatibility, preferences and strategies of involved actors as well as administrative capacities. In this context, the question of whether and under what conditions the implementation of policies can be characterized as rather effective or ineffective can hardly be answered by a mono-causal explanation but needs to take into account a complex configuration of different aspects.

Finally, it should be emphasized that different policy designs and governance approaches should not be interpreted as a panacea to overcome all problems causing implementation deficits in the EU. None of the discussed approaches will avoid the common practice of 'creative compliance' in the Member States; this practice of avoiding the intention of a law without breaking the terms of the law, constitutes a common problem for all modes of regulation (see Cohn 2002; McBarnet and Whelan 1991). Moreover, it should not be overlooked that the design of a European policy is the result of often long-winded negotiations among the member states. As a result, policy proposals are often watered down (by making use of exception clauses or vague formulations) or are enriched with elements that are in the interests of certain member states. Implementation deficits to a considerable degree are simply the result of inconsistent and ambiguous European policies. This basic deficit applies to all forms of European governance. The deliberate choice of European policy design therefore only allows for partial improvements of the implementation performance; the design of policies for effective implementation is constrained by the need to accommodate the diverse interests of the member states.

Note

1   Krasner (1988) differentiates between two dimensions of institutional anchorage. Institutional depth refers to the extent to which institutional arrangements are embedded in normative orientations and dominant belief systems. Institutional breadth, in turn, refers to the extent to which institutional arrangements are interlinked with their institutional environment.

References

Baier, V.E., March, J.G. and Sætren, H., 1990. Implementierung und Ungewißheit. In: J.G. March, ed. *Entwicklung und Organisation. Kritische und konstruktive Beiträge, Entwicklungen und Perspektiven*. Wiesbaden: Gabler, 170–184.

Blauberger, M., 2009. Compliance with Rules of Negative Integration: European State Aid Control in the New Member States. *Journal of European Public Policy*, 16 (7), 1030–1046.

Börzel, T.A., 2000. Why There Is no Southern Problem. On Environmental Leaders and Laggards in the EU. *Journal of European Public Policy*, 7 (1), 141–162.

Börzel, T.A., 2001. Non-Compliance in the European Union. Pathology or Statistical Artefact? *Journal of European Public Policy*, 8 (5), 803–824.

Cerych, L. and Sabatier, P., 1986. *Great Expectations and Mixed Preferences: The Implementation of European Higher Education Reforms*. Stoke on Trent: Trentham Books.

Cohn, M., 2002. Fuzzy Legality in Regulation: The Legislative Mandate Revisited. *Law and Policy*, 23 (4), 469–497.

DiMaggio, P.J. and Powell, W.W., 1991. The Iron Cage Revisited. Institutionalized Isomorphism and Collective Rationality in Organizational Fields. In: P.J. Di Maggio and W.W. Powell, eds. *The New Institutionalism in Organizational Analysis*. Chicago: Chicago University Press, 63–82.

European Commission, 2006. *23rd Annual Report from the Commission on Monitoring the Application of EU Community Law (2005)*. Brussels: Commission of the European Communities.

European Commission, 2010. *27th Annual Report from the Commission on Monitoring the Application of EU Community Law (2009)*. Brussels: Commission of the European Communities.

European Commission, 2011. *28th Annual Report from the Commission on Monitoring the Application of EU Community Law (2005)*. Brussels: Commission of the European Communities.

Featherstone, K. and Papadimitriou, D., eds. 2008. *The Limits of Europeanization. Reform Capacity and Policy Conflict in Greece*. Basingstoke: Palgrave Macmillan.

Falkner, G., Treib, O., Hartlapp, M. and Leiber, S., 2005. *Complying with Europe? Theory and Practice of Minimum Harmonisation and Soft Law in the Multilevel System*. Cambridge: Cambridge University Press.

Goggin, M.L., Bowman, A., Lester, J.P. and O'Toole, L.J.J., 1990. *Implementation Theory and Practice: Toward a Third Generation*. Glenview: Scott/Foresman/Little/Browns.

Gunningham, N. and Grabosky, P., 1998. *Smart Regulation, Designing Environmental Policy*. New York: Oxford University Press.

Hall, P.A. and Taylor, R.C., 1996. *Political Science and the Three New Institutionalisms*. MPIFG Discussion Paper 96/6. Köln: Max-Planck-Institut für Gesellschaftsforschung.

Hartlapp, M., 2009. Implementation of EU Social Policy Directives in Belgium: What Matters in Domestic Politics? *Journal of European Integration*, 31 (4), 467–488.

Hill, M.J., 2009. *The Public Policy Process*. Harlow: Pearson.

Hille, P. and Knill, C., 2006. "It's the Bureaucracy, Stupid": The Implementation of the Acquis Communautaire in EU Candidate Countries, 1999–2003. *European Union Politics*, 7 (4), 531–552.

Hjern, B., and Porter, D.O., 1981. Implementation Structures: A New Unit of Administrative Analysis. *Organization Studies*, 2 (3), 211–227.

Holzinger, K., Knill, C. and Schäfer, A., 2006. Rhetoric or Reality? "New Governance" in EU Environmental Policy. *European Law*, 12 (3), 403–420.

Ingram, H. and Schneider, A.L., 1990. Improving Implementation through Framing Smarter Statutes. *Journal of Public Policy*, 10 (1), 67–88.

Ingram, H. and Schneider, A.L., 1997. *Policy Design for Democracy*. Lawrence: University of Kansas Press.

Jordan, A.J., 1999. The Implementation of EU Environmental Policy: A Policy Problem Without a Political Solution? *Environment and Planning C (Government and Policy)*, 17 (1), 69–90.

Kaeding, M., 2008. Lost in Translation or Full Steam Ahead: The Transposition of EU Transport Directives Across Member States. *European Union Politics*, 9 (1), 115–143.

Knill, C., 1998. European Policies: The Impact of National Administrative Traditions on European Policy Making. *Journal of Public Policy*, 18 (1), 1–28.

Knill, C., 2001. *The Europeanisation of National Administrations: Patterns of Institutional Change and Persistence*. Cambridge: Cambridge University Press.

Knill, C., 2008. *Europäische Umweltpolitik. Steuerungsprobleme und Regulierungsmuster im Mehrebenensystem*. Wiesbaden: VS.

Knill, C. And Lehmkuhl, D. (2002): The National Impact of EU Regulatory Policy: Three Europeanization Mechanisms. *European Journal of Political Research*, 41 (2), 255–280.

Knill, C. and Lenschow, A., 1998. Coping with Europe: The Impact of British and German Administration on the Implementation of EU Environmental Policy. *Journal of European Public Policy*, 5 (4), 595–614.

Knill, C. and Lenschow, A., 1999. Neue Konzepte – alte Probleme? Die institutionellen Grenzen effektiver Implementation. *Politische Vierteljahresschrift*, 40 (4), 591–617.

Knill, C. and Lenschow, A., 2000. *Implementing EU Environmental Policy: New Directions and Old Problems*. Manchester: Manchester University Press.

Knill, C. and Liefferink, D., 2007. *Environmental Politics in the European Union. Policy-Making, Implementation and Patterns of Multi-level Governance*. Manchester: Manchester University Press.

Knill, C. and Tosun, J., 2012. *Public Policy: A New Introduction*. London: Palgrave Macmillan.

König, T. and Luetgert, B., 2008. Troubles with Transposition? Explaining Trends in Member-State Notification and the Delayed Transposition of EU Directives. *British Journal of Political Science*, 39 (1), 163–194.

Krämer, L., 2000. *EC Environmental Law*. London: Sweet & Maxwell.

Krasner, S.D., 1988. Sovereignty: An Institutional Perspective. *Comparative Political Studies*, 21 (1), 66–94.

March, J.G. and Olsen, J.P., 1989. *The New Institutionalism: Organizational Factors in Political Life*. New York: The Free Press.

Mastenbroek, E., 2005. EU Compliance: Still a 'Black Hole'? *Journal of European Public Policy*, 12 (6), 1103–1120.

Matland, R., 1995. Synthesizing the Implementation Literature: The Ambiguity-Conflict Model of Policy Implementation. *Journal of Public Administration Research and Theory*, 5 (2), 145–174.

May, P.J., 2003. Policy Design and Implementation. In: B.G. Peters and J. Pierre, eds. *Handbook of Public Administration*. Thousand Oaks: Sage, 223–233.

Mayntz, R., 1983. *Implementation politischer Programme II*. Opladen: Westdeutscher Verlag.

McBarnet, D. and Whelan, C., 1991. The Elusive Spirit of the Law: Formalism and the Struggle of Legal Control. *Modern Law Review*, 54 (6), 848–873.

O'Toole, L.J.J., 2003. Interorganizational Relations in Implementation. In: B.G. Peters and J. Pierre, eds. *Handbook of Public Administration*. Thousand Oaks: Sage, 234–244.

Pressman, J. and Wildavsky, A., 1973. *Implementation*. Berkeley: University of California Press.

Pridham, G. (1994). National environmental policy-making in the European framework: Spain, Greece and Italy in comparison. *Regional and Federal Studies*, 4 (1), 80–101.

Sabatier, P.A., 1986. Top-Down and Bottom-Up Approaches to Implementation Research. *Journal of Public Policy*, 6 (1), 21–48.

Salomon, L.M., 2002. The New Governance and the Tools of Public Action: An Introduction. In: L.M. Salomon, ed. *The Tools of Government: A Guide to the New Governance*. Oxford: Oxford University Press, 1–47.

Skjærseth, J. B. and Wettestad, J., 2008. Implementing EU Emissions Trading: Success or Failure? *International Environmental Agreements: Politics, Law and Economics*, 8 (4), 275–290.

Steunenberg, B., 2007. A Policy Solution to the European Union's Transposition Puzzle: Interaction of Interests in Different Domestic Arenas. *West European Politics*, 30 (1), 23–49.

Steunenberg, B. and Toshkov, D., 2009. Comparing Transposition in the 27 Member States of the EU: The Impact of Discretion and Legal Fit. *Journal of European Public Policy*, 16 (7), 951–970.

Thelen, K. and Steinmo, S., 1992. Historical Institutionalism in Comparative Politics. In: S. Steinmo, K. Thelen and F. Longstreth, eds. *Structuring Politics: Historical Institutionalism in Comparative Analysis*. Cambridge: Cambridge University Press, 1–32.

Thomson, R., 2009. Same Effects in Different Worlds: The Transposition of EU Directives. *Journal of European Public Policy*, 16 (1), 1–18.

Torenvlied, R., 1996. Political Control of Implementation Agencies: Effects of Political Consensus on Agency Compliance. *Rationality and Society*, 8 (1), 25–56.

Toshkov, D., 2008. Embracing European Law: Compliance with EU Directives in Central and Eastern Europe. *European Union Politics*, 9 (3), 379–402.

Treib, O., 2003. Die Umsetzung von EU-Richtlinien im Zeichen der Parteipolitik: Eine akteurszentrierte Antwort auf die Misfit-These. *Politische Vierteljahresschrift*, 44 (4), 506–528.

Weale, A., 1992. *The New Politics of Pollution*. Manchester: Manchester University Press.

Weale, A., Pridham, G., Cini, M., Konstadakopulos, D., Porter, M. and Flynn, B., 2000. *Environmental Governance in Europe*. Oxford/New York: Oxford University Press.

Weiler, J., 1988. The White Paper and the Application of Community Law. In: R. Bieber, R. Dehousse, J. Pinder and J.H.H. Weiler, eds. *One European Market?* Baden-Baden: Nomos, 337–358.

Winter, S. C., 2003. Implementation Perspectives: Status and Reconsideration. In: B. G. Peters and J. Pierre, eds. *Handbook of Public Administration*. Thousand Oaks: Sage, 212–222.

Part IV

CHANNELS OF REPRESENTATION

Chapter 17

European elections and the European voter

MARK FRANKLIN AND SARA B. HOBOLT

Elections in democracy are supposed to perform the functions of holding governments accountable and representing voters' interests, thus legitimising the exercise of power. Elections to the European Parliament (EP), however, largely fail to perform these functions. The reforms introduced in the Maastricht Treaty (1993), and reinforced in the Amsterdam Treaty (1999) and the Lisbon Treaty (2009), gave the European Parliament a significant role in selecting the president of the European Commission. The result of these reforms is a quasi-parliamentary system for selecting this branch of the EU executive, whereby the Commission president is nominated by the member states and ratified by the European Parliament immediately following the EP elections.

Nevertheless, European elections have not until now set in motion a process of government formation in the same way as do national elections in the member states. Moreover, citizens generally have little knowledge of policies implemented or promised at the European level by parties, and parties themselves often use these elections as opportunities to test their standing with the public in terms of their domestic political agendas. But national governments do not stand or fall by European election results either, so the choices of voters have no immediately obvious repercussions on policy at either level. In the circumstances it is perhaps not surprising that many European citizens fail to take European elections seriously, and turnout is generally low. The low-level levels of public participation in European elections in turn raises questions in some minds about the legitimacy of the European Union as a democratic polity (Franklin 2014).

But the fact that European elections have limited consequences for government formation at the national or European levels does not mean that they have no effects. Indeed, the very failure of European elections to legitimate the exercise of power in the EU has consequences for the future of the European Union, and European elections do have many consequences – some of them unanticipated and unfortunate – for the politics of member states. They also determine the composition of the European Parliament which in turn has implications for policy-making, especially since the European Parliament has acquired and enhanced its co-decision-making powers with the Maastricht Treaty and with successive treaty changes thereafter.

In this chapter we do not examine consequences of European elections for policy, since they are hardly apparent to voters, but instead focus on voting behaviour in European Parliament elections and the effects of these elections on national politics. We also evaluate the role of these elections in creating a 'crisis of legitimacy' for the European Union.

European Parliament elections

The introduction of elections to the European Parliament (EP) in June 1979 was a deliberate attempt by European leaders to give citizens a direct voice in the policy-making activities of the (then) European Economic Community and to strengthen its democratic credentials. The same aim of strengthening democracy at the European level has led to the transformation of the EP from a weak consultative assembly into a genuine parliament with co-legislative powers in the policy-making process (Rittberger 2005).

European Parliament elections are organized separately in each EU member country. In 1979 nine elections were held in the (then) nine member states with a tenth election two years later when Greece became a member. Such elections have been repeated in all member states in June of every fifth year thereafter, meaning that by June 2014, 145 separate elections had been conducted. While we can speak broadly of Europe-wide elections, there are significant variations in the way in which these elections are conducted in member states. For one thing, they are not all conducted on the same day. Some European countries traditionally go to the polls on Sundays while others have favoured midweek voting. These traditions have been maintained for European Parliament elections that, however, are all held in the same week in June (or May in 2014) every fifth year.

European elections also differ in terms of when they are held in the national electoral cycle. Since European elections are held in the same week but national elections are not, it follows that European elections occur at different times relative to national elections in different countries (and in the same country at different European elections). Sometimes the European elections will occur shortly after a national election, sometimes only after the elapse of a number of months or years, and sometimes they will occur in the shadow of national elections that are known (or felt) to be imminent.

Another difference between countries is the electoral system employed. Although legislation on uniformity of electoral procedures in EP elections was enacted in 2003 –according to which all national elections to the EP shall be held under a proportional representation electoral system – there has been, and continues to be, considerable variation in ballot structure and district magnitude across countries (Farrell and Scully 2007). Except in the British Isles, list-system proportional representation has been universal since 1979, but in England, Scotland and Wales plurality voting was used until and including the election of 1994, after which a list-proportional system came into use; while in Ireland and Northern Ireland a Single Transferable Vote system continues to be employed.

Equally important are the differences between the system used in any particular country for European elections and that used for national elections in the same country. As already mentioned, Britain and Northern Ireland have quite different electoral systems for European elections than for national elections. In other countries the system may be superficially similar in both types of election, but there are always differences in practice, such as constituency sizes and the number of votes required to get any candidate elected (which is always greater in European elections). To the extent that certain types of parties are advantaged or disadvantaged by these different electoral arrangements in European elections this can have important consequences for national politics, as discussed in the following.

In many ways, the legislative process in the European Parliament operates very much like in any national legislature, since members (MEPs) are organized in political groups. These groups consist of one or more European political parties, so-called Europarties, so they constitute alliances among national party families operating transnationally in Europe. The largest political group and Europarty in the 2014–2019 EP is the centre-right European People's Party (EPP) and the second-largest group is the centre-left Progressive Alliance of Socialists and Democrats (S&D), which is led by the Party of European Socialists (PES). These groups are the central mechanism for structuring debate over and support for legislation, and they decide vital political issues. Similar to parties in national parliaments, there are high levels of group cohesion in the EP and voting patterns operate on two broad dimensions: the left–right dimension and the pro-/anti-integration dimension (Hix *et al.* 2006, 2007).

However, despite the presence of traditional party politics at the European level, voters are generally unaware of this, and Europarties have traditionally played a limited role in EP election campaigns. This is not least due to the fact that, unlike national parliamentary systems, these elections are not contests between competing government alternatives and over incumbent performance records. While Europarties produce electoral manifestos, the extent to which the national parties use these manifestos in their own campaigning has traditionally been minimal. Instead, European election campaigns have tended to focus on domestic political matters and be dominated by national political actors. In between EP elections, the European Parliament is largely ignored by national media (Norris 2000; Peter and de Vreese 2004). It is therefore unsurprising that citizens have limited knowledge of the workings of the EP. In 2007 Eurobarometer asked citizens across the EU whether MEPs sit in the EP based on their nationality or their political affinities. Only a third of respondents realised it was the latter. Indeed, in that same survey in 2007 fewer than half were aware that MEPs were actually directly elected, and only 1 in 10 knew that the next EP elections were to be held in 2009.

There are some indications that this lack of interest in the EP may be slowly changing. Significantly, media studies of consecutive EP campaigns have shown that the media in recent elections pays more attention to European politics during the election campaigns. In 2009, more than a fifth of all TV news coverage across countries in the three weeks leading up to the election was dealing with the EU or the EP election specifically. Indeed, Europe was the third-most important news issue in television and newspapers, following the economy and crime. Comparing this to previous EP elections, we can see that coverage has been increasing (De Vreese *et al.* 2006; Schuck *et al.* 2011; Hobolt and Tilley 2014b). However, more than half of the actors appearing in stories on Europe were domestic political actors, suggesting that news about Europe continues to be viewed through national political lenses. Another reason for increased salience of the EU is the European sovereign debt crisis and the subsequent crisis of the eurozone, which has unfolded since 2009. This crisis has highlighted the importance of the EU to ordinary voters in both creditor and debtor states and has increased the salience of the EU in national elections. There remains significant variation across countries with highest EU coverage in Greece and Malta in 2009 and lowest in Belgium and the Czech Republic. These variations also influence how voters decide whom to vote for in EP elections, as we discuss in the next section.

Voting behaviour in European elections

Europeans vote differently in national and European elections. Notwithstanding the increasing importance of the EP since the first direct elections in 1979, studies have demonstrated three broad patterns of empirical regularities repeated in all seven EP elections (see e.g. Reif and Schmitt 1980; van der Eijk and Franklin 1996; Marsh 1998; Hix and Marsh 2007, 2011). First, levels of turnout are lower than in national elections. Second, citizens favour smaller parties over larger ones compared to national elections. Third, parties in national governments do worse in EP elections than in national elections. More recently, research has also shown that Eurosceptic parties perform better in EP elections, even when taking into account party size.

These different patterns of voting in national and European elections means that some parties are winners and others are losers in EP elections. Figure 17.1 shows the average performance of party family across EP elections between 1979 and 2009. It clearly shows that large governing party families – Socialists, Conservatives and Liberal (but surprisingly not the Christian Democrats) – are the losers in the elections, while smaller parties are the winners. Anti-European parties and Green parties have performed relatively well in EP elections, gaining on average 6.7 per cent of the votes and 2.5 per cent of the votes, respectively, compared to their performance in preceding national general elections. In contrast, socialist parties seem to have been the main losers in European Parliament elections, losing on average 3.5 per cent of their votes compared to national general elections.

There are two reasons why some parties lose and others win in EP elections: voters defect from the parties that they normally vote for in European elections and higher levels of abstention may affect some parties more than others. In practice, differential turnout has little effect (van der Eijk and Franklin 1996), so we focus on party switching. Table 17.1 shows that on average about a quarter of all voters at EP elections cast their ballot for a different party in the EP election than they did in the last national election. There is considerable variation across countries, however, driven mainly by the fact that in some countries at EP elections parties have disappeared since the time of the previous national election. If a party is no longer available to be voted for then of course, if one is going to vote at all, one must switch to another party. This has been a particular issue in France and Italy among West European countries, and in countries of East-Central Europe, with high levels of party system change over time. However, even in countries where party systems are relatively stable, such as Sweden and Ireland, we see high levels of switching between national and European elections. Looking over time, we see that switching in established democracies has increased slightly since the first elections.

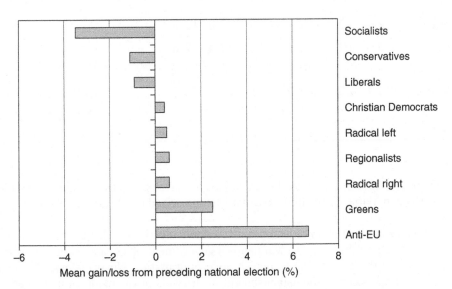

Figure 17.1   Winners and losers: party performance in European elections, 1979–2009
Source: Hix and Marsh (2011).

Table 17.1 Voting differently in EP elections than in previous national elections

(a) Established democracies							(b) Transitional democracies			
Country	1989	1994	1999	2004	2009	Mean	Country	2004	2009	Mean
Austria			26.9	28.0	32.0	29.0	Bulgaria		33.8	33.8
Belgium	11.0	19.6	9.6	26.9	23.5	18.1	Estonia	45.9	32.3	39.1
Britain	22.4	18.9	30.2	44.9	45.6	32.4	Czech Republic	39.0	12.0	25.5
Cyprus				20.9	12.1	11.0	Hungary	57.0	19.4	38.2
Denmark	36.1	33.0	42.0	34.1	36.4	36.3	Latvia	44.0	60.3	52.1
Finland			18.2	17.6	23.4	19.7	Lithuania	0.0	20.4	10.2
France	57.6	40.2	46.8	26.5	37.7	41.8	Poland	53.7	18.9	36.3
Germany	16.4	10.4	23.9	24.6	27.1	20.5	Romania		20.1	20.1
Greece	2.5	9.7	22.2	12.5	20.8	13.5	Slovakia	15.2	19.2	17.2
Ireland	24.6	18.9	32.6	36.4	43.1	31.1	Slovenia	39.3	30.4	34.9
Italy	47.6	42.8	68.5	28.8	15.2	40.6				
Luxem-bourg	9.0	5.9	11.2	33.4	25.7	17.0				
Nether-lands	20.9	22.0	22.0	36.7	37.0	27.7				
Portugal	9.0	10.9	8.2	14.1	21.2	12.7				
Spain	20.0	10.3	12.4	7.7	13.4	12.8				
Sweden			30.2	36.6	38.8	35.2				
Mean	23.1	20.2	25.3	26.9	28.3	23.1		36.8	26.7	30.7
Grand mean								26.8	26.7	26.2

There are different theoretical explanations for these patterns of voting in EP elections. Hix and Marsh (2007:495) have neatly summarised the debate as follows:

> The standard theory of European Parliament elections is that they are mid-term contests in the battle to win national government office, and so voters primarily use these elections to punish governing parties. Nevertheless, this is not the impression of the establishment in Brussels or the media in many national capitals, who identify falling turnout and support for anti-European parties as indicators of protest against the EU.

In other words, are defecting voters preoccupied with punishing national governments or do European issues matter to them? In answering this question we take advantage of one of the valuable contributions that European elections make in presenting themselves as unique laboratories for a truly comparative study of why people vote and why they vote the way they do and how this is conditioned by the domestic context.

The 'standard theory' referred to above is what political scientists call the 'second-order national election' approach which argues that differences in voting behaviour between national and EP elections are due to the fact that less is at stake in such elections. As a consequence turnout is expected to be lower and voters are expected to base their choices on domestic political concerns, not least the performance of the national government. In the seminal article in which Reif and Schmitt (1980) coined the term *second-order national election*, they highlighted the similarity between European elections and local and regional elections, where voting patterns also tend to reflect national political trends (see also van der Eijk and Franklin 1996; Ferrara and Weishaupt 2004; Hix and Marsh 2007). At first-order national elections, the formation of a government is a primary concern for voters, who therefore bear in mind strategic considerations especially regarding party size (small parties have little influence on policymaking) and experience in government. Such considerations matter less in second-order elections, and consequently voters are expected to vote more 'sincerely' for parties that are attractive to them on ideological grounds. This will benefit smaller parties who are disadvantaged at national elections by their small size and lack of government experience. Moreover, some voters may be motivated by a desire to punish national governments. Given that government office is not at stake in second-order elections, they offer an opportunity to express dissatisfaction with the performance of incumbent governments without actually kicking them out.

In other words, the second-order model offers three sets of motivations that may lead to different behaviour in EP elections: indifference that may lead to abstention, voting with the heart that may lead to defection to smaller parties and punishment of the government that may lead voters to vote for an opposition party. The balance among these motivations appears to differ across voters and across countries. We start with voters.

Explanations for voter behaviour based on the second-order model are supported by voting patterns, as shown in Figure 17.1. But these patterns of voting in EP elections are consistent with a different view: one that stresses the importance of voter attitudes towards the EU (Hix and Marsh 2007). Since at EP elections voters can 'vote with the heart', we are more likely to see them express their 'true preferences', which in many instances lead them to vote for Eurosceptic parties and parties that emphasize the European issue. Effectively the second-order nature of EP elections permits dissatisfaction with the positions of mainstream parties on the subject of European integration to show itself (Weber 2009). This view of EP elections has been characterized as involving 'arena-specific' (or 'Europe matters') motivations for voting (Marsh 2007; Hobolt *et al.* 2009; de Vries *et al.* 2011; Hobolt and Spoon 2012). While dissatisfaction with the progress of European integration is not per se higher in EP elections, there is evidence that such attitudes play a role for many voters when they go to the ballot box. We know from work on party competition and public opinion that mainstream political parties in Europe generally adopt very pro-European attitudes, and are more in favour of further integration than their voters (Hooghe *et al.* 2002; Hooghe 2003; Hobolt *et al.* 2009). So when voters feel free to express negative opinions on Europe they do so by abandoning these mainstream parties. Voters who have positive opinions have no need to abandon their parties since those parties generally share their pro-European attitudes.

Looking at aggregate patterns of EP electoral behaviour it is hard to separate punishment of governing parties from Eurosceptic preferences. Evidence from six EP elections show that large parties tend to lose votes in EP elections regardless of their position on European integration (Hix and Marsh 2007). However, the same study also finds some electoral gains for anti-EU parties and parties that emphasise the European issue (see also Hix and Marsh 2011). Other studies using individual-level data have shown that attitudes toward Europe play a considerable role in voters' decision to defect and abstain, particularly those who hold more Eurosceptic attitudes than mainstream parties (Marsh 2007; Hobolt *et al*. 2009; de Vries *et al*. 2011; Hobolt and Spoon 2012).

While the 'second-order' and 'Europe matters' views of the electoral process at EP elections are often presented as competing, it is perfectly plausible that some voters are concerned with the national government, while others with Europe (see Hobolt and Spoon 2012). Which behaviour we see depends in part on the degree of prominence and the politicization of the EU issue in the national political debate. Recent work on electoral behaviour in Europe has argued that the issue of European integration is becoming increasingly politicised as we are witnessing public contention over European matters in referendums, party competition and media reporting (Tillman 2004; de Vries 2007; Kriesi *et al*. 2008; Hobolt *et al*. 2009; Hooghe and Marks 2009). However, the level of politicisation of European issues varies considerably across countries and specific electoral contests. In some countries there is a high degree of party polarisation on Europe, for example in countries with prominent Eurosceptic parties, such as Denmark, France, Great Britain and the Netherlands, and in such countries European attitudes play a greater role in determining vote choice. Equally, there is considerable variation in the amount of media coverage and that has also been shown to make Europe matter more to vote choice, especially among those who are more politically sophisticated (Hobolt *et al*. 2009; de Vries *et al*. 2011; Hobolt and Spoon 2012).

Another important aspect of the context that has been shown to affect vote choice in EP elections is their timing in the national electoral term. Punishment of national governments is greatest around midterm, thereafter this tends to level off as the cycle continues (van der Eijk and Franklin 1996; Marsh 1998). As the national electoral cycle advances and the next national election comes closer, two things happen to affect the behaviour of voters should a European election take place. The first is that politicians and commentators increasingly regard the outcome as a 'marker' or barometer for the relative standing of national parties going into the next national election campaign. By this time the marker set by the previous national election has become obsolete. The second is that, with the approach of a national election, party leaders are motivated to take account of any signals that the electorate manages to send by means of its electoral choices. Taking account of such signals could improve their parties' chances when the national election comes. Voters seem well aware of this, since this is the context in which protest voting appears most prevalent and when smaller parties do best. Clearly voters do not suppose that their votes will cause such parties to gain office, but they evidently hope that the parties they normally support will take note of the protest and adapt their policies accordingly, and consequently they 'vote with the boot'. Similar midterm effects have been found in US elections.

Variation in national political context also leads to variation in turnout in EP elections, a topic to which we now turn.

Turnout variations

One of the most evident differences between European and national elections has always been the low and apparently declining turnout recorded in European elections. Average turnout in the nine EC member states participating in the 1979 EP election was 62 per cent (67 per cent when Greece is included). By 2014, turnout across the 28 EU member states had dropped to just 42 per cent. Many commentators have suggested that low turnout indicates lack of legitimacy for the European Community (EC)/EU, since citizens appear by their failure to vote to be withholding their support for European institutions. Table 17.2 shows the development in turnout across all EC/EU member states between 1979 and 2014.

Table 17.2 reveals considerable cross-national variation in turnout, ranging from an average of just 16 per cent in Slovakia to 91 per cent in Belgium. These variations cannot easily be explained with reference to the degree of Euroscepticism in different countries. Other contextual factors, however, play an important role. One contextual feature that we have not yet mentioned has been widely noted in the literature: the first European election ever held in established member countries saw generally higher levels of turnout than later elections. The exceptions are the compulsory voting countries, Belgium, Italy, Greece and Luxemburg (where turnout was maintained at a high level in subsequent elections because of the compulsion to vote) together with Britain and Denmark where initially low turnout remained low or even increased in subsequent elections. But in 10 other countries the inauguration of European elections evidently generated a level of interest that could not be sustained. Indeed, the decline in turnout over the course of seven European elections has appeared to be continuous, fuelling concerns about a democratic deficit in the conduct of EU affairs.

These concerns are probably misplaced. There is certainly a democratic deficit in the governance of the European Union (Føllesdal and Hix 2006) and the low turnout in European elections is at least partly due to the fact that European elections do not provide European voters with meaningful choices that would give them a real say in the future direction of European policy-making (van der Eijk and Franklin 1996: chap. 19). However, the decline in the average level of turnout across the EU as a whole in successive elections to the EP was not a sign that this deficit was increasing. Rather, it was primarily an artefact of the accession to the EU of new countries with characteristics that were different from those of the original member countries, and the evolution of these countries from first-time participants to seasoned members. In the 2004 and 2009 elections, among established member countries, turnout was actually higher at 57 and 54 per cent, respectively, than in 1999 (53 per cent). The long decline and recent rise in turnout in these countries can most easily be explained in the context of an analysis of the determinants of turnout across all EP elections held to date.

Just a few contextual factors can explain most of the variation in turnout, at least until 2004. This is shown in Table 17.3 that seeks to explain cross-national and over time (1979–2009) variation in turnout. Taken together, four variables explain 70 per cent of the between election turnout variations. The most powerful predictors of turnout at European elections appear to be compulsory voting, the length of time yet to elapse before the next national election, whether the election was the first election to the European Parliament ever held in the country concerned and whether the country is a

Table 17.2 Turnout (per cent) in European Parliament elections by country, 1979–2014

(a) Established democracies

Country	1979[a]	1984[b]	1989	1994[c]	1999	2004	2009	2014	79-'14
Austria[c]				67.7	49.4	42.4	46	45.7	50.2
Belgium[d]	90.4	92.2	90.7	90.7	91	90.8	90.4	90	90.8
Cyprus[d]						71.2	59.4	44	58.2
Denmark	47.8	52.4	47.2	52.9	50.5	47.9	59.5	56.4	51.8
Finland[c]			60.3		31.4	41.1	40.3	40.9	42.8
France	60.7	56.7	48.8	52.7	46.8	42.8	40.5	43.5	49.1
Germany	65.7	56.8	62.3	60	45.2	43	43.3	47.9	53.0
Great Britain	32.2	32.6	36.2	36.1	24	38.8	34.7	34.2	33.6
Greece[a,d]	78.6	77.2	79.9	71.2	75.3	63.2	52.6	58.2	69.5
Ireland	63.6	47.6	68.3	44	50.2	59.8	58.6	51.6	55.5
Italy[d]	84.9	83.4	81.5	74.8	70.8	73.1	65.1	60	74.2
Luxembourg[d]	88.9	88.8	87.4	88.5	87.3	89	91	90	88.9
Malta						82.4	78.8	74.8	78.7
Netherlands	57.8	50.6	47.2	35.6	30	39.3	36.9	37	41.8
Portugal[b]		72.4	51.2	35.5	40	38.6	36.8	34.5	44.1

(b) Transitional democracies

Country	2004	2009	2014	04-'14
Bulgaria		39	35.5	37.3
Croatia			25.1	25.1
Czech Rep	28.3	28.3	19.5	25.4
Estonia	26.8	43.9	36.4	35.7
Hungary	38.5	36.3	28.9	34.6
Latvia	41.3	53.6	30	41.6
Lithuania	48.4	21	44.9	38.1
Poland	20.9	24.5	22.7	22.7
Romania		27.7	32.1	29.9
Slovakia	17	19.6	13	16.5
Slovenia	28.3	28.3	20.9	24.6

Spain[b]	68.9	54.6	59.1	63	45.1	45	45.9	54.5		8
Sweden[c]		41.6		15	37.8	46	48.8	42.6		10
N	10	12	12	15	15	17	17	115		8	10	11	29
Mean*	67.1	65.0	62.9	58.0	52.9	55.7	54.4	53.1	57.6	31.6	32.2	28.1	30.1
Weighted EU mean**	62.0	59.0	58.4	56.7	49.5	45.5	43.0	43.1	52.1	45.5	43.0	43.1	52.1
Grand EU mean*										50.8	46.2	43.3

*All countries weighted equally.

**Countries weighted by electorate.

[a] The first election for Greece was held in 1981.

[b] The first elections for Spain and Portugal were held in 1987.

[c] The first elections for Austria, Finland and Sweden were held in 1996.

[d] Compulsory voting country (Italy only until 1993).

Table 17.3 Effects on turnout of contextual factors, all EU countries, 1979–2009*

VARIABLE	b	PCSE	SIGF
(CONSTANT)	63.0	5.4	0.00
Compulsory voting in country[a]	30.0	10.1	0.01
Years until next national election (where no compulsion)[b]	-3.3	0.9	0.00
First EP election held in country (where no compulsion)[b]	12.2	2.5	0.00
Transitional democracy	-17.6	8.2	0.00
Transitional * first EP election	-12.2	4.9	0.02
Adjusted variance explained	*0.7*		
N	*116*		

Notes: *The data for this analysis are taken from Table 17.2 (1979–2009). When country indicators are used to enforce fixed effects, the compulsory voting coefficient is somewhat reduced and R2 rises to 0.9, but other coefficients are hardly changed. A trend variable, if included, does not prove significant. Nor does an interaction between transitional and years to the next election, indicating that transitional democracies are not different from established democracies in this respect.

[a]Coded 0 or 1 except in Italy after 1993, when its effect can be expected to have diminished in proportion to the share of the electorate new since 1993. There it is coded 0.875 in 1999, 0.75 in 2004, and 0.625 in 2009. This mechanism explaining effects of institutional change validated for Italy by Scervini and Segatti (2012).

[b]Compulsory voting countries coded 0 because the compulsion to vote should override this effect.

transitional democracy. Countries with compulsory voting on average see turnout that is 30 per cent higher than those in which voting is strictly voluntary. Turnout is generally lower by over 3 per cent for each year that is still to elapse before the next national election, and the first EP election in each of these countries saw turnout higher by 12.2 per cent on average than later elections, except in the transitional democracies of East-Central Europe where the "first election boost" does not appear to play any role. With each successive EP election since 2004, the weight of these countries relative to established democracies increases and 2009 is really the last year in which the model can be said to summarize overall patterns. For later elections we need to know much more about individual countries in order to explain EP election turnout.

Focusing first on the historical pattern, it is well known that compulsory voting raises turnout. The surprise is to find it having so great an effect, but the reason is that turnout in EP elections would otherwise be so very low. In low-turnout elections, compulsory voting shows its power to greatest advantage (Franklin 1999). This fact alone explains much of the decline in turnout over the 25 years of EP elections, because the countries taking part in the elections of 2009 are very different countries from those that took part in the elections of 1979. In the first elections, almost half the countries taking part (4 out of 10) did so under conditions of compulsory voting. Today there are three countries with compulsory voting (Italy having abandoned compulsory voting in 1993), but these are now 3 of 28 – little more than a tenth. Because of the large effect of compulsory voting, this drop of almost 30 per cent in the proportion of countries with this characteristic would lead us to expect a drop of 10 per cent in turnout as a pure mathematical consequence (30 per cent of 33 per cent). Moreover, in elections to the Parliament of 1979–1984, 6 of the 10 countries were eligible for the 12.2 per cent first-election turnout boost, whereas none of the countries that acceded to the EU in 2004 received a similar boost. These two effects go a long way towards accounting in a rather prosaic fashion for the overall decline in turnout since 1979 (Franklin and Hobolt 2011).

Of course, Table 17.3 shows that individual countries have seen big changes in turnout that cannot be accounted for by the factors so far discussed. From this perspective, more interesting is the –3.3 per cent per year effect of time until the next national election. As already mentioned, European elections gain a surrogate importance from their role as barometers of the standing of national parties. Evidently this role is more important as national elections approach; but again the surprise is to find so great an effect. In a country with five-year parliaments, position in the electoral cycle could make a 16.5 per cent difference to European election turnout (5 times 3.3 per cent). With four-year parliaments, position in the electoral cycle could make a 13.2 per cent difference. Given the largely random position of European elections within national election cycles (except for Luxemburg, which has always held both elections on the same day), this one factor explains much of the variation seen in Table 17.2 from election to election within particular countries. Indeed, over the EU as a whole, we would have expected a fall in turnout of some 2 per cent in 1999 simply because of the fact that in that year, on average, EP elections were held seven months earlier in the electoral cycles of member countries than had been the case for earlier EP elections.

So while the fact of low turnout at European Parliament elections is a matter for some concern (see Franklin and Hobolt 2011), the apparent decline in EP turnout is not. Indeed, when we correct for the factors listed in Table 17.3, turnout actually appears to have increased after 1979 to a peak about six points higher in 1989 and then to have fallen off in 1994 – a fall that continued in 1999 to a point about level with the 1979 starting position, which was more or less maintained in subsequent elections – even in 2004 and later for those countries that were already EU members before 2004. However, turnout variation in the transitional democracies that became members of the EU in 2004 is really not accounted for by this model.

Why are the transitional democracies that joined since 2004 so different in the ways in which we observe them to be? This question was explored by Wessels and Franklin (2009). These authors found the reasons to centre on low levels of partisanship and low mobilization in these countries, and explain why these features are to be expected in countries where party systems have not had time to become established. In countries where a kaleidoscope of changing parties prevent voters from becoming attached to any of them it is difficult for leaders to call on established loyalties to bring their supporters to the polls – indeed, in such circumstances it is hard to speak of leaders as having supporters.

Consequences for national politics

The consequences of European elections for national politics are of three kinds. In the first place, national parties may be led to take various actions as a result of extrapolating the outcome to a national election situation. Sometimes a government party may be led to call an early national election, as in Spain in 1989, to capitalise on the popularity they see themselves enjoying (del Castillo 1996). Sometimes such a party may be led to adapt its policies, as in Germany in the same year (when a much harsher policy towards Eastern European migration was briefly adopted) in order to defuse the apparent appeal of an extreme party (Schmitt 1996). These reactions may or may not have the effect that the party intended, depending on how accurately the European election outcome reflects the true situation in the national political arena, but there will always be a tendency for miscalculations to occur exactly in proportion to the extent of the interest taken in the European election outcome. This is because, to the extent that party leaders and commentators take notice, voters behave differently than they would have done had nobody been watching – behaviour that is different again from what it would have been had national political power been truly at stake.

The second type of consequence is more insidious. European election outcomes differ from the outcomes that would occur in national elections for more reasons than that voters behave differently than politicians expect. Small parties are often advantaged for technical reasons as well, having to do with differences in the electoral system under which European elections are held. For both these reasons a party system can progressively change due to the impact of successive European elections, as small, and sometimes extreme or single issue, parties perform well in EP elections (Ysmal and Cayrol 1996; Schmitt 1996). This is primarily because the different electoral rules under which EP elections are conducted can benefit small parties and give them a toehold in national politics that they can later build on to establish themselves in their national political arenas. This has happened for Green parties in several countries, for the Front National in France, and may yet prove to have happened for the British UK Independence Party.

The third type of consequence results more directly from the fact that European elections are not exclusively, or even primarily, employed as opportunities to put forward or oppose policies related to the European arena. Keeping such policies off the national agenda seems to be a preoccupation of national politicians (see Franklin *et al*. 1996; De Vries and Hobolt 2012). Occasionally, however, such issues break through to become salient in national terms. When this happens, the results can be quite devastating for individual parties or leaders. European elections would be the proper venue for such matters to be discussed, if only such elections could be fought by different parties than fight national elections. Under such circumstances it would not be possible to employ European elections as markers even while they could be used to provide an airing for real European issues. So long as EP elections are not uncoupled in this way from national politics they will remain something of a sword of Damocles that national parties hang over their heads, apparently unknowingly, because of the potential that European issues have for splitting national parties into pro- and anti-European factions.

Consequences for the future of the EU

Democratic representation and accountability are associated with the notion of free elections. However, in order for elections to fulfil these functions, a number of conditions must be met which are not necessarily provided by the simple institution of elections per se. The logic of democratic elections presupposes that the political verdict of electorates can be construed as emanating from the political preferences of voters – preferences that are relevant to the decision-making arena concerned. If this condition is met, elections can be considered simultaneously (1) to legitimise power allocated by the elections (and therefore also to legitimise policies which may be devised with this power), (2) to exert electoral control by holding officeholders accountable and (3) to represent groups of citizens and their interests in the political process (thus showing sensitivity to their concerns). In order for elections to function in these ways, electorates must have some awareness of the political stance and record in the arena under consideration of those who are contending for their votes.

It is evident that these conditions are lacking in the present-day EU. Voters have on the whole never been encouraged to develop preferences for different European policies that would permit them to choose among candidates and parties in a European election in such a way as to legitimate and control the exercise of power at the European level. Indeed, the policies with European relevance that are regularly put forward by candidates and parties are seldom communicated to voters by national party leaders and national press corps that take little interest in European affairs. By failing to present voters with meaningful choices, national party leaders also miss the chance to educate them about European affairs. This failure is primarily due to the fact that the parties that select candidates and dominate the domestic campaigns at European elections are not European parties but national parties, and these parties generally treat European elections as opportunities to test their own relative popularity in the national arena. National elections tend to offer even less of a forum for discussion of European matters. Although there have been recent elections where Europe was indeed the most important issue, such elections are still rare (however, see Tillman 2004; de Vries 2007). So neither in their choice of national leaders who compose the Council nor in their choice of MEPs who hold the Commissioners accountable have voters been given much of an opportunity to have any input into the conduct of European affairs.

This lack of proper democratic accountability and control in European affairs is a grave problem, potentially amounting to a crisis of legitimacy for the European Union. MEPs as well as many professional observers of European integration have diagnosed a democratic deficit in European representative institutions. To their eyes, this deficit has in the past been seen in terms of a lack of power on the part of the EP to assert itself in relation to the Commission and the Council of Ministers. But it should be evident from a reading of this chapter that the democratic deficit felt by MEPs actually results from the fact that European elections are fought primarily on the basis of national political concerns, rather than on problems relevant to the European arena. Even to the extent that some European voters are concerned about EU matters, as recent studies have suggested, their votes will tend to express a protest against the Union project as a whole, rather than a vote for a particular European policy platform and direction. Most of the decisions taken in the EP do not concern large constitutional decisions about 'more or less EU', but rather more conventional left–right debates about what kind of Europe is being constructed: Should Europe protect businesses or consumers? Promote growth or the environment? Enforce greater austerity or seek to increase demand? and so on. For voter preferences to be represented at the European level, elections should present such questions about the future direction of European policy-making.

What the European Parliament lacks most today is not more legislative power – that has been expanded by successive treaty reforms – but a mandate to use that power in any particular manner. It lacks that mandate because of the way in which European elections have been conducted, not least due to the lack of any real contestation over alternative policy agendas of the sort that we observe in national elections. Moreover, since European elections do not directly lead to government formation, voters also cannot punish the EU-level institutions for policies or performance with which they are unhappy. While citizens increasingly attribute responsibility to the EU for policy outcomes in areas such as the economy, they are not able to use EP elections to hold EU representatives to account for these outcomes, since the link between their vote and policies is unclear (Hobolt and Tilley 2014a). This means that rather than holding a specific 'European government' to account for their actions, European citizens may well be losing faith in the European project and the legitimacy of the EU is threatened (Hobolt and Tilley 2014b).

It was hoped that things would be different in 2014. In that year, for the first time, the Europarties proposed rival candidates, the so-called *Spitzenkandidaten* (lead candidates), for the most powerful executive office in the EU – the Commission president – prior to the elections. This change was rooted in a modification of the procedure for choosing the Commission president. Whereas the president was previously chosen by a consensus of European leaders in the European Council which was approved by the EP, the Lisbon Treaty stipulates that the European Council shall nominate a candidate "taking into account the elections to the European Parliament", by qualified majority, and the parliament in turn must "elect" the nominee with an absolute majority (Article 17 of the Treaty on European Union). However, the European lead candidates played a limited role during the 2014 election campaign and most citizens were not aware of the candidates, at least outside their home countries (Hobolt 2014). Nonetheless, the election of the Commission president was transformed by the campaign: after the elections where the EPP remained the largest political group, the EP successfully persuaded Europe's reluctant leaders to nominate the EPP's lead candidate, Jean-Claude Juncker, as the next Commission president. The Parliament thereby set an important precedent for future elections of a strong link between the electoral outcome and the Commission presidency.

Discussion

Historically, the EU was built by national governments with little input by their citizenry, on the basis of what has been called a 'permissive consensus' regarding successive moves towards European unity (Inglehart 1971). The consequence of this permissive consensus has been to free national parties from the need to coherently address and articulate European policy concerns – often a difficult matter for parties whose origins lie in the aggregation of quite other sorts of interests and concerns. Instead of defending their participation in European decision making on the grounds of fulfilling an electoral mandate, ruling parties have consistently defended such actions on the grounds that they have done their best to protect national interests, thus casting European politics as a zero-sum game between the member states and undermining their efforts in other spheres to stress the positive-sum aspects of European integration. Sometimes, of course, their 'best' is not enough, and unpopular consequences seem to flow from European developments.

This 'permissive consensus', allowing European leaders to take decisions without consulting their citizens and yet count on their continued support, has been eroding for some time (Hooghe and Marks 2009). A variety of developments has increased the salience and visibility of European policies to individual citizens. The increasing politicization of Europe was amply demonstrated as long ago as the early 1990s by the Danish and French referendums regarding the Maastricht Treaty. A similar dynamic was evident in Ireland when that country came to ratify the Treaties of Lisbon and Nice (Hobolt 2009). More recently, the sovereign debt and eurozone crisis has become one of the most salient issues across Europe. The crisis has not only had economic and political consequences that have led to the fall of several national governments, but it was also linked to a question about the ability of European leaders to take decisions and the solidarity of European peoples in standing behind those decisions. A period of constant readjustments of European governance has involved EU institutions in increasing numbers of fiscal policy decisions, at least for debtor states, that were previously the exclusive domain of national parliaments and governments. However, this transfer of powers from the national level to the European level has not been matched by mechanisms for ensuring representation and accountability at the EU level.

Politicians often place their hopes in the EP as the primary institution that will ensure that decisions taken at the EU level are perceived to be democratically legitimate. However, the link between EP elections and the decisions taken by European leaders in regular (and irregular) summits is far from clear. The fact that European elections have so far failed to provide voters with means for making their concerns known, or for compelling attention by policy-makers to these concerns, further threatens the legitimacy of European policy-making and further enhances the possibility of repercussions at national elections. In the absence of well-established alternatives regarding the substantive direction of such policies, leading to a debate within each country (or across Europe as a whole) regarding what type of EU the people want to live in, criticism is moving from a focus on 'what Europe' to 'whether Europe'. This could yield unpredictable consequences for European political systems. The failure of governments to acquire mandates from voters for their support of "more integration" could result instead in a growth in Euroscepticism. This was clearly demonstrated in the 2014 EP elections, where parties who advocate withdrawal or at least repatriation of powers from the EU topped the polls in a number of countries, including Great Britain (UK Independence Party), France (Front National), Denmark (Danish People's Party) and Greece (Syriza).

Greater contestation over the future of Europe in national and EP elections as we are currently witnessing may thus significantly slow down the pace of unification, lead to more differentiated integration and even to some countries leaving the EU. But continued lack of consultation could ultimately be much more damaging to the European project. The proper place for consultations of this kind would be in the context of European election campaigns, but European elections have never yet been used for such a purpose. The reform that resulted in designated nominees for Commission presidents with alternative policy platforms in the 2014 EP elections may, in time, transform these elections by strengthening the link between vote choices and the future policies of the Union. Yet, after just one election with no "incumbent" candidate to vote against, it is too early to tell whether this institutional innovation will eventually enhance the accountability mechanism and thus the European content of campaigns, perhaps leading to more salient elections with higher turnout.

References

del Castillo, P. (1996) 'Spain: A Dress Rehearsal', in van der Eijk and Franklin with Ackaert *et al.* (1996) *Choosing Europe? The European Electorate and National Politics in the Face of Union.* Ann Arbor: University of Michigan Press.

De Vreese, C.H., Banducci, S., Semetko, H.A. and Boomgaarden, H.A. (2006) 'The News Coverage of the 2004 European Parliamentary Election Campaign in 25 Countries'. *European Union Politics* 7(4), 477–504.

de Vries, C.E. (2007) 'Sleeping Giant: Fact or Fairytale? How European Integration Affects Vote Choice in National Elections'. *European Union Politics* 8(3): 363–385.

de Vries, C. and Hobolt, S.B. (2012) 'When Dimensions Collide: The Electoral Success of Issue Entrepreneurs'. *European Union Politics* 13(2), 246–268.

de Vries, C., van der Brug, W., van der Eijk, C. and van Egmond, M. (2011) 'Individual and Contextual Variation in EU Issue Voting: The Role of Political Information'. *Electoral Studies* 30(1), 16–28.

Farrell, D.M. and Scully, R.M. (2007) *Representing Europe's Citizens? Electoral Institutions and the Failure of Parliamentary Representation* Oxford: Oxford University Press.

Ferrara, F., and Weishaupt, J.T. (2004) 'Get Your Act Together: Party Performance in European Parliament Election'. *European Union Politics* 5(3), 283–306.

Føllesdal, A. and Hix, S. (2006) 'Why There is a Democratic Deficit in the EU: A Response to Majone and Moravcsik'. *Journal of Common Market Studies* 44(3), 533–562.

Franklin, M. (1999) 'Electoral Engineering and Cross-National Turnout Differences: What Role for Compulsory Voting?' *British Journal of Political Science* 29: 205–216.

Franklin, M. (2014) 'Why Vote at an Election with No Apparent Purpose: Voter Turnout at Elections to the European Parliament'. *European Policy Analysis* (2004:4), available at www.sieps.se/sites/default/files/2014_4epa_version2_0.pdf

Franklin, M. and Hobolt, S. B. (2011) 'The legacy of lethargy: How elections to the European Parliament depress turnout'. *Electoral Studies* 30 (1), 67–76.

Franklin, M., van der Eijk, C. and Marsh, M. (1996) 'Conclusions: The Electoral Connection and the Democratic Deficit', in: van der Eijk, C. and Franklin, M., with Ackaert, J. et al. (1996) *Choosing Europe? The European Electorate and National Politics in the Face of Union.* Ann Arbor: University of Michiga Press.

Hix, S., and Marsh, M. (2007) 'Punishment or Protest? Understanding European Parliament Elections'. *The Journal of Politics* 69(2), 495–510.

Hix, S. and Marsh, M. (2011) 'Second-Order Effects Plus Pan-European Political Swings: An Analysis of European Parliament Elections across Time'. *Electoral Studies* 30(1), 4–15.

Hix, S., Noury, A., and Roland, G. (2006) 'Dimensions of Politics in the European Parliament'. *American Journal of Political Science* 50(2), 494–511.

Hix, S., Noury, A. and Roland, G. (2007) *Democratic Politics in the European Parliament.* Cambridge: Cambridge University Press.

Hobolt, S. B. (2009) *Europe in Question. Referendums on European Integration*. Oxford: Oxford University Press.

Hobolt, S.B. (2014) 'A Vote for the President? The Role of Spitzenkandidaten in the 2014 European Parliament Elections'. *Journal of European Public Policy* 21(10), 1528–1540.

Hobolt, S. B. and Spoon, J.-J. (2012) 'Motivating the European Voter: Parties, Issues and Campaigns in European Parliament Elections'. *European Journal of Political Research* 51, 6, 701–727.

Hobolt, S. B, and Tilley, J. (2014a) 'Who's in Charge? Voter Attribution of Responsibility in the European Union'. *Comparative Political Studies* 47(6), 795–819.

Hobolt, S.B., and Tilley, J. (2014b) *Blaming Europe? Responsibility without Accountability in the European Union*. Oxford: Oxford University Press.

Hobolt, S. B., Spoon, J., and Tilley, J. (2009) 'A Vote against Europe? Explaining Defection at the 1999 and 2004 European Parliament Elections'. *British Journal of Political Science* 39(1), 93–115.

Hooghe, L. (2003) 'Europe Divided? Elites vs. Public Opinion on European Integration'. *European Union Politics* 4(3), 281–305.

Hooghe, L. and Marks, G. (2009) 'A Postfunctionalist Theory of European Integration: From Permissive Consensus to Constraining Dissensus'. *British Journal of Political Science* 39(1), 1–23.

Hooghe, L. Marks, G. and Wilson, C. J. (2002) 'Does Left/Right Structure Party Positions on European Integration?'. *Comparative Political Studies* 35, 965–989.

Inglehart, R. (1971) 'Public Opinion and European Integration', in L. Lindberg and S. Scheingold (eds), *European Integration*. Cambridge, MA: Harvard University Press, 160–191.

Kriesi, H., Grande, E., Lachat, R., Dolezal, M., Bornschier, S. and Frey, T. (2008) *West European Politics in the Age of Globalization*. Cambridge: Cambridge University Press.

Marsh, M. (1998) 'Testing the Second-Order Election Model after Four European Elections'. *British Journal of Political Science* 28, 591–608.

Marsh, M. (2007) 'European Parliament Elections and Losses by Governing Parties'. In van der Eijk, C. and van der Brug, W (Eds) *European Elections and Domestic Politics: Lessons from the Past and Scenarios for the Future*. South Bend, IN: University of Notre Dame Press.

Norris, P. (2000) *A Virtuous Circle: Political Communications in Postindustrial Societies*. Cambridge: Cambridge University Press.

Peter, J. and De Vreese, C. H. (2004) 'In Search of Europe – A Crossnational Comparative Study of the European Union in National Television News'. *Harvard Journal of Press/Politics* 9(4), 3–24.

Reif, K. and Schmitt, H. (1980) 'Nine Second-Order National Elections: A Conceptual Framework for the Analysis of European Election Results'. *European Journal of Political Research* 8(1), 3–44.

Rittberger, B. (2005) *Building Europe's Parliament: Democratic Representation beyond the Nation-State*. Oxford: Oxford University Press.

Scervini, F. and Segatti, P. (2012) 'Education, Inequality and Electoral Participation', *Research in Social Stratification and Mobility*, 30 (4) 403–413.

Schmitt, H. (1996) 'Germany: A Bored Electorate', in van der Eijk and Franklin with Ackaert *et al.* (1996).

Schuck, A., Xezonakis, G., Banducci, S. and De Vreese, C.H. (2011) 'Party Contestation and Europe on the News Agenda: The 2009 European Parliamentary Election'. *Electoral Studies*, 30, 41–52 *Choosing Europe? The European Electorate and National Politics in the Face of Union*. Ann Arbor: University of Michigan Press.

Tillman, E.R. (2004) 'The European Union at the Ballot Box: European Integration and Voting Behaviour in the New Member States'. *Comparative Political Studies* 27(5), 590–610.

van der Eijk, C. and Franklin, M., with Ackaert, J. *et al.* (1996) *Choosing Europe? The European Electorate and National Politics in the Face of Union*. Ann Arbor: University of Michigan Press.

Weber, Till (2009) 'When The Cat Is Away the Mice Will Play: Why Elections to the European Parliament Are about Europe After All'. *Politique européenne* 28(2): 5–71.

Wessels, B. and Franklin, F. (2009) 'Turning Out or Turning Off – Do Mobilization and Attitudes Account for Turnout Differences between New and Established Member States at the 2004 EP Elections?' *Journal of European Integration* 32(5), 609–26.

Ysmal, C., and Roland Cayrole, R. (1996) 'France: The Midwife Comes to Call', in C. van der Eijk and M. Frankline (eds), *Choosing Europe? The European Electorate and National Politics in the Face of Union*. Ann Arbor: University of Michigan Press, 115–136.

Chapter 18

Shooting where the ducks are

EU lobbying and institutionalized promiscuity

Sonia Mazey and Jeremy Richardson

Introduction: the inevitability of lobbying

Lobbying, if not the oldest profession, has ancient origins. It is a natural political phenomenon. All systems, even totalitarian regimes, exhibit the phenomenon to some degree. Developed democracies all have very highly developed lobbying systems. Indeed, providing opportunities for lobbying is one of the hallmarks of a democracy. To be sure, there are debates about biases in lobbying systems, most notably that those interests with the most resources exploit the system to the disadvantage of those organized interests less well resourced or even not organized at all. However, our main concern in this chapter is with the development and nature of the European Union (EU) lobbying system, not with whether it is a 'good thing'. Suffice to say that we do not believe there is a consistent bias in the sense that one set of interests (such as business) always wins. Thus, 'no single actor can control a game with so many different players, or deliver the desired payoff' (Richardson 2000: 1015). Different sets of actors have different attributes. For example, environmental groups seem adept at agenda setting in the EU, whereas business groups are more adept in the detailed technical processing phase of policy-making (Mazey and Richardson 1992). Our (benign) view appears to be confirmed by Klüver's study of a very large number of EU decisions. She found 'no evidence for a bias in lobbying success across interest group type' (Klüver 2012: 1130). Thus, *'win a few, lose a few'* is probably the motto hanging above the entrance of every lobby organization in Brussels!

Our starting point is that once the EU came into existence, the emergence of an EU lobbying *system* was inevitable. As we argued in the preface to our early work on EU lobbying (Mazey and Richardson 1993: v), groups understand what is probably the first rule of lobbying; namely *it is best to shoot where the ducks are*! As we put it,

> as always, shifts in power are noted and acted upon by interest groups, who act as a type of weather-vane for the locus of political power in society. They quickly *re-target* their influence, once they realize that power to take decisions which affect them has moved to a new institution or to new actors.
>
> (Mazey and Richardson 1993: v)

Whilst at that time not using the term *policy-making state*, we drew attention to some fundamental shifts in the relationship between the EC (as it then was) and the member states. In particular, we emphasized the importance of the Single European Act (SEA) as the cause of a step change in lobbying activity at the European level. Thus, 'the impact of the SEA on EC policy-making is thus twofold: the scope of Community policies has been extended to include policy areas which were previously the responsibility of national governments; and reform of the EC decision-making process has weakened the policy-making influence of national governments at the EC level' (Mazey and Richardson 1993: 3). Our main conclusion was that the changes in the distribution of power within the EC had prompted a proliferation of interest group lobbying at the EC level. Our hypothesis was that the more powerful European-level institutions became, and the more that public policy came to be decided at the European level, the more groups would shift at least some of their activity (and resources) to that regional level. Thus, explaining the emergence and continued development of an EU lobbying system is not rocket science. Indeed, a really difficult research question would have arisen if the EU had *not* developed a vibrant and dense lobbying system. If the lobbying dog had not barked, that would have been unusual in political systems, to say the least!

Luckily, there seems to be a broad consensus that what we now see before us was, indeed, inevitable. Thus, we ourselves were heavily influenced by the pioneering work of Ernst Hass and Leon Lindberg. Haas suggested that two of the six conditions for a 'community settlement' to emerge were that

> [i]nterest groups and political parties at the national level endorse supranational action and preferences to action by their national government . . . (and) interest groups and political parties organize beyond the national level in order to function more effectively as decision-makers *vis á vis* the separate national governments or the central authority.
>
> (Haas 1958: 9–10)

Lindberg, writing shortly afterwards, was somewhat sceptical of the view that a European-level lobbying system would be significant. His caution was partly based on the fact that, at that time, 'the vital interests of the relatively few are as yet not directly affected by decisions of the Community institutions' (1963: 99). However, he went on to argue that groups might be forced to emphasize collective needs rather than national differences if '. . . the central institutions of the EEC become more active, as the types of actions taken involve the harmonization of legislation and the formation of common policies . . .' (Lindberg 1193: 101).

Now some decades on from those early observations, there is ample evidence of the 'shoot where the ducks are' thesis at work. Broscheid and Coen found that the greatest level of lobbying activity clusters around the regulatory domains of the Commission (2007: 361). More generally, Mahoney and Baumgartner argue that '. . . as the EU's competences expanded with the adoption of successive European Treaties, the number of groups increased as well' (2008: 1528). Similarly, Dür and Mateo suggest that '. . . the Europeanization of interests may increase as competences shift towards the EU level . . .' (Dür and Mateo 2014: 19). Of course, one might expect car manufacturers for example to mobilize at the European level when EU car safety rules might be introduced, but this mobilization is also evident in literally hundreds of issue of low political salience. For example Pallis has documented the mobilization of maritime transport groups since the mid-1970s. He notes that the EU has, since 1974, been trying to develop a Common Maritime Transport Policy and that the scope and depth of the policies has shifted from minimalist to an approach that considers comprehensive EU policies. As a result of this power shift to the EU level 'a variety of stakeholders has identified a new level of power, and has formed EU-level interest groups seeking to "shoot where the ducks are"' (Pallis 2005: 6).

Our central thesis is that once the EU began to develop into a significant venue or arena for public policy-making in Europe, a certain trajectory of institutionalized interaction between the EU and interest groups was likely. We base this prediction on three theoretical assumptions:

- First, *bureaucracies have a tendency to construct stable and manageable relationships with interest groups in each policy domain as a means of securing some kind of 'negotiated order' or stable environment.*

- Second, *interest groups generally exhibit a preference for state bureaucracies as a venue for informing themselves about and influencing public policy.*
- Third, *interest groups will seek to exploit new opportunity structures or venues as a means of maximizing their capacity to shape public policy to their own advantage.*

We suggest that different types of actors have associated behavioural patterns – or at least exhibit *procedural ambitions* (Richardson and Jordan 1979) which condition and structure their behaviour in the real world. Moreover, because many of these procedural ambitions are deeply embedded in the political cultures of the majority of the member states, it should be no surprise to see the gradual emergence of a 'European policy style' emphasizing group intermediation (Mazey and Richardson 1995: 337–59).

The European Commission as a bureaucracy: the art of strategic group politics

Our theoretical starting point is bureaucracy and the particular behavioural traits that modern bureaucracies exhibit. In his classic study of bureaucracies, Anthony Downs formulated many hypotheses concerning bureaucratic behaviour. Two of his central hypotheses are especially relevant to a discussion of Commission/group relations. He assumed *rational behaviour* on the part of bureaucrats – 'they act in the most efficient manner possible given their limited capabilities and the cost of information' (Downs 1967: 2). He also hypothesized that '[e]very organization's social functions strongly influence its internal structure and behaviour, and vice versa' (Downs 1967: 2). If we apply these two hypotheses to the Commission (which certainly has limited resources and an especially great need for information from across the 28 member states), we can assume that it will structure itself in ways that facilitate efficient policy formulation – its 'social function' under the Treaty of Rome. We can also assume that it will adopt behavioural patterns that maximize its ability to interpret the external world to facilitate efficient policy formulation. If we regard the Commission as a relatively new or *adolescent* bureaucracy when compared to most national bureaucracies such as the British civil service (Mazey and Richardson 1995), then another of Downs's observations seems valuable – namely that the 'generation of . . . external support is particularly crucial for a new bureau'. He suggests that a new bureau's survival strategy includes continually demonstrating that its services are worthwhile to some group with influence over sufficient resources to keep it alive (Downs 1967: 7). Initially, the external sources of support are said to be 'weak, scattered and not accustomed to relations with the bureau. The latter must therefore rapidly organize so that its services become very valuable to the users' (Downs 1967: 7–8). Once the users of the bureau's services get used to the gains they secure from it 'and *have developed routinized relations with it*', the bureau then can rely on a degree of inertia to maintain the external support (Downs 1967: 8, emphasis added.). This rather clientelistic relationship itself leads to *institutionalization* in the form of rule making, he predicts. Thus, 'many of the decisions of bureaux covered by *formalized rules* involve interactions with people outside the bureau' (Downs 1967: 60, emphasis added.). In the case of the Commission, it has developed sets of informal and formal 'rules' which emphasize the key role that consultation with interest groups plays in policy-making. Thus, from what we know about bureaucracies generally, we might predict the emergence of 'normal' bureaucratic/interest group politics in the EU.

All of these hypotheses and observations seem to fit the Commission perfectly. It has acted rationally as a 'purposeful opportunist' (Klein and O'Higgins 1985; Cram 1994) in expanding its policy domains and creating new ones (extending its 'territoriality' in Downs's terms). It has also practiced the art of 'strategic group politics' – the capacity of a policy-maker to 'regulate their interactions with outside constituencies in a way that fulfils their strategic objectives' (Peterson 1992: 612). In particular, it has recognized the utility of interest groups as sources of (a) information, (b) support and (c) legitimacy in its key policy-making roles. Finally, like all 'state' bureaucracies, it has recognized that *institutionalizing* consultation (Mazey and Richardson 2001) with interests is a classic form of *risk reduction*. By seating the appropriate stakeholders at the appropriate seats, bureaucrats both reduce likely resistance to their policy proposals at other venues and avoid the blame for subsequent policy failures or fiascos. Moreover, in the context of the EU, the need to construct complex advocacy coalitions (Sabatier 1988, 1998) in favour of policy innovation is especially pressing for the Commission, which has the power to *propose* but not *dispose*. Faced with intense institutional competition for policy space, it has every incentive to seek and nurture and construct coalitions which can cross institutional boundaries in the complex EU policy process.

Interest groups: exploiting multiple venues and allocating resources rationally

From what we know about interest groups in Western democracies, we can expect groups to seek to establish close relations with state bureaucracies and regulatory agencies. Interest groups are capable of allocating resources rationally as between possible lobbying targets – be they institutions (see Bennett 1997, 1999; Coen 1997, 1998, 2009; Broscheid and Coen 2003; Bouwen 2004a, 2004b; Broscheid and Coen 2007; Dür and Mateo 2014) or indeed the public at large (Dür and Mateo 2014). Moreover, the EU lobbying system is not new. It has existed in some form since European integration was first started by the founding fathers of the EU. Thus, deciding on lobbying strategies is no longer a shot in the dark. As Coen argues, 'at the EU level, it became apparent to the first wave of business lobbyists that those who wish to exert a direct lobbying influence on the European public policy system would have to marshal a greater number of skills than merely monitoring the progress of European directives and presenting occasional positions to the Commission' (2007: 337). His study of firms as lobbyists found that firms were politically sophisticated and were able to recognize and construct alliances with rival firms and countervailing interests (Coen 1997: 91; see also Coen 2009). One of the skills needed for successful lobbying relates to information. Thus, it is well known that the supply of reliable information is a crucial aspect of EU lobbying. As Chalmers found, access to EU decision-makers is 'largely related to the presumed informational needs of decision-makers . . .' (Chalmers 2013: 54). Perhaps surprisingly, he also found that the way information was conveyed was more important than the content of information (Chalmers 2013: 55).

Within the EU, groups were quick to recognize the formal and informal powers of the Commission as an agenda setter. Lobbying resources allocated to this early stage of EU agenda setting are likely to produce bigger policy payoffs than are resources allocated to lobbying later in the policy process. As a senior Commission official put it, at the beginning of the policy process a Commission official '. . . is a very lonely official with a blank sheet of paper, wondering what to put on it. Lobbying at the very early stage therefore offers the greatest opportunity to shape thinking and ultimately to shape policy' (Hull 1993: 83). Similarly, groups know that lobbying is not just about influencing or changing public policy – it is also about minimizing their surprises. Hence, knowing what is going on may be just as important to an adaptive interest organization as trying to influence what is going on. In that sense, participation is perfectly rational even if no policy payoff results. Finally, the increasing technical content of policy and the 'unpacking' of broad policy problems into more manageable, low-salience, technical issues, so familiar in Western democracies, further increases the incentive for groups to form 'policy partnerships' with Commission bureaucrats in (preferably) closed policy-making structures. Here we see, yet again, the Commission exhibiting generic traits long familiar to those working on the sociology of organizations. Thus, we might be able to better understand what is always described as *sui generis* system if we use as a starting point what we already know about organizations and institutions more generally. For example Richardson and Jordan drew upon the notion of 'negotiated order', originally developed by the sociologist Strauss (1978) in his study of psychiatric hospitals in order to understand why government departments and groups were so close in Britain (Richardson and Jordan 1979: 101). The desire on the part of both bureaucrats and groups for some kind of negotiated order (stability) drives a continuous process of trade-offs in what Jordan and Richardson described as a process of *'mutual exchange'* between bureaucrats and groups (Jordan and Richardson 1982). Drawing on this idea of exchange, we ourselves argued that 'a system of *exchange relationships* with bureaucrats must be developed, based upon *mutual trust* developed over time' (Mazey and Richardson 1995: 345) and somewhat later argued that such a system had, indeed, come about. Thus, the result of Commission initiatives in response to increased group mobilization, had produced 'an often *symbiotic relationship* (though rarely genuinely corporatist) between the Commission and interest groups' (Mazey and Richardson 2006a: 280); however, see Grugel and Lusmen 2013 for an example of the *breakdown* of a symbiotic relationship). In fact, the notion of mutual exchange between groups and EU policy-makers is now part of the conventional wisdom of EU lobbying studies. Also drawing on exchange models developed by sociologists, Bouwen has argued that 'the key to understanding the lobbying activities of business interests in the European institutions is to conceive of the relations between these private actors as an *exchange relation* between two interdependent organizations' (2004b, 339, emphasis added.). Groups and the Commission thus have an especially acute mutual interest in trying to form stable policy communities and policy networks over time.

Making policy communities and networks work can be difficult, however, even at the national level (Richardson 2000). Many exogenous factors intervene – including new ideas or 'frames' (Schön and Rein 1994), the structure of institutions, the arrival of new interests in a policy area and the sheer number of interests to be accommodated. The EU is a classic example of the appearance of a new opportunity structures (Kitschelt 1986) whose emergence has brought the possibility of a different stakeholder bias in terms of institutional power. Thus, our third hypothesis, reflecting the work of social movement theorists and interest group analysts alike, is that interest groups will seek to exploit (and sometimes create) new opportunity structures, or venues, which they believe will maximize their chances of public policy payoffs (for a sophisticated discussion of opportunity structures in the EU see Princen and Kerremans 2008). The EU as a polity presents an American-style plethora of opportunity structures to which interest groups can go. The creation of the EU has, therefore, created a quite new opportunity for what Baumgartner and Jones term 'venue shopping' by national and cross-national interest group actors in Europe (not all of whom, of course, are 'European'). As Baumgartner and Jones suggest, political actors are capable of strategic action by employing a dual strategy as follows:

> On the one hand they try to control the prevailing image of the policy problem through the use of rhetoric, symbols and policy analysis. On the other hand, they try to alter the roster of participants who are involved in the issue by seeking out the most favourable venue for consideration of these issues.
>
> (1991: 1045)

Although Baumgartner and Jones developed the 'venue shopping' thesis from their study of nuclear energy politics in the US, its relevance to the EU is clear. Like the US, the EU is a system of multiple access points. Thus, venue shopping is now normal in the EU, just as it is in the US. As each venue, or opportunity structure exhibits its own bias, this creates '. . . incentives for advocates to push issues towards the venue with the greatest receptivity to their own point of view' (Baumgartner 2007: 484).

We believe that the creation of a maturing system of interest group intermediation at the European level has both transformed national policy-making systems and fundamentally changed the roster of actors who constitute the power elites in Europe. This transformation is due to the simple fact that national governments have, for whatever reasons, ceded sovereignty over large areas of public policy-making to the EU level. Once public policy started to be made at the supranational level, groups were bound to allocate increasing amounts of lobbying resources to that level. There are, as Mahoney notes, both *supply* and *demand* factors at work in the creation of the EU lobbying system. She argues that scholars have tended to overlook the role of governments in influencing the behaviour of interest groups. Thus, 'the central governing body draws interests to it by increasing its attention to and control of certain policy areas' (Mahoney 2004: 440).

Whether caused by supply or demand factors, the very involvement of interest groups in transnational settings, such as the EU, in turn contributed to a further reduction of national sovereignty, whether or not states (individually or collectively) wanted that. In their study of activists beyond borders Keck and Sikkink argue that 'by thus blurring boundaries between a state's relations with its own nationals and the recourse both citizens and states have to the international systems, advocacy networks are helping to transform the practice of national sovereignty' (1998: 1–2). Although their study focuses on a particular type of transnational actor (such as environmental, human rights and women's groups), much the same conclusions could be reached by studying the behaviour of more conventional groups, such as firms (e.g. see Coen 1997, 1998; Broscheid and Coen 2003; Broscheid and Coen 2007; Kurzer and Cooper 2013; Dür and Mateo

2014; Rasmussen 2014) in the EU. A central theme in the Keck and Sikkink thesis, and in ours, is the autonomy from states which transnational action can deliver to activists and interest groups. As Keck and Sikkink suggest, the 'two-level game' metaphor developed by Putnam (1988) is useful in pointing out the role played by domestic interests in shaping national preferences. Putnam sees 'international relations as a two-way street, in which political entrepreneurs bring international influence to bear on domestic politics at the same time that domestic politics shapes their international positions' (Keck and Sikkink 1998: 4). This is precisely our argument in the case of the EU as an 'international system'. It is incredibly open and permeable to interest group lobbying compared with even the most pluralistic member states. The permeability of the Commission, and other EU venues such as the European Parliament (EP) and European Court of Justice (ECJ), to interest groups weakens the ability of states to control and steer national interest groups and, indeed, to control their national policy agendas. Insofar as groups become 'activists beyond borders', to borrow Keck and Sikkink's terminology, they both weaken the power of states in the process of transnational governance and may become an independent source of integration.

This does not mean, of course, that *all* groups trying to influence EU public policy operate at the EU level. As Grossman notes, 'not all groups are equally well equipped to benefit from multi-level policy making . . .' (Grossman 2004: 647). However, it appears that lobbying of Brussels by national associations is very common '. . . possibly allowing the EU to claim input legitimacy' (Dür and Mateo 2012; 983). The problem is that there is variation in the amount of lobbying across national associations such that the system of EU representation via this channel is best seen as '. . . a form of elite pluralism' (Dür and Mateo 2102: 983). Even for those well-informed and well-resourced national interests, such as multinational companies, the national route will not be ignored. Indeed, Grossman is a sceptic regarding the thesis that economic interests have played a decisive role in the path of European integration, arguing that integration '. . . continues to be a very political process in the sense that political institutions, such as elected governments and, to a lesser extent, European institutions, remain the central actors . . .' (Grossman, 2004: 650: see also Schneider and Baltz 2004). However, Grossman also notes that even if groups do not play a key role in issues having major institutional implications, they may well play such a role in regulatory policy-making concerning their particular areas of economic activity. This suggestion is in fact confirmed by the findings reported from a study of lobbying activity and group creation in the EU by Broscheid and Coen, who found that distributive policy domains had fewer groups than regulatory policy domains (2007: 346). Thus, it is important to remember that European integration is not just about grand bargains, and the high politics of history making decisions. Increasingly it is about technical regulations and soft law. At this level of policy-making, interest groups may well be better informed on specific (and often very technical) policy issues and policy proposals than national governments and may sometimes be disinclined to share information with them.

The rational and independent exploitation of new EU opportunity structures by interest groups exists alongside a less tangible process of identification with the new Euro-level structures in which these interests participate – especially if the structures deliver valuable policy payoffs. Transnational lobbying, particularly as it becomes institutionalized in the EU, can have long-lasting effects on the perceptions and behaviours of actors. The newly created institutional structures can be seen as 'meaningful objects of identification' (Breton 1995: 40). Following Breton's analysis, some kind of path dependency in the EU might therefore be postulated. Transnational organization expands in virtually all domains. The expanding scope and diversity of players is accompanied by increased institutionalization; the critical institutions are those established for collective decision-making, mobilization of resources, circulation of information, coordination of activities and control of free riders. The corresponding ideologies are those that legitimize particular institutional arrangements; the experience of interdependence in turn tends to generate a 'community fate' identity, a pragmatic solidarity (drawn from Breton 1995: 40–2). We see, therefore, a similar phenomenon in the European policy-making process and in the long-established traditions of national policy-making in Western Europe – namely a high degree of interest group integration into the policy process, based upon the twin 'logics' of organization and negotiation. It is to the seemingly inexorable trajectory of this mobilization process that we now turn.

The emergence of a European interest group system: from undersupply to oversupply of representation?

However the EU lobbying system is characterized, of one fact we can be absolutely sure: the number and the range of interest groups active at the European level have increased enormously over the history of the EU.

One of the earliest systematic studies of the emergence of a European interest-group system was Kirchner's (1980a) analysis of interest group formation at the EU level. This study cites Meynaud and Sidjanski's earlier study of European pressure groups, which found that many of these groupings established themselves at the Community level in response to the formation of a new centre of decision-making and as a result of advantages expected from Community action (Kirchner 1980a: 96–7). Sidjanski's study suggests that some of the groups were formed as the EEC's own institutions were created, others when it became clear that the EEC's regulatory powers could significantly affect different interests in society (1970: 402). Moreover, the Commission, particularly, has always been keen to nurture and develop a system of group intermediation. For example Mazey suggests that the Commission has continued to foster the development of women's networks in order to justify expanding the EU gender policy agenda beyond the workplace (2012: 135). Indeed, she points out that the European Women's Lobby was actually founded by the Commission, which continues to provide the bulk of its funds (Mazey 2012: 135). We return to the question of Commission funding of cause or diffuse interests later, but it is important to note that the Commission has as much interest in nurturing the business lobby. For example Cowles describes the role of the Commission in the setting up of the European Round Table, representing some of the largest companies within the EU. She records that 'the first list of potential industry members was drawn up in 1982 in the Commission's Berlaymont building by Volvo and Commission staff' (Cowles 1997: 504).

Kirchner notes that another phenomenon familiar from studies of national interest groups systems was evident in the early years of the Union – namely that groups beget more groups. Once one set of interests is mobilized and organized to influence decision-makers, those interests in society who have not yet organized will see the need to do so; if they do not, they are leaving policy space exclusively occupied by rival interests. Interest group mobilization is at least a means of 'risk avoidance' in the manner first suggested by David Truman in 1951. In an attempt to defend pluralism in the US (surely, now the defining characteristic of the EU interest group system), he argued that over time interest group power would tend to reach some kind of equilibrium. This was partly because society was full of what he termed 'potential groups' which, when threatened by the successes of those interests already organized, would themselves become organized to defend their own objectives (Truman 1951: 31). Kirchner suggests that the mobilization of trade unions at the European level is a classic example of this phenomenon (1977: 28). A similar risk-avoidance strategy has been noted even for powerful multinational companies. McLaughlin and Jordan suggest that a 'negative incentive' is at work for firms when deciding whether to join the relevant European association for their industry. If a firm does not join, the Euro association in question may produce 'unwelcome group decisions' (McLaughlin and Jordan 1993: 155). The danger of *not* participating in a European association is that the Commission might take the Euro association's view as the definitive view of the industry as a whole, to the detriment of the non-participating firm. So many incentive structures are at work, making increasing group mobilization inevitable. It would take a brave (or more likely foolish) interest group to deliberately shun the opportunity to join the Brussels game.

It would be quite wrong, however, to explain the emergence of a European interest-group system solely in defensive terms. As Kirchner notes in the case of trade unions, there were also perceived *positive* benefits from European-level organization. He suggests that one of the aims of the trade unions in mobilizing at the Euro level 'is to promote, at the European level, the interests which become increasingly difficult to achieve at the national level' (Kirchner 1980b: 132). Increasingly, this is a major motivation underpinning the continuation and further development of the EU interest-group system, consistent with neo-functionalist theory; that is groups increasingly see positive benefits from Euro-level solutions. This is particularly the case for groups concerned with trans-frontier problems, such as environmental groups and even companies bearing heavy costs due to the proliferation of different national regulations. At a more theoretical level, Stone Sweet and Sandholtz (1998) posit a demand/supply model of European integration, similar to Deutsch's (1957) transaction theory. They argue that the Community's rules for organizations favour 'economic actors with a stake in cross-border transactions (trade, investment, production, distribution). Rising levels of transnational exchange trigger processes that generate movement toward increased supranational governance' (Stone Sweet and Sandholtz 1998: 2). Transnational interests demand more Euro-level regulation because it facilitates efficient (and increased) transnational exchange. The development of the EU and the development of the EU interest-group system went hand in hand.

The story since the early 1980s has been one of steady growth in the number of groups operating at the European level. In 1985 Butt Philip was reporting that there were almost 500 Europe-wide groups (Butt Philip 1985: 88). Berkhout and Lowery estimate that by 1996 the population of EU lobby organizations '... included about 2200 interest organizations, a bit over half of which are professional associations or interest *groups*' (2010: 455). Wonka *et al.* have estimated that the total interest group population in 2007–8 was 3,700 (2010: 466). The Commission itself set up a voluntary Register of Interest Group Representatives in 2008, and by late 2013 it had attracted some 3,000 entries. Thus, it seems reasonable to assume that at any one time, between 2,000 and 3,000 groups are active in some way at the EU level. The Berkhout and Lowery data show that the boom years were probably in the early 1990s and that 'during the late 1990s the number or organizations that were active in the EU remained nearly constant' (2010: 457). Interestingly, they also found that the EU system is surprisingly volatile, even over short periods. Thus, they found that

> [f]ar from being a stable, persistent community of organized interests, the EU interest system is one in which interest organizations come and go before both the Commission and the Parliament. There is a large contingent of 'tourists' who visit Brussels presumably to influence 'more specific and/or timebound issues, and lack either the means or interest in establishing a more permanent presence before the Commission or EP. On the other hand there appears to be a core set of interests that might reasonably be labeled permanent representatives untouched by the volatility observed among 'tourists'.
>
> (Berkhout and Lowery 2011: 12)

One of the problems in trying to calculate the number of interest groups active at the EU level is that there are many sub-systems clustered around particular policy problems. For example up to 300 groups were identified on the field of EU water policy (Richardson 1994: 144). Even though such large numbers are undoubtedly common for very many policy areas and, indeed, for specific issues, there is often a 'core' of groups that matter most. However, as issue expansion takes place (another common and normal phenomenon in the EU), even the core can expand as new entrants demand and achieve legitimacy as key players. For example the drafting of the original Drinking Water Directive (80/778) during the 1970s included virtually no formal consultation with water suppliers, whereas nowadays, EUREAU, the representative association of the industry, is a core group (Richardson 1994: 156–7). Undoubtedly, many Brussels-based groups will be small-scale operations – mere 'listening posts' whose function is to simply gather information about funding opportunities or new EU-level policy initiatives. However, it is also possible to argue that the true size of the Brussels-level lobbying industry could actually be *higher* than any of these estimates, because it is impossible to know how many *ad hoc* and unrecorded visits lobbyists based in the member states make to Brussels in order to try to influence EU policy-making and implementation.

In theory, the Commission has a preference for consulting Euro associations, but in practice it is probably unusual to find examples of Commission officials relying solely on Euro associations in the consultation process. Commission officials also habitually go directly to the source of technical expertise on which the Euro associations themselves rely. For example Eising reports that '... political leaders in the EU prefer dealings with large firms rather than with business associations' (2007: 399). Whilst being in a Euro association might be a cheap insurance policy, there is probably no substitute for having an office in Brussels if a group has an ongoing and long-term interest in European public policy.

Individual members of Euro associations (such as national associations and individual firms) have increasingly spread their lobbying resources in a risk avoidance strategy. Brussels might be a policy-making maze, but groups learn their way round it. The more complex the multi-venue Euro-policy game becomes, the greater the need for flexibility and maneuverability by interest groups if they are to create policy win situations.

Concentrating resources on one EU institution is a very risky strategy and likely to fail. Creating *ad hoc* coalitions, sometimes between groups that might oppose each other on different issues, is also a sensible strategy, particularly when multiple opportunity structures (each having a different institutional bias) present themselves. For example, the formation of EU water policy has been characterized as a process involving uncertain agendas, shifting networks and complex coalitions' (Richardson 1994: 139). As we know from studies on national lobbying, groups look around for allies, knowing the common sense rule of safety in numbers. The EU is no different. For example Long and Lörinczi document the emergence of a coalition of ten environmental groups in Brussels, the so-called Green Ten (G10). The purpose of the coalition is to promote a message of strength, unity and professionalism to the key targets, the European institutions (Long and Lörinczi 2009: 172). More generally they note that non-governmental organizations (NGOs) in the environmental field build 'alliances and coalitions not only with other environmental groups in Brussels but with consumer groups, health groups, women's associations, retailing businesses, and trade unions' (Long and Lörinczi 2009: 176). That lobbying is (as it always was) often a *collective* enterprise has been underlined by recent research by Klüver who argues that what matters for lobbying success, '. . . is the sum of the characteristics of all lobbying camp members rather than the individual properties of a few powerful interest groups' (2013: 73).

Promiscuity, institutionalization, e-consultation, and venue shopping

The EU policy system, both in terms of institutional design and informal rules, positively encourages interest groups (and other actors) to behave promiscuously. However, there are attempts, especially by the Commission, to structure and institutionalize promiscuous behaviour. The Commission has not only been a 'purposeful opportunist' in terms of policy expansion. It has also been opportunistic in creating new institutions as a means of locking diverse interests into the *ongoing* process of Europeanization. It has been a strategic actor in constructing constellations of stakeholders concerned with each of the Commission's policy sectors. This construction process takes place both as a means for the Commission to create new Europeanized policy areas and, once established, for the long-term management of established European policies. It is important to stress, however, that each institutional innovation is linked to a broad *organizational culture* which has become embedded in most parts of the Commission. This culture is clearly outlined in the Commission's 1992 definitive publication *An Open and Structured Dialogue* (Commission of the European Communities 1992) and further developed in publications subsequent to the Cardiff European Council of 15/16 June 1998. The latter document stressed the need to bring the Union nearer to its citizens by making it more transparent, more understandable and closer to everyday life. In practice, this has meant even greater emphasis on interest group accommodation by the Commission in the following decade and a half.

In its 1992 document the Commission had argued that it 'has always been an institution open to outside input. The Commission believes this process to be fundamental to the development of its policies. It is in the Commission's own interest to maintain open access since interest groups can provide the services with technical information and constructive advice' (Commission of the European Communities 1992: 1). Over time, the Commission has introduced a number of measures designed to increase openness and transparency, consistent with its embedded policy style. These include earlier publication of the Commission's legislative programme, a commitment to ensure that target groups are aware of any new policy initiatives, and greater use of Green (consultative) Papers.

Since 2000, the use of the internet has become an increasingly important characteristic of the Commission's interest group management strategy. In a sense, e-governance has arrived at least in the form of e-consultation. In April 2001, the Commission adopted a Communication on Interactive Policy Making (C(2001) 1014). The so-called Interactive Policy Making (IPM) initiative involved the development of two internet-based mechanisms to assist the consultation processes: a feedback facility, to allow existing networks to report to the Commission on a continuous basis, and an online consultation tool, designed to receive and store rapidly reactions to new initiatives. Quittkat reports that the use of online consultation (OC) has increased steadily since 2000, when nine OCs were held, to 130 in 2006, with a total of 554 by 2007 (Quittkat 2011: 658). Critics, such as European Civil Society organizations, see OCs as mere box-ticking exercises (Quittkat 2011: 654) or what we termed 'sham consultation' (Mazey and Richardson 2006b: 257). Quittkatt appears to have at least some doubts, however. On the positive side, she argues that the introduction of OC '... can be considered a success insofar as OC contributes to better informed policy-making through the involvement of a wide range of different actors' (2011: 670). However, amongst a number of concerns which she sets out, we see as especially worrying her view that 'the Commission's weak record on publishing OC contributions and reports ... with publication being the exception rather than the rule' (Quittkat 2011: 671) because this prevents any proper assessment of the *outcomes* of this form of consultation.

There are constant criticisms of bias in the whole panoply of consultation process in the EU, particularly an alleged bias in favour of business groups. However, for many years the Commission has helped to fund European public-interest lobbies such as the European Women's Lobby, as we noted earlier, and organizations such as the European Environmental Bureau. In an attempt to allay public fears about the EU's democratic deficit, the Commission has, since the early 1990s, redoubled its efforts to achieve a more balanced institutionalization of interest group intermediation, mainly through the construction of a series of inclusive social networks such as the Social Policy Forum. As Mahoney suggests, this 'can be seen as an effort by the EU to promote wider civil society participation, working to lessen some of the endemic biases inherent in the patterns of mobilization of different sectors of society' (2004: 446). As long ago as 1997, the Commission adopted a Communication, *Promoting the Role of Voluntary Organizations and Foundations in Europe*, which stressed the need for NGOs to be consulted more widely and more systematically. As the Commission noted in 2002 (COM(2002) 704), this initiative underlined its intention to 'reduce the risk of the policy-makers just listening to one side of the argument or of particular groups getting privileged access'. The increasing institutionalization of NGO–Commission relations is also reflected in the considerable financial support that NGOs receive from the Commission as part of its broader constituency mobilization strategy. For example Salgado's study of the Commission's funding of Civil Society Organizations (CSOs) found that in 2009 the Commission funded more than 3,000 CSOs to the tune of $1.4 billion, with some CSOs, such as the

European Network Against Racism, receiving more than 80 per cent of their funding from the Commission (Salgado 2014: 338). Space does not permit a discussion of the merits or otherwise of a policy-making institution, such as the Commission, funding groups which then lobby that very same institution. However, we have no reason to doubt Salgado's general conclusion that such funding appears not to result in a loss of autonomy for those groups in receipt of funding and that the funding plays an important role in addressing power and resource imbalances in the EU lobbying system (Salgado 2014: 350).

The Commission's need to demonstrate openness and transparency in policy formulations is paralleled by its need to mobilize a consensus in favour of technically sound and politically feasible policies. In the end, policies have to 'work'. These potentially conflicting objectives are typically achieved through different institutional structures used at various stages of the policy-making process. Broadly speaking, the Commission employs two different strategies for involving groups in the policy process: large, open gatherings (including consultations via the internet as outlined earlier), and more restrictive committees, forums and myriad bilateral meetings. Although it is impossible to generalize about the relative importance of these two types of interest aggregation within the Commission, our own research suggests that there might be a pattern emerging. In the early stages of the policy process, consultative structures tend to be open and inclusive, bringing together all potential stakeholders in an open forum, a seminar or a conference. Generally, the purpose of this form of consultation is to inform potential stakeholders, to try out new ideas and to obtain early feedback on proposals. It is a form of 'kite flying' or political mapping familiar in most national capitals.

However, the subsequent formulation and implementation of detailed proposals usually takes place within the myriad formal and informal advisory committees and working parties in the Commission, which comprise group representatives and technical experts. Formal committees include so-called expert committees composed of national officials and experts, who are nominated by government departments. In practice, however, these nominees tend to perceive their role as being that of technical experts rather than national government agents. Generally, the Commission *must* consult the relevant expert committee or committees during the policy formulation process (though it is under no obligation to respond to the advice offered by the experts). The more broadly based 'consultative committees' represent sectoral interests and are composed of representatives of Euro associations and national groups. Though the Commission has a procedural ambition to deal primarily with the Euro associations, the latter are not always able to provide the level of expertise (and cross-national knowledge) required. The *raison d'être* of all these committees is to advise the Commission on the technical details of its proposals. The importance of these committees in the policy process is considerable. In addition, the Commission frequently sets up informal, high-level groups or working parties to consider a specific problem. In practice, it is possible to distinguish between rather open and 'thin' institutions, such as very large conferences and seminars, and the more restricted 'thick' institutions, where only the key players are present. Coen, observing this trend with respect to business interests, refers to the emergence at the EU level of 'the creeping institutionalisation of forum style politics' (1999: 16). This process is described as the Commission acting as both policy entrepreneur and *political* entrepreneur in response to the further explosion of lobbying after the Maastricht Treaty. The lobbying system is so vast that capturing its essence under one label is a tough task. To be sure, it is pluralistic, though Richardson and Coen argue that it is 'chameleon pluralism' due to its changeable nature (2009: 346–480; see also Coen and Katsaitis [2013: 1104–19] for a discussion of different types of pluralism).

The intensity and scope of lobbying have itself become a problem in need of regulation of some kind for both the Commission and the EP. The outcome of a very long process to decide on the form of regulation has been a system of voluntary registration and codes of practice, with recently a joint registration list maintained by the Commission and EP (for a comprehensive review of the process leading to this voluntary regulation involving registration and codes of conduct, see Cini 2013: 1146–49). In reality, the register and codes of conduct are supplementary to some rather important informal, but unwritten, rules and norms which facilitate exchange among individuals. However, controlling or over-regulating access is unlikely to be a strategy adopted by the Commission (or, indeed, by the Parliament); consulting as many stakeholders as possible is rational behaviour, given the need to obtain the best information and knowledge. It is also a good way of avoiding the dangers of asymmetric information supplied by lobbyist. Even if the broadening of consultations produces no new (or usable) information, it does strengthen the Commission's position in inter-institutional battles. As we suggested earlier, the functional logic for bureaucracies, and indeed legislatures, to behave in this way is compelling. In addition, the Commission needs to get ever closer to groups as it knows that groups have other, attractive, EU venues where they can influence the policy process, such as the EP.

The European Parliament has steadily secured for itself a greater role in the EU policy process (see Rittberger and Winzen, in this volume). As a result of this shift in the balance of power between EU institutions, the EP has moved up the rank order of lobbying targets, depending on the issue at hand. In fact, the EP has, for a very long time (and long before the more recent increases in its powers) attracted a great deal of lobbying activity – so much so, in fact, that the question of regulating lobbying has been a key issue within the EP for several years (as suggested earlier). There are three obvious explanations for this apparent inconsistency. First, expressing a preference for one opportunity structure over another does not preclude some lobbying of less-favoured structures. Secondly, it seems likely that in the past the EP attracted a disproportionate amount of lobbying from certain types of groups (environmentalists, women, consumers, animal rights) who, historically, may not have enjoyed such easy access to the Commission and/ or their national governments. Third, the EP's power in the EU policy process varies across policy sectors both because of the Treaties and because of the internal political dynamics of different policy sectors. Where there are effective EP committees, and (in the now wide range of policy areas) where legislative power is shared between the Council and the Parliament under co-decision making procedures, lobbying of the EP is likely to be more intense. The steady expansion of the EP's legislative role since 1986 has changed the calculation of the logic of influence by groups. As Kohler-Koch suggested as long ago as 1997, 'reflecting the new role of the EP as an important institution in the European decision-making process, the Parliamentarians are becoming a decisive target group for lobbyists, and lobbyists have to cope with the institutional structure, the procedures, and the policy style within the Parliament' (1997: 10). As she argued, changes in the Parliament's role, and in its relationship with groups, seem to be shifting the EP in the direction of a US Congress-type legislature. Typically, the public hearings of the EP's committees attract the relevant stakeholders, all interested in pressing their view on the Parliament. As Bouwen and McCown note, 'since the Treaty of Maastricht, the codecision power has provide the European Parliament with real veto power in the legislative process' (2007: 424). Few interests now dare risk leaving the parliamentary arena to their opponents and, hence, parliamentary hearings attract the full *melange* of stakeholders. Wessels, for example, produced data showing that there are probably some 67,000 contacts between the EP and interest groups annually (Wessels 1999: 109). Following Kohler-Koch, he concluded that 'the more the EP becomes a veto player, the more attention it receives' (Wessels 1999: 109). Similarly, Grant notes that business interests have realized that more attention needs to be paid to the EP, citing the example of the chemical industry's Euro association, CEFIC, which appointed a full-time EP liaison officer in 1990 (Grant 2000: 118). Bouwen's study found the supply and demand model (in this case the demand and supply for 'access goods') useful for explaining interest group access to the EP. The access goods in question all relate to information, namely *expert knowledge, information about the European encompassing interest (i.e. the needs of the particular policy sector under discussion at any time) and information about the domestic encompassing interest.* His central thesis is that the crucial access good supplied to the EP by interest groups is not technical information (the access good that we stress for Commission/group relations) but the European encompassing interest. This access good provides MEPs with the European perspective which they need if an agreement is to be forged within the transnational groups in the EP (Bouwen 2004a: 476–80). In addition, in order to increase their chances of re-election, MEPs also need the third access good, namely information on national needs and preferences. Thus, both European and national associations gain access to the EP by supplying goods which the EP demands, albeit sometimes rather different goods to those demanded by the Commission. Clearly, the Commission remains a key target for groups. As Lehmann argues, it still plays a 'pivotal' role. However, he goes on to argue that '. . . with the extension of its legislative powers over the past 20 years the European Parliament has become an equally important addressee of companies, trade associations, public affairs consultants, and citizens' action groups' (Lehmann 2009: 39). Rasmussen also argues that 'with its elevation to a genuine co-legislator following the Lisbon Treaty, the EP has become an important lobbying addressee for business and diffuse interests alike' (2014: 1). Rasmussen also echoes the argument we put forward above, namely that no interest can sit back having 'won' in one venue and assume that all will be well in the next venue. As Rasmussen argues 'today, interest groups lobby the EP regardless of whether or not they are successful in leaving their fingerprints on the European Commission's proposal. If they are successful at the Commission stage, they lobby Members of the European Parliament . . . to make sure that their inputs are not removed' (2014: 2). Thus, interest groups find themselves in a situation akin to a football team in the Group stage of the World Football Cup where a team can have a glorious victory in the first match, yet has more matches to play in order to be sure of entering to the next stage, where they can still be knocked out of the tournament! The 'more powerful EP = more lobbying' thesis, whilst supported by the evidence, needs a slight qualification, however. Thus Burns *et al.* argue that the emergence of early agreements between the EP and the Council under the co-decision procedure '. . . has led to an efficiency-democracy trade off as smaller groups of actors take decisions behind closed doors' (Burns *et al.* 2013: 943). Similarly, Andlovic and Lehmann express some concern about the effect of early agreements. In their case study of the influence of the aviation industry on the emissions trading system, they found some evidence that business groups seemed to adapt better to the more 'secluded setting' of early agreements (Andlovic and Lehman 2014: 802). Here we see what we term 'the iron law of increased EU complexity' at work, namely that nearly every reform seems to make the EU decision-making process ever more complex. Thus, extension of co-decision was supposed to be a democratizing measure. As Burns *et al.* point out '... codecision has clearly had an effect upon the EU as a political system by institutionalizing new rules and norms and opening up policy-making to a wider set of demands, but the operation of decision-making has in some areas limited the extent to which those demands can be met' (Burns *et al.* 2013: 943). A similar problem has been identified by Rippoll Servant, who argues that 'the combination of constraints on both *how* the EP negotiates and on *what* it negotiates is leading to a slow process of depoliticization' (2013: 983).

The increasing attention that interest groups pay to the EP is a direct reflection of its power as an institution. Similarly, the ECJ's attractiveness as a venue relates to its position in the EU's institutional hierarchy. Here, again, we see the EU interest intermediation system exhibiting some familiar features. In those political systems which accord the judiciary a major role in the interpretation of legal and constitutional arrangements, recourse to the courts has long been a standard 'lobbying' strategy. As McCown points out, courts can be very appealing venues for minority interests to challenge rules (McCown 2009: 89). In the EU, once the ECJ had acquired for itself a major role in the EU policy process it was inevitable that interest groups would devote more attention and resources to influencing Court rulings, on the principle of shooting where the ducks are. As courts acquire power in the field of public policy so they present groups with a new option, namely a litigation strategy. The ECJ represents a perfect example of the 'venue shopping' theory of Baumgartner and Jones, cited earlier. When groups fail to gain satisfaction at the national level, the Commission, the EP or Council of Ministers, they have the option – albeit a costly one – of trying to bring a case before the Court, or of persuading the Commission to bring a case before the Court.

Women's and environmental groups (and trade unions) have been adept in securing favourable ECJ decisions which have been extremely important in prompting policy change. Mazey argues that the ECJ, in particular, has been a very important opportunity structure or venue in supporting the plight of working women and forcing national policy change (1998: 136; 2012: 132). At a more general level, Stone Sweet and Brunell have portrayed the Court as a 'supplying institution – supplying integrative decisions in response to the demands of transnational actors such as businesses and individuals . . . who need European rules and those who are advantaged by European law and practices compared with national law and practices' (1998: 72). Dehousse (1998) also argues that the expansion of EU competence, particularly in the areas of environmental and social policies, has prompted much greater use of the ECJ by individuals and groups, who perceive the ECJ as an ally. Bouwen and McCown have analysed the conditions under which groups choose between litigation and lobbying strategies. The attraction of litigation (usually via the preliminary reference process) is that the activist case law of the ECJ provides 'interest groups with potentially powerful legal tools for promoting policy change' (Bowen and McCown 2007: 426). This strategy can bring about long term policy change as 'interest groups that successfully litigate in order to shape EU policy, not only effect the removal of national rules, on the basis of EU law, but also typically shape the form of future legislation' (Bouwen and McCown 2007: 426). Thus, if case law can be influenced, this is equivalent to policy change. As McCown puts it, '[t]he ECJ's case law, *heavily influenced by organized interests*, significantly structured or even created areas of EU law ranging from intellectual property rights to gender equality' (2009: 90). A common interest group strategy appears to be serial litigation, taking advantage of the ECJ's:

> ... tendency towards precedent based decision-making ... so that rulings become integrated immediately into EU law and, eventually, if they are used as precedents in later rulings, form an ever more firmly entrenched part of the relevant law ... more organized litigation strategies entail plans to bring multiple cases, either in sequence or simultaneously ...
>
> (McCown 2009: 95)

Schmidt has developed a path-dependent model of how lobbyists use litigation by transferring legal arguments from one area of rights (goods) to the next (citizens), in a process of positive feedback to the Court (Schmidt 2012: 8). Thus, 'the support of litigants provides legitimacy to the Court ... by showing that there is a positive response to the individual rights it has itself created (Schmidt 2012: 12; see also Schmidt, in this volume). Thus, once rights have been granted on one area, litigants act (often successfully) to get them extended to another area.

An intergovernmental theorist would argue that, in theory, the Council of Ministers should be the main European-level opportunity structure to be targeted by interest groups. This should be especially so in the light of Costello and Thomson's findings that, though it has strengthened the EP position in relation to the Commission, co-decision has not given the EP parity with the Council (2013: 1025–1039; see also Thomson, in this volume, and Naurin, in this volume). Yet, it is the least *directly* accessible of all EU institutions. As with Cabinets in Western democracies, lobbying has to be rather indirect. Nevertheless, as Hayes-Renshaw and Wallace suggest, although groups 'have no formalised relationship with the Council, their influencing efforts pervade the atmosphere in which the Council works' (1997: 22). There are three main channels of indirect lobbying of the Council. First, interest groups routinely lobby the national delegations in Brussels, that is those national officials who are members of the so-called Permanent Representations based in Brussels. These officials participate in the Council working groups, of which there are approximately 200 (Van Schendelen 1998: 6), and prepare the ground for meetings of the Committee of Permanent Representatives (COREPER) and the ministerial Councils. Where possible, these officials try to reach consensus and compromise between their respective national governments, leaving only the most contentious points to be resolved when the ambassadors meet in COREPER I and II (or, ultimately, the ministers in the Council meetings). As the national representatives (i.e. the ambassadors and deputy ambassadors to the EU) in COREPER play such a key role in the Council process (some 80 per cent of legislative proposals are adopted at COREPER level), national groups make sure that they lobby 'their' national officials, who (the interest groups hope) will then ensure that their views are represented in the COREPER meetings – hence the description of members of COREPER as the 'lobbied lobbyists' (Spence 1993: 48). As Saurugger argues, COREPER, along with national governments themselves is a major contact point for interest groups (2009: 105). Hayes-Renshaw, whilst emphasizing that the Council is difficult to lobby directly, highlights the importance of domestic interest groups as an influence on the position that member states adopt at the European level. Thus, she argues:

> ... in defining its national position...each member of the Council engages with those (usually domestic) groups that can provide information about the national interest in the area involved. When they then operate in the context of the Council, national ministers and officials are in effect intervening as the delegates of the national interest groups whose interests they have chosen (or been persuaded.) to defend.
>
> (Hayes-Renshaw 2009: 78)

Euro-groups and those national associations and firms who really understand the importance of intergovernmentalism in EU policy-making typically lobby a range of national delegations in Brussels – particularly of those member states who are known to hold strong positions on any given policy issue. For example Boessen and Maarse highlight the way that the tobacco industry forged links with several national governments in its fight against a ban on tobacco advertising (2009: 212–32). Bouwen's comparative study of the business lobbying of EU institutions sheds some light on the lobbying of the Council. Thus, he finds that national associations and individual firms, rather than European associations, have the highest degree of access to the Council. Indeed, it appears that national associations have better access to the Council than to either the Parliament or the Commission (Bouwen 2004b: 358). He explains this bias by reference to his access goods theory (cited earlier). Basically, the Council needs information on the 'domestic encompassing interest i.e the aggregate needs and interests of a sector in the domestic markets' (Bouwen 2004b: 358).

A second common means of lobbying Council is for interest groups to lobby members of the many Council working groups. Rather like COREPER, this form of institutionalized 'issue processing' presents opportunities for detailed, technical arguments to be presented and for national representatives to be won over. The working groups are one of the boiler rooms of European integration. Composed of national officials 'congregating in their thousands every working day in Brussels, they [constitute] the backbone of the European system of integration ... they are performing the vital and frequently time-consuming technical groundwork for what will eventually become a piece of European legislation or policy' (Hayes-Renshaw and Wallace 1997: 98). For example if a Council working group on vehicle pollution is meeting and contains a civil servant from the Swedish government, the civil servant will certainly have been lobbied by Volvo and Saab and will be fully aware of the ways in which the Swedish motor vehicle industry might be affected by any proposed EU legislation.

The third and most obvious means of influencing the Council is, of course, directly via national governments. Several authors see national governments as, in fact, the *main* opportunity structure for interest groups, not just as a means of influencing the Council but also as the key opportunity structure through which groups can influence the EU policy process as a whole. For example Grant has long been sceptical of the thesis that Brussels is the most effective lobbying arena (2000: 106–15). Similarly, Greenwood describes the 'national route' as the 'tried and tested ground for many organised interests' (1997: 32). Wessels also argues that 'a European route of interest intermediation is clearly not dominant' (1999: 117). Bennett's survey data on the lobbying strategies of British business associations confirms this view of interest group behaviour. He found that the national route was the preferred Euro lobbying strategy of the majority of associations (except federations). He, too, argues that this is perfectly rational: '[T]he preference for this route can be explained by its relative cheapness and its continuity of use of traditional channels of information and exchange that have developed from the period before European economic integration' (Bennett 1997: 85). Schneider and colleagues have also echoed 'the primacy of the national route' thesis. Indeed, Schneider and Baltz go so far as to suggest that the system is largely étatist and that groups are, therefore, generally weak in relation to national governments. Thus, they conclude that 'although governments have to respect the interests of their stakeholders to some extent, they possess ample and largely uncontrolled discretion in EU affairs' (Schneider and Baltz 2004: 25). Clearly, the importance of national governments as an opportunity structure varies according to the policy issue, the type of interest group, the time, and the nature of the national government itself (see Saurugger [2009] for a discussion of cross-national variation in relations between national governments and groups). However, the continued extension of qualified majority voting in the Council is likely to erode still further the traditional ties between interest groups and national governments and to force interests to develop strategies independent of 'their' governments. Even when an interest group and its national government are on the same side in a policy development debate (often not a reasonable assumption), the group cannot rely on its national government being able to deliver the desired policy objective under QMV. Moreover, as cross-sectoral trade-offs between member states are not uncommon in last-minute bargaining, a national government may choose to 'dump' an interest group in favour of some other policy goal.

Conclusion: the politics of uncertainty

In their analysis of the origins of the Single Market, Sandholtz and Zysman suggest that process was characterized by uncertainty – 'neither the pay-off from nor the preferences for any strategy were . . . clear' (Sandholtz and Zysman 1989: 107). We conclude on this note of uncertainty. It is an affliction suffered by all players in the EU policy process. In such situations those policy actors possessing certain 'decisional' and 'attitudinal' attributes may have particular advantages in constructing 'win' situations in a series of nested games. Two such attributes might be, first, the development of a long-term view of Europe and its place in the globalization process, and, second, an ability to change preferences readily in response to changing circumstances. At least *some* European interest groups appear to possess these attributes; for example the large multinational companies do, indeed, take a European and global view; they may also have a more flexible decision-making process and preference-formation processes than, say, member states, or those interest groups exclusively 'anchored' in national interest group systems. As Heinz and colleagues argue in their study of US interest groups, 'interest representation involves learning. A group's understanding of its interests may change as a result of improved analysis or reflection on past experience' (Heinz *et al.* 1993: 392). Much more research is needed, but it seems reasonable to hypothesize that organisations such as multinationals and interest groups such as Greenpeace, Friends of the Earth and Worldwide Fund for Nature are probably less constrained in their lobbying strategies and have more flexible preference-formation processes than, for example, governments. If, as Heinz *et al.* suggest, uncertainty begets uncertainty, it would be rational for all interest groups wishing to influence the European policy process to avoid becoming locked into any one set of relationships (e.g. with 'their' national government) or into just one 'advocacy coalition' (Sabatier 1988) or any one policy community or policy network, hence our argument central argument that *promiscuity* is perfectly rational and has become accepted as the norm.

Thus, we conclude by suggesting that lobbying in the EU is likely to remain pluralistic (albeit chameleon pluralism), unpredictable and favouring those actors who can mobilize ideas and knowledge in order to influence the 'framing' of public policies, who can manage a series of multilevel and shifting coalitions, and who can reformulate their preferences rapidly and consistent with the long-term goals of their organization. The practical reality of the EU interest-group intermediation system is that more and more groups participate in more and more institutions of intermediation. However, we do not suggest that these institutions are necessarily stable or, indeed, neutral. All institutions have a bias and create winners and losers. The central paradox is that institutionalisation and promiscuity go hand in hand. In a sense, institutionalisation is an attempt to constrain promiscuity. The fact that there are so many different venues for group lobbying means that the EU is an inherently *disjointed* policy process. Deals done at one institutional site can get undone at another. At best, therefore, we might see a process of serial institutionalization of group intermediation in each EU venue, leaving as problematic the ambition for joined-up governance in the European Union. Even more problematic, of course, is the question of who gains what, if anything, from this now dense process of group participation in the EU policy process. Clearly, participation does not necessarily equal the exercise of power over policy-making, but it is a necessary condition for the exercise of power. Whether the policy payoff from interest group participation in the EU policy process is high or low, we seem set to see more participation rather than less.

References

Andlovic, M. and Lehmann, W. (2014) 'Interest Group Influence and Interistitutional Power Allocation in Early Second Reading Agreements: A Re-examination of Aviation Emission Trading', *Journal of European Public Policy*, 21(6): 802–21.

Baumgartner, F. (2007) 'EU Lobbying: A View from the US', *Journal of European Public Policy*, 14(3): 482–88.

Baumgartner, F. and Jones, B. (1991) 'Agenda Dynamics and Instability in American Politics', *Journal of Politics*, 53(4): 1044–73.

Bennett, R. (1997) 'The Impact of European Integration on Business Associations: The UK Case', *West European Politics*, 20(3): 6–90.

Bennett, R. (1999) 'Business Routes of Influence in Brussels: Exploring the Choice of Direct Representation', *Political Studies*, 47: 240–57.

Berkhout, J. and Lowery, D. (2010) 'The Changing Demography of the EU Interest System since 1990', *European Union Politics*, 11(3): 447–61.

Berkhout, J. and Lowery, D. (2011) 'Short-term Volatility in the EU Interest Community', *Journal of European Public Policy*, 18(1): 1–16.

Boessen, S. and Maarse, H. (2009) 'A Ban on Tobacco Advertising: The Role of Interest Groups', in Coen, D. and Richardson, J. (eds.), *Lobbying in the European Union: Institutions, Actors, and Issues*, Oxford: Oxford University Press, 212–32.

Bouwen, P. (2004a) 'The Logic of Access to the European Parliament', *Journal of Common Market Studies*, 42(3): 473–96.

Bouwen, P. (2004b) 'Exchange Access Good for Access. A Comparative Study of Business Lobbying in the EU Institutions', *European Journal of Political Research*, 43(3): 337–69.

Bouwen, P. and McCown, M. (2007) 'Lobbying versus Litigation: Political and Legal Strategies of Interest Representation in the European Union', *Journal of European Public Policy*, 14(3): 422–43.

Breton, R. (1995) 'Identification in Transnational Communities', in Knop, K., Ostry, S., Simeon R. and Swinton, K. (eds.), *Rethinking Federalism: Citizens, Markets, and Governments in a Changing World*, Vancouver: University of British Columbia Press, 40–58.

Broscheid, A. and Coen, D. (2003) 'Insider and Outsider Lobbying of the European Commission: An Informational Model of Forum Politics', *European Union Politics*, 4(2): 165–90.

Broscheid, A. and Coen, D. (2007) 'Lobbying Activity and for a Creation in the EU: Empirically Exploring the Nature of the Policy Good', *Journal of European Public Policy*, 13(3): 346–65.

Burns, C., Rasmussen, A. and Reh, C. (2013) 'Legislative Codecision and its Impact on the Political System of the European Union', *Journal of European Public Policy*, 20(7): 942–52.

Butt Philip, A. (1985) *Pressure Groups in the European Community*, London: University Association for Contemporary European Studies (UACES).

Chalmers, A. (2013) 'Trading Information for Access: Informational Lobbying and Interest Group Access to the European Union', *Journal of European Public Policy*, 20(1): 39–58.

Cichowski, R. (1998) 'Constrained Court or Autonomous Policy-maker? The European Court of Justice and Integration', *Journal of European Public Policy*, 5(3): 387–405.

Cini, M. (2013) 'EU Decision-Making on Inter-Institutional Agreements: Defining (Common) Rules of Conduct for European Lobbyists and Public Servants', *West European Politics*, 36(6): 1143–58.

Coen, D. (1997) 'The Evolution of the Large Firm as a Political Actor in the European Union', *Journal of European Public Policy*, 4(1): 91–108.

Coen, D. (1998) 'The European Business Interest and the Nation-State: Large-Firm Lobbying in the European Union and Member States', *Journal of Public Policy*, 18(1): 75–100.

Coen, D. (1999) 'Business Lobbying in the European Union', in Coen, D. and Richardson, J. (eds.), *Lobbying in the European Union: Institutions, Actors, and Issues*, Oxford: Oxford University Press, 145–68.

Coen, D. (2007) 'Empirical and Theoretical Studies of EU Lobbying', *Journal of European Public Policy*, 14(3): 333–45.

Coen, D. (2009) 'Business Lobbying in the European Union', in Coen, D. and Richardson, J. (eds.), *Lobbying in the European Union: Institutions, Actors, and Issues*, Oxford: Oxford University Press, 145–68.

Coen, D. and Katsaitis, A. (2013) 'Chameleon pluralism in the EU: an empirical study of the European Commission interest group density and diversity across policy domains', *Journal of European Public Policy*, 20(8): 1104–19.

Costello, R. and Thomson, R. (2013) 'The Distribution of Power among EU Institutions: Who Wins under Codecision and Why?', *Journal of European Public Policy*, 20(7): 1025–39.

Cowles, M. Green (1997) 'Organizing Industrial Coalitions: A Challenge for the Future?', in Wallace, H. and Young, A. (eds.), *Participation and Policy-Making in the European Union*, Oxford: Clarendon Press, 116–40.

Cram, L. (1994) 'The European Commission as a Multi-Organisation: Social Policy and IT Policy in the EU', *Journal of European Public Policy*, 1(1): 195–218.

Dehousse, R. (1998) *The European Court of Justice*, Basingstoke: Macmillan.

Deutsch, K. (1957) *Political Community at the International Level: Problems of Definition and Management*, Garden City: Doubleday.

Downs, A. (1967) *Inside Bureaucracy*, Boston: Little, Brown.

Dür, A. and Mateo, G. (2012) 'Who Lobbies the European Union? National Interest Groups in a Multi-level Polity', *Journal of European Public Policy*, 19(7): 969–87.

Dür, A. and Mateo, G. (2014) 'Public Opinion and Interest Group Influence: How Citizen Groups Derailed the Anti-counterfeiting Agreement', *Journal of European Public Policy*, 21(8): 1199–217.

Eising, R. (2007) 'The Access of Business Interests to EU Institutions: Towards Elite Pluralsim?', *Journal of European Public Policy*, 14(3): 384–403.

Grant, W. (2000) *Pressure Groups in British Politics*, Basingstoke, Macmillan.

Greenwood, J. (1997) *Representing Interests in the European Union*, Basingstoke: Macmillan.

Grossman, E. (2004) 'Bringing Politics Back In: Rethinking the Role of Economic Interest Groups in European Integration', *Journal of European Public Policy*, 11(4): 637–56.

Grugel, J. and Lusmen, I. (2013) 'The European Commission as Guardian Angel: The Challenge of Agenda Setting for Children's Rights', *Journal of European Public Policy*, 20(1): 77–94.

Haas, E. (1958) *The Uniting of Europe: Political, Social, and Economic Forces 1950–57*, Stanford: Stanford University Press.

Hayes-Renshaw, F. (2009) 'Least Accessible but not Inaccessible: Lobbying the Council and the European Council', in Coen, D. and Richardson, J. (eds.), *Lobbying in the European Union: Institutions, Actors, and Issues*, Oxford: Oxford University Press, 70–88.

Hayes-Renshaw, F. and Wallace, H. (1997) *The Council of Ministers*, London: Macmillan.

Heinz, J. P., Laumann, E. O., Nelson, R. L., Salisbury, R. H. (1993) *The Hollow Core: Private Interests in National Policy Making*, Cambridge, MA: Harvard University Press.

Hull, R. (1993) 'Lobbying in Brussels: A View from Within', in Mazey, S. and Richardson, J. (eds.), *Lobbying in the European Community*, Oxford: Oxford University Press, 82–92.

Jordan, G. and Richardson, J. (1982) 'The British Policy Style or the Logic of Negotiation?', in Richardson, J. (ed.), *Policy Styles in Western Europe*, London: George Allen and Unwin, 80–110.

Keck, M. E. and Sikkink, K. (1998) *Activists Beyond Borders*, Ithaca: Cornell University Press.

Kirchner, E. (1977) *Trade Unions as Pressure Groups in the European Community*, Farnborough: Saxon House.

Kirchner, E. (1980a) 'International Trade Union Collaboration and the Prospect for European Industrial Relations', *West European Politics*, 3(1): 124–37.

Kirchner, E. (1980b) 'Interest Group Behaviour at the Community Level', in Hurwitz, L. (ed.), *Contemporary Perspectives on European Integration*, London: Aldwich.

Kitschelt, H. P. (1986) 'Political Opportunity Structures and Political Protest: Anti-nuclear Movements in Four Democracies', *British Journal of Political Science*, 16(1): 57–85.

Klein, R. and O'Higgins, M. (1985) 'Social Policy after Incrementalism', in Klein, R. and O'Higgins, M. (eds.), *The Future of Welfare*, Oxford: Blackwell.

Klüver, H. (2012) 'Biasing Politics? Interest Group Participation in EU Policy-Making', *West European Politics*, 35(5): 1114–33.

Klüver, H. (2013) 'Lobbying as a Collective Enterprise: Winners and Losers of Policy Formulation in the European Union', *Journal of European Public Policy*, 20(1): 59–76.

Kohler-Koch, B. (1997) 'Organised Interests in the EU and the European Parliament', paper presented to the International Political Science Association XVIII Congress, Seoul, 17–21 August.

Kurzer, P. and Cooper, A. (2013) 'Biased or not? Organized Interests and the Case of EU Food Information Labeling', *Journal of European Public Policy*, 20(5): 722–40.

Lehmann, W. (2009) 'The European Parliament', in Coen, D. and Richardson, J. (eds.), *Lobbying in the European Union: Institutions, Actors, and Issues*, Oxford: Oxford University Press, 39–69.

Lindberg, L. (1963) *The Political Dynamics of European Integration*, Stanford: Stanford University Press.

Long, T. and Lörinczi, L. (2009) 'NGOs as Gatekeepers: A Green Vision', in Coen, D. and Richardson, J. (eds.), *Lobbying in the European Union: Institutions, Actors, and Issues*, Oxford: Oxford University Press, 169–85.

McLaughlin, A. and Jordan, G. (1993) 'The Rationality of Lobbying in Europe: Why Are Euro-groups so Numerous and so Weak? Some Evidence from the Car Industry', in Mazey, S. and Richardson, J. (eds.), *Lobbying in the EC*, Oxford: Oxford University Press, 27–46.

Mahoney, C. (2004) 'The Power of Institutions: State and Interest Group Activity in the European Union', *European Union Politics*, 5(4): 441–66.

Mahoney, C. and Baumgartner, F. (2008) 'Converging Perspectives on Interest Group Research in Europe and America', *West European Politics*, 31(6): 1253–73.

Mazey, S. (1998) 'The European Union and Women's Rights: From the Europeanisation of National Agendas to the Nationalisation of a European Agenda?', *Journal of European Public Policy*, 5(1): 131–52.

Mazey, S. (2012) 'Policy Entrepreneurship, Group Mobilization, and the Creation of a New Political Domain: Women's Rights and the European Union', in Richardson, J. (ed.), *Constructing a Policy-Making State? Policy Dynamics in the EU*, Oxford: Oxford University Press, 125–43.

Mazey, S. and Richardson, J. (1992) 'Environmental Groups and the EC: Challenges and Opportunities', *Environmental Politics*, 1(4): 109–28.

Mazey, S. and Richardson, J. (eds.) (1993) *Lobbying in the European Community*, Oxford: Oxford University Press.

Mazey, S. and Richardson, J. (1995) 'Promiscuous Policymaking: The European Policy Style?', in Rhodes, C. and Mazey, S. (eds.), *The State of the European Union*, vol. 3: *Building a European Polity?* Boulder: Lynne Rienner, 337–59.

Mazey, S. and Richardson, J. (2001) 'Institutionalising Promiscuity: Commission/Interest Group Relations in the EU', in Fligstein, N., Sandholtz, W. and Stone Sweet, A. (eds.), *The Institutionalisation of Europe*, Oxford: Oxford University Press, 71–93.

Mazey, S. and Richardson, J. (2006a) 'The Commission and the Lobby', in Spence, D. (ed.), *The European Commission*, London: Harper, 279–92.

Mazey, S. and Richardson, J. (2006b) 'Interest Groups and EU Policy-making. Organisational logic and venue shopping', in Richardson, J. (ed.), *European Union. Power and Policy-making* (3rd Edition), Abingdon: Routledge, 247–68.

McCown, M. (2009) 'Interest Groups and the European Court of Justice', in Coen, D. and Richardson, J. (eds.), *Lobbying in the European Union: Institutions, Actors, and Issues*, Oxford: Oxford University Press, 89–104.

Pallis, A. (2005) 'Maritime Interest Representation in the EU', *European Political Economy Review*, 3(2): 6–28.

Peterson, M. A. (1992) 'The Presidency and Organized Interests: White House Patterns of Interest Group Liaison', *American Political Science Review*, 86(3): 612–25.

Princen, S. and Kerrimans, B. (2008) 'Opportunity Structures in the EU Multi-Level System', *West European Politics*, 31(6): 1120–46.

Putnam, R. (1988) 'Diplomacy and the Logic of Two-level Games', *International Organisation*, 42: 427–60.

Quittkat, C. (2011) 'The European Commission's Online Consultations', *West European Politics*, 49(3): 653–74.

Rasmussen, M. (2014) 'The Battle for Influence: The Politics of Business Lobbying in the European Parliament, *Journal of Common Market Studies*, doi:101111/jcms.12156.

Richardson, J. (1994) 'EU Water Policy: Uncertain Agendas, Shifting Networks, and Complex Coalitions', *Environmental Politics*, 3(4): 139–67.

Richardson, J. (2000) 'Government, Interest Groups and Policy Change', *Political Studies*, 48(5), 1006–25.

Richardson, J. and Coen, D. (2009) 'Institutionalizing and Managing Intermediation in the EU', in Coen, D. and Richardson, J. (eds.), *Lobbying in the European Union: Institutions, Actors, and Issues*, Oxford: Oxford University Press, 337–50.

Richardson, J.J. and Jordan, A.G. (1979) *Governing under Pressure*, Oxford: Martin Robertson.

Ripoll Servant, A. (2013) 'Holding the European Parliament Responsible: Policy Shift in the Data Retention Directive from Consultation to Codecision', *Journal of European Public Policy*, 20(7): 972–87.

Sabatier, P. (1988) 'An Advocacy Coalition Framework of Policy Change and the Role of Policy-oriented Learning Therein', *Policy Sciences*, 21: 129–68.

Sabatier, P. (1998) 'The Advocacy Coalition Framework: Revisions and Relevance for Europe', *Journal of European Public Policy*, 5(1): 98–130.

Salgado, R. (2014) 'Rebalancing EU Interest Representation? Associative Democracy and EU Funding of Civil Society Organizations' *Journal of Common Market Studies*, 52(2): 337–353.

Sandholtz, W. and Zysman, J. (1989) '1992: Recasting the European Bargain', *World Politics*, 42(1): 95–128.

Saurugger, S. (2009) 'COREPER and National Governments', in Coen, D. and Richardson, J. (eds.), *Lobbying in the European Union: Institutions, Actors, and Issues*, Oxford: Oxford University Press, 105–27.

Schmidt, S. (2012) 'Who Cares about Nationality? The Path-dependent Case Law of the ECJ from Goods to Citizens', *Journal of European Public Policy*, 19(1): 8–24.

Schneider, G. and Baltz, K (2004) 'Paying the Piper, Calling the Tune: Interest Intermediation in the Pre-Negotiations of EU Legislation'. Paper presented at the Pan-European Conference of International Relations, The Hague, 9–11 September.

Schön, D.A. and Rein, M. (1994) *Frame Reflection: Toward the Resolution of Intractable Policy Controversies*, New York: Basic Books.

Sidjanski, D. (1970) 'Pressure Groups and the European Economic Community', in Cosgrove, C. and Twitchett, K. (eds.), *The New International Actors: The United Nations and the European Economic Community*, London: Macmillan, 222–36.

Spence, D. (1993) 'The Role of the National Civil Service in European Lobbying: The British Case', in Mazey, S. and Richardson, J. (eds.), *Lobbying in the European Community*, Oxford: Oxford University Press, 47–73.

Stone Sweet, A. and Brunell, T. (1998) 'The European Court and the National Courts: A Statistical Analysis of Preliminary References, 1961–95', *Journal of European Public Policy*, 5(1): 69–97.

Stone Sweet, A. and Sandholtz, W. (1998) 'Integration, Supranational Governance, and the Institutionalisation of the European Polity', in Sandholtz, W. and Stone Sweet, A. (eds.), *European Integration and Supranational Governance*, Oxford: Oxford University Press, 2–26.

Strauss, A. (1978) *Negotiations, Values, Contexts, Processes and Social Order*, London: Jossey-Bass.

Truman, D. (1951) *The Governmental Process: Political Interests and Public Opinion*, New York: Knopf.

Van Schendelen, M.P.C.M. (1998) 'Prolegomena to EU Committees as Influential Policymakers', in Van Schendelen, M.P.C.M (ed.), *EU Committees as Influential Policymakers*, Aldershot: Ashgate, 3–22.

Wessels, B. (1999) 'European Parliament and Interest Groups', in Katz, R. and Wessels, B. (eds.), *The European Parliament, the National Parliaments, and European Integration*, Oxford: Oxford University Press, 105–28.

Wonka, A., Baumgartner, F., Mahoney, C. and Berkhout, J. (2010) 'Measuring the Size and Scope of the EU Interest Group Population', *European Union Politics*, 11(3): 463–76.

Chapter 19

Bypassing the nation-state?

Regions and the EU policy process

MICHAEL KEATING, LIESBET HOOGHE AND
MICHAËL TATHAM

European integration and regionalism have both altered the architecture of the Western European political order. They have opened up new spaces above and below the nation-state, created new forms of politics and generated three-level interactions. Much has been written on the Europe of the regions (Petschen 1993), which some observers think, or hope, will rival or even displace the Europe of states. Others have discerned new forms of 'multilevel governance' (Hooghe and Marks, 2001; Jachtenfuchs and Kohler-Koch, 1995; Marks, 1993; Piattoni, 2010; Scharpf, 1994, 1999) or third-level politics (Bullmann, 1994; Jeffery, 1997). In this chapter we examine the emergence of the region in the context of the state and of the European Union (EU). Then we look at the links between regions and the EU and the influence of regions in EU policy-making. We find that, rather than a new and ordered territorial hierarchy, authority is diffused across multiple territorial levels. Policy-making continues to be centred primarily on the state, but national governments increasingly share decision-making with European and regional actors.

Regions and regionalism in Western Europe

The emergence of the region, like that of the EU itself, is a response to functional, political and institutional developments, which have had varied impacts in different places. Functionalist analyses stress the links between territory and economic change and the rediscovery of the region as the motor of economic development (Scott, 1998; Storper, 1997). Together with the decline of national diversionary regional policies and planning, this has led to an emphasis on endogenous development and self-help and to increased competition among regions for investment, markets and technology (Keating, 1998). Regions are defined not merely by economics but also by culture and history, which define their boundaries and shape social relations within them and by the outcome of political leadership and competition (Keating, 2013). In some parts of Europe, territory has become a significant political cleavage, and regions have emerged as political spaces, sustaining a debate about the common interest and sustaining a distinct political agenda. Regions have also emerged as institutions, an intermediate level of government between states and municipalities, but taking different forms, from the fully fledged federalism of Germany, Belgium and Austria, to the weak, administrative regionalism of France. This has produced a heterogeneous pattern across Europe, according to whether the various meanings of the region coincide or not, and to the degree of institutionalisation of regional government. In some places, like Scotland or Catalonia, the economic, cultural and political regions (or rather stateless nations) coincide and are endowed with important institutions with legislative and administrative competences. Some of the other Spanish autonomous communities and many German Länder have a much weaker sense of political and cultural identity, although still possessing autonomous institutions. French regions were designed to suppress rather than encourage political and cultural identity and rarely constitute political spaces or a primary reference point for political debate. In some of the smaller states there are no elected regional governments and, at best, a system of functionally specific agencies for economic development. In some cases, the most important level for economic, social and political mobilisation is not the region but the city.

As a polity, the region has much in common with the EU itself. It is complex, patchily institutionalised and contested. Arenas and actors vary across policy areas and policy-making is organised through networks, which may be functionally or territorially based. As in Europe (Hooghe and Marks, 1999), there is a constant struggle between those who see the region as primarily an economic entity, driven by competitive market considerations locked in a neo-mercantilist competition for economic advantage, and those who favour a stronger social dimension (Keating, 1998, 2013). As in the European Union, concerns of economic competitiveness have usually trumped the concept of the region as a basis for social solidarity. In a few regions, strong regional governments are able to impose coherence on the array of local actors and define a common territorial interest. In other regions, development coalitions have emerged to promote a vision of the region's place in European and global markets but without an overall social project. Yet other regions are a political no-man's land, fought over by rival political and social interests, often with different territorial bases.

Regions and European integration

European integration has further enhanced the importance of regions, in the political and economic domains, and produced a new dynamic. In the economic domain, the opening of markets has produced a new territorial hierarchy. At one time, it was thought that integration would concentrate development in the central regions of the 'golden triangle' to produce a new centre–periphery cleavage, but it is clear now that matters are more complex. Some French economists replaced the analogy of the golden triangle with that of the 'blue banana', and others have favoured the analogy of the mosaic, with pockets of underdevelopment even in the booming regions. Later research suggests that several changes are happening at once to reshape the European economic space (Amendola *et al.*, 2004). There has been some convergence among states, as poorer peripheral states in southern and East-Central Europe catch up with the advanced north-west. Yet this conceals an increase in disparities within states as regions adapt differently to changing market conditions (European Parliament, 2007; Geppert and Stephan, 2008). In Germany, Belgium, Italy and Spain, there is a clear regional division, but elsewhere in western Europe the pattern is more complex, with contrasts between metropolitan areas and rural ones. In central and eastern European states there are also divergences between national capitals and the rest of the state, and an east–west gradient, with regions closer to western Europe doing better. It is this conceptualization that has informed national and EU spatial policies, although a more fine-grained analysis will often show significant disparities within regions and metropolitan areas (Mackey, 1993). The needs of national competitiveness together with EU rules have increasingly prevented states from intervening to correct these disparities through diversionary policies. EU competition policy may disadvantage marginal regions, through preventing cross-subsidisation of communications services and opening public procurement. Other EU policies, including agriculture and research spending, also tend to benefit the more developed regions (Cheshire *et al.*, 1991; Commission of the European Communities, 1996; Strijker and de Veer, 1988). The single-market programme has further disarmed national governments, while the economic and monetary union has removed their ability to manipulate exchange rates and interest rates or to run budget deficits, all instruments used for regional as well as national purposes.

Politically, European integration has also served to enhance the salience of regions. On one side, European integration has had a positive mobilization effect on regions. As economic regulation has shifted to the EU, a key argument against regional decentralization – that it risked dividing the market – has lost its relevance. The EU, not national states, regulates a single economic market, including setting interest and exchange rates, deciding on investment conditions, settling trade disputes and internalizing negative externalities. European market integration has lowered the bar for regions desiring political autonomy by reducing the economic costs of decentralization (Alesina and Spolaore, 2003; Marks and Hooghe, 2000). Yet European integration has also mobilized regions against Europe. Competences transferred to the EU include matters in which regions have a direct interest (Bourne, 2003; Fleurke and Willemse, 2006, 2007). This not only removes power to Europe; it also serves to increase centralization within states, since it is the member state governments who compose the Council of Ministers.

There have been two types of reaction at the regional level. A rejectionist regionalism opposes European integration fearing a further loss of democratic control, more remote government and the triumph of market principles. This reaction was common in many regions in the 1970s, is still visible in Scandinavia, and has recently become more apparent in some core autonomist regions including the Flemish region (Vlaams Belang), Northern Italy (Northern League), and some German Länder (De Winter and Gomez-Reino Cachafeiro, 2002; De Winter and Türsan, 1998). A second type of regionalism seeks to use Europe as a supplier of political and economic resources, if necessary against the state itself. Most obviously this involves economic development issues, but Europe has also been seen as a source of support for minority cultures and languages threatened within large states (Cardús, 1991; De Witte, 1992; Jolly, 2014). Hence, regional interests have sought new mechanisms to get into the European policy game.

Europe has provided a new arena for the expression of regional and minority nationalist aspirations. Some minority nationalist movements note that European integration has reduced the cost of national independence, and propose simply to join the list of member states; this is the case of the Scottish National Party and some Basque and Catalan nationalists. Others want to replace the existing Union with a federation of regions and small nations, abolishing the existing states; this is the policy of the Welsh nationalist party Plaid Cymru and of many Basque nationalists. Others again are more pragmatic, seeing in Europe an arena in which their nationalist aspirations can be expressed and legitimised, while seeking to exert influence at whatever points are available (Hepburn, 2010). In its most advanced form, this takes the form of post-sovereignty arguments in which nationalists abandon the search for a nation-state in favour of the construction of a pluralist and multilevel Europe, often calling in older, pre-state traditions of authority to support them (Keating, 2001).

European integration is ambivalent for regions. It provides the opportunity to open up a 'second front' for regions to challenge the national state; yet it may also threaten deeply held regional values and fundamental territorial interests when it constrains local choice. The effect of European integration on regions has also changed over time: as European integration has deepened from market integration to political integration, opportunities for regional empowerment have turned out to be less than transformative and constraints on local choice more binding.

This affects regionalist politics in profound ways. Territorial and autonomist parties as a group have become less pro-European. Expert data on party positioning on European integration, which track parties at the time intervals of 1984 through to 2010, provide a clear read on this. On a seven-point scale ranging from 1 (strongly opposed to European integration) to 7 (strongly supportive), autonomist parties have dropped from a maximum of 5.81 in 1996 to 5.11 in 2010. This party family is now virtually indistinguishable from average party families in its position on European integration.[1] Until 1996, autonomist parties were more than one point more supportive than the average party family, but since 1999 the difference has been consistently under a half point. In 2010, they were just 0.31 more supportive, a difference that was statistically insignificant. Territorial or autonomist parties are *less* pro-European than Christian Democrats, Socialists, Liberals, and the Greens, though more pro-European than Conservatives, the radical right, and radical left. However, there is great variation among territorial parties. Compared to other party families, they tend to hold more diverse views, and they are more likely to shift position over time (Elias, 2008, 2009; Hepburn and Elias, 2011). While some nationalist and autonomist parties, such as the Catalan *Convergència i Unió* (CiU), the Scottish SNP, the Welsh Plaid Cymru or the Flemish Volksunie/Nationaal-Vlaamse Alliantie, have been consistently pro-European, others, such as the Irish Sinn Fein, the Basque Herri Batasuna and its successors or the Flemish Bloc/Belang, have been consistently Eurosceptical, and yet others have switched over time, such as the Northern League (which switched to Euroscepticism) or the Finnish *Svenska folkpartiet i Finland/Suomen ruotsalainen kansanpuolue* (SFP/RJP, which switched to pro-European position).[2]

European integration and regionalism are Janus-faced phenomena. On one hand, they appear to weaken the nation-state. On the other hand, they represent attempts to create new political arenas to try to recapture control over state functions. The shape of these arenas will condition the politics that is possible within them, hence a series of conflicts over the character of the European Union: the social versus the market vision; the unitary versus the federalist vision; and the role of regions. In the next section, we review the channels by which regional interests have sought to influence Europe. Then we examine how the European Union has itself sought to use regions in pursuit of its own policy objectives. The result has been a dynamic interplay of interests at three levels, among regions, the EU and nation-states. This has spawned a considerable literature examining the ways in which regions can influence policy in the EU (Donas and Beyers, 2013; Hooghe, 1996; Jeffery, 1997, 2007; Jones and Keating, 1995; Le Galès and Lequesne, 1998; Tatham, 2013a, 2014a).

Channels of access

Formulating an interest

Regions are not merely actors but also political arenas, containing a plurality of interests. Their first problem in seeking access to European decision-making is formulating a regional interest. In some cases, such as the German Länder, the Belgian regions or the Austrian Länder, strong regional governments are able to formulate a regional interest, given legitimacy by democratic election. In others, such as the French regions, regional governments are institutionally weak and rivalled by powerful political figures rooted in the cities and departments as well as in a territorial bureaucracy of the central state. Some states have no regional governments at all.

A number of territories have a capacity to mobilise territorial lobbies encompassing both governmental and private actors (Keating, 2013). Despite the lack of elected institutions before 1999, Scotland showed a consistent ability to mount a territorial lobby encompassing business, trade unions, municipal governments, religious and other social leaders, and the deconcentrated arms of the central bureaucracy itself (Midwinter *et al.*, 1991). In the historical Spanish regions of Catalonia, the Basque Country and Galicia, regional governments are able to draw on a sense of historical identity to legitimise a regional interest, although with varied results. In some French regions, powerful notables are able to mobilise a lobby around themselves, despite the fragmentation of the system of political representation, with its three levels of subnational government. In England, there is no general level of regional governments and the capacity to organise lobbies within civil society is rather low. Italian regional governments have traditionally been institutionally weak, dominated by national political parties and poorly linked to civil society (Fargion *et al.*, 2006; Triglia, 1991); this has undermined their ability to formulate a regional interest.

There are some interests common to regions within the EU. These include institutional matters, the design of partnerships in policy implementation and the general principle of subsidiarity and its interpretation. There are also common interests in inter-regional cooperation and cross-border initiatives. Yet regions are also in competition with each other, to attract public funding and private investment and to shape EU policies to suit their particular interests. So there is a constant tension between promotion of regionalism in general, and the pursuit of regions' individual concerns. Regions have a multiplicity of channels for the pursuit of these collective and individual matters, of varying efficacy depending on the subject to be pursued and the political context. There is not, nor can there be, a single mode of representation of 'regional' interests in the EU.

Access via the national government

The most important channel of influence is via national governments. Generally, the more effectively regional interests are integrated into the national policy-making system, the better they will be looked after in Brussels. The strongest mechanism is provided by Article 203, originally introduced in the Maastricht Treaty, which allows a state to be represented by a minister of a subnational government in the Council of Ministers. This clause, which stipulates that representatives must have ministerial status, was designed for federal states such as Austria, Germany and Belgium or federalising ones such as Spain and the UK and not for countries with administrative regions such as France. It does not, it must be emphasised, allow regions to represent themselves at the Council of Ministers. A regional minister appearing there represents the state, and there needs to be a prior agreement among the regions and the state as to what their interest is (Tatham, 2008). The clause has been used in Germany, Belgium, Italy, Spain and the UK, but in rather different ways (Mabellini, 2005; Noferini, 2012; Tatham, 2011). In the German case, the Länder negotiate an agreement through the Bundesrat, and one of them then presents the common position. The Belgian regions, communities and federal government have laid down by special law detailed arrangements on federal–subnational representation and decision-making in Council of Ministers machinery. Each level represents the Belgian position and casts the vote in matters exclusively under its own jurisdiction, while both are involved in matters of joint competence, with one taking the lead. In contrast to the German collective approach, Belgian regions and communities minimise the need for prior agreement by taking turns in assuming the lead responsibility for the Councils on matters within their jurisdiction. The distinction between the collective and the individual approach rests on fundamentally different premises. The German approach accepts that regions are the third level in a multilayered European polity and that they are ultimately nested in a national arena. The Belgian approach minimises the national mould. Europe is seen as a polity with multiple actors at multiple levels who interact directly with European institutions on matters within their competencies. In the UK, the devolved administrations are allowed into the delegation to the Council of Ministers at the invitation of the central government and must follow the overall UK line. This has allowed them considerable information and the status of insiders but at the loss of a capacity publicly to take their own line.

Regions may also be involved in the process of treaty revision, to secure their own rights. As a condition of the ratification of the Maastricht Treaty in the Bundesrat, the Länder obtained a provision that the Bundesrat would have to approve all further transfers of sovereignty, even those that do not impinge on Länder competencies. In Belgium, treaty changes need the approval not only of the Senate, which is the federal chamber, but, where regional competencies are involved, of each regional and community assembly separately as well.

Elsewhere, regions have only a consultative role in European matters. France, however, provides another model of influence via the national state, through its integrated bureaucracy which links local and national policy-making, and the cumulation of mandates, by which politicians may simultaneously hold national and local office. To some degree, this unitary system with territorial influence has been extended to the EU (Balme, 1995), but it is uneven in its incidence. While the presence of local politicians in the national parliament provides a powerful institutional lever for local government in France, there is no powerful lobby for the defence of these institutional interests in Europe.

Generally, there is a positive association between devolution levels and the formal involvement of regions in shaping their member state's position on EU affairs. Figure 19.1 represents this relationship by using data gathered by Hooghe, Marks, Schakel (2010) to measure devolution levels across EU countries and data by Tatham (2011) to measure 'institutionalised regional involvement in the domestic EU policy-shaping process', an index aggregating eight dimensions of involvement, from participation in Council meetings to regional financial penalties for non-compliance with EU obligations. As illustrated in Figure 19.1, this relationship is far from linear. Devolution only implies a formal input beyond a certain threshold situated above the EU-wide average. Moreover, such a relationship is also often diachronic, in the sense that a substantial time lag can be observed between the initiation of a devolution process and its repercussions for EU involvement. In some cases, the lag was negligible (Bulmer et al., 2002). In others it was much greater (Beltrán García, 2012; Fargion et al., 2006; Noferini, 2012). Today, while highly devolved regions in Belgium, Italy, Austria, Germany and Spain and a few special status territories (Scotland, Wales, Northern Ireland, the Azores, Madeira or Åland) have some input in their member state's position, regions in most other EU countries have to rely on non-formal means, as exemplified earlier by the French case.

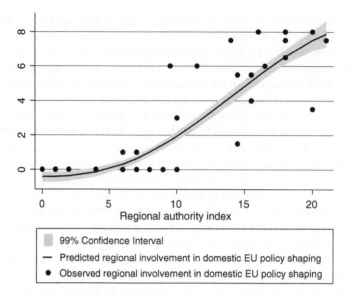

Figure 19.1 Regional authority and regional involvement in domestic EU policy-shaping

Source: Based on data from Tatham (2011).

Individual regional interests may also be projected through national governments via partisan links. This is particularly important in southern Europe. Successive Spanish governments in the 1990s and 2000s have needed the support of territorial parties to govern. This provides these parties access to national policy-making and thence to Europe. Similar dynamics have been observed in Italy where the Lega Nord has been able to exert some pressure on central government towards greater inclusion of its (regionally defined) interests during domestic EU policy shaping. In Belgium too, regional interests have access to the federal government through party networks.

Direct access: subnational offices

Recent years have seen a spectacular growth in direct links with the EU. These take a variety of forms. Regional and local governments make frequent visits to Brussels to lobby Commission officials, and they often engage the services of consultants to help them make a case and find their way through the bureaucracy. Many have opened permanent offices in Brussels. In the twenty-five years to 2010, the number of these grew from just 2 to well over 200 (Moore, 2008b: 520; Wonka *et al.*, 2010: 467). Stronger regions have their own offices. Thus one finds every German Land, all three Belgian regions and all but one Austrian Länder represented in Brussels along with most Spanish autonomous communities and Italian regions. In countries with a weaker regional tier, representation usually consists of a mixture of local and regional units. In France, most offices represent regions, but several *départements* also have offices. In the United Kingdom, local authorities, regional agencies, regional enterprise organisations, national local authority organisations, universities and elected regional assemblies fund offices representing individual local authorities, regional groupings of local authorities and a national local authority organisation, alongside offices representing the North of England, Northern Ireland, Scotland and Wales. In unitary systems, such as the Netherlands and Scandinavia, local governments (or associations of local governments) predominate.

The status of these offices differs considerably. Some are public–private consortia concerned with economic issues, while others are political representatives of the regional government. Catalonia has maintained the public–private formula with the Patronat Català Pro-Europa, while the Basque government has chosen to establish a direct political presence. Scotland has both forms, Scotland Europa, founded in 1992 as a platform for Scottish interests, and Scotland House, the representative of the Scottish government, housed together. The legal status of the offices also differs according to domestic law. Spanish and Italian regions had to go to court to challenge national bans on opening Brussels offices and the French regions had to tread carefully around the constitution. The German federal government only recognised the Länder offices in 1993. Particular sensitivity is aroused by ventures across national borders; the Italian government long resisted a proposal for a joint office between the region of Alto-Adige and its Austrian neighbour Tyrol. On the other hand, cross-border joint lobbying in Brussels is specifically encouraged in the Northern Ireland peace agreements as a way of defusing conflict.

These offices are sometimes portrayed as forms of direct representation in EU decision-making, yet the Commission is tied by regulations in deciding on matters like the allocation of regional funds, while political decision-making is in the hands of the Council of Ministers and the European Parliament. Regions do try, and occasionally succeed, to influence European policy, but such influence is usually confined to narrowly circumscribed issues and tends to be the privilege of the larger, politically autonomous and resourceful regions. Large-N research underlines that regional influence in Brussels is modest and that some variance can be accounted for by a region's demographic weight and degree of embeddedness within the EU. Populous regions and those frequently interacting with EU institutions report higher levels of influence. Decentralisation plays a conditioning role, magnifying the effect of other factors (Tatham, 2013b). Other factors such as leadership, entrepreneurship, social capital, perceived legitimacy (Greenwood, 2011; Jeffery, 2000) or cultural traits (Soldatos, 1990; Tabellini, 2007) also play a role.

Most offices, however, concentrate on the more subtle roles of information exchange and of liaising. In the first place, they provide information to regions on upcoming policy initiatives, allowing them to lobby their national governments, and they provide information and regional viewpoints to Commission officials, who are otherwise dependent on national governments for information. In the second place, they serve a symbolic role in projecting regions and regional politicians in the European arena and presenting them as participants in the policy process. This allows regional politicians to take credit for EU initiatives and even for funding that they would have received in any case under existing regulations. The open bureaucracy of the Commission encourages lobbying, while the opacity of the political decision-making process and the funding regulations allows a whole variety of actors to take credit for the outcomes (Dellmuth, 2011; Marks et al., 2002).

Regional lobbies are rarely powerful on their own in Brussels. Where they can work with a national government, they can achieve more. Thus, the Spanish regions as well as the French regions regularly meet collectively with their respective national permanent representations to exchange information and discuss strategy. The Scottish and Welsh representatives are described as part of the 'UKREP family', closely tied to the British permanent representation. Although there have been suggestions that regions bypass their member states by representing their interests directly in Brussels, surveys of regional offices in the European capital tell a different story. In their interest representation activities, European regions tend to cooperate with their member state (i.e. work together to achieve common policy outcomes) much more frequently than they bypass it. Such patterns have been relatively stable across policy areas with similar findings reported for general interest representation as well as for environmental affairs exclusively (Tatham, 2010, 2012). Meanwhile, conflicting interest representation – understood as representing interests which differ from the position taken by the national government – appears to be carried out even less frequently (Tatham, 2013a). Hence, when operating in Brussels, regions cooperate with their member state more frequently than they bypass it and only rarely lobby for incompatible policy objectives. Regions with greater autonomy and regions with the same parties in government as at the national level are more inclined to cooperate, while regions with less autonomy or where different parties are in power than at the national level are less inclined to cooperate (see also Bauer, 2006; Jeffery, 2007).

Regional lobbies may also be effective when linked with powerful sectoral interests, such as a major corporation based in the region, or a sector with links into the Commission directorates. The best examples are in Germany, where sectoral interests are often linked into the system of territorial government in the Länder.

European-wide lobbies

Several organisations lobby for regions as a whole at the European level. The International Union of Local Authorities and the Council of Communes and Regions of Europe are both wider in scope than the Community and have been closely associated with the Council of Europe, which they persuaded to establish a Conference of Local Authorities in 1961. Since 1975, the Conference also includes regional authorities, and in 1994 it was renamed into the Congress of Local and Regional Authorities and given the competence to initiate policy. In 1986, the organisation opened an office to deal with the EC. In 1985, the Council (later Assembly) of European Regions was launched, with 107 members including eleven Swiss cantons. It has pressed for involvement of regions in European decision-making, for the principle of subsidiarity, and for institutional changes. Other regional organisations seeking to influence policy-making in Brussels are the Conference of Peripheral Maritime Regions, the Association of European Frontier Regions, the Working Group of Traditional Industrial Regions, and a number of transnational frontier organisations.

Regions have been involved in trans-regional associations to varying degrees. Some general patterns have emerged, however. Affluent regions, regions with higher self-rule (i.e. autonomy) and lower shared rule (i.e. input in national decision making), and regions with strong territorial parties are more actively involved in trans-regional associations (Donas and Beyers, 2013).

Consultative mechanisms: committee of the regions

The establishment of formal rights of consultation with the Community owed a great deal to the pressure of the European Parliament, which in the course of the reforms of the regional fund stressed the need for greater involvement of regions. In 1988, the Commission created a Consultative Council of Regional and Local Authorities with consultative rights over the formulation and implementation of regional policies as well as the regional implications of other Community policies. Its 42 members were appointed by the Commission on the joint nomination of the Assembly of European Regions, the International Union of Local Authorities and the Council of Regions and Communes of Europe. The Maastricht Treaty replaced this with a stronger Committee of the Regions (CoR), which the Commission, the Council of Ministers and, since the Amsterdam Treaty, the Parliament are obliged to consult. It has the same status and powers as the Economic and Social Committee. It can also issue opinions on its own initiative and forward these to the Commission and Council. More ardent regionalists had hoped for a regionally based second chamber of the European Parliament or even of the Council of Ministers; what they got was a great deal less. In addition to its purely consultative status, several factors weaken the Committee (Farrows and McCarthy, 1997). Its membership is decided by national governments, some of which, like France, have exercised strong control, while others, including Belgium, Germany, Spain and the UK (for Scotland and Wales), have left the matter to regions themselves. National politics is also felt in the allocation of committee chairs and memberships and even in the allocation of own-initiative opinions by national quotas. The Committee includes not just regions but municipal representatives, with different institutional interests. The German Länder, who might be a powerful presence, have a more promising channel through their national government. Finally, the Committee has the task of representing regions as a whole, which may limit it to institutional matters where a common interest can be discerned, though even here the regional–local division may cause problems. In the early 2000s, tensions developed with the emergence of a group of strong 'regions with legislative powers' (RegLeg), who argued that their task in applying EU directives gave them a role analogous to national governments and different from that of municipalities and ordinary regions. They did not manage to convince CoR as a whole of their case but continue as an organized group, while still participating as individual regions within the CoR.

Literature since the Lisbon Treaty has been less pessimistic when analysing the Committee. It has underlined that despite having merely advisory functions, the Committee has nonetheless meaningfully assumed and performed its representational functions (Carroll, 2011; McCarthy, 1997). Recent research has also shifted its focus from general assessments of the CoR to more specific questions such as the conditions under which the CoR manages to exercise influence on Commission proposals (Domorenok, 2009; Neshkova, 2010). More generally, the speed with which the Committee produces recommendations, the quality of these recommendations and their resonance with the addresses' prior beliefs have been shown to increase its influence over EU policy outputs (Hönnige and Panke, 2013). Meanwhile, the new instruments provided by the Lisbon Treaty bring some potential for greater influence (Tatham, 2014a). Since December 2009, the policy areas in which CoR consultation is compulsory have been further extended to include civil protection, climate change, energy, and services of general interest while it is now also obligatory for the EP – and not just the Commission – to consult the CoR. The CoR now also has the right to question the Commission, the EP and the Council if they fail to demonstrate that they considered its opinion, and it can also call for a second consultation if the initial proposal is substantially modified during the legislative process. Of primary interest, however, is the Committee's new right to challenge EU legislation in the European Court of Justice on the basis of a breach of subsidiarity. How this new and untested instrument will be used will be consequential for the impact of the Committee on the EU policy process.

The Commission and the regions

Traffic between regional interests and the EU is not one-way. The Commission has itself played an important role in mobilising regional interests, establishing new networks and creating a dialogue among regions, states and itself. The main stimulus for this has been the EU's regional policy, now subsumed under the structural funds. These funds now account for a third of the EU budget, less than agricultural spending but far more than any other item. Elsewhere (Hooghe and Keating, 1994) we have explained the development of regional and structural policy as the product of converging logics. A policy logic, whose guardian is the Commission, combines with a political and distributive logic, located in the Council of Ministers and intergovernmental negotiations. The policy logic for EU regional policy is similar to that for national regional policies of the 1960s and 1970s. It is a mechanism for rectifying the territorial disparities produced by market integration and for achieving allocative efficiency, it is a social compensation for losers in the process of economic restructuring and it is a device to legitimise the European project in regions where support might otherwise be lacking. The political logic is the need to redistribute resources among member states. Initially, this meant compensating Britain for its disproportionately large net contribution to the Community budget in the 1970s. Later, the policy was extended to compensate the southern European countries for the effects of the single market programme and EMU. These different logics produced conflicts between the Commission and member states from the inauguration of the European Regional Development Fund (ERDF) in 1975. In order to gain the consent of member states, the ERDF was divided into fixed national quotas; all regions that were eligible under national regional policies were eligible for ERDF funding. Funds were administered by national governments, which almost invariably refused to treat them as additional to national spending but rather as a reimbursement to themselves for their own regional policy spending. Consequently, the policy was a way of dressing up an interstate transfer mechanism as a European policy.

Over the years, the Commission has sought to increase its own influence over the framing and implementation of the policy, to convert it to a genuine instrument of regional policy, and to ensure that spending is additional to national spending programmes. From the late 1980s, it also sought to co-opt regional interests as partners in designing and implementing programmes. This has produced a three-level contest for control of the policy instrument, among the Commission, member states and regions themselves. In 1988, there was a major reform, again guided by both political and policy logics. The political logic was provided by the need to compensate the countries of southern Europe and Ireland for the adoption of the single market programme measures in the period to 1993. The policy logic was the Commission's desire to convert the ERDF and other structural funds into a genuine policy. The funds doubled and the three main ones, the ERDF, the European Social Fund (ESF) and the Guidance Section of the European Agricultural Guidance and Guarantee Fund (EAGGF) were brought together (Armonstrong, 1995; Hooghe, 1996). Community-wide objectives were laid down and for the first time, the Commission drew up its own map of eligible areas, using Community-wide criteria. Funds were disbursed only to projects within approved Community Support Frameworks (CSFs), apart from 9 per cent, which was reserved for Community Initiatives sponsored by the Commission. CSFs were negotiated between the Commission and member states, with the involvement of regions themselves. Additionality was laid down as a general principle so that spending would be over and above national spending. The whole policy was guided by the notion of subsidiarity, with the greatest possible involvement of regional and local interests and the social partners in the world of business, labour and voluntary groups. The regulations prescribed an integrated approach to regional development: as this links spatial policy to technology, environmental policy, education, public procurement and competition policy, it was intended to bring regions into contact with a range of EU policies and directorates. The Commission, in line with contemporary thinking on development policy, also sought to move from infrastructure to human capital, productive investment and indigenous development. This, too, implies a more active and participative role for regional actors of various sorts.

These changes potentially paved the way for greater regional involvement in policy-making and for stronger direct links between the Commission and regional interests. To a significant extent, this has happened (Hooghe and Marks, 2001). Those states without regional structures have been obliged to create them, or at least a substitute for them, in order to be eligible for funds. This is the case in Greece, Ireland and even Sweden. There has been a great deal of political mobilisation around the funds. Some English regions have even constituted lobbies in the absence of regional governments, in order to face the European challenge (Burch and Holliday, 1993). The belief that there is a pot of gold in Brussels is one reason for the explosion of regional lobbying and offices in the EU capital. Regional actors have been brought into contact with Commission officials, and its thinking on development policy has diffused through the mechanism of partnership.

The institutional machinery of partnership, oiled by a considerable budget, strengthened features of multi-level governance (Ansell *et al.*, 1997; Hooghe, 1998). In a 1999 report, the Commission concluded that 'as an institution, the delivery system developed for the structural funds is characterised by multi-level governance, i.e. the Commission, national governments and regional and local authorities are formally autonomous, but there is a high level of shared responsibility at each stage of the decision-making process. The relationship between these is, accordingly, one of partnership and negotiation, rather than being a hierarchical one' (Commission of the European Communities, 1999: 143). There is no doubt that the initial reform constituted a direct challenge to state-centric governance in that European institutions set general rules, regions participated in making decisions and the three parties were thrown in a relationship of mutual dependency rather than hierarchy.

However, the effect of partnership on territorial relations should not be overstated. To begin, partnership has never applied evenly across all phases of decision-making. It has traditionally been strongest in the implementation stage of structural programming, but weak in the strategic planning stages. Furthermore, the Commission itself does not have a consistent definition of what a region is. Its NUTS (Nomenclature of Territorial Units for Statistics) table consists of three levels, each of which is an aggregation of national administrative units. Nor does it limit itself to regional authorities, however defined. Sometimes its initiatives involve local governments; others are aimed at the private sector or civil society. The Commission's main objective is to get programmes going, to spend the funds in the most effective way possible and to involve whatever partners are appropriate for the task at hand.

National governments have also found their way back into the act. While the Commission has succeeded in concentrating funds on the neediest regions, it still has to make sure that everyone gets something in order to keep national governments on side. While there are officially no national quotas, there was an understanding that Britain, for example, would get a large share of the funds for industrial areas, while France would do well in the rural category. The map of eligible areas is negotiated between states and the Commission, a practice that was formalised in 1993.

The concept of territorial cohesion has emerged as the rationale for regional policy, entrenched in the Lisbon Treaty, while ever more emphasis has been placed on competitiveness and linking policy successively to the Lisbon Agenda and Europe 20/20. There is an inherent ambiguity in the notion of territorial cohesion, which is open to a number of interpretations. Competitiveness is similarly ambivalent since, if the term is taken literally, it is not possible for all regions to improve their competitive standing (competitiveness being a relative term). This has allowed the EU to retain a redistributive element in cohesion policy, while justifying it on purely economic grounds. Enlargement more than doubled the disparities between the 10 per cent most prosperous and the 10 per cent least prosperous areas, calling for massive transfers if the policy were to operate on the same lines as in the past. The British government and some German Länder took the opportunity to argue that EU regional policy should be restricted to the new member states, leaving them to manage their own programmes while limiting their contribution to the budget. Subsequent reforms did not go this far but provided for further concentration of funding, decentralization to Member States and a simplification of policy instruments. The Commission proposals for the funding period starting in 2014 call for some two-thirds of spending to go to 'less-developed regions', mostly in central and eastern Europe, with a sixth for 'more developed regions' and the rest for transitional areas. The whole would represent about a third of the EU budget. There has also been a consistent emphasis on simplification and evaluation.

The retreat from interventionist regional policy since 1988 reflects general political pressures to contain the role and power of the Commission. It also stems from a concern within the Commission that an active role was too costly in time and resources and ineffective in control; regional funds featured in the mismanagement scandals that erupted in the late 1990s (Hooghe, 1998). The rules now encourage more partners (not only subnational authorities), greater adjustment to national practices, and greater separation of responsibilities, and as a consequence, partnership rules may no longer provide regional authorities an entitlement for participation in EU decision-making.

So, while structural policy has stimulated increased regional activity, this has followed distinctly national lines. Where regional governments have a strong institutional position in the domestic arena, they have become important actors. Where they are weak domestically, states have largely retained their central role concerning links to the Commission and control of regional policy implementation.

Beyond regional policy and its implementation, regional civil servants have displayed rather pragmatic attitudes towards the role and future of the European Commission. A study of regional senior officials in five countries and 60 regions indicates that these officials are only moderately in favour of a stronger, more powerful and independent Commission. If their own central government or even the CoR are perceived as helpful allies in the Brussels policy game, then these regional élites may actually favour a weaker and less independent Commission. Although regional elites express stronger supranationalist views when they consider that EU integration has benefited their country, when the region's inhabitants identify highly with the EU or when a territorial party is present in the region, regional elites' attitudes towards the Commission come across as much more varied and far less supportive than one could have expected (Tatham and Bauer, 2014). While the Commission long appeared a natural ally for regional actors, this relationship has become more nuanced and diverse as integration deepened. The Commission remains a prime lobbying target and access point into EU policy shaping, but its honeymoon period with regional actors has morphed into a more lucid – sometimes sour – relationship.

Enlargement

Regional issues featured quite prominently in the accession negotiations of the countries of Central and eastern Europe. In the early years, the impression was given that, to be a modern European country, it was necessary to have regional government on the western model. As there is no single western model, this was a great simplification, but the idea persisted that regions of a critical 'European' scale are essential for economic competitiveness.

Another widespread belief was that regional government is needed in order to receive and manage Structural Funds (Hughes *et al.*, 2003, 2004). There is no written record of the Commission having laid this down, but this impression seems to have been given by Commission officials and consultants, and taken up in domestic debates by those pressing for reform for their own reasons. Around 2000, the Commission clarified that the only formal requirement for the Structural Funds was that accession countries should have a level of administration at the NUTS2 level. It then proceeded to lay down a highly centralized model for the planning and management of Structural Fund programmes. Its motive appears to have been worries about the lack of capacity at the regional level and of clientelism and corruption, together with the need to spend the Structural Fund allocation for the remainder of the programming period 2001–7 in the mere three years available after accession (Keating, 2003). So the Commission pressed for as few sectoral and territorial programmes as possible, a single paying authority, and strong National Development Plans as the basis for the future Structural Fund programmes. A third of the funding was to be given through the Cohesion Fund, which does not have a regional dimension. In a further departure from its own practice, it insisted that a large part of the funds should go to hard infrastructure rather than the 'soft' development measures, such as human capital and entrepreneurship, now favoured by regional policy in the west. In subsequent rounds, there has been more decentralization of policy implementation but the weakness of regional governments in central and eastern Europe has limited their impact in the EU.

The result has been a de-linking of European policy from the domestic politics of regionalism in the new member states. Only Poland has a level of regional government corresponding to NUTS2 regions, and these do not control the Structural Funds. In the Czech Republic, the regions are too small and need to come together in consortia to form NUTS2 units. In Hungary, the planning regions are at NUTS2 level but were never elected governments and have now been largely dismantled. The weakness of the regional tier in the new member states means that they are unlikely to be among the protagonists of a stronger regional presence (Tatham, 2014a). There are for example no regions with legislative powers among them.

Regions from the new member states have nonetheless mobilised in Brussels and – much like their Western counterparts – opened representational offices there. Although these tend to be less staffed than EU15 offices, they have been geared towards policy influence and raising the profile of their region in Brussels (Mbaye, 2009; Tatham, 2014b). Given time, however, these behavioural differences in Brussels seem destined to fade as recent regional offices seem eager to learn from their established peers. Indeed, case study analyses already indicate convergence between new EU13 regions and some institutionally weaker EU15 regions (Moore, 2008a; Scherpereel, 2007, 2010). Estonian patterns, for example, are not so different from those present in other small, unitary-centralised EU15 countries (Tatar, 2011) while Kettunen and Kull go as far as to argue that this country's 'experience is very similar to that in Finland' when it comes to behavioural attributes in Brussels (2009: 128). Hence, a time might come when regional mobilisation from EU15 countries such as Ireland, Portugal, Greece, Sweden, Denmark or Finland might not significantly diverge from that observed from some EU13 countries.

Overall, enlargement has had a paradoxical effect on regional interests in Brussels. On one hand, enlargement intensified the disparity in status between countries and regions. Small and very small countries are now entitled to be represented in the Union with full voting rights in the Council, their own Commissioner, a quota of Commission staff, their own members of the European Parliament and their language as an official language of the EU. Meanwhile, as the European Parliament Committee on Constitutional Affairs observed, a number of historic regions 'with several million inhabitants, which make a major contribution to the economic dynamism of the Union and to the funding of its budget [are] still . . . unrecognised by the European treaties' (2002: 24). On the other hand, enlargement has decreased the saliency of the regional question in the EU. Indeed, the last enlargement waves have meant that the EU is currently at a federal low: if one calculates the EU's regionalisation level as a weighted average of the regionalisation of its member states, the EU28 is less regionalised than it was when it consisted of 6 or 15 member states (Tatham, 2014a).[3] In sum, whilst new member states have to some extent regionalised at home and mobilised in Brussels, enlargement has reduced the relative salience of the regional level in the EU.

Conclusion

Regionalism and European integration have changed the national state in important ways. It is difficult, however, to isolate these from other factors pointing in the same direction – the internationalisation of markets, capital mobility, the rise of transnational corporations and neo-liberal ideology. Territorial politics in the EU is complex. We have not seen the rise of a homogeneous regional tier of government in the EU. Instead, variety in forms of territorial mobilisation has persisted: historic nations; large provincial regions; units in federal or quasi-federal states; cities and city-regions. Regions also differ in their social and political constitution. In some cases, the region can be identified with a structure of government; in others, civil society or private groups are more important in defining and carrying forward a regional interest.

We have not seen the rise of a new territorial hierarchy. The national state has not been bypassed in favour of a Europe of the regions and remains the primary actor in the EU. This does not mean, however, that policy-making in this field can be explained simply by interstate bargaining. The intergovernmental perspective on EU policy-making presents national politics as a closed, domestic game, where the national interest is formulated before being taken to the EU, where a second game commences, characterised by intergovernmental bargaining (Moravcsik, 1993). In fact, national politics is penetrated by European influences, through law, bureaucratic contacts, political exchange, the role of the Commission in agenda setting and, to a greater or lesser extent according to the state, through regional influences. So we are witnessing both a Europeanisation and a regionalisation of national policy-making.

Both the institutionalisation of the regions and the interest of the Commission in an active and interventionist role peaked around the early 1990s, and since then there has been consolidation. Regions have continued to seek a role in Europe, but access and influence are unevenly distributed (Donas and Beyers, 2013; Tatham, 2013b). The regions that are best equipped institutionally and that have the best access to their national governments are advantaged in the new setting. They also tend to be the most economically and technologically advanced. EU initiatives through the structural funds have attempted to offset these advantages for resource-rich regions by concentrating resources on the poorer regions and encouraging partnership and administrative modernisation, especially in southern Europe. As we have seen, these efforts have been partially successful. Furthermore, the practice of multilevel governance seems now entrenched in European policy-making: the previously dyadic relationship between European institutions and national governments has been transformed into a three-way one – among regions, national states and European actors. Keeping the 'second' relationship going enables each party in the triad to retain strategic autonomy (Ansell *et al.*, 1997). Regions, even in southern or eastern Europe, are unlikely to be blocked from access by their national governments.

A Union of 28 members contains vastly more territorial diversity than that for which the regional instruments and policies were designed in the 1980s and 1990s. Territorial disparities will continue to be a major concern for Europe and regional policy will remain a major spending priority. It still has an economic rationale, in helping poorer regions contribute to European and national competitiveness, a social role as one of the few real measures of solidarity at the EU level, and a political one, in showing the potential losers that there is something for them in the European project. Pressures from stronger regions for constitutional recognition and greater involvement in European policy-making will also persist. So both weak and strong regions will continue to press on the EU policy agenda.

Notes

1   We prefer the label 'autonomist' or 'territorial' parties over the label 'regionalist' on account of the fact that it captures more accurately that these political parties' primary political objective is to deepen political autonomy, or gain independence, for their territorial community.

2   These data are extracted from consecutive Chapel Hill party expert surveys on European integration conducted by Leonard Ray (1999), Marco Steenbergen and Gary Marks (2007), Liesbet Hooghe, *et al.* (2010) and Ryan Bakker *et al.* (2012). For further information, see www.unc.edu/~hooghe.

3   The aggregate regionalization level of the EU was estimated as follows: the regional authority scores calculated by Hooghe, Marks, Schakel. (2010) were averaged out for each country for every period between enlargements. The ensuing scores were multiplied by the country's Council voting weight for every period. All country scores for each period were summed up and divided by the total number of votes for each period. The final score measures the EU's aggregate regional authority over time taking into account the differential weight of each country consequent to successive enlargements and voting weight readjustments. For more details, see Tatham (2014a).

References

Alesina, A. and Spolaore, E. (2003) *The Size of Nations*, Cambridge, MA: MIT Press.

Amendola, A., Caroleo, F.E. and Coppola, G. (2004) 'Regional Disparities in Europe', CELPE Discussion Papers 78, Centro di Economia del Lavoro e di Politica Economica, Università di Salerno, Italy.

Ansell, C., Parsons, C. and Darden, K. (1997) 'Dual Networks in European Regional Development Policy', *Journal of Common Market Studies* 35(3): 347–375.

Armonstrong, W.H. (1995) 'The Role and Evolution of European Community Regional Policy'. In B. Jones and M. Keating (eds.), *The European Union and the Regions*, Oxford: Clarendon.

Bakker, R., de Vries, C., Edwards, E., Hooghe, L., Jolly, S., Marks, G., *et al.* (2012) 'Measuring Party Positions in Europe: The Chapel Hill Expert Survey Trend File, 1999–2010', *Party Politics*. doi:10.1177/1354068812462931

Balme, R. (1995) 'French Regionalization and European Integration: Territorial Adaptation and Change in a Unitary State'. In B. Jones and M. Keating (eds.), *The European Union and the Regions*, Oxford: Clarendon.

Bauer, M.W. (2006) 'The German Länder and the European Constitutional Treaty – Heading for a Differentiated Theory of Regional Elite Support for European Integration', *Regional & Federal Studies* 16(1): 21–42.

Beltrán García, S. (2012) 'Is There a Real Model in Spain for Autonomous Communities to Participate in the Council of the European Union or Is It Only a Mirage?', *Journal of Contemporary European Studies* 20(4): 423–440.

Bourne, A. (2003) 'The Impact of European Integration on Regional Power', *Journal of Common Market Studies* 41(4): 597–620.

Bullmann, U. (1994) *Die Politik der dritten Ebene. Regionen im Europa der Union*, Baden-Baden: Nomos.

Bulmer, S., Burch, M., Carter, C., Hogwood, P. and Scott, A. (2002) *British Devolution and European Policy-Making: Transforming Britain into Multi-Level Governance*, Basingstoke: Palgrave Macmillan.

Burch, M. and Holliday, I. (1993) 'Institutional Emergence: The Case of the North West Region of England', *Regional Politics and Policy* 3(2): 29–50.

Cardús, S. (1991) 'Identidad cultural, legitimidad politica e interés económico'. In *Construir Europa*, Catalunya, Madrid: Encuentro.

Carroll, W.E. (2011) 'The Committee of the Regions: A Functional Analysis of the CoR's Institutional Capacity', *Regional and Federal Studies* 21(3): 341–354.

Cheshire, P., Camagni, R., Gaudemar, J.-P. and Cuadrado Roura, J. (1991) '1957 to 1992: Moving toward a Europe of Regions and Regional Policy'. In L. Rodwin and H. Sazanami (eds.), *Industrial Change and Regional Economic Transformation: The Experience of Western Europe*, London: HarperCollins, pp. 268–300.

Commission of the European Communities. (1996) *First Report on Economic and Social Cohesion 1996 (preliminary edition)*, Luxembourg: Office for Official Publications of the European Communities.

Commission of the European Communities. (1999) *Sixth Periodic Report on the Social and Economic Situation and Development of the Regions of the EU*, Brussels: Commission of the European Communities.

Committee on Constitutional Affairs. (2002) *Report on the Division of Competences between the European Union and the Member States*, Strasbourg: European Parliament.

De Winter, L. and Türsan, H. (Eds.). (1998) *Regionalist Parties in Western Europe*, London: Routledge.

De Winter, L. and Gomez-Reino Cachafeiro, M. (2002) 'European Integration and Ethnoregionalist Parties', *Party Politics* 8(4): 483–503.

De Witte, B. (1992) 'Surviving in Babel? Language Rights and European Integration'. In Y. Dinstein (ed.), *The Protection of Minorities and Human Rights*, Dordrecht: Martinus Nijhoff Publishers, pp. 277–300.

Dellmuth, L.M. (2011) 'The Cash Divide: The allocation of European Union Regional Grants', *Journal of European Public Policy* 18(7): 1016–1033.

Domorenok, E. (2009) 'The Committee of the Regions: in Search of Identity', *Regional and Federal Studies* 19(1): 143–163.

Donas, T. and Beyers, J. (2013) 'How Regions Assemble in Brussels: The Organizational Form of Territorial Representation in the European Union', *Publius: The Journal of Federalism* 43(4): 527–550.

Elias, A. (2008) 'From Euro-enthusiasm to Euro-scepticism? A Re-evaluation of Minority Nationalist Party Attitudes towards European Integration ', *Regional & Federal Studies* 18(5): 557–581.

Elias, A. (2009) *Minority Nationalist Parties and European Integration*, London: Routledge.

European Parliament. (2007) *Regional Disparities and Cohesion, What Strategies for the Future*, Strasbourg: Directorate General Internal Policies of the Union – Policy Department Structural and Cohesion Policies.

Fargion, V., Morlino, L. and Profeti, S. (2006) 'Europeanisation and Territorial Representation in Italy ', *West European Politics* 29(4): 757–783.

Farrows, M. and McCarthy, R. (1997) 'Opinion Formulation and Impact in the Committee of the Regions', *Regional and Federal Studies* 7(1): 23–49.

Fleurke, F. and Willemse, R. (2006) 'The European Union and the Autonomy of Sub-national Authorities: Towards an Analysis of Constraints and Opportunities in Sub-national Decision-making', *Regional & Federal Studies* 16(1): 83–98.

Fleurke, F. and Willemse, R. (2007) 'Effects of the European Union on Sub-National Decision-Making: Enhancement or Constriction?', *Journal of European Integration* 29(1): 69–88.

Geppert, K. and Stephan, A. (2008) 'Regional Disparities in the European Union: Convergence and Agglomeration', *Papers in Regional Science* 87(2): 193–217.

Greenwood, J. (2011) 'Actors of the Common Interest? The Brussels Offices of the Regions', *Journal of European Interation* 33(4): 437–451.

463

Hepburn, E. (2010) *Using Europe: Territorial Party Strategies in a Multi-level System*, Manchester: Manchester University Press.

Hepburn, E. and Elias, A. (2011) 'Dissent on the Periphery? Island Nationalisms and European Integration', *West European Politics* 34(4): 859–882.

Hönnige, C. and Panke, D. (2013) 'The Committee of the Regions and the European Economic and Social Committee: How Influential Are Consultative Committees in the European Union?', *Journal of Common Market Studies* 51(3): 452–471.

Hooghe, L. (Ed.). (1996) *Cohesion Policy and European Integration: Building Multi-Level Governance*, Oxford: Oxford University Press.

Hooghe, L. (1998) 'EU Cohesion Policy and Competing Models of European Capitalism', *Journal of Common Market Studies* 36(4): 457–477.

Hooghe, L. and Keating, M. (1994) 'The Politics of European Union Regional Policy', *Journal of European Public Policy* 1(3): 367–393.

Hooghe, L. and Marks, G. (1999) 'The Making of a Polity: The Struggle Over European Integration'. In H. Kitschelt, P. Lange, G. Marks and J.D. Stephens (eds.), *Continuity and Change in Contemporary Capitalism*, Cambridge: Cambridge University Press, pp. 70–97.

Hooghe, L. and Marks, G. (2001) *Multi-level Governance and European Integration*, Oxford: Rowman & Littlefield.

Hooghe, L., Marks, G. and Schakel, A.H. (2010) *The Rise of Regional Authority: A Comparative Study of 42 democracies*, Abingdon: Routledge.

Hooghe, L., Bakker, R., Brigevich, A., de Vries, C., Edwards, E., Marks, G. , et al . (2010) 'Reliability and Validity of Measuring Party Positions: The Chapel Hill Expert Surveys of 2002 and 2006', *European Journal of Political Research* 42(4): 684–703.

Hughes, J., Sasse, G. and Gordon, C.E. (2003) 'EU enlargement, Europeanisation and the Dynamics of Regionalisation in the CEECs'. In M. Keating and J. Hughes (eds.), *The Regional Challenge in Central and Eastern Europe: Territorial Restructuring and European Integration*, Brussels: Peter Lang, pp. 69–88.

Hughes, J., Sasse, G. and Gordon, C. (2004) *Europeanization and Regionalization in the EU's Enlargement to Central and Eastern Europe. The Myth of Conditionality*, Basingstoke: Palgrave Macmillan.

Jachtenfuchs, M. and Kohler-Koch, B. (1995) 'Regieren im dynamischen Mehrebenensystem'. in M. Jachtenfuchs and B. Kohler-Koch (eds.), *Europäische Integration*, Opladen: Leske & Budrich, pp. 15–44.

Jeffery, C. (Ed.). (1997) *The Regional Dimension of the European Union. Towards a Third Level in Europe?* London: Frank Cass.

Jeffery, C. (2000) 'Sub-National Mobilization and European Integration: Does it Make Any Difference?', *Journal of Common Market Studies* 38(1): 1–23.

Jeffery, C. (2007) 'A Regional Rescue of the Nation-State: Changing Regional Perspectives on Europe', *Europa Institute Mitchell Working Paper Series*(5): 1–16.

Jolly, S.K. (2014) 'Strange Bedfellows: Public Support for the EU Among Regionalists'. In A.C. Gould and A.M. Messina (eds.), *Europe's Contending Identities. Supranationalism, Ethnoregionalism, Religion, and New Nationalism*, New York: Cambridge University Press, pp. 81–99.

Jones, B. and Keating, M. (Eds.). (1995) *The European Union and the Regions*, Oxford: Oxford University Press.

Keating, M. (1998) *The New Regionalism in Western Europe. Territorial Restructuring and Political Change*, Cheltenham: Edward Elgar.

Keating, M. (2001) *Plurinational Democracy:Stateless Nations in a Post-sovereignty Era*, Oxford: Oxford University Press.

Keating, M. (2003) 'Regionalization in Central and Eastern Europe: The Diffusion of a Western Model?'. In M. Keating and J. Hughes (eds.), *The Regional Challenge in Central and*

Eastern Europe: Territorial Restructuring and European Integration, Brussels: Peter Lang, pp. 51–68.

Keating, M. (2013) *Rescaling the European State. The Making of Territory and the Rise of the Meso*, Oxford: Oxford University Press.

Kettunen, P. and Kull, M. (2009) 'Governing Europe: the Status and Networking Strategies of Finish, Estonian and German Subnational Offices in Brussels', *Regional & Federal Studies* 19(1): 117–142.

Le Galès, P. and Lequesne, C. (1998) *Regions in Europe*, London: Routledge.

Mabellini, S. (2005) 'Italy'. In Instituto di Studi sui Sistemi Regionali Federali e sulle Autonomie (ed.), *Procedures for local and regional authority participation in European Policy Making in the Member States*, Luxembourg: Committee of the Regions, pp. 197–207.

Mackey, R.R. (1993) 'A Europe of the Regions: A Role for Nonmarket Forces?', *Regional Studies* 27(5): 419–431.

Marks, G. (1993) 'Structural Policy and Multilevel Governance in the EC'. In A. Cafruny and G. Rosenthal (eds.), *The State of the European Community: The Maastricht Debates and Beyond*, London: Lynne Rienner, pp. 391–410.

Marks, G. and Hooghe, L. (2000) 'Optimality and Authority: A Critique of Neoclassical Theory', *Journal of Common Market Studies* 38(5): 795–816.

Marks, G., Haesly, R. and Mbaye, H. (2002) 'What Do Subnational Offices Think They Are Doing in Brussels?', *Regional and Federal Studies* 12(3): 1–23.

Mbaye, H. (2009) 'So What's New? Mapping a Longitudinal Regional Office Footprint'. In Brussels, *European Union Studies Association*, Marina del Rey, CA: European Union Studies Association, pp. 1–16.

McCarthy, R.E. (1997) 'The Committee of the Regions: An Advisory Body's Tortuous Path to Influence', *Journal of European Public Policy* 4(3): 439–454.

Midwinter, A.F., Keating, M. and Mitchell, J. (1991) *Politics and Public Policy in Scotland*, London: Palgrave Macmillan.

Moore, C. (2008a) 'Beyond Conditionality? Regions from the New EU Member States and their Activities in Brussels', *Comparative European Politics* 6(2): 212–234.

Moore, C. (2008b) 'A Europe of the Regions vs. the Regions in Europe: Reflections on Regional Engagement in Brussels', *Regional & Federal Studies* 18(5): 517–535.

Moravcsik, A. (1993) 'Preferences and Power in the EC: A Liberal Intergovernmentalist Approach', *Journal of Common Market Studies* 31(4): 473–524.

Neshkova, M.I. (2010) 'The Impact of Subnational Interests on Supranational Regulation', *Journal of European Public Policy* 17(8): 1193–1211.

Noferini, A. (2012) 'The Participation of Subnational Governments in the Council of the EU: Some Evidence from Spain', *Regional and Federal Studies* 22(4): 361–385.

Petschen Verdaguer, S. (1993) *La Europa de las regiones*, Barcelona: Generalitat de Catalunya, Institut d'Estudis Autonòmics.

Piattoni, S. (2010) *The Theory of Multi-Level Governance. Conceptual, Empirical, and Normative Challenges*, Oxford: Oxford University Press.

Ray, L. (1999) 'Measuring Party Orientations towards European Integration: Results from an Expert Survey', *European Journal of Political Research* 36(2): 283–306.

Scharpf, F. (1994) 'Community and Autonomy: Multi-level Policy-making in the European Union', *Journal of European Public Policy* 1(2): 219–242.

Scharpf, F. (1999) *Governing in Europe: Effective and Democratic?*, Oxford: Oxford University Press.

Scherpereel, J.A. (2007) 'Sub-National Authorities in the EU's Post-socialist States: Joining the Multi-level Polity?', *Journal of European Integration* 29(1): 23–46.

Scherpereel, J.A. (2010) 'EU Cohesion Policy and the Europeanization of Central and East European Regions', *Regional & Federal Studies* 20(1): 45–62.

Scott, A.J. (1998) *Regions and the World Economy: The Coming Shape of Global Production, Competition, and Political Order*, Oxford: Oxford University Press.

Soldatos, P. (1990) 'An Explanatory Framework for the Study of Federated States as Foreign-policy Actors'. In H. Michaelmann and P. Soldatos (eds.), *Federalism and International Relations. The Role of Subnational Units*, Oxford: Clarendon Press, pp. 34–53.

Steenbergen, M.R. and Marks, G. (2007) 'Evaluating Expert Judgments', *European Journal of Political Research* 46(3): 347–366.

Storper, M. (1997) *The Regional World: Territorial Development in a Global Economy*, New York and London: Guildford.

Strijker, D. and de Veer, J. (1988) 'Agriculture'. In W. Molle and R. Cappellin (eds.), *Regional Impact of Community Policies in Europe*, Aldershot: Avebury, pp. 26–44.

Tabellini, G. (2007) *Culture and Institutions: Economic Development in the Regions of Europe*, Working Paper. Milan: Bocconi University.

Tatar, M. (2011) 'The Impact of the European Union on Sub-National Mobilization in A Unitary State: The Case of Estonia', *Journal of Baltic Studies* 42(3): 379–407.

Tatham, M. (2008) 'Going Solo: Direct Regional Representation in the European Union', *Regional and Federal Studies* 18(5): 493–515.

Tatham, M. (2010) 'With or Without You? Revisiting Territorial State-bypassing in EU Interest Representation', *Journal of European Public Policy* 17(1): 76–99.

Tatham, M. (2011) 'Devolution and EU Policy-shaping: Bridging the Gap between Multi-level Governance and Liberal Intergovernmentalism', *European Political Science Review* 3(1): 53–81.

Tatham, M. (2012) 'You Do What You Have to Do? Salience and Territorial Interest Representation in EU Environmental Affairs', *European Union Politics* 13(3): 434–450.

Tatham, M. (2013a) 'Paradiplomats against the State: Explaining Conflict in State and Sub-state Interest Representation in Brussels', *Comparative Political Studies* 46(1): 63–94.

Tatham, M. (2013b) 'Regional Voices in the in the European Union: Sub-national influence in multi-level politics', ECPR General Conference. Bordeaux.

Tatham, M. (2014a) 'Limited Institutional Change in an International Organisation: Accounting for the EU's Shift Away from "Federal Blindness"', *European Politicial Science Review* 6(1): 21–45.

Tatham, M. (2014b) 'Same Game but More Players? Sub-national Lobbying in an Enlarged Union', *Regional and Federal Studies* 24(3): 341–361.

Tatham, M. and Bauer, M.W. (2014) 'Support from Below? Regional Élites, Governance Preferences and Supranational Institutions', *Journal of Public Policy* 34(2): 237–267.

Triglia, C. (1991) 'The Paradox of the Region: Economic Regulation and the Representation of Interests', *Economy and Society* 20(3): 306–327.

Wonka, A., Baumgartner, F.R., Mahoney, C. and Berkhout, J. (2010) 'Measuring the Size and Scope of the EU Interest Group Population', *European Union Politics* 11(3): 463–476.

Chapter 20

Political representation and democracy in the European Union

SANDRA KRÖGER

Introduction

In everyday language, democracy is usually associated with representation, even though this link has been understood in various ways. For example scholars have not only differentiated between delegate and trustee models of representation but also descriptive, symbolic, anticipatory, promissory, discursive, and advocacy representation, and disputed their respective merits (Pitkin 1967; Mansbridge 1999; Urbinati 2000; Dovi 2002). All of these different approaches to representation reveal a common understanding that modern democratic politics is linked to representation and perceive of representation as the most appropriate means to serve the goal of political equality for every citizen and to render the exercise of political authority legitimate. Indeed, by and large it is accepted today that political representation is a *sine qua non* for the legitimacy of any democratic political system, the EU included.

Conceptually and empirically, however, this link is not self-evident: 'Through much of their history both the concept and the practice of representation have had little to do with democracy or liberty' (Pitkin 1967: 2). The close linkage of representation with democracy was a product of contingent historical developments, more specifically of the gradual emergence of territorially confined nation-states (Hobson 2008). The French Revolution offered the intellectual and political context in which democratic government came to be envisioned and institutionalized as representative government (Urbinati 2004; Hobson 2008). Indeed, Abbé de Sieyès considered the establishment of representative government as the 'true object of the revolution' (Hobson 2008: 453). For him, representation was a means of reactivating democracy in the context of territorial nation-states. From such a perspective, 'democracy *is* possible and *it is* desirable precisely because it *is* representative' (Hobson 2008: 466), instead of being merely a second-best solution to direct democracy.

However, contemporary democracies are evolving in ways that increasingly undermine the adequacy of the standard model. The modern territorial state, and with it the link between democracy and representation, is challenged through a variety of 'diversification' processes, including those of supranational (European) integration, that have led to a diversification of competences, of actors and arenas, which have contributed to the dilution of traditional representative politics (Warren and Castiglione 2004; Kröger and Friedrich 2012). In the European Union (EU), the relationship between representation and (national) democracy is particularly challenged, given the number of competences that have been transferred to it, and its densely structured multilevel politics, both of which weaken the ability of national democracies to keep decision-making authority in their hands. It is this unsettled and contested nature of the EU and the quest for the right balance between a supranational and an intergovernmental political order and the institutional arrangements that go with it that have provoked fierce debate concerning its alleged democratic deficit.

This chapter seeks to provide a good understanding of the issues involved when we speak about representation and democracy in the EU. In order to do so, it first looks at the concept of democratic representation as an expression of the norm of political equality and representative government as the institutional translation of that norm. In the following section, it will be shown how the political system of the EU relates to political representation. As we will see and as is discussed in more detail in other chapters in this handbook (see Chapters 5–6 and 17–19), representation occurs in different channels and at different levels. Against this background, I then review the debate around the alleged democratic deficit of the EU and discuss ways in which the current crisis of the EU may have sharpened this deficit. In conclusion, I discuss in how far compound representation in the EU works in favour of democratic representation and therefore the democratic legitimacy of the EU.

Democratic representation and representative government

Democracy is here understood as a value, a right, a procedure, and a set of practices with the purpose of achieving collectively binding decisions. Political procedures and practices are democratic if they are firmly based on *political equality* as the 'foundational idea' of democracy (Christiano 2003). This idea stipulates that 'no compelling justification for democracy could oppose the view that people ought to be treated as political equals' (Saward 1998: 15). Scholars generally agree that each individual is of equal moral worth, a position that ultimately dates back to the tradition of natural law and social contract theory as developed by Hobbes, Locke, and Rousseau. They all postulated that individuals, in their natural condition, possess equal rights, a position also reflected in the categorical imperative of Kant, who likewise defended the postulate of universal equal human worth. To say 'this much is merely to say that the principle of political equality is integral to the meaning and practice of democracy' (O'Flynn 2010: 283).

The substantive equal worth of all citizens translates, on the one hand, into citizenship rights that guarantee the right to participate in public lawmaking and to control the decision-makers. On the other hand, it establishes obligations for the government to secure and respect the principle of political equality of its citizens and publicly to account for them. Hence, all those who are bound by collective decisions are entitled to an equal say in their making and in controlling the rulers and the administration. Governments are democratic if they recognize the principle of political equality and treat all citizens and their interests with equal concern and respect. Democratic representation thereby became the institutional translation of the principle of political equality.

Democratic representation in the context of nation-states was to be realized through two institutions: (1) regular, free and fair elections, based on the rule of one person, one vote (OPOV) which expresses the norm of political equality, and (2) a representative government that follows from the results of these elections and which publicly aggregates societal interests into a political program. Elections serve as the start and end points of political representation: through them, the represented authorize their representatives and through them, the former hold the latter to account. For the limited span of an electoral cycle, political authority is delegated to elected representatives. Normatively, electoral cycles imply that power is conditional and that its abuse can be sanctioned. Democratic representation has thus been understood as a way of establishing the legitimacy of representative institutions and of creating institutional incentives for governments to be responsive to citizens. Representative government so conceived has been shown to be a practically feasible and normatively justifiable version of democracy (Hobson 2008: 451).

Standard accounts of political representation thus describe and justify political representation in the context of nation-states. Their main, if not exclusive, aim is to perfect its territorially based electoral forms. However, contemporary democracies are evolving in ways that increasingly undermine the adequacy of these standard accounts. The modern territorial state, and with it the link between democracy and representation, is challenged through a variety of diversification processes, including those of the supranational (European) integration, of competences, actors, and arenas, which have contributed to the increasing dilution of traditional representative politics (Warren and Castiglione 2004; Kröger and Friedrich 2012). Given the transfer of competences to the EU, its fragmentation and its densely structured multilevel politics, all of which weaken the ability of national democracies to keep decision-making authority in their hands, the relationship between representation, democracy and the nation-state in the EU is particularly strained. What is more, the nation-state's apparently clear demarcation of the *demos* that can or should be represented is increasingly dissolving and there is no clear institutional centre of authority anymore given the delegation of competences to a multitude of non-state or semi-state actors. In the light of these developments, it has subsequently been argued that representation cannot be restricted to electoral representation or to representation in the nation-state alone anymore, for such a conceptualization no longer seems to grasp political reality (Rehfeld 2006; Lord and Pollak 2010).

Indeed, European integration brings about a transformation of political authority by which the state loses its monopoly on collectively binding decision-making. The result is a transformation of national sovereignty which is occurring empirically and which scholars are struggling to come to terms with conceptually. Since it took on its modern meaning, national sovereignty provided an account of legitimate rule, within a confined territory and associated to defined functions, in which political authority was 'singular and supreme' (Goodhart 2007: 573). What scholars are struggling with, then, is to detach the notion of sovereignty – and thereby representation – from boundaries that bind together territory, *demos* and the idea of righteous rule of that *demos* within those defined boundaries, leading some to speak of 'methodological nationalism' (Zürn 2001) which does not question the Westphalian state as its point of departure when thinking of normative democratic standards today.

Scholars have tried to come to grips with the changing nature of representative democracy, devising new terminologies in the process. They speak of a 'post-national constellation' (Habermas 2001), 'audience democracy' (Manin 1997), 'post-democracy' (Crouch 2004), and the like to highlight what in their view characterizes contemporary Western types of democracies. However, this is not the place to review recent developments in representation theory in detail, given that the focus should here be on political representation in the EU and that those developments are often not conceptually linked to EU studies.

Representation in the EU

Representation is also a central concept in the way in which the EU understands its democratic legitimacy. In Title II on 'Provisions on Democratic Principles', the Lisbon Treaty highlights two key principles. First, Article 9 states the normative basis for democracy in the EU, namely political equality. Second, Article 10 asserts 'the functioning of the Union shall be founded on representative democracy'. Thus, political equality and representative democracy are the self-proclaimed democratic 'meta-standards' of the EU (Lord and Pollak 2010: 126). More concretely, the Treaty stipulates in Title II, Article 10:

1   The functioning of the Union shall be founded on representative democracy.
2   Citizens are directly represented at Union level in the European Parliament. Member states are represented in the European Council by their heads of state or government and in the Council by their governments, themselves democratically accountable either to their national Parliaments, or to their citizens.
3   Every citizen shall have the right to participate in the democratic life of the Union. Decisions shall be taken as openly and as closely as possible to the citizen.
4   Political parties at European level contribute to forming European political awareness and to expressing the will of citizens of the Union.

In Article 11, the Lisbon Treaty states that the European institutions shall give citizens and associations 'the opportunity to make known and publicly exchange their views in all areas of Union action' and to maintain a regular and open dialogue with them. It also introduces the European Citizen Initiative whereby a group of at least a million EU citizens may petition the European Commission to further actions that fall within its competences. The Lisbon Treaty thus distinguishes (four) different channels of representation.

The *electoral* channel works via national parliaments (NPs) and via the European Parliament (EP) and the parties that campaign for the respective elections. The principal object of political equality in the electoral channel is the individual citizen. NPs are mentioned in the main text of the treaty for the first time, thereby continuing a trend going back to the Maastricht Treaty and the debate on the EU's democratic deficit that have seen the empowerment of NPs in EU affairs as one possible mechanism for tackling this issue. Previous measures included a legally binding 'Protocol on the Role of NPs in the European Union' which accorded NPs the right to receive information on EU affairs, demanded that there be a six-week period between issuing a legislative proposal and its adoption by the Council, and introduced rules for the cooperation between NPs and the EP, not least in the context of COSAC.[1]

Most notably, Article 12 now details the basic rights and functions of NPs in EU matters and introduces an 'Early Warning Mechanism' (EWM) that assigns national legislatures the right to scrutinize proposed EU decisions and initiatives for compliance with the principles of subsidiarity and proportionality. Furthermore, NPs can have a collective legislative influence in that a majority of them may force, by way of a so-called orange card, an early vote on an EU legislative proposal in the Council and the EP. They are also now involved in the evaluation of measures taken within the area of freedom, security and justice (Articles 70, 85, 88), may block treaty changes under the simplified revision procedures (Article 48) and must be informed of new applications to join the EU (Article 49). NPs have therefore become actors in their own right in EU policy-making.

Regarding the EP, formally speaking, the equal access of citizens seems realized. Universal suffrage in the elections for the European Parliament (EP) is valid for all who possess EU citizenship, also in other member states than their own. Yet, not every vote counts equally in EP elections. For instance, the Luxembourgian vote counts for about 80 times more than the German vote. This deviation from a strictly proportionate distribution of seats reflects the principle of 'degressive proportionality', with a minimum threshold of 6 seats for the smallest member state and a maximum of 96 for the largest (Art 14.2 TEU). The official rationality behind this arrangement has been to ensure that the range of political opinion found in even the less populous member state is represented. Contrary to NPs, the EP does not possess the right to initiate legislative proposals which originate in the European Commission. Co-decision procedures with the Council of the EU over these proposals is the rule by now (March and Mikhaylov 2010).

The *territorial* channel of representation materializes through the Council of the EU and the European Council.[2] The principal object of political equality in the territorial channel is the nation-state. The European Council brings together heads of state or government. It does not legislate but 'defines the general political directions and priorities' of the EU (Treaty of the European Union Article 15 para. 1). The Council of the EU meets in diverse sectoral configurations, bringing together the respective ministers of national governments. It is the main European legislator, even though most laws are now passed under the co-decision procedure with the EP. Even though qualified majority voting (QMV) is formally the default for decision-making, in practice it operates through consensus wherever possible. Moreover, the planned double-majority rule for QMV from 1 November 2014, involving 55 per cent of member states representing at least 65 per cent of the population, is designed to ensure that decisions must balance the interests of large and small states by preventing the former imposing a decision on the latter and vice versa.

Functional representation has mainly addressed the European Commission, even though more recently and with increasing competences, the EP has also become the addressee of lobbying strategies of civil society organizations (CSOs). There is by now a distinguished system of interest representation in place in Brussels (Coen and Richardson 2009; Wonka *et al.* 2010; Greenwood 2011; Fairbrass and Warleigh 2013). Exactly how this system works and what its central characteristics are remains disputed. Mostly, scholars have been interested in issues of access and influence and in explaining why either of them existed or not (Klüver 2013), however, with inconclusive results. Whether the specific system of interest representation that exists in Brussels is supportive of the overall democratic quality of the EU has attracted considerably less attention in the literature on interest groups – more so in the literature that frames the related questions more in terms of civil society organizations.

As the initiator of legislation and its role in agenda setting, the Commission is still the most important contact partner of interest groups (Kröger 2008a). Both supranational actors are understaffed and therefore dependent on external expertise (Bouwen 2002; Broscheid and Coen 2003). A substantial part of European legislation touches upon new areas with a quite complex character, and the European institutions are keen on gaining expert knowledge. The interactions between the Commission, the EP and CSOs are thus structured by the informational needs of the former and their concern to avoid overload (Bouwen 2002; Broscheid and Coen 2003). But also, both institutions work towards more system integration (Cram 1993), not least by consulting CSOs and thereby supposedly lending their proposals greater legitimacy. To support its aims, the Commission has actively promoted and cultivated Euro-groups of all kinds.

The *direct* channel of representation as expressed in the European Citizens' Initiative (ECI) is the fourth channel of representation. It is also the most recent channel which was introduced with the Treaty of Lisbon and only came into force in April 2012. Its legal basis is set out in Article 11, para. 4 of the Treaty of the European Union and in Article 24, para. 1 of the Treaty on the Functioning of the European Union. By way of an ECI, European citizens can invite the European Commission to propose legislation on matters where the EU has competence to legislate. The ECI has to be backed by at least one million EU citizens, coming from at least 7 of the 28 member states. Once officially registered, the organizers of the ECI have one year to collect signatures. After that, the Commission examines the initiative and decides whether to take action. If it decides to put forward a legislative proposal, the normal legislative procedure is in place and, if adopted, becomes law.

The Lisbon Treaty thus distinguishes between an electoral, a territorial, a functional, and a direct channel of representation, but it does not clarify the relationship between them. The meaning of the concept 'representative democracy' and the relationship between representation and democracy in the EU therefore in both theoretical and practical remains unclear. This is not least so as its normative core, political equality, in the Lisbon Treaty refers to two different political subjects: individuals and states (Kröger and Friedrich 2013) and to two kinds of political community, 'political solidarism' and 'political singularism' (Bellamy and Castiglione 2013). These two kinds of subjects have different reference points: self-determination or a putative common good of a European people, on one hand, and sovereignty, or a vision of the EU as an agreement between states based on mutual self-interest, on the other. While the former points towards an integrated European polity with state-like characteristics, the latter treats the EU as an advanced intergovernmental organization. However, the EU is neither a liberal democracy nor an international organization. It lacks the preconditions for the former (Kielmannsegg 2003) while it has too far-reaching competences and impacts on its members to be properly characterized as the latter. Instead, there is a coexistence of both forms of subjectivity:

1   If one follows the liberal tradition of democratic theory, a system of democratic representation that is based on the political equality of individuals emphasizes the emancipative value of self-determination: 'The idea of democracy derives its power and significance . . . from the idea of self-determination' (Held 1995: 145). Self-determination comprises two aspects. First, it refers to individual self-rule, that is the individuals' ability reflexively to decide on their own life. Second, it requires the capacity to participate equally in the making of collective decisions, that is to be included in collective self-determination (Christman 2008).

2   Instead, a system of representation based on the equality of states as subjects of political action, is founded on the principle of sovereignty. At the internal level, the core of sovereignty relates to the ultimate authority-holding power within a given territory. Furthermore, the task of the state is not (only) to deliver government *for* the people, but to secure government *by* and *of* the people at home. At the external level, it refers to the relation between states and describes the states' aspiration for survival, the absence of higher authorities and the equality between them. This understanding of sovereignty, on which Realism and classical international law are grounded, has been dubbed 'sovereign equality' (Kelsen 1944; Kokott 2004).

In the earlier phase of European integration, the EU was institutionalized as an international organization (IO), implying that member states were the subjects of political equality, realized through employing unanimity as the decision-making rule and through a limited transfer of competences. Over time, and with the transfer of ever more competences to the EU, the individual as the normative subject of political equality became more important. This change was reflected in the increased competences of the EP and the increased attention paid to CSOs. The development went hand in hand with the weakening of the political equality of states, particularly through the increased use of qualified majority voting. The latest developments in the Lisbon Treaty do not resolve the tension between both subjectivities. While representative democracy and political equality are fully embraced, a clear division or hierarchy of competences is absent. Instead, both subjects and visions of political community continue to exist in parallel and cause difficulties regarding the achievement of democratic representation in the EU as we shall see in more detail in the following.

The democratic deficit debate

What scholars will perceive as a democratic deficit of the EU depends on how they conceive of democracy in the first place, and, how they perceive of the EU. The more the EU diverges from the models respective scholars put forward, the more likely are they to perceive a democratic deficit of the EU. By way of example, while Robert Dahl (1998: 107) considers the mere size of international organizations as a barrier to democratic government as it decreases the possibilities of citizen participation, David Held (1995) contends that the nation-state is not the appropriate locus of democratic processes anymore, given the interconnectedness of policies and politics and their implications for citizens beyond national territories and national citizenship. Be that as it may, in general the debate around the EU's democratic deficit revolves around questions of democratic representation that I now address.

Ever since the Maastricht Treaty (1992), an intense debate about what is now called the EU's 'democratic deficit' has been growing, and there is no sign of it ceasing. The EU's policy-making is seen as distant, non-transparent and not corresponding to institutional checks and balances present within the member states. The peoples of Europe are felt to have little or no say on the EU's institutional development, its policy-making, and future objectives, while their lives are increasingly affected by European integration. In this debate, then, there are broadly speaking four different positions that scholars take: no deficit (liberal intergovernmentalism), institutional deficit (supranationalism), structural deficit (no *demos* thesis), and domestic deficit (republican intergovernmentalism). I look at them in turn now.

No deficit

According to the first view, liberal intergovernmentalism, there is no democratic deficit (Majone 1996; Moravcsik 2006, 2008), certainly not one that would be specific to the EU. From this perspective, the democratic deficit is at best an optical illusion which grounds on wrong expectations towards the EU. For Andrew Moravcsik, the main defender of this position, liberal democracies in general should detract issues of human rights and of technical expertise from the democratic process, and the EU certainly complies in this regard. Furthermore, competencies can be neatly divided between the EU and its member states, with the EU handling issues that member states are not capable of handling well on their own anymore. The EU is responsible for the creation of the internal market and can be justifiably isolated from partisan politicization and electoral competition to achieve this objective. The salient issues of European integration continue to be crucially dependent on democratically authorized member states' governments. The need for democratic oversight of EU policy-making in general is therefore marginal at best – and where it exists, the EU compares favourably with national democracies. Institutional checks and balances are even more developed than in member states, and the pluralist policy-making of the EU is more open to interest representation and minority protection than are many national systems (Moravcsik 2002: 605). In sum, 'contemporary Europe rests on a pragmatically effective, normatively attractive and politically stable European constitutional settlement' (Moravcsik 2006: 221).

A similar though not identical view has been defended by Giandomenico Majone (1996) who sees the EU as a 'regulatory state'. As in the previous model, efficiency provided through technical and insulated expertise is also here viewed as the primary source of legitimacy. The delegation of competences to the EU is legitimate so long as it produces Pareto-efficient policies from which EU citizens will benefit. A democratic deficit does not exist in Majone's view as the peoples of Europe do not want more integration anyway and do not expect it to be a democratic polity. Speaking of a democratic deficit thus misses the EU's nature and scope in the first place (Majone 2006: 620).

These perspectives rest on a thin notion of the EU's legitimacy which assumes that as long as market creation is efficiently and effectively organized and realized and has been legitimized by national elites as in the national interest, the agent of that project will itself be legitimate, particularly since voters anyway would not really care about deliberating about the EU (Moravcsik 2002: 614). The same group of authors sees the international constraints on national democracies as paralleling the domestic constraints adopted by most constitutional democracies (Keohane *et al*. 2009). Government for the people need not require government by the people – indeed, the second can, on occasion, subvert the first, and the EU operates primarily in areas where this proves to be the case (Scharpf 1999) and where technocratic governance is perceived as a safeguard against government ineffectiveness. Citizens are in any event indirectly represented as peoples or states through their government.

An institutional deficit

For the majority of scholars, however, there is a democratic deficit of the EU of some kind. Firstly, there exists the view that the deficit is mainly an *institutional* deficit at the EU level, and would that the flaws and omissions in the institutional design of the EU be undone, would the democratic deficit smoothly dissolve? This view typically compares the EU institutions with national democratic institutions and their underlying norms of democratic representation.

It defends that the EU has the capacity to enact norms which create rights and obligations both for its member states and their nationals, to take decisions with major impact
on the social and economic orientation of public life, to engage the Community in international agreements, and to spend significant amounts of public funds (Eriksen and Fossum 2000). However, there is a mismatch between taking policy decisions increasingly
at the EU level while politics still mainly operates at the national level. It is argued that
democratic government should move more consistently to the EU level, in particular
to the EP, to be responsive and accountable at the level where the policy decisions are
taken. Accordingly, it is criticized that the direct link between citizens and their representatives is too weak, suggesting that the EP should be further strengthened, not least
by giving it the power to elect a European president (of the European Commission),
that the European party and electoral system needs reform so that European elections
become first-order elections, and that the institutional infrastructure for accountability
is insufficient, specifically as regards the transparent meetings of the Council. What is
the background against which such reform proposals are formulated?

Despite the steady growth of the competences of the EP, it is argued that important
caveats remain. Above all, the main function of a democratic parliament, that of initiating
and passing laws, is still not within the powers of the EP. MEPs can only – and not in
all cases – veto legislative proposals made by the Commission. Also, crucial and highly
distributive policies, such as the Common Agricultural Policy, are still not fully incorporated into the co-decision competences of the EP, nor are issues of high politics such
as taxation or security and defence. Thus, resource intensive policies and issues with
identity-forming power are excluded from the realm of the EP (see Hurrelmann and
de Bardeleben 2009). Furthermore, it is not always clear where EU lawmaking occurs,
or where legislation ends and administration begins, as exemplified in the work of the
multiple comitology committees (Lord 2011: 13). In sum, the EP lacks the lawmaking
capacity that national parliaments have.

The unequal translation of votes into seats in the EP is also troublesome. Although
some commentators argue that some degree of unequal translation of votes into seats
is a usual problem of any federally structured political system (Lord and Pollak 2013),
it would be insufficient to extrapolate from federal nation-states to the EU level. In the
former, each subjectivity – citizens and territorial units – is institutionalized in an independent legislative body, such as the Senate and the House of Representatives in the
U.S. or the Bundesrat and the Bundestag in Germany. In the EU political system there
is only one directly elected legislative institution, the EP, which is simultaneously built
upon both subjectivities, as expressed by the specific method of distribution of seats in
the EP. Consequently, the EP neither possesses the characteristics of a full parliament
nor is its distribution of seats organized in proportion to the size of national populations.

Other problems relate to the elections of the EP and the way parties are organized
therein. In a democracy, elections are not an end in themselves, but a means to select
representatives who represent the various interests of the electorate, to shape the political agenda, and to allow for majoritarian politics. As the pioneering work by Reif and
Schmitt (1980) revealed, European elections are largely conceived of as second-order
elections. Candidates do not offer European programs, and voters are not guided by
European preferences. Linked to this, the party system of the EU is still organized
along national lines (Höreth 1999), a fact that is mirrored in the electoral programs of
the Euro-parties (Sigalas and Pollak 2012). The Euro-parties are epiphenomena, rather

than full parties, and unable to fulfil the aggregative functions of parties (Lord 2010). The EU has therefore so far failed to develop a form of political competition which is relevant to the exercise of political power in its own arena. Voter turnout in turn has been steadily declining. Voters 'tend to see the elections primarily as an opportunity to sanction unpopular national governments (Hurrelmann and de Bardeleben 2009: 231). However, as long as European elections are to some significant degree 'second order', the link between the citizen and its representative is very weak, and the public control of EU policies is accidental and not systematic. Worse, it even becomes part of the democratic deficit as MEPs are not directly authorized for what they do (because of the second-order problem).

A central arena for executing the control (accountability) function is the parliamentary plenary itself and the struggles between opposition and governmental majority therein. The functioning of the EP, however, is still dominated by an informal 'grand coalition' between the two largest groups in the EP, the European People's Party and the European Socialist Party. A consequence is that the 'big moments' of politics, such clashes between the governmental majority and its opposition, are absent. This makes it difficult for citizens to detect alternative political programs. Scholarly disputes remain over whether there has recently been some politicization along the ideological left-right divide (Hix and Noury 2009) or whether this should be interpreted as a 'façade politicization' (Bartolini 2005, chap. 6; Lord 2010: 8).

Additionally, the crucial function of sanctioning a government is restricted. Neither the intense hearings by the EP of nominated EU commissioners at the EP nor the EP's ability to issue a vote of no confidence with regard to the whole EU Commission are entirely convincing exercises of this function. The EP's lack of competences to elect a European government, or at least the Commission, makes one of the most important, publicly visible competences of parliaments not applicable, namely contestation over leadership (Follesdal and Hix 2006: 554). Furthermore, voting is neither an evaluation of rival programs for a forthcoming EP nor an appraisal of the relative performance of parties in an outgoing EP. Thus, both *ex ante* and *ex post* mechanisms of public control seem to be lacking.

Central functions of electoral representation at the EU level are therefore only rudimentarily developed or are lacking *tout court*. The EP does not enjoy full lawmaking capacity, it mixes the political equality of citizens and that of states by way of its progressive seats distribution, and some of the main ex ante and ex post possibilities of electoral authorization and control are lacking. Citizens in turn do not perceive that they authorize their representatives to represent them on European matters, or to hold them accountable for what they do. In other words, there is no electoral connection between citizens and their representatives and therefore a disconnection between European citizen's preferences and EU decisions. In essence, the democratic deficit therefore lies in the lack of possibility for a majority to exercise its power, to hold representatives to account and to actually influence policy decisions (Mény 2002: 9).

Territorial representation via the diverse Council formations and in the European Council does not necessarily compensate what electoral representation cannot at present achieve in terms of democratic representation. On one hand, the EU level functions to some extent as an international organization that upholds the principle of equality between sovereign states. This might increase the governments' ability to (co-)decide on policy issues that they cannot control any longer alone. On the other hand, the broad use of QMV, as well as the growing importance of the other channels of representation, weakens this traditional notion of sovereignty. Thus, although the territorial channel of representation focuses on the subjectivity of the state, it effectively establishes a mixture of shared and independent components of sovereignty, thereby illuminating a transformation of democratic sovereignty in the EU. The normative prospects of this transforming sovereignty are precarious, because the political equality of sovereign nation-states is questioned and not replaced by a consistent different logic, such as that of a federal chamber. It undermines the states' realization of the interests of their national constituencies, weakens the national channels of electoral representation, and is detrimental to the individual subjectivity of representation (Kröger and Friedrich 2013).

More concretely, the complexity of the decision-making system in the EU offers national governments significant leeway to play two-level games (Putnam 1988). It is very difficult for citizens to follow the policy processes (Hurrelmann and de Bardeleben 2009: 232), although there have been attempts to increase the availability of Council documents and to live-broadcast Council meetings (see Friedrich 2011: chap. 4). Yet, the comitology system in which national experts rather than political actors decide and the preparatory meetings in the COREPER are undermining these attempts for more transparency. It is almost impossible for the public to be aware of competing political alternatives, as long as the national media tend to focus on the position of their respective national representative. Equally at the national level, following the logic of two-level games, scapegoating is still a prominent game by the members of both the European Council and the Council of the EU, rendering it difficult for the public to trace the positions of the diverse governments and therefore to hold them to account.

In response, scholars who perceive of the democratic deficit as being an institutional deficit encourage the further politicization and political integration of the EU (Follesdal and Hix 2006; Mény 2002). Most of the proposals focus on the EP (Follesdal and Hix 2006; Crum and Fossum 2009) and the (more) direct election of a European president (Decker 2002: 261; Hix 2002). The lack of a European-wide party system and the absence of a clearly recognizable parliamentary opposition at the EU level are perceived as the greatest hindrances to the development of European democracy (Follesdal and Hix 2006). The idea is that with increasing competition at the EU level, voters will become more aware of what their MEPs are doing in the EP, and therefore be more interested in having a say come the next elections. From this perspective, democratic practice is enough to further the development of a European demos. Overall, proposals that go in this direction seek to strengthen the political equality (and influence and control) of individuals at the cost of the political equality of states.

Other proposals against the institutional democratic deficit focus more on governance architectures (Schmitter 2007; Sabel and Zeitlin 2008), networks, deliberation, and organized civil society (Ruzza 2007). So-called strong publics as 'a sphere of institutionalized deliberation and decision-making' (Eriksen and Fossum 2002: 402) have been one way of tackling the institutional deficit, and scholars have investigated whether they existed in for example the comitology system (Joerges and Neyer 1997) or the Open Method of Coordination (OMC) (Kröger 2008b). Given the lack of political will of member states to parliamentarize the EU further, networks have been seen as another way of including citizen participation in decision-making (Jachtenfuchs 1997: 12), not least by the European Commission who has strongly supported and contributed to the establishment and continued existence of European networks and umbrella groups. However, the democratic deficits of these networks and instruments are by now well documented (Héritier 2003; Kröger 2007; Tsakatika 2007), and there is today broad consensus that they can *at best* complement representative institutions, rather than legitimizing the EU in and of themselves (Héritier 1999: 280). Some go further and argue that this kind of governance is itself undemocratic and therefore exacerbates the democratic deficit of the EU (Tsakatika 2007).

A structural deficit

Other authors, and second, perceive of the democratic deficit as being structural. This is known as the 'no-demos' thesis (Höreth 1999). As the two previous perspectives, this one also evaluates the EU's democratic legitimacy against standards known from national democracies and concludes that the EU does not fulfil the criteria we associate with democratic government in nation-states (Mair 2006). That is so because the EU lacks the fundamental features of nation-states which enable citizens to collectively govern themselves: a demos, a public sphere for debate, and therefore an authoritative channel of representation. Because there are no demos and no shared identity, not least due to the absence of a shared language, the necessary intermediary structures are lacking (Grimm 1995; Kielmannsegg 2003; Sifft *et al.* 2007). These intermediary structures – political parties and a media-based public sphere – however, are necessary preconditions to integrate different political, economic and social interests into the political process of a democracy (Scharpf 1999: 187). They are necessary in that they mediate between politicians and citizens. The institutional consequence of the lack of a demos and intermediary structures is that there is not a single centre of authority which would allow for common debate and political control and thereby for democratic politics. Seeking to enforce further political integration in the EU without the necessary democratic substructure may indeed be dangerous both for the EU and for the national democracies that compose it (Schmitter 2000: 115). In sum, citizens from such a perspective cannot be represented at the EU level because there is no common demos.

However, not all scholars sharing the no-demos thesis are sure it cannot be overcome. Either, they defend that the EU ought not to be compared against the standards of national democracies and seek to identify other parameters for legitimate European governance (Sabel and Zeitlin 2008; Cheneval and Schimmelfennig 2012). Or they argue that the creation of a European demos is possible indeed. Generally, the latter set their hopes in the creation of a common public sphere, to be constructed through a vibrant civil society, be it in more or less organized forms, in Brussels, or transnationally (Habermas 2001). From this perspective, the EU is perceived as the space – ideally a multinational federal state or a consociational polity – through which achievements of the national welfare states could be upheld and even more (political, economic, and social) progress may be achieved. Why should a democracy-building process not also be possible at the supranational level if given enough time? After all, national democracies are the results of long historical processes as well. Particularly, Jürgen Habermas (2001) has developed and embraced such a post-national position. He argues that citizenship and democracy are not confined to the nation-state. Instead, constitutional rights, mediated through a European public sphere, can generate a shared political identity.

Other commentators focus more on organized civil society as the actor and locus of further democratization of the EU (Friedrich 2011). Indeed, there is a large literature arguing that a dense and pluralistic web of civil associations balances out deficiencies in political representation and that it contributes to the creation of social capital which is required to sustain a living democracy. The hope is that CSOs and their interactions and input into policy-making could provide for the mutual trust that is needed under circumstances of mutual (inter-)dependence as we find them in the EU as well as for more legitimate governance of the EU itself as it expands its competencies.

The normative background to the focus on non-electoral representation is the increasing plurality and heterogeneity of Western societies, the value attached to diversity and its representation in societal institutions, and the attention paid to minorities. Some authors would also argue that party politics is in some structural sense exclusive and that therefore additional forms of representation are required (Mansbridge 1999; Young 2000). From this perspective, functional representation, according to some authors, could contribute to the realization of political equality if it brings weak interests into the political process (Young 2000).

The empirical background to this focus is that the traditional representative institutions no longer seem to fulfil completely the promise of political equality of all citizens. If they did so, then citizens would not disengage from electoral representation and engage in other forms of political mobilization as they do. Indeed, whilst the traditional institutions of representative democracies are facing declining voter turnout, a massive drop in party membership, and declining overall trust, other forms of political action coming from civil society, both unorganized and organized, have firmly established themselves in the political arena.

Concretely, the European Commission has actively engaged in a systematic attempt to promote and develop 'societal representation' at the EU level (Kohler-Koch and Finke 2007; Bellamy and Castiglione 2010; Saurugger 2010), something reflected in the much debated White Paper on Governance (2001), where the Commission argued that 'its legitimacy today depends on involvement and participation' (European Commission 2001: 11). Indeed, since the early 1990s, it has massively invested in the creation and survival of some large, non-profit seeking European umbrella organizations, thereby also seeking to increase the legitimacy of its proposals and to contribute to the construction of a transnational demos (Kröger 2013). The EU more generally has also accorded CSOs an important role in its policy-making, culminating in the Lisbon Treaty which establishes as a legal duty to consult with them.

The related conceptual focus has been on the link between a social constituency and active citizenship and on the creation of a demos-equivalent outside the framework of the nation-state (Eriksen and Fossum 2000; Trenz 2009). From this perspective, the EU is in need of direct legitimacy, a necessary condition of which is an (emergent) political community and a European public sphere, to which CSOs could possibly contribute. Empirically interested scholars have asked whether CSOs can act as a 'transmission belt' that brings the interests and values of citizens to the EU (Nanz and Steffek 2004). From this perspective, the role attributed to civil society is to 'mediate between the national and the supranational, thereby connecting national society to transnational governance' (Rumford 2003: 32). However, whilst there is a pluralist consultation regime in place in the EU (Hüller 2010; Kohler-Koch and Quittkat 2010), the participating CSOs tend to not stand for the European citizenry (Greenwood 2010; Kohler-Koch and Quittkat 2010:

161ff; Kröger 2013; Smismans 2012) but are instead professionalized élites who are defending their respective interests or at best a cause (Maloney 2007). Their egalitarian potential at the European level therefore seems limited.

A domestic deficit

Other scholars, finally, are less optimistic about the possibilities to democratize the EU further, and the democratic deficit to them is mainly domestic. To them, the EU's democratic legitimacy is 'borrowed' legitimacy, borrowed from its member states, and will remain so in the foreseeable future (Scharpf 2009). Therefore, it is important that democracy be defended back home (Offe 1998; Bartolini 2005; Schmidt 2006). From this perspective, the locus of democracy and of the welfare state is the nation-state, and it cannot be reproduced at the EU level, given the lack of a demos, of a common language and of common representation of that (lacking) demos. Worse, the European integration process in fact seems to undermine the capacities of its member states to remain democratic.

This position, which one might coin 'republican intergovernmentalism', has been defended most prominently and consistently by Fritz Scharpf (1999, 2009). He argues that not only is the range of available policy options restricted in favour of a conservative bias at the EU-level, because of the joint-decision trap which implies that decisions will be based on the lowest common denominator. Also, the progressive realization of the internal market, due to the effect of supremacy of EU law and its direct effect, is increasingly constraining citizens in the range of their democratic choices, not least the choice for a welfare state. 'Negative integration' from this perspective undermines democracy[3] which entails commitments to de-commodification from the market which would then allow for democratic citizenship. Structurally, then, these problems cannot be overcome because of the lack of a European public sphere and, of course, the no-demos problem.

While not always as concerned with the repercussions European integration has on national welfare states as Scharpf is, a number of authors are similarly concerned with the potentially damaging effects of European integration on domestic democratic politics, and on national parliaments in particular. Parliaments have a public mandate from voters to legislate and to control the executive. *De facto*, their institutional core consists of the government (which controls the agenda and formulates policy proposals), the parliamentary majority (which accepts or rejects these proposals), and the parliamentary opposition (assuring public deliberation, the generation of political alternatives and control). Democratic legitimacy is created through the competition between the different parties who form the majority and the opposition, publicly offering different programs to the electorate and being accountable for their actions.

In the context of the EU, however, the domestically, rather clear role distribution becomes blurred. Neither the Parliament nor the government has direct influence over the European agenda. Governments hardly ever have electoral authorization for specific EU policies nor can they or the parliaments initiate legislation. Meanwhile, the powers of accountability of the opposition as well as of Parliament more generally are weakened. Not surprisingly then, the 1990s witnessed the emergence of a 'deparliamentarization' thesis (Raunio and Hix 2000). This thesis seeks to capture the transfer of policy-making powers to the EU and the resulting loss of power and influence of domestic parliaments – and with them those of the electorate which exercises these functions indirectly through its representatives – as well as the strengthening of executives in EU policy-making which results in informational asymmetries between the legislature and the executive (Raunio and Hix 2000: 145; Auel and Benz 2005: 373). As a result, national parliaments have no direct control over European policy-making and 'suffer from a lack of authoritative power over transnational policymaking' (Schmidt 1999: 25). Instead, executives have become the 'gatekeepers' in EU policy-making. National parliaments have, therefore, often been called the main 'losers' of European integration (Maurer and Wessels 2001). Let's have a closer look at why that is so (see Bellamy and Kröger 2012).

First, the transfer of competences to the EU leaves parliaments, governments and parties little to decide in these areas. Member states have to adopt the *acquis communautaire*, and they have to comply with ECJ law. In this respect, the EU has played a major role in limiting the available 'policy space' for competing parties (Mair 2007) and governments.

Second, the constitutional bias in the Treaties gives priority to the completion and realization of the internal market (Scharpf 1999: 54–58). Consequently, the 'policy repertoire' available to parties – and governments – has been diminished, thereby reducing the possibilities for them to disagree and propose alternatives (Mair 2007). The EU thereby also restricts the range of policy options that are possible within those fields that can still be influenced by domestic politics. As a result, parliaments, governments, and parties are being transformed into mere agents of the state and its treaty obligations, obliged to engage in responsible administration rather than developing and implementing their own priorities as set in response to the voters.

Third, because of the supremacy and direct effect of EU law as interpreted and upheld by the ECJ, parliamentary attempts to disagree with the integration process risk becoming *de jure* unreasonable. Parliaments have no choice but to adapt to and implement EU law, even in those cases where ECJ interpretations may be thought to extend EU competences in ways that appear to run counter to the directives approved by national governments, as has sometimes happened in areas related to EU citizenship or freedom of movement (Scharpf 2009). The net effect of these three factors is that governments and parties can offer ever fewer political alternatives to voters which in turn decreases party competition. As a result, elections become less decisive, and their value decreases. In turn, parties, vote seeking as they are, attempt to avoid the politicization or debate of EU affairs given that under the conditions I have sketched it is hardly an attractive electoral issue.

Fourth, the increased use of qualified majority voting in the Council and bargaining in the Council and the European Council make it difficult for national parliaments to force governments to enter into detailed *ex ante* commitments before taking decisions at the European level (Raunio 2009: 327). Parliamentary authorization of the executive gets proportionately diminished as in EU affairs, their traditional veto power has passed to ministers in the Council and is therefore non-existent.

Fifth, national governments represent their countries in EU negotiations, resulting in informational asymmetries between the executive branch and the legislature that likewise constrain parliamentary control and influence.

Sixth, parliaments – and particularly the opposition – do not debate government actions in EU-related affairs to the same degree as in conventional domestic politics.

Plenary debates of EU-related issues are rare (Raunio 2009: 320). The latter tend to be delegated to the European Affairs Committees, rendering it impossible for the electorate to follow the debates given they are not accessible to the public as 'cooperation takes place behind closed doors' (Auel and Benz 2005: 390). Such non-transparent cooperation contributes to the blurring of responsibilities between opposition and majority parties. To strengthen the national negotiation position, consensus is sought in camera, implying that the public are not offered political alternatives (Auel and Benz 2005: 379). Opposition parties, in turn, are unlikely to demand plenary debates about the EU given that they either have similar preferences to those of the government or lack more coherent approaches to the EU (Raunio 2009: 320).

Last but not least, there is a reduction in the policy instruments that national governments – and thereby parliaments and parties – can employ, or, put in other words, an increased use of instruments and actors over which they possess less control than they enjoy over traditional domestic policy instruments. These include governance modes such as the OMC or the informal political dialogue, in which the European Commission, but potentially non-elected third parties (experts, CSOs) as well, play an important role. In soft-law instruments, such as the OMC, national parliaments play no legislative role. They are, despite their official description, typically intergovernmental and rather informal in nature. Research indicates that, by and large, they escape national parliamentary scrutiny and that lines of accountability become increasingly blurred due to unclear chains of delegation and a lack of transparency (Kröger 2007; Dawson 2009). The space for partisanship and alternative policy options is thereby drastically reduced, as is the possibility for those concerned to hold the respective institutions to account.

From this discussion, one can see that there is no easy answer to the question of whether there is a democratic deficit of the EU and what its essence is if it exists. There is likely to be a continued divide in the interested community over which normative standards should be applied to the EU regarding its democratic quality. Indeed, the EU is a problem for democratic theory insofar as it cannot be democratic on modern accounts of democracy. On one hand, why indeed should we expect institutions and norms of democracy which were developed, in the national context, to retain their meaning if translated to a fundamentally different supranational context? Given the historical contingency of territorial boundaries and the decreasing congruence between the people affected by political decisions and nation-state boundaries, democratic theory is not well advised to treat the identity of a people as given (Goodhart 2007). On the other hand, it would be unacceptable to not be guided by normative standards when evaluating the democratic quality of the EU, and citizens are likely to be inspired in their assessment from what they consider to be democratically legitimate in their respective national contexts.

Either way, the question of whether citizens or people are democratically represented in the EU rests on a satisfactory resolution of the identity questions, that is the question of which *body politique* should be represented, at which level, and of whether that political community accepts the respective representation as legitimate. The door back to a sovereign nation-state seems foreclosed, and it is important to recognize, paradoxically as it may seem, that supranational integration and cooperation indeed are necessary for nation-states to retain some sovereignty over their territorial affairs and interests (Bellamy 2013).

483

One recent attempt of coming to terms with the apparently unsurmountable divide between a stress on the political equality of states, on one hand, and the political equality of citizens, on the other, in EU studies has been to think of the EU as a *demoicracy* (Nikolaidis 2004) which stresses 'the horizontal and mutual opening between peoples in a shared polity. It assumes that Europe is not constituted by separate demoi nor demoi-made-into-one but by distinct political demoi progressively opening to each other and to each other's democratic systems' (Nikolaidis 2012: 252). It not only argues that national representative democracy should remain at the centre of European democracy but also sees the EU as a way of perfecting rather than dissolving national democracies. It argues in favour of some degree of supranationality and the respective loss of national sovereignty, but also holds that there should be a 'right to exit' which federalists would not foresee (ibid.), thus perceiving of European integration as an open-ended process. In sum, then, in a *demoicracy*, peoples 'govern together but not as one' (ibid.: 254).

Most recently, other scholars have started to pick up the term and develop if further both conceptually and normatively. Francis Cheneval and Frank Schimmelfennig (2012: 3) argue that we are witnessing the 'emergence of a new form of polity, which requires and generates a concomitant transformation of democracy'. This new kind of democracy would ask for a change in methodology which would not extrapolate nation-state models of democracy – and with them the idea of one single demos – to the EU. They contend that national demoi will continue to 'possess the strongest collective identities, public spheres and political infrastructures, and enjoy the strongest legitimacy and loyalty on the part of individual citizens' (ibid.: 3) and that these elements are prerequisites of a legitimate democracy. Therefore, from their perspective, multiple *demoi* are indispensable as bearers of negative and positive rights of protection and participation. *Demoicracy*, they argue, equally takes into account the rights and demands of both citizens and 'statespeoples'. On this ground, Cheneval and Schimmelfennig propose four principles to assess the democratic quality of a *demoicracy*: the *sovereignty of the statespeoples' pouvoir constituant regarding entry, exit and basic rules of the political order of multilateral democracy, non-discrimination of statespeoples and citizens, equal legislative rights of citizens and statespeoples* and *supremacy of multilateral law and jurisdiction* (ibid.: 9–10) which they start briefly assessing for the EU context. They argue that the demoicratic quality of the EU is established not only at the EU level but also at member state level (ibid.: 13–14), implying that the EU level 'ought not to bear the full burden of ensuring democratic participation and accountability'. Their brief 'empirical' assessment of the four principles leads them to think that the EU has actually approached demoicratic standards whilst important deficits would exist at the national level, resulting from 'the uneven and weak implementation of demoicratic norms in the Member States and the uneven and weak adaptation of national democratic institutions to the tasks they need to fulfill in a demoicratic system' (ibid.: 2). As a consequence, they suggest democratic reforms should focus on the national level.

The most recent attempt to develop the notion of *demoicracy* further comes from Richard Bellamy (2013). His contribution is yet more fine-tuned as to which conditions need to be met in order for us to speak of a 'people' and governments being representative of a people. Introducing the notion of republican intergovernmentalism, he shows the benefits of states forming an 'association' of states, as he describes the EU, not least to 'guard against the domination of one people by another by preserving the capacity of the associated peoples for representative democracy' (ibid.: 499). In a more detailed manner than his forerunners, he then shows that the EU's system of representation corresponds to the principles of a *demoicracy* and as such 'facilitates mutual respect and fair terms of cooperation between the peoples of Europe' (ibid.: 499). Any move away from the current setting towards more political integration is deemed to decrease the democratic legitimacy of the EU, as Bellamy seeks to show by way of the example of the management of the current euro and debt crisis and the way in which the Fiscal Pact and the EU's Six-Pack regulations effectively institutionalize a system of domination of the creditor over the debtor states.

The crisis and the sharpening of the democratic deficit

Certainly, the current debt and euro crisis has ensured that the issue of the democratic deficit remains on the political and academic agenda. It has even arguably exposed if not sharpened the democratic shortcomings of the EU. The EU has opted in favour of a depoliticized, technocratic and more intergovernmental form of governance rather than recurring to parliaments and public debate at a moment where the very core of these institutions – budgetary policy – was at stake.

Indeed, the primary representative institutions – parliaments – have been quite sidelined in the handling of the crisis. The EP has been completely sidelined. Whilst there is a Euro-group working in the Council, there is no counterpart of it in the EP. In fact, one could hardly notice voices from the EP relating to the crisis since it first began. The de-parliamentarization thesis has found new support through the transfer of some budgetary competences from national parliaments to the European Commission. The latter now can assess the budgetary plans of governments and may ask for amendments even before they are discussed in the European Parliament, which is a major intrusion into the primary competence of national parliaments, that is the competence over the national budget. This is particularly worrying as the Commission's decisions are dominated by quasi-automatic rules set by the Commission itself in close collaboration with another non-elected institution, the European Central Bank. Whilst most member states' parliaments had to approve of governmental responses to the crisis (with the few exceptions of those member states where a referendum had to be held), discussion of political alternatives was by and large sealed off with the all too simple 'argument' that there 'is no alternative' to what was being proposed (Puntscher Riekman and Wydra 2013), thereby foreclosing a central feature of political equality, namely the possibility of reasonable disagreement (Bellamy and Kröger 2012), and also sidelining political parties competing for power by offering political alternatives.

At the time of writing, therefore, much suggests that the future of the EU and its member states may look like Italy or Greece in 2011–12 – member states governed by technocrats rather than by party government. Governments may no longer be enforcing partisan electoral promises, but implementing budgetary, economic, and other policies decided at the EU level, either in the European Council or, worse, in the Euro-group, rendering national elections almost irrelevant. Whether a member state has a right-wing or a left-wing government no longer seems to make much difference for the choice of core policies. What has been said to characterize the EU – policies without politics – may be becoming the dominant governance form in member states, too. The euro crisis has certainly increased the opportunity structure for the further hollowing out of national democracy without establishing democratic government at the EU level.

The sidelining of parliaments and parties has benefited governments and technocratic bodies. Intergovernmental governance has been strengthened by moving from the 'Community Method' to what German chancellor Merkel has called the 'Union method', which puts national governments centre stage. However, not all governments were on equal footing in the handling of the crisis. Rather, Germany (and, to a lesser degree, France) has dominated fiscal policy over the last few years, whilst Greece in particular, and to a lesser degree also other southern member states and Ireland, were forced to accept the austerity measures that the German chancellor was so keen on. National governments, specifically those of the highly indebted states, have proved powerless to change the underlying fiscal approach, which has been decided in Berlin and Frankfurt.

Technocratic governance has been increased by creating the Frankfurt group and letting it become the main driving body of fiscal policy as well as by supporting the establishment of technocratic governments in both Italy and Greece. A consequence of politics moving towards technocratic governance is that political alternatives are hardly present at the EU level – as effectively in member states. Indeed, the notion of opposition does not even exist with the Union, implying that citizens do not have the feeling that they can change the direction of policy.

The handling of the crisis is all the more severe as the fiscal treaty constitutes a significant deepening of European integration in the economic and budgetary sphere without at the same time strengthening either the national or supranational representative institutions and thereby lending democratic legitimacy to the current and future fiscal policy. The euro and debt crisis has thereby amplified an existing problem – the lack of a transparent, open political process at the EU level which would be in the hands of democratic representative institutions and therefore, in the last resort, of the European peoples and citizens. Instead, peoples have been represented in a non-transparent manner by their governments, but not all governments have weighted equally, and therefore have not all citizens and peoples been represented equally. The consequence has been that not only have citizens had no (direct) input into decision-making, but also there was no public space in which political alternatives could have been discussed. In short, the fiscal treaty and the different rescue measures lack the democratic legitimacy they so urgently need.

One consequence of the handling of the crisis has been that national electorates throughout the EU have kicked out of office their governments unusually often since 2009, signaling the severe discontent of electorates with their governments. Also, recent electoral results show worrying support for far-right parties – think for example of Geert Wilders in the Netherlands, Golden Dawn in Greece, the Front National in France, and United Kingdom Independence Party (UKIP) in the UK. These parties are all too eager to exploit the prevailing sense of disconnect between the national and the EU levels and of national politicians being powerless vis-à-vis the EU and its technocrats. They structure their politics around opposition to the EU. But hostility towards the EU has also moved from the fringes and closer to the centre more generally.

Conclusion

In this contribution, I first reviewed the historical fusion of representation and democracy in the context of the nation-state and how this historically contingent fusion is today challenged by a number of diversification processes. It was then shown that the EU also thinks of itself in terms of representative democracy and thereby political equality, without however clarifying the relationship between the equality of individuals and the equality of states that it mixes in its different channels of representation which were briefly laid out. Against this background, the debate around the democratic deficit of the EU was reviewed, dividing it into four streams, that is no deficit (liberal intergovernmentalism), institutional deficit (supranationalism), structural deficit (no-demos thesis), and domestic deficit (republican intergovernmentalism).

Even if not in agreement with any of these four streams in particular, one can see from the discussion that there is a tension, in the EU's system of representation, between the supranational and the intergovernmental logic of integration which manifests itself in channels of representation which mix these different logics within themselves. This is not the place to resolve that tension – if it can be resolved at all.[4] What seems clear from the discussion, however, is that there does not exist a channel of representation in the EU that clearly works in favour of political equality and that people can clearly identify with. All the channels, to a greater or lesser degree, are not transparent and are distant or even unknown, such as territorial and at times functional representation. Or they are known, such as electoral representation, but do not enjoy the recognition they deserve (EP) or seem to be the losers of European integration (NPs).

From a normative perspective, it is at best an unresolved question whether the EU's current system of representation provides the EU with democratic legitimacy, the ambivalence of the assessment stemming from the unresolved issue of which normative standards should apply to the EU in the first place – those known from the domestic sphere or other ones. However, some scholars of course arrive at less pessimistic conclusions about the democratic quality of the EU than the present contribution (Zweifel 2002). Either way, different levels and channels of representation only make for democratic representation if they succeed in realizing the norms of political equality and public control. So far, democratic representation such conceived has not been realized at the EU level, which is precisely why the governance discourse has been as successful in the EU. Therefore, and for the time being, achieving democratic legitimacy for the EU seems to remain dependent on functioning domestic representative institutions and them having a strong voice in EU affairs. From an empirical perspective, not much speaks in favour these days of a strong democratic legitimacy of the EU, with ever more people protesting and voting against it, and with the EU having resorted, in the context of the crisis, to even more technocratic, non-transparent governance as had already been the case hitherto.

However, it is important to note that there is more generally an existential problem with the state of representative democracy at all levels in Europe, it is not simply about the EU and its institutions. It is about a gap between citizens' preferences and the ability of elected representatives to respond to those preferences. Linked to this is a decline in respect for representative institutions more generally and in trust in the capacity of the state to solve problems, and we surely cannot exclusively blame the EU for this crisis of representative democracy.

Acknowledgements

Sandra Kröger acknowledges the support for her research of a Marie Curie Intra European Fellowship within the 7th European Community Framework Programme (call reference FP7-PEOPLE-2010-IEF).

Notes

1 Conférence des Organes Parlementaires Spécialisés dans les Affaires de l'Union des Parlements de l'Union Européenne.
2 And, to a lesser degree, through the Committee of the Regions (Piattoni 2012). However, given its low political salience in EU policy-making, it is left out here.
3 Similarly, Stefano Bartolini (2005) has argued that European integration would undermine national democracy by undermining their boundaries. In contrast to Scharpf, however, he focuses more on the weakening of shared identities and cultural loyalty.
4 For a more detailed analysis of this tension, see Kröger and Friedrich (2013).

References

Auel, K. and Benz, A. (2005) 'The Politics of Adaptation: The Europeanisation of National Parliamentary Systems'. *The Journal of Legislative Studies* 11(3–4), 372–393.

Bartolini, S. (2005) *Restructuring Europe. Centre Formation, System Building and Political Structuring between the Nation-state and the European Union*. Oxford: Oxford University Press.

Bellamy, R. (2013) '"An Ever Closer Union among the Peoples of Europe": Republican Intergovernmentalism and *Demoi*cratic Representation within the EU'. *Journal of European Integration* 35(5), 499–516.

Bellamy, R. and Castiglione, D. (2010) 'Democracy by Delegation? Who Represents Whom and How in European Governance'. *Government and Opposition* 46(1), 101–125.

Bellamy, R. and Kröger, S. (2012) 'Domesticating the Democratic Deficit? The Role of National Parliaments and Parties in the EU's System of Governance', *Parliamentary Affairs*. Published electronically 23 August 2013. doi:10.1093/pa/gss045.

Bellamy, R. and Castiglione, D. (2013) 'Three Models of Democracy, Political Community and Representation in the EU'. *Journal of European Public Policy* 20(2), 206–223.

Bouwen, P. (2002) 'Corporate Lobbying in the European Union: The Logic of Access'. *Journal of European Public Policy* 9(3), 365–390.

Broscheid, A. and Coen, D. (2003) 'Insider and Outsider Lobbying of the European Commission: An Informational Model'. *European Union Politics* 4(2), 165–189.

Cheneval, F. and Schimmelfennig, F. (2012) 'The Case for Demoicracy in the European Union'. *Journal of Common Market Studies* 51(2), 334–350.

Christiano, T. (2003) 'An Argument for Democratic Equality'. In Christiano, T. (ed.) *Philosophy & Democracy*. Oxford: Oxford University Press, 39–67.

Christman, J. (2008) 'Autonomie'. In Gosepath, S. Hinsch, W. and Rössler, R. (eds.), *Handbuch der Politischen Philosophie und Sozialphilosophie*. De Gruyter: Berlin, 96–102.

Coen, David and Richardson, Jeremy (2009) (eds.) *Lobbying in the European Union: Institutions, Actors and Issues*. Oxford: Oxford University Press.

Commission of the European Communities (2001) *European Governance: A White Paper*, COM (2001) 428 final.

Cram, L. (1993) 'Calling the Tune Without Paying the Piper? Social Policy Regulation: The Role of the Commission in European Community Social Policy'. *Policy and Politics* 21(1), 135–146.

Crouch, C. (2004) *Post-democracy*. Cambridge: Polity.

Crum, B. and Fossum, J. E. (2009) 'The Multilevel Parliamentary Field: A Framework for Theorizing Representative Democracy in the EU'. *European Political Science Review* 1(2), 249–271.

Dahl, R. A. (1998) *On Democracy*. New Haven, CT: Yale University Press.

Dawson, M. (2009) 'EU Law "Transformed"? Evaluating Accountability and Subsidiarity in the "Streamlined" OMC for Social Inclusion and Social Protection'. In Kröger, S. (ed.) *What We Have Learnt: Advances, Pitfalls and Remaining Questions of OMC Research*. Special Issue, *European Integration Online Papers*, 1(13).

Decker, F. (2002) 'Governance beyond the Nation-state. Reflections on the Democratic Deficit of the European Union.' *Journal of European Public Policy* 9(2), 256–272.

Dovi, S. (2002) 'Preferable Descriptive Representatives: Or Will Just Any Woman, Black, or Latino do?' *American Political Science Review* 96(4), 745–754.

Eriksen, E. O. and Fossum, J. E. (eds.) (2000) *Democracy in the European Union: Integration through Deliberation?* London: Routledge.

Eriksen, E. O. and Fossum, J. E. (2002) 'Democracy through Strong Publics in the European Union'. *Journal of Common Market Studies* 40(3), 401–424.

Fairbrass, J. and Warleigh, A. (2013) *Influence and Interests in the European Union: The New Politics of Persuasion and Advocacy*. London: Europa Publications Limited.

Follesdal, A. and Hix, S. (2006) 'Why There Is a Democratic Deficit in the EU: A Response to Majone and Moravcsik'. *Journal of Common Market Studies* 44(3), 533–562.

Friedrich, D. (2011) *Democratic Participation and Civil Society in the European Union*. Manchester: Manchester University Press.

Goodhart, M. (2007) 'Europe's Democratic Deficits through the Looking Glass: The European Union as a Challenge for Democracy'. *Perspectives on Politics* 5(3), 567–584.

Greenwood, J. (2010) 'Regulating NGO Participation in the EU; a De-Facto Accreditation System Built on 'Representativeness'?' In Steffek, J. and Hahn, K. (eds.) *Evaluating Transnational NGOs: Legitimacy, Accountability, Representation*. Basingstoke: Palgrave, 200–219.

Greenwood, J (2011) *Interest Representation in the European Union* (3rd edn.). Basingstoke: Palgrave Macmillan.

Grimm, D. (1995) 'Does Europe Need a Constitution?' *European Law Journal* 1 (3), 282–302.

Habermas, J. (2001) 'Why Europe Needs a Constitution'. *New Left Review* 11 (September–October), 5–26.

Held, D. (1995) *Democracy and the Global Order. From the Modern State to Cosmopolitan Governance*. Cambridge: Polity Press.

Héritier, A. (1999) 'Elements of Democratic Legitimation in Europe: An Alternative Perspective'. *Journal of European Public Policy* 6(2), 269–82.

Héritier, A. (2003) 'Composite Democracy in Europe: The Role of Transparency and Access to Information'. *Journal of European Public Policy* 10(5), 814–833.

Hix, S. (2002) 'Why the EU Should Have a Single President, and How She Should be Elected'. Paper for the Working Group on Democracy in the EU for the UK Cabinet Office, October. http://personal.lse.ac.uk/hix/Working_Papers/Why%20the%20EU%20Should%20Have%20a%20Single%20President.pdf, accessed 22 January 2013.

Hix, S. and Noury, A. (2009) 'After Enlargement: Voting Patterns in the Sixth European Parliament'. *Legislative Studies Quarterly* 34(2), 159–174.

Hobson, C. (2008) 'Revolution, Representation and the Foundations of Modern Democracy'. *European Journal of Political Theory* 7(4), 449–471.

Höreth, M. (1999) 'No Way Out for the Beast? The Unsolved Legitimacy Problem of European Governance'. *Journal of European Public Policy* 6(2), 249–268.

Hüller, T. (2010) 'Playground or Democratisation? New Participatory Procedures at the European Commission'. *Swiss Political Science Review* 16(1), 77–108.

Hurrelmann, A. and deBardeleben, J. (2009) 'Democratic Dilemmas in EU Multilevel Governance: Untangling the Gordian Knot'. *European Political Science Review* 1(2), 229–247.

Jachtenfuchs, M. (1997) 'Democracy and Governance in the European Union'. *European Integration Online Papers* 1(2). http://eiop.or.at/eiop/texte/1997–002a.htm, accessed 3 February 2013

Joerges, C. and Neyer, J. (1997) 'Transforming Strategic Interaction into Deliberative Problem-Solving. European Comitology in the Foodstuffs Sector'. *Journal of European Public Policy* 4(4), 609–625.

Kelsen, H. (1944) 'The Principle of Sovereign Equality of States as a Basis for International Organization'. *The Yale Law Journal* 53(2), 207–220.

Keohane, R. O, Macedo, S. and Moravcsik, A. (2009) 'Democracy-Enhancing Mulitilateralism'. *International Organisation* 63(1), 1–31.

Kielmannsegg, P. G. (2003) 'Integration und Demokratie'. In Jachtenfuchs, Markus and Beate Kohler-Koch (eds.) *Europäische Integration* (2nd edn.). Opladen: Leske und Budrich, 49–84.

Klüver, Heike (2013) *Lobbying the European Union: Interest Groups, Lobbying Coalitions, and Policy Change*. Oxford. Oxford University Press.

Kohler-Koch, B. and Finke, B. (2007) 'The Institutional Shaping of EU-Society Relations – A Contribution to Democracy via Participation?' *Journal of Civil Society* 3(3), 205–221.

Kohler-Koch, B. and Quittkat, C. (2010) *Die Entzauberung partizipativer Demokratie. Zur Rolle der Zivilgesellschaft bei der Demokratisierung von EU-Governance*. Frankfurt am Main: Campus.

Kokott, J. (2004) 'Souveräne Gleichheit und Demokratie im Völkerrecht'. *Zeitschrift für ausländisches öffentliches Recht und Völkerrecht* 64, 517–533.

Kröger, S. (2007) 'The End of Democracy as We Know it? The Legitimacy Deficits of Bureaucratic Social Policy Governance'. *Journal of European Integration* 29(5), 565–582.

Kröger, S. (2008a) 'Nothing but Consultation: The Place of Organised Civil Society in EU Policy-making across Policies'. European Governance Papers (EUROGOV) No. C-08-03. www.connex-network.org/eurogov/pdf/egp-connex-C-08-03.pdf, accessed 3 February 2013.

Kröger, S. (2008b) *Soft Governance in Hard Politics. European Coordination of Anti-poverty Policies in France and Germany*. Wiesbaden: VS Verlag.

Kröger, S. (2013) 'Creating a European Demos? The Representativeness of European Umbrella Organisations'. *Journal of European Integration* 35(5), 583–600.

Kröger, S. and Friedrich, D. (2012) 'Representation in the EU: The Second Transformation'. In Kröger, S. and Friedrich, D. (eds.) *Representation in the European Union: Coping with Present Challenges to Democracy?* Houndmills: Palgrave Macmillan, 3–20.

Kröger, S. and Friedrich, D. (2013) 'Democratic representation in the EU: Two kinds of subjectivity.' *Journal of European Public Policy* 20(2), 171–189.

Lord, C. (2010) 'The Aggregating Function of Political Parties in EU Decision-Making'. *Living Reviews in European Governance* 5(3). www.livingreviews.org/lreg-2010–3, accessed 16 January 2013.

Lord, C. (2011) 'Problems of Compound Representation in the European Union after Lisbon'. Unpublished manuscript presented at the concluding RECON conference, Oslo, December.

Lord, C. and Pollak, J. (2010) 'The EU's Many Representative Modes: Colliding? Cohering?' *Journal of European Public Policy* 17(1), 117–136.

Lord, C. and Pollak, J. (2013) 'Unequal but Democratic? Equality according to Karlsruhe'. *Journal of European Public Policy* 20(2), 190–205.

Mair, P. (2006) 'Ruling the Void? The Hollowing of Western Democracies'. *New Left Review* 42, (November–December), 25–51.

Mair, P. (2007) 'Political Parties and Party Systems'. In Graziano, P., and Vink, M. P. (eds.) *Europeanization: New Research Agendas*. Basingstoke: Palgrave Macmillan, 154–166.

Majone, G. (1996) *Regulating Europe*. London: Routledge.

Majone, G. (2006) 'The Common Sense of European Integration'. *Journal of European Public Policy* 13(5), 607–626.

Maloney, W. (2007) 'The Professionalization of Representation: Biasing Participation'. In Kohler-Koch, B. de Bièvre, D. and Maloney, W. (eds.) *Opening EU Governance to Civil Society: Gains and Challenges*. Manneheim: Connex Report Series, 5, 69–86.

Manin, B. (1997) *The Principles of Representative Government*. Cambridge: Cambridge University Press.

Mansbridge, J. (1999) 'Should Blacks Represent Blacks and Women Represent Women? A Contingent "Yes"'. *Journal of Politics* 61(3), 628–657.

Marsh, M. and Mikhaylov, S. (2010) 'European Parliament elections and EU governance'. *Living Reviews in European Governance* 5(4), available at www.livingreviews.org/lreg-2010-4.

Maurer, A. and Wessels, W. (eds.) (2001) *National Parliaments on their Ways to Europe: Losers or Latecomers?* Baden-Baden: Nomos.

Mény, Y. (2002) 'De la démocratie en Europe: Old Concepts and New Challenges.' *Journal of Common Market Studies* 41(1), 1–13.

Moravcsik, A. (2006) 'What Can We Learn about the Collapse of the European Constitutional Project?' *Politische Vierteljahreszeitschrift* 47(2), 219–241.

Moravcsik, A. (2002) 'In Defence of the Democratic Deficit: Reassessing Legitimacy in the EU'. *Journal of Common Market Studies* 40(4), 603–624.

Moravcsik, A. (2008) 'The Myth of Europe's 'Democratic Deficit'. *Intereconomics: Journal of European Economic Policy* (November–December), 331–340.

Nanz, P. and Steffek, J. (2004) 'Global Governance, Participation and the Public Sphere'. *Government and Opposition* 39(2), 314–335.

Nikolaidis, K. (2012) 'The Idea of European Demoicracy'. In Dickson, J. and Eleftheriadis, P. (eds.) *Philosophical Foundations of European Union Law*. Oxford: Oxford University Press, 247–274.

Nikolaidis, K. (2004) 'We, the Peoples of Europe . . .' *Foreign Affairs* 83(6), 97–110.

Nikolaidis, K. (2013) 'The Idea of European Demoicracy'. In Dickson, J. and Eleftheriadis, P. (eds.) *Philosophical Foundations of European Union Law*. Oxford: Oxford University Press, 247–274.

Offe, C. (1998) Demokratie und Wohlfahrtsstaat: Eine europäische Regimeform unter dem Streß der europäischen Integration'. In Streeck, W. (ed.) *Internationale Wirtschaft, nationale Demokratie. Herausforderungen für die Demokratietheorie*. Frankfurt am Main/New York: Campus, 99–136.

O'Flynn, I. (2010) 'Democratic Theory and Practice in Deeply Divided Societies'. *Representation* 46(3), 281–93.

Piattoni, S. (2012) 'The Committee of the Regions and the Upgrading of Subnational Territorial Representation'. In Kröger, S. and Friedrich, D. (eds.) *The Challenge of Democratic Representation in the European Union*. Houndmills: Palgrave Macmillan, 59–73.

Pitkin, H.F. (1967) *The Concept of Representation*. Berkeley: University of California Press.

Puntscher Riekmann, S. and Wydra, D. (2013) Representation in the European State of Emergency: Parliaments against Governments?' *Journal of European Integration* 35 (5), 565–582.

Putnam, R. (1988) 'Diplomacy and Domestic Politics: The Logic of Two-Level Games', *International Organization* 42(3), 427–460.

Raunio, T. (2009) 'National Parliaments and European Integration: What We Know and Agenda for Future Research'. *The Journal of Legislative Studies* 15(4), 317–334.

Raunio, T. and Hix, S. (2000) 'Backbenchers Learn to Fight Back: European Integration and Parliamentary Government'. *West European Politics* 23(4), 142–168.

Rehfeld, A. (2006) 'Towards a General Theory of Political Representation'. *Journal of Politics* 68(1), 1–21.

Reif, K.-H. and Schmitt, H. (1980) 'Nine Second-order National Elections – a Conceptual Framework for the Analysis of European Election Results'. *European Journal of Political Research* 8(1), 3–44.

Rumford, C. (2003) 'European Civil Society or Transnational Social Space? Conceptions of Society in Discourses of EU Citizenship, Governance and the Democratic Deficit: An Emerging Agenda'. *European Journal of Social Theory* 6(1), 25–43.

491

Ruzza, C. (2007) 'Conclusion. Linking Governance and Civil Society'. In Della Sala, V. and Ruzza, C. (eds.) *Governance and Civil Society in the European Union: Exploring Policy Issues*. Manchester: Manchester University Press, 139–154.

Sabel, C. F. and Zeitlin, J. (2008) 'Learning from Difference: The New Architecture of Experimentalist Governance in the EU'. *European Law Journal* 14(3), 271–327.

Saurugger, S. (2010) 'The Social Construction of the Participatory Turn: The Emergence of a Norm in the European Union'. *European Journal of Political Research* 49: 471–495.

Saward, M. (1998) *The Terms of Democracy*. Cambridge, Oxford: Polity Press.

Scharpf, F. (1999) *Governing in Europe. Effective and Democratic?* Oxford: Oxford University Press.

Scharpf, F. (2009) 'Legitimacy in the Multilevel European Polity'. *European Political Science Review* 1(2), 173–204.

Schmidt, V. (1999) 'European "Federalism" and its Encroachments on National Institutions', *Publius*, 29(1), 19–44.

Schmidt, V. (2006) Democracy in Europe: The EU and National Polities. Oxford: Oxford University Press.

Schmitter, P. (2000) *How to Democratize the European Union . . . And Why Bother?* Oxford: Rowman & Littlefield.

Schmitter, P. (2007) 'Can the European Union Be Legitimized by Governance?' *European Journal of Legal Studies*, no. 1 (April).

Sifft, S., Brüggemann, M., Königslöw, K.-V, Peters, B. and Wimmel, A. (2007) 'Segmented Europeanization: Exploring the Legitimacy of the European Union from a Public Discourse Perspective'. *Journal of Common Market Studies* 45(1), 127–155.

Sigalas, F. and Pollak, J. (2012) 'Political Parties at the European Level: Do They Satisfy the Condition of Programmatic Convergence?' In Kröger, S. and Friedrich, D. (eds.) *The Challenge of Democratic Representation in the European Union*. Houndmills: Palgrave Macmillan, 23–40.

Smismans, S. (2012) 'Interest *Representation* in the EU, Is There Any? A Top-down Perspective.' In Kröger, S. and Friedrich, D. (eds.) *The Challenge of Democratic Representation in the European Union*. Houndmills: Palgrave Macmillan, 209–225.

Trenz, H.-J. (2009) 'European Civil Society: Between Participation, Representation and Discourse'. *Policy and Society* 28(1), 35–46.

Tsakatika, M. (2007) 'Governance vs. Politics: The European Union's Constitutive "Democratic Deficit"'. *Journal of European Public Policy* 14(6), 867–885.

Urbinati, N. (2000) 'Representation as Advocacy: A Study of Democratic Deliberation'. *Political Theory* 28(6), 758–786.

Urbinati, N. (2004) 'Condorcet's Democratic Theory of Representative Government'. *European Journal of Political Theory* 3 (1), 53–75.

Warren, M. and Castiglione, D. (2004) 'The Transformation of Democratic Representation'. *Democracy and Society* 2(1), 5–22.

Wonka, A., Baumgartner, F. R., Mahoney, C. and Berkhout, J. (2010) 'Measuring the Size and Scope of the EU Interest Group Population'. *European Union Politics* 11(3), 463–476.

Young, I. M. (2000) *Inclusion and Democracy*. Oxford: Oxford University Press.

Zweifel, T. D. (2002) '. . .Who Is Without Sin Cast the First Stone: The EU's Democratic Deficit in Comparison'. *Journal of European Public Policy* 9(5), 812–840.

Zürn, M. (2001) 'Politik in der postnationalen Konstellation. Über das Elend des methodologischen Nationalismus'. In Landfried, C. (ed.) *Politik in einer entgrenzten Welt*. 21. wissenschaftlicher Kongreß der Deutschen Vereinigung für Politischen Wissenschaft. Köln: Verlag Wissenschaft und Politik, 181–203.

Index